MARXIST POLITICS

MD. AYUB MALLICK

R Routledge
Taylor & Francis Group

LONDON AND NEW YORK

AAKAR

First published 2023
by Routledge
4 Park Square, Milton Park, Abingdon, Oxon OX14 4RN

and by Routledge
605 Third Avenue, New York, NY 10158

Routledge is an imprint of the Taylor & Francis Group, an informa business

Print edition not for sale in South Asia (India, Sri Lanka, Nepal, Bangladesh, Pakistan or Bhutan)

British Library Cataloguing-in-Publication Data
A catalogue record for this book is available from the British Library

ISBN: 9781032393957 (hbk)
ISBN: 9781032393964 (pbk)
ISBN: 9781003349532 (ebk)

DOI: 10.4324/9781003349532

Typeset in Palatino
by Sakshi Computers, Delhi

AAKAR

Dedicated to
My Father

Contents

Introduction

Politics is a social activity, a relational approach to power characterized by co-operation, competition and conflict, by individual and group behaviour and activities. In this work, I have tried to analyze Marxist politics unlike the non-Marxist interpretation of 'politics' as the authoritative allocation of values. Non-Marxist politics is the organized dispute of power and the use of power, the ways and means of exercising power, the manner in which decisions are made and factors influencing those decisions, which are enforceable, associated with the attainment of social goals, are reached through information, recommendation, prescription, invocation, application, appraisal and termination. Conflict over scarce resources and values are institutionalized in politics. Institutionalization of resources and values and also of social mobility has reduced the violent character of class conflict to a minimum in industrial society, which is composed of representative democracy and economic rationalism. To the Marxists, all societies are class societies, characterized by class domination, where politics is the superstructure, subsidiary and epiphenomenal character of the socio-economic base of the society. This does not mean that politics is only the derivative and by-product of economics. Politics presupposes class conflict and class domination, which cannot be resolved through institutionalization within the same system unlike the belief of Liberal theorists. Politics is relatively autonomous. Politics is the expression of conflict and State is the pivot and expression of politics. To the Marxists, as a rule, the State of the most powerful, economically dominant class through the medium of the State becomes the politically dominant class, thereby acquiring the means of holding down and exploiting the oppressed class, which, in turn, retaliate against this oppression, where interests are fulfilled by employing power. In the production process, relations of production become conflicting, where capitalists hire labour in exchange of wages and non-owners have no choice except selling labour power. Labour becomes commodity and labour is exploited. The conflict is really between capital and wage labour, when the rate of exploitation is defined by the relation between wages paid and surplus value. Relative autonomy of the State for Marx and Engels is justified where the executive power of the State is exceptionally strong, but not completely independent. It is relatively independent. The State serves the interests of the ruling class and the ruling class dominates the subjugated class by means of State power, economic power and cultural apparatus. Politics is the striving to share power among States, or groups within a State, for certain aims and for power's sake. Domination is power and politics is the striving to share power. Human emancipation, among other things, is the end of politics, according to Marx and Marx sees politics in terms of class and power relations, which is itself is a relationship between domination and subjugation. As a rebellious off-spring of 19th century liberalism, Marxism believes that changes in power relations between classes actually means changes, first, at the political level, and then at the social, cultural and economic levels. According to Marx, capitalist class relations can be changed or altered through establishing socialist society and finally after the gradual process of reaching at the level of communism, where there will be end of politics. Now, the task is the overthrow of the capitalist society through revolution, which would be permanent, until all possessing classes have been forced out of their position of dominance. In the process of change there is conflict — conflict between the forces and relations of production — and class conflict. Relations of production are basically class relations. Changes in class relations or power relations can be made through changes in the relations of production. In order to make a balance, the capitalist depends less on labour through capital accumulation and technological rationality and makes few concessions to labour. The capitalist State helps capitalists in this aspect in order to avoid further power conflict. Labour aristocracy is another means to avoid further conflict. At this stage of State-monopoly capitalism, the fusion between monopoly houses, finance capital and State machinery becomes a possibility. However, State-monopoly capitalism aggravates the crisis situation leading to inflation, unemployment, further concentration of capital, and greater and larger conflict between the forces of production and relations of production, which, in turn, leads to the establishment of socialism and then the establishment of communism. In communist society, there would be the end of politics, where emancipation of humanity becomes a possibility. Working class is the agent of this social transformation, when this class is transformed from 'class-in-itself' to 'class-for itself' in its struggle for power. The working class has to be organized to free itself from 'false consciousness' and embourgeoisment process and to make revolutionary transformation of society.

In chapter two, I have tried to analyze Marxism — its essential parts and sources. The proletarian society can be realized through proletarian struggle, where the party acts as the vanguard of the proletarian class, according to Marx. Transformation of the society is due to revolution where forces of production make it inevitable following Marxist dialectic —thesis, anti-thesis and synthesis. Following this dialectic, according to Marx, trading capital is transformed into money capital. According to Marx, the principal contradiction of the capitalist social system is between social form of production and the capitalist form of appropriation. Workers are impoverished under capitalism; however, extensive social security measures and labour welfare laws have improved their conditions. Against the Marxist paradigm of classless society, Weber justifies capitalism on the basis of maximization of power; Macpherson reconstructs maximization of individual's extractive and developmental power. Pareto regards that rational and logical actions of men are determined by the pursuit of power, which is the care of politics. Further, Schumpeter's economic theory of democracy and entrepreneurship, Durkheim's anomie, C. Wright Mills's power elite, Sorel's myth and Hilferding's organized capitalism and realistic pacifism all go against Marxist mainstream—two discoveries of materialistic conception of history and of capitalistic production through surplus value. In fact, Marxism is a science of society, an interpretation of the past history, an analysis of the socialist society, a prediction of the future society—its making is a historical process, which has both a beginning and an end. Its development, in fact, has no end. According to Marxists, the development of history is associated with the development of production, which makes the existence of classes in society. Marx registers his concept of historicity with the development of the concept of dialectics. He makes use of Feuerbach's philosophy and his knowledge of economic development, which brings within his ideas the materialist conception of history. Marx radicalizes Hegel's philosophy and makes an atheistic conclusion. He travels from revolutionary democracy to proletarian communism. Marx was influenced by Adam Smith and David Ricardo in his critical-historical analysis of bourgeois political economy. He makes his contributions in the analysis of surplus value and its transformed forms like profit, average profit and ground rent. Examining the state of the society and dictatorship of the proletariat he explores the concepts of class struggle, bourgeois revolution and worker-peasant alliance. He, in fact, teaches us philosophy, political economy, and socialism and humanism associated with the emancipation of humanity and the development of human potentialities in production and consumption. It is the realization of man's inherent capabilities free from objectification. He makes two theoretical contributions—a positive theory of production relations and a normative theory of alienation and emancipation. Marx's and Engels's works are both naturalist and materialist, which are depicted from their views on human evolution and existence, materialist approach to history, man-nature symbiotic relationship and man's mastery over nature. Marx and Engles apply natural laws into social laws. Besides the economic laws of motion of modern society, Marx puts forward few elements of humanism and few elements naturalism. According to Marx, man is not to choose their productive forces, the basis of all historical processes. Material relations are the bases of all relations. In determined relations both Marx and Engels always defend philosophical materialism, but do not stop at the materialism of the 18th century. They enrich it with the acquisitions of German philosophy, especially of the Hegelian system, which lead to the materialism of Feuerbach. Feuerbach's materialism is based on empiricism and sensationalism, and for that, Engels, in his work, *Lundwing Fenerbach* says that Feuerbach is correct in pointing out that natural-scientific materialism is the foundation of the edifice of human knowledge, but he does not take care in bringing the science of society into harmony with the materialist foundation. Hegel's idealistic principle of identity of thought and being serves to substantiate the unity of laws governing the external world and the thinking is directed against Kant's agnosticism—something is outside, on the one hand, and things-in-itself is unknowable, on the other[1]. The nature of things is unknowable to human knowledge. While making materialist inversion of Hegel, Marx accepts history as the self-creation of man, historical development of social institutions and dialectical forms of development. The Hegelian method inspired Marx. Marx and Engels realize the importance of bourgeois democracy in developed capitalism and the immature character of the revolutionary proletariat in bourgeois democracy. Marxism gets inspiration from Young Hegelians and from the Western tradition and French and German enlightenment, from Spinoza to Gothe and Hegel. The interpretative framework of Marxism is not idealism, the substantiation of morals, but the substantiation of socio-historical and economic foundations for the development of a capitalist mode of production and substantiation of socialist reconstruction through the unity and union between the science of historical materialism and revolutionary practice. Marxist philosophy is certain and critical assimilation of

German philosophy, English political economy and French socialism, studies materialist interpretation of history, historico-materialist critique of capitalist economy and historico-materialist substantiation of socialism. Socialist reproduction, *i.e.,* reproduction of material wealth, reproduction of labour power and reproduction of production relations—all these are characterized by a planned process of constant renewal and growth of social production—production of the means of production and production of the means of consumption. Marx analyzes capitalistic reproduction in terms of organic composition of capital, rate of surplus value, exchange of commodities and the social product in the form of wages, rent, profit and interest. However, influenced by the British classical economy, Marx criticizes it since this type of economy that treats value as external to the nature of the commodity and does not take into account necessary labour time. According to Marx, value is a social reality, labour becomes commodity, and commodity becomes money. When Ricardo welcomes capitalism on the ground of capitalist investment in the form of revenue, Marx criticizes the system on the ground of exploitation, which is determined by the rate of surplus-value. Marx sketches the development of capitalism from commodity economy to exchange economy to large-scale production based on exchange economy in terms of large-scale circulation of capital, *i.e.,* capital within capitalism rules the world as a prelude to the triumph of labour over capital. Marx here realizes the importance of class struggle, class politics, class interest, class ideology, class institutions unlike the Utopian Socialists in the reconstruction of the new society. Marx is critical about Utopian Socialists on the ground of mysticism and non-revolutionary approach; combination of Christianity and socialism, of liberalism and socialism, and labour stratification of Charles Fourier. When Saint-Simon is for the abolition of unearned income, Fourier goes against Marxist principle 'from each according to his ability to each according to his needs' and puts forward 'from each according to his capacity to each according to his labour, capital and talent'. However, Fourier is much closer to Marx than Saint-Simon and Robert Owen, and Marx criticizes Owen's method of social revolution, which is different from Marx and is devoid of class struggle and revolutionary violence. Marx's discoveries of materialist conception of history and the revelation of the capitalist mode of production by means of surplus value have made socialism science. Marxism, in fact, is based on the principles of historical materialism and class struggle with the application of dialectical method.

Chapter three analyzes dialectical and historical materialism, the philosophy and action, and the theory and practice of Marxism. Practice of Marxism is Marxist approach to politics. In essence, the theory of history and the theory of economics are the foundations of philosophical materialism, which later developed as dialectical materialism, the theoretical basis of the laws of motion of society. Through the dialectical method we arrive at truth of knowledge generating a synthesis through the unity and struggle of opposites. Seen like that, dialectical progression of history is a scientific attempt to reach at the truth. Nothing happens accidentally in the process of socio-historical development, it is dialectically progressive. Therefore, historical materialism is inseparable from philosophical materialism, and dialectical materialism is science, where generalized laws are made with the help of dialectics. Marxism is a revolutionary practice and the Marxist approach to politics is an attempt to this end. Dialectical logic investigates development of thought and historical development of human practice. Self-conscious use of dialectical categories or forms of reality like negation, quantity and quality, necessity and relation make changes in human history. Marx differs from the Personian synthesis of the common whole of all contradictions in human history, and historical programs as a natural historical progress governed by natural-historical laws, is nothing but anti-intellectualist positivist tradition. Marxist dialectic is the comprehension and affirmation of existing state of things and also the recognition of the negative state of things. It is also the recognition of the investigation of the laws of social motion, where fact is the starting point. Comparison and confrontation of facts with others and not comparison and confrontation of facts with ideas is the essence of Marxist dialectic, which characterize the combination and confrontation of forces or production and relations of production, through which human society is studied. Therefore, production is the determining element of social change. The dialectics of historical materialism regard dialectical relation of unity and struggle of opposites and contradictory relation between classes and between forces of production and relations of production. Marxism speaks of the struggle and unity of opposites, both in nature and society. Marx applies natural laws in the study of social history. Natural necessity can best be understood as historical necessity, according to Marx. Therefore, Marx's methodological understanding of history and society is historical realism, a combination of history, materialism and realism. However, natural laws are not historical laws. It is the historical understanding of nature, but not the naturalization of history. Both natural and social relations are determined by society's mode of production and historical continuity of mode of production in the social production process. This historical continuity is the result of contradiction between the forces of production and relations of production. Human history and history of humanity represent domination-subordination relationship, where the State acts as the instrument of domination and revolution as an instrument to end this form of intercourse or domination-subordination relationship. According to Marx, man is the product of society and society is the product of the production process. Critics find a problem in economic determinism and confusion in Marx's application of the term 'economic' as mode or social mode of production. However, entrepreneurial activity, knowledge, technology, science and labour skills should also be included in the category of the mode of production. The factors of mode of production do not change simultaneously and with similar intensity. Further, geographical and biological factors should also be included in this category of factors for social change. Psycho-physical factors and relations play important responsibility in the historical progress of society. Again, it is said that in the base-superstructure relationship 'natural terrain' exercises over man before and after the formation and development of 'artificial terrain'. The concept of superstructure can also be understood non-mechanically. However, Engelsian tradition of Marxism envisages not only the dialectical or reciprocal relationships between structure and superstructure but also the relative autonomy of superstructure, which is understood through empirical observation. Engels's materialism is not only socio-economic, but also natural following Darwinian historicity of nature and this is also followed by matured Marx in *Capital*. Materialist dialectic, to Marx and Engels, is referred as objective laws, but not laws of thought projected through objective reality and projected through empirical observations. Lenin says that Marx and Engels's dialectical method is like the scientific method in sociology, an analysis of the relations of production constituting social formation and investigation of the laws of functioning and development of society. Matter is in motion and consciousness is the highest form of reflection of matter, the product of nature, which attributes supernatural properties to 'Spirit' or 'Idea'. There is a reciprocal interconnection between matter and consciousness, where the former is the primary and the later is the secondary as consciousness reflects the matter through brain, the highly organized matter. The sum total of the images of reality or matter reflected through human brain makes up man's knowledge about the world. Like that of labour, language plays an important role in the formation of consciousness. Labour and consciousness together produce language, which is connected with reality through human thought. However, unlike the Marxist analysis Gramsci asserts the importance of the subject's will and voluntarism in social action and looks into reality not from above, but from below. In his conception of culture politics and hegemony Gramsci makes a synthesis between culture and politics, between consent and coercion and points out that counter-hegemony does not crop up from political action in the traditional Marxist sense but from politicization of the cultural sphere, and henceforth moves from politics to culture, from political organization to socio-cultural formation, and from political action to socio-cultural action. Hegemony is spontaneous consent to pre-dominant power as tradition, institutions, ideas, beliefs and ideologies are manned by the pre-dominant class, their everyday practices and operations. Gramsci provides importance to the superstructure, for example consciousness, and tries to analyze the base through the superstructure. To the Marxists, knowledge arises in man's consciousness. The Marxist method of knowledge revolves round three aspects—generic scientific realism, specific qualified naturalism and particular dialectical materialism. Cognition is the reflection of reality and when knowledge correctly reflects the reality, and then it becomes truth. Knowledge moves from lower to higher *i.e.* from perception to abstract, from abstract to theory, and then from theory to practice. According to Lenin, the splitting of the single whole and the cognition of its contradictory parts is the essence of dialectics, which is the property of all human knowledge, the science of the general laws of motion, and the development of human society and thought. The lower stage is negated to reach the higher stage. Unlike the laws of formal logic—law of identity, law of contradiction, law of excluded middle and the law of sufficient reason, Marxist dialectic operates within three laws—the law of unity and struggle of opposites, law of negation of the negation and the law of transformation of quantity into quality. Critical theory regards negative, romantic and undialectical conceptions about capitalism, science and technology, and criticizes Marx's conceptions about labour, objectivism and scienticism. It also rejects Lukacs's absolute historicism. However, historical materialism is also a social scientific theory. Classes are related with the historical phases of production. The class struggle leads to the dictatorship of the proletariat, which in turn leads to the abolition of classes, where government of persons is replaced by the administration of things and the direction of the process of production. The State, according to the Marxists, is represented as the concentration of class power and relative autonomy of the State is represented as relationship between classes and functionaries of the State, which relationship is the basis of the dictatorship of the proletariat, from which socialist reconstruction is started with the abolition of old repressive machinery. According to Gramsci, the proletarian revolution can be identified with the development and activity of revolutionary organizations arising from the spheres of bourgeois political liberty and the relation of oppression between actual producers and owners of the means of production. Gramsci here stresses the importance of ideological and political means, *i.e.*, intellectual functions of the organic intellectuals and political functions of the party. In his concept of hegemony Gramsci uses and analyzes how the State apparatus of political society is supported by and supporting a specific economic group. This economic group can coerce via the institutions like law, police, army and prisons etc. for the maintenance of the *status quo*. Power, according to Gramsci, is not imposed from, but depends on the consent from below, which is produced and reproduced in the everyday interaction of life. According to Gramsci, the transition of power is necessary where the proletariat would have to depend on State power for the transformation of civil society and final re-absorption of political society by the civil society in a classless society. Marxism educates workers' Party, educates the Party as the vanguard of the proletariat, which is capable of assuming power. Althusser provides the importance of leadership at the superstructural level and differentiates Repressive State Apparatuses (RSAs) and Ideological State Apparatuses (ISAs). The role of the State is of cohesion and regulation.

In chapter four an analysis has been made on the role of the State, which acts as an intermediary for all community institutions. According to the Marxists, the State is the organizing activity of the political society, which is based on the contradiction between public life and private life, cannot, henceforth, resolve the contradiction between the aims and intensions of administration and means and resources of administration. Law is the expression of the will of the State, protects order preferred by the dominating class, and becomes the politically dominant class. Different from the capitalist State, the proletarian State protects the interest of the working class. The proletarian State, according to Engels, is a bourgeois State without the bourgeoisie, where the dictatorship of the proletariat is the guiding force to fight against bourgeois onslaughts. Stalin says that along the path of the consolidation and higher development of the proletarian State the withering away of the State takes place when classes disappear, dictatorship of the proletariat dies and the party also dies out. There will be no more political power properly so-called, as political power is precisely the official expression of antagonism in civil society. Modern representative State isolates politics from the material factors of civil society, and civil society isolates political being from the real life. The Commune is the reabsorption of State power by the civil society. In communist society there will be the end of politics, lies in the basic conflicts in the human society of production, the conflict over the modes of productive activity. To Miliband, the modern capitalist State simply cannot be treated as an instrument of the ruling class, rather it maintains law and order, fosters consensus, economic development and advancement of national interests. Miliband says that governments can and do press against the structural constraints by which they are beset. However, to recognize the existence and importance of these constraints is also to point to the limits of reform, of which more later, and to make possible a strategy of change which attacks the mode of production that imposes the constraints. Poulantzas says about the objective structures and relations, which determine the State — this does not signify the absence of relative autonomy of the State, which is compelled by the structural constraints, where the notions of objective structures and relations are the interests of the ruling class. However, Miliband finds problem in Poulantzas's account of 'structural super determinism', from where Poulantzas cannot state about the 'relative autonomy' of the State. Like Balibar, Poulantzas believes that the structure of the whole is determined by the economic does not mean that the economic always holds the dominant role in the structure, rather the unity of objective structures and relations in dominance implies that every structure or relation has a dominant level, but economic is, in fact, dominant as it regulates the shift of dominance. If the relations of production take primacy over the forces of production, then the relations of production, possession and economic property find expression in powers emanating from the sites delineated by the relations of production. The State exists as an institutionalized political power. Power is concentrated and marginalized by the State, according to Poulantzas following the structural approach unlike the post-structural approach (functional and institutional approach) of Foucault and Deleuze, who underestimates class and class struggle, says about pluralism of micro powers, where power is scattered and diluted. The exceptional State in association with the reorganization of the State system needs radical changes in the ideological State apparatuses in their relationship to the repressive State apparatuses. Classical Marxists basically centres on the repressive State apparatuses unlike the Gramscian ideological State apparatuses. According to Poulantzas, Althusser underestimates the economic role of the State apparatuses. Ideological State Apparatuses holds State power, according to Althusser. Poulantzas finds that hegemonic class controls the Repressive State Apparatuses. The alliance of the dominant class is the nucleus of the State power. Non-hegemonic class controls few of the branches of the State. The State apparatuses perform the role to maintain law and order, unity and cohesion of a social formation.

The subject's role in history has been formulated by Gramsci in his presentation of the role of intellectuals, who are the dominant group's deputies serving for holding, creating and increasing the hegemonic area. In Gramscian dimension Althusser considers the concept of hegemony. Gramsci makes a close relation between the political moment and economic moment and divides the political moment into three steps — (1) group unity on professional basis, where political consciousness does not exist. It is the economic-corporate level (2) unity of classes in class struggle within the structure of the State corresponding to trade-union struggle and reformist politics and (3) class unity reaching towards political struggle and gaining the level of hegemony. It is class hegemony, the sum total of economic and political aims. It is the expansion of class in the sphere of the State, the concrete form of a determinate system of production, where the struggle for power and struggle for new mode of production coincides with each other and dominant class becomes politically and economically dominant. Following the Leninist line Gramsci puts forward hegemony as class domination and class leadership. Hegemony is also the function of the working class in power. Both Lukacs and Gramsci deviate from Marxist positivism and economism and besides treating proletariat as an autonomous and organized political force and dialectic between class situation and class consciousness, they evaluate political initiative of the proletariat. History proceeds through happenings and nothing happens without conscious purpose, according to Lukacs. According to analytical Marxist, Adam Przeworski deviating from functionalist and instrumentalist approach sees the State as an institution where strategic interactions concerning political affairs take place, and where parties, pressure groups, bureaucracies and classes etc. act as rational actors. Like that, Elster finds common class interest developed by co-operative class strategy *vis-à-vis* individual interest developed by conflicting class strategy, where the State provides co-operative solution. The State makes a compromise with the interests of the capitalists and workers. That is, the State has special entity and interests of its own. It is a class compromise State, which is different from the hegemonic State of Gramscian style. The workers and capitalists make compromises without government intervention. Thus the State keeps itself free from the influence of the capitalists, from the structural dependence on capital. Through welfare State policies the State makes a positive response to desired income distribution without damaging the interests of the capitalists and capital.

In chapter five an analysis has been made on the class struggle. Every struggle is a class struggle, the bourgeoisie has simplified class antagonism — antagonism between the proletariat and the bourgeoisie, when proletarians are organized into a class and then into a political party. Marx, here, provides few important conditions for the creation of classes. These may be stated as economic conditions, domination of capital, class in relation with capital, common situation, common interest, mass unity, class-in-itself, class-for-itself, community of interests, national bond and political organization etc. Apart from economic conditions few psychological dimensions of class unity have been stressed by Marx and Engels as common interest, common consciousness and common battle; organizational motivation to unity and identity of commonality. The ideological forms like legal, political, religious, aesthetic or philosophic are reflection of contradiction between the forces of production and relations of production. Ruling class ideas are ruling ideas always and the class which controls the material means of production controls the mental means of production. Estates are social groups with different and opposite interests. Marx says about class struggle and revolutionary practice. Society is characterized by class struggle and not by individuals. History goes through the struggle of opposites. In the inescapable struggle economic factors play a determining role and non-economic factors make conditioning influences. Class consciousness of the masses and class consciousness of the leadership both are necessary for improved consciousness of the working class. Class consciousness is not an automatic or mechanical response to objective conditions, rather subjective elements provide important sources for the potentially improved consciousness as Wilhelm Reich tries to make a balance between objective sociological consciousness and subjective consciousness, consciousness of the revolutionary leadership and consciousness of the masses. Revolution is required to free the means of production from capitalist control and direct these means to the reconstruction of society for the better fulfilment of human needs. In this State of proletarian dictatorship elements like anti-authoritarianism, anti-bureaucracy, egalitarianism, representation, working class-rule rather than bureaucratic State of affairs, universal suffrage, recall of representatives, mandates on the representatives—all are subsumed under proletarian dictatorship. However, Marx emphasizes the necessity of subordination of the State to society for the promotion of individual freedom in a society of non-exploitation. The overcoming of the old by the new is the necessary pre-condition of superstructural changes and to overcome the old relations of production in conformity with the new productive forces, a corresponding transformation of views and institutions is necessary. For this transformation stubborn and organized class struggle is necessary. Social revolution, according to Marx, is the highest form of class struggle. Lukacs's 'revolutionary realpolitik' provides the importance of class struggle in Marxist analysis. The aim of Lenin's realism, his *realpolitik*, is the final elimination of all utopianism and the concrete fulfilment of the content of Marx's programme—theory becomes practical. In contrast, bourgeois theorists argue in favour of class collaboration. Cohen accepts classical Marxist thesis of historical development, *i.e.*, history develops through class struggle, which is the immediate driving force of history, but does not accept it as the most fundamental. To Levine and Wright, class interests are not exclusively determined by the forces of production and class interests do not determine class capacities unlike the classical Marxist considerations. In fact, to them, both class interests and class capacities are determined by forces of production, relations of production and superstructural considerations. According to Cohen, class structure is determined by economic structure and forces of production. Roemer like Cohen accepts the technological dimension of historical development. However, Roemer traces evolution of class exploitation in terms of property relations. The course of historical development is determined by economic base, property relations and exploitation, according to Cohen, Roemer and Wright unlike Robert Brenner's emphasis on class struggle, class structure and class power. Wright analyzes class relations in the process of social production, the objective basis of exploitation in terms of class structure, class formation, class consciousness and class struggle in interrelated forms. To him, the concept of class is based on the concept of exploitation (ownership exploitation, organizational exploitation and credential exploitation). Class structure emerges from exploitation, which emerges from unequal distribution of ownership of the means of production. Przeworski considers that classes are not considered by objective positions like economic structure, property relations, class structure, relations of exploitation, rather they are structured by the totality of economic, political and ideological relations.

Chapter six on 'Party and Revolution' goes through the Marxist-Leninist theory of proletarian party and revolution. The working class will substitute for the old society, *i.e.*, the bourgeois society in the course of development. The proletariat is raised to the position of the ruling class. They (working class) win the battle of democracy, control the production process in society and suppress the power hold of the bourgeoisie. The proletariat needs the State power. The party here becomes the guide, leader and also the teacher of the proletariat, who first wins political power, second attains political supremacy, and third transforms itself as the ruling class. The working class wages their struggle first at the economic level and then transforms it at the political level. The Social Democrats must take up actively the political education of the working class and the development of its political consciousness. Lenin says about the mutual correspondence between political capacity of working class and ideological capacity of the intellectuals. Intellectuals produce ideology, the party inculcates it and working class becomes politically conscious for revolutionary socialist movement. Lenin accepts the political capacity of the workers, the ideological capacity of the intellectuals and the mutual correspondence between these two. The party will introduce proletarian class consciousness. According to Lenin, the task of Russian Social Democracy is the establishment of revolutionary democratic-dictatorship of the proletariat and the peasantry. Lenin's strategy lies between Plekhanov's 'two-stage revolution' and Trotsky's 'permanent revolution'. Spontaneous revolutionary self-education and self-consciousness of the masses should be supplemented by party agitation and propaganda. The party prepares revolution, prepares the proletariat for ideological, tactical and organizational tasks. That is, the party is both the producer and product, pre-condition and result. There is a dialectical unity between these two. Trade union struggle, in opposition, is bourgeois, economic and not socialist. Here, the role of the party is important, which transforms trade union struggle into a socialist revolution, trade union consciousness into socialist consciousness and economic consciousness into political consciousness. Lenin puts forward the theory of democratic decentralization through which the party practices broad democracy, democracy and central control, participation and leadership. At the organizational level Lenin stresses the importance of command, co-ordination and control. Dictatorship of the proletariat is the dictatorship of the party. Soviets in the former Soviet Union were the direct expression of the dictatorship of the proletariat. Lenin has been criticized for centralization of power, however. Centralization of power is a distortion of Marxism, according to the critics. Trotsky emphasizes that revolution throughout Europe, which is a unique and continuous process unlike the Leninist theory of revolution that revolution in one country is a typical case and revolution in other countries is a rare exception. Lenin finds that the progression to capitalism is essential for building of socialism, where the role of the peasants is important as a social and political factor. On the basis of common interests, the peasants form alliances with the proletariat. The proletariat carries the democratic revolution to completion, allying to itself the mass of the peasantry in order to crush the autocracy's resistance. The working class leads the bourgeois revolution. The degree of economic development, the objective condition and the degree of class consciousness and organization of the broad masses of the proletariat, the subjective condition, which is inseparably connected with the objective conditions, which make the immediate complete emancipation of the working class impossible. A socialist revolution is out of question unless the masses become class conscious, organized, trained and educated. Trotsky says about 'permanent revolution' *vis-à-vis* Lenin's two revolutions theory. Trotsky says that dictatorship of the proletariat appears not after the completion of the democratic revolution. It appears on the basis of bourgeois revolution, because there is no other power and no other way to solve the tasks of the agrarian revolution. This opens up the prospect of a democratic revolution growing over into socialist revolution. Lenin here criticizes Trotsky's bourgeois character of revolution and merging of bourgeois and socialist revolutions. Lenin does not agree with Trotsky's 'uninterrupted revolution' that after bourgeois-democratic revolution socialist revolution would continue to be uninterrupted. Lenin does not regard Trotsky's argument that the formal bourgeois democratic stage can be avoided. Lenin says that proletarian revolution is impossible without the forcible destruction of the bourgeois State machine and substitution for it of a new one. Kautsky criticizes Lenin's seizure of power and the equation of proletarian democracy and proletarian dictatorship. According to Luxemburg, Kautsky upholds bourgeois democracy and Lenin and Trotsky uphold bourgeois dictatorship. Lenin, however, does not accept Trotsky's workers' State concept. It is workers' and peasant's State. Bukharin contributes to the defense of Soviet regime on the ground of proletariat's role as the ruling class. In between the revolutionary-democratic dictatorship of the proletariat and peasantry and proletarian revolution there comes the stage of imperialism, where the nations are divided into oppressor and oppressed. It is the monopoly stage of capitalism. Lenin rejects Kautsky's definition of imperialism, which inaccurately connects the national question with industrial capital and arbitrarily pushes into the forefront the question of annexation of regions. According to Luxemburg, the capitalist's greed for surplus value, enhanced by competition and the automatic effects of capitalist exploitation, lead to the production of every kind of commodity, including means of production, and also a growing class of proletarianized workers becomes generally available for the purposes of capital. In opposition to Hobson, Luxemburg justifies imperialism with the realization of surplus value and untrammeled capitalist accumulation. Schumpeter considers imperialism as the outcome of the pre-existing forces, but not of capitalism. Therefore, accordingly,

Luxemburg's analysis is closer to Marxist analysis than that of Hobson and Schumpeter. According to Lenin, imperialism forces the masses into tremendous struggle by sharpening class contradictions. The domination of finance capital and capital in general is not to be abolished by any reforms of political democracy. Imperialism helps to explain the reasons for the revolutionary movement of the working class. Socialism means political power wielded by the party. Stalin calls for value pattern or weightage of Russian revolutionary sweep and American efficiency for the reconstruction of socialism. However, Stalin has been criticized for excess use of power and totalitarianism. As a continuation of Leninism, Stalinism is a culmination of several factors—heritage of Bolshevik revolution, heritage of old Russia, personality of Stalin, rural revolution, mass collectivization and industrialization. Trotsky criticizes Stalin as a man of Thermidor[2], inspires Left opposition, and opposes the bureaucratically formation of Soviets and one-party democracy. Trotsky is also against Stalin's adventurist industrialization and forced collectivization at the expense of both workers and peasants. Trotsky is in favour of industrialization at the expense of the Kulaks for the benefit of both the workers and peasants and voluntary collectivization of agriculture. Stalin's constitution of 1936 is a betrayal of Bolshevism. Buick, Lock and Althusser say about the Stalinist deviation at the transitory level, which cannot be called the socialist mode of production as goods are produced for the market, as there is State and class society, composed of two contradictory modes of production: capitalist and communist. The Stalinist era is characterized by bureaucratic deformation and degeneration. In this respect Mao's New Democracy is based on People's Democratic Dictatorship, which is democratic as the People's Democratic Dictatorship constitutes democracy for the people and dictatorship of the people over the reactionaries. The Proletarian Cultural Revolution is necessary both for the establishment of democracy and dictatorship. The Revolution is based on dialectical materialist foundation. The contradiction exists in the process of development of all things and movement of opposites exists from the beginning to the end in the process of development of each thing. Contradictions within capitalism at its higher stage can be resolved through the Proletarian Cultural Revolution under resolute proletarian leadership. Success of the proletarian struggle depends on the work of the Communist Party in raising the level of political consciousness and organization of the proletariat, of the peasantry and of the urban petty bourgeoisie. The task of revolution in China is to fight imperialism and feudalism, and socialism is out of the question until the task is completed. Revolution cannot avoid two steps — first, New Democracy and second, Socialism. The Cultural Revolution is the ideological reflection of political and economic revolution, which cannot go without proletarian leadership and culture cannot go without proletarian ideology and proletarian culture. The chief targets of the Proletarian Cultural Revolution are imperialism and bourgeoisie of the imperialist countries and feudalism and landlords of the Chinese society. However, the Marxist-Leninist theory of revolution has been criticized by analytical Marxists, like Elster that revolution is the expression of pure potentiality, the power and fecundity of social community. Strategic rationality, a useful method in analyzing revolutionary class dynamics is derived from distribution of productive property and social rules specifying the use of productive property. Establishment of communism on a wider scale cannot be possible and cannot compete with communism. Revolution is a collective action, which can be explained in terms of individual action and rational decision-making. Roemer says that strategic rationality is the focal point of the game of revolution, the game between Leninist strategy and Tsarist strategy, revolutionary strategy and counter-revolutionary strategy, and income distribution and penalty schedule. To them, classical socialism is repressive and inefficient. They urge revolutionary changes to the transformation of the social system towards capitalist market economy. The need is radical socio-economic and political reforms. The process of transition to democracy to State socialism will start from first, the liberalization process, second, extrication from power, and third, construction of new political institutions. It is transition to social democracy with the aspects of socialism and without the socialization of the means of production. It is not market socialism of Miller, which has been criticized by Cohen and Roemer. Roemer's market socialism is like the successful capitalist economy, where publicly owned industries should be managed by individual managers, who would maximize their profits at market prices. The State intervenes only in the affairs of investment, but not management. Transition to communism needs socialism for political reasons, according to Eric Wright.

Chapter seven discusses critical theory in a short and precise manner. Horkheimer criticizes both existing capitalist system and Soviet socialism. It provides an alternative path for social development, *i.e.*, society without suppression and domination. It sees conscious human interests and human possibilities in the rational organization of human activity and it is concerned with metaphysical humanism. For the realization of a rational society he (Horkheimer) integrates philosophy with science while making an inter-disciplinary approach to this end. Horkheimer regards the potential development of the working class, the needs of the working class, and a rational society free from contradictions emerging from struggle against all contradictions and domination of technical rationality in all its forms. Horkheimer acknowledges less and less importance to the proletarian class struggle, the notions of rationalization and instrumental reason. He and Adorno regard the state of capitalist order and not of socialism. Mass culture reinforces privatization pattern and consumption orientations, establishes close liaison between public and private interests, undermines working class culture and increases domination of instrumental reason. To them, knowledge is power and technology is the basis of knowledge. Technological rationality is the coercive nature of the society. Culture brings itself within the sphere of administration. Culture industry takes people as customers. Politics in this society is the business; business motives have become absolute, where there is domination and concealment of domination in production. Society is adapted to technological development and the dialectic of Enlightenment is transformed into delusions. Proletarian existence has lost its revolutionary character in contemporary society of mass culture industry. Critical theory seeks to understand society in terms of subjective ground. Free subjectivity is the character of consciousness. Consciousness assumes the character of free subjectivity. To Adorno, social being or the masses are not subjects, but objects of social process and do not necessarily create class consciousness. For free subjectivity there is the need for close relationship between identification, ego and super ego. The essential shift from instrumental domination to rational domination, integrates all human characteristics towards free subjectivity. In connection with this concept of domination Herbert Marcuse emphasizes Marx's early work on *Economic and Philosophical Manuscripts* on alienation, division of labour and anarchic civil society. Culture industry in an advanced capitalist society has abolished revolutionary radical needs of the hour, destroyed the soil for revolution. The development of forces and relations of production is criterion of the development of human potentiality, which can be realized in a rational society. Marcuse applies instincts in the formation of a relation between individual and society. Satisfaction of instincts of human being is grounded on human labour. To him, Eros is the essence of human being, human potentiality and satisfaction of human instincts. Instrumental reason or science and technology should be applied to liberate man. In advanced industrial society one-dimensionality has become the universal means of domination. Human is spontaneously accepting domination. Technological rationality involves greater liberty, which also involves contraction of instinctual needs. Election is a mechanism for the maintenance of democratic order, stability and *status quo* in advanced industrial society. It legitimizes domination and technological rationality protects the legitimacy of domination. Historical rationality is the process of liberating potentialities and for the attainment of consciousness. Then, it is freedom. Consciousness becomes free for higher historical rationality. Negation of capitalism occurs when the proletariat becomes conscious. Revolutionary agents are Negative Subjects. The path of development is proletarian socialist revolution. Habermas argues for radical democratization of the society. He has transformed the conceptual framework of philosophy of consciousness into the conceptual framework of a theory of language and communicative action. Against Marx and Max Weber, Habermas presents universalist morality and universalist law showing the emergence of capitalism and the conception of modern democracy representing a rationality different from bureaucratic rationality. Against Horkheimer and Adorno, Habermas regards rational organization of society based on free agreement among the members of the society. A rationalized life would subject the systemic mechanisms to the needs of social individuals, rather the world be subjected to the imperatives of system maintenance. The structure of consciousness consists of three types of rationality *i.e.*, cognitive-instrumental, moral-practical and aesthetic-practical. Instrumental reason dominates human thought structure. Domination is distorted communication and reaffirmation of the necessity of self-reflection for self-understanding is essential for human emancipation from domination. Human emancipation is dependent both on theory and practice. Human evolve through labour and interaction, are essentially non-contradictory. In advanced capitalism a new form of legitimization is essential to secure mass loyalty to the system, to secure private utilization of capital and overall to secure a rational society defined by technocratic consciousness, efficiency, economy and sustained growth. Human emancipation depends on development of the productive forces, technical progress, overcoming of distorted communication, and development of ego formation. Human interests and activities assume empirical status. Habermas recognizes self-formation and self-understanding, effective historical consciousness, historicity, communication and understanding. Advanced capitalism is susceptible to crisis, which can be resolved through liberation of subjects and social integration. The crisis may be stated as system crisis and identity crisis, economic crisis and rationality crisis, and legitimating crisis and motivation crisis. The need is rational reconstruction of the society, rationalization of purposive-rational actions and rationalization of communicative actions. Habermas regards autonomous political sphere and State domination is legitimized through rationally motivated agreement or consensus. He justifies consciousness by and through language and consensus is reached in *an ideal speech situation*. System crisis can be stalled through State intervention, where system integration and social integration meet together. To Habermas, proletarian consciousness is the agent of enlightenment. When Habermas constructs the ideal speech situation model, Marcuse develops the human instincts model. Horkheimer and Adorno go against technocratic consciousness. Struggle against authoritarianism, contemporary culture and bureaucracy is the thrust of critical theory, which makes no insight into the constitutive elements of rational society and conditions of unfulfilled possibilities of Adnorno. Horkheimer, however, does not explore the relation between rationality of interests and rational society. Drawing inspiration from Marx, Hegel and Freud, Marx realizes human potentiality through historical development.

NOTES

1. Kant does not reject the objective existence of matter, but considers it unknowable by nature, calling it a 'things-in-itself'. By admitting the objective reality or 'things-in-itself' exits independently of consciousness, he tries to combine or reconcile materialism or idealism. When Kant assumes something outside us, a 'things-in-itself', corresponds to our ideas, he is materialist. And when he declares this 'things-in-itself' to be unknowable, transcendental and other-sided, he is an idealist.
2. Thermidor means eleventh month of French Revolutionary calendar, July 19–August 17 and men of Thermidor means participator in fall of Robespierre on 9th Thermidor.

1

About Marxist Politics

Politics encompasses the social, which comprises of at least three elements: interests, conflict of interests and resolution of conflicts. Therefore, it is not an independent phenomenon. On the contrary, it looks into social and political institutions and variables and attempts at social power, social progress and social change. The concept of politics is dynamic in content and essence dealing with power, sharing power, distribution of power and influencing distribution of power. As a social process politics is characterized by individual and group behaviour and activities, human relations in society characterized by co-operation, competition and conflict, decision-making and finally, authoritative allocation of values. Here, values, means, interests and objectives of the individual and group members of the society are allocated in an authoritative way for the divergences and conflict among the members of society. Therefore, it is both politics of conflict and consent, politics of adjustment and distribution. Politics, in essence, is benefits who get, when they get and how they get—a process of interaction between divergent interest groups and the authority in terms of distribution of social rewards. Not only group or individual interests, conflict of interests, 'negotiation, argument, discussion, application of force, persuasion' (Myerson and Banfield, 1955 : 304-05), agitation, settlement and resolution of conflicts, which politics presupposes that needs to be accompanied with authoritative decision-making in the context of an organizational framework. Robert Dahl justifies politics in terms of power, rule and authority (Dahl, 1963). Politics is 'a social process characterized by activity involving rival and co-operation in the exercise of power, and culminating in the making of decisions for a group (Bluhm, 1965 : 5). There is incorporation of power or authority within politics and legitimate use of force is the thread that runs through the inputs and outputs (Almond, 1965), when politics is a 'natural reflex of the divergences between the members of the society' as 'a matter of expression, advocacy, settlement and modification of disagreements' (Miller, 1965 : 17). Therefore, politics is a continuous process, which denotes the role of all those agencies, both State and non-State, have their role in the decision-making process. Some kind of authority, whether State or non-State is necessary for the settlement or modification of disagreements. The government 'has to solve these conflicts by whatever means are at its disposal, the only limitation being that in so doing it must prevent the break-up of the polity. Politics ceases where secession, and indeed civil war begins, as, at that point, there is no longer an authoritative allocation of values, but two sides allocating their values differently.' (Blondel, 1969 : 7). Therefore, making of decisions is an interpersonal process and power as participation in the decision-making process is also an interpersonal relation. Politics is a case where power is exercised and brought into being from influence to authority, from authority to force and from force to coercion. Henceforth, politics is 'organised dispute about power and its use, involving choice among competing values, ideas, persons, interests and demands. The study of politics is concerned with the description and analysis of the manner in which power is obtained, exercised, and controlled, the purpose for which it is used, the manner in which decisions are made, the factors which influence the making of those decisions, and the context in which those decisions take place.' (Curtis, 1968 : 1). A political action has the character of a decision taken by some actors, public and private, which is referred to two aspects. Firstly, who takes the decisions and secondly, how are the decisions taken in the interactive processes. Power is a crucial component in the interactive process, where 'values are authoritatively allocated in society through the process of the conflict of groups' (Hagan, 1958 : 40) or group interests. Therefore, politics is concerned with the attainment of social goals and it is the sphere in which the decisions are made with respect to the whole society, and these decisions are enforceable (Deutsch, 1967). Therefore, to him the core area of politics is equal to area of enforceable decisions and the essence of politics is equal to dependable co-ordination of human efforts for the attainment of the goals of society. As politics is dependent phenomenon, so are the enforceable decisions, which to Lasswell are reached through seven functional stages: information, recommendation, prescription, invocation, application, appraisal and termination. These are psychological factors affecting the decision-making process (Lasswell, 1958). The social factors like manipulation, negotiation, bargaining, mutual adjustments, centralization and decentralization of leadership—all these have been provided due weightage in the decision-making process or have been taken into account in discussing how and why decisions are made by the social scientists like Almond stressing on interest articulation and aggregation, Riker on coalition formation, Bently on group interaction, Boulding on data information through the feedback and communication process, Deutsch on cybernetics, Dahl on hierarchy and polyarchy and Lindblom on bargaining and price mechanism.

Previously, I have mentioned that politics is composed of conflict of interests and resolution of conflicts and conflict is conceptualized as an outcome of exchanges between individuals or groups in the form of competition for the attainment of goods and values. In industrial society conflict over scarce resources and values are institutionalized. 'Industrial enterprise is an imperatively co-ordinated association' (Dahrendorf, 1959 : 17). With the advent of democratic decision-making process and institutionalization of social mobility, industrial society has reduced the violent character of class conflict to a minuscule. An industrial democracy whose another name is representative democracy presupposes authority structures and organizations of conflicting interest groups mitigating the intensity of violence, representative institutions and democratic decision-making process, interest articulation and mediation of conflicts, workers' participation in industrial management etc. Economic rationalism presupposes capitalism with fixed capital oriented towards production on which depends consumers' interests, appropriation by capital owners of the material and organizational means of production, division of labour and emergence of a new middle class of bureaucrats and white-collar workers, institutionalization of social mobility, long-run profit orientation in the production process, orientation to opportunities open to the market, a rational organization of labour, labour discipline and rational work culture, and rational technology. In connection with the regulation of conflicts among various groups and quasi-groups, Ralf Dahrendorf maintains that parties in conflict and their interests are institutionally recognized within the framework of society at large. Secondly, representative institutions try to bring conflicting parties to the negotiating table. Thirdly, decisions and discussions on various problems and issues are made on the basis of rules of the game. Fourthly, a third party often acts as a mediator if autonomous and normal process of reconciliation breaks down. Fifthly, the judicial system tries to arbitrate the unresolved disputes if representative machinery of negotiation and reconciliation breaks down.

Conflict in industrial society is institutionalized and rationalized, where laws are binding on everyone. People accept this domination as rational which is based on a belief in the legality of ordinances and the legality of the titles of those who exercise domination. The working class accepts these processes of constitutionalism and parliamentarism because first, constitutional method is more preferable to that of violent seizure of power and second, constitutional accession to power might be followed by a wholesale recasting of State institutions. But reform within the capitalistic framework has become *sine qua non* of capitalistic victory or perpetuation by and through political manoeuvring in terms of legitimacy. But it is not capitalism of earlier tradition, but a complete break with it. It is a joint stock company which differentiates itself from capitalism characterized by sheer conflicts between capital and labour on the basis of close relation between manager and workers and isolation of capitalists as exploiters of workers from the mainstream production process, where the stock holders become the owner and executive the manager. New types of conflicting groups, issues and patterns of conflict emerge from the womb of decomposition of capital and differentiated role structures. Like that of decomposition of capital, labour also becomes decomposed and differentiated on the basis of occupations and interests, for example, agricultural labourers, industrial labourers, mining labourers, skilled, semi-skilled and unskilled labourers.

To the Marxists, all societies in the history have been class societies, societies composed of contending and conflicting classes from freeman and slave, patrician and plebeian, lord and serf, guildmaster and journeyman to bourgeoisie and proletariat in the epoch of capitalism which have stood in constant opposition to one another (Marx and Engels, 1976). All these class societies are characterized by class domination based on a particular mode of production. Politics may be conceived as specific articulation of class interest and class domination. To the Marxists, politics is the superstructure, based on socio-economic base structure of the society. Politics and economics, and culture and ideology are intertwined inseparably. Politics is determined and conditioned, provides politics a derivative, subsidiary and an epiphenomenal character. To Marx, 'In the social production of their existence, men enter into definite, necessary relations, which are independent of their will, namely, relations of production corresponding to a determinate stage of development of their material forces of production. The totality of these relations of production constitutes the economic structure of society, the real foundation on which there arises a legal and political superstructure and to which there correspond definite forms of social consciousness. The mode of production of material life conditions the social, political and intellectual life-process in general.' (Marx, 1976 : 3). Politics is a social activity, characterized by diversity, divergences and conflict. In the *Communist Manifesto*, Marx says that the history of all hitherto existing society is the history of class struggle. Politics is class conflict. To this end, Marx asserts three propositions:

1. that mode of production constitutes the forces of production and relations of production determine the whole of superstructure;
2. that independent changes in the mode of production lead in time to the destruction of old property relations and the creation of a new one; and
3. that the dialectic has offered contradictions in history through the medium of the struggle of the economic classes, which is sharpening under capitalist production system, can end only in revolutionary victory of the proletariat. And after the final synthesis of communist victory there will be the end of politics. Historical materialism allows us to understand the necessary conditions of that change.

The concepts like 'social dynamics', 'contradiction', 'incorporate tension', 'unresolved problems' are starting points of Marxist politics. The inherent contradiction between capital and labour determines the relationship between the ruler and the ruled in capitalist society. To Engels, at a certain stage of economic development and class cleavages the stage became a necessity. Created by particular socio-economic milieu the State comes out as a necessity following the growth of productive forces and resultant differentiation into the social classes. It is a society, to Engels, in which the family system is entirely dominated by the property system, and in which the class antagonisms and class struggles, which make up the content of all hitherto written history, now freely develop. (Engels, 1884). Here lies the role of State and non-State agencies in the process of politics. The class struggle necessarily creates a situation, when and where all human relations become disturbed and uncertain, when and where property owners become insecure in the hands of the oppressed few, when law and order situation is at stake, then the State comes into being. For example, the executive of the modern State or modern representative State is nothing but 'a committee for managing the common affairs of the whole bourgeoisie' (Marx and Engels, n.d. : 44). Graphically, we may see the sequence like this ('→' means leading to or moving towards): class formation after private property relations → divergent class interests → class conflict between haves and have-nots → creation of social inconvenience after class conflict → haves think about social order for peaceful wealth accumulation and self-protection → the emergence and existence of the State as manager and protector of bourgeois class interest. The State is an instrument of class rule, an 'executive committee' of the dominant economic class. The executive committees are the decision-makers, who serve the class interest of the dominant economic class. Therefore, the State is an instrument of class domination.

Politics is an activity linked with relations between classes, nations and other social groups, centered on the seizure, retention and use of State power. The relations between classes, and hence their policy, which expresses their fundamental interests, arise from their economic position. Political ideas and institutions corresponding to them constitute the superstructure on the economic basis. This does not mean that politics is the passive result of economics. Politics correctly reflects the needs of the material life of society. Politics is a matter of conflict between classes in society and is rooted in it. To the Liberals, there are various types of conflicts in society, irrespective of class conflict. To them, conflict can be resolved and politics reconciles conflict in society through adaptation, integration and overall socialization process. To the Marxists, conflicts cannot be resolved within the same system. Class conflict gives birth to other conflicts, but not politics reconciles conflicts, politics is the expression of conflict. The State is the core or pivot of politics or the super expression of politics. Engels in *The Origin of the Family, Private Property and the State* points out that as a rule the State of the most powerful, economically dominant class, through the medium of the State becomes also the politically dominant class, and thereby acquires the means of holding down and exploiting the oppressed class. Secondly, he points out that capitalists and workers are blamed against each other and equally cheated for the benefit of the impoverished Prussian cabbage junkers. Economically, the dominant power tries to establish domination over the other. Further, other classes try to snatch the power of the dominant and to become powerful. This power conflict between the dominant and subjugated classes is generated by means of social position and social prestige. According to Marx, those who own the means of production are economically powerful and try to subjugate the non-owners. How conflict arises from domination according to Marx? It is quite simple. A graphic representation explains the process (Figure 1)

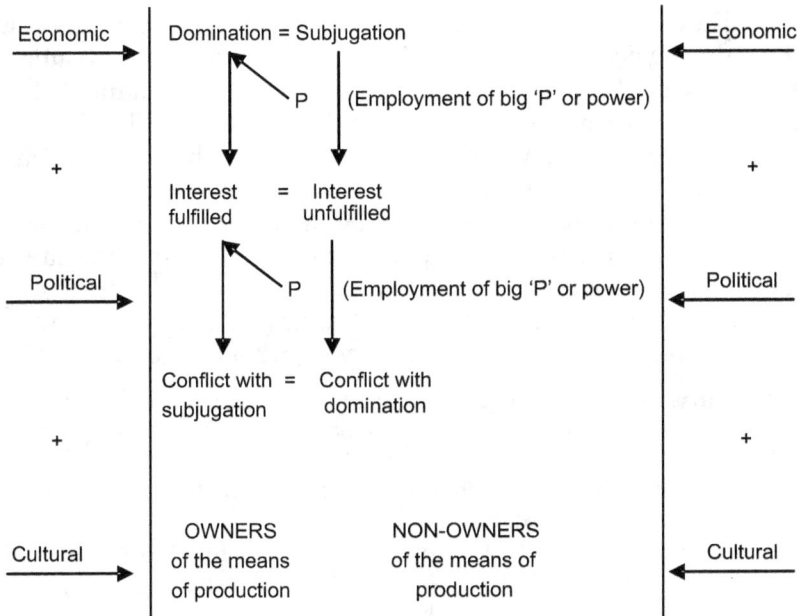

Economic	Domination = Subjugation	Economic
	P (Employment of big 'P' or power)	
+	Interest = Interest fulfilled unfulfilled	+
Political	P (Employment of big 'P' or power)	Political
+	Conflict with = Conflict with subjugation domination	+
Cultural	OWNERS of the means of production NON-OWNERS of the means of production	Cultural

Figure 1

Interests are fulfilled by employing power. However, it may be employment or threat of employment. In economic, political and cultural spheres the owners try to dominate over the interests of the non-owners and non-owners try to make some relief from that, resulting in conflict between the two classes, where power and interest are the interesting focal points. The class which dominates economically also dominates the ownership of the means of production. The other issue is how they dominate? Those who own the means of production dictate the terms and conditions of workers and the relations of production, which are hierarchical. Co-operative effort in the production process is one of the aspects of the relations of production. The co-operative effort is actually not found in the production process. As non-owners have no choice except the production, they have only to sell labour power. The capitalists hire the labour in exchange of wages. The class which owns the means of production is dominant in relations of production and hence, dictates the terms and conditions. In response, workers resist that tension between owners and non-owners prevails. To Marx, capitalist mode of production is more powerful than that of other modes of production. Labour is exploited in the production process. The social productiveness of labour is manifested in the produced productive forces, the value of production, the conditions of production, magnitude of accumulated productive capital, portion of total capital laid out in wages. The capitalists accumulate profit by increasing the surplus-value or by reducing necessary labour time and by decreasing the quantity of labour-power. Labour becomes commodity in the hands of the bourgeoisie, the capitalists in essence. Marx explains the theory of surplus value in *Capital*, where he tries to point out the law of capitalist accumulation: competition for resources among capitalists → accumulation of capital → labour-saving machinery for decreasing the quantity of labour-power and for more production, the law of concentration of capital: more competition among capitalists → capitalism leads to monopoly, and the law of increasing misery: replacement of labour force by machinery → increasing misery. To Marx,

Total mass of surplus-value = (is equal to) Total mass of profit,
Value of any commodity : (is proportional to) Quantity of average human labour,
Value of any commodity = (is equal to) Value of any labour,
Labour becomes a commodity.
Wage = (is equal to) Labour time necessary to produce a value,
Wage < (is less than) Actual duration of labour time,
Wage = (is equal to) Necessary labour time,
Surplus labour time = Surplus-value = Profit.

The rate of exploitation is defined by the relation between the wages paid and surplus value. At this stage, the conflict is between capital and wage labour. Therefore, to Marxists, politics is all pervasive and an articulated form of class conflict. In his 'Preface' to *A Contribution to the Critique of Political Economy* and *Capital* Marx says about economy or economic domination as the source of all dominations, political and cultural. Economy determines politics. It is not the consciousness of men that determines their being, but, on the contrary, their social being that determines their consciousness. The unpaid surplus-labour is pumped out of direct produces, which determines the relationship of rulers and ruled.

Domination by nature is political as it is closely related with politics and power conflict. Economic domination is political in that sense. The State, according to Marxists, serves the ruling class interest to perpetuate economic domination, with an exception of relative autonomy of the state. A mention here may be made that Marx and Engels discuss the State's relative independence or autonomy mainly in connection with regimes where the executive power is exceptionally strong. But this does not mean complete independence of the State. Marx says that the State power does not hover in mid-air and the Bonapartist State represents a class, the numerous class of French society, the small proprietors. The ruling class, in fact, dominates the subjugated class by means of State power, economic power and cultural apparatuses. Then, what is the nature of class domination in culture? Generally, the cultural domination is ideological domination. Each class has more or less an ideological orientation. Material interests are transformed into an ideology organized within a system, which actually represents the material interest of a class in question. The ruling classes have an ideology which dominates over the other classes. It justifies cultural domination. In the world of values, norms, ethics, philosophy, art, morality etc. the ruling class wants to make or tries to make domination over the other. So, culture is determined by ruling class interest, which captures culture and the whole culture is determined by ideology. Marx and Engels in *German Ideology* say that the ideas of the ruling class are the ruling ideas. This ruling force is the ruling intellectual force, has the means of material production at its disposal, and has control over the means of mental production; and those who do not own the means of material production at their disposal, have no control over the means of mental production, are subject to ruling ideas. But, why is cultural domination a necessity? So to say, if culture is captured and conquered, it is essay to capture individual personality, men's way of life and overall their consciousness. It is a psychological make-up of the whole classes within the society to subjugate them voluntarily; and ideology denotes cultural homogeneity. Cultural domination facilitates political and economic domination as a self-corrective to the ruling class to operate the class character of that class throughout the whole society, for example, by and through parliamentary democracy, electioneering proceedings and democratic values in the political sphere and work-ethic, work-values, work-efficiency, work discipline in the economic sphere. In the cultural sphere there is conflict and divergence among different forms of culture. So, there is cultural conflict, where the dominant culture undermines the subjugated. It is affirmative culture, which is 'meant that culture of the bourgeois epoch which led in the course of its own development to the segregation from civilization of the mental and spiritual world as an independent realm of value that is also considered superior to civilization. Its decisive character is the assertion of a universally obligatory, eternally better and more valuable world that must be unconditionally affirmed.' (Marcuse, 1968 : 95). How does cultural domination come into being? And by what means does it take its recourse? It is by means of economic power. Culture is produced by the economically more powerful owners, who own the necessary means of production and also the necessary means of propagating culture, such as printing and other machineries, radio, TV, newspaper, internet, etc. Wealth is an important factor in the production of ideas, values and norms. Hence, economically ruling class becomes culturally ruling class ideas. Those who own the means of production of economy also own the means of production of culture. Economically dominant class also becomes dominant in the cultural sphere. Secondly, the downtrodden sections of the society, the working classes are dominated by the economically dominant class and culturally dominant ideas. Such as, the employees of the newspaper office are dominated by the policies determined by the owner of the newspaper. Thirdly, no culture is sustained in the long run unless they are aided by the government, patronized by State power. So, to promote and strengthen culture State power is necessary. Therefore, those who control State power would automatically determine culture with the help of Repressive State Apparatus and Ideological State Apparatus as defined by Althusser. These people are the owners of the means of production. Is it possible for the ruling class to dominate in the cultural sphere all the time? No, is the answer. The graphic representation makes the answer clearer. The representation shows (Figure 2) that there is variation in 'cultural craftsmanship'—ruling and subjugated. There is resistance from the subjugated class for domination by the ruling class. Naturally, the ruling class with the help of their economic and political power generates 'cultural craftsmanship' faster than that of the subjugated class. The ruling class also faces another challenge: problem of continuously innovating culture with the help of instituted artists. There is the transition from social relations of a regular institution to social relations of conscious exchange. In the process of continuously innovating of culture, transition to specialism and professionalism, direct retaining and commissioning of artists, sponsorship and commercial sponsorship have all become the dominant factors, where culture has become a commodity in the commercial market and public is treated as patron, i.e., the deliberate maintenance and extension of culture as a matter of general public policy. This is the phase of corporate professionalism, where culture is produced not only for the market, but improved and strengthened with important development in the means of cultural production, especially the use of new media and advertising. Furthermore, every innovation like this bears an economic cost which is maintained by the owners of the means of production. There is another problem: problem of presentation to invoke generality in order to escape the bitter taste of exploitation. It is mixed in character. The more it is mixed, the more it becomes general. Culture is produced in a generalized form. It is the mixing-up and compromise exercise of both cultures, ruling and subjugated and between the both classes, owners of the means of production and non-owners of the means of production. It is the politics of culture making and highlighting the capitalist culture. The invention and development of the material means of cultural production is remarkable. No socio-political analysis can replace either general history or more specific individual studies. Another problem is: creation or making use of traditional culture through replication, formal production and reproduction, innovation, transition, change and recognition etc. Another problem: there is a conflict or conflict situation within ruling class ideologies or culture or sub-cultures. There is also the problem of introducing or reintroducing, influencing or re-influencing directly or indirectly the intellectuals and the ideas of intellectuals in the production of culture. There may be a lag in the ideas of the intellectuals. Intellectuals from the lower echelons of society do not conform to ruling ideas in few some cases; hence, there remains a gap between the ideas of the intellectuals and the ruling class. Another problem is the problem of unity among intellectuals. They are not consciously identical. The main reason for this disunity or the root of this division lies in the division of labour and specialization. Internal specialization creates problem for the ruling. There is the problem of 'uncommitted intelligentsia', because of (1) conditions of asymmetry between capitalist market and bourgeois social order, (2) conditions of internal institutional reproduction, and (3) conditions of oppositional and alternative social class interests. In association with this, there is also the problem of creating traditional culture and making use of it.

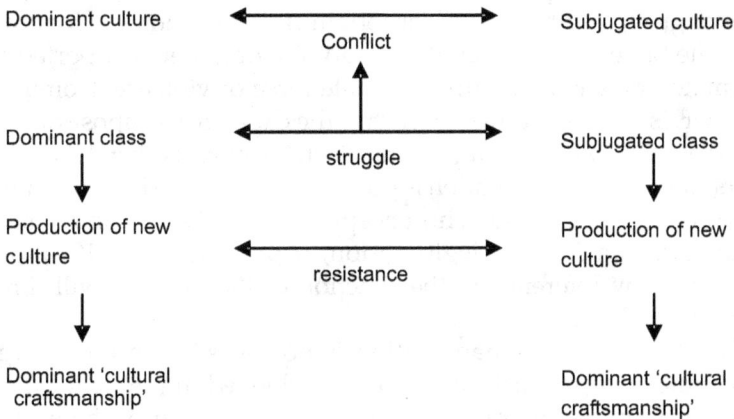

Dominant culture	⟵ Conflict ⟶	Subjugated culture
Dominant class ↓	⟵ struggle ⟶ ↑	Subjugated class ↓
Production of new culture ↓	⟵ resistance ⟶	Production of new culture ↓
Dominant 'cultural craftsmanship'		Dominant 'cultural craftsmanship'

Figure 2

There are cultural producers in all societies. Both the degrees of specialization and consequent social relations of the cultural producers are historically determined, in spite of the problem of 'uncommitted intelligentsia'. In capitalist society there is indeed no lack of examples of radically independent thinkers and artists under certain conditions of asymmetry between the capitalist market and a bourgeois social order, conditions of internal institutional reproduction developing the criteria of independent intellectual work, and conditions of dominant social order, which does not exclude important organizations based on different, alternative or oppositional, social and social class interests. Althusser has also accepted the cultural autonomy. Despite this cultural autonomy, culture is determined by economic and political factors in the society. In fact, culture in society cannot be analyzed without considering the class character of the material means of production. We have to remember first and foremost the relations between the material means of production and specific social forms, which depend on the specific production system, and second, the specific social forms are manifest cultural production and reproduction. Beyond professional specialization, and beyond the internal class division within social forms of cultural production, there remains ultimately the controlling form of ownership and management within which other forms operate. Within the centralized systems of advanced technologies every worker, cultural and productive becomes an employee of an owner or manager who need not be directly concerned with cultural production at all (Williams, 1982). Therefore, owners of the means of economic and cultural productions dominate the cultural sphere with the help of political power despite certain problems of cultural production and cultural domination.

To Max Weber, politics is the striving to share power either among States or groups within a State for certain aims and ends and for power's sake. The State is a relation of men dominating men, supported to be legitimate or combined with legitimate force or violence. Domination, to Weber, is a form of power, which is the capacity to impose one's will over another without having resistance on the part of other. Here, Weber differs from Marx. Domination is power. It is an authoritarian command over the subject people who accept it as legitimate and justified. Democracy is a form of legitimation, it provides a justification for domination by reference to the sanction of the popular will through formal procedures.

To Marx, human emancipation is not possible in the bourgeois democratic set-up, which can never be achieved in the political realm alone but requires the revolutionary transformation of the economic and social order. Human emancipation means, among other things, the end of politics. In industrial democracy man is not free from alienation. Alienated labour is the product of industrialization and market economy. The concept of alienation is primarily concerned with estrangement of labour. Marx articulates the presence of alienation in the philosophic and political dimension. According to Marx, alienation is a process whereby man forfeits something what is essential to his nature. 'This is based on a distinction between existence and essence on the fact that man's existence is alienated from his essence he is not what he ought to be and he ought to be that which he could be.' (Fromm, 1966 : 47). Marx describes the estrangement of labour or alienation of labour in three forms—alienation of labour from its product, alienation of labour from the act of production, and alienation of man from nature. (Struik, 1964 : 46-47). Man is dehumanized and transformed into a commodity with the process of objectification of labour. The alienation of the object of labour is nothing but the alienation of the work activity itself—labour becomes external to the worker, labour is imposed on the worker and worker takes labour as a means of mere subsistence, and the worker accomplishes the work, which is appropriated by others. Therefore, the worker is self-alienated in the process of production. There is another alienation, *i.e.* alienation of man as a species being or alienation of man from man. 'Consciousness which man has from his species is transformed through alienation so that species life becomes only a means for him ... What is true of man's relationship to work, to the product of his work and to himself, is also true of his relationship to other men, to their labour and to the objects of their labour.' (Fromm, 1966 : 103). Marx's delineation of the process of alienation may be presented in a cyclic graphic form:

> labour is a commodity → or commodification of labour → worker sinks into the level of commodification → labour becomes the more miserable commodity → increased misery of the workers with the power and volume of production → competition among the capitalists for greater accumulation of profit → accumulation of capital in few hands → restoration of monopoly → broader class division of the society into owners and non-owners →

Marx as an economist proposes few proportional dimensions in the process of estrangement and alienation of labour—a graphic representation of which is like below (Figure 3):

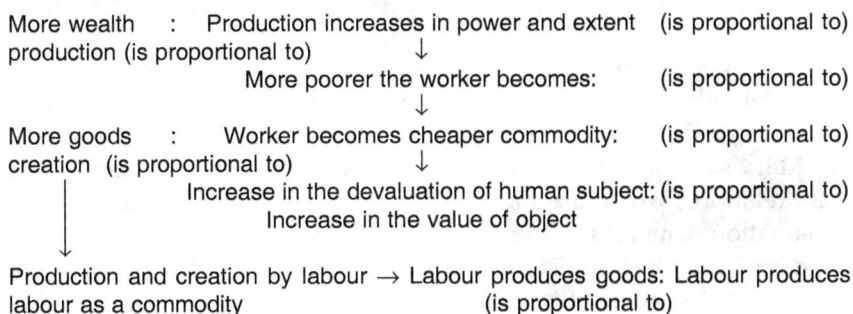

More wealth : Production increases in power and extent (is proportional to)
production (is proportional to) ↓

　　　　　　　　　　More poorer the worker becomes: (is proportional to)
　　　　　　　　　　　　　　　　↓

More goods : Worker becomes cheaper commodity: (is proportional to)
creation (is proportional to) ↓

　│　　　　　Increase in the devaluation of human subject: (is proportional to)
　│　　　　　　　Increase in the value of object
　↓

Production and creation by labour → Labour produces goods: Labour produces labour as a commodity　　　　　　　　　　(is proportional to)

Figure 3

Herbert Marcuse's study of alienation is in conformity with Marx's delineation of alienation, where he addresses the perversion of reason and alienation of man as a species-being. In his concept of 'one-dimensional man' he puts that domination-administration of modern industrial society is totalitarian and irrational resulting in diminution of man's inner self. It is one-dimensional society, represented by one-dimensional thought, dominated by technological rationality, derailment of reason and repression of freedom, resulting in one-dimensional man (Marcuse, 1964). The sequence is: from one-dimensional society to one-dimensional thought to one-dimensional development, and then to one-dimensional man. It is domination by alienation. Following Marcuse, Philip Slater (1970) suggests that man is alienated from his desire for community, desire for engagement, and desire for dependence in advanced industrial society dominated by technology, economic rationality and scarcity of resources. 'One-dimensionality is another term for alienation which we have defined as the repression of certain aspects of human nature, especially the non-rational dimensions of human existence. Western man is alienated from important "parts" of himself, because multi-dimensionality of his existence has been reduced to the dimensions of technology and the economy?' (Weisskopf, 1971 : 189-90). Mehring suggests that to Marx 'human self-consciousness was the supreme godhead' (Mehring, 1951 : 503). Here, human is being alienated from humanness, nature of love, beauty, truth, and man. Here, further he follows Hegel's self-conscious life activity as goal of most worthy in nature. In his *Economic and Philosophical Manuscripts* Marx says that the outstanding achievement of Hegel's Phenomenology is that Hegel grasps the self-creation of man as a process. The *real* active orientation of man to himself as a species-being is only possible so far as he really brings forth all his species-powers (Fromm, 1966). Marx here justifies the need of man for society. In *Economic and Philosophical Manuscripts* he brings about the notion of 'human sensibility'. Marx points out that in order for men to act as human beings certain socio-economic conditions are necessary. Human production is possible when man is free from physical need and free to create in accordance with the laws of beauty, and also free from domination and alienation, which negate 'human sensibility'. The need is to change the conditions of domination and alienation.

Marx sees politics in terms of class relations and changes in the class relations, which itself are relationships between domination and subjugation. Changes in the given class structure of the society is the most fundamental Marxist concept, which is different from non-Marxist concept of change: conflict can be resolved within the system, conflict is an unending process and conflict is institutionalized within the society. Marx finds fundamental change in the value system, change in the dominant mode of production and regime change. In fact, without socio-economic change and change in the redistribution of social power political change is not possible. Marxist concept of change is comprehensive. Marxism is the illegitimate and rebellious off-spring of the nineteenth-century liberalism. Changes in the power relations between classes actually mean changes at the political level, but it is also social and cultural. Again, without capturing political power socio-economic and socio-cultural changes cannot be possible. In essence, 'a political revolution is a social revolution when it involves the conflict of social classes'. (Miliband, 1977 : 154). Marx in his *Theses on Feuerbach* says that philosophers have so far interpreted the world; the question is how to change it. Engels while evaluating Marx says that Marx's mission of life is to overthrow the capitalist society and the State institutions for the liberation of the proletariat. Quoting Marx and Engels Miliband says, 'It is in our interest and task to make revolution permanent, until all more or less possessing classes have been forced out of their position of dominance, until the proletariat has conquered State power, and the association of the proletarians, not only in one country but in all the dominant countries of the world, has advanced so far that competition among the proletarians of these countries has ceased and that at least the decisive productive forces are concentrated in the hands of the proletarians. For us the issue cannot be alteration of private property but only its nihilation, not the smoothening over of class antagonism but the abolition of classes, not the improvement of existing society but the foundation of a new one.' (op. cit. Miliband, 1977 : 158).

How, can the class relations in capitalism or in capitalist society be changed or altered? It would be after establishing socialist society and finally after the gradual process of reaching at the level of communism, where there will be end of politics, end of all classes and class conflict and where the State will wither away and will die a natural death. To Marx, (a) the existence of all classes is only bound up with particular historic phases in the development of production, (b) the class struggle necessarily leads to the dictatorship of the proletariat, and (c) this dictatorship itself constitutes the transition to the abolition of all classes and to a classless society. What are the forces responsible for making changes in capitalist society? Conflict between the forces of production and relations of production reflect changes both in the superstructure and infrastructure. In this conflict there is another conflict, *i.e.* class conflict and relations of production are basically class relations. Changes both in the forces of production and relations of production facilitate change to socialism. Production becomes social in capitalist society. Concentration of the means of production in few hands, whereby they cease to appear as property of the immediate labourers and turn into social production capacities, two, organization of labour itself into social labour through co-operation and division of labour, and three, creation of the world market—these are the features of capitalist production. The way to socialized production process is the formation of joint stock company, where the means of production is owned by collectivity of individuals, which means plurality of ownership. But the capitalist system does not change and what changes is the change in ownership of the means of production, as capitalists individually cannot develop their economy and there is sharp competition between entrepreneurs. A sense of collectivity crops up. Capital in itself rests on a social mode of production and means of production and labour presuppose a social concentration. With the enormous expansion of the scale of production and of enterprises actually functioning, capitalists are being transformed into a mere manager or administrator and owner of capital into a mere owner. The capitalists invest not only from their own capital, but also from social capital, such as capital in banking system dealing with public money. There is dependency on social capital. The production process becomes much more social, where goods and commodities are produced by labour in co-operation with each other, and where there is increasing dependency of different sectors of production and different techniques of production. The search for the international market is another avenue to the process of market socialization in order to absorb the whole community internationally on the part of the actually functioning capitalists (administrators and managers) and capital owners. But, what are the basic contradictions of capitalism which facilitate changes in the capitalist production system? There is contradiction between the social character of production and the private capitalist form of appropriation of the products of labour. As the modern productive forces develop, production becomes concentrated and there is further social division of labour and further economic ties between various enterprises and industries. As the processes of production and labour are increasingly socialized, production belongs not to the working people, but to the private owners or capitalists and their monopoly houses, who extract profit for their own interests and not in the interest of the society as a whole. In the race for more profit, the capitalists expand production, expand market, promote and innovate market mechanisms and increase the exploitation of workers. The basic contradiction is between the lines, wage labour and capital. The demand for products among the people is limited by value of labour power and permanent mass unemployment. The basic contradiction in the capitalist society is the cause of periodic economic crisis of over production, which at the imperialist stage of capitalism is deepened further. The social character of modern capitalist production is contradicted by State regulation. The socialization process of production punctuated by scientific and technological revolution is contradicted by discrepancy between opportunities opened up by the technological revolution and obstacles created by imperialism in the utilization of these opportunities. Capitalism breeds not only the basic contradiction between capital and wage-labour, but also creates objective and subjective conditions to resolve it. Most of the working class is concentrated in large enterprises and industrial centres—this condition facilitates their unification in the struggle against the bourgeois class. Capitalists try to make a balance between increasing misery of labour and workers' unification against capitalist order and for socialist order, based on public ownership of the means of production and appropriation by the working class of all the products of collective labour. Depending less on labour, the capitalists try to make a balance between increasing misery of labour and consequent labour unrest and development of capitalism through capital accumulation, greater technological rationality and mechanization, and overall the lessening of production cost. Less dependence on labour is directly proportional to the weakening of the working class. Not only that. Capitalists try to make some concessions and provide the working class some economic benefits, such as bonus, housing benefit, uniform etc.; few political rights, such as right to vote, right to press, right to form trade unions despite their (capitalists) non-participatory, patronized, alienated and opportunistic tendency towards the working majority; few socio-cultural rights, such as right to profess any religion though they have created tensions, competition and a gap between the higher-ups and lower-downs in the rank of the workers. But conditions of labour remain unchanged, are impoverished in nature. Labour is exploited and generated through the international market. Sharp competition for resources and capital tones down the capitalists in number. Big enterprises, firms or amalgamations or unions appropriating much of the production and marketing of a certain product and dominating the market in order to obtain monopoly super profit. The appearance of the monopolies is a logical result of the concentration and centralization of production and capital. The nature of the monopolies predetermines the extraction of monopoly super profit, which includes an excess of surplus value created at the monopolies enterprises, part of the value of labour extracted from the workers by paying for his labour at lower prices, part of the surplus value produced at non-monopoly enterprises but appropriated by the monopolies etc. Monopoly yields super profits (Lenin, *Collected Works*, Vol. 23 : 114). The drive for monopoly super profit leads to heightened antagonisms in the world capitalist economic system not only between the monopoly bourgeoisie and the working class, but also between non-monopoly bourgeoisie. A graphic representation may be sketched below (Figure 4):

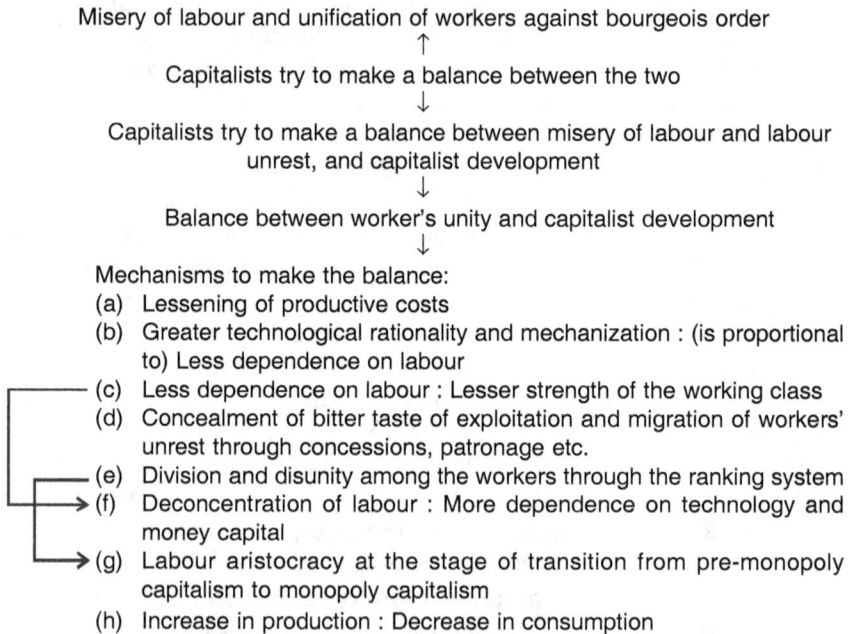

Misery of labour and unification of workers against bourgeois order
↑
Capitalists try to make a balance between the two
↓
Capitalists try to make a balance between misery of labour and labour unrest, and capitalist development
↓
Balance between worker's unity and capitalist development
↓
Mechanisms to make the balance:
(a)   Lessening of productive costs
(b)   Greater technological rationality and mechanization : (is proportional to) Less dependence on labour
(c)   Less dependence on labour : Lesser strength of the working class
(d)   Concealment of bitter taste of exploitation and migration of workers' unrest through concessions, patronage etc.
(e)   Division and disunity among the workers through the ranking system
(f)   Deconcentration of labour : More dependence on technology and money capital
(g)   Labour aristocracy at the stage of transition from pre-monopoly capitalism to monopoly capitalism
(h)   Increase in production : Decrease in consumption

Figure 4

The working class is suppressed and naturally it loses the buying and consumption capacity. Discrepancy between production and consumption begins with the movement of capitalist business from boom to slump, the stage of quicker returns from customer goods than that of investment goods, and the stage of lesser investment on investment goods than that of consumption goods. Capitalism tries to make a balance (pointed out earlier) and the capitalist State helps capitalism so that further decay would not create disharmony in a capitalist system. The ruling classes of capitalist countries use workers of a bourgeois tint to fracture the unity of the working class, corrupt its consciousness, and weaken its position. The formation of labour aristocracy is a feature of capitalism at its highest stage of development. Labour aristocracy is the principal social support of the bourgeoisie.

The relatively thin and usually highly skilled upper crust of the working class, which is bribed by the monopoly bourgeoisie with a share of super profits obtained through heightened exploitation of the working people. The bribery takes various forms—higher wages, improved living conditions, cozy jobs in State administration, war industry enterprises, reactionary trade unions, co-operatives and other organizations. Shares of capitalist companies are sold to them at lower rates etc. These working people of the upper category are the 'real agents of the bourgeoisie in the working class movement, the labor lieutenants of the capitalist class' (Lenin, *Collected Works*, Vol. 22, p. 194). It is at the stage of State-monopoly capitalism, where the State intervenes in the economic life on a large scale. The growing concentration and socialization of production and centralization of capital allow the monopolies to control the country's economy through the intermediary of the State. State-monopoly capitalism takes shape with its characteristic fusion of the major monopolies, finance capital and the bourgeois State machinery in order to extract high monopoly profits and to combat crisis phenomena. The State regulates capitalist economy in various ways: through State-owned property, State enterprise, mixed State and private operations, the programmed target-oriented method, regulation of capital investment, stimulation of consumer demand, subsidizing of research, financing of nature conservation measures etc. The public sector in the economy grows through nationalization of some branches of the economy either because of these industries becoming unprofitable, or under the pressure of the class struggle. The State intervenes in the economic and social life mainly in the interests of finance capital and at the expense of the working class. The crisis of capitalism grows deeper. The characteristic features of State-monopoly capitalism are chronic inflation, unemployment, and crises affecting the economy and other aspects of society. Leading to further concentration of production, State-monopoly capitalism aggravates the basic contradictions of capitalism—contradiction between the forces of production and relations of production and thus brings closer the end of the capitalist system—it is the complete material preparation for socialism and there is no intermediary rung between state-monopoly capitalism and socialism (Lenin, *Collected Works*, Vol. 25). Whatever may be the character of contradictions, Marx sees emancipation of the working class as the prime goal, when emancipation includes emancipation of humanity as a whole, and then communism or the establishment of communistic society is the final goal. 'It follows from the relation between alienated labour and private property, that the emancipation of society from private property, from servitude, takes the political form of the emancipation of the working class, not in the sense that only the latter's emancipation is involved, but because this emancipation includes the emancipation of humanity as a whole. For all human servitude is involved in the relation of the worker to production, and all types of servitude are only modifications or consequences of this relation.' (Bottomore and Rubel, 1961 : 184-85).

Why does Marx take into account the working class as the major agent of social change? To Marx, working classes are worst sufferer, alienated from the mode of production, from the fruits of their own production, from their own labour and from humanity and human society at large. Alienation in capitalist society is the alienation of the working class, which is the most potent force in changing society. Secondly, with an increasing scale the working class is being transformed into a majority with the process of concentration of capital, de-concentration and generation of labour through international market. The capitalists turn into a minority status in this process. Thirdly, the working class is the universal and radical force, able to change capitalist society drastically or able to make a total social transformation. This class force has no vested interest in capitalist society and can make or try to make a society universal in character in the interest of humanity at large. This role of working class derives from its objective place in the system of large-scale social production, whose development leads to the growth of the numbers, organization and solidarity of the working class and helps it to understand its own interests, which means that the working class is transformed from 'class-in-itself' to 'class-for-itself'*. Figure 5 shows —

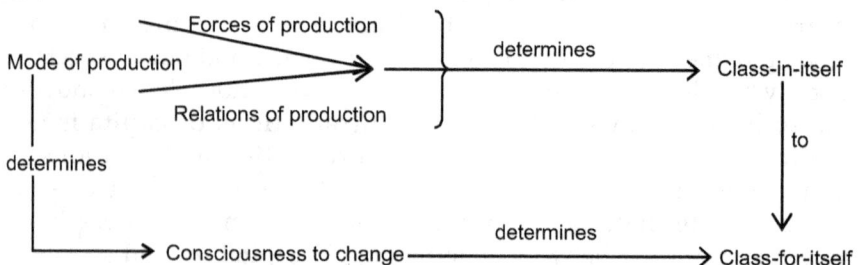

Figure 5

----

* Working and living conditions under capitalism engender in the working class such qualities as staunches, courage, organization, solidarity, endurance etc., *i.e.* the revolutionary qualities necessary for the successful liquidation of capitalism and for the building of a socialist society. Monopoly capital exerts increasing pressures on the classes and social

The working class has to be transformed from 'class-in-itself' to 'class-for-itself'. It is the consciousness of the working class about own class position in the relations of production, position of being exploited and alienated. Secondly, the capitalist system is totally responsible for that exploitation and alienation and for this the capitalist order is to be demolished and to be replaced by a new one. Thirdly, as an agent of social transformation, the working class must be conscious of its own responsibility of making and remaking of history, its own historical position and its own destiny, its own working interest of self-emancipation and emancipation of the impoverishment of labour. Thereby class solidarity comes into being. To Marxists, the understanding and active pursuit of the common interest of the whole class can often come into conflict with the particular interests of the individual workers or group of workers, *i.e.*, conflict between short-term and short-sighted interests of individual skilled workers and the long-term and broader common interest as a whole. For this reason particularly great importance is attached to class solidarity. Differentiation in wage structure and temptation of increasing affluence in industrialized societies has brought about weakening of class solidarity and class consciousness among the working classes. The working class must be aware and cautious about that. All these constitute working class consciousness of Marxist in nature and content, breaking through C. Wright Mill's 'labour metaphysic', Gramsci's 'common sense' and Rousseau's 'General Will'.

What is the role of ideology in the transformation of capitalist order? Marxists like Lenin and Lukacs regard ideology as necessary for transformation of capitalism to socialism unlike Bernstein, who considers that ideological struggle is not as necessary for transformation from capitalism to socialism as it is necessary for transformation from feudalism to capitalism. Ideological struggle of the working class against the bourgeois class interest, culture and ideology is necessary due to

---

groups that are carried over from former socio-economic formations, for example the peasantry, artisans and craftsmen etc. Many of these classes occupy positions close to the working class. The alliance of the working class with the non-proletarian strata of the working people is an imperative condition for the victory of the socialist revolution. The revolutionary political forces are formed on the basis of mass political experience. The party of the working class cultivates a socialist consciousness in the working class movement, educates, trains and organizes the masses and works out its strategy and tactics for the class struggle. The revolutionary party exercises political leadership of the revolutionary movement. In this process 'class-in-itself' is transformed into 'class-for-itself'.

few constraints towards reaching at the goal of proletarian liberation and labour emancipation: proletarian class interest is not easy to comprehend unlike the capitalist one, proletariats are more interested in concessions and reforms as the cost of revolution is greater than that of reform, capitalist order is survived through the strength of its own continuous ideological penetration, and working class may develop 'false consciousness' among themselves in the complex process that they would survive and satisfy themselves within the capitalist order. The process is not only complex but subtle too. Graphically, it is a process like input → output → feedback → input (Figure 6):

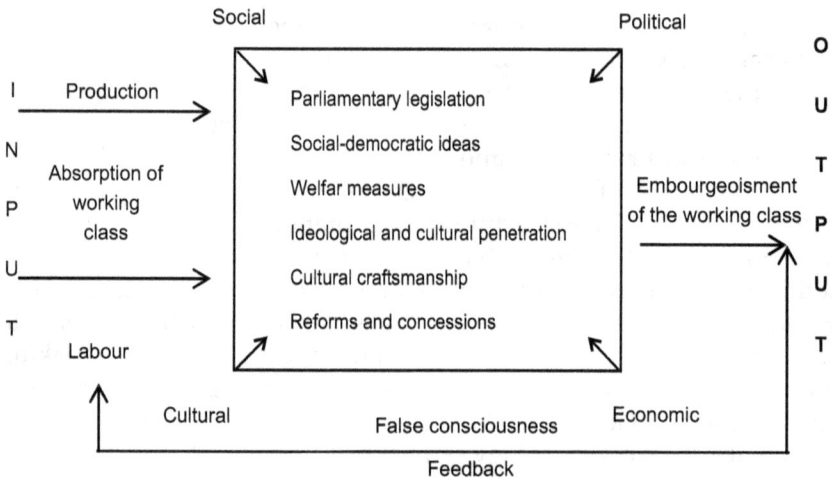

Figure 6

Hence, the working-class has to be organized along class political lines by means of vanguard party, where and when class-party interaction becomes collaborative and the party will act to break the resistance of landlords and capitalists, to rally all the working people around the proletariat, and to arm revolution. Depending on all these conditions of the level of development of the productive forces, national peculiarities, the general cultural level of the people, historical tradition, alignment of the class forces, the revolution may be peaceful or violent. The sharpness and intensity of class struggle depend on the strength of resistance offered by the reactionary bourgeoisie to the majority of the people, on the degree of violence bourgeoisie resorts to the proletariat. Marxists try to tone down violence, but if there is no way out to get rid of bourgeois violent onslaught in capturing power, then there is the need of violence.

REFERENCES

Almond, G. 1965. 'A Developmental Approach to Political Systems', *World Politics*, Vol. XVII, No. 2, January.

Blondel, J. (ed.). 1969. *Comparative Government* (London: Macmillan).

Bluhm, William. 1965. *The Theories of the Political System* (New Jersey: Prentice-Hall).

Bottomore, T.B. and M. Rubel. 1961. *Karl Marx* (London: Penguin Books).

Byrnes, Robert E. 1983. *After Brezhnev* (London: Frances Pinter).

Curtis, M. 1968. *Comparative Government and Politics* (New York: Harper and Row).

Dahl, R.A. 1963. *Modern Political Analysis* (Englewood Cliffs: Prentice-Hall).

Dahl, R.A. 1969. 'The Behavioural Approach in Political Science' in Gould and Thursby (eds.), *Contemporary Political Thought* (New York: Rinehart and Winston, Inc.).

Dahrendorf, Ralph. 1959. *Classes and Class Conflict in Industrial Society* (London: Routledge and Kegan Paul).

Deutsch, Karl. 1967. 'Nation and World' in Ithiel de Sola Pool (ed.), *Contemporary Political Science: Towards Empirical Theory* (New York: McGraw Hill).

Fromm, E. 1966. *Marx's Concept of Man* (New York: Frederick Ungar).

Hagan, Charles. 1958. 'The group in Political Science' in Ronald Young (ed.), *Approaches to the Study of Politics* (Northwestern University Press).

Lasswell, H. 1958. *The Political Writings of Harold Lasswell* (New York: Free Press).

Lenin, V.I. 1964-70. *Collected Works* (Moscow: Progress Publishers).

Marcuse, H. 1964. *One-Dimensional Man* (London: Routledge and Kegan Paul).

Marcuse, H. 1968. 'On the Affirmative Concept of Culture' in *Negations: Essays in Critical Theory* (Boston: Beacon).

Marcuse, Herbert. 1968. *Negations: Essays in Critical Theory* (Boston: Beacon).

Marx and Engels. 1976. *Selected Works* (Moscow: Progress Publishers).

Marx, Karl. 1976. 'Preface' and 'Introduction' to *A Contribution to the Critique of Political Economy* (Peking: Foreign Language Press).

Miliband, Ralph. 1977. *Marxism and Politics* (Oxford: Oxford University Press).

Miller, J.D.B. 1965. *The Nature of Politics* (London: Gerald Duckworth and Co.).

Myerson, M. and E.C. Banfield. 1955. *Politics, Planning and the Public Interest* (New York: Free Press).

Struik, K.J. 1964. *The Economic and Philosophical Manuscript of 1844* (New York: International Publishers).

Williams, Reymond. 1982. *Culture* (London: Fontana).

2

Marxism, Essential Parts and Sources of Marxism

Marxism is not a lifeless dogma, not a completed, ready-made and immutable doctrine, but a living guide to action. It is the science of socialism, stands in a much more original and direct relationship than that of the whole of sociology of Comte and Spencer. Marx treats bourgeois society as historical and finds in it the inherent tendencies leading to its revolutionary overthrough, *i.e.,* the objective tendency in the economic basis of the bourgeois society and subjective tendency in the social and economic division of classes, arising from the economic base and not from politics, law and ethics etc. The bourgeois society is the assumed civil society, where there is class cleavage and the bourgeois class controls other classes economically, politically and culturally. Marx recognizes the class war of the oppressed and exploited wage labourers to be war for suppression of the present structure of society by a new one, which is a highly developed form of society. To Marx, proletarian struggle is the practical instrument to bring about the realization of the proletarian society. To Marx, at a certain stage of development, the material forces of production come into conflict with the existing relations of production. From forms of development of the forces of production, these relations turn into their fetter, then comes the period of social revolution and with changes in the economic foundation the entirely superstructure more or less is rapidly transformed. Forces of production make revolution inevitable—this is true at every stage of development and in all revolutions from primitive communism to final communal State of society following the Marxist politics from thesis to synthesis. Every synthesis is a thesis until and unless the final State of perfect society is reached. Graphically, the process is spiral (Figure 7).

Therefore, every synthesis is thesis, which contains conflict between its parts, *i.e.* the anti-thesis. Applying the principle, Marx says about the transformation of previously independent forms of trading capital into money capital. All capitalist production remains essentially a production for sale. Production is sold as a commodity and each form of capital enters into the market—the commodity market, the labour market or the money market. In *Capital* Marx sees that industrial capital gives to production its capitalist character, which includes class antagonisms between capitalists and labourers to the extent that it assumes control over social production, the social organization of labour and techniques of production are revolutionized and with them the economic and historical type of society. Marx defines capitalism in *Capital* in terms of use of wage labour and private ownership of the means of production and he implies in *Critique of the Gotha Programme* that if wage labour continues even in State-owned means of production, then it is not socialism, but State capitalism. Thus while discussing capitalism, Marx proposes to treat history; the internal structure of bourgeois society consisting of social classes, capital, landed property, wage labour, relations between the classes based on capital, landed property and wage labour, circulation and credit; and the world market and crises. In *Communist Manifesto* Marx not only criticizes the bourgeois society, but also repudiates the bourgeois onslaught that communists want to abolish private property, freedom, individuality and culture. He points out:

1. Abolition of private property is not the distinctive feature of communism.
2. All property relations are subject to historical change consequent upon the change in the historical conditions.
3. French revolution is a bourgeois revolution on the ground that it abolishes feudal property in favour of the bourgeoisie.
4. Abolition of bourgeois property is the distinctive feature of communism, not the property in general.
5. Modern bourgeois private property is the final and most complete expression of production and appropriation of products, which is based on class antagonism.
6. It is the exploitation of labour of many by few.
7. Abolition of private property is not the transformation of personal property into social property.
8. Social character of production undergoes a change and it loses its class character.
9. When labour can no more be transformed into capital, money, rent or into a social power capable of being monopolized, the

bourgeoisie says that freedom and individuality are being destroyed. This individuality must be destroyed.

10. There can no longer be any wage-labour when there is no longer any capital.

11. To the bourgeoisie the disappearance of class property is equal to the disappearance of production itself and disappearance of class culture is equal to the disappearance of all cultures.

12. There appears a sequential paradigm here—abolition of class property → abolition of class individuality → abolition of class freedom → abolition of class power → abolition of class culture → abolition of class ideology.

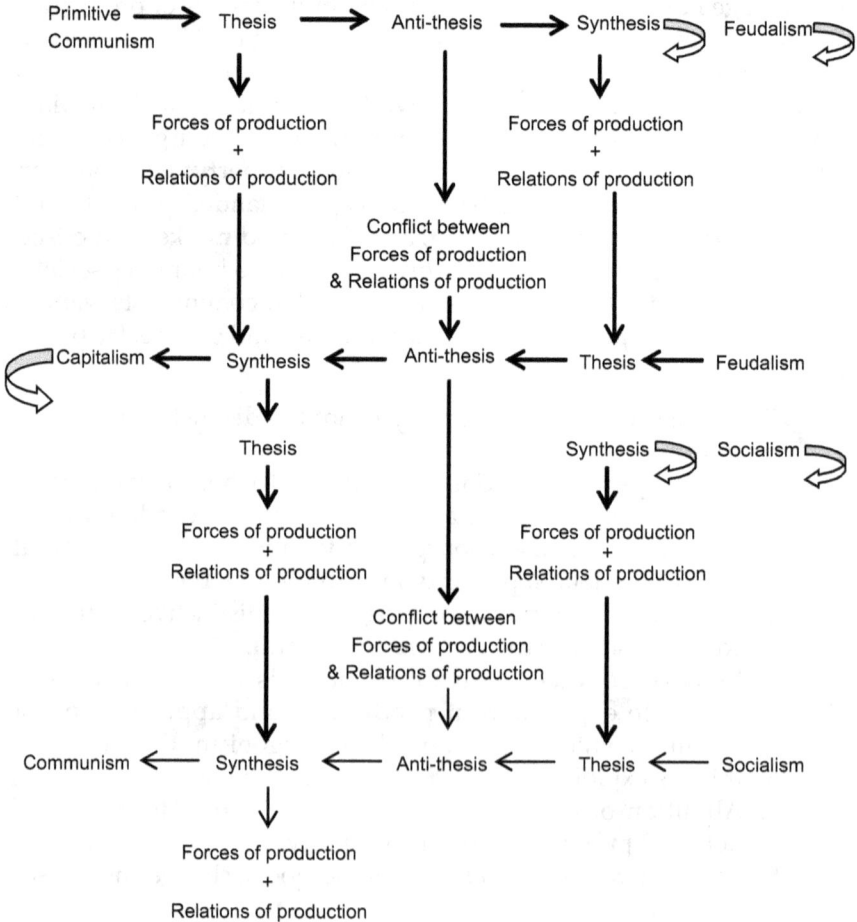

Figure 7

13. Communist revolution is the most radical rupture with bourgeois property relations and therefore its development involves the most radical rupture with traditional ideas. Ruling ideas of age have ever been only the ideas of the ruling class.
14. Communist society is a classless society, in which the free development of each is the condition for the free development of all.

Besides, Marx also highlights a few positive contributions of capitalist development, for instance, better economic sweep through revolutionizing the means of production and co-operative and social mode of production, internationalization of labour and capital*, and urbanization. However, he rejects capitalism for exploitation of labour, inequality and consumerism leading to commodity fetishism. This is the materialization of production relations between people under the conditions of commodity production, which is based on private ownership of the means of production. Commodity fetishism has both objective and subjective aspects. The social links between private commodity producers are manifested on the market in the process of exchange. This type of social relations is objectively conditioned by commodity production based on private ownership. The labour of each commodity producer constitutes part of aggregate social labour. Subjectively, commodity producers accept such materialization of the relations of production. The products of man's labour are presented as independent things, endowed with a life of their own and entering into definite relations with people and one another. Money and capital are the highest products of the development of commodity exchange. So, commodity fetishism is embodied most fully in money and capital. Commodity fetishism is eliminated when the private ownership of the

---

* Internationalization of capital and labour—in recent decades, against the background of the overall internationalization of economic life, there is an increase in foreign investment within the group of developed capitalist countries. All foreign investments are made by industrial and banking monopolies, which use long-term capital investments to capture key positions in various sectors of the economy. With the internationalization of economic life inherent in modern imperialism, the centralization of capital has occupied an important place in the expansion of international industrial and bank monopolies. The formation of monopolies is accompanied by increased international expansion of the highly developed capitalist countries. 'The surplus of capital', cannot be applied or yield adequate profit at home, is exported to backward countries where 'the price of land is relatively low, wages are low, raw materials are cheap.' (Lenin, *Collected Works*, Vol. 22 : 241).

means of production is eliminated and when social ownership of the means of production is established. Marx's analysis of capitalism is followed by few predictions—there would be concentration of capital and de-concentration of labour with the process of monopoly capital and the process of urbanization, wages for the workers would remain at the subsistence level, the rate of profit would fall with the process of over-production, collapse of capitalism would be due to internal contradictions of capitalism, and proletarian revolution would necessarily be in industrially advanced countries (Singer, 1980). The main contradiction of the capitalist social system is between the social character of production and private capitalist form of appropriation, which is revealed in the anarchy of production and lagging in society's effective demand. The crises and periods of economic stagnation would impoverish small producers, which would increase the dependence of hired labour on capital and the deterioration of the economic and social position of the workers. First, over-production would bring about economic crises, when productive forces are destroyed on a mass scale, second, unemployment sharply increases, third, people are deprived of productive labour, and fourth, machinery becomes idle and is even destroyed. With the sharpening of contradictions within it, capitalism would collapse like a pricked balloon.

But, present day capitalist society is more stabilized, more cautious about the possible danger of decay. Marx's capitalism is not twentieth century capitalism, where extensive social security measures and labour welfare laws have improved the conditions of the workers. They are now proprietors (Dahl, 1986 and Djilas, 1990). But, these are the subtle mechanisms to contain the bitter taste of exploitation following Parsons's methods of pattern maintenance, tension management, goal attainment, adaptation and integration. Marx's materialist conception of history should be left aside on the ground that Marx never looks forward the distinction between tradition and modernity in nationalism, which is the embodiment of primordial entities and nation-State, which is an expression of power over time and space and also the basic features of advanced capitalist democracy. His analysis of capitalism as decaying, unequal and exploitative is true, but the attainment of true democracy and full communism in replacing the old one is impractical and unaccommodative in accordance with the present needs of the world capitalist system, which is becoming increasingly differentiated, stratified and functionally specialized, and overall globalized. Against the Marxist paradigm of classless Stateless society, Weber puts forward that society is stratified, there is love for power and status insecurity syndrome among human, so there would be power, politics, class, status and stratification everywhere. Classless society is an impossibility (Giddens, 1995; Berlin, 1939 and Max Weber, 1958). To Weber, where there is interest, there is class; where there is class, there is status; where there is status, there is stratification; where there is interest, there is conflict of interests; where there is conflict of interests, there is politics; and where there is politics, there is domination. There is politics everywhere. Unlike Marx, Max Weber finds that class is determined by market relations. Weber speaks of class when a number of people have in common a specific causal component of their life chances, when this specific component is represented exclusively by economic interests in the possession of goods and opportunities for income, which is represented under the conditions of commodity or labour markets. Unlike the economic one, Weber justifies the importance of concepts and values for they play an important role in society. Weber also criticizes Marx for imprecise economic categories. But, Marx's disciples point out the 'economic' term in four distinct senses in defense of (1) desire for wealth or money, or for social status and power, which can be significantly possible by means of wealth or money; (2) presence or absence of land and raw materials necessary for production; (3) techniques, forces and powers of production including tools and machineries, skill and knowhow; (4) mode of production or the social relations of production—the institutional rules and processes that govern the production and distribution of wealth. However, Weber criticizes Marx for not providing due importance to non-economic factors, such as ideas, motives and rationality, and ethics and values and also for treating technology as economic base of the society. Again, Pareto maintains that economic rationality will be indispensable and for that reason, many of the characteristics of the capitalist economy must continue even after socialist revolution. He rejects Marx's conception of labour value as outmoded and regards the theory of economic equilibrium in terms of individual choice and theory of distribution of income according to mathematical laws. He justifies private ownership and competition on the basis of economic rationality and efficiency. Both Pareto and Weber accept the Marxist conceptions that there is a privileged class in capitalist society which takes over greater portion of common wealth, capitalist regime will evolve in the direction of socialism; but both reject the theory of surplus value and exploitation, and socialist economy differs fundamentally from capitalist economy with regard to organization of production and distribution of income. Likewise, C.B. Macpherson in his *Theory of Possessive Individualism* regards the presence of net transfer of power in liberal market society, where there is the accumulation of the material means in the hands of a set of people, which is the result of two factors: society's decision to set up a right of unlimited individual appropriation and natural inequality of individual capacities. Like that of Max Weber, he is also doubtful about the coming of a classless society. But, he considers the goodness of a socialist society. When Max Weber justifies capitalism and capitalist democracy on the basis of maximization of power, Macpherson tries to reconstruct the claims of maximization of individual powers—extractive and developmental power. Pareto says that competition and private ownership are economic institutions favourable to the increase of wealth, and the growth of bureaucracy and spread of State socialism would in all probability bring on a decline of the whole economy. Weber, on the other hand, puts the emphasis on rational organization and bureaucracy, which he believes that far from being weakened, would be strengthened in the event of a transition to socialism. But, both are critical to Marxist ideas. Max Weber's study of sociology of religion is an empirical refutation of historical materialism. Pareto regards that logical and rational actions of men are determined by pursuit of power. Residues actually motivate men. Classes are relatively constant. History does not move towards universal reconciliation—history moves in the cycle of mutual dependence. Further, J.A. Schumpeter's study of democratic theory or economic theory of democracy, is different from the Marxist economic analysis of democracy, but bears a corollary with Marx in discussing the historical relation between capitalism and democracy. He says that democracy is the rule of the politician, but does not prescribe dissolution of class politics. He treats political parties as analogous to business concerns, who are engaged in a competitive struggle for power and profit. There is competition for political leadership. While criticizing Marx for neglecting the proper role of entrepreneurship in capitalist democracy, Schumpeter identifies the continuous existence of profit with innovation and entrepreneurship, and dismisses the value theory of Marx. Durkheim's ideas are in conscious opposition to Marxist theory of society while studying socialism and abnormal forms of division of labour. He finds that social life is not explained by the notion of those who participate in it by the Marxists, but by more profound causes not perceived by consciousness, in other words, by economic factors and class struggle, is secondary phenomenon arising from the lack of regulation of industrial society and division of labour. C. Wright Mills (1952) also differentiates political from economic and prefers the term 'power elite' instead of ruling class. Another criticism is also made by both Sorel and Hilferding. Sorel (1908) sketches Marxism as deterministic science and basic tenets of Marxism as myths or images, which influence the working class in their struggle against capitalism, such as strike action. He follows the polices and practices of political reformism and democracy, supports working class morality, trade union and co-operative movement by the working class. Hilferding in his conception of 'organized capitalism' criticizes Marx's approach to capitalist society, the contradictions within the society and the final solution to communism through socialist revolution on the grounds that the basic characteristics of capitalism have been changed and capitalism as a socio-economic change has been stabilized with some developments within. These are: dominance of large banks and corporations, State regulation through economic planning, necessary changes in the relation between the working class and the State in an organized and a planned manner. To him, twentieth century capitalism is an era of organized capital and 'realistic pacifism'. However, whatever may be the stages of capitalist development the law of capitalist accumulation remains as theorized by Marx (Baran and Sweezy, 1966 and Mandel, 1976). However, there is a slight difference between them over the scheme of periodization of capitalism. Graphically, see Figure 8.

	Cause	Effect
Marx :	Changes in the relations and forces of production due to contradiction in the mode of production.	Transition from competitive capitalism characterized by law of capitalist accumulation.
Baran and Sweezy :	Changes in the laws of accumulation, changes in the market structure and market relations.	Transition from competitive capitalism to monopoly capitalism, and from monopoly capitalism to State monopoly capitalism characterized by capitalist law of accumulation due to basic contradictions of capitalism.
Mandel :	Laws of capitalist accumulation, contradictions of accumulation and structural relations	Transition from competitive capitalism to monopoly capitalism, then to State monopoly capitalism, and finally to late capitalism, which is characterized by division of labour, financing and State activity as an integrated whole.

Figure 8

Whatever may be the criticisms raised against Marxism, for example the criticisms as mentioned above, as 'an interpretation of past history' and as an independent exploratory method of analysis, which is dead now (Kolakowski, 1978), it has produced an explanatory power to analyze some unresolved problems of the society, such as conflict, change and conflict again, exploitation and accumulation etc. and generated a body of rational norms and understanding for a socialist society, which as a whole, or as an integrated whole, throws serious challenges to modern modes of thought. Marxism has digested the advances of social thought before it, blended philosophy and political economy, blended social ideals and historical process, and kept away all utopian ideas. It studies social development with reference to economic substantiation, philosophic conceptualization, historical premises and political understanding. It is a science of society and history. 'The making of Marxism is a historical process which has a beginning and an end, while the development of Marxism, which naturally starts from the time of its origination, has no end.' (Oizerman, 1981 : 12). Engels in his *Socialism: Utopian and Scientific* says: 'These two discoveries, the materialistic conception of history and the revelation of the secret of capitalist production through surplus value, we owe to Marx. With these discoveries socialism becomes a science.' (Engels, 1984 : 180). The material conception of history starts from means of production for human life to production and next to exchange of products is the basis of social structure, which appears in history in the manner like distribution of wealth and division of class depending on production— what is produced, how it is produced, and how the products are exchanged. The final causes of social and political changes can be traced in the changes in mode of production and exchange. The contradiction between socialized production and capitalistic appropriation is manifested as the antagonism between proletariat and bourgeoisie. The proletariat seizes the public power and by means of this, transforms the socialized means of production. The socialized production upon a predetermined plan becomes possible. The development of production makes the existence of different classes of society—anarchy of production, and as anarchy vanishes, the political authority of the State dies out, and man becomes the master of his own. Universal emancipation is the historical mission of the proletariat and becomes the historical necessity. For Marx, there is no contradiction between the historicity of knowledge and the reality of their objects; rather they are two aspects of the unity of known objects. Marxism uses the concept of dialectic to register the historicity of its subject matter and that of materialism to indicate the scientificity of its approach. Graphically, it is, dialectic → historicity of social and material objects → scientificity. 'To thoroughly comprehend historical conditions and thus the very nature of this act, to impart to the now oppressed proletarian class a full knowledge of the conditions and of the meaning of momentous act it is called upon to accomplish, this is the task of the theoretical expression of the proletarian movement, scientific socialism.' (Ibid, 1984 : 198). How Marxist approach becomes scientific? Graphically, the process can be shown as follows:

> Human values and motivations appropriate to human needs → certain socio-economic conditions necessary for the fulfilment of these needs → action taken for the production of the appropriate socio-economic conditions as man makes their own history → man as an actor is conscious about historical process and his position in history → knowledge and consciousness about social and historical facts → careful and scientific study of socio-historical facts.

Critics find in Marxism historicity, economism and an image of utopianism, when Marx says or predicts about the possibility of classless Stateless society. However, Marx's reconciliation between objectivity and personal values does not preclude his approach towards scienticism. In fact, 'the contribution Marx has made in his role of what might be termed philosopher-utopian, we need also to acknowledge the indelible mark which he has left as a social scientist—especially, perhaps, an inspirer of policy-science approach: science in the service of policy formulation and action.' (Arora, 1967 : 313-14). Social scientists very often criticize Marx's methodology and suggest his over emphasis on the role and significance of economic factors in socio-historical change. They very often stress on the impact of ideas and word-symbols, which have played more important role in the determination of social change than Marx had to admit. 'Marx, as a man, was both scientist and prophet, sociologist and revolutionary. If he had been asked whether these two attitudes are separable, I personally think he would have answered that in the abstract they are. In my opinion, he was too scientifically oriented to admit that his interpretation of capitalism was bound up with a moral decision.' (Aron, 1965 : 154).

The starting point of Marx's spiritual evolution is Hegel's philosophy, its left orientation supporting most consistently revolutionary democratic ideas both in theory and practice. In spite of his idealism, Marx in his doctoral work on *Difference between the Democritean and Epicurean Philosophy of Nature* (1841) he draws from Hegel's philosophy very radical and atheistic conclusions. Marx understands and investigation clashes head-on with Hegelian philosophy and understanding because of its conciliatory and political conclusions and of the discrepancy between theoretical principles and actual social relations. The philosophy of Feuerbach and his own knowledge of economic development bring about within his ideas a materialist conception of history taking a final revolutionary shape in his class stand and his passage from revolutionary democracy to proletarian communism. He makes it clear or relies on the matter that economic relations play a decisive role in the formation and development of society and State. He criticizes Utopian Socialism of Proudhon, Cabet and others and arrives at the theoretical substantiation of communism and turns it into science. Marxism becomes the scientifically based system of philosophical, economic and socio-political views, a doctrine of cognition and transformation of the world in the hands of both Marx and Engels. Marx's new stand finds expression in *Contribution to the Critique of Hegel's Philosophy of Law* and *On the Jewish Question*. Marxism is consistent and scientifically integrated doctrine, is made up of three elements—philosophy of dialectical and historical materialism, political economy and scientific communism. The determining role of the production in social development allows Marx to make important studies on wage labour and capital, and capitalist development characterized by capitalist exploitation and accumulation. The results of scientific studies and the principles of the theory developed are generalized in the works like *Economic and Philosophical Manuscripts* (1844), *The Holy Family* (1845), *The German Ideology* (1845-46), *Theses on Feuerbach* (1845), *The Poverty of Philosophy* (1847) and *The Communist Manifesto* (1848) and *Wage, Labour and Capital* (1849). Between 1850 and 1857, Marx made a historico-critical analysis of bourgeois political economy influenced by the works of William Petty, Adam Smith and David Ricardo. Marx's manuscript of 1857-58, *Outlines of a Critique of Political Economy* makes a revolution in political economy. In *A Contribution to the Critique of Political Economy* (1859) Marx studies the theory of value and the theory of money. The second issue of this work (1961-63) Marx makes his contribution in the field of surplus value and its transformed forms: profit, average profit and ground rent, productive labour, reproduction and economic crises. The experiences of bourgeois revolutions of 1848-49 in Europe was of great importance for the development of theory or theories by Marx—theory of socialist revolution and class struggle, theory of dictatorship of the proletariat, proletarian tactics in bourgeois revolution and worker-peasant alliance, for example his works like *The Class Struggles in France* (1848-50), and *The Eighteenth Brumaire of Louis Bonaparte* (1852).

Examining the experiences of Paris Commune in *The Civil War in France* (1871) Marx discovers the State form of dictatorship of the proletariat and analyzes the measures adopted by the proletarian State. He further develops the theory of scientific communism in *Critique of the Gotha Programme* (1875). Marxism is an integral theory—an integration of three forms of theory—theory of philosophical understanding of society, theory of political economy and the theory of scientific communism, where Marx formulates key laws of communist economy and communist organization of labour: the law of time saving, law of free time under communism, all round development of the individuals etc. In all of his works, Marx comprehensively discovers the theory of knowledge, dialectical understanding of society and applies these principles to the materialist understanding of history and society. To Lenin, the genius of Marxism lies in the fact that he furnishes answers to questions which have already engrossed the minds of humanity and his teaching arises as a continuation of the teachings of philosophers, political economists and socialists. The Marxist doctrine is omnipotent, true, complete, harmonious and integral and irreconcilable with any form of superstition, reaction, bourgeois opposition, and defense of bourgeois order and oppression (Lenin, 1943, *Collected Works*, Vol. XI). It is the legitimate successor of 19th century humanism in the shape of German philosophy, English political economy and French socialism (Ibid, 1943).

Then, what is about humanism? To the Marxists, socialist humanism is genuine, based on the necessity for struggle by the working class and other working people, and creates conditions essential for the triumph of man's humanistic ideals. Hyppolite (1969) claims Marx as Hegelian and tries to find elements of idealism in Marxism. He discusses alienation and especially the relationship between alienation and objectification both in Hegel and Marx. Marx describes his position as naturalist humanist, *i.e.* a unity of naturalism and humanism. Humanism is the view that man as a being of praxis changes nature and creates him. Marx envisions few intrinsic goods of communist social individuality, such as political community, development of human productive powers, friendship and artistic achievement etc. Communism as fully developed naturalism equals itself with humanism as fully developed humanism equals itself with naturalism. It is a genuine resolution of conflicts between man and nature, and man and man. It is also the resolution of conflicts between existence and essence, between objectification and self-confirmation, between freedom and necessity, and between individual and the species (Marx, 1944). To him, private property is the material sensuous expression of estranged human life.

The realization of man is the sensuous revelation of production and consumption, where religion, family, State, morality, art and science are particular modes of production. Man is not lost in his object only when the object becomes for him a human object or objective man. This becomes possible when the object becomes social for him, society becomes being for him. All objects become for him the objectification of himself, which confirm and realize his individuality. That is, man himself becomes the object. That is, man is affirmed in the objective world. Only through the objectively unfolded richness of man's essential being, the richness of subjective human sensibility is either cultivated or brought into being. Not only the five senses, but also the mental make-up—the practical senses, in a word, human senses—the humanness of the senses, which comes to be by virtue of its object, by virtue of humanized nature. In this way the objectification of human essence both in its theoretical and practical aspects is required to make man's sense human, as well as to create the human sense corresponding to the entire wealth of human and natural substance. In this connection, Roemer (1985) analyzes 'rational choice' of Marxism on raising question like where is there room for social formation of the individual. To answer, he considers the materialist description of the historical processes of two categories of interests'—forces and relations of production representing R_t at time t and individuals and their preferences representing P_t at time t. At time t there is constellation $\{R_t, P_t\}$ giving rise to production, distribution, exchange and invention and so on. This is called the solution process, comes into existence at the next time period, (t+1). Thus the process is represented as $\{R_t, P_t\} \rightarrow \{R_t + 1, P_t + 1\}$. The second important process is social formation process, *i.e.*, social formation of preferences members of a new generation are born each time period and their preferences are formed by the State of the world, R_t. The process can be represented as $\{P_t, R_t\} \rightarrow \{P_t+1, R_t+1\}$. 'Thus individuals are formed by society, and these individuals react rationally to their environments to produce tomorrow's environment, which in turn produces individuals who think somewhat differently from before, and react in their environment to bring about yet a new equilibrium.' (Roemer, 1985: 1440). Marxism makes two great contributions—a positive theory of property relations, technical change and class struggle and a positive and normative theory of alienation and exploitation. Starting from negative consequences of division of society into rich and poor, Marx points out to an ethical resolution of conflict, *i.e.*, the abolition of exploitation and the uniting of mental and manual labour. Lenin in his *State and Revolution* adopts a realistic interpretation of Marx's critique of earlier conception of equality and regards Marx's theory of the phases of communism in *Critique of the Gotha Programme* as a redefined conception of justice. The first phase of communism does not provide justice and equality—differences in wealth persist. Marx shows the cause of development of communist society, which is compelled to abolish at first only the 'injustice' of the means of production seized by individuals and which is unable at once to eliminate the other injustice which consists in the distribution of consumer goods according to the amount of labour performed and not according to the needs (Lenin, 1943, *Collected Works*, Vol. 25). Marx's arguments on exploitation and equality like his conceptions of freedom, friendship, individuality and political community are components of ethical picture, is contender for moral truth, and these components play important political role in the conflicts over the development of working class movement and maintenance of socialism. Both Marx and Engels overstress the importance of scientific theory at the expense of moral argument (Gilbert, 1981 and Gilbert, 1982). The development of the working class movement and the maintenance of socialism is the humanist task for the proletariat, to Marx. In his *Holy Family* Marx says that the propertied class and the class of the proletariat present the same human self-alienation while the former finds in this self-alienation its confirmation of power, a semblance of human existence and the latter finds in it its own powerlessness and reality of an inhuman existence. Therefore, the proletariat has a humanist role to play, necessarily driven by contradiction between its human nature and inhuman conditions of life. It cannot abolish conditions of its own life without abolishing conditions of the life of society today. Therefore, change is the natural necessity and motivations to change are the essential human property. Marx and Engels's works can be treated both as naturalist and materialist. They regard human emancipation as natural, the naturalistic implications of Darwinism in the evolutionary debate. The materialist view of history is unequivocally naturalistic—men inevitably enter into definite social relations which are indispensable and independent of their will. Labour is not the source of all wealth. Nature is as much the source of use values as labour, which is the manifestation of a force of nature, human labour power (Marx and Engels, 1875).

In *Capital* Marx puts man-nature symbiotic relationship and nature-imposed conditions of human existence. Labour process is a human action, and in *Economic and Philosophical Manuscripts* he again tries to make a connective links between man and nature, when he says that man lives on nature and nature is man's inorganic body and man is a part of nature, and man produces their means of subsistence, depends first of all on the nature. In *Socialism : Utopian and Scientific* Engels remarks that the conditions of man or of life environment of man administer and rule man, who becomes the master of his own natural environment, lord of his own nature. Therefore, Benton considers Marx's abstract concept of labour process is a transhistorical condition of human survival. He underrepresents the significance of non-manipulatable natural conditions of labour-processes and over represents the role of human intentional transformative power *vis-à-vis* nature. Consequently, Marx is prevented from adequately theorizing the necessary dependence of all forms of economic life on the naturally given preconditions. Rather, dependence of politically important form and its related striking features on specifically capitalist accumulation, Marx takes into account, where the elementary factors of labour process are work itself, subjects of work and instruments for work (Benton, n.d. : 65-65). Where Marx and Engels express nuanced judgements on Darwinism, their theoretical interpreters rely on it as the theory linking conceptions of humanity and society to the methods and assumptions of science. Marx refers to Darwinism as the basis in natural history, where the basic law of human history is analogous to Darwin's law of organic evolution like that of Haeckel's 'adaptation and heredity', where the individual development of an organism, *i.e.*, autogeny is analogous to the development of a particular form in the course of evolution, *i.e.*, phylogeny. To Engels, Darwin's theory of evolution is the practical proof of Hegel's account of inner connection between necessity and change. To him, Darwin's mistake in lumping together in natural selection, and the survival of the fittest, the two separate things—firstly, selection by the pressure of overpopulation, where the strongest survives in the first place, but can also be the weakest in many respects and secondly, selection by greater capacity of adaptation to altered circumstances, when this adaptation as a whole means progress as well as regress. In other words, each advance in organic evolution (progress thy name is) is at the same time regression, fixing one-sided evolution and excluding the possibility of evolution in many other directions—this is the basic law, the unity of opposites. The struggle for life is struggle for existence or survival of the fittest. 'The whole Darwinian theory of the struggle for existence is simply the transference from society to organic nature of Hobbes' theory of *bellum ominum contra omnes* (struggle of all against all) and of the bourgeois economic theory of competition, as well as the Malthusian theory of population ..., it is very easy to transfer these theories back again from natural history to the history of society, ... these assertions have been proved as eternal natural laws of society.' (Engels, 1982 : 207-8).

Malthus in his *An Essay on the Principle of Population* formulates an extra-historical law of population, according to which the population increases in geometrical progression, while the means of subsistence grow only in arithmetical progression—hence, there is contradiction in social development, which can be or may be overcome by restricting marriages, childbirth and regulating it through hunger, epidemics, and wars etc. The ideas of Malthus have been further developed by neo-Malthusianism by spreading the theory of optimum population. According to this theory, every social mode of production has its own specific law of population, there are no eternal and natural social laws, relative surplus population or unemployment in capitalist society is not the consequence of the general law of capitalistic accumulation, growth of population is analogous to further ecological crisis and further exacerbation of capitalist contradictions, and poverty is natural, especially in less developed countries. Population growth is the prime factor—this is the Malthusian trap.

Marx and Engels regard the recognition, transformation and application of natural laws into social laws—'When Hegel makes the transition from life to cognition by means of propagation (reproduction), there is to be found in this the germ of the theory of evolution, that, organic life once given, it must evolve by the development of the generations to a genus of thinking beings.... What Hegel calls reciprocal action is the organic body, which, therefore, also forms the transition to consciousness, *i.e.,* from necessity to freedom, to the idea.' (Engels, 1982: 309). There is an element of naturalism in Marxist thought and ideas together with an idea of humanism associated with a spiritual element of motivation to change environment or nature. This motivation to change is also nature gifted or nature given, therefore; there is an element of naturalism in humanism, consisting of values and motivations.

Marx in his *Economic and Philosophical Manuscripts (1844)* says that the production costs of a commodity consist of only two sides: the natural objective side like land and human subjective side like labour and the spiritual element of invention and of thought along side the physical element of labour. Then, we have two elements of production in operation—man, the human element and nature, the non-human element. Besides the economic laws of motion of modern society, Marx puts forward few elements of humanism, few elements of naturalism, for example rationalism and romanticism (reason and violent emotion) like that of Rousseau, natural human motivations and criticism of the civil society and transformation of the society. Colletti (1978) finds, '... revolutionary political theory, as it has developed since Rousseau, is already foreshadowed and contained in *The Social Contract*; ... that so far as political theory in the strict sense is concerned, Marx and Lenin had added nothing to Rousseau, except for the analysis of the 'economic bases' for the withering away of the State.' (Colletti, 1978 : 158). Besides, Marx develops dialectical method of knowing and doing, and the materialist interpretation of history. Armed with necessary knowledge and the requisite organization workers can destroy the ruinous effects of the natural laws of capitalist production and replace them with the spontaneous action of the laws of social economy of free and associated labour. They can change the historical laws of their own behaviour through their relations with man and nature (Marx, 1982).

There is moral realism in Marx's analysis of humanism. He is not pragmatist or instrumentalist, but realist, humanist and naturalist (Kolakowski, 1968; Gilbert, 1984; Shaw, 1981). Powers are attributed to natural agents in material relations with natural agents. Human beings are endowed with natural powers and their essence is revealed in the ensemble of social relations. In history we find a dialect of the powers of the forces and the relations of production. In political economy we find labour-power, which identifies and causally explains the nature of production under the social relations of capitalism.

Therefore, Marxism is an integrated whole, consisting of naturalism, humanism, materialism, economism and historicism (isms associated with nature, human beings, material world, economy and history). Marxism is dynamic both in content and essence over time and space. The cyclic process can be presented as such or the dynamic character of Marxism graphically can be formulated below:

Marxism = (Naturalism + Humanism + Materialism + Historicism) Economism at particular time and space.

or, Marxism (M)

at particular

time (t) and space (s) = $(N + H + M_1 + H_1)$ E at particular time and space, where time can be presented as 't' and space as 's'.

$$M_{t,s} = \{(N_{t,s}) + (H_{t,s}) + (M_{1t,s}) + (H_{1t,s}) (E_{t,s})\}$$

$$M_{t+1,s+1} = \{(N_{t+1,s+1}) + (H_{t+1,s+1}) + (M_{1t+1,s+1}) + (H_{1t+1,s+1}) (E_{t+1,s+1})\}$$

$$M_{t+2,s+2} = \{(N_{t+2,s+2}) + (H_{t+2,s+2}) + (M_{1t+2,s+2}) + (H_{1t+2,s+2}) (E_{t+2,s+2})\}$$

$$M_{t+...n,s+...n} = \{(N_{t+...n,s+...n}) + (H_{t+...n,s+...n}) + (M_{1t+...n,s+...n}) + (H_{1t+...n,s+...n}) \times (E_{t+...n,s+...n})\}$$

Marxism is a dynamic theory, and not a static dogma, consisting of naturalism and humanism, materialism and historicism, multiplied by economism. Marx can be treated both as philosopher and sociologist, as political theorist and economist, where none can be treated in isolation. Marxist approach to politics is an interpretative framework, where philosophy, sociology and political economy each is treated as organic part, without which the study of Marxism becomes an impossibility. The whole structure of Marxism or Marxist theory is dialectical, which cannot be understood without the dialectical, self-contradictory and interrelated nature of its parts from naturalism to economism: man is both human and natural at the same time, *i.e.,* humanly natural and naturally human at the same time, human progress is both material and historical at the same time, *i.e.,* materially historical and historically material at the same time, and human progress and development each is both political and economic at the same time, *i.e.,* politically economic and economically political at the same time. Marxism is both policy-science and human science, where 'human' is the basic category when 'transcendence of labour's self-alienation' provides the essential link with the totality of Marx's work. From this standpoint, I do not agree with Robert Tucker's formulation that Marx is neurotic who after experiencing the inner drama of his own proud and ambitious personality, darkly in nature and expressing the same in his original psychological system—Marx himself succumbs to total self-deception and mythically projects his inner drama on the outside world, misleading the people into believing that alienation is not an entirely individual matter but primarily social problem with possible social solutions to it (Tucker, 1961). Tucker equates original psychological system of Marx with original Marxism of self-alienation, projection of inner drama on the outside world with projection of self-alienation on the social screen as like social division of labour, *i.e.,* projection of original Marxism on mature Marxism, alienation with individual problem and division of labour with social problem—and these equations are inconsistent and highly misleading.

In *Philosophy and Myth in Karl Marx* (1961) Tucker's representation of Marxism, its transformation from original to mature, from psychological to apparently sociological, from self-alienation to division of labour is nothing but psychological caricature of Marxism. Further, the concepts of 'money worship' and 'egoistic need' are treated as unconscious projections of the psychological urge for 'self-aggrandizement' and competition is treated as the source of 'acquisitive mania' and the whole system collapses without the hunger for surplus labour or value as the primary underlying postulate—all these understandings of Tucker are distorted, mistranslated and misunderstood. Following the line of same understandings Daniel Bell (1965) does not see capitalism in a negative sense, what he criticizes is the 'inner man' of the isolated individual under capitalistically reified social relations of production, subject to 'forced labour', which is only 'a force of the self'. This study of Bell is quite misleading, a search for justification of capitalistic understanding of man and reality. Bell and Tucker misinterpret Marx and demonstrate Marxist ideas as meaningless. Bell in his *The End of Ideology* says, 'The irony, however, is that in moving from 'philosophy' to 'reality', from phenomenology to political economy, Marx himself had moved from one kind of abstraction to another. ..., self-alienation becomes transformed: man as 'generic man' becomes divided into class of men.' (Bell, 1965 : 365-66)— this statement about Marx is quite misleading. Another thing which misleads us about Marxist outlook is that the social reality in Marxist sense is not 'Man', not the 'individual' but the 'economic classes', and individuals, and their motives, count for naught. But to Marx, man is a natural being directly—he is an active natural being with some natural tendencies, abilities and impulses—he is conditioned and limited by nature and natural objects, which are objects of his need, *i.e.*, manifestation and confirmation of his essential powers. To Marx, a non-objective being is a nullity and is a non-being. As everything natural has to have its beginning, man too has an act of coming-to-be— and history has an act of coming-to-be it is a conscious self-transcending act of coming-to-be. The nature which comes to be in human history, the genesis of human society is man's real nature. Human self-consciousness is the consciousness of a specific natural being, which is sensuous consciousness. Sensuous consciousness is not the abstractly sensuous consciousness but a humanly justified sensuous consciousness. Objectification is only the possible mode of existence for a natural being—the social being, which provides life-giving power to humanly natural being, forms the essence of the human, is equal to nature outside it, is equal to social mode of existence of the human being. Therefore, objectification is not equal to alienation or estrangement. Graphically (Figure 9),

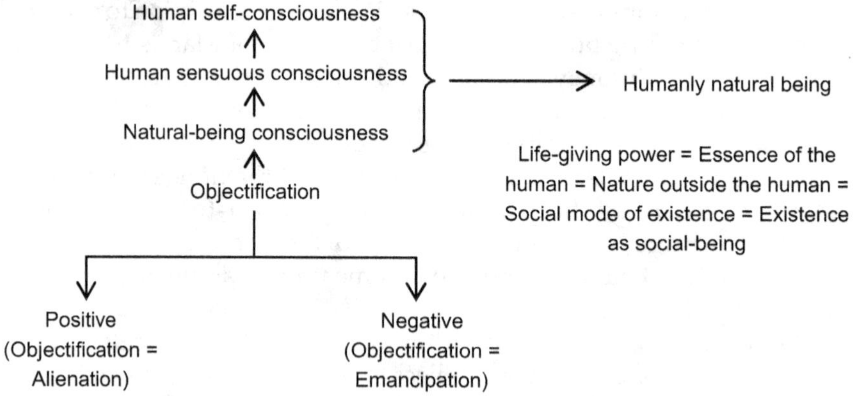

Figure 9

Controversy crops up over the issue of alienation, over the issue of early Marx and mature Marx claiming that Marx "drops out" his concept of alienation from his later writings. But, previous analysis does not testify this argument. Further, Marx justifies his concept of alienation or estrangement with reference to social practice. The concept of alienation is not abstract and static, rather practical and dynamic—the whole process is conceived as a process of self-estrangement of man through the evolutionary process of consciousness as it has been magnified in *The German Ideology*. In *Manuscripts of 1844* Marx establishes direct spiritual link between abstract man and real man by representing consciousness. He says about actual estrangement of real man and establishes link between philosophical man and social man, generic human and real man, generic consciousness and real consciousness. In *Introduction to the Critique of the Hegelian Philosophy of Right* preceded by *The German Ideology* and *The Economic and Philosophical Manuscripts* Marx categorically points out that man, being squatted outside world, is not abstract, but is concrete in the world of man, State and society. Marx never alienates or drops out his concept of alienation from his various parts of study. From the Marxist perspective both alienation and transcendence of alienation must be defined in terms of the objective necessities. The necessity of alienation is defined as a necessity inherent in self-development and self-mediation, *i.e.*, self-realization of human potentialities and its transcendence is also defined so. The necessity of alienation is, therefore, a historical necessity and it is bound to be superseded through concrete historical development (Meszaros, 1975)— development of productive forces, development of social contradictions under capitalism, insights of human beings and radical transformation of education. Marx in *Poverty of Philosophy* points out that men are not free to choose their productive forces, the basis of all human history. Every productive force is an acquired human force, the product of human activity and practical human energy. This human energy is conditioned by circumstances in which men find themselves, which is conditioned by the productive forces and consequent social relations. Every succeeding generation finds itself in the possession of the productive forces won by the previous generation, which serve the succeeding generation the raw material for new production. In human history an interconnection arises. There is a history of humanity which has become all the more a history of humanity since the productive forces of man and therefore his social relations have been extended. Therefore, the social history of man is nothing but the history of their individual development, whether they are conscious of it or not. Their material relations are the bases of all their relations, where the material and individual activity is realized (Marx, 1982). Following the same line of thought, which I have stated earlier that Marxism is an integrated whole, I can point out that Marx's conception of human and or real man is an integrated concept, a lens through which the self-realization process of man can be visualized from different angles, philosophical (P), social (S), historical (H) and economic (E) or is like a prism through which the different realities from philosophic to economic can be projected. See Figure 10.

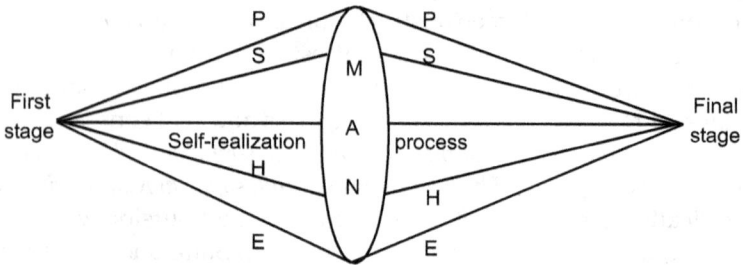

Figure 10

Therefore, self-realization is a socio-historical process, which is continuous and unending over time (t) and space (s), when man becomes philosophic, social, historical and economic at the same time. For classification a formula can be put up to this end. It follows like

Man (M) = Entity (Philosophic + Social + Historic + Economic)

$$M = E (P + S + H + E_1) \ldots\ldots\ldots (1)$$

$$M_{t, s; t+1; s+1; t+2; s+2; \ldots t+n, s+n} = E\{(P_{t, s; t+1, s+1; t+2, s+2; \ldots t+n, s+n}) + (S_{t, s; t+1, s+1; t+2, s+2; \ldots t+n, s+n}) + (H_{t, s; t+1, s+1; t+2, s+2; \ldots t+n, s+n}) + (E_{1t, s; t+1, s+1; t+2, s+2; \ldots t+n, s+n}) \ldots\ldots\ldots (2)$$

The philosophy of Marxism is materialism. Marx and Engels always defend philosophical materialism. Marx did not stop at the 'eighteenth century materialism', but enriched it with the acquisitions of German philosophy, especially of the Hegelian system, which in its turn led to the materialism of Feuerbach. During the long period from Descartes to Hegel, and from Hobbes to Feuerback, philosophers were impelled by the force of pure reason, and progress of natural sciences and industry, to move towards materialism. In his philosophical outlook, Feuerbach realizes fantasy and ideal in Hegelian pre-existence of absolute idea and logical categories before the existence of the world. Feuerbach comes to the conclusion that the existence of extra-mundane creator, God and belief in pantheism that God is everything and everything is God are non-perceptible. Our consciousness and thinking are conditioned and determined by the perceptible world, material and bodily organs. Therefore, the non-perceptible world is the product of perceptible world, mind is the product of matter and materialism is the foundation of the edifice of human essence and knowledge. Feuerbach says that which does neither reject Hegelian philosophy nor rejects theology and Absolute Idea is a rational expression of theology. He revolts against

Hegelian idealism, but does not re-examine Hegelian dialectics from the materialist point of view. Thinking as a function of man's brain or human brain and also as a property of it inherently links the spiritual and material, where the latter is the primary and the former acts as secondary. Feuerbach bases his thought structure on man and nature, where man is an integral part of nature. The philosophical system makes man including nature as the basis of man, the universal subject of philosophy. To Feuerbach, thinking or consciousness is an attribute of 'Nature', where 'Man' is a part of it. However, Feuerbach does not realize the importance of societal and material conditions of life besides the physiological properties and processes in the body.

Thus the Feuerbachian man is alive and sensuous, linked with nature, but isolated from concrete socio-historical conditions. In *Essence of Christianity* (1841), *Basic Propositions of the Philosophy of the Future* (1842) and *Preliminary Theses for the Reform of Philosophy* (1843) he rejects monarchism, the claims of Absolute Reason and of religion as illegitimate attempts to abstract human powers from man, to substitute thought for man's thinking, and to set up these to dominate man. He realizes the inherent interconnection between sensation and thinking, between sensuous and rational world, and finds the essence of man as the one and only universal and supreme subject matter of philosophy. But, he does not pursue a consistently materialist line on this question because he takes man as an abstract individual, as a purely biological being. He applies the principles of empiricism and sensationalism and opposes the agnosticism of Kant in the process of cognition. Feuerbach wants sensible objects really distinguished from the objects of thought, but does not understood human activity as objective activity. However, he does not deny the importance of thought in the process of cognition; rather he tries to examine the object in connection with the activity of the subject. He supposes the social nature of human knowledge and consciousness, but on the whole does not overcome the contemplative nature of pre-Marxist materialism. His understanding of history remains idealist.

Marx in his book *Theses of Feuerbach* (1845) criticizes Feuerbach on the ground that he does not grasp the significance of revolutionary and practical-critical activity, but changing circumstances of human activity can only be grasped through revolutionary practice. In spite of his dissatisfaction with abstract thought and search for empirical observation, he does not conceive practical human sense activity. Feuerbach sets out from the fact of religious self-alienation, and duplication of the world into religious and secular and resolving the religious into secular. But he does not find effective means of combating religion, but advocates a new religion—the principles of morality from man's intrinsic striving for happiness—every man rationally limits his requirements and loves other. Therefore, Feuerbach resolves the essence of religion into the essence of man. In essence, the essence of man is equal to the real nature of man, which in turn is equal to the totality of social relations.

But Feuerbach's human is an abstraction from the socio-historical process and the nature of human is an inner and universal quality which unites the individuals in a purely natural way—Marx formulates. Feuerbach does not consider religious sentiment as a social product. His abstract individual belongs to a particular form of society. All social life is essentially practical and rational solution of any problem can be made only through human practice and comprehension of that practice—which Feuerbach does not take into account. Feuerbach's materialism only observes the world. His materialism does not conceive sensuous existence as practical activity, is the observation of particular individuals and of civil society. The standpoint of Feuerbachian materialism is civil society and the standpoint of new materialism is human society or social humanity, which needs change (Marx, 1845). The first premise of all human history is the existence of living human individuals. The first fact is the physical organization of these individuals and their consequent relation to the rest of nature. The change of human society must always set out from these natural bases and their modification in the course of history through the action of men, who can be distinguished from creatures and animals by consciousness, by ability to produce their means of subsistence. The way in which men produce their means of subsistence depends on the nature of the actual means of subsistence they find in existence and have to reproduce. It is a definite form of activity of these individuals, a definite form of expressing their life, a definite mode of life on their part (Marx and Engels, 1847). The nature of change depends on what they produce and how they produce and the nature of individuals depends on the material conditions determining their production. Feuerbach is not a systematic philosopher, but his non-atomistic empiricism, his theory of mind and criticism of religion deserve attention. Feuerbach's philosophical development is of great significance for dialectical understanding of the progress of thought (Kamena, 1970 and Wartofsky, 1977). According to Marx, Feuerbach has a serious and critical relation to the dialectic of Hegel, who has made real discoveries in the fields of genuine materialism and positive science and philosophy, which is nothing more than religion brought into thought and developed by thought to be condemned as another form and mode of existence of human alienation (Marx,1844). To Feuerbach sense experience is the basis of all science. Irrespective of the many drawbacks in Feuerbach's philosophy, it undoubtedly deserves praise for having influenced by the subsequent development of philosophy and for reinstating the principles of materialism. Engels in *Ludwing Feuerbach* himself points out that Feuerbach is quite correct in asserting that the exclusively natural-scientific materialism is indeed the foundation of the edifice of human knowledge, but he does not take into account that one must bring the science of society into harmony with the materialist foundation and in constructing the foundation of that society upon that materialist foundation. His materialist foundation is bounded by traditional idealist fetters. For example, in his study of Christianity, Feuerbach sets out to equate the essence of religion with the essence of man. This is projected outside himself, the powers and capacities of God, with the powers and capacities of man, and the divine law with the law of man's own nature.

A much more important part in Marxist thought is played by the Hegelian idea of alienation. The concept is fundamental in the Hegelian account of mind. Marx criticizes Hegel for the imaginative reconstruction of the idea of real transformation of society, whose moral aspect would be the reacquisition of the natural qualities by man and rehabilitation of man as a social being liberated from enslaving alienation. To Hegel, labour and the alienation of labour, both are spiritual, which are overcome by the dialectical process of 'sublimation', which takes place on the level of abstract thought, and left unchanged the existing social institutions. The 'sublimation' process takes place in the forms like: sublimation of abstract right in morality, sublimation of morality in the family, sublimation of family in civil society, sublimation of civil society in the State and finally the sublimation of the State in world history. To Hegel, all phenomena in nature and society are based on 'absolute idea', 'world reason' and 'world spirit', where the principle is self-cognition and the process of cognition, which itself is an activity passes through three stages of development—development of idea in the element of pure thinking, *i.e.,* Logic or logical categories, development of idea in the form of 'other-being', *i.e.,* Philosophy of Nature and development of the idea in thought and spirit, *i.e.,* Philosophy of Mind. In *Economic and Philosophical Manuscripts* (1844) Marx tries to show the abstract demonstration of abstract thought—abstract thought is nothing-in-itself and abstract idea is nothing-in-itself, and Nature is something. Hegel turns human subject into predicate of thought. So, if human does not exist, his manifestation of life cannot be human and thought cannot be grasped as manifestation of the life of man as human, as natural subject and as being living in society, world and Nature. At the final stage of Philosophy of Mind, absolute idea conceives in different forms of human consciousness and activity. The idealistic principle of identity of thought and being serves to substantiate the unity of laws governing the external world and thinking is directed against Kant's agnosticism. Lenin in connection with this puts inconsistency in Kant's philosophical outlook that Kant's philosophy is reconciliation between idealism and materialism. When Kant assumes that something is outside, then he is materialist. When he declares things-in-itself is unknowable, he is idealist (Lenin, 1943, *Collected Works*, Vol. 14). This study has led Kant to agnosticism—that the nature of things as they exist in themselves is in principle inaccessible to human knowledge. Knowledge is possible only through 'phenomena', *i.e.*, the means through which things reveal themselves in our experience. Therefore, Kant's philosophy is the captive of dualism, agnosticism and formalism. Graphically (Figure 11):

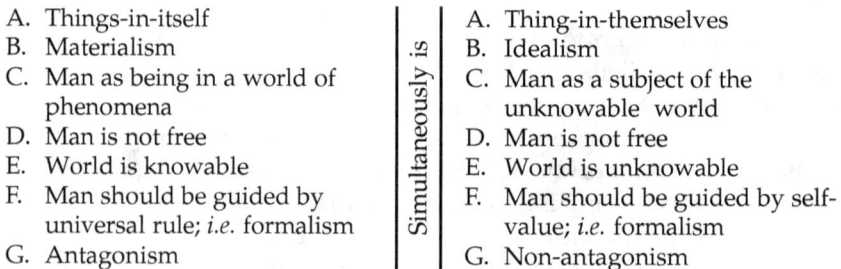

A. Things-in-itself B. Materialism C. Man as being in a world of phenomena D. Man is not free E. World is knowable F. Man should be guided by universal rule; *i.e.* formalism G. Antagonism	Simultaneously is	A. Thing-in-themselves B. Idealism C. Man as a subject of the unknowable world D. Man is not free E. World is unknowable F. Man should be guided by self-value; *i.e.* formalism G. Non-antagonism

Figure 11

There is dualism in Kant's philosophy and dialectical relation between the philosophical categories on the basis that each category is simultaneously the other and at the same time manifests in other way—for example, man is simultaneously not free as a being in a world of phenomena and free as a subject of the unknowable world at the same time, and for knowledge the world is indemonstrable and at the same time it is the necessary postulate of faith. Kant likewise teaches us on the antimonic nature of reason, which serves as the basis of dualism and agnosticism giving an impetus to the development of positive dialectics in classical German philosophy. In connection with this, Colletti (1973) remarks that Marx's materialist inversion of Hegel is an understandable look as a return to the materialist elements in Kant's philosophy, where reconciliation between materialism and idealism is likely to crop up. The Marxists like Marx, Engels and Lenin evaluate Kantian theory as a-historical and *a-priori* in the construction of knowledge, a mind-mingled and mind-determined phenomenon *vis-à-vis* their own understanding of knowledge, where cognitive power is subject to historical transformation and development. Therefore, Kant locates *a-priori* conditions of objective knowledge in human mind, whereas Marxism locates the a-priori conditions in socio-historical practices—the boundary line between 'phenomena' and 'things-in-themselves' is not absolute, but relative historically and the potential knowability is independent and prior to human subject. However, switching from spontaneous materialism to idealism and then to a reconciliation between the two, Kant makes a breach from metaphysics first. The socio-historical practices, in Marxist sense, are conditions of objective knowledge, 'sociological knowledge ... the science of the laws of social life and its causal development' (Adler, 1925 : 136). Adler remarks that causal relations in social life is not mechanical, but is mediated by consciousness, *i.e.*, socio-historical process is conditioned by both material and mental and the category of knowledge is conditioned by both reason and experience of the material world. Marx has made a positive contribution in the formation of genuine science of society, where the starting point is from society to individual and social determinism of economic phenomena. Marx, while criticizing Hegel accepted history as self-creation of man and historical development of social institutions, and dialectical process of development. To Hegel, the Absolute Idea is inherently contradictory—it constantly develops itself and will continue to develop until the absolute idea exhausts itself. The Absolute Idea initially takes the form of mechanical forces, then of chemical compounds, and finally begets nature, life, and then men and human society, assumes a material objects and phenomena, *i.e.*, Nature. In opposition to empiricism of Locke and Hume, that reality is limited to fixed world of objects and man has no power to reshape it, Hegel accepts few propositions that go beyond the crude empiricism of Locke and Hume. Hegel believes:

(1) that man is a thinking being, powerful enough to organize reality on the basis of rational thinking and to bring the fulfilment of his own potentialities as well as the potentialities of the external world, and to establish a unity between man himself and the Nature—man and his empirical world—rationalism and empiricism;

(2) that the integrated nature of the external world cannot be comprehended only through our sense organs, rather one has to go in the metaphysical plane through idealism, is beyond the empirical experiences;

(3) that there is antagonism between subject and object of knowledge, which finally is resolved through the identity between subject and object, which is achieved by reason or

spirit, which transforms both the subject and object of knowledge into a unity or universality;

(4) that the antagonism between subject and object of knowledge arises when object of knowledge conditions our knowing or subject of knowledge and the subject of knowledge does not want the bondage of the objective world of sense experience and likely tries to make a transcendence over it;

(5) that there is contradiction between the essence and existence of a thing—they are not similar—the existence is one and the essence is another, but they form a totality, when the essence is fully grasped and its potentialities are fully realized through reason and rationality—things become real, real becomes rational and rational, the real—therefore, things become rational and real both, when the essence and existence form an unified totality;

(6) that reason or spirit passes through the history of mankind, when history is the progress in the consciousness of freedom and freedom is the essence of mind;

(7) that everything must be understood not only in terms of things what they are and what they are not—contradiction in terms and reality—being and non-being at the same time—negation of negation—from thesis, the existence of a thing to anti-thesis, the essence of a thing to synthesis, the totality or universality of a thing;

(8) that dialectical method sees nature, society and knowledge in motion and development through dialectical process, where contradiction becomes universal, which requires that thought should develop in conformity with real processes and continuous changes in the realty.

Hegel's philosophy is important in two respects for Marx, *i.e.*, Marx himself is influenced by Hegel's philosophy of history and his critique of Kant, and Marx's dialectical materialism is a comprehensive form of Hegel's dialectical method and Marx applies the method in explaining the socio-historical process of development. While criticizing Kant, Hegel points out the flaws in Kantian analysis that Kant restricts human claims to knowledge to the level of 'appearance'—human beings can know only the 'appearance', thought Kant accepts that knowledge is the product of intuition inherent in the knowing subject and externally produced senses in combination. Hegel finds that 'appearance' and 'essence' necessarily belong together, and reality necessarily corresponds with human spirit. Like Hegel, Marx interprets world history as a dialectical progression, where material labour becomes the essence or so to say self-validating essence of humanity. In *Capital* Marx says that his dialectical method is not fundamentally different from Hegelian dialectical method, but is in direct opposition to it. The thought process, which Hegel calls as 'idea' is the creator of the real, is the outward manifestation of the idea, which is nothing, in his view, other than the material when it has been transposed and translated inside the human head. With the help of dialectical method of cognition Marx develops his theory of knowledge in considerations of economic structure of the society—its development as a natural historical process, social antagonisms within capitalist relations of production, exploitation arising from natural laws of capitalist production, relations of production and social intercourse arising from it. Mention here may be made that the dialectic of productive forces and production relations affects historical progress in contrast with Hegel's dialectic of world spirit. In place of Hegel's constitutional bourgeois State and Hegel's State as a march of God on earth, Marx puts forward his concept of 'free association of producers', where capitalism takes place, social order is maintained through exploitation, classes are determined by the laws of mode of production, production will be directed towards satisfying the interests of the producers. Hegelian process of spiritualization and liberation of the 'spiritual being' is nothing but bourgeois practice of reconciliation of class interests. In fact, Hegel tried to meet the urgent needs of the contemporary bourgeoisie. Thus he justifies the State. Sequentially, we can deduce Figure 12.

I. *The State occupies the superior power,* → (sequentially moves forward)

II. *Occupying superior power the State ensures the fulfilment of the common interests of the people,* → (sequentially moves forward)

III. *The State is whole by nature with its superior power,* → (sequentially moves forward)

IV. *The State as a whole by nature is rational,* → (sequentially moves forward)

V. *As a whole by nature the State is universal,* → (sequentially moves forward)

VI. *Universal is rational, rational is universal,* → (sequentially moves forward)

VII. *Rational is real, real is rational,* → (sequentially moves forward)

VIII. *Therefore, the State is universal, rational and real,* → (sequentially moves forward)

IX. *Individuals as parts surrender to the capacity and authority of the State as a whole* → (sequentially moves forward)

Figure 12

In this way, Hegel justifies the domination of the State machinery. Marx probably realized the possible danger in it. Whatever may be the criticism, the Hegelian method inspired Marx and for that Marx in *Economic and Philosophical Manuscripts* (1844) says that Hegel's outstanding contribution in *Phenomenology* is the idea of self-creation of man as a process. Lenin regards that Marx does not stop at the materialism of the eighteenth century, rather advances further towards materialist philosophy—enriches the philosophy with the acquisitions of German classical philosophy, especially of the Hegelian practices, which in its turn lead to materialism of Feuerbach. Dialectic is one of the acquisitions, *i.e.*, the doctrine of development in its fullest and deepest form, free of one-sidedness—the doctrine of the relativity of human knowledge, which provides us with a reflection of eternally developing matter.

The latest discoveries of natural science have remarkably confirmed Marx's dialectical materialism, despite the teachings of bourgeois philosophers with their new reversions to old and rotten idealism (Lenin, 1943, *Selected Works*, Vol. 11). According to Lenin, Marx and Engels are the first to realize bourgeois democracy in the countries with developed capitalism at any rate and the immature character of the revolutionary proletariat in the passing away phase of bourgeois democracy. While Hegel advocates constitutional monarchy with bourgeois political domination, Young Hegelians proposes republican ideas devoid of revolutionary action against aggressive reaction. Young Hegelians are critical of feudal relations, orthodox pietism and absolutist feudal reaction. 'Young Hegelian idealism, on the one hand, and revolutionary democracy, on the other, should be regarded not only as the outcome of earlier development in philosophical and socio-political thinking in Germany, but also as a definite phase in the ideological development of Marx and Engels.' (Oizerman, 1981 : 38). Though Althusser (1965) depicts the influence of liberal-rationalistic humanism of Kant and Fichte on Marx, but Marx himself explicitly denies and approves the influence of Hegel and Young Hegelians in his doctoral dissertation of 1839-41. Few like Bekker (1940) and Cornu (1934) believe that before reaching the stage of Hegelianism, Marx crossed the stage of enlightenment first and then of romanticism. However, this belief is not conducive to our other critics' points of view.

Young Hegelian, M. Hess lauds Marx in a letter to B. Auerback on September 2, 1841 that—"Dr. Marx – that is my idol's name – is still a very young man; he will deliver the final blow at medieval religion and politics. He has the most profound philosophical gravity, combined with the subtlest wit. Just imagine Rousseau, Voltaire, Holbach, Lessing, Heine and Hegel blended in one individual; I say blended, not mixed," (Oizerman, 1981 : 101). In relation with the above—'profound philosophical gravity' and blending of the ideas or philosophies of Rousseau and Hegel and others, Lenin regards Marx's philosophy as 'consummate'. Mention here may be made that Hess, the Young Hegelian following the lines of Gans, the founder of Young Hegelian movement considered Hegel's principles with the conception of jurisprudence and the political conceptions of bourgeois radicalism and Feuerbachianism, and sought to provide and developed the philosophical interpretation and ideas of utopian socialism and communism. Marxism gets inspiration not only from Young Hegelians, but also from humanistic philosophy of Western tradition, and French and German enlightenment. There is an element of humanism in Marxism, which I have said earlier, which runs from Spinoza through French and German enlightenment to Goethe and Hegel. Marx realizes man and potentialities of the human. But, I do not say that Marx's interpretation of history is an anthropological interpretation or cannot treat Marxism as the humanistic protest against oppression and enslavement of the human being only, rather the protest is humanistic and the interpretation is materialist and economic, positive and dialectical.

The re-emphasis of Hegelianism or Hegelian elements in Marxism is laid by Lukacs, who attempts to show that the goal of history is the true realization of the very absolute, which Hegel sought in his contemplative philosophy, which Marx finds in his political economy of the destiny and role of the proletariat as the identical subject-object of history. 'In his youth, Marx had detected an ambivalence in his master Hegel, and the same ambivalence was present—not surprisingly—in the disciple. For each was a dialectical thinker, and the Marxist dialectic in particular was open-ended: being a unity of subjective and objective factors, both the theory and the practice were constantly interacting and evolving. Marx himself had changed and developed his views, both political and economic during his lifetime.' (Mclellan, 1998 : 2). To Lukacs, it is not the primacy of economic motives which constitutes the decisive difference between Marxism and bourgeois thought, but the point of view of totality, which Marx takes from Hegel (Lukacs, 1971). However, the differences between Hegel's ontology and Marx's ontology cannot be ignored here. Marx rejects Hegel's realized idealism or Hegelian absolute, the figure of constellational identity, *i.e.*, reduction of matter and being into spirit and thought though reified idealism, differentiates himself from Hegelian totality or spiritual monism on the ground that his concept of totality is subject to empirical confirmation and not to speculative subjective confirmation, and separates his causal teleology, is limited to human praxis and whose appearance elsewhere is rationally explained, from Hegel's immanent teleology, which is conceptual.

Is Marxism devoid of idealism? Critics justify Marxism on the ground that Marxist philosophy is in maximum dependence on ideology. Marx produces his philosophical opinion before the period of producing his mature works. But, Marx's philosophical opinions in his early period get substantial modifications in the later writings, and the proposition of this critique is absurd on the ground that Marx also develops his philosophy as a practical critical outlook. Furthermore, besides the presence of idealism and humanism, and ethics and values in his early writings, Marx's philosophical propositions are not mere 'opinions', (Rodinson, 1969) but are substantiated with socio-historical propositions in terms of totality, causal teleology and human praxis—which have been transposed into his mature writings. In fact, there is no philosophy without ideology, and no ideology without philosophy. Both are inseparable and non-antagonistic. What is really important in this connection is philosophical function of ideology and ideological function of philosophy. Again, Marx essentially deals with human, human science, and he is a social scientist. Human science is social science, and social science is policy-science—science of behaviour—individual behaviour and human actions, where value-free analysis is utopia. A social science cannot exist without philosophy which expresses definite social interests, values and requirements. Rodinson says that Marx starts from preliminary ideological choice rooted in a definite tradition of the eighteenth century—and the values of freedom, equality and brotherhood have been chosen. Rodinson's critique of Marx is motivated one due to his (Marx) socialist ideological orientation of the radical improvement of the society. Rodinson criticizes Marx's ideological orientation on the basis of his opposite ideological orientation, *i.e.*, bourgeois ideological orientation of man's slow improvement by means of education, moral enlightenment and technical progress.

There is ideology in Marxism, but this does not mean that Marxism is non-science or unscientific. The basic foundation of Marxism and its interpretative framework is not idealism as an improvement over Hegelianism. Is it purely scientific and non-ideological examination of Marxism? It can be said that as a social science it is not and impossible. Another critic of Marxism, Rubel (1957) denies the scientific character of Marxism on the grounds that without providing economic proof for the inevitability of socialism—whether it is economically viable or not, whether it would provide radical improvement of the society or not, whether it would liberate the proletarian class, Marxism criticizes the capitalist system and that Marx regards proletarian movement via ethical vocation. This is not true. Marx's critique of capitalism both in his early and mature writings is not the substantiation of morals, rather the substantiation of socio-historical and economic foundations for the development of the capitalistic mode of production and scientific substantiation of the inevitable socialist reconstruction. Following Rubel's idea of moralizing substantiation E. Fromm (1966) regards Marxism from a humanistic point of view.

Marx and Engels regard the predominant social forms as unreasonable, which come into conflict with man's rational nature and also with the totality of historically changing relations. Marx and Engels show the bourgeois content of both English classical political economy and German classical philosophy which proclaim social progress in terms of reason, freedom and humanism. Marx's and Engels's mission of socialist transformation and socio-historical orientation are not only practical-political, but also theoretical, *i.e.*, both their mission and orientation both are based on the totality of theory and practice—unity of theoretical and practical consideration of socio-historic facts, figures and processes. The philosophical conceptions of historical materialism as a science, the unity and union between the science of historical materialism and revolutionary practice have made possible positivism and neo-positivism. In this way Marxism bears corollary with Comtean positivism, but Marx and Engels differ from him on the basis of his subjective idealism and agnosticism. Comte (op. cit., Mill, 1961) does not regard the transformation of bourgeois system by revolutionary means. Capitalism, to Comte, crowns man's historical evolution and social harmony can be achieved by propaganda of a new religion, religion of humanity. Comte regards that all societies need religion because they need spiritual power, which at once sanctifies and shapes the temporal power—this view is in opposition with the Marxist point of view.

The formation of Marxist philosophy includes formation of Marxist political economy and formation of scientific communism. The fact is that Marxist philosophy is created through the critical assimilation of classical German philosophy, English political economy and French utopian socialism. Without economic studies working out on historical materialism or laws of historical development become impossible, for example, historically transient character of capitalist mode of production and the inevitable march to socialism cannot be studied or analyzed without directly involving the studies on bourgeois political economy, the correspondence between the forces of production and relations of production in capitalist economy and laws of socialist economy etc. Not only the critical analysis of bourgeois political economy but also the critique of utopian socialism played important formative role in the shaping of Marxism. Marx and Engels through their philosophical and economic studies—materialist interpretation of history, historico-materialist critique of capitalist economy and historico-materialist substantiation of socialism—have made the transformation of utopian socialism into science possible, for example, scientific relation between social consciousness and social being, socio-economic formation of the society based on causal teleology, causal relation between the forces of production and relations of production and the identification of fundamental relations, *i.e.*, production relations in the socio-economic formation of the society—the totality of the relations of production forms the economic structure of the society, which represents the real foundation of a society on which grows the legal and political superstructure of society and which conditions definite forms of social consciousness. Marx never offers a readymade alternative model of society. He offers the logic and validity of the need to replace the existing order—capitalist order, where he finds fundamental contradiction between capital and labour within it, is precipitating its final goal.

Developing philosophical materialism, Marx extends the knowledge of nature to knowledge of human society. Marx develops strikingly integral and harmonious scientific theory—shows the consequence of the growth of productive forces—out of one system of social life another and higher system develops. Lenin says that Marx's philosophy is finished philosophical materialism, which provides humanity and especially the working class with powerful instrument of knowledge. Marx provides especial attention to economic analysis. In continuation of the works of Adam Smith and David Ricardo of the school of classical political economy laying the foundation of labour theory of value, Marx develops his theory of surplus value, where the value of every commodity is determined by the quantity of socially necessary labour time spent on it. Material, human and social reproductions constitute a single whole, which Marx finds and classical political economy has a good deal to say about it. Reproduction is assumed as continuous repetition and uninterrupted renewal of the social process of production. Marx investigates reproduction of the different parts of aggregate social capital, which is not merely the reproduction of value, but also material reproduction. Every type of social reproduction includes reproduction of material wealth, reproduction of labour power and reproduction of relations of production. The type of reproduction, whether expanded or simple, depends upon the dominant relations of production, whether the process of production is to be reproduced in ever increasing volume, or the process of production is to be reproduced every year in the same volume. Capitalism is characterized by expanded reproduction, which is interrupted by economic crises regularly. Socialist reproduction is characterized by planned process of the constant renewal and growth of social production. The expanded form of reproduction constitutes two forms of reproduction, extensive and intensive, when the former is based on additional employment of labour and natural resources, fixed assets and turnover funds and the latter on increasing rate of power-worker ratio and asset-worker ratio, labour productivity and technological updating. Capitalist reproduction constantly reproduces material wealth—the aggregate social product, labour power and capitalist relations of production, where simple production is the starting point as a part of the expanded reproduction, which not only includes production, but also distribution, exchange and consumption. Marx in his *A Contribution to the Critique of Political Economy* says that production and consumption are mutually dependent—there is no consumption without production and no production without consumption. It is only consumption that consummates the process of production, since consumption completes the product as product by destroying and consuming its independent concrete form. Hence, Marx divides social production into two parts—production of the means of production and production of the means of consumption. Capitalist reproduction is different from the normal reproduction process, while the former is characterized by profit and market orientation, and the latter by reproduction corresponding to the needs of the society both in quality and quantity. Marx discovers the conditions under which the aggregate social product can be realized—these are constant capital, variable capital and surplus-value. To Marx,

I. aggregate social product = constant capital + variable capital + surplus value or profit;
II. annual social product = annual (production of the means of production + production of the means of consumption or consumer articles).

There is exchange between two types of production—production of the means of production and production of the means of consumption—the means of production go to the means of consumption in exchange for the articles of consumption brought by the workers and capitalists. Marx prescribes that means of production to be produced in the required quantity and means of consumption to be produced in the acquired quantity—this is required for balanced development of social production and complete realization of all output from both processes of production. Capitalist expanded reproduction differs from simple reproduction on the basis that in the former surplus-value is turned into capital, which brings about accumulation of capital. Parts of this accumulated surplus value are used to buy more producer goods and more labour power. The proportion according to which accumulated surplus value increases is determined by the average social composition of capital. To Marx,

    I. total surplus value = labour value of the physical surplus
    II. total profit = price of the physical surplus

The value composition of capital reflects changes in the technical composition as it is determined by technical composition. The relation between the means of production (c) and labour power (v) characterize the technical composition of capital (*i.e.* constant capital and variable capital). The value of capital is determined by the relation between the value of the means of production and value of labour power. To Marx,

    I. changes in the value composition of capital : (is proportional to) changes in the technical composition of capital (determined by technological conditions of production).
    II. organic composition of capital = (is equal to) value composition of capital.

Organic composition of capital increases under capitalism in antagonistic forms, and involves the increase in the rate of surplus value, relative surplus population, the growing army of unemployed, and the deterioration of the conditions of the proletariat. Marx in his *Theories of Surplus Value* (1968) and *Capital* (1967) says that if profits as a percentage of capital are to be equal over a period, then capitals of equal size yield equal profits in the same period of time, and then prices of the commodities must be different from their value. To Marx,

    I. sum total of the cost prices of all commodities = sum total of the values of all commodities; and,
    II. total profit = total surplus value.

The determination of surplus value itself arises only out of the determination of value by labour-time and without this average profit is the average of nothing. An average profit cannot be anything but profit on the average social capital, whose sum is equal to the sum of surplus-value. Therefore, the sum total of average social capital is equal to the sum total of surplus-value, and average profit is equal to sum total of surplus-value. It is the total realized unpaid labour. Marx, therefore, tries to analyze capitalistic reproduction of both capital and labour in terms of equal and constant organic composition of capital, rates of surplus value, exchange of commodities in terms of value, constant productivity and disposing of unlimited labour power by the capitalists. Lenin says that the doctrine of surplus value is the cornerstone of Marx's economic theory. The basic problem before Marx is the problem of deviation of natural prices from the values of labour, *i.e.,* the exchange of commodities in terms of value, which like David Ricardo receiving inspiration from Adam Smith terms it as relation of things unlike the Marxist notion of relation of men or human relations. The exchange of commodities expresses tie by which individual producers are bound through market. 'Money' signifies that this tie is becoming closer and 'capital' signifies further development of the tie through the commodification of human labour, selling of labour power in exchange of wage to the owner of the means of production. The worker uses one part of his labour in a day to cover the expenses for maintaining himself and his family or family members, and the other part is expensed for the profit of the owners of the means of production, creating surplus-value for the capitalist. This part of labour the worker toils without any remuneration or exchange.

According to Ricardo, the basic determination of the relative prices of commodities is the amount of labour in the course of production directly and the current production period indirectly. In this production process, the physical surplus of commodities is distributed among capitalists, landlords and workers in terms of profits, rents and wages. Ricardo believes that the rate of distribution of annual physical surplus of commodities which have direct relation with the fluctuation in rates of profit and wages should have no effect on the relative prices of commodities. The division and distribution of physical surplus of commodities have nothing to do with how much labour power is necessary in producing its component parts. But, the conviction of Ricardo is not correct—natural prices deviate from labour values in capitalist economy due to variation in use of labour and use pattern of labour power in production. Marx stipulates that all sectors in production exhibit the same organic composition of capital. Profit is the offspring of the aggregate advanced capital and surplus-value takes the converted form of profit (Marx, 1978, *Capital*, Vol. 3). Rent is one of the forms of income received regularly from landed property and others, which does not involve participation business and business activities. As a result of monopoly of private ownership of land the share of surplus is appropriated by the landowners. To Marx,

I. absolute rent = share of surplus value from land;
II. surplus value – average profit = excess surplus value → absolute rent (lower organic composition of capital)
III. surplus value – average profit = excess surplus value → differential rent (created because of the higher productivity of labour of agricultural labourers on better land and the higher productivity of additional invested capital)

Absolute rent is produced by surplus labour of hired agricultural workers and reflects their exploitation by capitalist entrepreneurs and landowners. As distinct from differential rent absolute rent is received from all lands and which indeed is not dependent on variations. Wage form of labour in capitalist economy is paid to the workers for their mere subsistence, *i.e.*, labour is sold in terms of wage, which may be of two types—time wage—the amount of the worker's pay depends on the actual time he works and piece wage—the amount of worker's pay depends on the number of articles produced. In capitalist society, social product is distributed in the form of wages, rents, profits and interests. Adam Smith (1937) in his *Wealth of Nations* produces his natural price theory, where he says that when the price of any commodity is neither more or less than what is sufficient to pay the rent of the land, the wages of labour and the profits and when the commodity is sold at the natural rate, then the price of this commodity is called natural price, which exactly covers natural profit, natural rent and natural wage. He justifies natural profit as a component part of natural price in a free and competitive market. The actual price of any commodity is its market price, which is determined by demand and supply in the market. However, Smith finds that natural prices are the centres of gravity as it is determined by objective laws of nature like the physical laws of nature, rational socio-economic structure and reasons governing human motivations and desires.

According to Ricardo, profits depend on the price, rather than on the value of food (Figure 13). To the Marxists, the law of value is manifested as law of prices, and price is an expression of value in the form of money. It is also an expression of the socially necessary labour on production of commodities—value of labour operates within the commodity—as commodities are exchanged, equal amount of labour value are exchanged. Therefore, Marx's theory of value is simultaneously the theory of money. In connection with this, Marx criticizes Adam Smith and David Ricardo on the ground that they treat value as something external to the nature of the commodity and do not take into account the socially necessary labour time. Marx regards that both the theorists treat value of the product of labour as the product of eternal and natural form of social production. To Marx, products of labour as commodities have both natural value and use value. Use value is the usefulness of a commodity. While use value is a necessary condition for a product to enter into exchange relations, hence, according to Marx, is to have exchange value. Therefore, value becomes a social reality. Commodity 'X' expresses its value in commodity 'Y'. Marx regards social relations in commodity exchange. The 'relative form of value' of commodity 'X' is expressed in commodity 'Y' as 'equivalent form of value'. The physical form of commodity 'Y' becomes the value form of commodity 'X'— it is the equivalence between different kinds of commodities and different kinds of value-creating labour embodied. The physical nature of commodity 'Y' is the objectification of labour and labour value of commodity 'X', *i.e.*, use value appears as value and concrete labour appears as abstract labour. Commodity 'Y' does not express its own value, which concrete labour produces becomes the form of appearance of abstract labour—and this labour is identical with other forms of labour, hence, becomes social labour. Further, labour embodied in commodity 'Y' is expressed in physical form in commodity 'Z' and in this way the process is expanded. This is the total or expanded form of value. In opposition to modern bourgeois political economy, Marx says that the magnitude of value of commodities regulates the exchange between commodities. The exchange value is expressed as commodity, and which is expressed in terms of money, the price—exchange value is determined by the substantive character of the commodity, abstract labour and necessary labour time—that is expressed by one and determined by another. How money arises as exchange value? Marx gives answer—money arises from contradiction between the general character of value and the material existence of a commodity, *i.e.*, product of labour becomes commodity, commodity becomes the exchange value and exchange value becomes the money.

According to Marx, the needs of the working class is determined by the level of civilization, conditions of living and living standards, the habits and expectations of the workers. This is unlike the Ricardian and Mathusian dimension where favourable conditions of excess demand for labour and labour's value around which its market price and wage fluctuate and wages are determined physically and naturally. Ricardo assimilates the problem of price determination with the determination of wage by means of Malthus's theory of population pressure on food supply. To Marx, the value of labour power depends on commodity producing necessary labour time and the reproduction. Marx believes that Ricardo does not understand what money really is, what labour value actually stands for, rather he takes money as a simple device of circulation, where price is determined by demand and supply of labour and circulating quantity of money in the market. According to Ricardo, labour is purchased or sold, may be increased or diminished in quantitative measure, has both natural and market price—natural price is necessary to enable the labourers to interact with one another, to subsist and perpetuate their race without either increase or diminution. The quantity of labour bestowed on the production of a commodity regulates the relative value of the commodity, modified by employment of machinery and other fixed and durable capital. Value of the commodity does not rise or fall with the rise and fall of wages, modified by unequal durability and unequal rapidity of capital with which it is returned to the employer. Ricardo here goes against the old idea that increase in wages causes increase in prices. To him, price rise or decrease depends on organic composition of capital, when it is below the average price rises and when it is above the average price decreases. However, he tends to forget the crucial importance of fixed capital in the determination of the rate of profit. Ricardo regards the closer correspondence between changes in the values and changes in the relative price, but does not explain the difference between value of production and price of production. However, he concedes that the employment of machinery may displace the workers, but capitalist accumulation process would absorb the workers or the reserve army of unemployed labourers. Here, Ricardo justifies the capitalist economic system and differs from Marx on that ground. Ricardo prescribes that economic development will come from capitalist investment in the form of revenue from the capitalist class and not from rental income, which is unproductively consumed. Population growth increases demand for food and consequently increases demand for cultivation in less fertile land, increases rents from land and decreases profit. Graphically, see Figure 14. The process is spiral. It is like this :

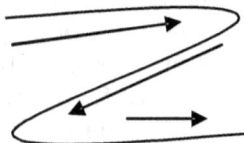

Figure 14

population increase → more demand for food → more pressure on land: fragmentation of land for cultivation, cultivation in less fertile land → increase in rents from land → decrease in the rate of profit → transfer of social surplus into unproductive consumption increases → decrease in new and productive investment → decrease in profit discourage the entrepreneurs to make new investment and to undertake simple reproduction.

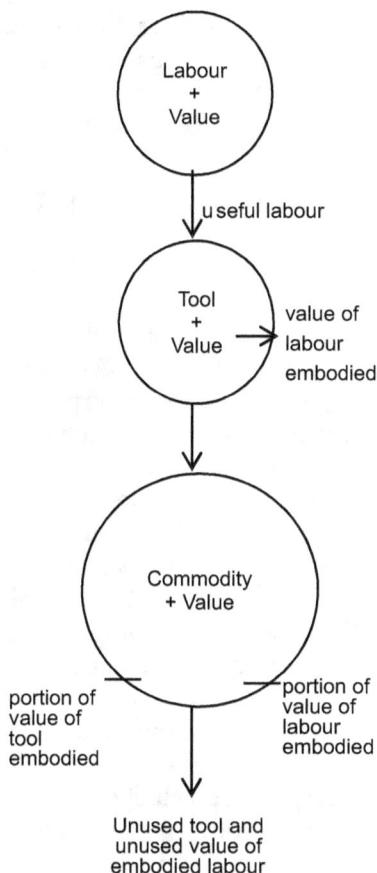

profit varies with price, ... (1)

profit does not vary with the value of food or commodity, ... (2)

things facilitating production reducing production cost will increase the rate of profit, ... (3)

things not facilitating production augmenting production cost will reduce the rate of profit, ... (4)

production facility will simultaneously increase profit and the amount of consumer durables or consumable commodities, ... (5)

value of commodity is determined by the labour power directly involved with the production of commodities and also by tools and implements of production on which labour is bestowed, ... (6)

a portion of value of a tool being transferred to the commodity, is produced with its assistance —as tool or implement wears out over the course of time, the value of labour bestowed upon the tool produced in the past is slowly shifted over to the commodities produced with the aid of the tool—as the tool ceases to be useful, its embodied labour or value of embodied labour also ceases to exist. .... (7)

Figure 13

Unlike Marx, Ricardo does not understand the technical advancement in agriculture, the consequences of scientific and technological innovations instead of Nature's niggardliness and the social relations that generate accumulation and technical progress, the difference between labour and labour power, and profit accumulation by the capitalists through surplus-value produced by the workers. Marx's critique of capitalism is exploitation. Exploitation is the extraction from productive input of more value than is contained within it. The labour power of the workers in capitalist economy is exploited. They are exploited in terms of surplus-value. The rate of surplus-value determines the rate of exploitation. The rate is determined by the ratio of surplus value extracted from the unit of labour power to the value of that power, labour power. Profits, which are produced by the workers and appropriated by the capitalists, are simply the surplus value of labour. Positive rate of profit gives birth to positive rate of surplus value. But economists like Schumpeter considers surplus-value as false—the appearance of profit is in direct contradiction with the essence of surplus value. Marx finds answer to this problem. To Marx, capitalism can not function under conditions of—

i.   rate of profit : (is proportional to) surplus value = average rate of profit (equal profit per equal capital) and,

ii. aggregate surplus value (is proportional to) : total social capital = average rate of profit,

which depends on the special rates of profit and on the relative share of industries with high and low organic composition of capital. Average rate of profit is the result of competition between different enterprises and different sectors of industries. Different enterprises and industries develop unevenly under capitalism having no parity in their level of technical development, which derives uniformity in the organic composition of capital. Then, equal amount of capital will yield unequal profits. Competition forces profit to tend towards an average rate. Where the organic composition of capital is lower, the same amount of capital will yield more profit than in industries with higher organic composition of capital. This situation cannot persist for long. In the quest for maximum profits, capitalists become involved in intense competition. As a consequence of spontaneous flow of capital from the industries with low rate of profit to those with a high rate, the rates of profit will level off at an average rate under normal conditions of production. There is no proportionality of the rate of profit to surplus value in each enterprise, but the aggregate surplus value of the economy as a whole is distributed among sectors in proportion to total social capital, constant and variable. Marx reconstructs the classical political economy, which constitute the extraction of surplus labour in production process, the realization of embodied surplus labour in commodities as surplus value and surplus value as profit in the process of circulation and the movement of surplus value, and also the distinction between labour and labour-power, which becomes the origin of profit and surplus value. Furthermore, labour is the substance of value—profit, rent and interest are surplus values—and total surplus value is equal to total profit, whose money rate equalizes itself with the natural price away from the labour value and equilibrates the price system in extracting surplus value. Competition and capitalists' pursuit of highest rate of profit distort the natural price of a commodity (where the labour becomes a commodity and the exchange value of a commodity is determined by quantity of abstract and socially necessary labour embodied in it) away from the labour value in order to extract a large amount of surplus value. Then, what becomes possible in the capitalist system is:

> highest rate of profit for the capitalist = aggregate quantum of surplus value = total unearned income = profits + money form of rent + interest appropriated by the capitalists and their dependent classes.

By employing the principle that labour becomes the commodity and distinguishing labour from labour power Marx distinguishes labour from all other commodities. The capitalists buy workers' labour power, and then antagonism between the workers and capitalists takes place over the issues of how much labour, of what intensity of labour and of what kinds of labour the workers will deliver and the capitalists will extract from the factory. In his early writings Marx views agricultural and industrial labour as painful, exhausting and alienating, which the working class is able to shun. Marx divides the workday into necessary labour time and surplus labour time, which the workers realize and hence labour-management struggle comes in the forefront. It is a historic struggle over the issue of working hours and working conditions—the story of alienation and resistance—capital's attempt to extract more labour from the labour power through its control over the work itself, work place and the work process, and labour's increasing efforts to resist capital's encroachment and relations of domination (Nell, 1982 and Bowles, 1983) in the work place. Lenin (1943) puts the consequences of capitalism, which can be presented graphically in serial sequences:

> capital is created by the labour of the worker and is pressed on the worker by running small capital and creating a reserve army of unemployed → capitalism spreads itself in agriculture → application of machinery in agriculture → peasant economy falls into the prey of money and declines or ruins due to its backward techniques → small-scale production is destroyed due to intervention of large capital → capital leads to an increase in labour productivity and to the creation of monopoly houses manned by big capitalists → production becomes much more social → expansion of social mode of production → more and more workers are bound together in an economic organism → collective production through or by and through collective labour → collective labour is appropriated by the capitalists due to their profit motives → appropriation of surplus value → competition over the occupation of market for more profit → overproduction and economic crisis → insecurity of existence of the mass of the population with the concentration of capital and de-concentration of the working class → dependence of the workers on capital → creation of great powers of united labour by the capitalist system

Marx traces the development of capitalism from commodity economy to exchange economy to large-scale production (from commodity economy based on exchange of commodity in terms of money to exchange economy in terms of money to large-scale production based on exchange economy in terms of wide-scale circulation of capital). That is capitalism, or capital within capitalism, rules the world as a prelude to the triumph of labour over capital.

With the overthrow of feudalism free capitalist society appears with a new system of oppression and exploitation warped in words like 'free', 'freedom' and 'choice' etc. Various socialist ideas emerged as a reflection and protest against this system of oppression. *Utopian Socialism* is the early one to go against this oppression and system of oppression—condemnation of the system, dream of destruction of the capitalist order with an alternative fancy of a better order in an endeavour to convince the rich about the immorality of oppression and exploitation (Lenin, 1943). This variety of socialists is influenced by optimistic ideals of human perfectibility and broadly humanitarian outlook, when they hope for an ideal social order devoid of revolution and class conflict through educational experimentation. Jean De Sismondi (1773-1842), one of the first of these socialists, who opposes the 'laissez faire' principle in the economy, growing use of machine power instead of hand labour or manpower in the factory, too much cost-benefit analysis rather than human happiness in the cold calculation of economic gains. Engels (1935) in his *Socialism : Utopian and Scientific* designates early socialism as 'utopian' because of the imaginative possibility of social transformation involving the elimination of individualism, competition and sway of private property without a recognition of class struggle and revolutionary role of the proletariat in the accomplishment of this transition. Lenin says that utopian socialism does not point the real way out. Lenin further points out—

> ... (Utopian Socialism) It could not explain the essence of *wage slavery* under capitalism, nor discover the *laws of its development*, nor point to the *social force* which is capable of becoming the creator of a new society.
>
> Meanwhile, the *stormy revolutions* which everywhere in Europe, and especially in France, accompanied the *fall of feudalism*, of serfdom, more and more clearly revealed the *struggle of classes* as the basis and the motive force of the whole development.
>
> Not a single victory of *political freedom* over the feudal class was won except against *desperate resistance*. Not a single capitalist country evolved on a more or less *free and democratic basis* except by a *life and death struggle* between the various classes of capitalist society.
>
> The genius of Marx consists in the fact that he was able before anybody else to draw from this and consistently apply the deduction that world history teaches. This deduction is the doctrine of the *class struggle*.
>
> People always were and always will be the stupid victims of deceit and self-deceit in politics until they learn to discover the *interests of some*

class behind all moral, religious, political, and social phrases, declarations, and promises. The supporters of reforms and improvements will always be fooled by the defenders of the old order until they realize that every old institution, however barbarous and rotten it may appear to be, is maintained by the *forces of some ruling classes*. And there is the only one way of smashing the resistance of these classes, and that is to find, in the very society which surrounds us, and *to enlighten and organize for the struggle*, the forces which can—and, owing to their social position, must—constitute a power capable of *sweeping away the old and creating the new* (Lenin, 1943 : 8).

Here, Lenin like the others, Marx and Engels realizes the importance of 'class struggle', class contradiction in social development, class as 'social force' unlike the early socialists in the course of socio-historical development, for example, transition from feudalism to capitalism and from capitalism to socialism. The utopians do not understand 'class politics', 'class interest', 'class State', 'class ideology' and 'class institutions' and so on and so forth in class terms in the reconstruction of the new society, rather they reconstruct new society from the womb of the old one without 'desperate resistance' and 'life and death struggle'. According to Lenin, transformation of the society, *i.e.*, 'sweeping away the old and creating the new' is the possible contradiction of world historical and social development can be resolved by another contradiction of the world history, *i.e.*, 'class struggle', which the early socialists fail to learn from world history. They do not realize the importance and role of the 'forces of some ruling classes' in the maintenance of the old order and hence, the advocates of reforms and improvements are being fooled by the defenders of the old order. Therefore, without powerful resistance smashing the resistance of the defenders social transformation is not possible—this lesson of 'class struggle' Marx learns from the history of 'stormy revolutions' in Europe and especially in France. The only way to make a resolute resistance or to make struggle against the defenders (the so-called ruling class) of the older 'stormy' is 'to enlighten and organize' the working class (the so-called class living in oppression and destitution) 'for the struggle'. Lenin further remarks about Marx's own realization of this fact, which cannot be traced in the writings of the early socialists—

> Independent organizations of the proletariat are multiplying all over the world, from America to Japan and from Sweden to South Africa. The proletariat is becoming enlightened and educated by waging its class struggle; it is ridding itself of the prejudices of bourgeois society; it is rallying its ranks ever more closely and is learning to gauge the measure of its successes; it is steeling its forces and is growing irresistibly. (Lenin, 1943 : 8).

Few regard that Marx borrows the concept of class struggle from

French historians and historical writings at the end of the eighteenth century and develops his idea of class division associated with particular phases of historical development, which in subsequent phase disappears through class struggle—the proletariat seizes the public power, and by means of this transforms the socialized means of production and socialized production slips into public property. The contradiction between socialized production and capitalistic appropriation now presents itself as an antagonism between the organization of production in the individual workshop and the anarchy of production in society generally—the proletariat uses this contradiction for the fulfilment of their mission. Aron (1965) categorically puts that Marx does not borrow his central idea of class struggle from Saint-Simonian ideas; rather he is familiar with these ideas. In Saint-Simonian ideas Marx finds the opposition between two types of society—military and industrial, application of science and technology in industry, renovation of production and production system, and the transformation of the world through industry. But the central question in Marxist thought is 'class struggle and contradictory character of capitalist industrial society', which is not Saint-Simonian or Comtist conception of industrial society. Both Saint-Simon and Comte (op. cit., Mill, 1961) do not believe in intrinsic contradictions in capitalist society, society is torn by class contradictions and conflict, and class conflict is the moving force of historical development. Aron (1965) is true with regard to class struggle and class conflict as non-Saint-Simonian. But this does not mean that he borrows nothing from the early socialists. There are some underlying common presuppositions beneath the linear surface of differences— the early socialists start from the ambition to construct a new science of human nature based on moral and ideological determinants of human behaviour, to make moral and ideological sphere of human nature as an object of science which will resolve the problem of social harmony, where the pre-existing moral, religious and political theory act as obstacle to the newly discovered laws of harmony. No distinction is made between physical and natural sciences. 'The influence of Saint-Simon upto his (Marx) own ideas is apparent from textual comparisons. In the first place, there is in both writers the same emphasis upon industry, upon society as a workshop in which man produces spiritual as well as material products, and it is probable that Marx's immediately critical attitude to Hegel's concept of labour as purely spiritual labour, sprang from his early reading of Saint-Simon. Secondly, there is the conception of the relation between society and the State, the State is (in certain circumstances) an obstacle to the development of industrial society, but also, that society (in particular the economic structure of society) is the basis of the State.' (Bottomore and Rubel, 1961 : 26; Gurvitch, op. cit.). Citing the opinion of Jean Piaget Bottomore and Rubel point out Marx's conception of ideology: 'The great merit of Marx is that he made a distinction, in social phenomena, between an effective basis and a superstructure which oscillates between symbolism and an adequate consciousness, in the same sense (and Marx himself explicitly says this) as psychology is obliged to make a distinction between actual behaviour and consciousness. ...The social superstructure stands in the same relation to its basis as does the individual consciousness to behaviour ...' (Bottomore and Rubel, 1961 : 63).

To Engels, the capitalist mode of production moves in antagonism between the organization of production in individual workshop and anarchy of production in society generally and Fourier finds 'vicious circle' in this production process, which is unable to make a further progress and which can not be destroyed. But Fourier cannot see in his lifetime that the circle is gradually narrowing—the movement becomes a spiral and must come to an end. It is the compelling force of anarchy in the production of society at large that more and more completely turns the great majority of men into proletarians and it is the masses of the proletariat again who will finally put an end to anarchy in production. The contradiction between socialized production and capitalist production ends in a violent explosion. The socialized organization of production develops so far that it has become incompatible with anarchy of production. The whole mechanism of the capitalist mode of production breaks down under the pressure of the productive forces, its own creations. Means of production, means of subsistence, available labourers—all the elements of production and of general wealth, are present in abundance.

But, the abundance, according to Fourier, becomes the source of distress and want as abundance prevents transformation of the means of production and subsistence into capital. As the productive forces grow more and more powerful against their quality as capital, the stronger and stronger their social character shall be recognized—this forces the capitalist class to treat them more and more as social productive forces so far the conditions under capitalist system permits. The period of industrial high pressure—the period of crisis—the inability of the bourgeoisie in managing the productive forces and establishment of joint-stock companies and trusts runned by salaried employees—all show the capitalists' inability to perform the social function further.

The solution to this problem lies in practical recognition of the social nature of the productive forces, in the harmonizing of the modes of production, appropriation and exchange with the socialized character of the means of production. This can come only through social possession of the means of production, when the social characters of means of production and of products are utilized by the producers with a perfect understanding of its nature. Mention here may be made of the fact that social character of the means of production under individual possession of means of the production reacts against the producers, periodically disrupts all production and exchange according to the law of Nature. The capitalist mode of production more and more transforms the majority of the population into proletarians and the proletariat seizes political power and turns the means of production into State property, *i.e.*, social possession of the means of production (Engels, 1935). This can be realized through 'revolution' or 'stormy revolution' or so to say through 'class struggle'.

The utopian socialists do not put emphasis on class struggle, rather go against it, who believe that private property is the result of human spirit's erring way to absolute truth and justice—this anti-historical approach is rejected by Marx on the ground of utopianism based on the logic of abstract anti-thesis between what exists and what ought to be. Engels in his critique of bourgeois democracy finds few negative tendencies of Saint-Simonism whose main defects are mysticism, non-revolutionary approach to economic problems and compromise with capitalist structure of society. Saint-Simonism is an outdated 'ism'— nobody now thinks of it and speaks about it. Fourier's socialism is also not free from mysticism though he tries to establish the axiom of 'social philosophy' instead of 'social poetry' of Saint-Simon, is devoid of scientific research and cool, unbiased systematic thought. Fourier says that if the inherent urge of the individual for some useful social activity is realized, then social parasitism becomes impossible. The strive for action is in human nature—there is no need to oblige the human to take a recourse to action from outside—the only need is to motivate action in right direction through individualistic social organization giving way to collectivism and association, but not through labour organization in class terms. However, Fourier develops his ideas from that of Saint-Simon, while the former locates the anti-thesis between labour and pleasure, town and country, the latter is identified in his anti-thesis between what is and what ought to be; while the former establishes the foundation of social philosophy, the latter turns his way to social poetry. Therefore, Fourier is more specific, more consistent and less abstract than that of Saint-Simon, instead of their mystic character.

However, like of Saint-Simon, Fourier prescribes a new testament with old teachings—non-abolition of private property and maintenance of old class relations through co-ordinated associations. It is on their part the early socialists unequivocally sound the revival of the old with a new dimension. They base their doctrines on religious teachings with possible combinations of Christianity and communism and Christianity and socialism, *i.e.*, of religiosity and community and religiosity and collectivity, which is unscientific and non-revolutionary. Henceforth, Engels favours French communists than that of the socialists on the basis of the communists' regard for social revolution, abolition of private property, proletarians' growing consciousness of appropriation and oppression, and for the idea that mere political transformation is a half-hearted attempt or more specifically a no attempt to liberate the oppressed masses. Instead, Engels finds no full-proof revolutionary idea among the communists of French tradition, for example, lack of revolutionary use of force and contradiction between conspiratorial tactics and organized mass revolutionary struggle. Saint-Simon follows a class collaborationist approach in his study of bourgeois capitalist society on the ground that he views bourgeoisie, proletariats and intellectuals as natural allies and co-beneficiaries of the new industrial society, where the technicians become the real leaders in recuperating the future industrial society by means of their wisdom and efficiency—and this view differentiates himself from that of Marx. In this way he justifies the class character of the bourgeois society and frees the society from the possible danger of class struggle.

In short, he is a humanist, where he bears a corollary with Marx. Drawing inspiration and teachings from Kant, Hegel, and Comte on the one hand, Bentham and Adam Smith, on the other, he tries to combine religion and humanity, and efficiency, economy and control,—by and through this combination he bears a corollary with Max Weber and differs from Marx. He makes a curious combination between liberalism and socialism. Is it possible? Actually it is not. In fact, he is in the middle of the two extremes to catch benefits from both sides. Predictably, he is an opportunist (Martel, 1968; Bowle, 1954; Litchtheim, 1969). Saint-Simon stands out in his failure to understand the historic role of the proletariat as the builder of a new society and of revolution as a means of transforming the old society, where history, scientific knowledge, morality and religion play an important role. However, he resolutely upheld determinism, extends it to the development of the human society and pays special attention to the positive role played by natural laws of history. Side by side, he develops the science of humanity and universal philosophy of history for the advancement of human beings with 'the greatest possible opportunity for the development of their faculties' (Manuel and Manuel, 1979 : 602) instead of their natural and organic inequality in terms of psycho-physical potentialities and socio-economic positions. Therefore, unlike Marx he is against the total leveling off process in society. Marx also differs from Saint-Simon, Fourier and Owen on the grounds of their ideas of antagonism, passion and charity as the sources of all social evils. However, Marx praises Fourier and Owen for their emphasis on reciprocal community life and virtues of co-operation, and on that grounds they differ from Marx as these are unattainable attributes within the capitalistic framework.

Fourier condemns the wastefulness of production and appeals to the material interests of men for order and harmony through passions of five senses: love; friendship; fellow feeling; ambition; and passions for planning, change and unity, *i.e.,* passions of planning, change and unity can be realized through the nine preceding passions of five senses and belongingness. Association is the principle of attraction among men, as gravitation is in the physical world. When Saint-Simon is for abolition of unearned income, Fourier gives argument in favour of the principle 'from each according to his capacity to each according to his labour, capital and talent' unlike the Marxist communistic principle 'from teach according to his ability to each according to his needs', when and where labour, capital and talent will get their share from industrial surplus in proportions of 5 : 12, 4 : 12 and 3 : 12 respectively. Labour should be attractive, free from monotony and overwork. A minimum income, according to Fourier, is necessary for all and should be guaranteed to all, with the surplus divided according to a fixed ratio. Further, Fourier stratifies labor into first, the necessary labour, second, the useful labour, and third, the agreeable labour according to role play, and wage and reward payment, which goes against Marxist communism and for liberal paradigm. He says that even in communistic society privacy would continue, private property, inheritance and economic inequality would be retained, class character would necessarily reorient the political economy, but they would lose their antagonistic character.

Marx finds ambiguity in this reconstruction. In fact, 'the longing for order which he depicted with such poignancy was a cry from the soul of the early industrial society' (Manuel and Manuel, 1979 : 644). Therefore, he justifies the foundation of the bourgeois capitalistic system. However, Robert Owen makes his contribution, is more developed than that of Saint-Simon and Fourier and is much more closer to Marx, *i.e.,* for example, his study of the consequences of bourgeois capitalist system and prescriptions to alleviate these consequences are good efforts to make a new moral world. In fact, he starts with Marxist dialectical assessment of capitalism and ends with reformism. As an idealist and a businessman he attempts to base the employer-employee relations on co-operation rather than competition and suggests reforms in order to make a halt in the exploitation of wage earners or to remedy the poverty and misery of the wage earners. He believes in man's natural goodness, but evils result from the capitalist system, private property, religion and institutions of marriage—which can be remedied through natural order and communal system where man's goodness can become free. He is a philanthropist and father of factory legislation, a rationalist, who believes in gradual progress of human self-knowledge and finds ignorance as the source of man's inhuman conduct. He conceives the future classless society as a free federation of self-governing communities. He lays emphasis on the distribution system of the classless society. Failing to understand the need and importance of social revolution in social transformation, he relies on the bourgeois governments to transform the society.

To this end, Marx criticizes Owen's efforts and methods of social transformation as too slow to work. Owen starts from the idea that changes in the mode of production affect the relations among producers and Industrial Revolution brings about a new kind of human being— an opportunity for the new moral world—an immense possibility of a new human in the midst of poverty, hunger and ignorance—a possibility for the enhancement of a sober, practical and human life based on psycho-physical well-being, recreation, good sense, civic ideas, order and sobriety (Williams, 1961 and Bowle, 1954). However, Owen's socialistic principles mainly are common ownership and labour; a combination of both physical and mental labour; psycho-physical development of all individuals; equal opportunity and equal rights; well-being and happiness of the poor through education and wider purchasing power; and increased productivity by means of scientific production, wealth and prosperity. Education should be universal, compulsory and moral, which brings about charity and benevolence in the minds of the human—the essential components of the new human. William Thomson, an ardent follower of Robert Owen, gives an importance to labour in the production process and labour produces all value in exchange and he is entitled to the full product of his labour. To this end, reconstruction of social institutions following Owen's prescriptions is necessary. William Thompson (1977) in his study on William Morris says that Morris supplies a moral dimension of socialism following Owenian tradition. Like that of Owen and Thompson, Morris's reconstructive socialism is devoid of class struggle and revolutionary violence that separates class from class, in spite of the fact that he does regard anti-parliamentary and anti-political movement and action for the transformation of the present capitalist society to a new one, when that transformation would necessarily be gradual. Here, Morris differs from Marx. But in another direction Marx borrows from Morris one particular dimension of the future society, *i.e.*, government of persons would necessarily be replaced by *administration of things*.

Therefore, Marxism is a curious mixture of teachings from German philosophy and ideology, English economics and French revolutionary and social thought. However, Marxism is an improvement over the past ideas and philosophy with few modifications and addition. Marxism rests first on the doctrines of historical materialism and class struggle with the application of dialectical method, which Marx derives from Hegelian philosophy. Secondly, Marx's theory of surplus and falling rate of profit are closely related with English classical economics, which Marx derives from David Ricardo. Thirdly, Marxism contains few elements of French Revolution and of French socialism in its theory of progress through revolt and its assumptions concerning the *withering away of the State*. Fourthly, in addition to the first source of influence from German philosophy, Marx gets inspiration from both Young Hegelians and Feuerbach. In *Theses on Feuerbach* Marx says that all social life is essentially practical and all mysteries find their rational solution in human practice and in the comprehension of this practice. That is the mysterious entity of the world or the mysteries of philosophy like absolute truth, reason and justice, which socialism deals with, can find solution in human practice, *i.e.*, social philosophy can comprehend itself in human practice. To the early socialists, socialism is the expression of absolute truth, reason and justice, and needs only to be discovered to conquer the world by virtue of its own power as absolute truth is independent of time and space and of the historical development of man. It becomes a mere accident, when and where it is discovered. At the same time, absolute truth, reason and justice are different for the founder of each different school, based on the subjective understanding, knowledge and intellectual training of the founder and his conditions of existence. From this nothing is emerged, but a kind of eclectic average socialism crops up. In order to make socialism into a science it has first to be placed on a real basis. But the old idealist conception of history knows nothing of class struggles based on material interests, of material interests itself, of production and all economic relations appear in the history of civilization (Engels, 1978). According to Engels, socialist movement becomes scientific by embracing the best philosophical achievements—materialism of the 18th century French philosophers and dialectics of the German philosopher Hegel. Philosophy, in its turn, fulfils itself and moves towards its own realization or withering away by identifying itself with the cause of the proletariat, the class that is destined to do away with classes. In this way, philosophy is realized through politics and politics is realized through philosophy. Marxist philosophy appears as objective, scientific and revolutionary, as world view and as the product of past history, as a method predicting future history, and as a practice, creating future history.

In *Poverty of Philosophy* Marx justifies his theory as science of society and history and equates the role of socialists and communists with that of the economists. Like that of economists, who are theoreticians of the bourgeois class, the socialists and communists are theoreticians of the proletarian class. According to Marx, theoretical justification is not sufficient for social transformation. Without practice theory becomes impossible: (1) the proletariat is not sufficiently developed to constitute itself as a class. (2) The struggle itself of the proletariat with the bourgeoisie has not yet assumed a political character. (3) The productive forces are not yet sufficiently developed to enable to catch a glimpse of the material conditions necessary for the emancipation of the proletariat and formation of a new society, and then the theoretical justification becomes an utopia. But, when the history moves forward and the struggles of the proletariat assume clear outlines, the theoreticians of the proletariat need not seek science in their minds. They have only to take note on what is happening before their eyes and to become the mouthpiece of this: (1) they look for science and merely make systems for it. (2) They are at the beginning of the struggle, they will not see in poverty its revolutionary and subversive side, but will see in it only poverty. Mention here may be made that the revolutionary and subversive aspect of poverty is its positive side, and poverty itself is its negative side, while the former overthrows the old society and the latter justifies it. From this moment, science, which is the product of historical movement and associating itself with the historical cause, has ceased to be doctrinaire and has become revolutionary.

Engels in *Anti-Duhring* points out two discoveries of Marx, *i.e.*, the discovery of the materialist conception of history and revelation of the secret of capitalist mode of production by means of surplus value as scientific and with these discoveries socialism has become science. This socialism reflects an actual conflict. The new forces of production have already outgrown the bourgeois form of using them. The bourgeois form here means bourgeois mode of production and conflict here means contradiction between new forces of production and old mode of production. This objective conflict is not like conflict between original sin and divine justice in man's consciousness. The conflict originates from objective conditions, which is independent of the will and purpose of the men. Modern socialism is nothing, but the reflex in thought of this actual conflict. Marx in his *Holy Family* says that within the anti-thesis between the proletariat and wealth, the private owner is the conservative side and proletariat is the destructive side, while from the former arises the action of preserving the anti-thesis and from the latter that of annihilating it.

REFERENCES

Adler, Max. 1925. *Kant under Marxism* (Berlin).
Althusser. L. 1965. *For Marx* (London: Allen Lane).
Aron, Raymond. 1965. *Main Currents in Sociological Thought*, Vol. 1 (UK: Penguin).
Arora, P. 1967. 'Marx: Utopian or Scientist', *Political Quarterly* (Vol. 38).
Baran, Paul and Paul Sweezy. 1966. *Monopoly Capitalism* (London: Penguin Books).
Bell, Daniel. 1965. *The End of Ideology* (New York: Free Press).
Benton, Ted.n.d. 'Marxism and Natural Limits', *New Left Review*.
Berlin, Sir I. 1939. *A Contemporary Critique of Historical Materialism* (London: Macmillan).
Bowle, J. 1954. *Politics and Opinion in the Nineteenth Century* (London: Jonathan Cape).
Bowles, Samuel. 1983. *The Production Process in a Competitive Economy* (Massachusetts: University of Massachusetts).
Colletti, Lucio. 1973. *Marxism and Hegel* (London: New Left).
Colletti, Lucio. 1978. *From Rousseau to Lenin* (Bombay: Oxford University Press).
Dahl, Robert A. 1986. *Democracy, Liberty and Equality* (Oslo: Norwegian University Press).
Djilas, M. 1990. 'Social Democracy in a Worldwide Movement', *Moscow News Weekly*, March 12.
Engels, F. 1935. *Socialism: Utopian and Scientific* (New York: International Publishers).
Engels, F. 1978. *Anti-Duhring* (Moscow: Progress Publishers).
Engels, F. 1982. *Dialectics of Nature* (Moscow: Progress Publishers).
Fromm, E. 1966. *Marx's Concept of Man* (New York: Frederick Ungar).
Gerth, H.H. and C. Wright Mills. 1958. *Max Weber: Essays in Sociology* (New York: Galaxy).
Gilbert, Alan. 1981. 'Historical Theory and the Structure of Moral Argument in Marx', *Political Theory*, Vol. 9.
Gilbert, Alan. 1982. 'An Ambiguity in Marx's and Engels's Account of Justice and Equality', *American Political Science Review*, Vol. 76.
Gilbert, Alan. 1984. 'Marx's and Moral Realism' in Ball and Farr (eds.), *After Marx* (Cambridge: Cambridge University Press).
Hilferding, R. 1981. *Finance Capital* (London: Routledge and Kegan Paul).
Kamenka, Eugene. 1970. *Marxism and Ethics* (London: Macmillan).
Kolakowski, Leszek. 1978. *Main Currents of Marxism* (Oxford: Oxford University Press).

Kolakowski, Leszek. 1968. *Towards a Marxist Humanism* (New York: Grove Press).

Lenin, V.I. 1943. *Selected Works* (New York: International Publishers).

Lenin. V.I., *Collected Works*.

Litchtheim, G. 1969. *The Origins of Socialism* (New York: Frederick A. Praeger).

Lukacs, G. 1971. *History and Class Consciousness* (Massachusetts: MIT).

Macpherson, C.B. 1962. *The Political Theory of Possessive Individualism* (Oxford: Oxford University Press).

Mandel, Ernest. 1975. *Late Capitalism* (London: New Left).

Mandel, Ernest. 1976. 'Introduction to Karl Marx', *Capital-I* (London: Penguin).

Manuel, E.M. and P.F. Manuel. 1979. *Utopian Thought in Western World* (Oxford: Basil Blackwell).

Martel, M.U. 1968. 'Saint Simon' in *International Encyclopedia of Social Sciences* (London : Macmillan).

Marx, K. 1978. *Capital*, Vols. I-III (Moscow: Progress Publishers).

Marx, K. and Frederick Engels. 1982. *Collected Works* (Moscow: Progress Publishers).

Marx, K. and Frederick Engels. 1875. *Contribution to the Critique of Gotha Programme*.

Marx, K. and Frederick Engels. 1847. *The German Ideology*.

Marx, K. 1967. *Capital*, Vol. 3 (Moscow: Progress Publishers).

Marx, K. 1844. *Economic and Philosophical Manuscripts*.

Marx, K. 1968. *Theories of Surplus Value*, Vol. 2 (Moscow: Progress Publishers).

Mclellan. D. 1998. *Marxism after Marx* (London: Macmillan).

Meszaros, I. 1975. *Marx's Theory of Alienation* (London: Merlin Press).

Mills, C. Wright. 1951. *White Collar* (New York: Oxford University Press).

Mill, John Stuart. 1961. *Auguste Comte and Positivism* (London: Cresset).

Nell, Edward. 1982. 'Understanding the Marxian Notion of Exploitation: The Number of One Issue', in George R. Feiwell (ed.), *Samuelson and Neo-classical Economics* (Massachusetts: Kluwer-Nijhoff).

Oizerman, T. 1981. *The Making of Marxist Philosophy* (Moscow: Progress Publishers).

On Historical Materialism. 1984. (ed.) (Moscow: Progress Publishers).

Pareto, V. *Lectures of Political Economy, Manual of Political Economy* and *Treatise on General Sociology* cited in Raymond Aron. 1967. *Main Currents in Sociological Thought*, Vol. 2 (London: Penguin Books).

Rodinson, M. 1969. 'Sociological Marxism vs. Ideological Marxism', in *Marx and Contemporary Scientific Thought* (Hague: Mouton).

Roemer, John E. 1985. "'Rational choice' Marxism", *EPW*, Vol. XX, No. 34, August 24.

Rubel, M. 1957. *Karl Marx* (Paris).

Schumpeter, J.A. 1976. *Capitalism, Socialism and Democracy* (London: Allen and Unwin).

Shaw, William. 1981. 'Marxism and Moral Objectivity' in Kai Nielson and Steven C. Patten (eds.), *Marx and Morality* (Guelph: Canadian Association for Publishing in Philosophy).

Singer, P. 1980. *Marx* (Oxford: Oxford University Press).

Smith, Adam. 1937. *Wealth of Nations* (New York: Modern Library).

Sorel, George. 1908. (1972). *Reflections on Violence* (New York: Macmillan).
Thompson, E.P. 1977. *William Morris: Romantic to Revolutionary* (London: Lawrence and Wishart).
Tucker, R.C. 1961. *Philosophy and Myth in Karl Marx* (Cambridge: Cambridge University Press).
Wartofsky, Marx W. 1977. *Feuerbach* (Cambridge: Cambridge University Press).
Williams, Reymond. 1961. *Culture and Society* (Harmondsworth: Penguin).

3

Dialectical and Historical Materialism

Marxist theory and Marxist approach to politics suggest both theory and practice, philosophy and action. This approach is different from the behavioural approach on the grounds that the former does treat politics in terms of class contradictions and not justify the present system as good, and so try to change the system by means of another contradiction or class struggle. However, like that of the post-behavioural approach Marxist approach takes into account both the facts and values. Henceforth, Marxism is treated as philosophy of praxis, which refers to free, creative and self-creative activity through which man creates and re-creates history—in this sense, man is a being of praxis. In *Economic and Philosophical Manuscripts of 1844* Marx elaborates his view of man as a free creative being of praxis, both in positive and negative form, *i.e.*, man as constructor of the objective world and man as a critic of human self-alienation. In *Theses on Feuerbach* Marx traces man as a self-conscious revolutionary. Marx essentially points out that the coincidence of the changing of circumstances and of human activity or self-changing can be conceived and rationally understood as revolutionary praxis—rational solution in human praxis and the comprehension of this praxis. This theory of praxis is a decisive argument against agnosticism—the criterion of 'truth' or 'knowledge'.

Science puts emphasis on 'truth' and it involves social values. In short, starting from observation of facts to generalization of working hypothesis and then to testing of the hypothesis via social values science, particularly social sciences comes to the conclusion. Scientific understanding proceeds by discussion, free competition of ideas, probabilities and probable suggestions. In case of social sciences, scientific neutrality on values is impossible. According to Marx, both history and society move according to the laws of motion of society. Following the theory of praxis, Marx proposes two important paradigms —or so to say theories: theory of historical materialism and theory of surplus value. Engels, Plekhanov and Lenin have since uphold the two Marxist theories, *i.e.*, the theory of history and theory of economics as foundation of philosophical materialism, which later on is developed as dialectical materialism, the theoretical basis of the laws of motion of society. However, critics point out that Marx's studies on capitalism and socialism are useless on the eve of great socio-economic and political changes in the world. Marx's laws of history and society are nothing but plausible statement of trends in socio-historical development.

All things are never equal in society. Social events and trends are too complex, too dynamic and too much open to outside influences— hence, no reliable prediction is possible in this case—I do agree with this. What is true in case of social sciences is also true for Marxism. Marx provides few conditions for socio-historical development—if the conditions remain equal, then they will give birth to few consequences *i.e.*, particular condition (which he learns from experiences) produces particular consequence—a particular cause provides a particular effect —this is not unscientific. Few say that Marx imposes dialectical necessity on historical development, makes abstractions to laws of motion of society, and implies conditions for social development selecting the favourable facts and ignoring the unfavourable ones. The path of science is littered with the debris of abstract ideas, therefore, the laws of historical development are abstraction of events—polarization of society with the disappearance of middle class, increasing impoverishment of the working class, economic crises, trade-union crises, decline of nationalism as a political force and its replacement by international class struggle, sharpening of class struggle, violent and revolutionary, however, which is more or less an automatic outgrowth of capitalism and industrialism.

The major drawback in Marxist theory is the equation of the laws of motion of society with that of nature, where the historical and social data are different from the natural one, and will and consciousness are the essence of socio-historical data. A mention may be made here that the movement of history and its law of causation are teleological or purposive, while it is different in case of nature. But, nature has its goal of being fulfilled and man as a natural being has desirable goal for society with the naturally inevitable. Nature has its own law of motion which bears a corollary with that of the society, for example, attraction and repulsion, action and reaction, with an exception of morals and values, which the society essentially justifies with its law of motion. In fact, the desires, motivations and values, which man as a natural being takes into account in their course of action, are Nature destined. Marxism contains moral judgement but is not unscientific in this sense.

The dialectical method is not a mere magical spell—it tries to infuse both the necessary and ethical substances. Marx uses the dialectic with a difference—reverses Hegelian dialectic that not ideas, but physical world reality is dialectical, *i.e.*, the reversal of dialectical idealism into dialectical materialism. To Marx, ideal is nothing more than the material when it has been transposed and translated inside the human head. Nature is dialectical, and the contradictions are formed in thought, are merely reflections of those that occur in nature. Engels and Plekhanov put dialectic in this way. According to Engels, dialectic is the process and dialectic of the concept is the conscious reflex of the dialectical motion of the real world, and the dialectic of brain is only a reflection of the forms of motion of the real world, both of Nature and history. In the moments when he (Marx) inclines towards a more 'activist' theory of knowledge, Marx puts dialectic in a different way— the truth within us and the real world outside us are in constant dialectical interaction— unity of thought and being and unity of subject and object. Knowledge depends on the interaction between man and Nature.

There is a difference between Marx and Engels, when the latter makes constant use of the concept 'matter', for example, 'materiality of all existence' and 'both matter and its mode of existence, motion are untreatable and ... therefore their own final cause' in his *Dialectics of Nature* and *Anti-Duhring*, which is foreign to Marx's work. However, Marx tends often to drop his activism and relapse into something simpler views of Engels and Lenin: mind is a reflection of a dialectical matter. Lenin in his *Materialism and Empirio-criticism* says that praxis should be the first and basic viewpoint of the theory of knowledge. Lenin develops philosophy of Marx and Engels according to the development of sciences, and primarily of natural sciences. Critics point out that by such a dialectical method we arrive at truth, and hence the dialectical must be replaced by critical.

The nature of dialectics—struggle and unity of opposites are difficult to conceive in ideas and to identify these in nature. Neither in ideas, nor in nature, it is true that opposites always generate a synthesis. The laws of nature are best regarded as generalizations about the behaviour of matter, derived from and supported by empirical investigations. Dialectic is not such a law. As a philosophy dialectical materialism is wholly dogmatic, beyond the reach of reason and critical examination. But, the criticisms cited against Marxist materialist dialectics are one-sided and motivated. If the scope of dialectic is broadened, then all the changes mean contradiction and then dialectic merges with the common scientific attitude of the Western world—this view is over-simplified. The awareness of conflict, process and change is fully incorporated into Western thought and needs no dialectic to support it—this over-simplified statement is not justifiable. Marx's understanding of dialectical progression of history from feudalism to communism is a good scientific attempt. Nature is dialectical and also historical—which is developing by the progressive movement from the lower to the higher, when the movements are all zigzag and with temporary setbacks—this truth of Nature is also applicable in the case of historical development. Engels points out that complex of processes, wherein the concepts go through an uninterrupted change of coming into being and passing away, in which, in spite of some seeming accidents and retrogression, a progressive development asserts itself in the end.

According to Stalin, there are no accidents in socio-historical development—all are subject to certain laws. Dialectic here becomes the algebra of revolution. Hence, in Marxist literature dialectic is the essential analytical tool in the study of history and society. Dialectical materialism postulates a material and self-sufficient nature, which moves by its inherent dialectical laws. I here argue that man cannot be totally excluded from that process. Secondly, in this process mankind in the mass will be subject to the impersonal and immanent laws as nature. I argue here again that mind cannot be totally excluded from that process. The argument here is based on a two-way process—from Nature to society and from society to Nature. History is viewed as dialectically progressive. Marxists assert that historical materialism is inseparable from philosophical materialism—in this way dialectical materialism is identical with science and dialectics are the most generalized laws possible.

According to Engels, which he anticipates that what still survives of all former philosophy is the science of thought and its laws—formal logic and dialectics. Everything else is merged in the positive science of Nature and History. Labriola (1904) and Gramsci (1971) call Marxism as philosophy of praxis, as method of considering various actions or aggregates of actions from the standpoint of their effectiveness. The method consists of practical and historical investigation, description of various habits and methods of work and identification of their integral elements. It studies history and undertakes concrete investigations of the work of collective bodies, analyzes forms of labour organization and the subjective factors changing the organization and degree of efficacy of labour. This method of praxis takes into account the interaction between individuals and also between the individual and the collective in the production process. Though Lukacs in his earlier period attacks Engels for his misunderstanding of the philosophy of praxis—for his belief that the behaviour of industry and scientific experiment constitutes praxis in the dialectical and philosophical sense, when it is the fact that scientific experiment is contemplation at its purest, but later on in his work, *History and Class Consciousness* (1971), preface to new edition, he criticizes himself for his own conception of revolutionary praxis and keeps authenticity in Marxist doctrine. Korsch (1970) treats Marxism as theory of social revolution and revolutionary philosophy, which is based on the principle of unity of theory and practice, unity of theoretical criticisms and practical revolutionary changes. These two are inseparable entities. Further, in his analysis of praxis Marcuse (1969) identifies Marxism as scientific, but not self-sufficient, as action, but not merely a philosophy, as theory of social activity, an historical action and more specifically a theory of proletarian revolution and revolutionary critique of bourgeois society. He treats praxis as doing and labour as specific form of praxis. Habermas (1970) makes a positive criticism of Marx's conception of social praxis on the ground that Marx himself has a tendency to reduce social praxis only to one, *i.e.,* the work, but social praxis, in reality, includes both work and interaction. He formulates the concept of praxis by making a distinction between work and interaction—between purposive rational action and communicative action—between instrumental action of rational choice governed by technical rules based on empirical knowledge and symbolic interaction governed by consensual norms. In tune with the Marxist notion of praxis Petrovic (1971) conceives revolution as radical change—change in terms of abolition of oppression and alienation of man by man and from man respectively, and in terms of creation of human person and human society—change of both human and human society.

Dialectic is the most prominent feature of Marxist logic. It is the logical teaching of dialectical materialism, science of the laws of motion of society, forms of mental reflection of the development of the objective world and of the laws governing the cognition of truth. The Marxist teaching on logic absorbs all valuable elements of formal logic and demarcates its limits. Formal logic is designed as the science of the laws and forms of reflection of constancy in thought and in the objective world. Dialectical logic is the study of reflection in the laws and forms of thought of the process of development, of internal contradictions of phenomena—their qualitative change, and the passage of one into another. As a science dialectical logic is possible on the basis of dialecticomaterialist method. Dialectical logic is the unity of both logical and historical, when each one interconnects and interpenetrates the other. Thought goes from the surface of objects to its essence, and it comprehends its real manifestation. Dialectical logic investigates the development of thought and the system of its categories changes with the historical development of cognition and human practice. Dialectical logic essentially entails contradictions—that poles of contradiction are within and internally related, that contradictions reflect the negativity of reality whereby multiplicity arises from unity, and that tension between unity and multiplicity is resolved through change. Engels in *Anti-Duhring* suggests that change is associated with the tendencies associated with each pole of contradiction or is associated with interaction between opposite tendencies is a negation of negation, when original negation is the positing of multiplicity within a whole and subsequent negation is the change out of tension between unity and multiplicity. To Marxists, the system of dialectical categories changes with the development of cognition and human practice. Then, what are the dialectical categories? These are negation, quantity, relation and necessity—forms of reality—and self-conscious use of these categories reflects change. Negation is a process of development of multiplicity from unity. Quantity here means parts outside the whole different from parts within the whole—and qualitative change arises from quantitative change. Relation here is relation between multiples within the whole and relations of production are relations between actors. Necessity here implies possibility, which is grounded in a tendency; hence, tendencies determine the necessities. System of dialectics changes with the development of human thought and action—they are parts of social existence.

Marx's theory of action is differentiated from that of Parsons (1966) to whom man's actions are determined not merely by self-interest, whether it is based on rationale or instinct, but primarily by social norms. When the rise of radical positivism is the negation of normativism, the rise of voluntaristic theory of action is treated as the negation of negation. Parsons incorporates both normative and non-normative elements in the theory of social action. He uses the dialectical conception of change with internal contradictions and the scheme like thesis, anti-thesis and synthesis in his analysis of social action with ends, means, conditions and guiding norms. Parsons tries to make a synthesis of an anti-thesis between radical rationalistic positivism, where the ends of human actors are governed by scientifically valid knowledge and radical anti-intellectual positivism, where human actors are driven by unknown forces—two-faces of utilitarianism, where ends sought by human actors are randomly chosen. This is the inherent dilemma or contradiction of utilitarianism. Parsons also criticizes Weber's voluntaristic theory of action with an idealist tradition, which ignores the factual and conditional elements in the analysis of action. What Parsons emphasizes in his work is on conceptualization of social action and not on interpretation of capitalism, but his main purpose or goal of conceptualization is the analysis of socialism and laissez-faire individualism and the maintenance of property of common value integration. A mention here may be made that Parsonian synthesis is an attempt to synthesize all class contradictions into a common whole, *i.e.*, the capitalist system. Here, he differs from Marx.

Marx treats the social movement as a process of natural history, which is governed by laws not only independent of human will and consciousness, rather determine that will and consciousness—this according to Parsons falls under the anti-intellectual positivist tradition, which keeps Marxist dialectic far away from Sartre's (1969) dialectical anthropology. A mention here may be made that Sartre moves from Marxist project to Kantian project of formal structures of history—from project of making history intelligible through a critique of historical reason, named after critique of dialectical reason (transformation of 'critique of historical reason' as original to 'critique of dialectical reason' as Marxist project) to the ontological solitude of being and nothingness as the foundation of historical anthropology, *i.e.*, the investigation of formal structures of history in their circularity. Unlike the Marxists, who posit that science is viewed as applied statistics, Lukacs (1971) says that dialectic exists only in humanistic and historical sciences as it is opposed to naturalistic studies of society. Sartre (1969) follows this line. To Sartre however,

> ..., philosophy is characterized as a method of investigation and explication. ..., philosophy remains efficacious so long as the praxis which has engendered it, which supports it, and which classified by it, is still alive. But it is transformed, it loses its uniqueness, it is stripped of its original, dated content to the extent that it gradually impregnates the masses so as to become in and through them a collective instrument of emancipation. (Sartre, 1969 : 232).

Here, Sartre like that of Marx treats philosophy as a living affair. Marx in his *Capital* regards his scientific analysis of capitalism as instance of dialectical method, which is not opposed to natural scientific analysis. Historical materialism as a science is dialectics in operation. Marx in *Capital* says that the Hegelian contradiction is the source of all dialectics, where the Marxist dialectic is naturalistic and Hegelian dialectic is spiritual. Professor Kaufmann reviews Marxist dialectics as in *Capital*:

The one thing which is of moment to Marx, is to find *the law of the phenomena*—with whose investigation he is concerned; and not only is that *law of moment* to him, which governs these phenomena, in so far as they have a definite form and mutual connection within a given period. Of still greater moment to him is *the law of their variation, of their development, i.e.,* of their transition from one form into another, from one series of connections into a different one. ... But it will be said, the general laws of economic life are one and the same, no matter whatever they are applied to the present or the past. *This Marx directly denies* .... On the contrary, in his opinion every historical period has law of its own.... Nay, one and the same phenomenon falls under quite different laws in consequence of the different structure of those organisms as whole, of the variation of their individual organs, of the different conditions in which those organs function... *The scientific value of such an inquiry lies in the disclosing of the special laws that regulate the origin, existence, development, death of a given social organism and its replacement by another and higher one.* (Marx, 1978: 27-28).

Marxist dialectic is the comprehension and affirmative recognition of the existing state of things and also the recognition of the negation of that state. Here, we have the concepts like totality, contradiction and negation, motion or process, qualitative change, scientific procedure, search for laws and empirical investigation—through which Marx investigates the laws of social motion. Here, facts serve as the fundamental starting points—comparison and confrontation of facts with another facts—not comparison and confrontation of facts with ideas. Here, Marx differs from Herbert Marcuse (1960, 1967) who is against the positivistic opposition to the principle that matters of fact and experience have to be justified before the court of reason and of the opinion that dialectical thought remains unscientific. To Marcuse, science comes to be associated with instrumental reason or interest, which is seen at least in the social sphere. This society is maximally technicized and bureaucratized community, which integrates the working class by drawing them into the orbit of false requirements. The driving force of social change—the great rejection of all social values, is the radical intellectuals and students as well as the unemployed and lumpens etc. To Lukacs, (1971) however, there remains a problem in the fact that capitalist society is predisposed to harmonize with scientific method. Science breaks up the whole into fragmented facts. It is essentially an expression of the reification endemic to capitalist society and by its totalizing method, historical materialism is counterposed to science. Dialectics characterize social determination as the combination of the forces of production and relations of production, *i.e.,* the mode of production through which historical materialism studies human society. According to Marx, individual produce in society and production is the determining element, whose relations assign ranks among individuals and influence of one to the others. The totality of production relations determine specific social relations, which are mutually determining and interacting with each other. In the production process, production itself, distribution, exchange and consumption are the interdependent and interacting elements, in which production is the determining element, and capital is both the starting point as well as the finishing point. The dialectics of historical materialism can be analyzed as the unity of the principles of totality, process, qualitative change and contradiction. This principle of contradiction refers to the principle of unity of opposites, which is the determinant instance. Social determination in terms of contradiction as discovered by historical materialism is referred by unity and conflict of opposites. Contradiction, here, is referred to contradictory relations between social classes and contradictory relation between the forces of production and relations of production. The relationships—relationships between classes and relationships between the forces of production and relations of production—the relationships of contradiction are different from Hegelian contradictions. But, in what sense? To Marx,

a) poverty is the negation of wealth, but proletariat is not the negation of the bourgeoisie;
b) wealth is the negation of poverty, but bourgeoisie is not the negation of the proletariat;
c) forces of production is not the negation of the relations of production; and
d) relations of production is not the negation of the forces of production; and
e) development of the proletariat along with the development of capitalism or bourgeois capitalist system is a supposedly pre-condition of proletarian revolution—diminishing number of industrial magnates or concentration of capital monopolizing all advantages of capitalist transformation from capitalism to monopoly capitalism gives birth to growth of mass misery, oppression, slavery, degradation and exploitation—and with this grows the increasing mass of the working class or de-concentration of capital in a disciplined, united and organized manner as like the process of capitalist production produces (Marx, 1978).

Marxist dialectic is a part of historical materialism, and the essence of dialectic has been applied in the field of historical development. The negation of negation is the means whereby Hegel dissolves the determinate being into infinity. Godelier finds that essentially there is no difference between the Marxian unity of opposites and Hegelian identity of opposites. However, there is a Hegelian tradition. The same Hegelian tradition of contradiction can also be found in Mao-Tse-Tung, Lenin and Trotsky, and even also in Western Marxists like Lukacs, Gramsci, Marcuse, Colletti etc. Mao-Tse-Tung following the line of contradiction distinguishes it into antagonistic and non-antagonistic, principal and secondary and combined and uneven nature of contradiction. More or less of Hegelian provenance is the dialectics of Lukacs—subject-object contradiction, of Gramsci—theory-practice contradiction, of Marcuse—existence-essence contradiction, and of Colletti—appearance-reality contradiction. However, they are not like the dialectical tradition of Marx, Engels and Lenin, which is also different from Benjamin's sudden and catastrophic aspect of history; Bloch's objective fantasy; Althusser's complex, pre-formation and over-determination of the whole, and Adorno's criticism and non-identity thinking. Not only from Hegelian tradition, but also from other dialectical traditions Marxist dialectics get inspiration and draw the necessary constitutive elements for its own formation. See Figure 15.

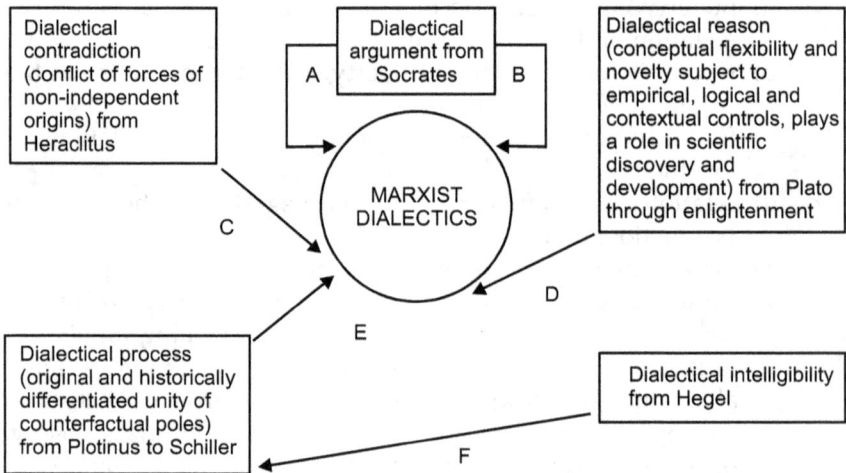

Figure 15

(Here, the graphic directions (→) are: 'A' means 'class struggle'; 'B' means 'ideal conditions as norms of truth'; 'C' means 'constitutive elements of capitalist mode of production'; 'D' means 'rationality of collective self-emancipation through material practices'; 'E' means 'systemic dialectics of commodity form and struggle for socialism'; and 'F' means 'social objects are causally related and historically specific).

Colletti (1985) refuses to accept Marxist dialectics as science and its application in the study of historical development. He differentiates opposition from contradiction that of all oppositions are not contradictory, but all contradictions are opposite in character. In other words, opposition without contradiction as object of science and opposition with contradiction as object of dialectics, which implies the unity of opposites, the negations to each other. In this connection, Herbert Marcuse (1960) traces Marxist dialectical origin from that of Hegel's negative character of reality. Colletti, henceforth, takes historical materialism as non-dialectical science, unlike the Marcusian labeling of non-scientific social philosophy. In his anti-scientific bias towards Marxist dialectics, Marcuse explains that the social facts like the alienation of labour, commodity fetishism, surplus value and exploitation—which Marx believes are not sociological facts. Surplus-value is an analytical concept of abstraction, but not a fact; alienation and exploitation are less negative than the social fact of crime and more ideological rather than a scientific critique of the society. Like that of Marcuse's use of non-scientific social philosophy of Marxism, Perry Anderson (1975) shows factual inaccuracies in the Marxist conception of Asiatic Mode of Production and theoretical and methodological problem of Marxism in separating and distinguishing juridical property from the relations of production as for juridical property can never be separated either from economic production or politico-ideological power, which becomes an outright and official fusion in pre-capitalist social formations.

Following the same non-dialectical science of Marxism, Colleti (1985) says, 'Marxism, while continuing to speak of conflicts and of objective oppositions in reality, no longer had to claim for itself (and worse, seek to impose on science) a special logic of its own—the dialectic —that was at variance with and opposed to the logic followed by the existing sciences. Further: Marxism could henceforth continue to speak of struggles and of objective conflicts in nature and in society, making use of the non-contradictory logic of science; and better yet, it would henceforth be a science and practice science itself.' (Colletti, 1985: 19). Della Volpe in *Logic as a Positive Science* (op. cit., Colletti, 1985) thinks that dialectical contradiction can be the rational instrument of objective thinking or real opposition. Pointing out the limits of Della Volpe, Colletti says that if Marx is to be treated as a scientist, then it is not possible to provide equal importance to other aspects of his work, *i.e.*, the theory of alienation and fetishism. Colletti finds that Della Volpe does not see two aspects of Marx's work—opposed and contrary aspects and he remains within the aporia that marks the history of these interpretations. When 'Marxism is a scientific theory of social development, it is for the most part a "theory of collapse", but not a theory of revolution; where, on the other hand, it is a theory of the revolution, *i.e.,* is exclusively a "critique of political economy", it runs the risk of becoming a utopian subjectivism. In more circumspect terms, this aporia reverberates within Della Volpe's work in the form of a radical uncertainty over the nature of Marxism as a social science.' (Colletti, 1985 : 23). Colletti further finds that conflict between capital and wage-labour is nothing other than real opposition, which should not be confused with dialectical contradiction. Marx becomes the scientist, who analyzes particular species characterized as historical, which constitute various types of society in succession of one another in the course of human endeavour. Colletti's argument in favour of non-dialectical science of Marxism may be provided again in the following words:

> The fundamental principle of materialism and of science, ..., is the principle of non-contradiction. Reality cannot contain dialectical contradictions but only real oppositions, conflicts between forces, relations contrariety. These assertions must be sustained, because they constitute the principles of science itself.
>
> On the other hand, capitalist oppositions are, for Marx, dialectical contradictions and not real oppositions.... this does not justify a rehabilitation of *Diamat*. For Marx, capitalism is contradictory not because it is a reality and all realities are contradictory, but because it is an upside-down, inverted reality (alienation, fetishism).
>
> All the same, if it is true that this does not rehabilitate *Diamat*, it is nonetheless true that it confirms the existence of two aspects in Marx: that of the scientist and that of the philosopher. (pp. 28-29).
>
> On the one hand, there is the Marx of the prefaces to *Capital,* who puts himself forward as the man who had developed and completed as a science the political economy founded by Smith and Ricardo. On the other hand, there is the Marx who is a critic of political economy, the man who intertwined (and over-turned) the arguments of Smith and Ricardo with a theory of alienation of which the economists know nothing. (pp. 21-22).

Therefore, according to Colletti, Marxists do not classify ideas on the subjects of contradiction and non-contradiction, contradictory opposition and non-contradictory opposition, while the former gives rise to dialectical opposition, and the latter the formal logic, but does not violate the principles of identity and contradiction.

In spite of Labriola's (1904) claim of 'naturalization of history' by Marxism and overcoming the abstractions of a theory of historical factors by Marxists—various analytic disciples illustrate that historical facts have ended by bringing forth the need for a general science, which will unify different historical processes. Marx does not propose natural laws of historical development, but discovers his own explanatory laws of motion of society based on economic foundation and historical interpretation. In terms of method, Marx follows positivistic interpretation of social sciences and causal explanation in historical social sciences. He analyzes capitalist society in terms of its functioning, structure and evolution. Like Comtean social physics, Marx undoubtedly believes that modern societies are industrial and scientific in comparison with the past military and theological societies. Unlike Comte, he does not regard the anti-thesis between modern industrial and scientific societies and past military and theological societies as the central concept, but he assigns the contradiction within the capitalist society the central place in his own methodological work. The antagonistic character of the capitalist society is inseparable from the fundamental structure of the capitalist society, and which is different from Comtean marginalization and easy correction of labour-management conflict. But there is the distance of Marxism from positivism as he grasps the idea that science does not precede by mere accumulation of facts, but by propagating theories and transference of non-observable items into scientific theories with reference to realities, for example, his theory of surplus-value and labour power. For Marx, powers and relations are the principal categories for the comprehension of human agents. Studying from his works like *Economic and Philosophical Manuscripts of 1844, German Ideology* and *Capital* a graphic presentation depicting Marx's study in historical social science may be sketched below (Figure 16):

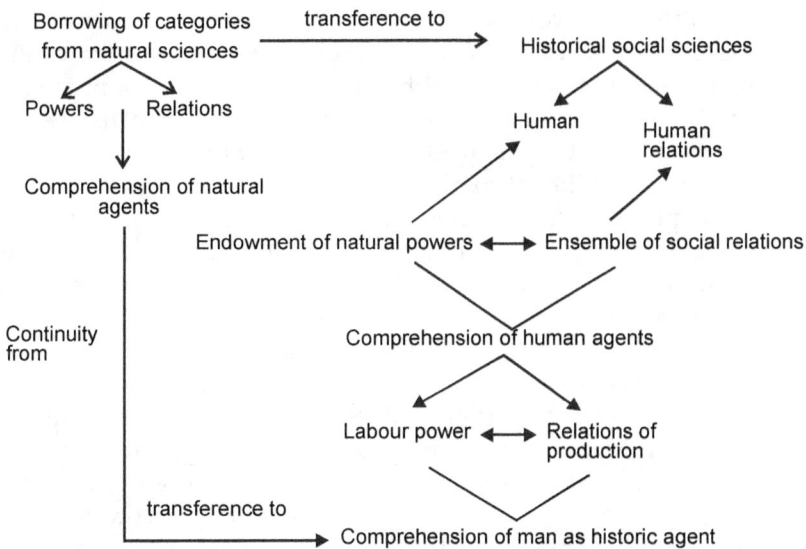

Figure 16

Therefore, human history is not natural history, and what we see in it the continuity from the latter to the former, transference of categories of the latter to the former, and application of natural laws in the study of social history. Therefore, Marx (1963) in *The Eighteenth Brumaire* says that men make their own history, but they do not make it just as they please; they do not make it under circumstances chosen by themselves, but under circumstances directly encountered, given, and transmitted from the past. The human agents act under certain circumstantial constraints, which may be called 'natural necessity', which is better understood in terms of 'historical necessity', as material and social constraints are characteristics of a particular period of historical development. In short, Marx's method may be characterized as historical realism—that is the fusion of materialism and realism in history. However, Raymond Aron (1965) finds historical interconnections between these and treats these interconnections as impossible both in philosophical and logical senses. To achieve a dialectical interpretation of history, it is necessary for all elements of a society to form a whole and for the transition from one of these totalities to another to be intelligible. These two requirements—totality and intelligibility of sequence seem to be linked to the human world. In the historical world, societies constitute total units and different aspects of collectivities are, in fact, related to one another. Different sectors of social reality may be explained in terms of one element regarded as essential—forces and relations of production. Aron raises questions with regard to the necessary relations between dialectical interpretation of natural necessity and socio-historical necessity or reality. To him, the connection between the dialectical philosophy of nature and class struggle, the central question of Marxist thought is neither apparent, nor real, or necessary. He locates historical orthodoxy in combining socio-historical reality with natural necessity, but this is possible somehow at the historical level. Whatever the possibility of combination at the historical level, logically and philosophically this is not possible—economic interpretation of history and class struggle have nothing to do with the dialectics of nature as propounded by Engels in his *Dialectics of Nature*. Furthermore, Aron doubts the interconnection between philosophy of capitalism and metaphysical materialism, which logically and philosophically is not possible, but has been established historically. In the philosophical sense of the world, a good revolutionary does require a materialist outlook, according to the Marxists, but Aron points out that logically, there is no doubt one may be a disciple of Marx in political economy without being a materialist in the metaphysical sense of the world. According to the Marxists, historical laws are not laws of history as such, but they are laws in history, which express with some validity the conditions and relations of a definite historically determined mode of production. The fusion of materialism and realism in history is evidenced from two essential laws of materialist interpretation of history:

a. the history of all hitherto existing society is the history of class struggle, and
b. the history unfolds itself and proceeds according to the dialectic of the concepts of productive forces and production relations.

A mention here may be made, in this connection, that Marx repeatedly distinguishes natural laws from historical laws, natural science from historical social sciences in several of his works, like *Grundrisse, Capital* and *Theories of Surplus Value:*

> first, eternal natural laws independent of history, at which opportunity bourgeois relations are then quietly smuggled in as the inviolable natural laws on which society in the abstract is founded, (*Grundrisse*), second, production relations are converted into entities, which become independent in relation to the agents responsible for production, and which appear to them as overwhelming natural laws ... (*Capital*) and, third, bourgeois mode of production and the conditions of production, and distribution which correspond to it are recognized as historical—natural laws of production vanishes and the prospect opens up of a new society—a new economic social formation is only the transition. (*Theories of Surplus Value*)

Therefore, Marx's laws are not the naturalization of history. Marx regards history primarily in terms of class struggle and productive forces, which largely provide historical understanding of nature through the concepts like totality and determination—which can be treated as methodology —one part determines it, the other parts and the totality, and at the same time it is itself affected by other parts. See Figure 17.

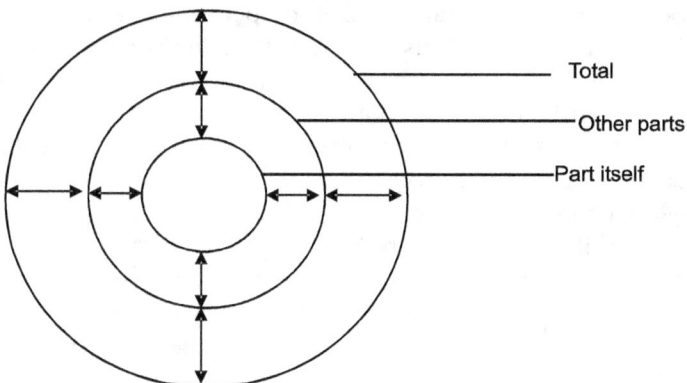

Total

Other parts

Part itself

Figure 17

Therefore, this conception is a part of dialectical method not only because of the use of the concept of totality, but because of particular kind of causality within the totality—which goes against the reductionist interpretation of economic determination. To Marx:

> The conclusion we reach is not that production, distribution, exchange and consumption are identical, but that they all form the members of a totality, distinction within a unity. Production predominates not only over itself, in the antithetical definition of production, but over the other moments as well. The process always returns to production begin a new.... A definite production thus determines a definite consumption, distribution and exchange as well as *definite relations between these different moments*. Admittedly, however, in its *one-sided form*, production is itself determined by the other moments.... Mutual interaction takes place between the different moments. This is the case with every organic whole (Marx, 1973: 20-21).

According to Marxists, the first historical act is thus the production of the means of production to satisfy the basic needs of human life. The second is that after the satisfaction of the first need, the action of satisfying and the instrument of satisfaction which have been acquired lead to new needs, *i.e.*, productions create needs, which in turn create further production (production → needs → production). The third basic fact is the propagation of social relations having a constant impact on the development of the society, and which become the subordinate relation determined by the development of social production. Graphically, it is production → needs → production → new needs → production. Therefore, social mode of production determines social needs and diverse social ties. Marxists believe that production of one's own in life and production of fresh life in procreation appear as a two-fold relation—on the one hand, as a natural and on the other, as social. Social in the sense that it needs co-operation and denotes co-operation in several dimensions—co-operation under what conditions, co-operation in what manner, co-operation to what respect and co-operation to what end. Both types of relation, social and natural are determined by society's mode of production and mode of co-operation, as the aggregate of productive forces determine the social conditions. Marx characterizes the dialectical nature of social determinateness as historical continuity in the social production process. 'The productive forces are ... the result of practically applied human energy; but this energy is itself conditioned by circumstances in which men find themselves, by the productive forces already acquired, by the social form which exists before they exist, which they do not create, which is the product of the preceding generation. Because of the simple fact that every succeeding generation finds itself in possession of the productive forces acquired by the previous generation and that they serve it as the raw material for new production, a coherence arises in human history, a history of humanity takes shape which becomes all the more a history of humanity the more the productive forces of men and therefore their social relations develop.'[1] (Marx, 1975: 30-31).

Marx and Engels see the progress of history in collisions, which have their root in the contradiction between the forces of production and relations of production or forms of intercourse. Firstly, the material production and its progress within the framework of relations of production which have historically outlived themselves turns the productive forces into a destructive element. Secondly, historically definite relations of production, which is antagonistic in character, determine the domination of one class by another—the domination-subordination relationships. The State here represents itself as an instrument of political form of domination and revolution is an instrument to end all forms of domination and exploitation—social, political and economic. Thirdly, all revolutions are not with the same characteristic features—the communist revolution differs from earlier social revolution, while the former does eliminate the private property and puts an end to the domination of the exploiting classes. Finally, the communist revolution means not only abolition of the old economic and political powers and relations, but also a massive change in the consciousness of men. Both for the production on a mass scale of this communist consciousness and for the success of the cause itself, an alteration of men on a mass scale is necessary—the alteration can only take place through revolution and this revolution is necessary for the alteration of men and their consciousness, for the overthrow of the ruling class.

The above study is the study of history of sociology, of dialectical relations in the social mode of production and of application of dialectical laws in the study of history, of historical materialism, and of technological foundation of social relationships and necessary fundamental social change. This study differs from Ogburn's (1964) cultural lag theory, where the driving force of history and social history is disguised economic interest, which is less important than that of the time factor. He comes to focus on the different tempos of change and maladjustments in different parts of manmade world of culture. Technological inventions occur before changes in the cultural spheres, and changes necessarily lag behind the technological innovations due to non-adaptiveness of the former. This leads to cultural maladjustments.

---

1.   Marx's letter to P.V. Annenkov in 1846.

Changes in different parts of culture are adjusted or readjusted with technological changes in the course of time. Graphically,

Technological inventions and cultural changes

i. technological inventions → cultural changes → changes in different parts of culture → mal-adjustment in changes between different parts, maladjustment of changes with technological inventions → cultural lag → adaptation and readjustment of culture and culture changes with technological inventions in course of time.	ii. technological inventions → cultural changes → further technological inventions → new cultural changes, *i.e.,* before every change in culture technological inventions usually occur—which probably bears a corollary with the Marxist analysis previously has been discussed, *i.e.,* production → needs→ production → new needs → new production.

According to Marx, man is the product of society, but not as legal relations of production because he is interested in explaining the character and development of the whole culture-complex as effects of the relations of production. Marx seeks to explain all major political and cultural changes in terms of development in the mode of production, but such changes cannot be explained and established without statistical information gathered through investigations of major political and cultural phenomena. Marx ignores the fact that economic basis of society at any given time is often compatible with more than one political form, which may be explained by other factors other than the factors of mode of production. Marxism confuses ultimate and proximate causation and forgets the fact that science is not concerned with ultimate causes. It minimizes the reciprocal relations among several factors, and declares the decisive influence of the economy. Marx summarizes the factors of responsibility—the mode of production in material life determines the social, political and intellectual life processes in general—this particular historical fact is the fundamental determinant of all history, which consists of purposive labour activity, materials and instruments on the one hand, and on a boarder scale, methods of exchange and the means of transport, nature of production, whether subsistent in nature or not. Marx ignores the entrepreneurial function in this category.

There is factorial ambiguity in Marx's thinking—whether factors like knowledge, technology, science and labour skills should be included in the category of modes of production or in the category of superstructure. What problem arises at this stage? (See Figure 18). Hence, there remains some ambiguity and uncertainty in Marxist concept of determination and factors of determination. Furthermore, the factors of modes of production, the independent variables in Marxist sense do not change simultaneously or may not change with similar intensity at a time. There may be variations and hence a lag. Marx does not consider this. Further, except the spontaneous changes in the modes of production, Marx does not mention and clarify the question—how changes occur in the independent variables? Marxist analysis is deficient in this respect. However, Marxists are right in affirming primacy to socio-economic conditions and structures while explaining social transformations and differentiations, which essentially are the consequences of changes in the economic structures and social environment, but not of geographical and biological environments.

To them, socio-economic conditions and structures constitute the base of human society and culture. Therefore, they divide humanity into social classes, which can explain history better than that of racial and rational conflicts, which in the ultimate analysis is the expression of disguised or diverted economic and social conflicts of different classes. This explains the methodological specificity of the Marxists. Development of society changes men's ways of feelings, pain, pleasure and other psycho-physical relations. There is nothing purely natural for humanity at large, which represents constitutive elements like private property, class divisions, adaptation with external and internal environments and biological entity of man. Man as a biological entity adapts with his own environments for the pursuit of happiness and for the fulfilment of his impulses. To the Marxists, biological is mediated through social—which historicists polemizes and which sometimes is called as idealist sophistry. Humanity is not made up of individuals who are equal in psycho-physical continuation, differentiated only by the social environment in which they find themselves. Besides the socio-cultural differences, biological differences also play important factors. Human history is continually crossed by natural history or accidents. While examining the base-superstructure relationships this conditioning must be examined—that 'natural terrain' exercises over man before the formation and development of 'artificial terrain' and even after the formation of it (Labriola, 1904 and even published in 1966). The reduction of cultural activities should not be reduced to a mere superstructure. Culture does signify not only the relations between men, but also between man and nature. Arts, science and philosophy not only are influenced by 'artificial terrain' but also by 'a natural terrain'. Arts, science and philosophy are determined by economic structures in large part and by indirect ways and in the works of art, religion and science and mediation between conditions and products which is fairly complicated. Men living in society do not cease to live also naturally. They are certainly not bound to nature as animals, but receive resources and material from it. Nature is the immediate subsoil of the artificial terrain of society. Techniques have interposed modifications and diversions of natural influences between man as social animal and nature. Our dependence on nature persists amidst our social life. The effects of nature with immediate sentiments result from these since the dawn of history, only through the angle of vision provided by social conditions (Labriola, 1904, 1966). Therefore, Labriola points out that Marx's materialist conception of history can be understood in terms of 'naturalization of history', which I have pointed out earlier, but this 'naturalization' process does not bear corollary with Marxist analysis.

The dependence of superstructure on the infrastructure or structure must not be conceived in simplistic way; therefore, it is necessary not to stop at point of generic refutations of simples and mechanism as Luporini does, but to proceed further towards the actual study of process of the interaction between superstructure and structure. The concept of superstructure can even be understood non-mechanically, which cannot include the totality of cultural activities. That is, we have to proceed from generic refutations of simples to mechanism to the actual study of processes (Timpanaro, 1975). That is, from the study of reciprocal action between structure and superstructure and dependence of the superstructure on the structure, only in the last instance to the study of the process by which the superstructure acquires autonomy over the structure within certain limits and exercises reaction on it, which will yet remain secondary in comparison with the action exercised on it by the structure. Therefore, what is primary and what is secondary depends on the nature of action exercised by one over another. Reduction of cultural activities to superstructures for all time mechanically is an approach to reductionism.

In Marxist tradition the distinction between structure and superstructure is more Engelsian than that of Marxian, where the structure is the combination of techno-economic domain and inter-subjective communications, come under the concept of social relations of production (Colletti, 1972). The difficulties inherent in the relationship between structure and superstructure cannot be resolved only through dialectical or reciprocal relations between structure and superstructure, but also through empirical observations of the relative autonomy of superstructure. Culture is determined not only by the structure of the society, but also by the antecedent culture and contemporary culture of different countries with different social structures. In his letter to Conrad Schmidt, Engels says that the economy creates nothing new, but it determines the way in which the thought material is found in existence, is altered and further developed and it is the political, legal, and moral reflexes which exert the greatest influence on philosophy. However, Engels does not look at the importance of cultural transmission in the determination of culture. Autonomy from the structure results not only from the character of cultural traditions but also from a process of increasing internal coherence. Marxism is an affirmation of decisive primacy of socio-economic conditions over juridical, political and cultural phenomena and affirmation of the historicity of the economy, which is viewed as the evolution of the economic formation of the society like the process of natural history. However, in the construction of materialism, Engels's contribution is much greater than that of Marx's equation of the evolution of economic formation of the society with the process of natural history in his mature work, *Capital*. Engels's materialism is not purely socio-economic, but also natural. He draws inspiration from Darwin's historicity of nature. Graphically, it may be presented in Figure 19.

If, sometimes

Knowledge, science, technology and labour skills

⎧ Marx's putative emphasis on
⎨ knowledge, science, technology
⎪ as factors within the modes of
⎩ production

Modes of production

Then,

⎧ Man makes their own history
⎨ is reduced to history, is made by
⎩ mankind working with Nature

Reduction of Marxist theory

If, sometimes

Knowledge, science, technology and labour skills

⎧ Marx's putative emphasis on
⎨ knowledge, science, technology
⎩ as factors of superstructure

Then,

Superstructure

⎧ Materials and tools depend for
⎨ the most part on knowledge is
⎪ deduced from knowledge,
⎩ depends on materials and tools

Deduction of Marxist theory

Figure 18

The task here is not to counterpose the historicity of society to a-historicity of nature, but is to make a linkage with distinction between historicity of nature and historicity of society. The process is vertical or

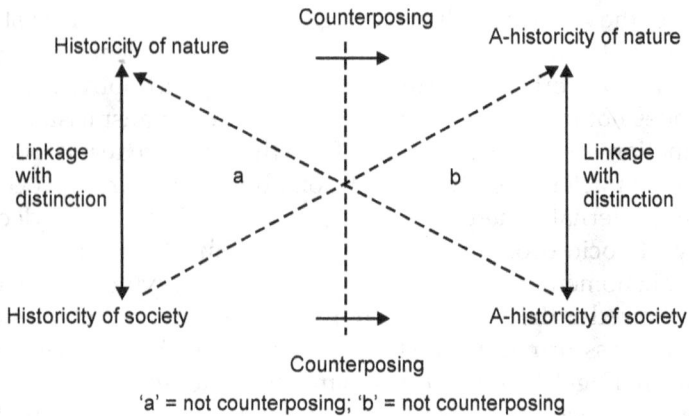

Counterposing

Historicity of nature   A-historicity of nature

Linkage   a   b   Linkage
with   with
distinction   distinction

Historicity of society   A-historicity of society

Counterposing

'a' = not counterposing; 'b' = not counterposing

Figure 19

it may be horizontal, but not diagonal. As a rule, historicity counterposes a-historicity, both in the spheres of society and nature. But this situation does not arise in cases of historicity in one sphere and a-historicity in another sphere. Therefore, both historicities are not the same. There is a difference. Henceforth, there cannot be either naturalization of social history or socialization of nature, accordingly. Materialism generally is understood as priority of nature over mind, of physical level over biological level, of biological over socio-economic and cultural—these conditionings through which nature exercises on man. Cognitively, the element of passivity, *i.e.*, external situation which we do not create imposes itself on us, does not claim to be the theory of knowledge. Engels does not regard the elements of passivity. He sought to oppose vulgar materialism and attempts to enlarge Marx's historical materialism into natural dimensions. Marx's 'guiding thread of history' (Carver, 1981) as discussed in *Critique of Political Economy*, becomes the materialist conception of history in Engels's hands, where he does treat subject as passive element and extends dialectical method beyond human action and beyond the institution explaining physical reality, as it has been discussed in *Anti-Duhring*. Engels develops a positivist notion of science which leads to the dialectical conception of nature, where he provides the laws of dialectics in the *Dialectics of Nature*. He argues that the theory of history and the subject matter of history if is applied in the order of dialectic, then dialectical materialism is exhibited. With legal and political superstructure of Marx, he introduces another ideological superstructure in addition with that of Marx's own. He understood that through labour man enters into social relationships and also into relationships with nature. Engels is in opposition to simplistic and crude features of materialism which primarily result from two factors—reduction of man's moral, cultural and political behaviour to biological activities without any mediation and thereby failure to take of the 'second nature' which labour confers to man within the animal realm to which man essentially continues to belong, and assessment of social inequalities and injustices as ills to be cured by science and thereby failure to regard the importance of class struggle (Timpanaro, 1975). Graphically (Figure 20),

Crude:

reduction into
Moral, cultural and political activities ----------➤ Biological activities
no mediation

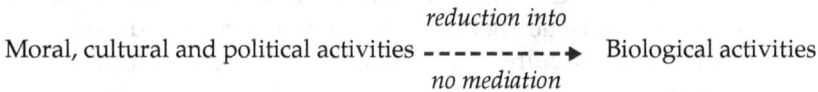

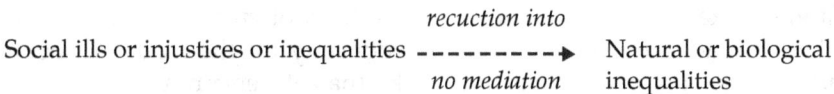

Alternative Marxist:

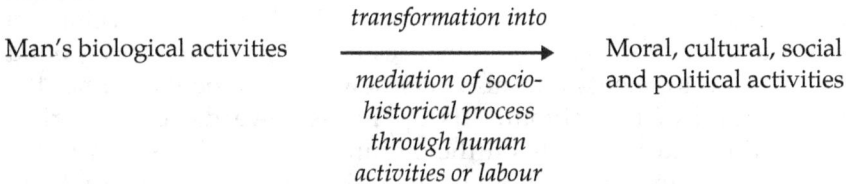

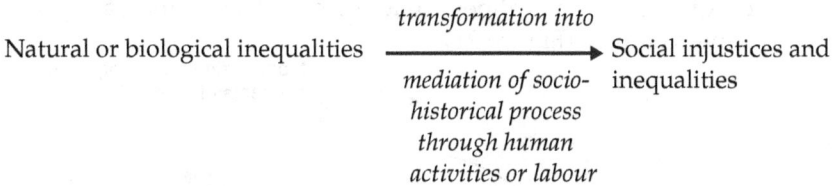

transformation into
Man's biological activities ————————➤ Moral, cultural, social
mediation of socio- and political activities
historical process
through human
activities or labour

Crude:

recuction into
Social ills or injustices or inequalities ----------➤ Natural or biological
no mediation inequalities

Alternative Marxist:

transformation into
Natural or biological inequalities ————————➤ Social injustices and
mediation of socio- inequalities
historical process
through human
activities or labour

Cure by class struggle

Figure 20

Therefore, the materialist dialectic, according to both Marx and Engels, refers to a few laws, objective laws or laws of objective existence, but not laws of thought projected through objective reality, and existence of objective laws in reality through empirical observations. 'In Gramsci's universe, matter in motion will find already existing matter present and in motion. Intellectual practices will find existing practices already present.... Gramsci not only tends to view reality as a field in motion occupied by various forces, no matter how invisible or visible in their immanence; he also proposes that these forces must be accounted for when making strategic cultural and political moves designed to change their overall arrangement.' (Holub, 1992: 73-74). Gramsci rejects the conception of historical reality that dependent on transcendent world and will create a new world imposing itself on the reality. This is Gramsci's historicism according to Esteve Morera (1990). Modernizing technologies change the instruments and mode of production, rationalizes the overall production process and also the relations of production. 'New ways of producing and processing material goods, new technologies, that is, also effect new ways of producing and processing cultural goods, unsettling the world of received norms and values. Whereas idealist aesthetics tended to measure, as did Croce, for instance, new forms of cultural production against received aesthetic norms, Marxist aesthetics, particularly Lukacsian version, tended to ignore new cultural formations when measuring art against a new set of aesthetics. Gramsci does both and more.' (Holub, 1992 : 74). Gramsci sets traditional norms or traditional aesthetics against the background of new developments and also sets new developments against the background of traditional. His openness towards technological production and its effects on the cultural sphere, places him in the modernist camp with Benjamin and Bretcht and away from emancipatory aestheticians and modernists like Adorno and Marcuse. Gramsci examines the operation and effects of culture industry and takes into account the elements of modernity for the study of socio-cultural and political programmes like that of Benjamin and Bretcht, but does not share with Marx the discontent with culture, the claims of autonomy of art, and the hopes to activate dialectic vindicating the effects of mass culture (Figure 21).

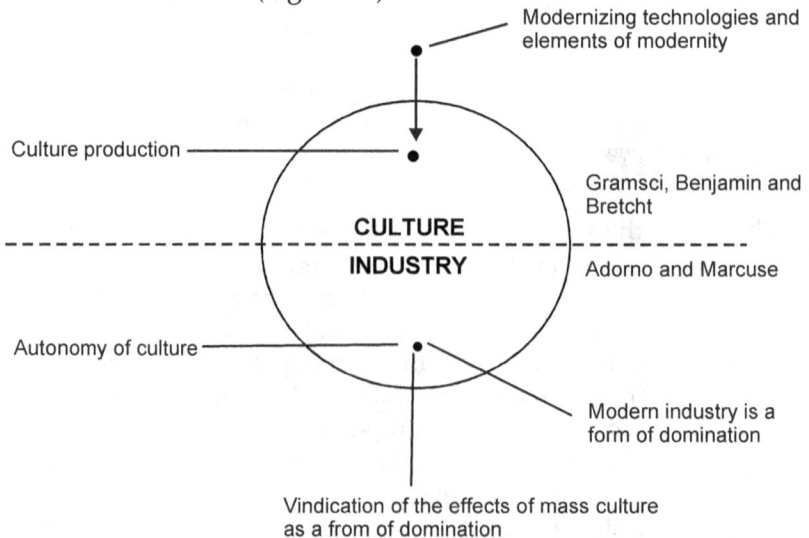

Figure 21

'These traces relate Gramsci to a theory of materialism and power, to a Foucaultian world order, perhaps to a phenomenological materialism, or to a phenomenological Marxism.' (Holub, 1992: 73).

The question of objective reality outside of human mind here is decided in favour of materialism, where the concept of matter epistemologically implies nothing but objective reality, which exists independently of the human mind and is reflected by it. Dialectical materialism insists on the concept of relativity: relative character of every scientific theory of the structure of matter and its properties, relativity of the boundaries of nature and transformation: transformation of matter into motion—from one state into another. Lenin says in his *What the Friends of the People Are* that what Marx and Engels call the dialectical method in contradistinction to the metaphysical method is nothing more or less the scientific method in sociology consisting of the premises like society is a living organism, which is in a constant state of development; an objective analysis of the relations of production, which constitute the social formation; and investigation of the laws of functioning and development. Engels in *Anti-Duhring* says that matter without motion is just an inconceivable as motion without matter. Conversion of matter to pure energy and pure energy to matter are possible under certain circumstances (Marshall, 1951). Motion is therefore indestructible. Lenin in his *Materialism and Empirio-Criticism* finds that matter is a philosophical category, which denotes the objective reality, which is given to man by his sensations. Scientific knowledge of matter is continuously developing. The essence of things is also relative. It expresses only the degree of profoundity of man's knowledge of objects. Matter incorporates recognition of infinity and inexhaustibility. The infinity of matter in motion implies the infinity of the basic forms of its existence, *i.e.* time and space. Matter is absolute objective reality outside which no existence is possible. Matter is infinite in its structure and in the multiplicity of its existence. Matter is infinite by virtue of its self-activity, self-motion and self-development.

Therefore, Marxist-Leninist philosophy of dialectical materialism as a method consists of two elements—dialectics and materialism. It is not a popular philosophy, but a philosophy of science and practice. Marxist philosophy is distinguished from the preceding philosophical system, which is not science above other sciences, but is an instrument of scientific investigation or a method penetrating all natural and social sciences. It is the negation of all preceding philosophies—the negation here signifies the continuity, absorption, critical reforming and unification of all preceding philosophical outlook. Engels in *Ludwing Feurerbach* says that dialectical materialism takes the materialist world outlook most consistently and resolves to comprehend the real world of nature and history. It sacrifices idealistic fantasies. Dialectical materialism is different from metaphysical materialism, and also from idealism. Metaphysical materialism emphasizes the role of sensuous experience, perception and empirical method in the cognition of reality, sees the world as a sum total of disconnected things at the foundation of which lay an immutable substance that do not undergo any genuine historical development. These materialists are unable to explain the reasons for changes in people's opinions and views and the role of objective economic conditions in their life. In opposition to dialectical materialism, which proposes that the world is logically moving matter and consciousness is a property of highly organized matter rather than that of all matters, metaphysical materialism comes to realize that the world is a motionless material substance and thought is the property of nature. According to the metaphysical materialism, consciousness is the passive contemplation of the world in contraposition to both idealism: consciousness determines matter and consciousness is the creator of the world and dialectical materialism: man's consciousness not only reflects the world, but creates it and the world does not satisfy man and man decides to change it by his own activity or activities. It is the alteration of nature by men, but not solely the nature as such, which is the immediate and essential basis of human thought. With the increase of intelligence man has learned from nature to change nature. Marxist-Leninist philosophy thus fights against idealism and mechanistic materialism. Stalin in his *Dialectical and Historical Materialism* (1938) focuses on contraposition of dialectical materialism to idealism, where former holds that world is material, develops in accordance with the laws of movement of matter; matter, nature, and being are objective realities existing independent of mind; matter is primary, the source of ideas, sensation and mind,—mind is secondary, a reflection of matter and being,—thought is the production of matter and of brain (a high degree of perfection of matter through development); world and its laws are knowable,—knowledge of the laws of nature tested by experiment and practice is authentic knowledge having the validity of objective truth, and the latter asserts that the world is the embodiment of 'absolute idea', 'universal spirit' and 'consciousness'; only mind really exists; and world and its laws are unknowable.

Mechanistic materialism considers that the world consists of unchanging material particles or atoms, interaction among or within these particles produces all the phenomena of nature. Nature works like the machines. Mechanistic materialism requires the conception of the Supreme Being, seeks to reduce all the processes to the cycle of mechanical interactions, and does not account for social development and human social activity. It is an abstract conception of human nature. Dialectical materialism corrects mechanistic materialism.

In *Philosophical Notebooks* Lenin says that motion is the mode of existence of matter. Equilibrium is only relative and only has meaning in relation to one or another definite form of motion. Matter without motion is unthinkable as motion without matter unlike the mechanistic materialism, which asserts that matter by nature is inert and no change happens to occur without external force and each particle is independent of everything else and relationships are merely external relationships. Engels in *Anti-Duhring* points out that motion is conceived as the mode of existence, the inherent attribute of matter, comprehends all changes and processes occurring in the universe, from mere change of place right to thinking. Dialectical materialism, therefore, considers various forms of motion of matter—their infinite diversity from one form into another, from simple to complex, from lower to higher. Matter in motion cannot move otherwise than that space and time—right and left, up and down, back and forth, and infinity. Matters and their properties by interacting with infinite space and time cause corresponding changes in each and other properties. Reflection is a universal property of the matter, which is also the ability of the material to reproduce. Qualitatively different material entities therefore reflect one and the same action in different ways. Reflection constitutes the corresponding change of the physical properties. Consciousness is the highest form of reflection of matter or reality. When idealists consider that consciousness is the primary element, which remains in opposite to the matter and attribute supernatural properties to the 'Spirit' and 'Idea', the materialists present soul as a body possessing consciousness and explains spiritual process with physical reasons *vis-à-vis* the dialectical materialists' standpoint of consciousness as a product of historical development of matter.

Consciousness is conditioned by the material life processes, which signifies the unity of the world—world is the objective reality, exists independently of man's consciousness, the world is governed by law of motion of matter in space and time, and matter develops itself through the world process. Consciousness is the product of Nature and is also the property of highly organized matter, *i.e.*, the brain. Consciousness is the generalized form of human thought structure. Marx in *Capital* says that the ideal is nothing else than that of the material world reflected by the human mind and translated into forms of thought. Lenin finds the anti-thesis between matter and consciousness to be incorrect. He, on the contrary, finds a reciprocal interconnection between the two.

Consciousness arises and develops under the influence of the matter, in the first place, and having arisen from the highly organized matter consciousness acquires some degree of independence or autonomy and influences actively the material world or the development of the material world, in the second place. Therefore, consciousness is the secondary in its origin and also secondary in its essence as it reflects reality through brain, the highly organized matter. Labour is the condition for transforming the psyche of the animals into human consciousness, where the psyche is the form of image of the phenomena, arising from human brain as a conditioned reflex and affecting the organism. Psychic is the result of the physiological activity of the brain. Animals passively adapt themselves to their environment, while man actively influences the environment with the help of tools made by them. Men make their own society with the help of their labour and develop that society with the help of the same. Therefore, men's consciousness is connected with labour and society.

Labour is here the social form of motion of matter. The existence and development of labour depend on the consciousness of the individual making up the society. Consciousness here is the awareness about the surrounding world or outside and inside environments or intra-societal and extra-societal environments, which is nothing but knowledge. Before conducting human activities, there is an image of outside world in the human brain as a resultant effect of man's interaction with the outside world. The sum total of these images reflects the reality, which in turn makes up man's knowledge. Through consciousness man understands his surroundings—what is happening in the outside world and human society recognizes and transforms the surrounding world, where individual as a subject expresses the essence of the society. Consciousness is the ideal reflection of the outside world or of the reality, which the subject possesses. Besides the possession of consciousness, man's greatest possession is labour. The development of labour is accompanied by advancement in man's consciousness. In the process of labour man acquires not only the consciousness to reflect the objective reality and but also self-consciousness to assess thoughts, ideas, sentiments, motives and values.

Like that of labour, language plays an important role in the formation of consciousness, on the one hand, and labour and consciousness together produce language, is the direct reality of thought. Language is connected with objective reality through human thought. There is unity between consciousness and language, but this does not ignore the differentiation between the two, where consciousness reflects the reality and language expresses this reflection, consciousness is the recognition of reality and language is the recognition of communication and understanding between people. Graphically, it may be presented in Figure 22.

Any social action presupposes the existence of an idea—and without this idea any social action cannot be accomplished. Idea is the motive force of practical social action, when it is transformed into an element of mass of consciousness. According to Marx, material forces must be overthrown by the material forces, and ideas take possession of the masses, then ideas become the material force, renders organization and purpose to practical action. This mass consciousness directs the people's will to the solution of material social problems, *i.e.,* mass consciousness directs mass psychology. Here, mass consciousness in correlation with social psychology gives birth to mass psychology. In this connection, Gramsci's view of consciousness may be stated, where he gives the importance to superstructure, tends to analyze the base through superstructure. Gramsci suggests that it would be a great mistake to equate ideas of Marx and Engels. Rejecting Plekhanov's theory of materialism Gramsci turns to the Marxist dialectical unity between materialism and idealism. Gramsci's relationship between organic intellectuals and their class is dialectical—drawing of material from the working-class experience on the one hand, and at the same time imparting to it a theoretical consciousness, on the other. Gramsci calls for collective consciousness of the organic intellectuals in the political, social and economic spheres, who have some degree of autonomy. The 'relationship between the intellectuals and the world of production is not as direct as it is with the fundamental social groups but is, in varying degree, "mediated" by the whole fabric of society and by the complex of superstructures, of which the intellectuals are, precisely the "functionaries"'. (Gramsci, 1971: 12). Gramsci does not take human consciousness as passive, but treats it as practical social activity.

According to Gramsci, man's identity disappears with the performance for the others. The identity of the subject can be realized through the subject's impulses and instincts and subject's struggle or determination to struggle. "'One's real nature' can be taken to be the sum total of one's animal *impulses and instincts,* and what one tries to appear as is the social cultural 'model' of a certain historical epoch that one seeks to become... It seems to me that 'one's real nature' is determined by the struggle to become what one wants to become." (Gramsci, 1985: 145). Here, Gramsci asserts the importance of subject's will and voluntarism in social action in his presumption of subjectivism and idealism unlike the Marxists. Gramsci stresses on rationalization and seems to overlook the effects of industrialization of culture and life-world on consciousness unlike Adorno, Marcuse and Horkheimer. Like Bretcht and Benjamin, Gramsci theorizes production of new culture under modern conditions of production with modern technologies— changes in the production processes affect changes in the cultural patterns and production, and needs and expectations of everyday life practices. In the production process, Gramsci looks into reality not from above but from below—people's involvement in the production process without which the capitalist production process in capitalist apparatus would collapse and popular culture ceases to function.

In his analysis of cultural politics, Gramsci finds problems in Marxist concept of dialectics, where base is dialectically related to various spheres of superstructure, such as politics, culture, ideology, law and various social practices, which are not directly involved with the production process, but are indirectly involved in the production process that legitimize capitalist appropriation. Here, the power of the predominant class operating the State extends beyond the sphere of State as such. Here, Gramsci's cultural politics is related with his theory of needs and aspirations and theory of hegemony. Therefore, the predominant class transcends its power from the limits of State or political society with the help of institutions like police, army and law to the civil society with the help of institutions like schools, churches, various cultural organizations and press, where ideological practices maintain the *status quo* guaranteed in the political society and legitimizes economic practices, such as concentration of capital and de-concentration of labour, profit motive, and accumulation of surplus value etc. It is domination via civil society. See Figure 23.

Gramsci in his conception of cultural politics and hegemony tries to make a synthesis between culture and politics, between consent and coercion and to point out that counter-hegemonies do not arise from political action in the traditional or Marxist dimension but from politicization of the cultural sphere, *i.e.*, he moves from politics to culture, from political organization to socio-cultural formation, from political action to social and cultural action. Gramsci equals hegemony with spontaneous consent to predominant power due to its constitutive elements like traditions, institutions, ideas, beliefs and ideologies manned by the pre-dominant class, and everyday practices and operations. Raymond Williams in his work *Marxism and Literature* follows the Gramscian line where he says that hegemony is a system of meanings and values and a sense of reality. Gramsci attempts to make a combination of purposive rational action with value rational action. In hegemonic cultural production Gramsci lays emphasis on relation of consumer to product rather than relation of producer to the product.

Various cultural products satisfy the needs of various social groups. The intrinsic principle of hopes and aspirations and the desire for change are the essential factors in motivating changes. Subjects can be changed in terms of cognitive, emotional and psychic structures. In the process of change Gramsci conceives of 'de-centring and autonomy of the different discourses and struggles, the multiplications of antagonisms and the construction of a plurality of spaces within which they can affirm themselves and develop, are the conditions *sine qua non* of the possibility that the different components of the classic ideal of socialism can be achieved ..... this plurality of spaces does not deny, but rather requires, the overdetermination of its effects at certain levels and the consequent hegemonic articulation between them.' (Laclau and Mouffe, 1985: 192). There are few standard Marxist positions which have been rejected in Laclau and Mauffe's work. These are:

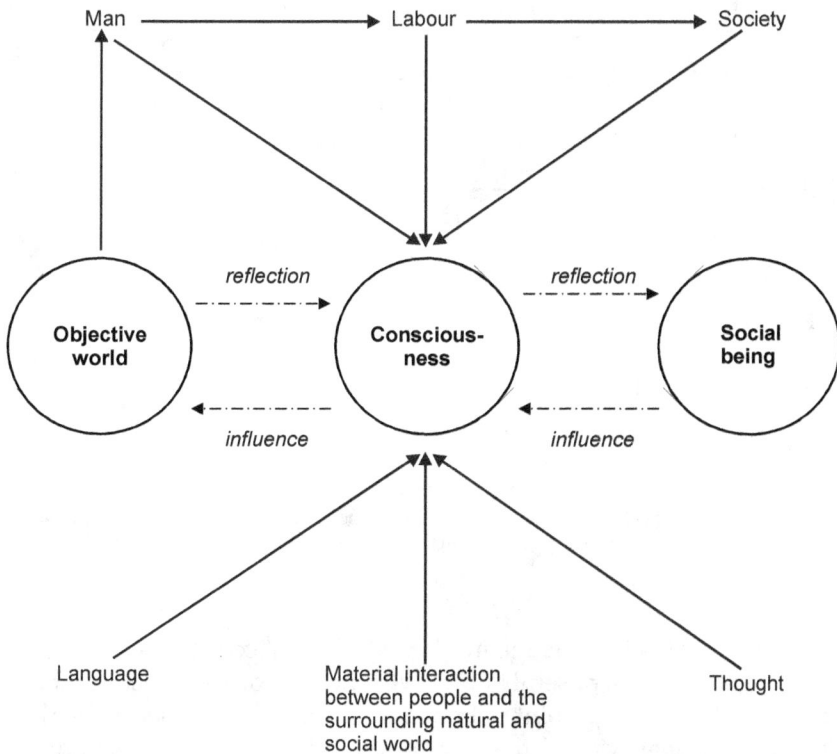

Figure 22

i. that class position, which may be treated as objective and structural, is the primary historical determinant or determinant of socio-political identities or alignments;

ii. that the relations of production enjoy the explanatory primacy or it may be said that economic structure is the primary factor responsible for social change;

iii. that politics, ideology and culture are the secondary factors responsible for social change;

iv. that base-superstructure relationship theoretically is a viable analytical tool;

v. that working class has objective interests in socialism;

vi. that there are few structural tendencies towards the unification of the working class for the achievement of the goal to socialism;

vii. that the achievement of socialism or the abolition of capitalist production relations is the crucial strategic goal of the working class for their own emancipation or for the advancement towards socialism or for socialist transformation, but not for what is termed as 'radical democracy' by Laclau and Mouffe; — working class's strategic goal is an epoch-making goal; and

viii. that socio-historical development can be studied within the unified framework of explanation and knowledge.

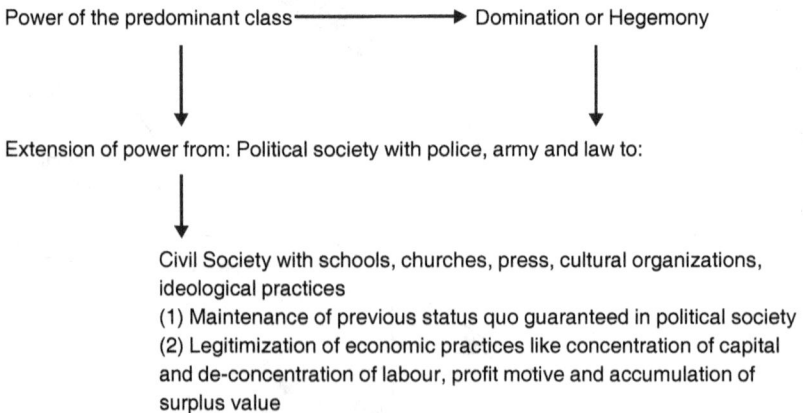

Power of the predominant class ⟶ Domination or Hegemony

↓   ↓

Extension of power from: Political society with police, army and law to:

↓

Civil Society with schools, churches, press, cultural organizations, ideological practices
(1) Maintenance of previous status quo guaranteed in political society
(2) Legitimization of economic practices like concentration of capital and de-concentration of labour, profit motive and accumulation of surplus value

Figure 23

Then, what is knowledge in Marxist ideas? According to Marxists, knowledge is the purposeful and active reflection of the objective world. Practice is the starting point of knowledge. Lenin in his *Materialism and Empiro-Criticism* says that the standpoint of life, of practice, should be the first and fundamental in the theory of knowledge, where practice includes material and productive, social and political, scientific and experimental. Knowledge arises in man's consciousness in the forms of sensations, ideas and concepts. Practical action differs from spiritual action in terms of man's material contact with natural objects and objectified social relations, the application of physical energy along with mental energy, and co-ordination of action with the essence and properties of the world, both natural and social. As a more important part of consciousness, knowledge is the endless process of approximate thought to the cognized objects, is the reflection of the properties and interconnection of these properties of cognized objects. Without practice knowledge becomes an impossibility, which becomes the material activity of the people aiming at changing and transforming the material world. Practice includes not only economic activity, but also social activity, particularly class struggle which changes and transforms the relations of production and thereby the entire social life process.

Lenin in his *Materialism and Empirio-Criticism* points out the essence of knowledge of dialectical materialism at first that things or objects exist independently of our consciousness, sensations and exist independently outside us. Second, there is definitely no difference in principle between the phenomenon and the thing-in-itself and there cannot be such difference. There is only the difference between what is known and what is not yet known. Third, as in every other sphere of science, in the theory of knowledge we must think dialectically. We must not regard our knowledge as ready-made and unchangeable, but must determine how knowledge emerges from ignorance, and how inexact and incomplete knowledge becomes more and more exact and complete.

The Marxist epistemology revolves round two concepts, objectivity and labour. According to Marx, men make their own history, but they do not make it at their own choices—they do it under the given circumstances transmitted by and through the past. Therefore, history is nothing, but the activity of men in the pursuit of their ends. The real foundation or the essence of man is the sum total of the forces of production, capital and forms of social intercourse. Therefore, human essence is the ensemble of social relations. Marx's method has three aspects—realism, naturalism and materialism; scienticism, criticism and dialectic; and generosity, specificity and particularism, *i.e.*, generic scientific realism, specific qualified naturalism and particular dialectical materialism. Marx's own epistemology revolves round scientificity and historicity. Engels's contribution in epistemology is a combination of positivism and pre-critical metaphysics of science, combination of non-reductionist cosmology and monistic dialectics, combination of dialectical ontology and reflectionist epistemology. Lenin's contribution gives more stress on practical activity. Theory reflects the world and generalizes the practical activity of man. In the process of cognition the unity of theory and practice is the major principle of Marxism-Leninism.

Knowledge, according to the Marxists, is not static, but it moves from a lower to a higher level, from perception to abstract thought to theory and then to practice. Lenin categorically puts emphasis on that from living perception to abstract thought, and from this to practice. This is the dialectical path of the cognition of truth.

What is truth, then? Dialectical materialists conceive truth as knowledge of things, but not things themselves or things as such. Cognition is the reflection of reality and when knowledge correctly reflects this reality, and then it becomes truth. This truth may be of two types—absolute and relative truth. While the former is characterized as complete knowledge and complete reflection of the objective world and the latter as approximate knowledge and approximate reflection of the objective world. Lenin in his *Materialism* and *Empirio-Criticism* regards that human thought by its very nature is capable of giving and generally does give absolute truth, which is compounded of a sum total of relative truths. Each step in the development of science, adds something new to the sum of absolute truth, but the limits of the truth of each scientific proposition are relative, now expanding, now shrinking with the growth of knowledge. Then, what are the forms and methods of cognition or scientific knowledge? These forms and methods reflect the aspects and connections of reality and the laws governing the development of scientific knowledge. These include: first, observation —purposeful and deliberate perception of the reality; second, experiment—subject's active interference in the field of phenomena; third, comparison—the study of similarities or differences between one form of phenomena under study and other forms of phenomena; fourth, hypothesis—a linkage between theoretical and empirical knowledge —transition from reflection of external aspects of phenomena under study to reflection of internal aspects of phenomena; fifth, analogy— an inference that makes possible the transition from empirical to theoretical knowledge; sixth, model-building—close connection between empirical and theoretical knowledge, transition from theoretical to the empirical are effected through model-building, which is the reproduction of certain properties of the object under study; seventh, inductions from particular to the general and deductions, from general to particular; eighth, from abstract to concrete leading to reproduction in man's consciousness of the essence of the objects under study through abstract concepts; and ninth, correspondence of logical to historical— this is the essential aspect of the dialectical method of cognition, particularly the method—from abstract to concrete—logical reproduces the historical—the chain of thought must begin with the same thing with which history begins. The purpose of scientific cognition is to assert the inner nature, the essence of objects and phenomena, and the laws governing their functions and development.

Development does not simply mean a mere process of growth, but also a process which passes from quantitative changes to fundamental qualitative changes. Here, we must consider things as interconnected, changing and moving—their coming into being and going out of being. The genuine dialectic is by means of a thorough and detailed analysis of a process in all its concreteness—there is no such thing as abstract truth and truth is always concrete. Everything in the world develops and human society is also developing. Engels in his *Dialectics of Nature* says that in nature, in a manner exactly fixed for each individual case, qualitative changes can only occur by the quantitative addition and subtraction of matter or motion. All qualitative differences in nature rest on differences of chemical composition or on different quantities of forms of motion. It is impossible to alter the quality of a body without addition or subtraction of matter or motion, *i.e.* without quantitative alteration of body concerned. The transformation of quantitative into qualitative changes occurs in the dialectical process, and which consist of struggle of opposites and also their unity.

Stalin in *Dialectical and Historical Materialism* says that dialectic holds that internal contradictions are inherent in all things and phenomena of nature—all these have negative and positive sides, a past and future, something dying away and something developing, something new and something old—all of these constitute struggle of opposites, the internal content of the process of development, the internal content of the transformation of quantitative changes into qualitative changes. The dialectical method, therefore, holds that the process of development, from the lower to the higher, takes place not as a harmonious unfolding of phenomena, but as a disclosure of the contradictions inherent in things and phenomena, as a struggle of opposite tendencies which operate on the basis of these contradictions. In the natural sphere, contradictions are manifested in attraction and repulsion, substance and field, particles and anti-particles, positive and negative sides, action and reaction, association and dissociation of atoms. In the sphere of life, contradictions are manifested in assimilation and dissimilation, life and death, and heredity and mutability. In society, or in the social sphere, contradictions are expressed in the contradictory relations between the forces of production and relations of production, between exploiters and exploited, socialism and capitalism etc.

According to Engels, dialectic is the science of the general laws of motion and development of nature, human society and thought. As per the laws of dialectics the source of development is the internal contradiction between properties and phenomena. The basic law of materialist dialectics provides us the development of the world, both organic and inorganic, the view of the cognition of the world and a picture of world transformation. There are three essential laws of dialectics: the law of unity and struggle of opposites—the sources and driving forces of development; the law of transformation of quantity into quality—the revolutionary change of the world like a leap; and law of negation of the negation—spiral like progressive development—these laws operate in the objective world—and laws are relations or connections between objects of the world—and these are essential and necessary interconnections for the development of world objects. The objectivity of the laws implies that they operate independently of the will and desires of man. Dialectical materialism attacks the idealist conception of law, fatalism and blind worship of laws etc. Man cannot abolish or create laws, but he is able to cognize them and utilize them in practical activity. It comprises the scientific method in cognizing the world. The laws of dialectics may be presented as such:

1. The law of unity and conflict of opposites: Dialectics is the teaching —it shows how opposites can be and how they happen to be or how they become identical and under what conditions they are identical, becoming transformed into one another,—why the human mind should grasp these opposites not as dead, rigid, but as living, conditional, mobile, and becoming transformed into one another. Development is the struggle of opposites, where a state of temporary equilibrium may exist between two opposites, when neither side predominates. Conflict alone is the source and the driving force of development. Diversity and difference give rise to contradiction or conflict. Difference involves divergence of trends—this manifests contradiction at first hand. Engels in his *Dialectics of Nature* points out that contradictoriness is universal, which is the source of motion. Motion by the continual conflict of opposites and their final passage into one another or into higher forms, determines the life of nature. The contradictions may be of various forms —antagonistic and non-antagonistic, basic and non-basic, internal and external, essential and non-essential. The contradictions may be stated thus:

antagonistic contradiction: contradiction between classes, whose interests are irreconcilably hostile, whose only solution can only be through social revolution;

non-antagonistic contradiction: contradiction between social classes and social groups, whose fundamental interests coincide, which cannot be solved through social revolution;

basic contradiction: decisive contradiction playing leading part in development and influencing all other contradictions;

non-basic contradiction: contradiction not playing leading part in development and not influencing all other contradictions;

internal contradiction: interaction of the opposite aspects inherent in one and the same phenomenon;

external contradiction: interaction of the opposite aspects inherent in different phenomena;

essential contradiction: interaction of opposite aspects of the essence of an object;

non-essential contradiction: interaction of the opposite aspects of accidental connections and relations.

Lenin in his *Philosophical Notebooks* explains the law of unity and struggle of opposites in the followings words—

the splitting of the single whole and the cognition of its contradictory parts are the essence of dialectics. The content of contradiction must be tested by the history of science. The identity of opposites is the recognition of the contradictory, mutually exclusive, opposite tendencies in all phenomena and processes of nature. The condition for the knowledge of all processes of the world in their spontaneous self-development, in their real life, is the knowledge of them as a unity of opposites. Development is the struggle of opposites. There are two basic conceptions of development—development as increase and decrease, as repetition, and development as unity of opposites. The unity—coincidence, identity and equal action of opposites is conditional, temporary, transitory and relative. The struggle of mutually exclusive opposites is absolute, just as development and motion are absolute. Marx in *Capital* first analyzes the simplest, most ordinary and fundamental, most common and everyday relation of bourgeois society —a relation that is encountered. The subsequent exposition by Marx shows the contradictions of the bourgeois society, development of these contradictions and development of this society. Consequently, the opposites are identical—the individual exists only in the connection that leads to the universal—universal exists only in the individual and through the individual. Every universal is an individual and every individual is universal. Universal comprises approximately all individual aspects and every individual enters incompletely into the universal. Dialectics is the property of all human knowledge. Natural science shows us objective nature with the same qualities, the transformation of the individual into universal, of the contingent into necessary, transitions, modulations and reciprocal connections of opposites.

2. The law of negation of the negation: Dialectical negation is objective, connected with development. It is negation of one qualitative state and formation of a new one—stems from the development of

internal contradictions, from the struggle of opposite forces of a phenomenon, and thereby links one state of development to another, *i.e.,* lower to higher. According to Lenin, not empty negation, not futile negation, not skeptical negation, vacillation and doubt is characteristic and essential in dialectics—which undoubtedly contains the element of negation. Marx in his book *Capital* goes on with the economic and historical investigation of accumulation of capital. Before the capitalist mode of production, petty industry exists on the basis of private property of the labourer in his means of production. The so-called primitive accumulation of capital consists in the expropriation of the immediate accumulation of capital, consists in the expropriation of the immediate producers, that is, in the dissolution of private property based on labour of its owner. This is possible because the petty industry is compatible only with a system of production, and a society, moving within narrow and primitive bounds, and at a certain stage of its development it brings forth the material agencies for its own annihilation. This annihilation, the transformation of the individual and scattered means of production into socially concentrated ones, forms the pre-history of capital. As soon as labourers are turned into proletarians, their means of labour into capital, as soon as the capitalist mode of production stands on its own feet, the further socialization of labourer and further transformation of land and other means of production, and further expropriation of private proprietors, takes a new form. Engles in *Anti-Duhring* further points out Marx's understanding in *Capital* of the law of negation of the negation, which may be presented as such—

> *expropriation*: what is to be expropriated is no longer the labouer working for himself, but the capitalist exploiting many labourers;
>
> *accomplishment of expropriation*: by action of the immanent laws of capitalist production itself by the centralization of capital—one capitalist always kills many;
>
> *concentration of capital and associated development*: development of co-operative form of the labour process on an increasing scale; the conscious technical application of science; methodical cultivation of the soil; transformation of the instruments of labour; economizing of all means of production by their use as the means of production of combined and socialized labour; monopolization of all advantages to this transformation of capital; growing of mass misery, oppression, slavery, degradation and exploitation; growing revolt of the working class with the de-concentration of labour; reorganization of the working class as disciplined and united;
>
> *expropriators are expropriated*: monopoly of capital becomes fetter upon the mode of production, which has sprung up and flourished along with and

under it. Centralization of the means of production and socialization of labour at last reach a point where they become incompatible with their capitalist integument. This integument is burst asunder. The death knell of capitalist private property sounds.

Engels further points out Marx's understanding of the negation of negation, as the result of the capitalist mode of production, which produces capitalist private property. This is the first negation of individual private property. But capitalist production begets, with the inexorability of a law of Nature, its own negation. It is the negation of the negation. Engels says that history proceeds also on the basis of the law of the negation of negation. All civilized people begin with the common ownership of land, which is being abolished, negated and transformed into private property after a long or shorter series of intermediate stages. But the demand for private property should be negated; it should once again be transformed into common property, which necessarily arises. But this demand does not mean the restoration of the old original common ownership, but the institution of a far higher and more developed form of possession, in which far from being a hindrance to production, on the contrary, for the first time frees production from all fetters and gives it the possibility of making full use of modern chemical discoveries and mechanical inventions. According to Engels, an extremely general and comprehensive law of development of nature, history and thought is the law of the negation of negation. Dialectics is nothing more than the science of the general laws of motion and development of nature, human society and thought. Therefore, negation of negation equals law of motion and development of nature, human society and thought, and dialectics equals science of motion and development of nature, human society and thought, hence, negation of the negation equals law of dialectics. This is one of the laws of dialectics. Negation does not indicate only 'no', but it is the condition of positive advance,—the old is abolished after preparing conditions for the transition to the new. To the liberals, development means a smooth and upward course proceeding through a series of small changes. But development does not take place in harmonious unfolding, but in the disclosure of contradictions—the lower stage is negated and the development which follows the negation of the lower stage is itself negated, therefore, higher stage is reached only as a result of double contradiction. This development takes in spiral forms, and not in a straight line. The law of negation of the negation also operates in socialist society—under socialism the old is negated by the new—there is continuous process of supplanting old machinery by the new—old forms of production and management are replaced by the new forms.

3. The law of transformation of quantity into quality: According to Engels, which he says in his *Dialectics of Nature* that all qualitative differences in nature rest on differences of chemical composition, on different quantities and forms of motion—change of form of motion takes place between at least two bodies, of which one loses a definite quantity of motion of one quality, while other gains a corresponding quantity of motion of another quality. Therefore, both quantity and quality mutually correspond to each other. Like that of laws operating in the development of inorganic bodies, the same laws operate in the organic bodies. Citing Marx, Engels in *Anti-Duhiring* says that not every sum of money, or of value, is at pleasure transferable into capital. To effect this transformation, a certain minimum of money or of exchange value must be presupposed in the hands of the individual possessor of money or commodities. The fact is that a sum of value can only be transformed into capital when it has reached a certain size, varying according to the circumstances. The whole of part IV of Marx's *Capital*, Production of Relative Surplus Value; Co-operation, Division of Labour and Manufacture, Machinery and Large Scale Industry—deals with quantitative change which alters the quality and qualitative change alters the quantity, *i.e.*, quantity is transformed into quality and *vice versa*. In materialist dialectics there is cause and effect relationships, where the cause is expressed as objective character of object's action on one another, cause necessarily produces effects, cause cannot be the result of its own effect, and there is temporal sequence of cause and effect. Unlike the laws of formal logic—law of identity, the law of contradiction, law of excluded middle, and the law of sufficient reason, Marxist dialectical logic operates within the three laws—law of unity and struggle of opposites, law of negation of the negation and the law of transformation of quantity into quality and *vice versa*. In formal logic, we find stability in the object of thought, while dialectical logic is thinking in terms of categories within the unity of opposites. Dialectical logic recognizes thought as developing—from appearance to essence, from external to internal, from particular to the general, from accidental to the necessary, from relative to the absolute truth. Methodologically, dialectical materialism is the most consistent and reasoned outlook about the world, about society and history. It is concerned with the law of change—the reality of the world. Both in inorganic and organic worlds, there is constant transformation with relative equilibrium position. This world of reality is characterized by a hierarchy of species-being, from lower to higher, from protozoa to modern man (protozoa → coelenterate → worms → cyclostomata → dipnoi → fish → amphibian → reptiles → birds → mammals → anthropoid apes → man → modern man), by a

sort of qualitative progression from inorganic nature to human world, and also by transformation of human society from primitive communism of initial period of humanity to socialist society and finally to communism ending with pre-history humanity.

This transformation or change, both natural and social occurs following certain laws mentioned earlier—transformation from lower to higher or qualitative transformation and contradiction. According to Karl Korsch, rather than the object of knowledge, dialectical materialism is the theoretical expression of the revolutionary movement of the proletariat. Gramsci puts up that Marxism is not just self-sufficient and all the fundamental elements of dialectical and historical materialism constitute a total and integral conception of the world. For Gramsci (1971), human history is not explained by atomistic theory but that reverse is the case and atomistic theory is a part of superstructure. It is not the primacy of economic motives that constitutes the decisive difference between Marxism and bourgeois thought, but the point of view of totality (Korsch, 1970, Gramsci, 1971 and Lukacs, 1971) is the basic differential. The critical theory modifies Lukacs's absolute historicism, emphasizes the relative autonomy of theory, and criticizes Marx's conception of labour, objectivism and scienticism.

Habermas like Horkheimer and Adorno rejects labour as the fundamental category of human activity, but he considers the implicit differences in Marx between labour and interaction, while the former is purposive rational action on an external world and the latter is communication between subjects. Habermas examines the philosophical presupposition, which allows the transformation of reason from an instrument of liberation to an instrument of domination. Marx tends to use natural science as a model for his study of society, which minimizes the role of philosophy. Horkheimer, Adorno and Habermas believe that Marxist theory can only be critical, if it restores the philosophical dimension in opposition to all forms of scienticism. Habermas agrees with the unresolved dichotomy in Marx between Marx's empirical theory of capitalism or capitalist economy and critical appraisal of revolutionary practice—Marx's theoretical categories are at times reductionist and even positivistic. The critical theorists say about the gradual de-centering of the role of the proletariat and loss of any historically grounded agency of human emancipation; revolutionary attribute of individuals rather than class expression; negative, romantic and un-dialectical conceptions about capitalism, science and technology; social theory as true repository of epistemology without bridging the gap between the present and future, holding future and showing no success. The critical theory remains negative in this respect.

Unlike Marx, Marcuse believes that human emancipation is possible only through sublimation of the work itself in sensuous manner, but not through rational regulation of necessary labour or not through creative work. Habermas points out the degeneration of the Russian revolution into Stalinism, technocratic social management, failure of revolution in Western countries, absence of class consciousness among the working class and collapse of Marxist theory as deterministic, objectivist, and pessimistic. Habermas attempts to combine the conception of human species as natural process with the conception of nature or reality, which is constituted by human activity. It leads to a dilemma—nature with transcendental status of a constituted objectivity cannot be the historical ground for constituted subjectivity, and the historical ground for constituted subjectivity of nature cannot simply be the constituted objectivity. It is the irreducibility of objectivity to subjectivity, which Adorno posits unlike the Marxist dialectical approach to the reduction of irreducible opposites, for example, consciousness and being, to the other.

Marxists apply the dialectical laws to the study of history. In *Economic and Philosophical Manuscripts of 1844*, Marx says that sense experience must be the basis of all sciences. Science becomes the genuine when it proceeds from sense experience—sense perception and sensuous need, that is, only when it proceeds from Nature. Man is an object of sense perception. History is a preparation for man for the development of human needs. It is the development of Nature into man. Consciousness of man is a social product. Social activity and social mind by no means exist only in the form of activity or mind, which is manifestly social. In his species-consciousness man confirms his real social life, and reproduces his real existence in thought, while species-being confirms itself in species-consciousness, conversely. Thought and being are distinct, but they also form a unity.

Historical materialism is the social-scientific theory—it designates the view that the course of history is the ultimate cause and moving force of economic development of society—changes in the mode of production and exchange, and also the cause and moving force of consequent division of the society into distinct classes and class struggle between the classes. The existence of classes is related with historical phases of development of production. This class struggle inevitably leads to the dictatorship of the proletariat and this in turn leads to the abolition of classes. How does the contradiction between the forces of production and relations of production give birth to class contradiction? See Figure 24. The mode of production should not only be regarded simply as the reproduction of the existence of individuals, but should also be regarded as a mode of life. Individuals express their life through the material conditions of their production. Marx in 'Preface' to *A Contribution to the Critique of Political Economy* summarizes the conception of historical materialism thus:

> In the social production which men carry on they enter into definite relations that are indispensable and independent of their will; these relations of production correspond to a definite stage of development of their material powers of production. The sum total of these relations of production constitutes the economic structure of society—the real foundation on which rise legal and political superstructures and to which correspond definite forms of social consciousness. The mode of production in material life determines the general character of the social, political and spiritual processes of life. It is not the consciousness of men that determines their existence, but, on the contrary, their social existence determines their consciousness. At a certain stage of their development, the material forces of production in society come into conflict with the existing relations of production, or what is but a legal expression for the same thing—with the property relations within which they had been at work. From forms of development of the forces of production, these relations turn into their fetters. Then, comes the period of social revolution. With the change of the economic foundation the entire immense superstructure is more or less rapidly transformed. In considering such transformation the distinction should always be made between the material transformation of the economic conditions of production which can be determined with the precision of natural science, and the legal, political, religious, aesthetic or philosophic—in short ideological—forms in which men become conscious of this conflict and fight it out. Just as our opinion of an individual is not based on what he thinks of himself, so we cannot judge of such a period of transformation by its own consciousness; on the contrary, this consciousness must rather be explained from the contradictions of material life, from the existing conflict between the social forces of production and the relations of production. No social order ever disappears before all the productive forces, for which there is room in it, have been developed; and the new higher relations of production never appear before the material conditions of their existence have matured in the womb of the old society. Therefore, mankind always takes up only such problems as it can solve; since, looking at the matter more closely, we will always find that the problem itself arises only when the material conditions necessary for its solution already exist or are at least in the process of formation. In broad outlines we can designate the Asiatic, the ancient, the feudal, and the bourgeois methods of production as so many epochs in the progress of the economic formation of society. The bourgeois relations of production are the last antagonistic form of the social process of production—antagonistic not in the sense of individual antagonism, but of once arising from conditions surrounding the life of individuals in society; at the same time the productive forces developing in the womb of bourgeois society create

the material conditions for the solution of that antagonism. This social formation constitutes, therefore, the closing chapter of the prehistoric stage of human society.

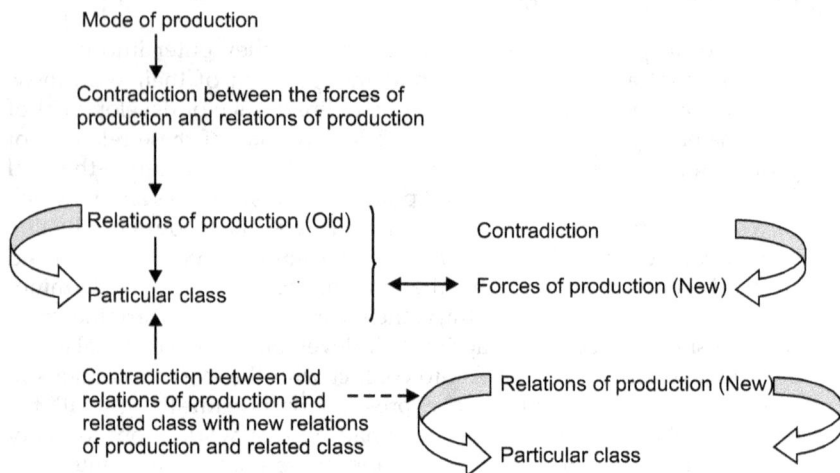

Figure 24

In *German Ideology* Marx says that in the development of the productive forces a stage is reached where productive forces and means of intercourse are called into being, under which the existing relations are no longer productive, but are destructive forces. The conditions under which determinate productive forces can be used are also the conditions for the dominance of a determinate social class, whose social power is derived from property ownership. The dialectic between the forces of production and relations of production implies the theory of revolution, is due to historical necessity and not an accident. According to the materialist conception of history, society is regulated by objective laws; development of the material basis of the society is the foundation on which views, institutions, political, ideological and cultural developments develop; and views, institutions and ideas also play an important and active role in the development of the material basis.

According to Stalin, the history of society ceases to be an agglomeration of 'accidents', but becomes the history of the development of society according to regular laws of society. Engels in *Ludwing Feuerbach* says that in the history of society the actors are endowed with consciousness, where the human act with deliberation or passion towards definite goals. Nothing happens without the intended goals or aims—numerous desired ends or goals cross and conflict with one another. Thus, the conflict of innumerable individual wills and actions in the domain of history produces a state of affairs entirely analogous to that in the realm of unconscious nature.

Many individual wills active in history for the most part produce results quite other than those they intended and often quite the opposite. The forces of production change and develop as the fundamental laws of the development of society. Change and development of production start with the changes and development of the instruments of production. First, the productive forces of society change and develop. Second, depending on these changes and in conformity with them, men's relations of production and their economic relations also change. Marx in his *Poverty of Philosophy* says that the productive forces are closely bound up with social relations. In acquiring new productive forces men change their mode of production and in changing their mode of production, in changing their way of living, they change all their social relations. The relations of production, or property relations and forms of ownership of the means of production, necessarily arise out of social production having their influence upon the development of productive forces. As the forces of production develop, and as the new relations of production are brought into being, corresponding to the development of the forces of production, classes too arise and develop. For society has always been divided into the exploiters and exploited. The exploiters, who are in the minority, exercise their domination over the majority by means of State power. Engels, points out in his book *Origins of the Family, Private Property and the State* that the State has not existed for all of eternity. There have been societies which have managed without it. They have no notion of State or State power. At a definite stage of economic development, which necessarily involves the cleavage of society into classes the State becomes a necessity because of these cleavages. Though the State arises from the need to keep class antagonisms in check, it is also in the thick of the fight between the classes. Thus it is normally the State of the most powerful economically ruling class, and so acquires new means of holding down and exploiting the oppressed class. The central link in civilized society is the State, which in all typical periods is without exception the State of the ruling class. The State, according to Lenin, is an organ of class rule and an expression of repression. The great majority of working class is exclusively absorbed in labour, according to Engels, which he expresses in *Socialism: Utopian and Scientific*. There remains a class, according to Engels, which is not directly involved with productive labour, but is involved with the management and direction of labour. It is the law of the division of labour which lies at the root of the division into classes. In *Anti-Duhiring* Engels says that so long as the working population is so much occupied in their necessary labour they has no time left for looking after the common affairs of society. The advance in industry creates the conditions under which the working class not only grows in number and organization, but prepares the working class for taking command over production. Marx in *Communist Manifesto* says that the history of class struggle forms a series of evolution in which a stage has been reached where the exploited and oppressed class cannot attain its emancipation from the sway of the exploiting class. At this stage, the socialist revolution is a historical necessary. For that, Marx, in his letter to Weydemeyer says that the existence of classes is only bound up with particular historical phases in the development of production. The class struggle leads to the dictatorship of the proletariat, and this dictatorship constitutes the transition to a classless society, where, according to Engels, it is government of the people, which is replaced by the administration of things and the direction of the process of production.

Marx says that men are not free to choose their productive forces, which are the basis of all their history. Every productive force is an acquired force, the product of former activity. The productive forces are, therefore, the result of practically applied human energy. This energy is conditioned by the circumstances in which men find themselves, by the productive forces already acquired, by the social forms, which is the product of preceding generation. Every succeeding generation finds itself in possession of the productive forces acquired by the previous generation, which serve as raw material for new production. A history of humanity takes place. The history of men is essentially the history of individual development. The material relations are the bases of all their relations, and material relations are the necessary forms in which their material and individual activities are realized. There is the law of correspondence between the relations of production and forces of production, which is essential for the functioning and development of social production. Though production relations are the forms of and conditions for the development of the productive forces in the first stage, in the second stage, a discrepancy emerges between production relations and the productive forces, and these two come into conflict. Then production relations act as a brake or constraint on the development of production. In the course of further development of production, the obsolete forms of production come into conflict with the new forces of production, giving rise to new forms of production relations. These new types of production relations gradually replace each other—in the place of an earlier form of intercourse, which has become a fetter, a new one is put, corresponding to the more developed productive forces, and hence, to the advanced mode of the self-activity of individuals. Every change in the social order, every revolution in property relations is the necessary result of the creation of new productive forces which would no longer conform to the old property relations. Private property itself arose in this way. See Figure 25:

Common ownership of the means of production, relations of production and mutual assistance among the people (determination by means of collective labour)
↓
Improvement of the primitive means of labour from stone to metal
↓
Application of means of labour from 'on communal basis' to 'on individual basis' for private production of material goods
↓
Communal ownership of the means of production is replaced by private ownership of the means of production $\xrightarrow[\text{historical necessity}]{}$
Private property appears and slave-owning production relations set in
↓
Conflict between slave-owning production relations and new forces of production $\xrightarrow[\text{historical necessity}]{}$
Slave owning production relations are replaced by feudal production relations
↓
Conflict between feudal production relations and new forces of production $\xrightarrow[\text{historical necessity}]{}$
Feudal production relations are replaced by capitalist production relations (based on wage labour, money and capital)
↓
Contradiction between the social character of production and the private capitalist form of appropriation emerged and developed
↓
Contradiction brings about:
↓
i. economic crises of over production
↓
ii. destruction of productive forces and means of subsistence created
↓
iii. chronic under-capacity of production
↓
iv. mass unemployment
↓
Conflict between capitalist production relations and new forces of production $\xrightarrow[\text{historical necessity}]{}$
Capitalist production relations are replaced by socialist production relations
↓
Social ownership of the means of production and social form of distribution of the material goods produced

Figure 25

Therefore, the economy is the determining factor and laws of economy are the fundamental laws of social and historical development. They are the objective laws operating independently of the individual's will—they are specific laws peculiar to particular socio-economic formation and general laws to all formations. People need changes in society through the utilization of these objective laws—the economic laws are determined by class relations and class interests. The progressive class utilizes economic laws for higher development, while the reactionary classes resist, when the former belongs to the majority and the latter to the minority. The majority working class in their achievement towards the goal of socialism utilizes the economic laws in the interest of the majority of society. The struggle for socialism is guided by scientific knowledge of these objective economic laws. The struggle for socialism and establishment of it are acknowledged with the full understanding of these laws. They are utilized to undertake the planned regulation of production in accordance with the needs of society in general, and of the individual as a part. The laws have already been mentioned. In short, development of production begins with a change in the productive forces, productive forces are instruments of production and people utilize these, the instruments of production within the framework of forces of production develop first, to lighten labour and to obtain more material wealth with minimum expenditure of labour people constantly improve the existing instruments and devise new and more efficient methods, and as the instruments of labour and the workers develop people's relations in the production process, the relations of production also change.

Engels in *Anti-Duhring* says that materialist conception of history starts from the principle that production and with production exchange of the products are the bases of every social order. The distribution of the products and division of society into different classes in every society, which appears in history, are determined by the nature of production —what is produced, how it is produced ad how the product is exchanged. Accordingly, the ultimate causes of all social changes and political revolutions are sought in the minds of men, in their increasing insights into eternal truth and justice, in changes in the mode of production and exchange, are to be sought not in the philosophy but in the economics of the epoch concerned. The growing realization is that existing social institutions are irrational and unjust, that reason has become nonsense and good deeds a scourge is only a sign that changes have been taking place quietly in the methods of production and forms of exchange with which the social order, adapted to previous economic conditions, is no longer in accord. The existing social order is the creation of the present ruling class. The mode of production peculiar to the bourgeoisie is called the capitalist mode of production, which is incompatible with the feudal mode of production. The bourgeoisie shatters the feudal system and on its ruins established bourgeois social order, the realm of free competition, freedom of movement, and equal rights for commodity owners. The capitalist mode of production freely develops, then. From the time when steam and the new tool making machinery begun to transform into a large-scale industry, the productive forces evolved under bourgeois direction, developed at a pace that was previously unknown, and to an unprecedented degree. As manufacturing and the handicrafts industry have been further developed under its influence, they have come into conflict with the feudal fetters of the guilds, so large-scale industry, as it develops more fully, comes into conflict with the barriers within which the capitalist mode of production holds it confined. The new forces of production have already outgrown the bourgeois from of using them—the conflict between forces of production and mode of production rises in thought, exists in the facts, objectively outside of us, independently of the will or purpose of the men, who brought it about. Modern socialism is nothing but the reflex into thought of this actual conflict, its ideal reflection in the minds first of all the class which is directly suffering from it—the working class. The solution consists firstly, in the recognition of the practice of the social nature of the modern productive forces, secondly, in bringing the mode of production, appropriation and exchange in accord with the social character of the means of production. This can only be brought about by society taking possession of the productive forces which have outgrown all control other than that of society itself. Thereby, the social character of the means of production and of the products,—which today operates against the producers themselves periodically, breaking through the mode of production and exchange. The forces working in society work exactly like the forces operating in nature. The treatment of the productive forces recognized by the society opens the way to the replacement of the anarchy of social production by a socially planned regulation of production in accordance with the needs of both of society and of each individual. See Figure 26.

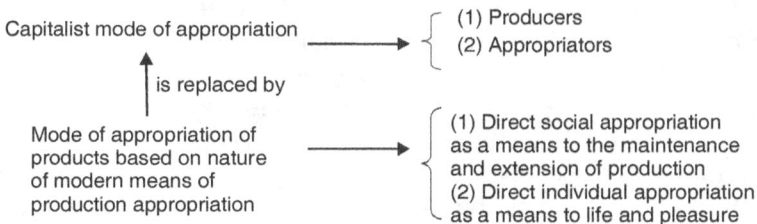

Capitalist mode of appropriation ⟶ { (1) Producers (2) Appropriators

↑ is replaced by

Mode of appropriation of products based on nature of modern means of production appropriation ⟶ { (1) Direct social appropriation as a means to the maintenance and extension of production (2) Direct individual appropriation as a means to life and pleasure

Figure 26

The division of society into exploiting and exploited class, ruling and oppressed class, is the necessary outcome of the low development of production. So long as the sum of social labour yields a product, which exceeds what is necessary for the bare existence of all and so long as almost all the time of the great majority of the members of society is absorbed in labour, then so long the society is necessarily divided into classes. Therefore, the law of division of labour in society is the root of the division of society into classes. If the division into classes has a certain historical justification, it has this only for a given period of time, and only for given social conditions. It is based on the insufficiency of production, which will be swept away by the full development of productive forces. It, therefore, presupposes that the development of production has reached a level at which the appropriation of means of production, of products, of political supremacy, the monopoly of education and intellectual leadership by a special class of society, has become not only superfluous, but also economically, politically and intellectually a hindrance to development. The expanding force of the means of production bursts asunder the bonds imposed by the capitalist mode of production. Release from these bonds is the sole condition necessary for an unbroken and constantly more rapidly progressing development of productive forces, and therewith a practically limitless growth of production itself. The appropriation by society of the means of production puts an end not only to the artificial restraints on production, but also to the positive waste and destruction of the productive forces and products, which is now inevitable accompaniment of production and reaches its zenith in crises. The seizure of the means of production by society puts an end to commodity production and to the domination of product over the producer. Anarchy in social production is reached by conscious organization on a planned basis. The struggle for individual existence comes to an end. Man enters into conditions which are really human. Man with full consciousness will fashion his own history. It is humanity's leap from the realm of necessity into the realm of freedom. This emancipating act of humanity is the historical mission of the proletariat. It is the task of scientific socialism. It is the theoretical expression of the proletarian movement.

Here, the economy is the base, which determines the superstructure. The mode of production in the material life determines the general character of the social, political and spiritual processes of life. Men are the producers of consciousness and ideas, the superstructure of society. Consciousness can never be anything else than conscious existence and social organization evolves directly out of production and commerce, which in all ages forms the basis of the State and of the rest of the idealistic superstructure. This viewpoint of Marx in *German Ideology* once more is reflected in his understanding of 'capital' in *Capital*. Lenin points out that Marx shows not only the capitalistic economic structure and its law of development, but also definite modes of consciousness. Marx takes the system of commodity production and the laws governing this system and development of formation of the capitalist society. Besides the analysis of the relations of production in capitalist society, Marx analyzes two questions—how the commodity organization of social economy develops and how it becomes transformed into a capitalist economy? While explaining the development of the capitalist formation of the society in terms of relations of production, Marx tries to analyze the response of the superstructure to these relations of production in exhibiting the capitalist social formation with manifestation of class antagonism inherent in the relations of production, bourgeois political superstructure, preserving the domination of the capitalist class, with bourgeois ideas of liberty, equality and fraternity, and even with bourgeois family relations. To Stalin, the base is the economic structure at a given stage of development and the superstructure is the political, legal, religious, artistic and philosophical views of the society, and political, legal and other institutions corresponding to them. The superstructure is the product of its base, which consists of economic structure of the society and the sum total of relations of production in society.

It is the relations of production and not the forces of production which are the bases of the superstructure. The superstructure is not directly connected with forces of production, production and man's productive activity. The superstructure reflects changes in the level of development of the productive forces not immediately and not directly, but only after changes in the base. Every base has its corresponding superstructure. The base of the feudal system has its superstructure, its political, legal and other views and the corresponding institutions; the capitalist base has its own superstructure; and so has the socialist base. If the base changes or is eliminated, then its superstructure changes or is eliminated. If the new base arises, then following this a new superstructure is raised corresponding to that base. The superstructure is the product of one epoch; in which given economic base exists and operates—it is eliminated and it disappears with the elimination and disappearance of the economic base. According to the materialist conception of history, production and reproduction of the real life— this factor is the determining element in history. The economic situation is the base, but the various elements of the superstructure also exercise their influence in the course of historical struggle and development.

The political, juridical, philosophical, religious, literary and artistic developments are based on economic development; react upon one another and also on the economic base. It is not the economic condition alone that is active, while everything else makes a passive impact on the historical development and production. There is interaction on the basis of economic necessity, which ultimately always asserts itself.

Determination by the economic base is operated by and through two fundamental mechanisms that are functionally intertwined—the systemic processes of reproduction and class struggle. According to Marx, every mode of production has certain specific laws of motion through which reproduction takes place, wherein external forces have their impact—the relationship between the conquering and conquered people. Marx in *Grundrisse* says that three things possibly happen in this case (1) the conquering people subjugates the conquered under its own mode of production; (2) it leaves the old mode intact and is contented itself with a tribute; and (3) a reciprocal interaction takes place whereby something a new or a synthesis arises. In all cases, the mode of production—mode of production of the conquering people, mode of production of the conquered and synthesized form of mode of production, is decisive for the new distribution. All these are determined by the interaction between mode of production of the conquering people and mode of production of the conquered. However, there is relative autonomy of the superstructure. The rise and development and abolition of class divisions are equally determined by the development of the productive forces and relations of production. The reciprocal determination of the base by the relatively autonomous superstructure means that class struggle is not only economic, but political and ideological as well. According to Engels, in a modern State, law must not only correspond to the general economic conditions and be its expression, but also be an internally coherent expression. However, in the reproduction of the totality the laws of motion of the superstructure are determined, conditioned and circumscribed by the base.

The determination of the political by the economic base has been formulated by Marx in the *Eighteenth Brumaire* where the State has been represented as concentration of class relationships, and State power as class power. The relative autonomy of the State denotes relationship of representation, relationship between the classes, and the functionaries of the State. Further, the relative autonomy of the State is the basis of the dictatorship of the proletariat from which starts a socialist construction with the abolition of old repressive State machinery and administrative apparatus and formation of a new one, which has been stated by Marx in *Civil War in France* and by Lenin in *State and Revolution*.

In *The Eighteenth Brumaire* Marx says that the whole of superstructure of different and specially formed feelings, illusions, and modes of thought, and views of life arises on the basis of the different forms of property, of the social conditions of existence. The whole class creates and forms these out of its material foundations and the corresponding social relations. According to Marx, relations of domination are only relations of production and ideas are formed and developed within class relations and class struggle. The economic basis has the determinative role in giving rise to superstructure and in changing the superstructure with changes in the socio-economic basis. Lenin in *Revolution Teaches* categorically states that changes in the superstructure become sharper and deeper when one economic basis supersedes another as a result of social revolution—the old is replaced by the new—the old superstructure falls apart and the new one is created by the independent action of the most diverse social forces. Revolution in the superstructure takes place when the old basis is ousted or replaced by the new. The new superstructure takes those elements from the old, which can serve classes of the new society. The ideas and institutions play important role in defending, protecting and strengthening the basis for fulfilling particular class interests. Therefore, production, base and superstructure are the key links and components of any socio-economic formation (Figure 27). Therefore,

I. *Socio-economic formation (F) = Production (P) + Base (B) + Superstructure (S)*

II. $(F_{1s,t} + F_{2s,t} + ...F_{3s,t}) = (P_{1s,t} + P_{2s,t} + P_{3s,t} + ...P_{ns,t}) + (B_{1s,t} + B_{2s,t} + B_{3s,t} + ...B_{ns,t}) + (S_{1s,t} + S_{2s,t} + S_{3s,t} + ...S_{ns,t})$

III. Graphically, $F = \leftrightarrow (P \leftrightarrow B \leftrightarrow S)$, where F is the whole and P, B and S are parts, and whole precedes the parts and parts precede the whole—the interactive whole within specific time and space ('t' and 's').

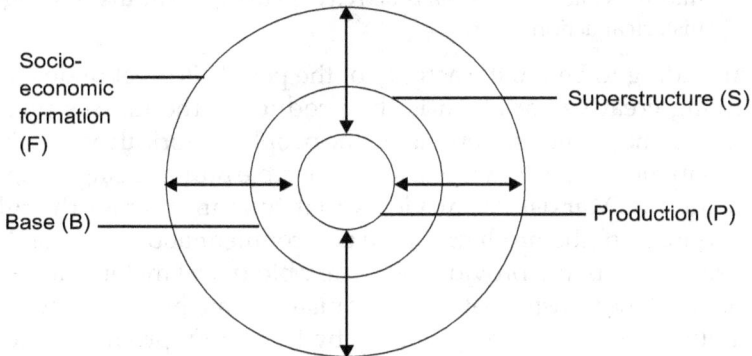

Figure 27

Production is characterized by forces of production, reproduction, distribution, and relations of production. Besides production, basis and superstructure, a socio-economic formation is characterized by other social features—specific human communities, mode of life, family, marriage, language, natural science and certain public organizations. These components are essential for any socio-economic formation. Like the components of production, base and superstructure, the components of human communities, mode of life, family, marriage, language, natural science and public organizations also change with the transition from primitive communism to feudalism, from feudalism to capitalism, from capitalism to socialism, and from socialism to communism. History is a law-governed natural historic process of replacement of one socio-economic formation by another. Lenin in *What the 'Friends of the People' Are and How They Fight the Social Democrats* says that only the reduction of social relations to production relations and of the latter to the level of the productive forces, provided a firm basis for the conception that the development of formation of society is a process of natural history. Material production is the basis of social life, the working people are the chief productive force, and hence they are the decisive force in social development and real makers of history. They do not make history at their own will, but make it in accordance with the objective conditions or laws or laws of mode of production which are historically determined. Graphically, the process may be explained as such:

> development of material production from lower to higher → changes in the people's historical role → progressive development of mankind → people's historical role rises → greater and deeper social transformation from primitive communism to feudalism, from feudalism to capitalism, from capitalism to socialism and finally from socialism to communism → larger number of people taking part in the historical process → greater activity of the people concerned is taking place → people's activity is turned into mass activity → mass activity increases with the thoroughness of historical action

According to Lenin, the activity of the people is great under socialism. Living creative socialism is the product of the masses themselves. Besides the greater importance to the people, historical materialism gives importance to the individual, to the concrete human being. In opposition to the pre-Marxist social views that human, human thoughts and emotions are the products of the environment and *vice versa*, Marxism asserts that nature provides necessary biological material for the rise of man, but the transformation of this material into human being is brought about by social factors, primarily by labour, by productive activity or activities. Labour creates man and finds its embodiment in the structure of the human body. The individual is humanized and socialized. Lenin regards that the idea of historical necessity does not in the least undermine the role of the individual in history and history is made up of active individuals, who are active historical figures or agents. According to Marxists, historical materialism proposes:

a. individual makes history by his labour;
b. man makes his own history through his political and conscious activity, will and reason;
c. the greater is social progress, the greater the influence of individual on society;
d. people participate in historical activities and individual plays increasing role in the historical process, in the material and spiritual life processes with the development of history and progress of science, technology and culture;
e. not a single class in history achieves power without producing its political leaders and prominent representatives who are able to organize movement and lead it;
f. working class all over the world is waging a hard and persistent struggle for their emancipation needs authorities;
g. the ruling class, which rules the material force of society is also the ruling intellectual force, where the dominant material relationships are grasped as ruling ideas (Marx and Engels, *German Ideology*);
h. the ruling class creates and forms sentiments, illusions, mode of thought and views of life out of the material foundations and corresponding social relations (Marx, *The Eighteenth Brumaire*);
i. the ruling class possessing the means of material production control the means of mental production (Marx and Engles, *German Ideology*);
j. the mental production is a process accompanied by the intellectuals consciously, but with false consciousness, where the real motives impelling the intellectuals remain unknown to him and he works with material thought or thought material, which he accepts without examination as the product of thought and does not investigate further for a more remote process independent of thought (Engels, *Letter to Mehring*, July 14, 1893, *Selected Correspondence*);
k. the existence of and struggle between classes are conditioned by the degree of development of their economic position, and the existence of revolutionary ideas presupposes the existence of revolutionary class (Marx and Engels, *German Ideology* and Engels, 'Preface' to *The Eighteenth Brumaire*);

1. contradiction and motion, struggle and change are the essence of development—nothing is unchangeable—nothing is sacred—this is the law of development. Therefore, revolutionary class needs revolutionary ideas. People always will be and are always to be the stupid victim of deceit and self-deceit in politics as long as they do not learn the interests of classes behind any moral, religious, political and social phrases, declarations and promises. The supporters of reforms will be fooled by the defenders of the old order as long as they will not realize that every old institution is kept in being by the forces of the ruling classes. There is only on the way of breaking the resistance of these classes, and that is to find, in the very society which surrounds us, and to enlighten and organize for the struggle, the forces which can and, by their social position, must form the power capable of sweeping away the old and of establishing new. (Lenin, *Three Sources and Three Component Parts of Marxism*).

Marxism stresses the positive role of the superstructure in social development—socialist State, institutions and views play important role in directing, organizing and mobilizing the people. Three important tasks are to be fulfilled at this stage—expansion of the socialist State industry; subjection of capitalist enterprise to strict State control—first directing the capitalist enterprise to socially useful channels, then gradual elimination of capitalist enterprise and replacement of capitalist enterprise by State enterprise and providing small producers with improved instruments of production and gradually persuading them to engage in the forms of co-operative production so as to raise their productivity and standards of living. Engels prescribes the relative autonomy of the superstructure in representing the reciprocal interaction between basis and superstructure. The superstructure evolves out of the economic basis, the superstructure has a relative autonomy, has its own structure and laws. In a few circumstances, and for a limited period, the superstructure determines the evolution of the basis, and in the long run, the superstructure determines the basis. History proceeds in the manner of a natural process and is subject to the laws of motion (Engels's Letter to Bloch, *Selected Correspondence*). Engels in *Anti-Duhring* says that as soon as there is no longer any class of society to be held in subjugation and as soon as along with class domination and the struggle for individual existence based on the former anarchy of production, the collisions and excesses arising from these have also been abolished, there is nothing more to be repressed which would make a special repressive force, a State, necessary. The first act in which the State really comes forward as the representative of society as a whole—the taking possession of the means of production in the name of society—is at the same time its last independent act as a State. The interference of State power in social relations becomes superfluous in one sphere after another, and then ceases on its own. The government of persons is replaced by administration of things.

Edward Bernstein says that materialist conception of history is not purely materialist and much less purely economic. Purely economic causes create first of all only a disposition of reception of certain ideas, but how these then arise and spread and what form they take, depends on techno-operation of a whole series of influences. The intellectual understanding and ethical values are important impulses to human action, and ideological and ethical factors have independent spheres of action (Bernstein, 1961).

Marx in his criticism of Stalin's *Economic Problems of Socialism in the USSR* says that Stalin gives no thought to man, no importance to people, but to things. Here, Stalin's concerns with Soviets, which are concerned with only the relations of production,—Soviets do not pay attention to the superstructure—Soviets do not pay attention to politics—Soviets do not pay attention to the role of the people. On the other hand, Mao asserts revolution in the sphere of ideas which affects the tempo and speed of economic development—developments in the superstructure which run parallel to the development of the base—the former also conditions the development of the latter. It is the relation between the people and subjective side of the revolutionary process. To Mao, class is a subjective notion in that it is more referred to a person's attitude than to his or her social origin. The party constantly uses the term 'proletariat', which has no specific class relations. Mao emphasizes the ideology in the substitution of the Party for an absent proletariat. According to Mao, it is impossible to separate the inner moral world from his outward behaviour and from the political realm as a whole. Things are not more important than people. Weapons are important factors in war, but not the decisive factor. Things are not the decisive factor, but people are decisive. The contest of strength is not only a contest of military and economic power, but also a contest of human power and morale. Military and economic powers are necessarily wielded by the people. Leaders play important role in history. They are the outstanding personalities, who can represent the will and interests of the people and stand in the forefront of the historical struggles,—hence, the role of the individuals cannot be denied. Mao continues the tradition as exemplified by Lukacs, Gramsci and later by Lenin.

According to Lukacs, study of history discloses the essential nature of man. With the possible exception of Labriola, Lukacs is the first of the Marxist thinkers who evaluate the role of Hegel in the formation of Marxist thought. According to Lukacs, in the history there is a dialectical relation between subject and object, and without this factor, dialectics ceases to be revolutionary, where the central problem is to change reality. History and class consciousness are the same and one thing. In spite of Marx's distinction between relationship to the means of production and consciousness of shared interest in his analysis of class relations in *The Eighteenth Brumaire*, Lukacs goes beyond the mere psychological dimension of consciousness. He says, consciousness of a class, means total awareness of the class and their own interests. Class consciousness consists of appropriate and rational reactions and condition, ascription, particular class position and the process of production. Therefore, historically significant actions of a class are determined by consciousness and these actions can be understood by consciousness, not by individual thoughts and feelings. According to Lukacs, consciousness of the proletariat must become the deed. In proletarian dialectics, consciousness is not knowledge of an opposed object, but the self-consciousness of the object. The act of consciousness overthrows the objective form of the object. Lukacs's distinction of class-consciousness into actual and ascribed consciousness bears a corollary with Lenin's distinction into trade union consciousness and socialist class consciousness. Revolutionary is the bearer of proletarian class consciousness and a developed class consciousness, a consciousness, which is able to point out the road along which the dialectics of history is objectively impelled, and consciousness of the proletariat will awaken to the consciousness of the process. This consciousness will make the proletariat become both the subject and object of history whose praxis would change reality. With an exception of idealistic fashion, Lukacs like Hegel, and unlike the classical Marxists, does not radically separate subject and object. History is the interaction between subject and object and the dialectics of history is, in fact, the dialectical relation between subject and object. Through ascribed consciousness the proletarian class is the only class, which can unite both subject and object, which is expressed in that class's subjective thought what the class is objectively doing in history. History is a dialectical interaction between subject and object, unity of subject and object, theory and practice, thought and reality. Practice is a union of thought and reality. Therefore, history is practical. Historical change is the root cause of changes in thought (See Figure 28).

According to Lukacs, the social relations become transformed into relations between commodities, both subjectively and objectively. Man becomes the object. In the reified world there are no subjects—this objectification and reification starting from economic division of labour and economic rationality, can be found in the modern State and modern bureaucracy. Besides the all-pervasiveness of objectivity, the evolution of capital has now reached a point where the proletariat can destroy reification and become the subject of the historical process. According to Lukacs, reality can be understood and penetrated as a totality. The subject is capable of this penetration and capable of transforming the reality through praxis, the dialectical unity between theory and practice. The subject is at once the cause and effect, mirror and motor of the historical and dialectical process. In an increasingly radical and conscious manner every proletarian revolution creates workers' councils. When this workers' council increases its strength or its power, then it becomes the organ of State. At this point the class consciousness of the proletariat reaches to the point where the proletariat overcomes the bourgeois outlook of its leaders. The proletariat stands on the threshold of its own consciousness and hence on the threshold of victory. The workers' council spells the political and economic defeat of bourgeois reification—the dictatorship eliminates bourgeois separation of the legislature, administration and judiciary, controls over administration, laws and justice, overcomes the fragmentation of the proletariat in time and space, and brings politics and economics together into a true synthesis of proletarian praxis or proletarian approach to unity of theory and practice, subject and object, thought and reality.

Antonio Gramsci shares with Lukacs the notion of totality and also with Council Communists' views—the political dimension of Marxism and the importance of ideological struggle in the process of socialist transformation. In consonance with his revolutionary approach, Gramsci stresses the importance of Internal Commissions elected by trade union members in matters of arbitration and discipline in factory, and which are to be turned into Factory Councils. See Figure 29.

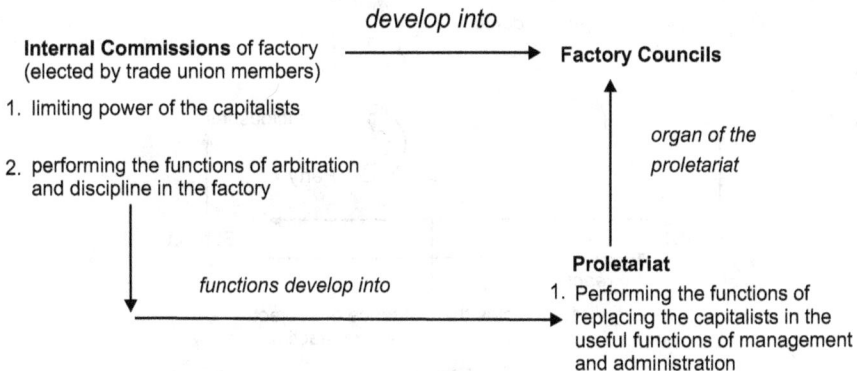

Figure 29

The actual process of proletarian revolution can be identified with the development and activity of revolutionary organizations of a voluntary nature, which arise in the sphere of bourgeois democracy and political liberty, and the process of that revolution arises in the sphere of production, where the relations between actual producers and the owners of the means of production are of oppression and exploitation, where there exists no freedom for workers and no democracy. The main task of the Council is to change the attitude of the mass of the workers from their attitude of dependence. The socialist State already exists potentially in the institutions of social life characteristic of the exploited working class. To link these institutions, co-ordinating and ordering them into a highly centralized hierarchy of competencies and powers, while respecting the necessary articulation and autonomy of each, is to create a genuine workers' democracy, which is an active and effective opposition to the bourgeois State. The working class is now prepared to replace the bourgeois State here and now in all

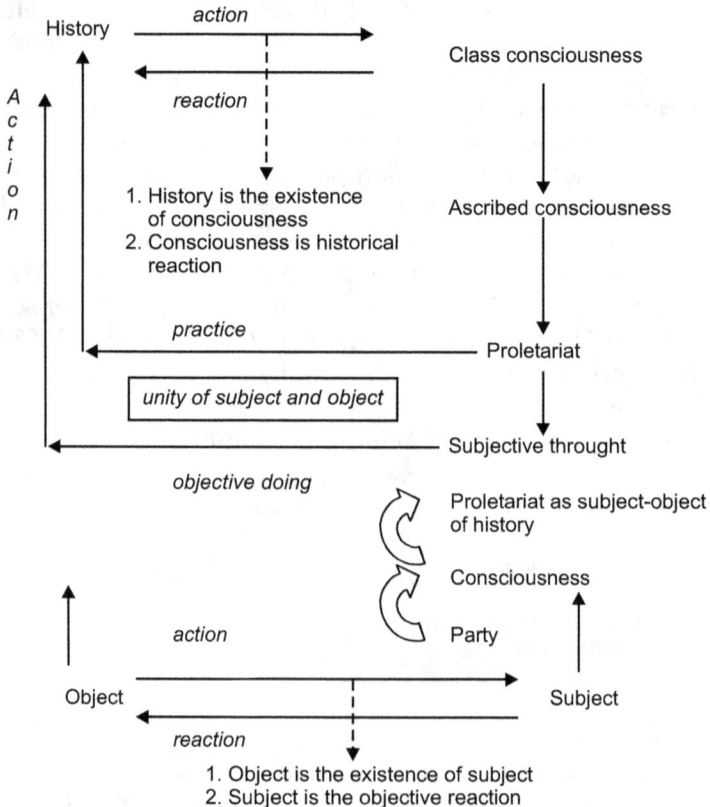

Figure 28

essential functions of administering and controlling national heritage.
See Figure 30.

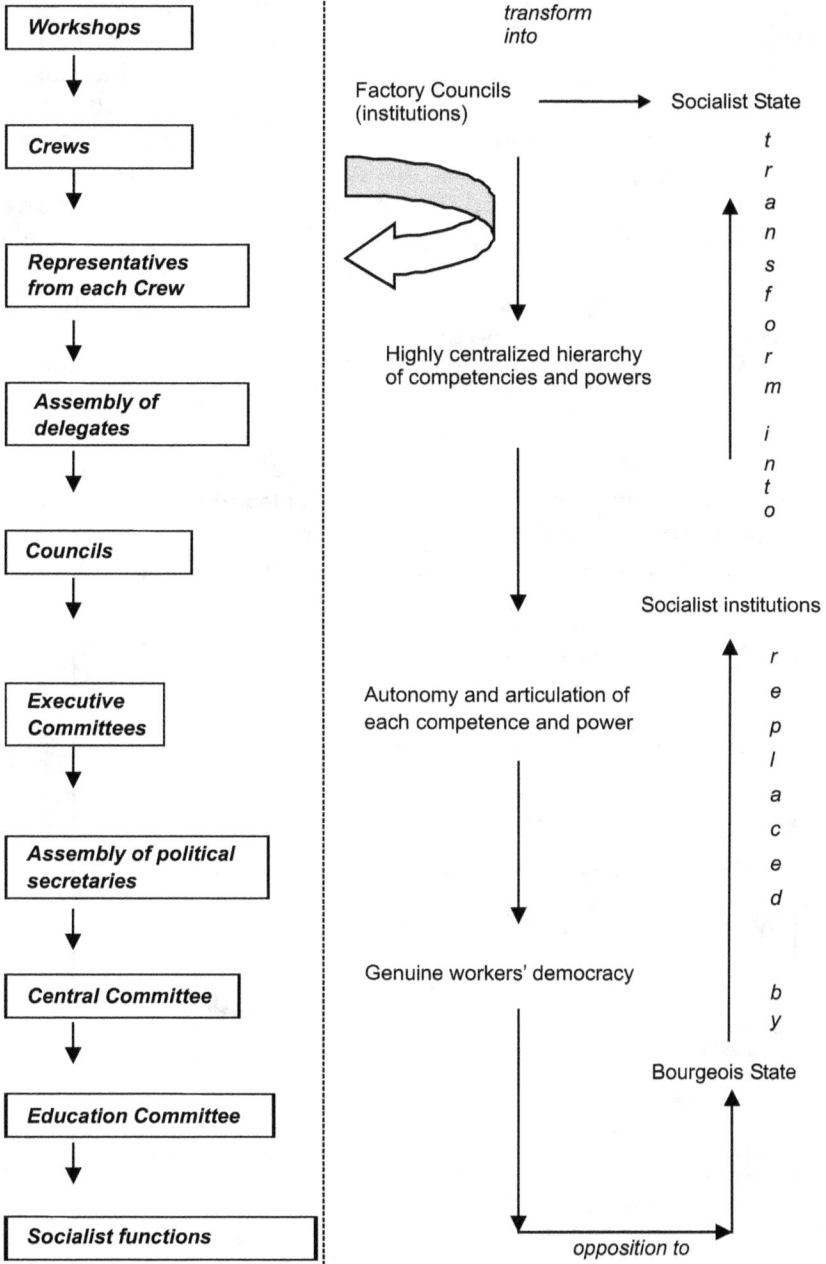

Workshops	*transform into*
Crews	Factory Councils (institutions) → Socialist State
Representatives from each Crew	
Assembly of delegates	Highly centralized hierarchy of competencies and powers
Councils	
Executive Committees	Socialist institutions
Assembly of political secretaries	Autonomy and articulation of each competence and power
Central Committee	Genuine workers' democracy
Education Committee	Bourgeois State
Socialist functions	*opposition to*

t r a n s f o r m i n t o

r e p l a c e d b y

Figure 30

The education committee performs the functions of organizing propaganda, drawing up work plans, approving projects and proposals from individual factories and individual workers, and finally giving general leadership to the whole movement. Following Lenin, Gramsci introduces the importance of the Communist Party in educating the masses with its own doctrine, tactics and rigid and implacable discipline, and in co-ordinating and centralizing the whole of proletariat's revolutionary action. The communist party would take the leadership position, where collective consciousness of the individual must be direct and active and where multiplicity is united by the rubbing together of individuals. There remains a dialectical relation between the leaders and masses—an organic centralism, but not directions and spontaneity. As a superstructural element, the Party performs its role in autonomy, *i.e.*, conscious leadership, but not consciousness from outside, and not directions to spontaneity. Then, what according to Gramsci, is spontaneity? It is not the task of politicization and socialization of the masses by the Party. Spontaneity is not the result of any systemic educational activity on the part of conscious leading group, but is the result of everyday experience illuminated by common sense. The Party only stimulates the masses and carries them into action. See Figure 31.

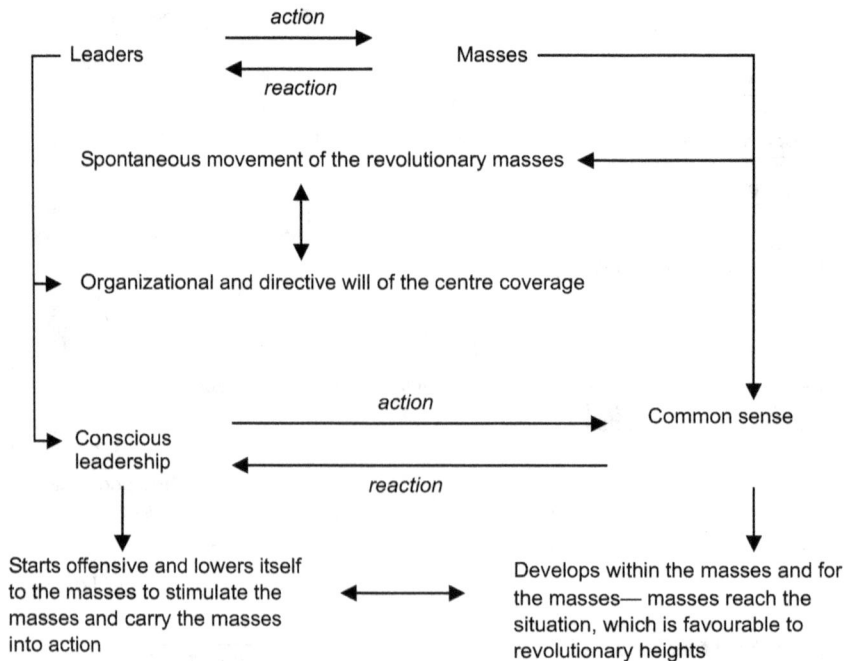

Figure 31

As a theoretician of superstructure, Gramsci stresses the role of intellectuals, and the importance of thought in the formation of society. According to Gramsci, all men are intellectuals, but do not have the function of intellectuals in the formation of society. The former is passive or less active than that of the latter, the former is concerned with traditional intellectuals and the latter is concerned with organic intellectuals, the former treats intellectuals as a man and the latter treats intellectuals as social class. Each man outside his professional activity is a philosopher, who brings into being new modes of thought, and each social class organically creates a homogenous entity performing functions not only in the economic, but also in the social and political fields. The organic intellectuals are members of the class or class organization and they articulate collective consciousness of their class in the political, economic and social spheres. Production of organic intellectuals is the precondition for any successful revolutionary movement. The proletariats in the struggle for dominance and in developing their dominance assimilate and conquer the traditional intellectuals ideologically and simultaneously elaborate the organic intellectuals. The quicker and more efficacious the assimilation and conquest become, the more the proletariats succeed in simultaneously elaborating their organic intellectuals. The Party is the organization of intellectuals, who are collective in nature, and as representative of collective will.

Gramsci's emphasis on the role of intellectuals led him to a subtler presentation of historical materialism. Gramsci's focus is less on economic sub-structure of society and more on the means by which the proletariat can attain to the understanding of the socio-economic relations of capitalist society (ideological or intellectual functions of organic intellectuals), and on the political means necessary to overthrow it (political functions of the party), *i.e.*, on ideological means and political means. In addition to ensuring the economic organization and political power of their class, the main function of organic intellectuals is to preserve the hegemony of their class over society as a whole by means of justifying ideology of which they are the agents. Hegemony is a concept, which helps to explain how the State apparatuses of political society are supported by and support a specific economic group, which can coerce via its institutions of law, police, army, prisons and the various strata of society into consenting to the *status quo*. On the other hand, hegemony is a concept that helps us to understand not only the ways in which a predominant economic group coercively uses the State apparatuses of political society in the preservation of *status quo*, but also how and where political society and, above all, civil society, with its institutions ranging from education, religion, contribute to the production of meaning and values which in turn produce, direct and maintain 'spontaneous' consent of the various strata of society to that same *status quo*.

Both Gramsci and Lukacs share the view that consciously or unconsciously the life-world is structured by modernity in relation with their emphasis on the superstructure rather than infrastructure, their understanding of ideology, their understanding of the diminishing revolutionary potential of Western capitalism. Gramsci in contradistinction to Lukacs, is against the realism of the past, and not to the modernism of the present, not to the reproducibility of cultural context, and not to powers emerging from modern technologies. Gramsci reflects the double-edged nature of the powers emerging from modern technologies—the possibility of manipulation and domination of the cultural sphere and the production and control of needs and desires designed for consumption of specific cultural and ideological goods. Gramsci's notion of complexity of modern reality transcends Lukacs's notion of realism. Gramsci relates the problems of realism and modernism to the transformations in the structure of the modern life world. Gramsci's notion consists of culture industry, production and manipulation of needs and desires, and consuming subjects that are unable to define their needs, which are subjected to the powers that manipulate the public into the acceptance of static *status quo*. Like Foucault, Gramsci believes that power is not imposed from above, but the operations of power depend on consent from below—power is produced and reproduced in the everyday interaction of life—power is ubiquitous.

Control of State power without hegemony in civil society is an insecure basis for a socialist programme. A social group can and must exercise leadership before winning governmental power—it subsequently becomes dominant when it exercises power and it will continue to lead as well if it grasps its hold firmly. Gramsci links force with the struggle for hegemony in civil society—persuasion and force are necessary in any civil society. Gramsci advocates that the Party is an educational institution, which offers a counter-culture, whose aim is to gain ascendancy in most aspects of civil society as opposed to directly political institutions before gaining State power. Gramsci treats civil society as a superstructure, an ensemble of organisms commonly called private, corresponding to the function of hegemony which dominant group exercises throughout society. This is in contrast to Marx's definition of civil society as a totality of economic relationships. According to Gramsci, civil society performs the functions of mediation between economic structure and the State through organization and technical means. In revolutionary strategies, the object of frontal attack should be civil society in developed countries. As capitalism develops, so 'war of position' is considered important. 'War of movement' becomes more costly for the working class, which should also be launched when it becomes absolutely necessary. To Gramsci, the Leninist strategy of revolution is not applicable in case of the West. However, Gramsci realizes that a transition is necessary and might be necessary where the proletariat would have to, and should have to rely on State power during the transformation of civil society, and final reabsorption of political society by civil society into a classless society.

Following Marx's Paris Commune model, Lenin declares that the task of revolution is to smash State power (Figure 32). According to Lenin, the government of people can give way to the administration of things which is a withering away process. The workers will organize large-scale production on the basis of what capitalism has created relying on the experience of the workers and discipline backed up by the State power of the armed workers, and reducing the role of the State officials to that of simply carrying out the instructions of workers as responsible, revocable and modestly paid foremen and accountants —the proletarians will accomplish these tasks after accomplishing proletarian revolution. After this, the gradual withering away process will start (Figure 33). In this process Party takes care in inculcating proletarian consciousness and in making a conducive environment to the order mentioned above. Marxism educates the masses and educates the Party as the vanguard of the proletariat, which is capable—

(a) of assuming power,
(b) of leading the whole people to socialism,
(c) of directing and organizing the new order,
(d) of being the teacher, the guide, the leader of all the workers and exploited in the task of building up their social life without the bourgeoisie and against the bourgeoisie.

The gradual shift from dictatorship of the Proletariat to the dictatorship of the Party, and the equivalence of the Party and the State are aided and abetted by factors like the growth of bureaucracy and the lack of an effective workers' voice. See Figure 34.

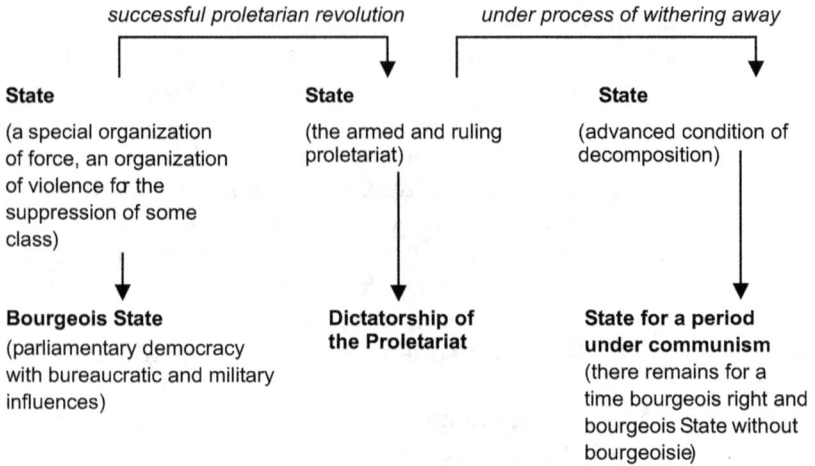

successful proletarian revolution   under process of withering away

State

(a special organization
of force, an organization
of violence for the
suppression of some
class)

State

(the armed and ruling
proletariat)

State

(advanced condition of
decomposition)

Bourgeois State

(parliamentary democracy
with bureaucratic and military
influences)

**Dictatorship of
the Proletariat**

**State for a period
under communism**

(there remains for a
time bourgeois right and
bourgeois State without
bourgeoisie)

Figure 32

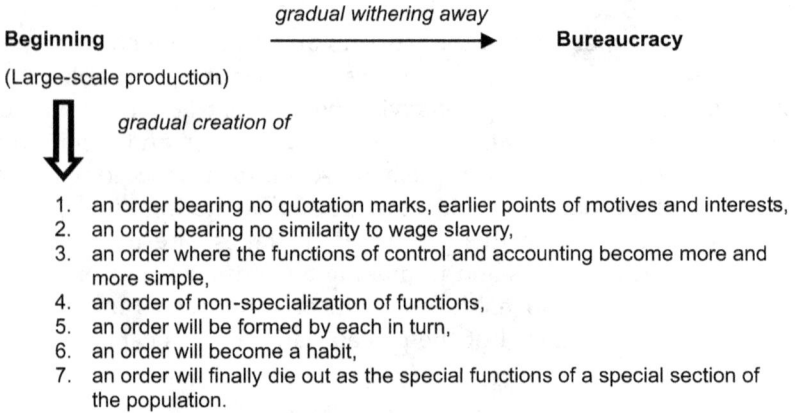

gradual withering away

Beginning

(Large-scale production)

Bureaucracy

gradual creation of

1. an order bearing no quotation marks, earlier points of motives and interests,
2. an order bearing no similarity to wage slavery,
3. an order where the functions of control and accounting become more and more simple,
4. an order of non-specialization of functions,
5. an order will be formed by each in turn,
6. an order will become a habit,
7. an order will finally die out as the special functions of a special section of the population.

Figure 33

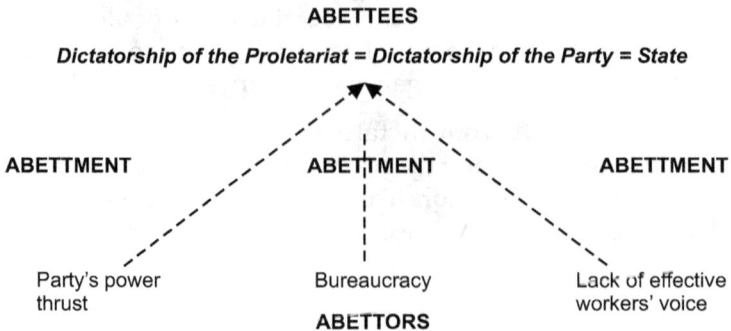

ABETTEES

Dictatorship of the Proletariat = Dictatorship of the Party = State

ABETTMENT   **ABETTMENT**   **ABETTMENT**

Party's power
thrust

Bureaucracy

Lack of effective
workers' voice

ABETTORS

Figure 34

This party domination is enhanced by suppression of opposition; bureaucracy is enhanced by an increased nationalization programme to suppress the workers' voice. In opposition to party's centralization of power, Mao says in his *Some Questions Concerning Methods of Leadership* that leadership, which is correct, is from the masses to the masses. This means that the party leadership takes the scattered and unsystematic ideas and concentrates interest to these ideas through study, and makes these into concentrated and systematic ideas. They then go to the masses, and propagate and explain these ideas, until the masses embrace them as their own, hold fast to them and translate them into action. The masses take ideas into action directly. Ideas are preserved in and carried through masses, concentrate ideas from the masses, and go to the masses. This is the task of actual and correct leadership. Soon, over and over again in an endless spiral, ideas are becoming more correct, more vital and richer each time. That is:

(a) ideas from masses (scattered and unsystematic ideas)	→ ideas to the masses (concentrated, systematic and action oriented ideas)	→ ideas from the masses (vital, correct and richer ideas) ↵ **enter**
(b) ideas from masses	→ ideas to the masses	→ ideas from the masses (more vital, more correct and more richer ideas) ↵ **enter**
(c) ideas from masses	→ ideas to the masses	→ ideas from the masses (more and more vital, more and more correct and more and more richer ideas ↵ **enter**

In fact, good leadership means good communication with the masses. Maoism emphasizes the importance of consciousness of the masses.

According to Althusser, Marx develops the concept of society as a totality—unity of economy, politics and ideology—unity of structures — all are united in a structure of structures. The structure is a combination of peculiar elements, which is not outside its effects. The effects are not outside the structure, but within it. In fact, the existence of structure consists of its effects. The causality is structural. Althusser rejects the idea that there is only one simple contradiction between forces and relations of production, between base and superstructure. See Figure 35.

Structure

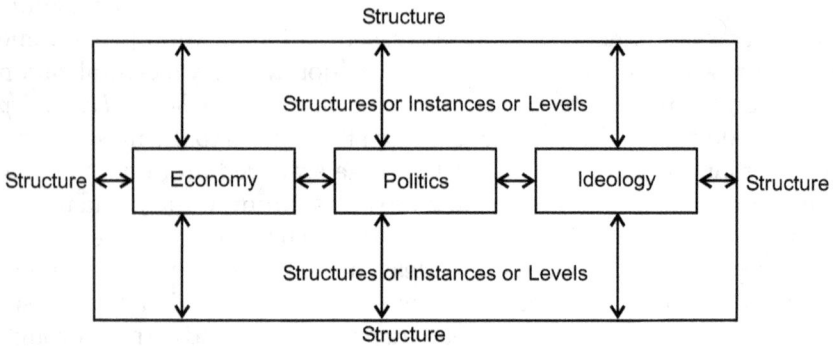

Figure 35

Althusser regards that each level or instance or structure has its peculiar time and rhythm of development, *i.e.* in terms of rhythm of development at a particular time the levels, instances, or structures are uneven. Each level or instance or structure contributes to determining the structure, as well as being determined by the structure. All levels or instances or structures are not dominant at the same time, where one or two becomes or become dominant and others remain as determinant. Dominant is determined by determinant—political at the dominant instance or level or structure is determined by economic instance or level or structure. There is always a dominant element—a structure in dominance. The determining role of the economy on this structure of dominance can never be isolated from the structure as whole. Therefore, according to Althusser, the notion of structural causality follows the conception of history as a process without subjects or subject. According to Marx, the individual subject is the ensemble of the social relations. The subject has an important role in the understanding of history through concepts like the forces and relations of production. Althusser regards that both the forms and relations of production have structures, but essentially no subject. In *Reading Capital* Althusser says that the structure of relations of production determines the places and functions occupied and adopted by the agents of production, who are not the occupants or functionaries. The true subjects are the definers and distributors of production, the relations of production: the political and ideological and social relations. But these relations cannot be thought within the category of subject. That is, the relations of production are the true subjects, but they are not in the category of subjects as such. Althusser contrasts with the tendency to see human as the active subject of history. However, it may be pointed out here, as the critics of Althusser find that Althusser separates theory from practice, philosophy from class struggle and his insistence on ideology and science serves to justify the existence of party and bureaucracy. For example, in *For Marx*, Althusser says that the 'cult of personality' refers exactly to the domain of superstructure and therefore to State organization and ideologies. Furthermore, it refers largely to this domain alone, which possesses relative autonomy as we learn from Marxist theory. Therefore, the leadership remains within the domain of superstructure. In his earlier work Althusser says almost nothing about the State; rather he distinguishes between Repressive State Apparatuses and Ideological State Apparatuses, and analyzes the role of Ideological State Apparatuses, such as trade unions, churches and schools as important sites of class struggle. The major attempt has been by Nicos Poulantzas in applying Althusser's ideas to classes and the State in his book *Political Power and Social Classes*. Poulantzas points out the relative autonomy of State and politics. The role of the State is of cohesion and regulation— cohesion between the levels of social formation and the regulation of global equilibrium as a system. The social formation is dominated by the capitalist class irrespective of political positions held by the representatives of that class. The State maintains the social formation. Following Althusser, Poulantzas excludes the reference to consciousness and rejects any form of economic reductionism in his work, *Classes in Contemporary Capitalism*. See Figure 36.

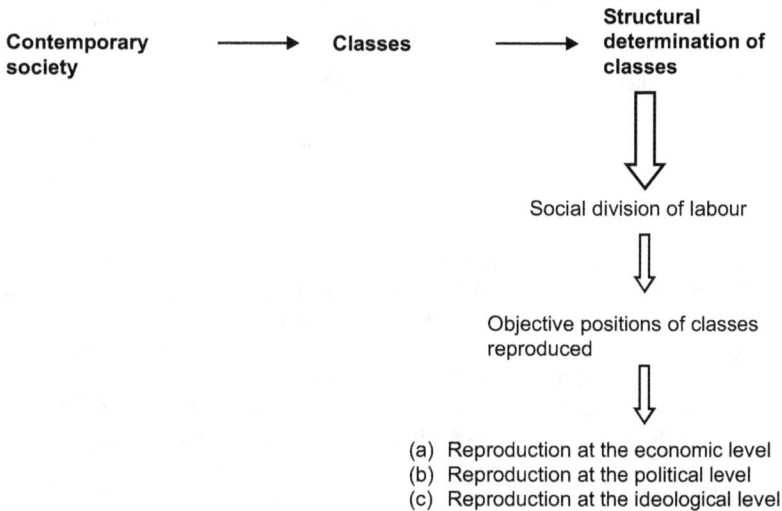

Contemporary society ⟶ **Classes** ⟶ **Structural determination of classes**

⟱

Social division of labour

⟱

Objective positions of classes reproduced

⟱

(a) Reproduction at the economic level
(b) Reproduction at the political level
(c) Reproduction at the ideological level

Figure 36

Poulantzas gives emphasis on political and ideological criteria rather than that of the economic in the reproduction of objective position of classes.

REFERENCES

Althusser, L. 1965. *For Marx* (London: Allen Lane).
Althusser, L. and E. Baliber. 1970. *Reading Capital* (London: New Left Books).
Anderson, Perry. 1975. *Lineages of the Absolutist State* (London: New Left Books).
Aron, Raymond. 1965. *Main Currents in Sociological Thought-I* (London: Penguin Books).
Bernstein, E. 1961. *Evolutionary Socialism* (New York).
Brecht, Arnold. 1959. *Foundations of Twentieth Century Political Thought* (Princeton: Princeton University Press).
Carver, T. 1981. *Engels* (Oxford: Oxford University Press).
Colletti, Lucio. 1985. 'Marxism and the Dialectic', *New Left Review* (No. 93).
Colletti, Lucio. 1972. *From Rousseau to Lenin* (London: New Left Books).
Engels, F. 1982. *Dialectics of Nature* (Moscow: Progress Publishers).
Engels, F. *Anti-Duhring* (Moscow: Progress Publishers).
Federn, Karl. 1939. *The Materialist Conception of History* (London).
Gramsci, Antonio. 1971. *Selections from Prison Notebooks* (London: International Publishers).
Gramsci, Antonio. 1985. *Selection from Cultural Writings* (Cambridge: Harvard University Press).
Habermas, H. 1970. 'Contribution to a Phenomenology of Historical Materialism', *Telos 4*.
Holub, Renate. 1992. *Antonio Gramsci* (London: Routledge).
Korsch, K. 1970. *Marxism and Philosophy* (London: New Left Books).
Korsch, K. 1970. 'Concerning Marxism in Linguistics', *Supplementary, New Times*, Vol. 26, June 28.
Labriola, Antonio. 1966 (1904). *Essays on the Materialist Conception of History* (New York).
Laclau, Ernesto and Chantal Mouffe. 1985. *Hegemony and Socialist Strategy* (Verso: London).
Lenin, V.I. *Materialism and Empirio-Criticism.*
Lenin, V.I. *Collected Works.*
Lukacs's opinion cited in Chatterjee, P. 1978.'On the Scientific Study of Politics: A Review of the Positivist Method' in Sudipta Kaviraj and Others (eds.), *The State of Political Theory* (Calcutta: Research India Publications).
Lukacs, G. 1971. *History and Class Consciousness* (Massachusetts: MIT).
Marcuse, H. 1960. *Reason and Revolution* (Boston: Beacon).
Marcuse, H. 1967. *One-Dimensional Man* (London: Routledge and Kegan Paul).
Marcuse, H. 1969. *Negations: Essays in Critical Theory* (Boston: Beacon)
Marshall, Roy K. 1951. *The Nature of Things* (New York).
Marx and Engels, *Collected Works.*
Marx, Karl and F. Engels. 1975. *Selected Correspondence* (Moscow: Progress Publishers).
Marx, Karl. 1963. *The Eighteenth Brumaire of Louis Napoleon* (New York: International Publishers).
Marx, Karl. 1971. *Theories of Surplus Value* (Moscow: Progress Publishers).
Marx, Karl. 1973. *Grundrisse* (Harmondsworth: Penguin).

Marx, Karl. 1978. *Capital-I* (Moscow: Progress Publishers).

Morera, Esteve. 1990. *Antonio Gramsci* (London: Routledge).

Myrdal, G. 1944. *An American Dilemma* (New York).

Ogburn, W. 1964. *On Culture and Social Change* (Chicago: Chicago University Press).

Parsons, Talcott. 1966. *The Structure of Social Action* (New York: Free Press).

Petrovic, Gajo. 1971. *Philosophie and Revolution* (Reinbek bei Hamburg: Rowohlt).

Poulantzas, N. 1978. *Classes in Contemporary Capitalism* (London: Verso).

Poulantzas, N. 1978. *Political Power and Social Classes* (London: Verso).

Sartre, Jean-Paul. 1969. 'Marxism and Existentialism' in J.A. Gould and V.V. Thursby (eds.), *Contemporary Political Thought* (New York: Holt).

Shah, A.B. 1964. *Scientific Method* (Bombay: Allied Publishers).

Stalin, J.V. 1938. *Dialectical and Historical Materialism* (New York: International Publishers).

Therborn, G. 1980. *Science, Class and Society* (London: Verso).

Timpanaro, S. 1975. *On Materialism* (London: Verso).

Williams, Raymond. 1977. *Marxism and Literature* (Oxford: Oxford University Press).

4

The Theory of the State

The more powerful the State, therefore, the more political a country is. According to Marx, the State is the structure of society. In so far as the State admits the existence of social evils, it attributes them to natural laws against which no human power can prevail. Administration is the organizing activity of the States. The contradiction between aims and intentions of administration on the one hand, and the means and resources on the other, cannot be resolved by the State as the State is founded upon this contradiction, contradiction between public and private life, contradiction between general interest and particular interest. The functions of administration are formal and negative. Power causes at the point where civil life begins. In *German Ideology* Marx says that the State is the form in which individuals of the ruling class assert their common interests, in which the whole civil society is epitomized. The State acts as an intermediary for all community institutions, which receive political form. The material life of individuals does not depend on the will of the individuals but rather on the mode of production and form of intercourse, and the reciprocal relations, between these two, are the real bases of the State. In the material life, division of labour, and private property, are necessary elements, which are not created by the State. Rather these elements condition the growth of the State. The individuals, who rule under these conditions, must give their will a general expression, as the will of the State, as law. Law is the expression of this will conditioned by their common interests. The State does not rest on a dominating will, but the State arises out of the material mode of life of individuals has the form of dominating will. See Figure 37.

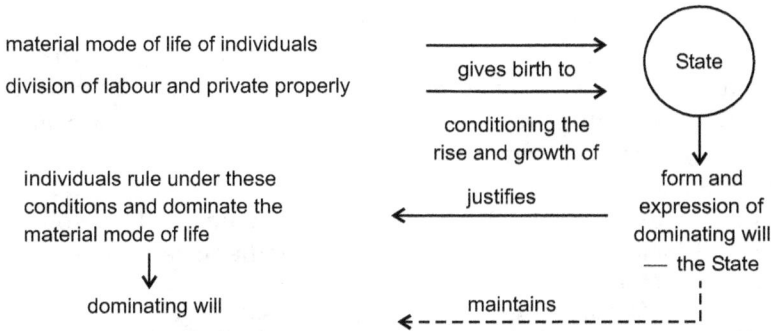

material mode of life of individuals

division of labour and private properly

gives birth to →

conditioning the
rise and growth of →

State

↓

individuals rule under these
conditions and dominate the
material mode of life

justifies ←

form and
expression of
dominating will
— the State

↓

dominating will

maintains ←

Figure 37

If the will loses its existence, then material existence and life of the individuals also change. Law and legislation have an autonomous evolution and have their own independent history.

According to the Marxists, the State is not introduced into society from outside, but is a product of society's internal development. Changes in the material mode of production bring about changes in the State system and succession of one material mode of production causes one form and expression of dominating will. With the emergence of classes society begins to disintegrate increasingly into groups with opposing interests. Class struggle between the exploiters and exploited also begins to start. The State is the structure of society, but itself is separated from society and stands above society, where the State acts as a machine protecting the order preferred by, and advantageous to the class that dominates the economy. Thereby this class becomes politically dominant class and acquires new means for the suppression and exploitation of the oppressed class. Territoriality, public authority with repressive State apparatuses, collection of taxes levied on, a wide network of ideological institutions, such as churches, schools etc., State intervention of economic matters, and State intervention in foreign affairs—all are the characteristic features of the modern State. The State is a machine for maintaining the rule of one class over another—it is the public authority which represents the interests of the economically dominant interests, but not the interests of the total population. Common interests represented by the State are nothing but the conglomeration of bourgeois class interests. Representative bodies, the bureaucratic administrative machine, police, army, courts, intelligence agencies, prosecutors, prisons —all are used for the maintenance of class rule. These are instruments of class rule and elements of public authority. As class contradictions deepen, class struggle intensifies and the State machine expands. The functions of the State increase with the expansion of its functional periphery, internally and externally, internally through economic compulsion, maintenance of exploitation of one class by another, and externally through seizure of foreign territories and defense of its own lands from foreign attack. The functions and power of the State are determined by the nature of the State or form of the State. This type or form of the State is determined by which class holds power and which production relations the State protects, maintains and consolidates. Historical materialism distinguishes types of the State as under:

Exploiting State	*Socialist State*
a. slave-owning State—slaves are exploited and slave-owners are exploiters	non-exploitative and non-coercive State—transition from capitalist State to socialist State via dictatorship of the proletariat
b. feudal State—peasants are exploited and feudal-lords are exploiters	
c. capitalist State—proletariats are exploited and bourgeoisie are exploiters	

Lenin categorically distinguishes several forms of the State—the slave-owning society has different forms of government—the rule of one man named after monarchy, the monarch or emperor at its head—elective rule named after the republic—the rule of a relatively small minority named after aristocracy and the rule of the majority named after democracy. Democracy of the capitalist society is a democracy for the negligible minority—democracy for the capitalists. It is the dictatorship of the capitalists. With the advent of imperialism, the bourgeois State directly turns towards reaction and assumes the historical role in defending the economic basis of imperialism. Lenin in *A Caricature of Marxism and Imperialist Economism* says that in its imperialist stage the State violates democracy through its domestic and foreign policy. Therefore, imperialism is the negation of democracy in general. At this stage, monopoly capitalism becomes widespread, power of the monopolies and the power of the State are combined with each other, the proletarian and national liberation movements are crushed in attempting to save the capitalist system. In a transition from capitalism to socialism, there lies the stage of dictatorship of the proletariat—the State here is nothing but the revolutionary dictatorship of the proletariat. This is the great beginning. In *A Great Beginning* Lenin says about the dictatorship of the proletariat, only a definite class,—the urban workers, and the factory, and industrial workers in general are able to lead the whole mass of the working and exploited people in the struggle to throw off the yoke of capitalism. One of the main functions of this proletarian State thus is to suppress the exploiting classes. The dictatorship is essential in overcoming the resistance of the bourgeoisie. According to Lenin, (who is in his *Left-wing Communism—An Infantile Disorder* says) dictatorship of the proletariat means the most determined and more ruthless war waged by the new class against a more powerful enemy, the bourgeoisie, whose resistance is increased tenfold by its overthrow. Further, in *A Great Beginning* Lenin points out the stage of dictatorship as a positive march towards socialism and communism—the dictatorship is not only the use of force against the exploiters, but also represents and creates a higher type of social organization of labour in comparison with capitalism. This is what is important; this is the source of strength and the guarantee that the final triumph of communism is inevitable. The socialist construction is not confined to the establishment of a socialist economy. The proletarian State guides the Cultural Revolution. The dictatorship of the proletariat is a qualitatively new type of democracy—it is democracy for the overwhelming majority. The alliance of the working class with the working people of the town and country is founded on the community of their basic political and economic interests. It is also founded on the common desire to abolish exploitation and build socialism. In this alliance, the working class or the proletariat plays the leading role. In this respect Lenin differs from Mao-Tse-Tung. The peasants and the urban bourgeoisie are inconsistent and often vacillate between the proletariat and bourgeoisie. Only the proletarians are the most advanced, consistently revolutionary, and organized class. The Party plays the leading role in overcoming the vacillation, if any vacillation creeps in. The Party leads the people along socialist lines. According to Lenin, all nations will arrive at socialism and this arrival becomes inevitable, but all will do so not in the same way, each will contribute something of its own to some form of democracy, to some variety of the dictatorship of the proletariat, to the varying rate of socialist transformations in different aspects of social life, which he says in his *A Caricature of Marxism and Imperialist Economism.*

Marx, in association with Engels says that the executive committee of the modern State is but a committee for managing the common affairs of the whole bourgeoisie. Form this it follows that the proletariat coming to power would necessarily constitute a class government. There would necessarily be dictatorship of the proletariat in place of the dictatorship of bourgeoisie, where the former would be more democratic than the latter, less oppressive than the latter—there would be no State as State, no State in proper sense of the word, no exploitation, but a half-State. Engels in *Principles of Communism* says that it (dictatorship of the proletariat) would be bourgeois State without the bourgeoisie, would establish a democratic constitution and a democratic republic. This democracy or democratic State would be established after the revolution, and not in the era of capitalism. According to Lenin, the dictatorship of the proletariat and the poor peasantry is an effective weapon against the provisional government, where according to Stalin, the proletariat is the guiding force and gradually the communist party becomes the instrument of the dictatorship of the proletariat with a view to seize power and force through industrialization, regardless of the wishes of the population, no matter how backward the country is. The dictatorship is justified on the grounds of majoritatian rule and the dangers of counter-revolution and also the dangers of outside bourgeois onslaughts. The dictatorship of the proletariat is thus identified with the dictatorship of the party. But critics like Sorel argue that class struggle is the essential feature of Marxism and do not regard Marx's emphasis on political. They rather concentrate entirely on direct action by means of the general strike, which necessarily goes against the Marxist notion that the class struggle necessarily leads to the dictatorship of the proletariat.

The proletariat seizes State power in the course of socialist revolution. The proletariat destroys the old machinery and creates a new one for the transformation of capitalist society into socialist society. In order to build and consolidate socialism, the proletariat must fulfil two-fold tasks—

1. it must by its supreme heroism in the revolutionary struggle against capital, win over the entire mass of the working and exploited people, organize them and lead them in the struggle to overthrow the bourgeoisie and utterly suppress their resistance;

2. it must lead the whole mass of the working and exploited people, as well as all the petty-bourgeois groups, on to the road of new economic development, towards the creation of the new social bond, a new labour discipline, a new organization of labour, which will combine the last word in science and capitalist technology with the mass of association of class-conscious workers creating large-scale socialist industry. Corresponding to this is also a political transition period in which the State can be nothing but the revolutionary

dictatorship of the proletariat. It is an instrument of non-coercion than that of coercion. The workers' State is an enemy of the landowners and capitalists and friend of the proletariat and the peasantry. In this process the first thing to do to win equality and genuine democracy for the working people, for the workers and peasants, to deprive capital of the possibility of hiring writers, buying up publishing house and bribing newspapers. Genuine democracy is impossible without socialism and socialism is impossible without steady development of democracy.

Lenin in his *State and Revolution* says that the State will be able to wither away completely when the society adopts the rule: from each according to his ability to each according to his needs—when people have become so accustomed to observing the fundamental rules of social intercourse and when their labour has become so productive that they will voluntarily work according to their ability. Marx and Engels say that the abrogation of the State has only one meaning—it is the necessary outcome of the abolition of classes, involves the natural disappearance of the need for the organizational power of one class to retain its domination over the other classes. Another precondition for the withering away of the State is the high cultural standards and consciousness of society's members'—work for society's benefit, communal behaviour of free individual will in the non-coercive social environment. Besides these, few external preconditions may be cited here for the withering away of the State. These are—the elimination of capitalism in all countries, the triumph of socialism and communism on a world-wide scale. The danger of foreign military attack necessitates the maintenance of army, State security organs and other State institutions. The withering away of the State proceeds gradually with the disappearance of external danger, the growing role of public bodies, people's increasing participation in the administrative affairs of the society, and the extension of public control. With this, State administration turns into a non-State administrative organization—society is ruled under *administration of things*. Stalin says that the communists are in favour of the State withering away, and at the same time, they stand for the strengthening of the dictatorship of the proletariat, which represents the most powerful and mighty authority of all forms of State which have existed up to the present day. The highest possible development of the power of the State: that is the Marxist formula. Is it contradictory? Yes, it is contradictory. But this contradiction is a living thing, and completely reflects Marxist dialectics (Stalin, *Selected Works*). Stalin in his *Foundations of Leninism* says that it is precisely along the path of the consolidation and higher development of the proletarian State that the withering away of the State takes place. Even the Party will wither away in time—when classes disappear, the dictatorship of the proletariat dies out, and the Party will also die out.

Critics find that the classless society is a utopia. A Stateless society will bring about completely a situation of anarchy. A classless Stateless society is a situation of organized anarchy. Marx approves of temporary force to end all forces, unlike the anarchists. Marx regards only the self-regulating automatic economic machine by accepting the economic planning in a classless society, as the government of persons is replaced by administration of things, and the direction of the processes of production. Marx gives little recognition to the problem of choice and alternatives, but does not provide useful suggestions to the solving of this problem in the world of unlimited wants and limited resources unlike the analytical Marxists. Marx and Lenin both do not take into account of the problem of allocation of resources and of the balancing of alternatives. The Marxists abuse Malthus's population theory and do not provide importance to Malthus's population-subsistence ratio. There is no need to worry about this ratio until the vacant lands of the earth are ploughed up. With regard to the Stateless society Marx does not accede to the Stateless programme of the anarchists; but Marx's socialism is Stateless in so far as the State is an expression of class society. Marx's account in *Poverty of Philosophy* may be cited as—the working class in the course of its development will substitute for the old civil society an association of classes and their antagonisms, and there will be no more political power properly so-called, since political power is precisely the official expression of antagonism in civil society. In a non-class sense, the socialism has a place for leadership, authority and politics. Marx and Engels say in *The Communist Manifesto* that the first step in the revolution by the working class is to raise the proletariat to the position of ruling class, to win the battle of democracy. The proletariat will use its political supremacy to wrest, by degrees, all capital from the bourgeoisie, to centralize all instruments of production in the hands of the State, *i.e.*, of the proletariat organized as the ruling class; and to increase the total of productive forces as rapidly as possible. Two important tasks—economic and political tasks have been placed by Marx and Engels in *The Communist Manifesto* in the process of transition from capitalism to socialism.

The economic tasks may be grouped as development of socialist mode of production, which includes the centralization of the means of production and credit in the hands of the State, abolition of the right of inheritance and of private property, heavy and progressive income tax and so on. The political tasks may be grouped as proletarian dictatorship, which includes the political supremacy of the proletariat through winning the battle of democracy and the gradual transcendence of politics in its class-struggle sense. Dictatorship corresponds to 'modern institutions of temporary State of siege, proclamation of martial law in a distress area, or some other form of crisis-and-emergency government' (Wolfe, 1967: 169). Marx in *Class Struggles in France* says that every provisional political set up following a revolution requires a dictatorship. Socialism is declaration of the permanence of revolution, the class dictatorship of the proletariat—the transit point to the abolition of class distinctions generally.

In *Communist Manifesto* Marx argues that the existing State must be used by the proletariat to implement its immediate objectives. In *Contribution to the Critique of Hegel's Philosophy of Law* Marx says that bureaucracy develops out of the anti-thesis between the State and civil society, separation of State from civil society, separation of general interest from particular interest. Bureaucracy embodies the State in its possession as its private property. In *The Constitutional Question in Germany* Engels says that from the moment, the State administration and legislature fall under the control of the bourgeoisie, the independence of the bureaucracy ceases to exist. In *The German Ideology* Marx finds that the independence of the State is only found nowadays in those countries where the estates have not yet completely developed into classes, where consequently no section of the population can achieve dominance over the others. Apart from the concept of the State as an instrument of class domination, the State has certain independence from the classes, while the former 'constitutes what might be called a primary view of the State', and the latter 'is to be found another view of the State in his work, which it is inaccurate to hold up as of similar status with the first, but which is none the less of great interest' (Miliband, 1973: 163-64).

Some theorists say that the two theories are incompatible—if the State becomes the instrument of class domination and class oppression (as Lenin discusses in his work *State and Revolution*), then anything that rises as superior to all classes is not the State. But if the State is a parasite superior to all classes in society, there is no reason for supposing that when society becomes classless, the State will disappear (Plamenatz, 1954). There is a way to reconcile these apparently conflicting views of State, if we can establish that there is only one theory of the State in Marx's political philosophy, of which the two views are nothing but expressions of the State. Hegel, Marx insists, inverts the proper relationship between State and civil society—family and civil society are the premises of State, not its products or the spheres of the concept of the State. According to Marx, Hegel correctly describes the separation of State and civil society and the hostility between these two spheres, but nevertheless expounds it as a necessary element of idea, as absolute rational truth. Marx rejects the necessity of this division. Marx's hostility to this division is based on the argument that modern man must effect a fundamental division within himself as a citizen of the State and as a member of civil society. Marx says in his *Contribution to the Critique of Political Economy* that the political State is the abstraction of civil society from itself and true universality consists in civil society raising itself to political being as its true, general and essential mode of being. Marx identifies proletariat as the universal class and has a universal character by its universal suffering. True universality must be achieved by human emancipation, by the abolition of the distinction between State and civil society. Modern State is the alienated expression of man's universal nature. What Marx believes may be expressed as below:

Socialism = True democracy = True unity of the general and particular ..... (I)

Abolition of the distinction between State and civil society = True universality .... (II)

Establishment of abstract sphere of generality ≠ Division of the State from civil society .... (III)

According to Marx, the proletariat would affect the transcendence of the State and civil society. Marx believes that the State could be overcome by the general interest actually becoming the particular interest, which in turn is only possible as a result of the particular actually becoming the general interest. That is, it means the transition from particular to the general and from general to the particular. See Figure 38.

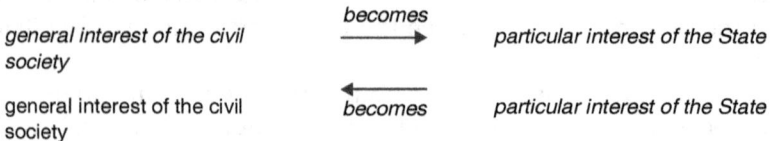

	becomes	
general interest of the civil society	——————→	particular interest of the State
general interest of the civil society	←—————— becomes	particular interest of the State

Figure 38

But, if particular interest of the civil society becomes the particular interest of the State and State defends that particular interest, the State perpetuates the alienated relationships through institutionalization; it is the transition from particular to the particular. Therefore, it is direct class influence on the State apparatus. Further, the State is relatively independent of that class influence. These two are the central questions of Marx's theory of the State. Marx's project regards the following matters:

1. emancipation of politics from the State and returning it to the emancipation of man;
2. Marx's sensivity to class rule and class dictatorship;
3. parliamentary democracy in bourgeois State is the most complete form of 'alien politics';
4. re-appropriation of politics in the transition to socialism;
5. modern State is the product of the relations between classes in civil society;
6. the State is not primarily an instrument of coercion and nor parliamentary democracy is a mask for this reality, rather there is an element of coercion in the existing State institutions and coercion is necessary for the transition to socialism. Unlike the anarchists, Marx does not regard the primacy of the element of coercion, the continued existence of coercion and politics as diversion, which goes against Tucker (1969)'s argument that Marx's position with regard to State is equal to anarchism.

According to Marx, class assumes an independent existence as against individuals. The modern representative State isolates politics from the material factors of civil society and isolates political being from the real life. Marx pays emphasis on the material and political preconditions of socialist revolution. 'For Marx, socialism grows out of contradictions inherent in bourgeois society and political liberalism. A socialism that would grow, like Lassallean socialism, out of an alliance with the Right after both have overthrown political liberalism, will necessarily carry with it some of the characteristics of its authoritarian ally.' (Avineri, 1972: 183). Marx in his book *The Civil War in France* says that the commune is the re-absorption of State power by society as its own living forces instead of as forces controlling and subduing it, by the popular masses themselves, forming their own force instead of the organized force of their suppression. It is the political form of the social emancipation, instead of the artificial force. The dictatorship of the proletariat is the transitory stage towards socialism—the notion of the dictatorship of the proletariat disposes much too easily and therefore, does not dispose at all of the inevitable tension that exists between the requirement of direction on the one hand, and of democracy, on the other (Miliband, 1977).

To Lenin, the State is a product and manifestation of the irreconcilability of class antagonisms. The State arises where, when and insofar as class antagonisms cannot be resolved objectively and conversely, the existence of the State proves the irreconcilable class antagonisms. The State is the creation of order, which legalizes and perpetuates class oppression by moderating conflicts between classes.

According to Engles, which he puts in his *The Origin of the Family, Private Property and the State,* Lenin cites as 'the state is, therefore, by no means a power forced on society from without; ..., it is a product of society at a certain stage of development; ... it has split into irreconcilable antagonisms which it is powerless to dispel. But in order that these antagonisms, these classes with conflicting economic interests might not consume themselves and society in fruitless struggle, it became necessary to have a power, seemingly standing above society, that would alleviate the conflict and keep it within the bounds, of 'order'; and this power, arisen out of society but placing itself above it, and alienating itself more and more from it, is the state.' (op. cit., Lenin, 1977: 10). Citing the proposition of Engels Lenin puts the State as a public power 'grows stronger, however, in proportion as class antagonisms within the State become more acute, and adjacent states become larger and more populous. We have only to look at our present day Europe, where class struggle and rivalry in conquest have tuned up the public power to such a pitch that it threatens to swallow the whole of society and even the State.' (op. cit., Lenin, 1977: 14). Furthermore, Engels says, 'The state, then, has not existed from all eternity. There have been societies that did without it, that had no idea of the State and State power. At a certain stage of economic development, which was necessarily bound up with the split of society into classes, the State became a necessity owing to this split. We are now rapidly approaching a stage in the development of production at which the existence of these classes not only will have ceased to be a necessity, but will become a positive hindrance to production. They will fall as inevitably as they arose at an earlier stage. Along with them the State will inevitably fall. Society, which will reorganize production on the basis of a free and equal association of the producers, will put the whole machinery of state where it will then belong: into a museum of antiquities, by the side of the spinning-wheel and the bronze axe.' (op. cit., Lenin, 1977: 18).

The proletariat seizes State power and turns the means of production into State property to begin with—this view Engels puts in *Anti-Duhring*, has been cited by Lenin in his *State and Revolution*. The State is not abolished, rather it withers away. However, the proletariat seizes the State and abolishes the State as State, *i.e.*, the State as an instrument of coercion in the hands of the bourgeoisie. That is the proletarian State is not abolished, but it withers away; and the bourgeois State does not wither away, but it is abolished. The State is a special coercive force. Hence, the special coercive force for the suppression of the proletariat by the bourgeoisie must be replaced by special coercive force for the suppression of the bourgeoisie by the proletariat. The proletarian State takes possession of the means of production in the name of society. Engels gives emphasis to violent revolution. Other than that of a diabolical power, force plays an important role in history, *i.e.*, the revolutionary role. Force is the midwife of history, of every old society, which is pregnant with the new. It is the instrument through which social movements make its way. Lenin believes that the suppression of the bourgeois State by the proletarian State is impossible without a violent revolution and the abolition of the proletarian State is impossible except through the 'withering away' process. So long as the State exists, there is no freedom, and when there is freedom, there will be no State. The State does not completely wither away so long as there remains the safeguarding of bourgeois law, which sanctifies actual inequality. For the State to wither away complete communism is necessary. What complete communism signifies?

Complete communism, in short, signifies the following:

1. absence of subordination of individual to the division of labour;
2. absence of anti-thesis between mental and physical labour;
3. labour becomes not only a livelihood but life's prime want;
4. productive forces increase with the all round development of the individual;
5. abundance of co-operative wealth flow; and
6. social law becomes 'from each according to his ability, to each according to his needs'.

Based on these ideas Tucker (1976) evaluates Marx. Marx believes that the sovereign political authority in society cannot under any circumstances be considered a rightful authority and State qua State is an evil. Marx's normative position with regard to the State is anarchism, which may be defined as that State power, which is evil in essence, which cannot possibly be legitimized. Tucker here fails to differentiate between the proletarian State and bourgeois State, when he says that the proletarian dictatorship is only a way to something different and something beyond a society without State. To this end of society without State, the dictatorship of the proletariat is desirable, but as a form of State it is not. As a State, the proletarian State would doubtless be less evil than any other in history, but it would be an evil itself. But Tucker does not realize the true nature or thrust of classical Marxist philosophy of the State and the dictatorship of the proletariat. The Anarchists do not propose to create the worker's State in the revolutionary process leading to the Stateless society; rather they view the dismantling of Statehood as part and parcel of the revolutionary process. Engels in his letter to Van Patten on April 18, 1883 that the Anarchists put things upside down—they declare that the proletarian revolution must begin by doing away with the political organization of the State. But to destroy it would be to destroy only organism by means of which the victorious proletariat can assert its newly-conquered power, hold down its capitalist adversaries, and carry out that economic revolution of society, without which the whole victory must end in a new defeat and in a mass slaughter of the workers similar to those after the Paris Commune. The Anarchists see the Paris Commune as the anti-statist revolution and classical Marxism as the first historical incarnation of the dictatorship of the proletariat. The classical Marxism does agree with the anarchists on the issue of abolition of the State as the aim. To achieve this aim, Marxism asserts the temporary use of the instruments, resources and methods of the State power against the exploiters. Marxism rejects State qua State as evil, and also rejects State as the prime source of all evils. However, to the Marxists,

  i. the prime source of all evils = the imprisonment of man within the division of labour in production.
 ii. the prime end = economic emancipation of labour via the overthrow of the relations of domination and servitude in economic relations.

According to Marx and Engels, man primarily becomes the subject of the sovereign State of capital, *i.e.*, the despotism of capital. Therefore, communism signifies, according to Marx—freedom:

   i. man's complete and perfect freedom in the life of production,
  ii. abolition of private property,
 iii. abolition of social division of labour,
  iv. abolition of slavery of specialization,
   v. abolition of capitalist mode of production and wage labour,
  vi. emancipation of the worker from the bondage to a particular form of specialized work,
 vii. shortening of the working hours and rotation of jobs,
viii. free association of producers etc.

According to Marx and Engels, politics is fundamentally about economics—modes and relations of production and their changes. The meaning of politics lies in the basic conflicts in the human society of production, the conflicts over the modes of productive activity. All political struggles are one of the forms of class conflicts. All political struggles are class struggles in ideological disguise. Ideological disguise of economic issues are political ones. The realm of the political may be defined as the realm of power and authority relations among the people.

Marx's economic interpretation of politics goes along with political interpretation of economics. The social relations of production form the foundation of society in every historical epoch are relations not simply of economic exploitation but also of domination and servitude. The capital-labour relation becomes the politico-economic relation of domination and servitude. The capitalist economic order appears as a supremely authoritarian private realm of the political. It is a special form of command economy where the capitalist qua capitalist acts as a tyrannical ruling authority comparable to the great oriental despots of antiquity. Marx says about the dictatorship of capital, autocracy of capital and despotism of capital. Marx in *The Eighteenth Brumaire* says that representatives of the small peasants appear as their masters, as authority over them, as an unlimited governmental power that protects them against the other classes and provides all benefits from above. Its final expression can be found in the executive power subordinating society to itself. Both for Marx and Engels, liberal parliamentary democracy is bourgeois or class dictatorship, where the methods of representative government and universal suffrage are subtle mechanisms to misrepresent the people. 'Marx rejected representative democracy because he wanted more democracy, liberalism because he wanted more liberty, and the laissez-faire because he wanted an economic system which would attain perfect retributive justice. ... It is the grievous gaps in his doctrine and the total lack of foresight which have turned Marxism into quite another thing.' (Sartori, 1973: 454). Marx's liberal democracy increases the likelihood of peaceful revolution and politics is important to Marx for the pre-revolutionary period, for the ultimate fulfilment of man's nature.

According to Miliband, Marx sees politics as a determined and conditioned activity, which is subsidiary and epiphenomenal in character. The primacy of the economic determines and conditions the political and other forms—this is circumstantial, specific and contingent, but there is also the other side—that is political forms and processes determine, condition and shape the economic forms and processes. Marx's own cost of mind is strongly anti-determinant. In the Marxist sense, conflict is inherent in class system, which cannot be resolved within the system—it promotes the development of one system into another, in this sense, conflict is revolutionary and positive, rather than disruptive and negative. Marxists regard that politics is class conflict— one class subjugates other classes and the latter class or other class tries to resist that—and conflict arises. In this class conflict, one class is dominant and one class is subjugated. Politics provides the necessary sanction and legitimization to all forms of domination, permits the relations between members of the society, between different classes, both inside and outside their relations of production. However, economy is the core of all social and political relations. The Marxists, according to Miliband argues that the State is the essential means of class domination. It is not a neutral referee arbitrating between competing and conflicting classes. Inevitably, it is deeply engaged in partisan politics. It is not above class struggles, but takes an important role in this struggle—intervenes in the affairs of the society, which is crucial, constant and pervasive. This intervention is conditioned by the characteristics of the State. The State fundamentally becomes the instrument of class domination (Miliband, 1977). Miliband regards that State coercion and repression must be integrated with the theory of domination comprising both with superstructural and infrastructural elements. As an instrument of class domination, the State manages the common affairs of the whole bourgeoisie. Necessarily, the State must have a certain degree of autonomy. Managing the common affairs means the mediation and reconciliation of conflicts arising out of the common affairs. The personnel of the State system are located in the executive, legislative, administrative and judicial branches, who tend to belong to the same class, which tend to dominate the strategic heights of the bourgeois society. They are State elites; share the ideological and political assumptions of the economically dominant class. That is, those who run State apparatus should

(a) at the very least be favourably disposed towards those who own and control the larger part of the means of economic activity;

(b) much better disposed towards the interest of those who own and control the largest part of the means of economic activity than towards any other interest or class;

(c) seek to serve the interests and purposes of the economically dominant class;

(d) likely to be persuaded to serve the interests and purposes of the economically dominant class, which in a sense, to serve the national interest.

Miliband (1977) argues that the capitalist enterprise is the strongest pressure group in capitalist society, able to command the attention of the State. But this is not the same thing as saying that the State is an instrument of the capitalist class. However, the pressure and influence of the business group may be decisive or not. The process of decision-making is complex. Many factors play their role in the decision-making process. Pressure of business groups is one of the important factors.

The pressure of the business group helps to explain the notion that the State is an instrument of class domination. Furthermore, according to the Marxists, because of structural, objective and impersonal kind of dimension, the State is an instrument of the ruling class. It means that the nature is determined by the nature and requirements of the mode of production. There is structural constraint and there is structural rationality, which no government and State can evade. The structural constraints' concept helps to understand (Figure 39)—

from: ⟶	actual	to:
pledging to far-reaching reforms before election	Why governments do act as they do? ↓	failing to carry out the pledged reform after being elected
	middle position or position between two extremes	

Figure 39

There is the problem in the concept of 'structural constraints', which fails to explain—how and in what way the 'structural constrains' limit the government to do what it desires to do, depriving the agents of the government the freedom to act, freedom of choice and manoeuvre and turning them into the bearers of objective forces. This is another form of determination. Miliband calls it as the hyper-structuralist trap. 'Governments can and do press against the 'structural constraints' by which they are beset. Yet, to recognize the existence and importance of these constraints is also to point to the limits of reform, of which more latter, and to make possible a strategy of change which attacks the mode of production that imposes the constraints.' (Miliband, 1977: 73).

The State is a class State—it enjoys the high degree of autonomy from the ruling classes and from the civil society at large. Marx and Engels acknowledge the relative autonomy of the State, which consists of degrees of freedom, is in direct relation to the freedom which the executive power and the State in general enjoy *vis-à-vis* institutions and pressure groups. The executive power is least constrained—in this situation the autonomy of the State is greatest. State is relatively independent, mainly in connection with regimes where the executive power is exceptionally strong. Engels uses the concept of equilibrium between contending social forces—this type of equilibrium is supposedly provided by the State. Miliband cites Engels, who says that economically dominant class becomes politically dominant and acquires the new means of holding down the oppressed class. In exception, periods occur in history where the warring classes balance each other. The State power as mediator of conflicting interests assumes a certain degree of independence. Such was the absolute monarchies of the seventeenth and eighteenth centuries balancing the nobility and class of burghers. Such was the case with Bonapartism of the First and Second French Empires, which played off the proletariat against the bourgeoisie and the bourgeoisie against the proletariat. Later on, there emerged the German Empire of the Bismarck nation where the capitalists and workers are balanced against each other and equally cheated for the benefit of the impoverished Prussian cabbage junkers. However, to Miliband, Engels does not regard the State for itself. Engels's theorization of the relative autonomy of the State is fairly misleading and inadequate. The relative independence of the State does not reduce its class character, on the contrary, relative independence makes possible for the State to play its class role in a flexible manner. The State simply cannot be treated as an instrument of the ruling class, and if it is treated so, then the State would be inhibited in the performance of its role and the State would loss the freedom for making the existing social order intact.

However, Marx in *The Eighteenth Brumaire* says that the bourgeoisie or bourgeois class confesses that its own interest requires its deliverance from the peril of its own self-government; that to establish peace and quiet in the country, its bourgeois parliament must first of all be laid to rest; that its political power must be broken in order to pressure its social power intact; that the individual bourgeois can only continue to exploit the other classes and remain in the undisturbed enjoyment of property, family, religion and order on the condition that his class is condemned to political insignificance along with the other classes. See Figure 40.

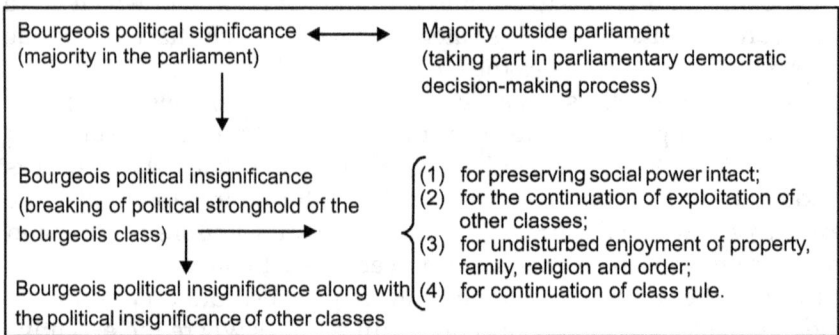

Bourgeois political significance ⟷ (majority in the parliament) ↓ Bourgeois political insignificance (breaking of political stronghold of the bourgeois class) ⟶ ↓ Bourgeois political insignificance along with the political insignificance of other classes	Majority outside parliament (taking part in parliamentary democratic decision-making process) (1) for preserving social power intact; (2) for the continuation of exploitation of other classes; (3) for undisturbed enjoyment of property, family, religion and order; (4) for continuation of class rule.

Figure 40

Modern capitalist State maintains its autonomy through the performance of its functions, namely—maintenance of law and order, fostering of consensus, economic development and advancement of national interest. Further, relative autonomy also ensures that—

1. the State represents as State for itself;
2. those who occupy leading position in the State system use their power to advance their economic interests;
3. enrichment of economic interests leads to the proliferation of diverse economic ventures and activities, and growth of new bourgeoisie having close connections with the State and agents of State organs;
4. it is not economic power which results in the wielding of political power and influences, shapes the political decision-making, rather it is political power, creates the formation of the economically powerful one;
5. the State is an instrument of economic power in the sense that those who own State power use it for their economic purposes and needs, but not in the sense that those who hold State power serve the interests of the economically dominant class separate from these power holders.

Miliband tries to understand the Marxist approach in terms of specificity of politics. In doing so, he avoids the implications of base-superstructure dichotomy and does not interpret politics in terms of historical materialism. According to Miliband, Marxism does not regard the specificity of politics as Marxism is led by historical materialism treating politics as conditioned and determined activity is without any substantial degree of autonomy. Conflict draws the central attention of Miliband—all manifestations of social life are permanently present in the permanent conflict of the capitalist society. He invites the discussion of the State in the context of 'stability' and 'legitimacy' of the bourgeois order, appreciates the importance of the State as an 'institution and like Marxist says that the State is an essential means of class domination. In his analysis of politics he uses the concepts like 'conflict', 'conciliation', 'domination', 'stability', 'State', 'defense of bourgeois order', 'legitimization', 'democratization', 'party', 'dictatorship of the proletariat', 'reform', 'revolution' and so on and so forth. See Figure 41.

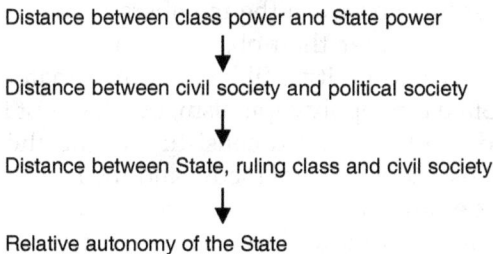

Distance between class power and State power

↓

Distance between civil society and political society

↓

Distance between State, ruling class and civil society

↓

Relative autonomy of the State

Figure 41

In fact, Miliband's idea of Marxist politics is Weberian, *i.e.*, bureaucratic—the notion that an emergent power in society is distinct from class society.

Mention here may be made that Poulantzas advances a very rigorous critique of contemporary Marxist theories. Poulantzas stresses the interlocked influences of State and society. He argues that the State plays an active role in the formation of classes. Class conflict is to be located not only in the society at large, but also within the apparatuses of the State itself. Poulantzas makes a distinction between State power and the general forms of class power. Poulantzas attacks Miliband's method of analysis—the method starts with assertions referring to reality, which is in contradiction with reality. According to Poulantzas, Miliband gives the impression that

1. social classes and the State are objective structures;
2. relations between social classes and the State are objective relations;
3. relations between social classes and groups are interpersonal relations;
4. State is reducible to interpersonal relations of the diverse 'groups' that constitute the State apparatus;
5. relations between social classes and the State are reducible to interpersonal relations of individuals composing social groups and individuals composing the State apparatus.

This study does not lead to the study of the objective co-ordinates that determine the distribution of agents into classes and the contradictions between these classes. In his analysis of bureaucracy Miliband cites only social origins and personal ties of bureaucracy with members of the ruling class, and not the objective function of bureaucracy. According to Poulantzas, the State apparatus forms an objective system of special branches. Miliband, on the contrary, makes a diversion from objective structures of the State to the personal motivations of their agents. According to Miliband, changes in the State or capitalist State, would be related to the ever closer links between the members of the ruling class and the State apparatus, rather than objective changes in the articulation between economy and polity. Miliband approximates the classical Marxist thesis of State monopoly capitalism, but does not look into ideas as objective and institutionalized consisting of the church, political parties, trade unions, schools, mass media and the family etc. Poulantzas talks about ideological State apparatuses along with repressive State apparatuses, such as law, police, army, court, administrative bodies etc. According to Poulantzas, the objective structures may be presented here (Figure 42)—

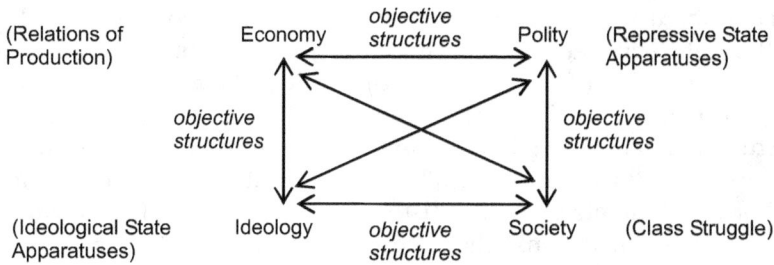

(Relations of   Economy   *objective*   Polity   (Repressive State
Production)   *structures*   Apparatuses)

objective structures   *objective structures*

(Ideological State   Ideology   *objective*   Society   (Class Struggle)
Apparatuses)   *structures*

Figure 42

According to Poulantzas, the State is determined by objective structures and relations. In this respect, critics cite that if the State is treated as a system of objective relations leading to structural superdeterminism, which prevents us from accepting the theoretical justification of the relative autonomy of the State. However, Poulantzas rejects the long Marxist tradition that the State is only the simple instrument of class rule manipulated by the ruling class at their will and stresses the relative autonomy of the State. According to Poulantzas, those who run the State are compelled by the structural constraints. A class may be considered as a distinct and autonomous force within a social formation when the economic level is reflected on the other levels by a specific presence and persistent effects. Poulantzas criticizes 'economism' of classical Marxism, on the one hand, and critics condemn Poulantzas for his structural determinism, which makes impossible to study the dialectical relations between State and the system. Miliband phrases this structural determinism as structural superdeterminism, which makes no difference between various forms of government and the bourgeois State, bourgeois democracy and the fascist State. Poulantzas presents Bonapatism as characteristic of all forms of capitalist State and rejects the belongingness of ideological State apparatuses to the system of the State. Sometimes, Poulantzas's method of structural superdeterminism is treated as structuralist abstractionism, which helps him further to reintroduce the concept of economic determinism of classical Marxism. According to Miliband, power is not located in the level of structure, but is an effect of the ensemble of these levels, levels of the class struggle. To him, Poulantzas does not make a distinction between class power and State power. Miliband says that State power is the main and the ultimate, but not the only means, whereby class power is assured and maintained—but one of the main reasons for stressing the importance of the notion of the relative autonomy of the State is that there is a basic distinction between class power and State power. According to Miliband, the structural superdeterminism prevents Poulantzas from correctly posing the problem of the relative autonomy of the State and there exists incompatibility between the objective characters of the relations existing between the bourgeois class and the State—between the structural constraints of the system and the relative autonomy of the State. But from Poulantzas's point of view there is no incompatibility—the relative autonomy would be in turn a structural element. The relative character of autonomy indicates that it belongs to a world of structural determinations. In *Fascism and Dictatorship* Poulantzas makes distinctions between various forms of the State. Poulantzas thinks that Miliband emphasizes the link between dominant class and elite in power, and concedes the relative autonomy of the State only in case of Fascism, on the one hand, and Miliband considers that Poulantzas is interested with regimes of exception and for that he has lost all interest in the bourgeois democratic form of State, on the other. According to Poulantzas,

1. the State has the general function of constituting the factor of cohesion of a social formation;
2. if the State is defined as the instance of maintaining the cohesion of a social formation, of producing the conditions of production of a social system, of maintaining class domination, the institution in question, *i.e.*, the ideological State apparatuses exactly do the same function;
3. the State constitutes the factor of cohesion between the levels of social formation;
4. everything that contributes to the cohesion of social formation pertains to the State, for example trade unions, social-democratic leaders etc.

Althusser speaks of 'ideological State apparatuses' and tries to defend this term. Althusser in his *Lenin and Philosophy and Other Essays* says that to his knowledge, no class can hold State power over a long period without at the same time exercising its hegemony over and in the State Ideological Apparatuses. A class cannot maintain itself in power for a long period of time without controlling ideological apparatuses. Like Poulantzas Althusser accepts that everything which serves to maintain the cohesion of a social formation forms part of the State. According to Miliband, Poulantzas's concept of class may be presented graphically,

a distinct and autonomous class → a social force within social formation → class and its connections with the relations of production or economic existence → reflection on the other levels by the specific presence of this class → class relation to the relations of production and the place in the production process are reflected on the other levels by the pertinent effects → reflection of the place in the process of production on the other levels.

Following Balibar, Poulantzas asserts that by mode of production, we should not designate what is generally marked out as economic but as a specific combination of various structures and practices which, in combination, appears as so many instances and levels, *i.e.*, as so many regional structures of this mode. Furthermore, the structure of the whole is determined by the economic does not mean that the economic always holds the dominant role in the structure. The unity constituted by the structure in dominance implies that every mode of production has a dominant level or instance, but the economic is in fact dominant only insofar as it attributes the dominant role to one instance or another, insofar as it regulates the shift of dominance which results from the decentration of the instances. Therefore, what distinguishes one mode of production from another and consequently specifies a mode of production is the particular form of articulation maintained by its level— this articulation is henceforth referred to the term matrix of a mode of production. Both Poulantzas and Balibar say that the economic decides which level is going to have the dominant role. Balibar says in *Reading Capital* that the economy is the determinant in that it determines that of the instances of the social structure, occupies the determinant place. Not a simple relation, but rather a relation between relations; not a transitive causality, but rather a structural causality.

Apart from the Miliband-Poulantzas debate, a mention here may be made about Poulantzas's theory of the State. The State does really exhibit a peculiar material framework that can by no means be reduced to mere political domination, which is inscribed in the materiality of the State. This materiality of the State is institutionalized. The State apparatuses are not exhausted in State power. The State is not created by the ruling class, nor is taken over by that class. State's actions are not reducible to political domination. The essential autonomy of the superstructural instances, *i.e.* the State and ideology would serve to legitimize the autonomy, self-sufficiency and self-reproduction of the economy. The position of the State *vis-à-vis* the economy has changed not only with the mode of production, but also with the stage and phase of capitalism. What is perfectly legitimate is the theory of the capitalist State which forces its specific object and concept—this is made possible by the separation of the space of the State and that of the economy in the capitalist mode of production. The specific autonomy of political space under capitalism—a circumstance that legitimizes theorizations of that space—is not the flawless realization of the State's supposed autonomy of essence, but the result of a separation from the relations of production that is peculiar to capitalism. A concrete State should be considered a simple realization of the state-of-the-capitalist-mode-of-production. Social formations are the actual sites of existence and reproduction of the modes of production. They are sites of the various forms of State. The State is bound up with the relations of production constitutes its primary relation with social classes and the class struggle. The capitalist State and its relative separation from the relations of production, which is produced by the relations themselves, is the basis of the State's organizational framework. Poulantzas considers:

1. production process is grounded on the unity of the labour process and the relations of production;
2. this unity is realized through the primacy of the relations of production over the labour process and production forces;
3. from this primacy flows the presence of political and ideological relations within the relations of production;
4. the relations of production like constituent relation of possession and economic property, find expression in class powers that are organically articulated to the political and ideological relations which concretize and legitimize them;
5. the State plays an equally specific role in organizing ideological relations and the dominant ideology;
6. the State cannot reproduce political domination exclusively through repression or force, but directly calls upon ideology to legitimize violence and contribute consensus among those classes, which are dominated from the point of view of political power;
7. ideology is always class ideology and ruling ideology is essentially ideology of the ruling class; and
8. dominant ideology is embodied in the State apparatuses.

The function of dominant ideology is to inculcate and reproduce social class, class domination and social division of labour. The ideological State apparatuses may include church, religious apparatus, educational apparatus, official information network, television, cultural apparatus, army, police, judicial system, prison and State administration etc. The State acts within an unstable equilibrium of compromises between the dominant classes and the dominated. The State adopts popular measures. However, to analyze the State solely with the categories of repression-prohibition and ideology-concealment obviously leads one to subjectivize the reasons for consent.

If the relations of production take primacy over the forces of production, then the relations of production, possession and economic property find expression in powers emanating from the sites delineated by the relations of production (Figure 43). Power comes down to objective positions rooted in the division of labour. Power is the capacity of each class to realize its specific interests in a relation of opposition to that capacity in other classes. Therefore, without economic relations power becomes impossible. However, powers relating to the social classes and the class struggle are not reducible to the State. Modern capitalist State concentrates various forms of power. At present, the relations between class powers and the State are becoming closer and closer. Class powers are not just economic ones, will stretch beyond the State. While considering Ideological State Apparatuses, the State's discourse does not exhaust all political discourses, yet it includes a class power in its structure. Similarly, the ideological power is never exhausted by the State, where the roots of the former lies beyond the latter and power consists of the relations of power. If class powers are not reducible to the State and outmeasures its apparatuses, and these powers have their roots in the social division of labour and in exploitation, these powers have primacy over the apparatuses that embody them, *i.e.*, the State. This State plays a constitutive role in the existence and reproduction of class power and also in the class struggle, persists in the relations of production. Where exists class struggle, the State exists as institutionalized political power and hence, there exists no State of society prior to the State. The State marks out the field of class struggle, the relations of power, relations of production—it organizes the market and property relations—it institutes political domination, establishes a politically dominant class, and justifies all forms of social division of labour within the framework of the class-divided society. The determining role of the relations of production or the primacy of class struggle over the State and its apparatuses does not take place mechanically, but chronologically and historically. Besides, the historical-chronological precedence over the State is inscribed in diverse temporalities and in historical forms marked by uneven development— a form of State may precede the relations of productions—the Absolutist State in Europe was predominantly capitalist while the relations of production were feudal. According to Poulantzas, Marxism proposes the following points—

1. class struggle is the motive force of all social formations;
2. class power is the cornerstone of power in all class-divided society;
3. inspite of the grounding of economic power and relations of production, political power is the primordial in the changes in its character that condition every essential transformation in other fields of power;

4. political power occupies a distinct and separate place in the fields of power in the capitalist mode of production;
5. however, various fields of power may intersect with each other;
6. inspite of this, political power is concentrated and marginalized by the State, is the central site of the exercise of power.

However, this view has not been accepted by Foucault and Deleuze, who suggest that power is scattered and diluted among various micro-situations, which has not been accepted by Poulantzas. See Figure 44.

Foucault and Deleuze	Poulantzas
Functional and institutional tradition ↓	Structural tradition ↓
Pluralism of micro powers—power is scattered and diluted ↓	Power is concentrated and marginalized by the State
Underestimation of classes and class struggle	

Figure 44

Poulantzas argues that all power, political, ideological and economic are materialized through political, ideological and economic apparatuses, which are not mere appendages of power, but play an important constitutive role in the formation of power, where the State organically presents itself in the generation of class powers (Poulantzas, 1980). Class struggles have primacy over the institutions or apparatuses and go beyond these in their relationship (Figure 45).

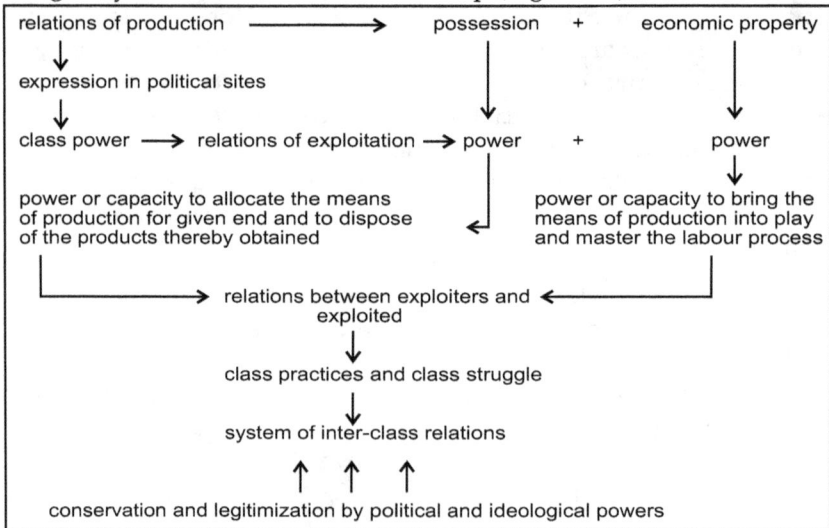

Figure 43

Therefore, in contradiction with the liberatarian viewpoint, Poulantzas says that the State plays a constitutive role not only in the relations of production and powers, but also in the totality of power relations and in contradiction with the statist theory, says that class struggles make up the primary field of power relations and which invariably have primacy over the State. Still relations of production play the determining role, but the primacy of struggle over the State goes beyond the sphere of the relations of production. However, these relations of production are the relations of power and struggle (Poulantzas, 1980).

In *Fascism and Dictatorship* (1979) Poulantzas describes that in case of growth of fascism no dominant class or class fraction seems to be able to impose its leadership on the other classes and fractions of the power bloc, whether by its own methods of political organization or through the parliamentary democratic State. But, generally, there cannot be an alliance of classes and fractions of equal importance—there is domination of one dominant class over another—there is hegemony of one fraction over another—there is leadership. But fascism characterizes the crisis of hegemony. In fascism the power bloc is unable to overcome the contradictions within the alliance, unable to impose hegemony within the power bloc by one class or fraction. Hence, the crisis of

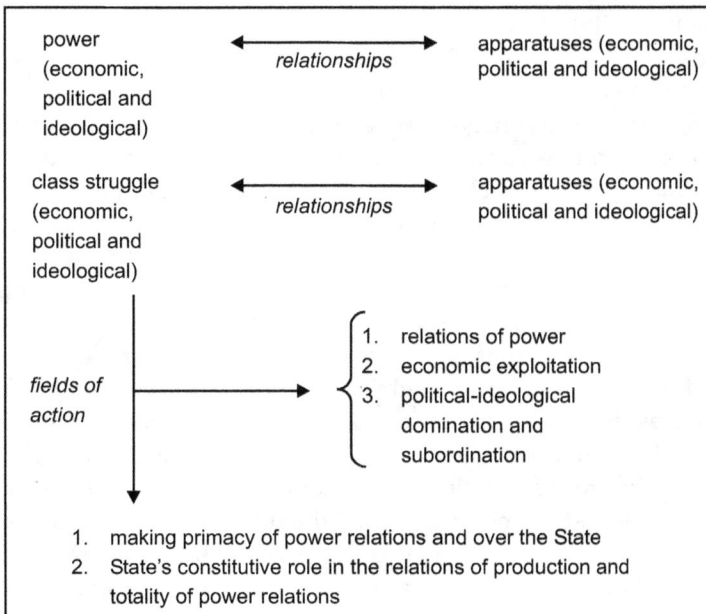

Figure 45

hegemony takes a recourse to this trend, *i.e.* the trend of modification of hegemony—modification of the relations of forces within the alliance, *i.e.* redistribution of respective weights and hegemony of finance capital or big monopoly capital. It is said that the fascist dictatorship is no different from the bourgeois democracy, which also achieves the dictatorship of the finance capital. It is the simple identification of economic domination and political hegemony by the Comintern. The process of modifications of hegemony, Poulantzas says is from the stage of evidently unstable hegemony to the stage of inability to assume hegemony and finally to the stage of hegemony of a fraction.

This shift of political hegemony, which is the function of fascism, has not been recognized by the Comintern. Further, 'conjuncture of fascism and the start of the growth of fascism correspond to a crisis of party representation as far as the power bloc is concerned ....' (Poulantzas, 1979: 73). Gramsci in *Prison Notebooks* says that the situations of conflict between represented and representatives reverberate out from the terrain of the parties throughout the State reinforcing the relative power of bureaucracy, of high finance, of the Church and of all bodies relatively independent of the fluctuations of public opinion. There is split between dominant classes and class fractions and political parties. However, characteristically fascism has a relative autonomy from both the power bloc and the fraction of big monopoly capital. It has relative autonomy from what? From internal contradictions among the classes and fractions of classes—the relative autonomy recognizes the power bloc of big monopoly capital and establish within it the hegemony of this power bloc or the fraction of big monopoly capital, and also from contradictions between dominant classes and dominated classes, while in the former the fascist State assumes autonomy from internal political crisis and in the latter it assumes autonomy from the political crisis of the ensemble social formation. Mention here may be made that the relative autonomy of the State in fascist formation is different from relative autonomy of the State in capitalist formation, where the State performs its functions within the framework of equilibrium of social forces and where the State acts as the mediator in the class struggle. The relative autonomy of the fascist State is different from the normal forms of capitalist State and is also different from the peculiar and particular form of autonomy of the Bonapartist forms of State. In this connection Poulantzas cites opinion of Miliband as—'It is in this perspective that must be understood the notion of independence of state power from all forces in civil society, to which Marx and Engels occasionally referred as possible in "exceptional circumstances", and of which fascism, in the context of advanced capitalism, may be said to provide further example. In this context, however, the concept is ambiguous in that it suggests a certain neutrality on the part of the state power .... Which actual experience bellies....' (Miliband, 1969: 93).

The exceptional State needs relative autonomy to recognize hegemony. The exceptional State in association with the reorganization of the State system needs radical changes in the ideological State apparatuses and in their relationship to the repressive State apparatuses. Institutions in the State system are apparatuses whatever the form of the State may be. The fascist State is akin to all other forms of the capitalist State. It is itself the exceptional capitalist State. In an exceptional State, the role of reorganizing hegemony implies the limitation of the distribution of power within the State system and strict control of the State system by one of the apparatuses in the hands of the class, which is struggling for its hegemony. The characteristic limitation of the relative autonomy of the ideological apparatuses in the exceptional State is also due to the ideological crisis which accompanies the political crisis. The specific intervention of ideology concentrates and increases repression against the popular classes. It legitimizes repression. When the ideology is in crisis, the ideological intervention becomes necessary. 'There is apparently paradoxical feature here. The exceptional State is characterized both by increased autonomy from the hegemonic class or fraction, and by a limitation of the relative autonomy of the ideological state apparatuses. The paradox was noted by Marx in his work on Bonapartism: the greater the relative autonomy of the state from the hegemonic class or class fraction, the stronger is its internal 'centralization'. But the paradox is only superficial: such relative autonomy from the hegemonic class or fraction is necessary precisely so that the state can establish its hegemony, by organizing and consolidating the power bloc. In this conjecture of crisis, this implies the restriction and radical control of the power 'game' which was previously sanctioned by the relative autonomy of the ideological state apparatuses. The class contradictions within the exceptional state, contradictions which it is in fact based on, take different forms.' (Poulantzas, 1979: 316). As for the exceptional State, the ideological and political crises lead to the hegemonic class losing its direct links with both its political and its ideological representatives. The State apparatuses are subject to internal ideology, which coincides with the dominant ideology, is the dominant apparatus. At this point,

militarization of society	$\rightarrow$	army is dominant
bureaucratization of society	$\rightarrow$	administration is dominant
clericalization of society	$\rightarrow$	church is dominant

The function of the exceptional State is thus the necessary means for reorganizing ideological hegemony. 'In fact, depending on the relation of forces and the distribution of class power within the State system, the dominant position may belong (a) to the repressive State apparatus and one of its branches—the army in military dictatorship, the civil administration in Bonapartism, the political police in the established fascist State; (b) to an ideological State apparatus—for example the party in the first period of fascist rule, or the Church in the clerical-military dictatorships like the Dollfuss regime in Austria.' (Poulantzas, 1979: 318). Besides the exceptional forms of the State, in other forms of the capitalist State, the repressive State apparatuses are dominant over the ideological State apparatuses. Here, the political parties perform the function principally as transmission belts. The indoctrination of ideology operates here normally. Within the State system the central nucleus of the State is really dominant.

Marxist classics basically centres on repressive State apparatuses, while according to Poulantzas, Gramsci develops his theory that ideological apparatuses belong to the State system. To Gramsci,

1. the State can be treated as a system;
2. the State has two aspects—coercive and persuasive;
3. the State has two roles—repressive and ideological;
4. the ideological apparatuses belong to the State system;
5. the State represented as public, includes organizations normally referred to as private, such as church, schools, trade unions, parties, news media etc.;
6. the State is the organizer of hegemony; and
7. ideological apparatuses can be treated as State apparatuses.

Poulantzas analyzes the theory that ideological apparatuses are State apparatuses and treats ideology not as mere conception, but accepts it as norms, customs, practices, and way of life in a social formation. Within social formation there exists institutions and apparatuses. According to Poulantzas,

> **institutions** = a system of norms or rules socially sanctioned;
> **ideology** = rules and norms;
> **political repression** = social sanctioning;
> **state apparatuses** = ideological apparatuses + political repression;
> **dominant ideology** = embodiment of ideological apparatuses within social formation, where, *religious apparatus* = churches, *political apparatus* = parties, *union apparatus* = unions, *educational apparatus* = schools and universities, *communication apparatus* = papers, radio, television, cinema etc.

These apparatuses are legally monopolized by the State and they are considered as ideological State apparatuses. Ideologies are class ideologies. Ideology consists of power relations essential to social formation. Again, political domination needs direct and decisive intervention of ideology. Dominant ideology in the form of ideological apparatuses is directly involved in the State apparatuses, which concentrates, guarantees and gives expression to political power. Repressive State Apparatuses do not generally intervene in the functioning of ideological apparatuses directly, but do present continually behind them. The direct economic functions of the State— reproduction of social conditions of production, intervention in the reproduction of production cycle, intervention in the detailed workings of the economy—all are articulated to the State's overall political role and carried out under repressive apparatuses and ideological apparatuses. In this connection, Poulantzas criticizes Althusser on the ground that he underestimates the economic role of State apparatuses by distinguishing reproduction of the relations of production, only where the State intervenes, from reproduction of the means of production and reproduction of labour-power. In *Lenin and Philosophy and Other Essays* Althusser says that the role of the repressive State apparatuses consist essentially in securing by force the political conditions of the reproduction of relations of production and here the role of the ruling ideology is heavily concentrated. To Poulantzas, apparatuses cannot be considered as State apparatuses alone. It also consists of ideology. In fact, State is equal to repression plus ideology. Following Gramsci, Poulantzas says that the 'firm' is not merely the 'unit of production', but provides important contribution to—

a. reproduction of the social conditions of production,
b. ideology,
c. relations of political domination,
d. relations of production,
e. relationship between social relations of production and political social relations, relationship between social relations of production and ideological social relations.

However, this economic apparatus, the technical basis of production, which contains production units, cannot be described as economic State apparatuses, although the State intervenes to maintain and guarantee the economic order. Unlike the State apparatuses, both the ideological and economic State apparatuses, cannot be smashed at the same time, and in the same way. The apparatuses are no more than the effects of the class struggle. The apparatuses relate to the relations of power. Poulantzas, in this respect, outlines Althusser's conception of the relative autonomy of the ideological State apparatuses, and the unity of the ideological State apparatuses on the grounds of ruling ideology, and ideology of the ruling class, which holds State power. Althusser, according to Poulantzas, abstractly formulates —

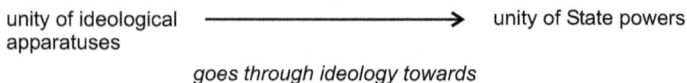

unity of ideological ────────────────→ unity of State powers
apparatuses

goes through ideology towards

This abstract and formalistic formulation in concrete terms does not take into account the presence and importance of class struggle in a social formation, the presence and importance of contradictory and antagonistic ruling ideology, and the dislocations of State power. State power, according to Poulantzas, is formed by an alliance of the dominant classes, so if the one class has hegemony, the other classes in power involve dislocations among the State apparatuses—between the ideological State apparatuses themselves and between ideological State apparatuses and repressive State apparatuses. The hegemonic class controls the repressive State apparatus as it is the nucleus of the State power and the non-hegemonic classes control some of the branches of the State.

Poulantzas (1978) considers that political unity of the power bloc under the protection of the hegemonic class means the unity of the State power—this is related to the interplay of the institutions of the capitalist State and to the unity and relative autonomy peculiar to it. The State derives its own unity from the plurality of dominant classes and fractions and the unity of State power is to be found in the univocal correspondence of the State to the specific interests of that class or fraction—in the co-existence of the relation between the State and the power bloc and the unitary functioning of the institutionalized power to the benefit of the hegemonic class. Though the capitalist class represents the interests of the power bloc as a whole, as a matter of fact, it has specific relation with the hegemonic class, and has to perform specific functions in the interests of that hegemonic class. Here lies the intrinsic unity and relative autonomy of the State. '...this relative autonomy of the state from the power bloc and the hegemonic class or fraction does not depend on an equilibrium of the force of the dominant classes and fractions, amongst which institutionalized power operates as arbitrator. In fact, as general rule, it is precisely that hegemonic class or fraction whose political organization is constituted by the state, which is preponderant amongst the other forces of the power bloc: but this privileged position which it occupies does not prevent the relative autonomy of the state from it.' (Poulantzas, 1978: 302-303). The State has the particular function of constituting the factor of cohesion. The

State system is the structure in which the contradictions of the various levels of a formation are condensed. A historically determined social formation is characterized by several modes of production, which are overlapping and sometimes contradictory. The State performs here the role of cohesion, the maintenance of the formation's unity, *i.e.* in Weberian terminology—maintaining the monopoly use of legitimate force, in Apter's formulation—maintenance of the boundaries, in Easton's and Deutsch's formulations—maintenance of the system of which it is a part, in Almond's formulation—maintenance of the system in terms of input-output-feedback analysis and also the formulation of lag, lead, load and gain analysis. In short, political is the factor for the maintenance of the formation's unity. However, Poulantzas is not functionalist, but a structuralist defining criterion of the State structure, as that structure which has the role of the cohesive factor of the system combined with that of monopoly of legitimate force. According to Marxist classics,

a. State + class struggle = political class domination,
b. relation of the State to political struggle = relation of the State to the ensemble of the levels of structure, therefore;
c. political struggle = ensemble of the levels of structure, and,
d. relation of the State to the articulation of interests = formation

Engels, therefore, in his *Origin of the Family, Private Property and the State* says that—

1. the State is the product of society at a certain stage of social formation or at the certain stage of social development;
2. society is entangled with insoluble contradictions and irreconcilable antagonisms;
3. society cannot be left in a fruitless struggle, so it becomes necessary to have power seemingly standing above society that would alleviate the conflict or neutralize it;
4. the State keeps the society within the bounds of order;
5. the State power is originated from society, but is placed above the society and more and more alienating from it.

Hence, the State has the function of order—it prevents political class conflict from breaking out and classes and society from consuming themselves. In performing the function of order, the State has to perform the techno-economic function at the economic level, political function at the level of political class struggle and ideological function at the ideological level, where the economic and ideological are determined by the political role, the global role of the State. In the ensemble of structures, the State is related to class society and necessarily to political class domination. The global role of the State is the factor of cohesion in the unity of a formation. 'The function of the state as the organizer of the labour process is only one aspect of its economic function, which also includes, for instance the function of the judicial system, *i.e.* the set (ensemble) of rules which organizes capitalist exchanges and provides the real framework of cohesion in which commercial encounters can take place. The state's function *vis-à-vis* the ideological consists of its role of education, teaching, etc. At the strictly political level, that of the political class struggle, this function of the state is the maintenance of political order in political class conflict.' (Poulantzas, 1978: 53).

By reproducing social relations or class relations and sanctioning and safeguarding class domination the State apparatuses perform the role to maintain the unity and cohesion of a social formation. The politico-ideological relations are material practices, materialized through political and ideological relations. The economic apparatus, for example, business or factory materializes the economic relations in their articulation with political and ideological relations. Social classes and their reproduction exist by way of relationship linking them to the State. State apparatuses do not possess power of their own, but materialize class relations, which embrace power. In fulfilling the economic, political and ideological functions the State power reproduces class relations, which is inscribed in the very structure of the apparatuses and the classes occupy the terrain of political domination. The role of the State apparatuses or the role of the State power is responsible for the cohesion and unity of the social formation, representation of class interests and the reproduction of social relations or classes. Therefore, the State power is essentially related with class struggle. In the process of socialist transformation the working class must not only transform the State power, but also the apparatuses of the State. The classes are structurally determined and this determination is not restricted to the economic situation alone, but is extended to the levels of social division of labour and the State apparatuses enter into the process of determining classes as the embodiment and materialization of the ideological and political relations (Poulantzas, 1978a). '...the fundamental reproductions of social classes do not just involve places in the relations of production. There is no economic self-reproduction of classes over and against an ideological and political reproduction by means of the apparatuses. There is, rather, precisely a process of primary reproduction in and by the class struggle at all stages of the social division of labour. This reproduction of social classes also involves the political and ideological relations of the social division of labour; these latter have a decisive role in their relationship to the relations of production. The reason is that the social division of labour itself not only involves political and ideological relations but also the social relations of production within which it has dominance over the "technical division" of labour. This is a consequence of the fact that within the production process, the production relations are dominant over the labour process.' (Poulantzas, 1978a: 30).

Poulantzas moves away from the Sartrean approach through Althusserian structuralism to revolutionary materialism. This is different in many respects from that of Marx, who moves from Law to the State, and then to Political Economy; from Hegel to Feuerbach, and then to revolutionary materialism; from radical bourgeois liberalism to petty-bourgeois humanism, then to communism. However, these changes are not separated from each other, but are closely interconnected. From an existentialist point of view, Poulantzas attempts to combine Althusserian and Gramscian positions within an essentially Marxist-Leninist outlook —without politics nothing would have happened and politics would not have found its theoretical expression without the philosophy of revolutionary materialism. Sartre identified the role of the State in transcending the internal divisions within the dominant classes, in pursuing national interest and in maintaining the established order serving the interest of the dominant classes and performing its relative autonomy. The State constitutes the function of mediation and arbitration between conflicts within the dominant classes, in so far as these conflicts run the risk of weakening the State. The State embodies and realizes the general interest of the dominant class over and above the antagonisms and conflicts of particular interests. The ruling class produces its State and its institutional structures will define themselves in terms of concrete reality. Sartre finds that

    a. the State acts as the mediator between the exploiting and exploited classes;
    b. the State without this mediating role cannot function;
    c. the State is determination of the dominant class, which is conditioned by class struggle;
    d. the State exists for the sake of the dominant class;
    e. the State posits itself in relation to class from which it originates;
    f. the State is the institutionalized, united and effective group, which derives its internal sovereignty from itself;
    g. the sovereign action of the State is essentially a national praxis;
    h. the State acts in the interests of the class from which it originates, and sometimes acts against their interests;
    i. there is a real contradiction of the State—it is a class apparatus pursuing class interests and State apparatus for itself as the sovereign unity of all (Sartre, 1968).

Following Sartre, Poulantzas is concerned with the State's role in forming a power bloc, the relative autonomy of the State, the State's role as a factor of cohesion and class unity of the State. Both Sartre and Poulantzas believe that the state is the totalizing ensemble and the factor of cohesion, where there is mutual separation and fragments among the members and within the classes of the society due to the alienated human conditions and structure of the society. See Figure 46. The influence of Althusser and Gramsci on Poulantzas is quite obvious in this respect. Althusser makes distinctions between two kinds of State apparatuses—one kind is repressive constituting of all political, administrative and judicial elements and the other kind is ideological, referring to all elements or institutions contributing to all ideological motivations, such as family, education, religion and culture. In the former kind violence is the primary constituent and in the latter, violence is the secondary constituent. According to Althusser, in the production process, human resources or skills continuously flow from family, places of residence, school, church etc. into larger society and into the production places for preservation, production and reproduction of human skills. Reproduction of labour power and production relations are closely related not only with the production process, but also with the ideological apparatuses. This production process is influenced by the ruling class ideology. The reproduction of labour power not only creates or reproduces skills, but also reproduces the subjection of the labour to the ruling ideology or practice of that ideology. It seems to me that according to Althusser, reproduction of labour power not only reproduces the forces of production, but also the relations of production. The ruling ideology is produced away from the production places. Althusser treats ideology in terms of reproduction of labour power and production and the practice of ruling ideology. Althusser accepts the reproduction of the conditions of existence of ideology by the ruling class ideology. Ideology as a superstructure holds its relative autonomy in interacting with the economic base, which controls or determines the superstructure. In the base-superstructure relationship Althusser introduces the reality of ideology. Althusser treats base as infrastructure and accepts integration and unity between various levels and instances. Accordingly,

i. infrastructural unity = forces of production + relations of production;

ii. superstructural unity = (politico-legal instances + ideological instances).

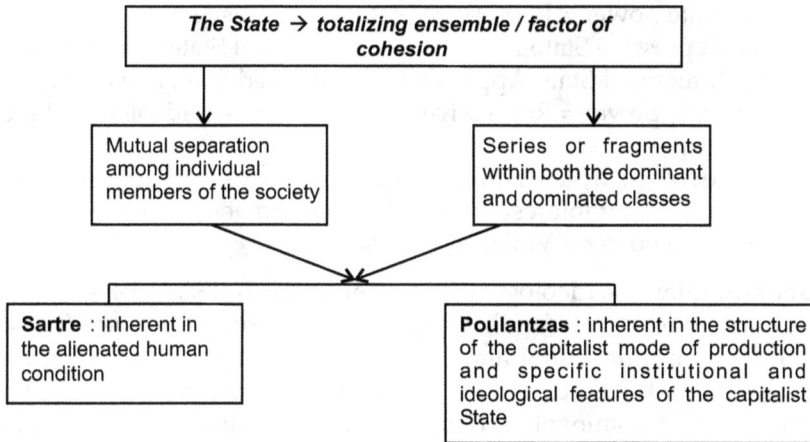

```
┌─────────────────────────────────────────────┐
│   The State → totalizing ensemble / factor of │
│                 cohesion                       │
└─────────────────────────────────────────────┘
```

┌──────────────────────┐   ┌──────────────────────────┐
│ Mutual separation   │   │ Series or fragments   │
│ among individual   │   │ within both the dominant │
│ members of the society│   │ and dominated classes   │
└──────────────────────┘   └──────────────────────────┘

┌──────────────────────┐   ┌───────────────────────────────────────┐
│ **Sartre** : inherent in │ │ **Poulantzas** : inherent in the structure │
│ the alienated human   │   │ of the capitalist mode of production   │
│ condition   │   │ and specific institutional and   │
│   │   │ ideological features of the capitalist │
│   │   │ State   │
└──────────────────────┘   └───────────────────────────────────────┘

Figure 46

However, Althusser distinguishes between ideological apparatuses and repressive apparatus, while the former is plural and diversified, private and non-violent, and the latter denotes or is characterized by singular and unified, public and violent. Following Marxist classics, Althusser says that the State apparatus characterizes or represents the State, as the repressive machinery for the execution and interference in the affairs of class contradiction, and class struggle between the bourgeoisie and the proletariat in the interests of the ruling class. This repression is tangible and this may occur in duality—visible and invisible, violent and non-violent, repressive and persuasive, physical and psychological. In ideological State apparatuses there is a dosage of repression, which may appear as concealed and symbolic. Althusser believes that the State power and the State apparatus must be differentiated, as the objective of the class struggle is State power and for this, classes use the State apparatus for holding State power. Thus the proletariat must seize State power for holding down the bourgeois State apparatus filling up the gap with proletarian one. Therefore,

i. the end of the State power 'X' = the end of the State apparatus 'Y'
ii. the establishment of the State power 'X' = the establishment of the State apparatus 'Y'

This does not means that the State power and the State apparatus are the same. They are different. To Althusser,

a. State power ≠ State apparatus, State apparatus = Repressive State Apparatus,

b. State power ≠ Repressive State Apparatus,
c. Repressive State Apparatus ≠ Ideological State Apparatuses,
d. Integrated State Apparatus ≠ Diversified State Apparatuses,
e. State power = Repressive State Apparatus + Ideological State Apparatuses,
f. Ideological State Apparatuses = Site of class struggle on which conflicting interests contend for supremacy,
g. State power = Violence + Ideology.

Out of multifarious Ideological State Apparatuses (ISAs), for example, religious, educational, familial, legal, political, organizational (trade-union), communicational and cultural, according to Althusser, the bourgeoisie upholds education as the dominant ISA in replacement of the previously dominant ideological State apparatus, *i.e.* the Church. However, I think that no ISA is unimportant, but the most powerful ISAs are education, culture, communication at present day times. Althusser believes that—

1. all State apparatuses do their functions both by repression and ideology predominantly and massively;
2. the repressive State apparatus, which does function by ideology is an integrated whole under the centralized commanding unity of the State power, where the politics of class struggle is applied by political representatives of the ruling classes in possession of the State power;
3. the ideological State apparatuses are diverse, distinct and relatively autonomous;
4. the unity of apparatuses: in case of repressive apparatus unity is so sought by execution of the politics of class struggle of the classes in power under the leadership of the representatives of the classes in power and in case of diversified ideological State apparatuses unity is sought by the ruling class ideology;
5. not only that. The role of the ruling ideology is heavily concentrated and it mediates between repressive State apparatus and ideological State apparatuses, harmonizes both the apparatuses and different ideological State apparatuses;
6. the ideological State apparatuses contribute to the reproduction of the relations of production or the capitalist relations of exploitation (Althusser, 2002).

According to Althusser ideology has no history. This means that 'ideology is nothing insofar as it is a pure dream .... ideology....., emphatically does not mean that there is no history in it, but that it has no history of its own .... Ideology represents the imaginary relationship of individuals to their real conditions of existence.... Ideology has a material existence.... And ... (1) there is no practice except by and in an ideology; (2) there is no ideology except by the subject and for subjects.... there is no ideology except for concrete subjects, and this destination for ideology is only made possible by the subjects: meaning by the category of the subject and its functioning .... the category of the subject is only constitutive of all ideology in so far as all ideology has the function (which defines it) of "constituting" concrete individuals as subjects .... individuals are always already subjects.... the mirror-structure of ideology ensures simultaneously: (1) the interpellation of "individuals" as subjects; (2) their subjection to the subject; (3) the mutual recognition of subjects and subject, the subjects' recognition of each other, and finally subject's recognition of himself; (4) ... the subjects recognize what they are and behave accordingly, ...' (Althusser, 2002: 186, 203).

The role of subjects in history has further been formulated by Gramsci in his role of intellectuals, who are dominant group's deputies serving for holding, creating and increasing the hegemonic area. See Figure 47.

According to Gramsci, the role of intellectuals in the production process is mediated and indirect one by the whole social fabric and complexes of superstructures in varying degrees, but not direct as they have their relationships with fundamental social groups. The intellectuals have two types of role in the whole fabric of the society and in the complexes of the superstructures—direct relationship with social groups and classes, where the members of the society largely agree with the norms and principles, and the members also accept the rules and laws formed by the dominant classes, indirect and mediated role in the productive process through creative-analytical-exploratory-persuasive and justified activities, and indirect and mediatory role in creating and expanding the hegemony at superstructural level of the dominant classes through common consent and classes. The intellectuals are organically connected with social groups, however, they are organically stratified—all intellectuals do not have the same organic quality; there are different strata among intellectuals; there is gradation among intellectuals in terms of their organic quality in the civil society, in terms of their functions, and in terms of their relations with the social classes in the civil society. There are two superstructural levels,—civil society or private level and political society or public level, which correspond to the function of hegemony exercised through civil society by the dominant classes and to the function of direct domination exercised through political society via State organs, respectively.

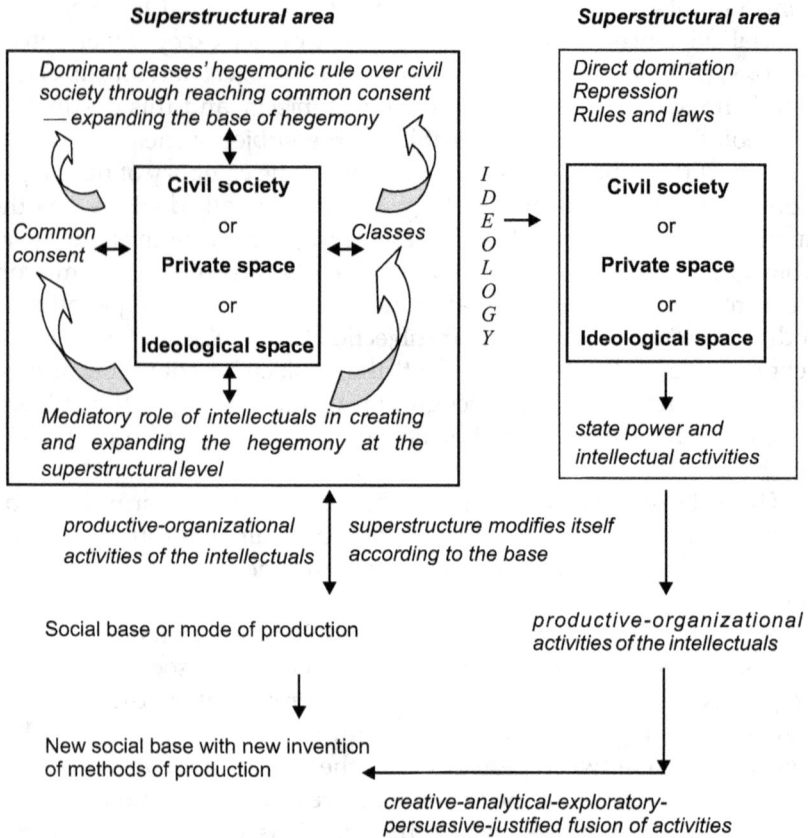

Superstructural area   **Superstructural area**

Dominant classes' hegemonic rule over civil society through reaching common consent — expanding the base of hegemony

Direct domination
Repression
Rules and laws

Civil society
or
Private space
or
Ideological space

Common consent ↔   Classes ↔

I D E O L O G Y →

Civil society
or
Private space
or
Ideological space

Mediatory role of intellectuals in creating and expanding the hegemony at the superstructural level

state power and intellectual activities

productive-organizational activities of the intellectuals | superstructure modifies itself according to the base

Social base or mode of production

productive-organizational activities of the intellectuals

New social base with new invention of methods of production

creative-analytical-exploratory-persuasive-justified fusion of activities

Figure 47

To Gramsci, (1) the intellectuals are dominant groups' deputies, (2) they perform two subaltern functions—social hegemony and political government—spontaneous consent by the great masses of the society is historically conditioned by the prestige the dominant classes enjoy due to their position in the world of production and the State legally enforces discipline on the non-consenting groups either actively or passively. 'Unity of the State in the differentiation of powers: Parliament more closely linked to civil society; the judiciary power, between government and Parliament, represents the continuity of the written law (even against the government). Naturally all three powers are also organs of political hegemony, but in different degrees: (1) Legislature; (2) Judiciary; (3) Executive. It is to be noted how lapses in the administration of justice make an especially disastrous impression on the public: the hegemonic apparatus is more sensitive in this sector, to which arbitrary actions on the part of the police and political administration may also be referred.' (Gramsci, 2002: 63-64).

In *Prison Notebooks*, Gramsci goes from the expansion of the concept of intellectuals to the expansion of the concept of the State, which to him means dictatorship plus hegemony or repression plus hegemony or repressive State apparatuses plus ideological State apparatuses. The State is a political society, which represents dictatorship or repressive State apparatus, is used to control the masses in conformity with the given structure of economy and production, but not to make a balance between civil society and political society, but a combination of both, where the civil society is represented by hegemony of the one social group over the entire nation through so-called private organizations, like church, school, trade-union, press etc. Gramsci in his *Political Writings* says that the old type of intellectual is the organizing element in a society with a mainly peasant and artisanal basis. The dominant class to organize State and commerce breeds a particular type of intellectual—the technical organizers, the specialists etc. In capitalist societies, the economic forces have developed in a capitalist direction and here have absorbed the greater part of national activity with all the characteristics of order and intellectual discipline. In the capitalist State, the proletariat needs intellectuals or leaders in order to enable the peasant masses to organize with an autonomous political leadership. It is certainly important and useful for the proletariat that one or more intellectuals individually should adopt its programme and ideas, and should merge into the proletariat. The intellectuals must not be taken to mean traditional intellectuals, but the whole social mass that performs the functions of organization in the realm of production, culture and administration. With the bourgeoisie, the intellectuals play a direct role in the constitution of the class and with the proletariat the intellectuals play an active role in organizing class consciousness of the proletariat, in uniting conscious leadership and spontaneity, where the party acts as collective intellectual. The formation of unitary collective consciousness requires various initiatives and conditions, which the party as collective intellectual organizes. In *Prison Notebooks* Gramsci notes that intellectuals do not form an independent class, but each class have its intellectuals.

Gramscian concept of hegemony operates through mechanisms that ensure the masses' consent to a class policy cannot be reduced to the Marxist notion of dominant ideology or to Weberian mechanisms of legitimacy which combine violence with the ends of social integration. In his analysis of hegemony Gramsci considers the function of ideology as agents of social unification, as a conception of world that is implicitly manifest in art, in law, in economic activity and in all manifestations of individual and collective life (Gramsci, *Prison Notebooks*). Ideologies are historically necessary. They have a validity which is psychological. They organize human masses. They create the terrain on which men move. They acquire consciousness of their position and struggle. Gramsci anticipates Althusser's conception that ideologies are not pure illusion, but bodies of representations existing in institutions and practices— they figure in the superstructure and are rooted in class struggle. From *Prison Notebooks* a mention here may be made about Gramsci's notion of the dominant class and concept of hegemony that a class is dominant in two ways, *i.e.* leading and dominant. It leads the classes which are its allies, and dominates those which are its enemies. Even before attaining power or class can and must lead, when it is in power it becomes dominant, but continues to lead as well. There can and must be a political hegemony even before the attainment of governmental power, and one should not count solely on the power and material force which such a position gives in order to exercise political leadership or hegemony.

However, Poulantzas in his work *Political Power and Social Classes* says that Gramsci introduces a theoretical break, a buffer between hegemony and domination. To him, a class can and must become the leading class before it becomes a politically dominant class and it can win hegemony before the conquest of political power. The notions— domination and hegemony are distinct phenomena according to Gramsci, but critics find these two are organically combined and inseparable and non-identical. Furthermore, according to Poulantzas, Gramsci has included the State structure in his concept of hegemony. Again, few negative effects in Gramsci's thought may be produced here —the primacy of ideological over the analysis of superstructures, the primacy of historical bloc over the relations of force and the State, and deviation of cultural idealist character in Gramscian analysis.

However, like Althusser, Gramsci discusses both hegemonic apparatuses and ideological State apparatuses. Gramsci, the theoretician, does not reduce State only to repressive State apparatuses, but also includes certain number of institutions from civil society, such a church, schools etc. Althusser proposes to add repressive apparatus. In Gramscian dimension Althusser considers the concept of hegemony— hegemony of the State power over and in State ideological apparatuses, are multiple, distinct, relatively autonomous and capable of providing an objective field of contradictions which express the effects of the clashes between the capitalist class struggle and the proletarian class struggle, as well as their subordinate forms. According to Gramsci, which in *Prison Notebooks* we find that State = Political Society + Civil Society; *i.e.* hegemony projected by the armour of coercion.

Hegemony undoubtedly presupposes that account, is taken of the interests and groups over which hegemony is exercised, a certain balance or compromise is formed, leading group makes sacrifices of a corporative economic nature. If hegemony is ethico-political, then it cannot but be economic, it cannot but have its basis in the decisive function that the leading group exercises in the key sectors of production. Gramsci establishes a close relationship between a non-economist interpretation of Marx and Leninist interpretation of the relations of force. The expansion of State concept is grasped in terms of relations of force and civil society is rived by class struggle from economic to the ideological level. A class is formed on the basis of its function in the mode of production, and the development and the struggle for power and conservation of power create superstructures, which determine the formation of the material structure of the superstructure. Ideology as the superstructure does not create social reality, but productive base as social reality creates ideology. Base and superstructures form a historic bloc, that is complex and conflicting set of superstructures is the reflection of the set of social relations of production. Every social group coming into existence on the original terrain of an essential function in the world of economic production creates with itself organically one or more strata of intellectuals.

Gramsci makes the point to the transition from the economic to the political by relating the economic to the degree of homogeneity, self-consciousness and organization that classes possess in relation to the State. Within the concept of relations of force, Gramsci makes a close relation between the economic moment and political moment. The political moment is divided into three steps—the economic and corporative, where the group unity is affected on the professional basis, where class consciousness proper does exist, but not political consciousness. This level is concerned with the economic-corporate level of the community concerned. The second step is concerned with unity of classes in the class struggle developing within the structure of the existing State system for winning the politico-juridical equality with the ruling groups and for claiming to participate in and to reform legislation and administration within the existing fundamental structures. This second step of class struggle and class unity is equivalent to or corresponding with the Leninist concept of trade-union struggle and reformist politics. The third step is a step of superseding the second level and reaching towards the goal of making a political level, establishing an integral relationship between class, State and society, and gaining hegemony. The third level is the level of class hegemony. In this way Gramsci moves from economic moment to political moment, from class consciousness to class unity and from class struggle to class hegemony. At this third phase or level of class hegemony, is purely political, where—

1. corporate interests of one's own become the interests of other subordinate groups;
2. the corporate limits of the purely economic class is transcended;
3. from economic structure to the complex of superstructures— a passage is made;
4. various ideologies come into conflict and confrontation with each other until a single ideology or a single combination of them tends to prevail and propagate itself throughout society. Class hegemony is the sum total of economic and political aims, expansion of class in the sphere of the State, which is taken as the organ of one particular group, designed to create favourable conditions for that particular groups' maximum expansion. The interest of general in character of the subordinated groups is co-ordinated with the interest of the dominant group. The process of the State is not static, but is a continuous process of formation and a process of superseding unstable equilibria. Gramsci identifies the State concept in two senses—the State in the strict sense, where the State is identified with government, class dictatorship, coercive and economic functions minus hegemony and the State in the integral sense, where the State means dictatorship plus hegemony even at the price of 'compromise equilibria' so as to safeguard its own political power or to safeguard the political power of the ruling class and to maintain and justify its dominance. To Gramsci, this 'compromise equilibria' is the historic basis of the State, the relation of contradictory forces. Therefore, according to Gramsci, State is the factor of social cohesion, integrating the other classes more or less successfully with compromises. Further, Gramsci points at the shift in the basis of the State, and it occurs when crisis at superstructures coincides with far reaching changes or movement at the base, the intervention of masses who are weakly organized and abandoned by their own political leadership takes place in the chaotic and disordered movement without leadership and without a precise and collective political will, certain social strata have an objective interest in social transformation take up an oscillating class position and they provide the mass basis for a new policy on the part of the leading classes, the middle classes

enjoy a function of command and responsibility during the war, the interests of dominant classes coincide with the interests of the middle bourgeoisie, and when the workers' movement is organizationally too weak to oppose this. Gramsci here puts forward the complex role of the superstructures in the period of crisis of hegemony. From *Prison Notebooks* it can be pointed out here that the State apparatus is far more resistant than is often possible to believe and it succeeds at the moments of crisis in organizing greater forces that remain loyal to the regime.

Gramsci outlines the concept of the State in articulating State, class and society. According to Gramsci, State-class articulation = war of movement and State-society articulation = war of position, and the State = balance between political society and civil society and the dialectic between base and superstructure. Further, in *Prison Notebooks* Gramsci establishes the base-superstructure relationship in analyzing the theories of State, historic bloc and hegemony. According to Gramsci, the State is the concrete form of a determinate system of production, where the struggle for power and struggle for new mode of production coincides with each other and dominant class becomes politically and economically dominant. Graphically (Figure 48),

The leading and dominant class is the historic bloc in power relations, who find their historic unification in the State. This State-class articulation is the result of State-society articulation, an articulation between political society and civil society. This articulation the bourgeoisie as a class makes in order to attain unity in the State, to eliminate opposing and antagonistic forces and obtain the active or passive consent of the others. In *Prison Notebooks* Gramsci also notes that structure and superstructure form the historic bloc, where the dominant class establishes their hegemony in and over the society in alliance with other classes and where the State is in complex and integral relationship with the masses and is based on relationship between the leaders and the masses. In terms of 'historic bloc' or 'historical bloc' Gramsci puts forward the concept of 'ensemble' and says that the complex and contradictory ensemble of the superstructures is the reflection of the ensemble of the social relations of production. The historic bloc is the dialectical and organic unity of base and superstructures, where economics becomes the determinant in the last instance, and politics has primacy over economics and it is in command over politics. The existence of a socialist historic bloc implies an organic alliance and solidarity between intellectuals and people, leaders and led, governors and governed. The alliance between the working class and the peasant masses and other social strata forms the conditions of the new historic bloc. The struggle of the working class and their allies against the capitalist-bourgeois system means the consolidation and expansion of working class hegemony, the revolutionary transformation of the base and superstructure, and construction of a new relationship between base and superstructure.

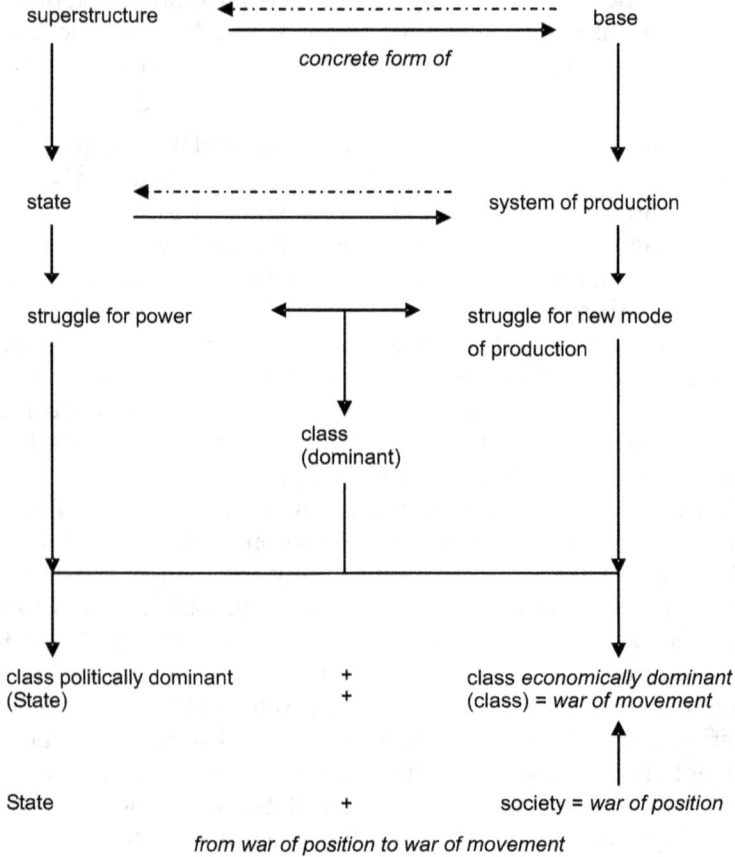

from war of position to war of movement

Figure 48

Following this argument, the hegemony protected by the armour coercion, Gramsci further says that the coercive element of the State withering away by degrees is the more conspicuous elements of the regulated society, *i.e.* ethical State or civil society. The historic basis of the State and the hegemonic apparatuses pare the way to the understanding of the State under socialism. The essence of proletarian dictatorship is not force alone, but the organization and discipline of the working masses with an objective to build socialism, which cannot be achieved by a single stroke, but through prolonged transition from capitalism to socialism. Gramsci finds the historical periodization of the State: first, the State synonymous with the government, second, the identification of State with civil society, third, the gradual withering away of the State as authoritarian and coercive, and fourth, the establishment of an ethical State. The socialist State is the organizer of mass consent. The establishment of socialism is the transitory State. Lenin likewise formulates the historic-organic process—organizational and hegemonic aspects of the dictatorship of the proletariat, the establishment of socialism at the transitory stage and the communist goal of establishing communism. This historic organic process of Lenin bears a corollary with Gramscian historic-organic-four stage process. Gramsci states the transition from the economic-corporate stage to class struggle stage and then to the political stage of the integral State. No State can avoid the passing through the phase of economic-corporatism. Hence, it can be said that the content of the State based on the political hegemony of the new social group must be of an economic order, *i.e.* the reorganization of the structure and the relation between men on the one hand and the system of production on the other. The superstructural elements of foresight and struggle will inevitably be a few planned elements, in number. The cultural policy will be critical, negating and criticizing the policies of the past.

Gramsci in his article of March, 1924, which appeared in *Ordine Nuovo*, says that the hegemony and the dictatorship of the proletariat both are closely related and this type of relationship is essential in the practice of class struggle—hegemony of the proletariat in the struggle for State power, and hegemony in the exercise of power, after the establishment of the State power. Revolution presents itself as the hegemony of the proletariat with its ally, the peasantry. Following the Leninist line, Gramsci says that hegemony is class domination and class leadership, where the working class, an independent and political force needs a vanguard party, an alliance with the peasantry based on long-term common interests. This class leadership will be won in the course of a struggle. Lenin in his *The Trade Unions, the Present Situation and Trotsky's Mistakes* distinguishes between hegemony of the proletariat and State form of the dictatorship of the proletariat. Hegemony is the function of the working class in power, the ideological and political leadership of the proletariat over society. The leadership of that class is essential for the transition from capitalism to socialism and finally to communism. Here lies the importance of proletarian hegemony. The working classes set up trade unions through which they exercise their hegemony—these people set up dictatorships and exercise coercion through the State. Through trade unions the proletariat cannot directly exercise proletarian dictatorship—it can be exercised by the vanguard party that has absorbed the revolutionary élan of the proletariat through State organization. However, the above relationships established are dialectical, concrete and organic. Graphically (Figure 49),

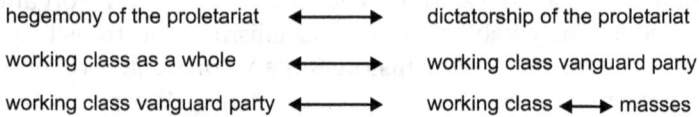

hegemony of the proletariat	←——→	dictatorship of the proletariat
working class as a whole	←——→	working class vanguard party
working class vanguard party	←——→	working class ←—→ masses

Figure 49

The party has decisive influence on and leadership over workers' organizations, trade unions, agricultural organizations and co-operatives and which seeks to realize hegemony through State organizations like the Soviets in Stalinist era. Gramsci uses the dictatorship of the proletariat as expansive, where the key problem is not the physical personification of the function of command, but the relations between the leaders and the party of the working class and the relations between the party and working class. The dictatorship of the proletariat is not repressive, but expansive—a continuous movement takes place from the base upwards, continuous replacement through all the capillaries of society, a continuous circulation of men, organic relationship between party and working class, not mere physical repression but spiritual repression by the proletariat, mass base of the proletarian dictatorship and dictatorship's ability to lead the alliance and dictatorship's implantation in the masses. Furthermore, the expansive character of the dictatorship of the proletariat may be visualized through graphic representation, where hegemony becomes the central point of attention (Figure 50)—

Here, 'a' = mass base of the proletarian State by and through the alliance formation with the workers, peasants and other social strata in an expansive mode, 'b' = resolving of contradictions between multiple allies by the proletarian State in order to preserve, 'c' = the long-term interests of the allies supporting the proletarian cause through the function of hegemony, 'd' = subjugation of the interests of the allies of non-proletarian in nature through the function of hegemony, 'e' = domination of the interests of dominant and leading class, 'f' = the leadership capacity of the proletarian party, 'g' = party's organic and concrete relationship with class and the masses, 'h' = democratic centralism and 'i' = bureaucratic centralism. The central question is hegemony, which does not mean only the relationship of domination of the proletariat over the bourgeoisie, but also the political relations between the proletariat and other non-capitalist classes, relationship of alliance, but not of political oppression. According to Gramsci,

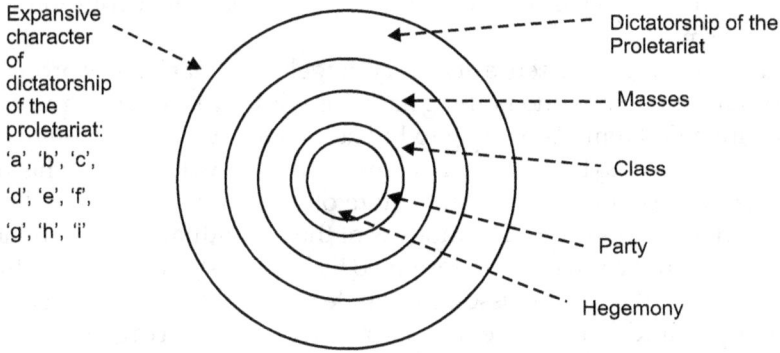

Expansive character of dictatorship of the proletariat: 'a', 'b', 'c', 'd', 'e', 'f', 'g', 'h', 'i'

Dictatorship of the Proletariat

Masses

Class

Party

Hegemony

Figure 50

i. hegemony ≠ practices of the dominant class;
ii. hegemony ≠ State power + governmental practices;
iii. hegemony ≠ political hegemony + exercise of leadership;
iv. hegemony ≠ alternative strategy of the proletariat in alliance formation, preservation of the long-term interests of the proletariat, and resolving the contradiction between dominant class interests and subordinate class interests;
v. hegemony = leading role of the working class in proletarian dictatorship;
vi. therefore, it is possible and necessary to launch political hegemony even before coming to government and governmental power.

In the name of the Leninist concept of hegemony, of the dialectic between the objective conditions of the balance of forces and the subjective conditions of political maturation Gramsci rejects the determinist conception of history. Lukacs's historicism differs less from Gramsci or bears a corollary with the Gramscian outlook, when Lukacs criticizes the Leninist conception of history as a field of struggle governed by law of tendency or tendencies. Lukacs in his understanding of Lenin says that Lenin's concept of organization, therefore, means a double break with mechanical fatalism; both with the concept of proletarian class consciousness as a mechanical product of its class situation, and with the idea that the revolution itself is the only mechanical working out of fatalistically explosive economic forces. Lukacs's Leninism is concerned with a break with economism and a break with Marxist positivism, evaluation of political initiative of the proletariat besides the treatment of the proletariat as an autonomous and organized political force and dialectic between class situation and class consciousness. Both Gramsci and Lukacs can be treated in terms of the Hegelian tradition, critique of positivism in the name of philosophy of revolution and historicism.

In analyzing the essence of history, Engels says that history proceeds through happenings and nothing happens without a conscious purpose or an intended aim. According to Lukacs, which he says in *History and Class Consciousness* that to Engels, many individual wills active in history for the most part produce results quite other than those intended and quite often the opposite. The motives of the individuals are secondary, and these motive forces are determined by some historical forces, which set in motion the great masses, the whole people and the whole classes of people and which create lasting action resulting in a great transformation. The historical forces are independent of man's consciousness. Lukacs finds that for a class to become ripe for hegemony means that its interests and consciousness enable the class to organize the whole society according to their interests. However, it must not be thought that all classes ripe for hegemony have a class consciousness with the same inner structure. Everything hinges on the extent to which they can become conscious of the actions they need to perform in order to obtain and organize power (Lukacs, 1971). The class consciousness of the bourgeosie may well be able to reflect all the problems entailed by bourgeois hegemony, capitalist transformation and penetration of total production. Bourgeois class consciousness is conditioned by critical realism, which is distinct from socialist class consciousness, conditioned by socialist realism. Lukacs makes a few points with regard to socialist realism side by side with critical realism—

1. '...that 'true consciousness', which socialist realism by definition possesses.'
2. 'Socialist realism differs from critical realism, not only in being based on a concrete socialist perspective, but also in using this perspective to describe the forces working towards socialism from the inside. Socialist society is seen as an independent entity ....'
3. In the seizure of power by the proletariat 'people will not be automatically transformed. Lenin once remarked that socialism had to be built by people who were moulded by capitalism. The truth is, people are only transformed when they participate in the transformation of reality. The progressive bourgeois realist must not be expected to embrace socialism the moment the proletariat seizes power. Some progressive intellectuals—even those who later on become socialists—may be driven into

the opposite camp by the experience of class struggle in its acutest form. And the upheavals to which a revolution gives rise may serious doubts even among long-standing supporters of socialism.'

4. 'As socialism develops, critical realism, as a distinct literary style, will wither away ...The critical realist will increasingly apply perspectives approximating the socialist realism. This will gradually lead to a withering-away of critical realism... Society will eventually achieve a condition which only socialist realism can adequately describe.' (Lukacs, 2002: 111, 117, 121, 131).

According to Lukacs the roots of naturalism lie in economic subjectivism, which contradicts with economic objectivism. Leadership generally imposes subjective requirements on production without actually realizing the laws of economic reality, for example Stalinism in Russia. This subjective consideration or leadership tendency is also manifested in the arena of politics. Lukacs finds dialectical relation between naturalism and revolutionary romanticism, when both are carried out at the core of economic subjectivism pursued and practiced in Soviet Russia in Stalinist era. In opposition to Bukharin's *Historical Materialism*, which discusses the problems of causation and teleology in a less profound way, both Lukacs and Gramsci treat Marxism as a philosophy of historical materialism characterized by a dialectical method employing a natural science method in contrast with sociology as a positive science. Lukacs speaks of in his article, 'Technology and Social Relations' that as a necessary consequence of Bukharin's natural-scientific approach sociology develops into an independent science with its own substantive goals or teleology. Natural scientific approach here means the theory of causation. The method of dialectic can do without such an independent substantive achievements. Dialectics' realm is that of the historical process as a whole, whose individual and concrete moments reveal its dialectical essence precisely in the qualitative differences between them and also in the continuous transformation of their objective structure. Totality is the territory of dialectic. In the opposite direction, scientific general sociology must have its own independent substantive achievements allowing only one kind of law —law of causality—regularities of social behaviour in causal laws.

In response to the classical Marxist theory of the autonomy of the State, Adam Przeworski (1990) develops the strategic concept of the State, through which he interprets the State as an institution within which strategic interactions concerning political affairs take place. Przeworski does not regard the functionalist interpretation of Nicos

Poulantzas and instrumentalist interpretation of Ralph Miliband. Przeworski points out the distinctive claims of Marxist political theory and does accept the view otherwise. Following Przeworski (1990) the claims of Marxist theory of the State are—

1. all governments must respect and protect the essential claims of the owners of productive wealth of the society under capitalism;
2. the capitalists in capitalist society are endowed with public power;
3. this public power, no formal institution, for example, the State can overcome;
4. in capitalist society the people have political rights, they vote or provide popular mandates, governments pursue popular mandates, State managers have interests and conceptions of their own, but the effective capacity of all governments to attain whatever goals is circumscribed by the public power;
5. public power is the power of capital; and
6. the nature of political forces that control the State institutions does not alter this situation, for it is structural—a characteristic feature of the system, not of occupants of governmental positions.

According to Przeworski, the State as an institution consists of structures, which conduct strategic political interactions, where the parties, pressure groups, bureaucracies and classes etc. act as rational actors. The political outcomes are public policy formulation, occupancy of public positions, transformation of the State or the institutional terrain and participation in politics. The strategic interactions organized by the State are guided in favour of some classes or against some classes. The interplay of political strategies provides special advantage to the capitalist class. Przeworski's conception of the State is like Elster's Prisoner's Dilemma model—common class interest developed by co-operative class strategy exists *vis-à-vis* individual interest developed by conflicting class strategy, where the 'task of the State is to provide a cooperative solution for the Prisoner's Dilemma faced by members of the economically dominant class, and, as part of this task, to prevent the members of the dominated class from solving their dilemma.' (Elster, 1985: 400). Three important theories—capitalist class abdication theory, capitalist class weakness theory and class balance theory with regard to State autonomy, have been developed by Przeworski and Elster. The capitalist class abdication theory makes it clear that the capitalists only want profit-making and control of the State by the capitalists would not make profitous to them.

Here, the pursuit of profit and abandonment of politics are correlated. They do not want to constrain them as it would make their profit-making unattainable. They want to see the State as autonomous neutral party for resolving conflicts between them and between the capitalists and workers. The neutral State would uphold the legitimacy of the State policy, which would make profit incentive for the capitalists' sounder. According to class weakness theory, the State becomes autonomous if the capitalist class is weak to govern. However, there is no essential correlation between the strong capitalist class and dependent State, and weak capitalist class and autonomous State. In fact, the State becomes customarily autonomous in capitalist society. As per class balance theory, State autonomy maintains class equilibrium in civil society, where neither the capitalists nor the workers can dominate over one another. Przeworski says that

> actual democratic conditions do not require State autonomy . . . (1)
> democratic State requires State autonomy . . . (2)
> State autonomy is required for best performance of State officials . . . (3)
> State autonomy is required for close monitoring of State officials . . . (4)
> State autonomy is required for making a balance between State officials' satisfaction from over-stated State activity and choices and demands of the public . . . (5).

According to Przeworski, political parties are the essential components of the democratic State, which may not be treated either as State or class. The parties are relatively autonomous from State or class, but they actually take part in State and class activities. See Figure 51. The leftist and socialist parties with the support of manual wage workers, who are the minority in terms of class composition in democratic capitalist societies, participate in elections with a little hope of winning the elections, and governing. Therefore, the leaders of the leftist and socialist parties make rational choices between the two,—homogeneity in class composition with a distinct and straight-forward class ideology with the little hope of winning elections and broad-based class orientation with a greater chance of winning elections. If the socialist and left parties opt for the second, become mass parties, they would reduce the importance of class politics and weaken the organizational appeal to workers, and also weaken the working class solidarity. However, the left and socialist parties remain the minority parties, even after becoming mass parties, and radical transformation of the society, through elections, becomes impossible. The formulation of Przeworski and Sprague (1986)'s formulation is relevant in this respect. The left and socialist parties are unlikely to win an overwhelming majority of votes. No political party can win elections overwhelmingly. The democratic capitalist society is heterogeneous. As the society is heterogeneous, no political party can win the support of all groups and sections. No party can win the support of everyone without losing the support of someone. The prospects of winning elections for the political parties are limited by the fact of the democratic capitalist society. The facts are existence of multiple groups and interests, conflicts of interests and values, and heterogeneous co-existence of social elements. Thus, no political party can win a clear mandate. Whether the left and socialist parties deliberately restrict their appeal to specific groups or attempt to win the support of the entire electorate, however, their opportunities are limited by the heterogeneous elements of the society. In fact, election cannot bring about radical transformation of society. Elected representatives are conservative as they merely represent the values and interests of heterogeneous in character. According to Przeworski, the State makes a compromise with the interests of the capitalists and workers. The working class's preference for socialism than that of capitalism would not improve their material well-being. The radical transformation of the capitalistic society would create serious socio-economic dislocations and make serious negative consequences for the worker's well-being. Under democratic conditions, workers' socialism is difficult to attain, and the 'valley' between capitalism and socialism must be traversed by the workers themselves, according to Przeworski. Both the workers and the capitalists in capital economy need investment —the workers do not want to seize all profits—the share of profits in capitalist market are decided by the strategic interactions between workers and capitalists. The share of profits depends on a few possibilities:

1. If the workers bag too large share of benefits, then the capitalists get less share of benefits from the profits—the capitalists take less interest in investment and entrepreneurial activities—the capitalists consume more from their income than investment—investment decreases.
2. If the workers take too small share of profit, then they are weakened in terms of income and capitalists bag more share of benefits from the profits—the capitalists take more interest in investment and entrepreneurial activities—the capitalists consume less from their income than investment—investment increases.
3. If the capitalists invest too high from their income, the production will grow more rapidly—this becomes the ultimate goal for both the capitalists and workers.
4. If the capitalists invest less from their income, the production will be extremely slow, economic progress will be at the low

ebb—workers will suffer from the disinvestment or low level of investment process—workers will be deprived of material gains from the less investment process and they will fight for larger share of profits. The decision of the working class with regard to the higher rate of wages depends upon two counts: the rate of capitalists' investment and the rate of workers' uncertainty about the future. The rate of uncertainty depends upon two counts: capacity of the social institutions, for example the State to defend class interests and capacity of the social institutions to protect class compromises between the capitalists and workers.

5. The strategic interactions between workers and peasants depend upon the conditions of uncertainty rate and cost-benefit analysis—if the rate of uncertainty of any class becomes high, then that class prefers to calculate short-term costs and benefits and if the rate of uncertainty of any class becomes low, then that class prefers to calculate costs and benefits on a long-term basis. Further, decision-making of both workers and capitalists depends on the following conditional possibilities—

   a. output growth from investment > rate of uncertainty of future of the working class → compromise policy of the working class allowing the capitalists for higher rate of profit;

   b. output growth from investment < rate of uncertainty of future of the working class → militant struggle by the working class for higher rate of profit;

   c. maximum output of profit form investment > rate of uncertainty of the future of the capitalists' → capitalists' incentive for more investment;

   d. minimum output of profit from investment < rate of uncertainty of the future of the capitalists → capitalists' incentive for disinvestment.

Przeworski's State is a class compromise State. Here lies the importance of State autonomy. It may be mentioned in this respect, the theory of structural dependence of the State. Under this theory, the State in capitalist society must protect the interests of the capitalists, *i.e.* making of more profits from investment. If the government restricts capitalists' profit incentives, then the capitalists will automatically reduce investment, economic growth will fall, and both the capitalists and workers will surely suffer. Conversely, if the government promotes capitalists' profit incentives, then the capitalists will increase their rate of investment, economic growth will go on increasing, and both the capitalists and workers will not suffer from lower incomes. The workers and capitalists make possible compromises without government intervention—it is a compromise between profit making from investment and wage rate from investment, compromise between wage share of national income and the rate of profit, and also a compromise between share of wages from national income and the rate of investment: the share of wages for the workers and the rate of investment on the part of the capitalists are inversely related. In the absence of State interference, the workers respect the capitalists' interests. Through its taxation policy, the State respects the capitalists' interests. But these aspects of structural dependence theory have not been accepted by Przeworski and Wallerstein. To them, taxes are imposed by the State not on the part of profit used by the capitalists for consumption purposes, but on the part of the investment. Therefore, the State keeps itself free from structural dependence on capital. Through taxation, the government collects revenue and may transfer this income to the wage share of the workers. Therefore, the State makes itself free from the influence of the capitalist, capitalist political organization and capitalist class consciousness. The State makes a positive response to desired income distribution, however, without damaging the interests of the capitalists and the mechanism of capital in the capitalist economy through various State welfare policies. Przeworski (1991) finds that all governments are to some extent dependent on capital but this dependence is not so binding as to make democracy as sham. A stable democracy does require that governments must be strong enough to govern effectively but weak enough not to be able to govern against important interests. Capitalist democracy, according to Bowles and Gintis (1986) involves a dynamic equilibrium between democracy and authoritarianism, between individual rights and capital expansion and between civil rights and property rights. This dynamic equilibrium establishes workplace democracy and community empowerment through democratic institutions as a counter balance between individual rights and State intervention, development of a democratic and participatory culture, democratic accountability of major rational economic actors, capitalists and workers and economic well-being of the society. This capitalist democracy may be called post-liberal democracy. Loyalty becomes important in a stable democracy, according to Przeworski.

Organization of class ⟶ Classes-in-struggle ⟶ Class struggle

⬆

Political parties ⟶ Participation ⟶ Participation in ⟶ State structure
in election constitution and
governing

⬆

Political
structure

Political parties
with leftist class
orientation and
parties with
broad-based
class
orientation

Political parties
with broad-
based class
orientation

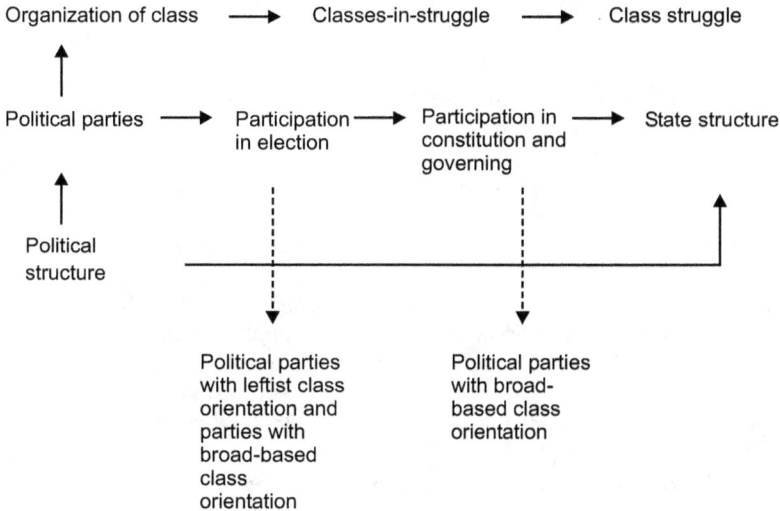

Democratic Capitalist Social Base

Figure 51

REFERENCES

Althusser, L. 2002. 'Ideology and Ideological State Apparatuses' in Anand Prakash (ed.) *Marxism* (New Delhi: Worldview Publications).

Althusser, L. *For Marx.*

Althusser, L. *Lenin and Philosophy and Other Essays.*

Althusser, L. and E. Balibar. *Reading Capital.*

Avineri, S. 1972. *The Social and Political Thought of Karl Marx* (Cambridge: Cambridge University Press).

Elster, John. 1985. *Making Sense of Marx* (Cambridge: Cambridge University Press).

Gramsci, A. 2002. 'The Formation of the Intellectuals' in Anand Prakash (ed.), *Marxism* (New Delhi: Worldview Publications).

Gramsci, A. *Political Writings.*

Gramsci, A. *Prison Notebooks.*

Lenin, *Collected Works.*

Lenin, V.I. 1977. *State and Revolution* (Moscow: Progress Publishers).

Lenin. V.I. *Collected Works.*

Lukacs, G. 1966. 'Technology and Social Relations', *New Left Review* (Vol.39).

Lukacs, G. 1971. *History and Class Consciousness* (Massachusetts: MIT).

Lukacs, G. 2002. 'Critical Realism and Socialist Realism' in Anand Prakash (ed.), *Marxism* (New Delhi: Worldview Publications).

Marx and Engels, *Collected Works.*

Marx, K. and F. Engels. *Selected Works.*

Miliband, R. 1969. *The State in Capitalist Society* (London).

Miliband, R. 1970. 'Reply to Nicos Poulantzas', *New Left Review*, No. 82 (Nov.-Dec.).

Miliband, R. 1973. 'Marx and the State' in S. Avineri (ed.) *Marx's Socialism* (New York: Lieber-Artherton).

Miliband, R. 1977. *Marxism and Politics* (Oxford: Oxford University Press).

Plamenatz, J. 1954. *German Marxism and Russian Communism* (London: Longman).

Poulantzas, N. 1969. 'The Problem of the Capitalist State', *New Left Review*, No. 58 (Nov.-Dec.).

Poulantzas, N. 1978. *Political Power and Social Classes* (London: Verso)

Poulantzas, N. 1978a. *Classes in Contemporary Capitalism* (London:Verso).

Poulantzas, N. 1979. *Fascism and Dictatorship* (London:Verso).

Poulantzas, N. 1980. *State, Power and Socialism* (London: Verso).

Przeworksi, Adam and Michael Wallerstein. 1988. 'Structural Dependence of the State on Capital', *American Political Science Review* (Vol. 82).

Przeworski, Adam and John Sprague. 1986. *Paper Stones: A History of Electoral Socialism* (Chicago: University of Chicago Press).

Przeworski, Adam and Michael Wallerstein. 1982. 'The Structure of Class Conflict under Democratic Capitalism', *American Political Science Review* (Vol. 76).

Przeworski, Adam. 1991. *Democracy and the Market* (Cambridge: Cambridge University Press).

Przeworski, Adam. 1990. *The State and the Economy under Capitalism* (Switzerland: Harwood Academic Publishers).

Sartori, G. 1973. *Democratic Theory* (Connecticut: Greenwood Press).

Sartre, J. P. 1968. *The Critique of Dialectical Reason* (London: New Left Books).

Thomas, P. 1980. *Karl Marx and the Anarchists* (London: Routledge and Kegan Paul).

Tucker, R.C. 1969. *The Marxian Revolutionary Idea* (New York: W.W. Norton).

Tucker, R.C. 1973. 'Marx as Political Theorist' in S. Avineri (ed.) *Marx's Socialism* (New York: Lieber-Artherton).

Wolfe, B.D. 1967. *Marxism* (London: Chapman and Hall).

5

The Theory of Class Struggle

The history of all hitherto existing society is the history of class struggles. Freeman and slave, patrician and plebian, lord and serf, guild-master and journeymen, in a word, oppressor and oppressed, were in constant opposition to one another. The class struggle carried on an uninterrupted fight that ended either in a revolutionary reconstruction or in the common ruin of the contending class each time. In all epochs of history and everywhere a complicated arrangement of society into various orders and manifold gradation of social rank—patricians, knights, plebeians and slaves in ancient Rome; feudal lords, vassals, guild-masters, journeymen, apprentices and serfs and other subordinate gradations in the Middle Ages. Sprouting from the ruins of the feudal society the bourgeois society has not done away with class antagonisms. It has established new classes, new conditions of oppression and new forms of struggle in place of the old ones. The present epoch of the bourgeoisie has simplified the class antagonisms — society as a whole is more and more splitting up into two great hostile camps, into two great classes directly facing each other, *i.e.* the bourgeoisie and the proletariat.

The proletariat goes through various stages of development. At first the struggle is carried on by individual labourers, then by the work-people of factory, then by the operatives of one trade against the individual bourgeoisie who directly exploit them. However, at this stage the proletariat attacks not against the bourgeois conditions of production, but against the instruments of production. At this stage, the labourers still form an incoherent mass. They are scattered over the whole country. They are broken up by their mutual competition. If they become able to unite, it is the result of the union of the bourgeoisie, but not the result of the active union of the proletariat. The bourgeoisie as a class to attain their political ends is compelled to set in motion the whole proletariat.

At this stage the proletariat reaches the stage of coherence from the stage of incoherence in their fight against the enemies of the enemies, *i.e.* the monarchs, landlords, non-industrial bourgeoisie, the petty bourgeoisie. The proletariat does not fight their immediate enemies, the bourgeoisie. The whole historical movement is concentrated in the hands of the bourgeoisie. With the development of industry the proletariat not only increases in number, but also becomes concentrated in greater masses. Its strength grows and it feels more strength. Various interests and conditions of life are being more and more equalized. Therefore, ranks among them are also being more equalized. Wages become more fluctuating with the growing competition among the bourgeoisie and the resulting commercial crises. Improvement of machinery makes the livelihood of the proletariat more and more precarious and the collision between individual workman and individual bourgeois take the form of collision between classes.

The workers begin to form an association and unions against the bourgeoisie in order to keep up the rate of wages and to mark provision beforehand for occasional revolts. The ever expanding union of workers is the result of occasional revolts. The union of the workers is expanded with the improved means of communications created and developed by modern industry. Further, developed means of communications also help in the centralization of various local struggles of the same character and transformation of these struggles into one national struggle between classes. Every struggle is a class struggle. The proletarians are organized into a class and then into a political party. When the class struggle nears the decisive hour of revolution, the process of dissolution goes on within the ruling class and in fact in the whole range of society. The proletariat is recruited from all classes of the population. The lower strata of the middle class, consisting of shopkeepers, small traders, handicraftsmen and peasants—gradually enters into the proletarian class, partly because their capital does not suffice for modern industry and is swamped in competition with the large capitalists, partly because their specialized skill is rendered worthless by new methods of production. The epoch of the bourgeoisie possesses the distinctive feature—it has simplified class antagonisms—society is splitting up into two great hostile camps—bourgeoisie and proletariat. Of all the classes that stand face to face with the bourgeoisie today, the proletariat alone is really a revolutionary class. The other classes decay and finally disappear in the face of modern industry. The proletariat is a special and essential product of the capitalist-bourgeois system. All historical movements are movements of minorities. But the proletarian movement is the self-conscious and independent of the immense majority in the interest of the immense majority. If the proletariat during its contest with the bourgeoisie is compelled by force of circumstances to organize itself as a class and by revolution or by means of revolution, it makes itself the ruling class and as such sweeps away by force the old conditions of production, then it will along with these conditions have swept away the conditions for the existence of class antagonisms and of classes generally and will thereby have abolished its own supremacy as a class. In *The Communist Manifesto* Marx and Engels put emphasis on a communist society. In place of the old bourgeois society there will have a society where there will be the free development of each, the condition for the free development of all.

Marx emphasizes the distinctive character of modern classes—the proletariat and the bourgeoisie in relation to earlier social groups such as feudal estates. In *Poverty of Philosophy* Marx says that economic conditions in the first place have transformed the mass of the people into workers. The domination of capital creates the common situation and is responsible for the creation of common interests of this class. This mass is already a class in relation to capital, a class-in-itself, but not yet a class-for-itself. After this stage, the mass unites and forms itself into a class-for-itself. This class fights for class interests and this struggle is definitely political struggle. In *18th Brumaire* Marx says that the small-holding peasants form a vast mass. The members of the small-holding peasants live in similar conditions without entering into manifold relations with one another. This is due to their mode of production. This mode of production isolates them from one another instead of bringing them in mutual intercourse. This is due to their economic conditions of existence that separate their mode of life, their interests and culture from those of other classes. They don't form a separate class as such. In so far as there is merely a local interconnections among the small land-holding peasants, and the identity of their interests begets no community, no national bond, and no political organization among them. Hence, they do not form a class as such. Form this it suggests that Marx says about two important contending classes—the proletariat and the bourgeoisie and provides few important conditions for the formation of classes, *i.e.* economic conditions, domination of capital, common interest, common situation, class in relation with capital, mass unity, class-in-itself, class-for-itself, community of interests, national bond and political organization etc. Based on economic criteria, Marx in his *Capital* says that the owners merely of labour powers, owners of capital, and landowners, whose respective sources of income are wages, profit and ground-rent. In other words, wage-labourers, capitalists and landowners, constitute the three big classes of modern society based upon the capitalist mode of production. See Figure 52.

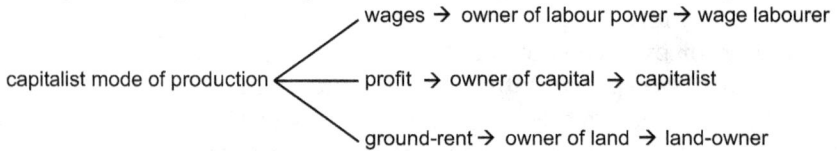

wages → owner of labour power → wage labourer

capitalist mode of production ← profit → owner of capital → capitalist

ground-rent → owner of land → land-owner

Figure 52

The law of development of the capitalist mode of production is to separate the means of production increasingly from labour and to concentrate the scattered means of production more and more into wage-labour and the means of production into capital. To this tendency, there corresponds the independent separation of landed property from capital and labour or the transformation of all landed property into a form which corresponds with the capitalist mode of production. Then, Marx asks the question—what constitutes wage-labourers, capitalists and landlords as the three great social classes? To him, classes are three social groups whose components, the individual members, live from wages, profit and rent respectively, that is, from the utilization of their labour power, capital and landed property. Apart from economic criteria, Marx sometimes introduces psychological criteria. When an aggregate group of people satisfies the economic criteria of a social class, then the members of the aggregate social group form a social class and the members of that social group are linked with class consciousness, consciousness of common interests and common class antagonisms arising out of psychological characteristics. In association with economic criteria, the psychological dimension has been touched upon. A few remarks of Marx and Engels may be cited here—

1. common interest, common consciousness and common battle: 'The separate individuals form a class in so far as they have to carry on a common battle against another class.' (*The German Ideology*)
2. organizational motivation to unity: Marx and Engels empha-size the importance of 'the organization of the proletarians consequently into a political Party.' (*The Communist Manifesto*)
3. identity of commonality: 'In so far as millions of families live. ... In so far as there is merely a local interconnection among these small-holding peasants, and the identity of their interests begets no community, no national bond and no political

organization among them, they do not form a class.' (*The Eighteenth Brumaire*).

Sociologically, according to Marx, the capitalist, petit bourgeoisie and the proletariat—these three classes lead to conflict with each other and Marx associates the concept of the proletariat with fundamental dichotomy—bourgeoisie and the proletariat. Each class, according to Marx, is determined by the relations of production. Marx in his letter to Weydemeyer on March 5, 1852 says that he does not demand any credit to him for discovering the existence of classes and struggle between the classes in modern society. Bourgeois historians had described the historical development of the class struggle and bourgeois economists described the economic anatomy of the classes before the description of Marx—the existence of classes is bound up with particular historical phases in the development of production, class struggle necessarily leads to the dictatorship of the proletariat, and dictatorship only constitutes the transition to the abolition of all classes and to a classless society. Following Marx, Lenin says in his book *A Great Beginning* that classes are large groups of people differing from each other by the place they occupy in a historically determined system of social production, by their role in the social organization of labour, and consequently by the dimensions of the share of social wealth of which they dispose of and the mode of acquiring it. Classes are groups of people one of which can appropriate the labour of another owing to the different places they occupy in a definite system of social economy.

Therefore, according to Lenin, (1) classes are groups of people; (2) classes are different from each other in terms of their position in the system of social production; (3) the system of social production is historically determined and therefore, classes are historically determined groups of people; (4) classes are determined by their role in the social organization of labour and therefore classes are associated with social production process; (5) classes are determined by the dimensions of the share of social wealth; (6) as production is a social process, so classes are social groups of people, where one group can appropriate the labour of another; (7) definite social groups or classes occupy different positions in the system of social production. Marx in *Capital* says that when an independent labourer, for example a small farmer, all three forms of revenue may here be applied, works for himself and sells his own product, he is first considered as his own employer or as capitalist, who makes use of himself as a labourer, and second as his own landlord, who makes use of himself as his own tenant. Therefore, on first account, to himself as wage-worker he pays wages; on second count, to himself as capitalist he gives the profit;

and on the third count, and to himself as landlord he pays rent. Therefore, three classes belong to the same class of an independent labourer, the small farmer. Assuming the capitalist mode of production and the relations corresponding to it to become the general basis of society—this assumption is correct. It is due to the ownership of the means of production, and not to his own labour, that he is in a position to appropriate his own surplus labour.

Therefore, Marx relates classes and class struggle with social relations of production, which are indispensable and independent of men's will and people enter into them in the social production of their material life. As soon as the economic structure of society changes, the laws, ideologies and class ideologies, political institutions and intellectual activities of the men also change, more or less rapidly. The members of the social groups of people stand in certain relations to one another. The relations may be co-operative and conflicting. According to Marx, conflict and contradictions arise from the economic basis of the society and the process of social development is dialectic. Human development proceeds through stages through contradictions. Relations of production become fetters on the forces of production. Relations of production are indispensable and men enter into them inevitably. These relations of production are determined by the forces of production. Relations of production are formally and legally expressed through the system of property, which essentially reflects the structure of classes. A society, according to Marx, becomes divided into classes in accordance with the system of property structure and relations of production. Society is divided into ruling and privileged class and the ruled and under-privileged, while the former tries to subjugate the latter and try to prevent changes in the existing relations of production. The ruling class disposes of the coercive power of the society. The ruling class appropriates the lion's share in the production process, and revolutionizes the methods of production. With the revolution of the methods of production the proletariat is increased in number and strength as a class. This class becomes revolutionary. By transforming the relations of production the proletariat resolves class contradictions and as well as transforms the whole superstructure.

The classical Marxist formulation of historical materialism does not speak about or does not seek to answer the questions—what are the forces responsible for the incompatibilities or contradictions between the forces of production and relations of production and how the incompatibilities come to an end. According to John Plamenatz, the 'present object is merely to establish two points: the first, that Marxism offers us no explanation of why the "relations of production" should not change with every change in the forces of production, to which they are said to "correspond", except that it is the interest of a ruling class that they should not, of a class having the power to prevent their doing so; and the second, that Marxism offers us no explanation of why the resulting incompatibilities should at last be resolved except the inevitable political victory of a revolutionary class, whose interest it is to destroy the old "relations of production" and replace them with new ones that are not fetters on economic progress. The gradual development of the forces of production and the discontinuous but more rapid changes in the "relations of production" do not, therefore, constitute an autonomous economic process. The conservatism of the ruling class and the revolutionary activities of the exploited class are not mere effects of that process; they are quite essential to it. It is not just a question of their having some influence on it, an influence that is only secondary, for, without them, the fundamental historical process, falsely called economic by the Marxists, would not even be "dialectical". It is the political activities of these classes, the use of their political power by the exploiters, and the revolutionary struggle of the exploited, which both cause the contradictions between the "forces" and "relations of production" and resolve them.' (Plamenatz, 1954: 32-33). Plamenatz also points out four statements of Karl Marx in connection with the gist of historical materialism and class struggle that there is a distinction between the material transformation of the economic conditions of production, which can be determined with the precision of natural science, and the legal, political, religious, aesthetic or philosophic — in short, ideological forms in which men become conscious of this conflict, *i.e.*, the conflict between the forces and relations of production and fight it out; that no social order ever disappears before all the productive forces for which there is room in it have developed, and new and higher relations of production never appear before the material conditions of their existence have matured in the womb of the old society; that there are so progressive epochs in the formation of society—Asiatic, ancient, feudal and modern bourgeois modes of production; and that the bourgeois relations of production are the last antagonistic form of the social process of production.

To Marx, the ideological forms like legal, political, religious, aesthetic or philosophic are reflection of contradiction between the forces of production and relations of productions and in all these ideological forms men become conscious of this conflict and try to fight it out. Ideologies are system of ideas to justify theory of action. Marx's theory is very much useful for the proletariat, for the advancement of society without class, oppression and domination. Morality is one of ideological forms. Engels in *Anti-Duhring* says about class antagonisms, class movement and class morality. All hitherto existing social movements are moved by the forces of class antagonisms. Morality is always class morality,—which either justifies class domination and class oppression of the ruling class or protects the interest of the ruling class. This may be called ruling class morality. On the other hand, as soon as the oppressed class gains strength and becomes powerful, then the oppressed class represents opposition to and struggle against the domination of the ruling class and for the interests of the oppressed. This may be termed as oppressed class morality. Therefore, it cannot be doubted like all other branches of knowledge that there has been progress in morality, on the whole.

But, we cannot pass beyond class morality. A really human morality transcends class antagonisms and their legacies in thought become possible only at a stage of society which has not only overcome class contradictions but has even forgotten them in practical life. Then Engels appreciates the presumption of Herr Duhring in advancing his claims that from the midst of the old class society, and on the eve of a social revolution, to impose on the future classless society an eternal morality independent of time and changes in the real world. Engels further says that the development of classes is bound up with the relations of production and the contradictions between the forces of production and relations of production. With the disappearance of the old common ownership of land, the natural division of labour within the family, cultivating the soil made possible. Production has been more developed. Labour power can produce more than that of the necessary means for its maintenance. Likewise the means of employing additional labour power, the means of maintaining additional labour power exist. Labour acquires a value. It is slavery that first makes possible the division of labour between the agriculture and the industry. There is no socialism without the slavery of antiquity.

> If, with his domination of man by man as a prior condition for the domination of nature by man, Herr Duhring only wanted to state in a general way that the whole of our present economic order, the level of development now attained by agriculture and industry, is the result of a social history which evolved in class antagonisms, in relationships of domination and subjection, he is saying something which long ago, ever since the *Communist Manifesto*, become a common place. But the question of issue is how were are to explain the origin of class and relations based on domination, and if Herr Duhring's only answer is one word "force", we are left exactly where we are at the start. The mere fact that the ruled and exploited have at all times been far more numerous than the rulers and exploiters, and that therefore it is in the hands of the former that the real force has reposed, is enough to demonstrate the absurdity of the whole

force theory. The relationships based on domination and subjugation have therefore still to be explained ... As men originally made their exist from the animal world—in the narrower sense of the term—so they made their entry into history: still half animal, brutal, still helpless in the force of the forces of nature, still ignorant of their own strength; and consequently as poor as the animals and hardly more productive than they. There prevailed a certain equality in the conditions of existence, and for the heads of families also a kind of equality of social position—at least an absence of social classes—which continued among the primitive agricultural communities of the civilized peoples of a later period. In each such community there were from the beginning certain common interests the safeguarding of which had to be handed over to individuals, true, under the control of the community as a whole: adjudication of a disputes; repression of abuse of authority by individuals; control of water supplies, especially in hot countries; and finally when conditions were still absolutely primitive, religious functions. Such offices...are naturally endowed with a certain measure of authority and are the beginnings of State power. The productive forces gradually increase; the increasing density of the population creates at one point common interests, at another conflicting interests, between the separate communities, whose grouping into larger units brings about in turn a new division of labour, the setting up of organs to safeguard common interests and combat conflicting interests. These organs which, if only because they represent the common interests of the whole group, hold a special position in relation to each individual community—in certain circumstances even one of opposition—soon make themselves still more independent, partly through heredity functions, which comes about almost as a matter of course in a world where everything occurs spontaneously, and partly because they become increasingly indispensable owing to the growing number of conflicts with other groups.... Here we are only concerned with establishing the fact that the exercise of a social function was everywhere the basis of political supremacy; and further that political supremacy has existed for any length of time only when it discharged its social functions. (Engels, 1978: 218-220).

In *German Ideology* Marx says that the ideas of the ruling class are in every historical epoch the ruling ideas. The class which rules the material force of the society also rules the intellectual force. The operation becomes simultaneous. The class, which controls the means of material production, controls the means of mental production. The ideas of those who lack the means of mental production are subject to it. The individuals composing the ruling class possess among other things the consciousness. They, therefore, think and rule as class, as thinkers, as producer of ideas, as producer and distributor of ideas. The ruling class justifies its rule, as they are the representatives of common interest, representatives of law and order and defenders of the common good. The ruling class makes revolution. The ruling class is opposed to a class, not as a class but as the representative of the whole of society. Its interest really is more connected with the common interest of all other non-ruling classes. Under pressure of conditions, its interests have not been able to develop as the particular interest of a particular class. Its victory benefits many individuals of other classes, which are not winning a dominant position, but only in so far as it now puts these individuals in a position to raise themselves into a ruling class. Every new class achieves hegemony on a broader basis than that of the ruling class previously. The opposition of the non-ruling class to the new class later is developed profoundly. Marx in his letter to Bolte dated November 23, 1871 says that the political movement of the working class has as its ultimate object, of course, the conquest of political power for the working class, and for this it is naturally necessary that a previous organization of the working class, arising from its economic struggle, should have been developed upto a certain point. Where the working class is not yet far enough advanced in its organization to undertake a decisive campaign against the collective power or collective political power of the ruling classes, it must at any rate be trained for this by continual agitation against the policy of the ruling classes and adopting an attitude hostile to it. Marx in *The German Ideology* says that history does not end by being resolved into self-consciousness, but that in it at each stage there is found a material result. A sum of productive forces, a historically created relation of individuals to nature and to one another, is handed down to each generation from its predecessor. A mass of productive forces, different forms of capital and conditions is modified by the new generation on the one hand and prescribes on the other for its conditions of life and gives it a definite development. In other words, circumstances make men just as men make circumstances. Therefore, Marx in his *Theses on Feuerbach* says that the materialist doctrine concerning the changing of circumstances and education forgets that circumstances are changed by men. This is the materialist doctrine of the previous period, overlooks the human revolutionary practice. Marx emphasizes the importance of revolutionary practice. To him, the coincidence of the changing of circumstances and of human activity can only be comprehended and rationally understood as revolutionary practice.

According to Marx, social division of labour plays important role in the appearance of classes. The development of the productive forces gave the people an opportunity to work in separate families, in isolation from the others. According to Engels, property distinctions between individual members of society undermined the old communist system. Therefore, the mode of production is the determining element in the formation of classes, for example the social status of the working class and the laws of the capitalist mode of production determine the continuous and extended reproduction of the proletariat and at the same time, the aggravation of contradiction between the proletariat and the bourgeoisie, is expressed in the intensification of class struggle. In the capitalist mode of production the bourgeoisie and the proletariat are the basic classes. In slave-owning mode of production, they are slaves and slave-owners and in feudal mode of production, peasants and landlords. Besides the existence of basic classes in a particular mode of production, there are certain non-basic classes with different socio-economic structures existing along with dominant mode of production. Graphically (Figure 53),

	Basic classes	Non-basic classes	Socio-economic structure of
Slave-owning mode of production	Slave and slave-owners	Artisans and free peasants	handicrafts and small-scale farming
Feudal mode of production	Landlords and serfs	Artisans and peasants	Socio-economic structure of handicrafts and small-scale farming
Capitalist mode of production	Bourgeoisie and the proletariat	Petty urban and rural bourgeoisie ↑	Socio-economic structure of industrial production
		Middle and intermediate classes including intelligentsia	

Figure 53

Apart from basic and non-basic classes, there exists the intelligentsia, such as researchers, engineers, teachers, doctors, artists, writers etc. These intellectuals come from various sections of the society—some of them serve the interest of the capitalist producers in the capitalist production and others take the side of the working class by propagating and elaborating ideology. Estates are social groups, connected with social classes. Estates form class distinction—the higher estates constitute the exploiting classes and lower estates make up the class of the exploited. Including the intelligentsia, Marxism-Leninism includes artisans, peasants, small traders, petty urban and rural bourgeoisie in the category of middle class—its intermediate position between the class of large capitalists, traders and manufacturers, the bourgeoisie properly so called, and the proletarian or industrial class determines its character. This class is extremely vacillating in character—vacillating between aspirations to enter into the rank of the higher class or estate and going down into the lower class or estate and the fear of entering into the rank of the second, between the hope of promoting their interests by conquering a share in the direction of public affairs and the dread of rousing by ill-timed opposition, the ire of a Government that disposes of their very existence. Different classes have different and opposite interests with different socio-economic positions, and hence, there is conflict. Take for example, the conflict between the bourgeoisie and the proletariat. See Figure 54.

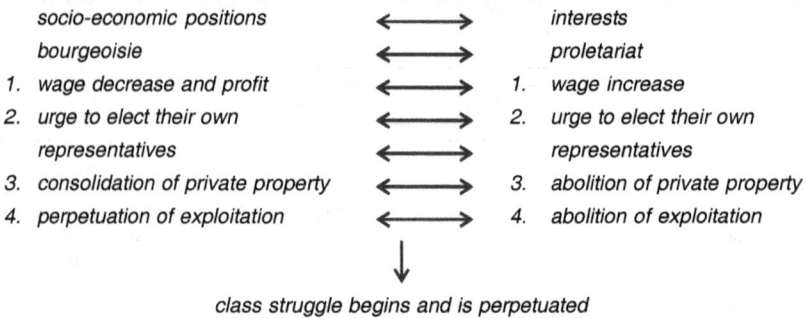

socio-economic positions	⟷	interests
bourgeoisie	⟷	proletariat
1. wage decrease and profit	⟷	1. wage increase
2. urge to elect their own representatives	⟷	2. urge to elect their own representatives
3. consolidation of private property	⟷	3. abolition of private property
4. perpetuation of exploitation	⟷	4. abolition of exploitation

class struggle begins and is perpetuated

Figure 54

This class struggle affects the development of the productive forces and improves the means of productive labour. It also affects production relations. Old production does not automatically change under the impact of new productive forces. The ruling class supports the old production relations. A powerful force is necessary to overcome the resistance of the ruling class, and hence class struggle starts. Class struggle becomes the motive force for progress in antagonistic society. Marx gives emphasis to the proletarian class struggle in all three directions—economic, political and ideological for radical transformation of the society and establishment of a classless communist society. According to Marx and Engels, abolition of classes means the development of production carried out to a degree, at which appropriation of the means of production and of the products and with this, of political domination, of monopoly of culture and of intellectual leadership by a particular class of society, has become not only superfluous but economically, politically, intellectually, a hindrance to development. According to Lenin, the abolition of classes, means placing all citizens on an equal footing with regard to the means of production, is belonging to society as a whole. It means giving all citizens equal opportunities of working on publicly-owned means of production, on publicly-owned land and at publicly-owned factories and so forth.

According to Marxists, in classless society, class conflict becomes absent. According to them, before attending classless society, society becomes characterized by and equipped with class conflict and relationship of domination and subordination. Conflict and domination are inherent in class societies and societies are characterized by classes and not by individuals as such. A graphic representation of class conflict in societies may be presented in Figure 55. From the above graphic representation the following points may be jotted down—

1. society is not composed of individuals, but of interrelations among individuals and classes—where classes remain irreconcilably divided;

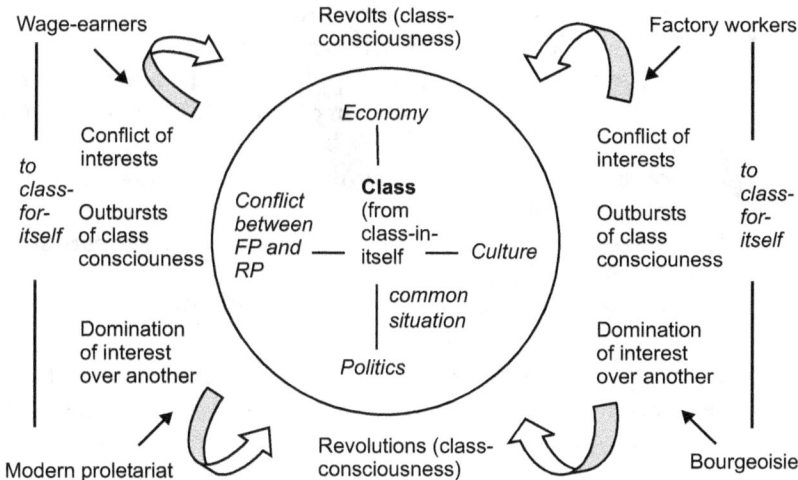

Figure 55

2. conflict is inherent in class system and cannot be solved within the same system of class mechanism;
3. conflict in society is not static, but dynamic, moves from lower to higher—there is seriality, from conflict → eruptions → revolts → revolutions;
4. conflict among classes in society assumes a sharp and sharper character and these conflicts may or might assume multiple forms of economic, political and cultural, and these are locked in the twin processes of domination and subjugation of economic, political and cultural in character;
5. these processes of domination and subjugation are taking shape with the total process of transformation of the mode of production;

6. domination and conflict are inherent in class societies resulting mainly out of conflict between the new forces of production and old relations of production, where the dominant classes' endeavour to maintain class domination and subjugated classes' endeavour to defend it, and where the dominant classes control the forces of production through accumulation of capital and the subjugated class try to defend it;

7. with the growth of expansion of accumulation of capital class conflict between the dominant and subordinated class becomes much more sharper, the conflict between social character of the forces of production and the individual character of the relations of production takes an acute form, which cannot be solved within the same system of mode production;

8. from domination conflict arises which have different and related aspects, *i.e.*, economic, political and cultural, where economy is the primary source of conflict, the prime mover of domination and conflict;

9. economic domination or accumulation of surplus value and capital is the cause and economic conflict is the effect. Politics legitimizes conflict through law, sanctions what is permitted —permitted relations between members of different and conflicting classes inside and outside the relations of production;

10. ideology justifies the relations of domination;

11. revolution is a political term, where class consciousness of the working class is transformed from class-in-itself, from consciousness of common situation to class-for-itself, to consciousness of common interest;

12. revolution is a political term, where the objectives of the modern proletariat, industrial wage earners and factory workers are to achieve their interests in opposition to those of the bourgeoisie, to do this through the abolition of private property and its replacement by community of goods, and to recognize no means of carrying out these objects other than a democratic revolution by force;

13. in revolution the proletarians are organized into class and consequently into a political Party under the leadership of the working class themselves, where proletarian class consciousness becomes revolutionary class consciousness;

14. the working class comes to acquire class consciousness in order to make a thoroughgoing revolutionary transformation of the capitalist society; and this role of the proletariat is not

determined by any extra-historical agency — it is determined by the nature of capitalism and by the concrete conditions which it imposes upon the working class and upon society at large.

The first premise of human history is the existence of living human individuals, according to Marx and Engels. The *Holy Family* tells us that history does nothing, possesses no immense wealth, and wages no battles. It is man that does all, makes history, possesses and fights. History is not a person apart, using man as a means for its own particular aims. History is nothing but the activity of man pursuing his aims. In *Theses on Feuerbach* Marx proposes the action-orientation of historical process, goes through struggles and contradictions, through circumstances of domination and subjugation, domination and conflict. *The Eighteenth Brumaire* shows us that men make their own history, but they do not make it just as they please—they do not make it under circumstances chosen by themselves, but under circumstances directly encountered, given and transmitted from the past. The history of circumstances is the history of class struggles.

In his study of class struggle, Marx in his *A Contribution to the Critique of Political Economy* says about the compositional relations and consciousness in society—social relations like religious, familial, military, political and economic and individual consciousness determined primarily by the economic relations. The economic conditions of production may change without rendering immediate changes in the legal and political orders. Ideological and political rhetoric should not be confused with the social productive processes. In *German Ideology* Marx and Engels say that the social structure and the State are continually evolving out of the life process of definite individuals, but of individuals, not as they appear in their own or other people's imagination, but as they really are—as they operate and produce materially. That is, there remains a distinction between conscious human activity and human consciousness, while the former aims at the creation and preservation of the conditions of human life and the latter furnishes reasons, realizations, modes of legitimization and moral justification (Avineri, 1970). However, there is a reciprocal relationship between conscious human activity and human consciousness. Likewise, Engels says that political, juridical, philosophical, religious, and artistic developments are based on economic development. But all of these react upon one another and also upon the economic basis. It is not that the economic situation is cause, solely active, while everything else is only passive effect. There is, rather, interaction on the basis of economic necessity, which ultimately always asserts itself (Letter to W. Borgius,

1894). Class relations find expression not only within the economic relations of production, but also in various forms elsewhere in society. The class relations may be examined via the legal statutes, dealing with property relations, through the State and political processes, in the sphere of morality and also in interactional and social- psychological forms. Although in Marxist theory the concept of class-in-itself occupies an important position, other developments and conditions must be present there for a class-in-itself to become class-for-itself, the more substantive and socially crystallized group. The conditions may be traced as under:

a. common position in the economic mode of production;
b. separate life style and cultural mode;
c. conflicting and hostile interests of opposing class;
d. social interconnection and social community across social and regional lines; *i.e.,* national and international class identity and unity;
e. application of class consciousness in society; and
f. political organization.

Following the last condition, Dahrendorf (1959) says that organization of the proletariat as a class, means its organization as a political party as well. For the working class to make an effective political struggle, requires the existence of a political Party under strong leadership as class struggle is essentially political in character. How does class struggle assume political character, or how does class conflict or class contradiction assume political character? To say, contradiction in the

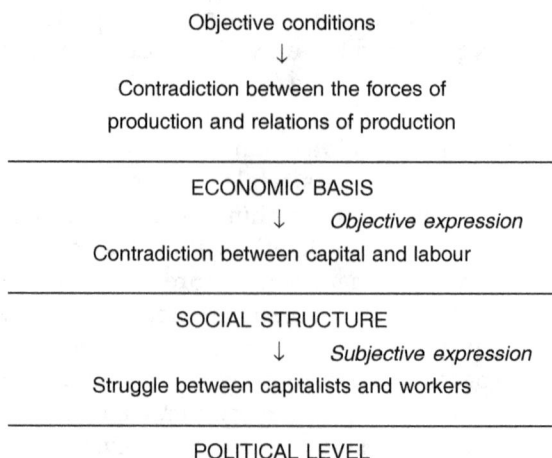

Objective conditions
↓
Contradiction between the forces of
production and relations of production

ECONOMIC BASIS
↓   *Objective expression*
Contradiction between capital and labour

SOCIAL STRUCTURE
↓   *Subjective expression*
Struggle between capitalists and workers

POLITICAL LEVEL

Figure 56

economic sphere is in parallel with contradictions both in the spheres of social and political. See Figure 56.

The class struggle is being fought out or controlled within the *status quo* at the philosophical, ideological and political levels of consciousness, where the movement of the forces and relations of production assert themselves with decisive force in the end. Here, we find, according to Marxists, the determining role of the economic and conditioning influences of the non-economic. Class consciousness in the proletariat is a consciousness of material reality, and a rejection of the rationalizations and the ideological creations of the old ruling class. Likewise, the fluctuations in capitalist production from prosperity to stagnation and then to decline, the class consciousness of the working class also fluctuates (Mandel, 1971). As objective conditions of decline, the class consciousness of the working class comes to the fore, and as the objective conditions are favourable, the class consciousness of the working class decline. Here, the favourable and unfavourable conditions are in respect with the development of capitalist system. As the capitalist system develops, and the conditions of the working class deteriorate, class consciousness of the working class is developed. And as the capitalist system is not developed, and the conditions of the working class are not so bad, class consciousness of the working class is falsified. Wilhelm Reich (1971) in his analysis of class consciousness considers two types of class consciousness—objective sociological consciousness and subjective consciousness, consciousness of revolutionary leadership and consciousness of the masses, and tries to make a balance between the two in order to abolish the distinction between the subjective and objective consciousness. To him, like that of Marx that class consciousness is not automatic or mechanical responses to objective conditions, there exits subjective discontents that provide important sources for the potentially improved class consciousness. To him, class consciousness equals everything that contains the probable conditions for making revolution, which contradicts bourgeois order. That element which supports and reinforced bourgeois order and tries to make a bond with it, that element impedes the process of formation of class consciousness.

According to Reich, objective class consciousness contains the knowledge of contradictions of the capitalist system, possibilities of socialist planned economy, need for social revolution, balance between the form of appropriation and form of production, balance between progressive and retrograde forces of history etc. The subjective consciousness contains everyday problems of the masses, for example, food, clothing, family relations, sexual satisfaction, fashion, and leisure etc. Here, revolution is required to free the means of production form capitalist control and direct them toward human needs. According to Marx, revolution is necessary not only because the ruling class cannot be overthrown in any other way, but also because only in a revolution the class can, which overthrows it rid itself of the accumulated rubbish of the past and become capable of reconstructing society. In reconstructing society there must have a transitional society between capitalist society and classless communist society. This transitional society is ruled under the dictatorship of the proletariat, which is moving towards classless Stateless society under communist rule. At the transitory stage the role of the State is nothing but the revolutionary dictatorship of the proletariat, a means whereby the vast majorities are in control of production and political life at the expense of the small and reactionary minority (Fromm, 1967). Here, at this stage, class struggle or class conflict between majoritarian proletariat and minority reactionary elements prevails. In his 'Introduction' to *Civil War in France* Engels categorically mentions that elements like anti-authoritarianism, anti-bureaucracy, egalitarianism, representation, working class's rule in running the affairs of politics and economy rather than bureaucratic State of affairs, universal suffrage, right of recall of representatives, binding mandates on the representatives, equal wages to representatives and workers—all of these are subsumed under proletarian dictatorship. That does not mean absence of total authority in the administration of affairs and presence of total autonomy to the individual members of the society in managing the affairs of their life, social, political, economic and cultural.

In dictatorship of the proletariat, there is authority, but not authoritarianism; there is organization, but not bureaucracy; there is individual freedom, but not total autonomy to individual actions; there is control from below, but not control from above. Engels is in favour of authority, but not authoritarianism both in industry and also in the spheres of the State and society. Engels in *On Authority* says that abolition of authority in industry means abolition of industry. On the ground of absence of authority in society, Engels criticizes Bakunin in his letter to T. Cuno in 1872 that in Bakunin's society there will above be no authority, for authority equals State, which is an absolute evil. Engels asks that how these people propose to run a factory, operate railways or steer a ship without having in last resort one deciding will, without single management, they of course do not tell us. The authority of the majority over the minority also ceases. Every individual and every community is autonomous. But as to how a society, even of only two people, is possible unless each gives up some of his autonomy, Bakunin again maintains silence. Therefore, according to Engels, absolute authority, no autonomy and absolute autonomy, no authority and management are impossible. There is the need to keep the balance between the two. In *Critique of the Gotha Programme* Marx rejects superimposition from the above and subordination to the below. That is, Marx rejects superimposition of the State over society and emphasizes the necessity of subordination of the State to society for the promotion of individual freedom in a society of non-exploitation.

In society of exploitation and of class conflict there remains superimposition of the State on the society, where the superstructure always reflects and serves the interest of the ruling class. There is a reciprocal relation between ruling ideas and the ruling class. The dominant views are of the ruling class, which are worked out and upheld by the ruling class intellectual representatives. In all revolutionary periods the revolutionary class formulates new revolutionary ideas and creates new institutions. At this stage, the superstructure serves the basis. Stalin in his *Concerning Marxism in Linguistics* becomes an exceedingly active force, actively assisting its basis to take shape and consolidate itself. The superstructure is created by the basis in order to serve it, to actively help and consolidate itself. The views and institutions reflect the given economic structure of society, the interests of the ruling class whose dominance depends on that economic structure.

In *German Ideology* Marx and Engels say that dominant material relationships are grasped as ideas. These ideas are ruling ideas as they are ideal expression of the dominant material relationships. As they are ruling ideas, they are ideas of dominance. Further, the class which is the ruling material force of society is at the same time ruling intellectual force —this intellectual force controls the means of mental production. Based on the social conditions of existence, Marx in *The Eighteenth Brumaire* says that there rises an entire superstructure of distinct and peculiarly formed sentiments, illusions, modes of thought and views of life—all these are produced out of the material foundation and the corresponding social relations. Therefore, ideological domination is essentially class domination. The intellectuals do not constitute separate class with separate class interests but function as the intellectual representatives of one or the other classes. Engels in his letter to Mehring says that ideology is a process accompanied by the so called thinker consciously but with a false consciousness. The real motives impelling him remain unknown to him. He works with mere thought material. He accepts thought material without examination as the product of thought. According to Marx, which he says in *The Eighteenth Brumaire* that what makes the intellectuals the representatives of the petty bourgeoisie is the fact that in their minds they do not get beyond the limits which the petty bourgeoisie do not get beyond in life, that they are consequently driven, theoretically to the same problems and solutions to which material interest and social position drive the petty-bourgeoisie practically. This is, in general, the relationship between the political and literary representatives of a class and the class they represent.

Marx and Engels in *Manifesto of the Communist Party* say that within the old society, the elements of the new, have been created and that the dissolution of the old ideas, keeps even pace with the dissolution of the old conditions of existence. The existence of revolutionary ideas presupposes the existence of revolutionary class—this view has been expressed by both the authors in *The German Ideology*. When the material forces of production come into conflict with the existing relations of production, the entire superstructure changes. This conflict gives birth to class conflict through which social transformation is effected. In the *Eighteenth Brumaire* Marx says that all class struggles, either political or religious or philosophical or some other ideological domain are more or less the expression of the struggle of social classes. The existence of classes and the existence of class struggle among classes are conditioned by the degree of development of their economic position. Therefore, in *Critique of Political Economy* Marx says that with the change of the economic foundation, the entire superstructure is more or less rapidly transformed. The overcoming of the old by the new is the necessary pre-condition of superstructural changes. To overcome the old relations of production in conformity with the new productive forces, a corresponding transformation of views and institutions is necessary. Marx is his letter to Annenkov, 1846 says that men never relinquish what they have owned. But this does not mean that they never relinquish the social form in which they have acquired certain productive forces. On the contrary, they are obliged to change all their traditional social forms, from the moment when the form of their intercourse no longer corresponds to the productive forces acquired. Lenin in his *Three Sources and Three Component Parts of Marxism* that people always have been the foolish victims of deception and self-deception in politics. They will be victims of deception and self-deception until they have learnt to seek out the interests of some class or other behind all moral, religious, political and social phrases, declarations and promises. The supporters of reforms and improvements will always be fooled by the defenders of the old orders until they realize that every old institution, however barbarous and rotten it may appear to be, is kept going by the forces of certain ruling classes. There is only one way so smashing the resistance of those classes, and that is to find, in the very society which surrounds us. The forces can do owing to their social position must constitute the power capable of sweeping away the old and creating the new and to enlighten and organize those forces for the struggle. Marx's philosophical materialism has shown the way out of spiritual slavery. Marx's economic theory alone has explained the true position of the proletariat in the general system of capitalism. Not a single victory of political freedom over the feudal class was won except against desperate resistance. Not a single capitalist country evolved on a more or less free and democratic basis except by a life and death struggle between the various classes of capitalist society. The genius of Marx lies in his having been the first to deduce from this the lesson world history teaches and to apply that lesson consistently. The deduction he has made is the doctrine of class struggle.

The Marxists regard that without class struggle there would be no social progress and society's progressive development becomes faster when the most stubborn and organized is the struggle of the exploited against the exploiters. The social revolution, which is believed to be the highest form of class struggle, plays important role in social progress resulting in destruction of the old and the establishment of the new. The social progress through class struggle at various stages of social development may be presented here. See Figure 57.

Thesis: *Primitive Communist Society*

Anti-thesis:

slave society and class struggle in slave society
1. class struggle between slaves and slave-owners,
2. mass involvement into this struggle — from disruption to mass upsurge.

    ↓ (movement towards a progressive society)

feudal society and class struggle in feudal society
1. intensification of class struggle than that of the previous one,
2. class struggle between peasants and feudal lords,
3. class struggle between peasants in alliance with artisans and feudal lords, *i.e.* struggle crosses the rural boundary,
4. peasants' war start with the involvement of large number of people,
5. mass uprising turns into mass war or peasants' war,
6. war spreads over vast territories,
7. uprising of the masses does not end exploitation,
8. the slave and peasant uprisings in conjunction play important and progressive part in the progressive development of capitalism.

    ↓ (movement towards a progressive society)

capitalist society and class struggle in capitalist society
1. class struggle between the bourgeoisie and the proletariat,
2. in search of profit bourgeoisie exploits the proletariat, who are in search of end of exploitation,
3. the struggle between the proletariat and the bourgeoisie becomes so intense in the epoch of imperialism,

4. the peasants and artisans join the ranks of the proletariat and majority of the intellectuals are reduced to the working class status, unable to influence top bourgeois intellectuals,

5. capitalist production helps unite, organize and educate the working class, emancipates all other working people and abolishes exploitation.

↓ (movement towards a progressive stage)

transitory stage between capitalism and socialism and class struggle at this transitory stage

1. transitory stage — transition between capitalism's crisis and the establishment of socialism,

2. conditions of capitalism's general crisis, crisis of world capitalism, favourable situation for working class movement, growing influence of the Communist parties, people's dissatisfaction with the reactionary policy of the imperialists, working class's reaction against the ideological bankruptcy of reformism and action in favour of socialist revolution,

3. struggle against bourgeois onslaughts,

4. more and more working people's involvement in socialist revolution and establishment of socialism,

5. proletarian struggle—struggle for peace, national independence, democracy and socialism through diverse methods like strikes, demonstrations, meetings, conferences, and various forms of parliamentary struggle,

6. bourgeoisie try to motivate the working people making use of their economic stronghold, and by using the former ties with the old intellectuals, businessmen, bureaucrats, officials and army leaders they try to disrupt the country's economy and functioning of the State institutions,

7. the proletariat seizes State power and establishes its revolutionary dictatorship,

8. at this stage proletarian struggle is waged against bourgeois onslaught, when the proletariat has political power and controls key positions in the economy—suppression of both overt and covert resistance of the bourgeois exploiters, struggle for emancipation of the peasants from the influence of the bourgeoisie under the leadership of the working class and inclusion of these peasants into socialist camp, enrollment of the bourgeois economist to work in the national economy and intellectuals to work for socialist spirit, struggle for socializing in socialist disciplines in various fields of society. Lenin in his 'Foreword' to *Deception of the People with Slogans of Freedom and Equality* says that the dictatorship of the proletariat is the end of the class struggle but its continuation in new forms. The dictatorship of the proletariat is class struggle waged by a proletariat that is victorious and has taken political power into its hands against a bourgeoisie that has been defeated but not destroyed, a bourgeoisie that has not vanished, not ceased to offer resistance but that has intensified its resistance.

↓ (movement towards progressive society)

Synthesis: Socialist Society and class distinction in Socialist Society

1. class distinction instead of class conflict,

2. class distinction between working class, collective-farm peasantry and intelligentsia,

3. with the process of evolution class distinction is erased in communist society.

Figure 57

Therefore, according to Marxists, history progresses through class struggle. G. Lukacs (1977) in his analysis of 'revolutionary realpolitik' provides us the importance of class struggle in Marxist analysis, particularly the analysis of Lenin. 'Lenin handled all problems of socialism during the dictatorship of the proletariat, which must win him the respect even of his bourgeois and petty-bourgeois opponents, is therefore only the consistent application of Marxism, of historical-dialectical thought, to problems of socialism which have henceforward become capital. In Lenin's writings and speeches—as, incidentally, also in Marx—there is little about socialism as a completed condition.... Concrete knowledge of socialism is—like socialism itself—a product of the struggle for it; it can only be gained in and through this struggle.... The aim of Lenin's realism, his *realpolitik,* is therefore the final elimination of all utopianism, the concrete fulfilment of the content of Marx's programme: a theory become practical, the theory of practice. Lenin handled the problem of socialism as he had done the problem of the State: he wrested it from its previous metaphysical isolation and embourgeoisment and situated it in the total context of the problem of the class struggle.' (Lukacs, 1977: 73-74).

In contrast with this Marxist analysis, bourgeois theorists argue in favour of class collaboration and co-existence and co-operation of multiple classes in bourgeois capitalist system. In capitalist societies, there is neither exploitation nor hostilities; there are only social groups and classes according to profession, education, and income etc. Property relations among social groups are harmonious. There is social mobility, both horizontal and vertical. Others agree that class distinctions in capitalist society are being eliminated and gradually transformed into the middle class. The workers are no longer proletarians: their standard of living is high, they save money from their earnings, buy company shares and get profits like factory owners. The activities of the factory owners and employers are restricted by welfare State laws. All are treated as workers and all their interests coincide at a particular point. Working people unite not according to their relation to the means of production but according to other considerations. Modern scientific and technical progress would automatically provide power and leverage to the working class without indulging in class struggle and revolution. The viewpoints of the critics may graphically be presented here. See Figure 58.

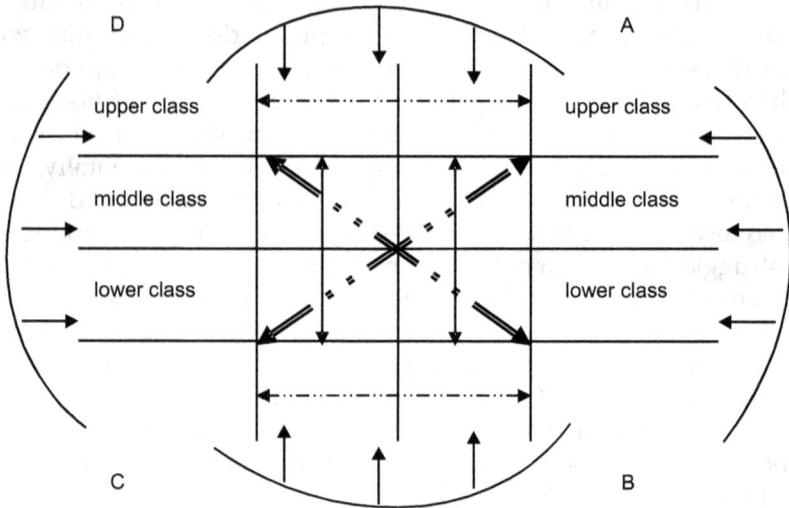

Figure 58

Here, 'A' = factory conditions of co-existence of workers and employers; 'B' = welfare State laws; 'C' = social mobility of social, economic and political character; 'D' = scientific and technical progress.

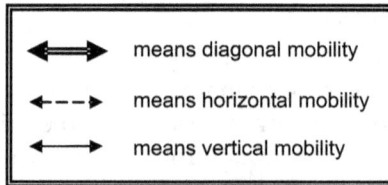

The working people have been absorbed in the industrial capitalist enterprise, parliamentary democratic debates. Their interests are co-ordinated through imperatively co-ordinated associations. All classes are transformed into a single class, the middle class with upper-lower-middle stratification.

According to Cohen (1988), Marxist theory of history is a process of liberation—liberation from scarcity imposed by nature and from oppression imposed by some people on others. The ruling and ruled classes share the cost of natural scarcity unequally and Marxism fights for the disappearance of society's class division. Loss of freedom, exploitation and indignity are the price which the mass of humanity must pay in creating material wherewithal of human liberation. With regard to the materialist interpretation of history, Cohen starts with two types of properties—material and social, the former designates the human interaction with nature and the latter designates human interaction with society, which is in response to the classical Marxist interpretation of forces of production and relations of production. Cohen's formulation may be presented here graphically. See Fig. 59.

Cohen's Categories and Mechanism of Historical Development

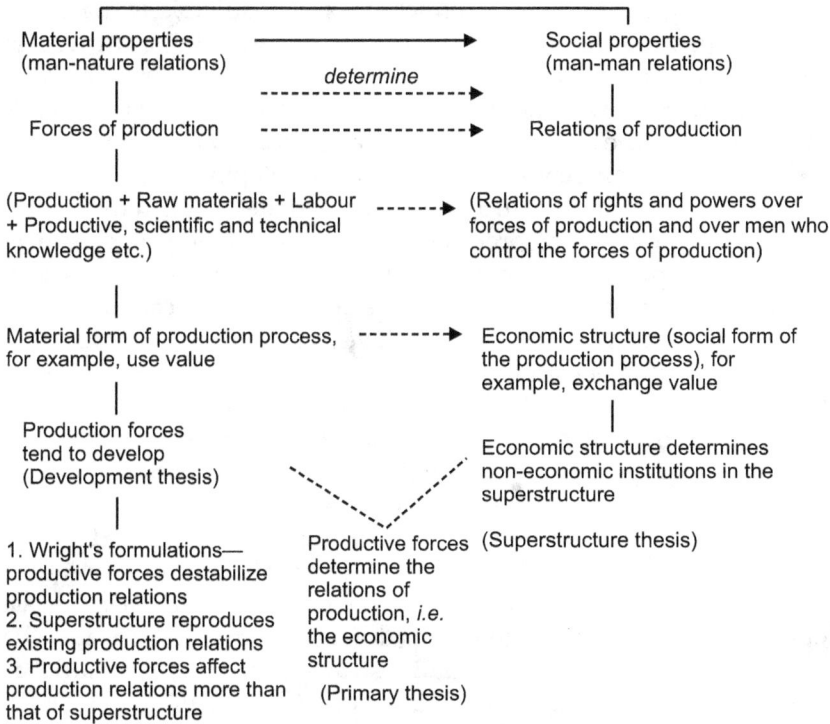

Material properties (man-nature relations) ⟶ Social properties (man-man relations)

determine

Forces of production ⟶ Relations of production

(Production + Raw materials + Labour + Productive, scientific and technical knowledge etc.) ⟶ (Relations of rights and powers over forces of production and over men who control the forces of production)

Material form of production process, for example, use value ⟶ Economic structure (social form of the production process), for example, exchange value

Production forces tend to develop (Development thesis)

Economic structure determines non-economic institutions in the superstructure

1. Wright's formulations— productive forces destabilize production relations
2. Superstructure reproduces existing production relations
3. Productive forces affect production relations more than that of superstructure

Productive forces determine the relations of production, *i.e.* the economic structure

(Superstructure thesis)

(Primary thesis)

Figure 59

Cohen says that productive forces develop throughout the course of human history and old productive forces and productive techniques are replaced by the new one. According to Erik Wright (1992) no particular group wants to reduce the productivity of labour, productive technology and productive knowledge evolve with the passage of time. In response to productive technology and productive knowledge, human requirements also evolve, and groups motivated to increase the productivity of labour always exist. Cohen accepts the classical Marxist thesis of historical development—history develops through class struggle, which is the immediate driving force of history and immediate explanation of historical development, but does not accept class struggle as the most fundamental. Cohen accepts the relationship between economic structure and productive forces as the most fundamental. For this, Levine and Wright (1980) criticize Cohen's incapacity to assess the capacity of classes in the transformation of society and point out that it is false to state that class interests determine class capacities and that class interests exclusively are determined by the forces of production.

To them, class interests and class capacities are not exclusively determined by the forces of production—it is justifiable to state that forces of production, relations production and superstructural considerations are all important in the formation of class interests and class capacities. Cohen (1978) finds that the class structure is determined by the relationship between economic structure and productive forces, and consequently by the development of production or the levels of surplus production. Cohen classifies economic structure according to the levels of productive development—no surplus level of production: pre-class economic structure, some or few surplus level of production: pre-capitalist economic structure or pre-capitalist class society, moderately high surplus level of production: capitalist economic structure or capitalist class society, and massive surplus level of production: post-class economic structure. According to Cohen, capitalism encounters crises, the development of productivity under capitalism needs non-class society, the working class understands the feasibility of socialism and they have the ability to transform society to socialism. '... the more severe a crisis is, the more developed are the forces whose progress it arrests. Therefore socialism grows more and more feasible as crises get worse and worse .... What is *de facto* the last depression occurs when there is a downturn in the cycle and the forces are ready to accept a socialist structure and the proletariat is sufficiently class conscious and organized.' (Cohen, 1978: 203-204).

Cohen mentions three important conditions from which contradiction results—(1) when society's economic organization becomes unable to optimally use and develop the accumulated productive power, (2) when the prospects opened by the productive forces of the economy are closed by the relations of reduction or when there arises tension between the use value and exchange value, and (3) when there is a bias of output expansion. Under advanced capitalism, competition and struggle for profit promote output expansion and reduce the possibility of reduction of toil.

Roemer (1981) specifies three modes of crisis of advanced capitalism in his crisis model—(1) profit squeeze crisis: workers consume more economic products and capitalists have insufficient incentive to accumulate, (2) realization crisis: production becomes higher than that of the existing demand, buying power of the workers becomes limited, and (3) fiscal crisis: taxation reduces capitalists' profits and their incentive to accumulate. In response to the capitalist crisis, Micha Kalecki

(1971) presents the capitalist business cycle, which may be presented here as a reference to Roemer's crisis model. See Figure 60. Roemer's ideas do not contradict with Cohen, rather he accepts Cohen's technological dimension of historical development, but traces the evolution of exploitation in terms of property relations in the course of historical development. Like Roemer, Eric Wright (1985) classifies four kinds of property—labour power, means of production, organizational assets and skills in his analysis of exploitation and social formation. Based on social formation, Wright classifies contending classes into lords and serfs, bourgeoisie and proletariat, bureaucrats and workers and contradictory classes into bourgeoisie, managers or bureaucrats, and intelligentsia or experts. Following Wright we may deduce the following table as

Types of Social Formation	Exploitation-Generating Asset Inequality				Historic Task of Revolutionary Transformation	Basic Contending Classes/Principal Contradictory Classes
	LP	MP	ORG	SKILL		
Feudalism	Yes	Yes	Yes	Yes	individual liberty	lords and serfs/ bourgeoisie
Capitalism	No	Yes	Yes	Yes	socializing of the means of production	bourgeoisie and proletariat/managers
Statism	No	No	Yes	Yes	democratization of the organizational control	bureaucrats and workers/ intelligentsia
Socialism	No	No	No	Yes	substantive quality	
Communism	No	No	No	No	self-actualization	

Note:
LP = Labour power
MP = Means of production
ORG = Organization
Source: Wright (1985)—Compiled and edited, pp. 89, 115.

When, Cohen, Roemer and Wright emphasize on economic base, property relations and exploitation as prime movers of historical development, Robert Brenner (1985) emphasizes on class struggle, on class structure, and on class power. This class factor will affect demographic and commercial changes, will affect the distribution of income and economic growth in the society. For that he criticizes Cohen's technological interpretation of historical development. '...productiveness of capitalism derives not from any particular productive force or technique, but is a consequence of the property relations themselves, it becomes just about impossible to see how the sort of argument Cohen makes for the primacy of the productive forces can be sustained ...no particular advance in technique—no increase in the productive forces

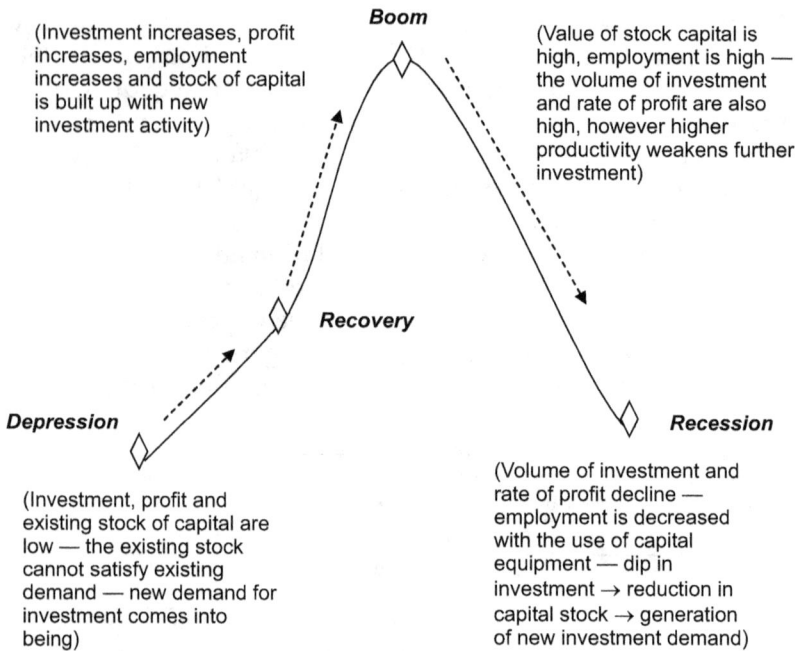

Boom

(Investment increases, profit increases, employment increases and stock of capital is built up with new investment activity)

(Value of stock capital is high, employment is high — the volume of investment and rate of profit are also high, however higher productivity weakens further investment)

Recovery

Depression

Recession

(Investment, profit and existing stock of capital are low — the existing stock cannot satisfy existing demand — new demand for investment comes into being)

(Volume of investment and rate of profit decline — employment is decreased with the use of capital equipment — dip in investment → reduction in capital stock → generation of new investment demand)

Figure 60

—is necessary to bring about either capitalist property relations or the tremendous increases in productiveness associated with them.' (Brenner, 1986: 47). According to Brenner, transition from pre-capitalist to capitalist property relations rarely occurs as a result of economically rational actions. Pre-capitalist property relations are maintained by pre-capitalist rational class actions. Transition to capitalist property relations is an unintended consequence and results from conflict between pre-capitalist classes.

However, Eric Wright (1985) says that class is a relational concept and class relations are rooted in the objective basis of exploitation, *i.e.*, the process of social production. As affluence is the cause of deprivation, so class relations are contradictory. Eric Wright (1985) treats class analysis in terms of class structure, class formation, class consciousness and class struggle in interrelated forms. Unlike the classical Marxist interpretation that class structure determines class formation, class consciousness and class struggle, Wright points out that class structure does not specify or determine social change, but only influences it and class structure only makes limitation or limits the variations that occur in class formation and class consciousness. According to Wright,

first, class structure limits variations in class formation,

second, class structure limits variations in class consciousness,
third, class formation limits variations in class struggle,
fourth, class formation selects class consciousness,
fifth, class struggle transforms class structure and class structure selects class struggle,
sixth, class struggle transforms both class formation and class consciousness,
seventh, class formation selects class consciousness,
eighth, class consciousness selects class struggle.

Wright's class analysis is based on the concept of exploitation, is the fundamental conflict of interests. His concept of exploitation is rooted in the relations of production. 'If class structure is understood as a terrain of social relations that determine objective material interests of actors, and class struggle is understood as the forms of social practices which attempt to realize those interests, then class consciousness can be understood as the subjective processes that shape intentional choices with respect to those interests and struggles.' (Wright, 1985: 246). Therefore, Wright's opinion may be clarified in Figure 61. Exploitation emerges from unequal distribution of ownership of the means of production in capitalist society and class structure of this society emerges from three forms of exploitation—ownership exploitation, organizational exploitation and credential exploitation, while ownership exploitation is the primary and the other two forms of exploitation are not unimportant. Both organizational exploitation and credential exploitation are not located in ownership, but are located in or within nine non-ownership locations—expert managers, expert supervisors, expert non-managers, semi-credentialed managers, semi-credentialed supervisors, semi-credentialed workers, uncredentialed managers, uncredentialed supervisors and proletarians. Organizational assets do not seem like productive property and credential assets also do not appear as such type of relationships. However, Wright does not devalue both types of assets, but gives weightage to these in class locations within the capitalist society ranging from '+' to ' > 0' to '–':

expert managers, expert supervisors, expert non-managers → +,
expert managers, semi-credentialed managers, uncredentialed managers → +,
semi-credentialed managers, semi-credentialed supervisors and semi-credentialed workers → > 0,
expert supervisors, semi-credentialed supervisors and uncredentialed supervisors → > 0,
uncredentialed managers, uncredentialed supervisors and proletarians → –,
expert non-managers, semi-credentialed workers and proletarians → –,
therefore, manager and expert groups → +,
supervisors and semi-credentialed groups → > 0,

and, uncredentialed and workers groups → –.

In this connection, Wright's class locations in capitalist society based upon intersection of three forms of exploitation may be presented here.

Activity	Owners of the means of production	Assets in the means of production Non-owners (Wage labourers)				Organisation assets
Owns sufficient capital to hire workers and not work	1 Bourgeoisie	4 Expert managers	7 Semi-credentialed managers	10 Uncredentialed managers	+	
Owns sufficient capital to hire workers but must work	2 Small employers	5 Expert supervisors	8 Semi-credentialed supervisors	11 Uncredentialed supervisors	> 0	
Owns sufficient capital to work for self but not to hire workers	3 Petty bourgeoisie	6 Expert non-managers	9 Semi-credentialed workers	12 Proletarians	–	
		+	> 0	–		

Skill/Credential assets

Source: Wright (1985), p. 88

A different class analysis has been developed by Adam Przeworski (1985)—classes are not considered by objective positions. Classes constitute the effects of class struggles, which are not uniquely determined by the relations of production; rather they are structured or determined by the totality of economic, political and ideological relations. Class struggles have an autonomous effect upon the process of class formation. Positions within the relations of production of classes and class formation are no longer viewed as being objective in the sense of being prior to class struggles. The success of political practice, *i.e.*, the class struggle for an example, depends upon certain limits, *i.e.*, positions of classes and class formation within social relations. However, the formation of classes-in-struggle within these historically concrete limits is determined by class struggles. Class struggles have formative effects on class formation. Therefore, class struggle is prior to class structure and class formation. Class is an important phenomenon. The working class is the potential proponent of the class image of the society. Political parties seek to organize workers as a class. When no political party seeks to organize workers as a class in opposition to all other classes, then the class image of the society becomes absent. Therefore, class struggle is important in the class formation and class structure of the society. Przeworski finds that the establishment of socialism is embarrassed due to underestimation of the organization of workers as a class by the socialist parties for participation in the electoral process and compromises between workers and capitalists. Therefore, class struggle is an essential concept in the transformation of society.

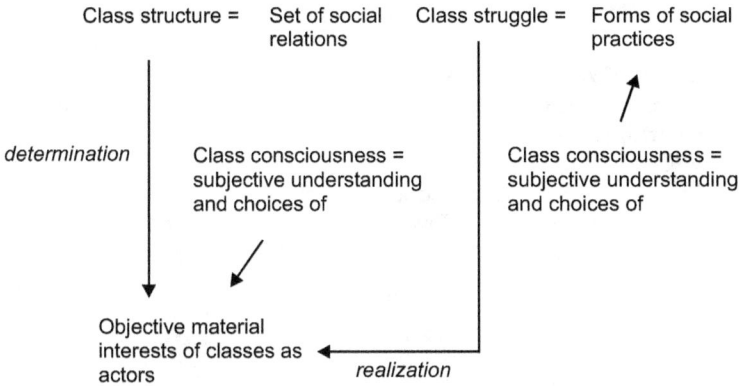

Class structure = Set of social relations   Class struggle = Forms of social practices

determination   Class consciousness = subjective understanding and choices of   Class consciousness = subjective understanding and choices of

Objective material interests of classes as actors   *realization*

Figure 61

REFERENCES

Brenner, Robert. 1985. 'Agrarian Class Structure and Economic Development in Pre-industrial Europe', *The Brenner Debate* (eds.) by T.H. Aston and C.H.E. Philpin (Cambridge: Cambridge University Press).

Brenner, Robert. 1986. 'The Social Basis of Economic Development', *Analytical Marxism* (ed.) by John E. Roemer (Cambridge: Cambridge University Press).

Cohen, G.A. 1978. *Karl Marx's Theory of History: A Defense* (Princeton: Princeton University Press).

Cohen, G.A. 1988. *History, Labour, and Freedom: Themes from Marx* (Oxford: Oxford University Press).

Dahrendorf, Ralph. 1959. *Classes and Class Conflict in Industrial Society* (Stanford: Stanford University Press).

Fromm, Erich. 1967. (ed). *Socialist Humanism* (London: Penguin Press).

Kalecki, Micha. 1971. *Selected Essays on the Dynamics of the Capitalist Economy*: 1933-1970 (Cambridge: Cambridge University Press).

Lenin, V.I. *Collected Works*.

Levine, Andrew and Eric Olin Wright. 1980. 'Rationality and Class Struggle', *New Left Review* (Vol. 123).

Lukacs, G. 1977. *Lenin* (London: Verso).

Makhov, A.S. and A.S. Frish (eds.). 1969. *Society and Economic Relations* (Moscow: Progress Publishers).

Mandel, Ernest. 1971. *The Formation of Economic Thought of Karl Marx* (New York: Monthly Review Press).

Marx, K. and F. Engels, *Collected Works*.
Marx, K. and F. Engels, *Selected Correspondence*.
Marx, K. and F. Engels, *Selected Works*.
Plamenatz, John. 1954. *German Marxism and Russian Communism* (London: Longmans, Green and Co.).
Przeworski, Adam. 1985. *Capitalism and Social Democracy* (Cambridge: Cambridge University Press).
Reich, Wilhelm. 1971. 'What is Class Consciousness?', *Liberation* (October).
Roemer, John E. 1981. *Analytical Foundations of Marxian Economic Theory* (Cambridge: Cambridge University Press).
Stalin, J.V. *Concerning Marxism in Linguistics*.
Wright, Eric Olin. 1985. *Classes* (London: Verso).
Wright, Eric Olin. 1992. 'State Employment, Class Location and Ideological Orientation', *Politics and Society* (Vol. 20: No. 2).

6

Party and Revolution

According to the Marxist-Leninist theory, the proletarian Party can lead the working people's struggle completely and combine all its forms properly. The Party's role particularly becomes important in the imperialist era, when the contradictions of capitalism are extremely aggravating and socialist revolution becomes the immediate practical tasks of the proletariat.

Marx is his *The Poverty of Philosophy* says that the working class, in the course of development will substitute for the old bourgeois society, an association which will preclude classes and their antagonism, and there will be no more political power proper since political power is precisely the official expression of class antagonism in bourgeois society. In the *Communist Manifesto* Marx and Engels point out that civil war breaks into revolution, where the violent overthrow of the bourgeoisie lays the foundation for the sway of the proletariat. The first step of this revolution of the working class is to raise the proletariat to the position of the ruling class and to win the battle of democracy. By using the political supremacy the proletariat seizes all capital from the bourgeoisie and centralizes all the means of production in the hands of the State. That is, the proletariat seizes the State power and thereby controls the production process in the society, suppresses the exploiters. By virtue of economic power, or the economic role that the proletariat performs, the proletariat is capable of being the leader of all the working and the exploited people and of waging an independent struggle for their emancipation from suppression and exploitation.

The theory of class struggle recognizes the overthrow of bourgeois rule and the becoming of the bourgeoisie as the ruling class. According to Lenin, who says in his work *State and Revolution* that the proletariat actually needs State power, *i.e.* a centralized organization of force and violence to vehemently resist the resistance of the exploiters and to lead the enormous mass of the population consisting of the peasants, the petty bourgeoisie and semi-proletarians. All these works are done in the interests of socialist system and organizing of the socialist economy, which is the immediate stage just before reaching the communist State. At this stage, which is said to be the transitory stage of social transformation, the workers' Party is being educated by Marxism. Marxism educates the vanguard of the proletariat, which is capable of assuming power and leading the whole people to socialism, of directing and organizing the new socialist system. Here, the Party becomes the teacher, guide and leader of the working and exploited people. The Party organizes their social life against the bourgeoisie. At this stage opportunism prevails. Few members of the workers' Party are said to be the true representatives of the better-paid workers. They get fairly well under capitalism. These opportunist elements renounce their role as revolutionary leaders of the people against the bourgeoisie. Dictatorship of the proletariat is the political rule of the proletariat and it is also integrally bound up with the revolutionary role of the proletariat. Both for Marx and Engels in *Communist Manifesto* the proletariat cannot overthrow the bourgeois rule without first, winning political power, second, attaining political supremacy, and third, transforming the State into the organized proletariat as the ruling class. Lenin has made two important additions to Marxism—theory of the organization of the Russian Social-Democratic Party and its relations to class interest which it wants to serve and theory of the proletarian Party that seeks to control bourgeois revolution and exploit this revolution in the interest of the proletariat. In *What is to be Done?* Lenin says that revolutionary movement of the proletariat does not arise spontaneously out of the working class's struggle against the bourgeoisie or their employers. At first, the working class wages their struggle at the economic level and then this struggle is waged at the political level.

ECONOMIC LEVEL: They create trade unions to protect themselves from exploitation, to get better wages and to improve their conditions of life and employment. The trade union activities are essentially connected with economy. The workers engage in trade union activities when there is large-scale concentration of capital and de-concentration of labour. The working class is subject to the same, their enemies are the same and the same remedies of sufferings occur to them. The workers, therefore, unite under the trade union banner. But this unionism does not solve all the problems before the workers, enable the workers to understand society they live in, and give birth to political and revolutionary proletarian movement. At this level of trade unionism, the proletariat cannot be considered as the revolutionary class. They are not politically consciousness and disciplined. They do not have knowledge of the general structure of society and laws of social development, which need to be inculcated by means of the revolutionary Party. They must be educated about their role in history, in theoretical understanding of revolution as there can be no revolutionary movement, discipline and unity of purpose without a revolutionary theory. To emancipate the workers, there is the need to wage class struggle on the political level.

POLITICAL LEVEL: The workers are uneducated. They cannot produce revolutionary theory that can make them a solid revolutionary class capable of waging class struggle politically. Mere economism would not solve their problems. Economism is a slavish cringing before spontaneity, which must not produce socialism, according to Lenin. Lenin accepts the development of capitalism in Russia and that the proletariat must lead the movement for the democratization and socialization of Russia. In *Development of Capitalism in Russia* that Russian capitalism is firmly based on large-scale enterprises of advanced capitalism. In *Iskra* news paper Lenin stresses two crucial ideas in his work, 'The Urgent Tasks of Our Movement': isolated from Social-Democracy, the working class movement inevitably becomes bourgeois and the revolutionaries must devote the whole of their lives to revolution. Lenin stresses the importance of political and strategic points against the opponents. Lenin's emphasis is on introducing socialist consciousness into the working class. The revolutionary class consciousness must be brought to the workers from outside by the intellectuals. In *What is to be Done?* Lenin says that the history of all countries shows that the working classes through their own efforts are able to develop trade-union consciousness only. The theory of socialism grows out of the theories elaborated by the educated representatives of the propertied classes, by the intellectuals. Therefore, social democrats must not confine themselves to economic struggle, is motivated by spontaneous trade union consciousness. Spontaneous development of the working class movement leads to the subordination of the bourgeoisie. The Social Democrats must take up actively in the political education of the working class and in the development of its political consciousness.

Lenin in *Our Immediate Tasks* says that working class consciousness cannot be a genuine political consciousness unless the workers are trained to respond to all cases of tyranny, oppression, violence and abuse, no matter what class is affected unless they are trained to respond from a

Social-Democratic point of view and no other. Lenin accepts the political capacity of the workers, the ideological capacity of the intellectuals and the mutual correspondence between them. However, Lenin does not have much faith in intellectuals, who perform the social function of producing ideologies. I do propose here that production of ideology is one and the inculcation of ideology is another, where the former is the function of the intellectuals and the latter is the function of the Party. Lenin wants a strong and disciplined Marxist Party consisting of both workers and intellectuals, capable of restraining the caprice of the intellectuals, and capable of providing the intellectuals a sense of responsibility by binding them to the workers in common loyalty to the cause of revolutionary socialist movement. The Party will wholeheartedly devote to the revolutionary theory and without comprehensive revolutionary social and political theory, the Party cannot be disciplined and the workers cannot be united under an ideological stronghold. Workers need both faith and discipline in this struggle for emancipation through revolutionary socialist movement. Lenin argues that it becomes necessary to form revolutionary socialist Party recruiting in it the active, ablest and bravest workers.

In *What is to be Done?* Lenin says that the consciousness of the working masses cannot be the genuine class consciousness, unless the workers learn from concrete and practical political facts and events to observe every other social class in all the manifestations of its intellectual, ethical and political life; unless they learn to apply in practice the materialist analysis and the materialist estimate of all aspects of life and activity of all classes, strata and groups of the population. Lenin asserts that no movement can endure without a stable organization of leaders to maintain continuity; that the wider the masses drawn into the struggle, the more urgent the need for such an organization; that the organization must consist of mostly of persons professionally engaged in revolutionary activities; that in an autocratic State, the more organizational membership is confined to professional revolutionaries, the more difficult it will be to destroy the organization; and that the greater will be the number of workers and members of other classes who will be able to join the movement and do active work in it. The Party should introduce proletarian class consciousness, the revolutionary socialist consciousness into the proletarian class. Lenin maintains that the strong bonds between Party as an organization and workers as organizational units must be secured through secrecy and mutual confidence.

Lenin in his *Two Tactics of Social Democracy in the Democratic Revolution* says that the Marxists are absolutely convinced of the bourgeois character of Russian revolution, which must provide rapid development of capitalism and of the working class, but not overstep the bounds of bourgeois social and economic relationships. But the political forms of the bourgeois system must be extended and stretched to the limit. Therefore, the task of Russian Social Democracy is establishment of revolutionary-democratic dictatorship of the proletariat and the peasantry, at this stage, according to Lenin. The revolutionary-democratic dictatorship, Lenin means to point out the victory of the revolutionary people—the proletariat and the peasantry over Tsarism. Here, Lenin gives emphasis on the peasant forces. Lenin in *The Agrarian Programme of Social-Democracy in the First Russian Revolution, 1905-07* firmly establishes the unique Bolshevik political strategy based on the potential of the peasant rebellion. The agrarian question is the basis of the bourgeois revolution in Russia. Peasants are disunited and their outlook is narrow. Therefore, peasant revolution is possible under the leadership of the proletariat, *i.e.,* the Social Democracy, whose tactics in Russian bourgeois revolution are determined by the task of supporting the fighting peasantry and not by the task of supporting the fighting peasantry. Lenin's strategy lies somewhat between Plekhanov's 'two-stage revolution' and Trotsky's 'permanent revolution' strategies and also lies on two features of Russian revolutionary tradition—a centralized Party of professional revolutionaries and peasantry as the material factor of the revolution.

This centralized Party of the professional revolutionaries is the political leader of the working class and the General Staff of the proletariat. Lenin says in *One Step Forward, Two Steps Backward* that the whole working class should act under the leadership of the Party and the whole class would be able to rise to the level of consciousness and activity of its advanced detachment, of its Social Democratic Party. No sensible Social-Democrat has ever yet doubted that under capitalism even the trade-union organizations are unable to embrace almost the whole of the working class. Formerly the Party was not a formally organized whole, but was only the sum total of separate groups, and therefore, no other relations expect those of ideological influence was possible between these groups. Presently, the Party is organized, which implies the establishment of authority, the transformation of the power of ideas into the power of authority, the subordination of lower Party bodies to the higher Party bodies. In *Left-wing Communism—An Infantile Disorder* Lenin says about iron discipline in Party organization with the support of the whole mass of the working class. The dictatorship of the proletariat is a stubborn struggle—bloody and bloodless, violent and peaceful, military and economic, educational and administrative—

against the forces and traditions of the old society. Without an iron disciplined Party tempered in the struggle and without a Party capable of enjoying the confidence of all, of watching and influencing the mood of the masses, it is impossible to conduct such a struggle successfully. Weakness in the iron discipline of the Party means aiding the bourgeoisie against the proletariat. In *The Terms of Admission into the Communist International* Lenin prescribes few qualifications for the Communist Party in performing its duty as organization of the Party in the more centralized manner, iron discipline bordering on military discipline prevails in it, Party centre—powerful and authoritative, wielding of wide powers and enjoying of universal confidence of the members of the Party.

According to Lenin, the Party is the vanguard of the proletariat, whose historical tasks are emancipation of their own from all ideological association with other classes, establishment of their own class-consciousness based on their own class position, and promotion and strengthening of their own independent class interests. Their basis of the leading role of waging a common struggle is their common position within the capitalist process of production. The spontaneous revolutionary self-education and self-consciousness of the masses should be supplemented by sound Party agitation and propaganda— which is enough to ensure the necessary development of ideological evolution of proletariat into its revolutionary practice. The Party is the centralized organization of the proletariat's most conscious elements. Party organization is the instrument of class struggle in a revolutionary period and which presupposes the activity of revolution. There is a difference between the proletariat and the Party. In the class struggle, the communist Party consisting of professional revolutionaries, brings to the fore the common interests of the proletariat and always and everywhere, the interest of the movement as a whole. Marx and Engels say in *Communist Manifesto* that the communists are the most advanced and resolute section of the working class, and they have over the great mass of the proletariat the advantage of clearly understanding the line and results of the proletarian movement. Lenin's idea of Party organization essentially contains two poles—selection of Party members on the basis of proletarian consciousness and total solidarity with and support for all oppressed and exploited within the capitalist society. See Figure 62 for dialectical unity between particular and universal as Lenin takes into account.

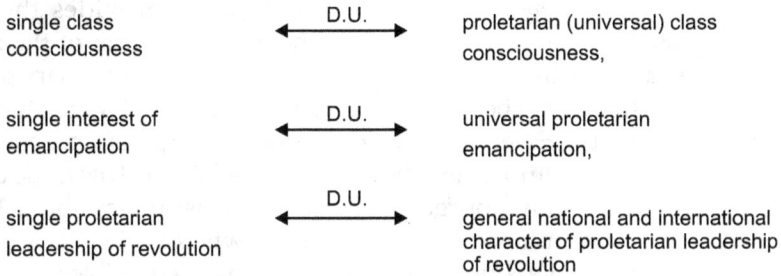

single class consciousness	←— D.U. —→	proletarian (universal) class consciousness,
single interest of emancipation	←— D.U. —→	universal proletarian emancipation,
single proletarian leadership of revolution	←— D.U. —→	general national and international character of proletarian leadership of revolution

Figure 62

Here, D.U. means dialectical unity. Lenin's organization theory is a double brake with mechanical fatalism—break with the concept of the proletarian class consciousness as a mechanical product of its class situation and break with the idea that revolution is the mechanical working out of fatalistically explosive economic forces (Lukacs, 1977). The Party, according to Lenin, prepares the revolution on the one hand, accelerating the matured revolutionary tendencies by action and on the other hand, preparing the proletariat for ideological, tactical and organizational tasks, *i.e.* Party acts as producer and product, pre-condition and result of revolutionary mass movement, which is in contraposition of Kautsky's and Luxemburg's views of Party that Party organization is the pre-condition of revolutionary action and Party organization is the product of revolutionary mass movement. Kautsky's and Luxemburg's study of Party organization and revolutionary mass movement is undialectical, but Lenin makes a dialectical unity between producer and product, precondition and result.

The Party's roles are that it foresees the trajectory of objective economic conditions of revolution, forecasts the appropriate action and prepares the proletarian masses tactically, materially, ideologically and organizationally. Party must learn through mass action, through class struggle. In revolutionary mass movement it makes adjustment between theory and practice, which becomes impossible without strict Party discipline. Without possible adjustment, the Party lags behind the masses, loses contact with the masses instead of leading. The Party must unite the spontaneous discoveries of the masses in class instinct with the totality of revolution and bring the masses into consciousness (Lukacs, 1977). In terms of organization, hierarchy and specialization of activity Leinin puts forward the Weberian style, which socialism needs to apply, *i.e.,* rationality, efficiency, specialization, continuity, operationalization, speed, precision, superordination-subordination relationships etc.

Organization is a part of Lenin's revolutionary praxis. That is, Lenin in his *State and Revolution* says that capitalism provides the pre-conditions that enable to take part in the administration of the State. However, as according to Lenin, organization is the revolutionary praxis, therefore, it should not be based on mere economism and trade unionism and spontaneity. Essentially, trade union struggle is an economic struggle geared for improving the conditions of labour. This trade union struggle is essentially bourgeois and not socialist (Hammond, 1957). For Lenin, trade union struggle is narrow, whereas the Party as the organization of professional revolutionaries makes possible for greater number of people from the working class and from other social classes and to join movement and perform active work in it—which he says in his work *What is to be Done?* Therefore, in his *The Reorganization of the Party* he prescribes widening of Party membership and says that the working class is instinctively and spontaneously social-democratic and more than ten years of work put in by social democracy the working class has done a great deal to transform this spontaneity into consciousness. Lenin says that the history of all countries shows that the working class by their effort can develop only trade-union consciousness, which is spontaneous. Here lies the importance of Party organization, which is able to transform trade union consciousness to socialist consciousness, economic consciousness to political consciousness.

Further, with regard to the decision-making in the Party organization, Lenin puts forward his theory of democratic centralism, where Lenin stresses the need for centralized control of the Party. However, Lenin is not in favour of broad democracy, which he designates as a useless and harmless toy, useless or unuseful as no revolutionary organization can use broad democracy in their practice and harmful because (1) that this practice of board democracy will facilitate the work of police in carrying out large-scale raids, (2) that it will divert the thoughts of the workers from serious and imperative tasks of becoming professional revolutionaries, and (3) that it will perpetuate the prevailing amateurism. Then, what Lenin means by democratic centralism. By 'democratic' Lenin seems to realize that (1) decisions should be resolved and reached according to the majority vote of the central committee of the Party, (2) all Party members should have the right to participate in the general Party policy making, (3) Party Congresses should be supreme over policy, (4) there should be periodic elections in the Party, (5) there should be collectivist membership, (6) there should be unity over the goals of revolutionary socialism. By 'centralism' Lenin means that after taking general decision generally agreed on all should be done centrally—(1) day-to-day dealings of the

Party should be decided centrally, (2) all information are gathered centrally, (3) Party leadership is located at the central level, (4) decision at the central bodies are binding on the local bodies. Therefore, democratic centralism is a synthesis between democracy and central control, participation and leadership. At the organizational level, Lenin stresses the importance of command, co-ordination and control. According to Lenin, the 'Party is in a position in which the strictest centralization and the most stringent discipline are absolute necessities. All decisions of higher headquarters are absolutely binding for the lower. Every decision must first of all be executed, and only after that an appeal to the corresponding Party organ is permissible. In this sense, outright military discipline is indispensable in the Party at the present time.' (Cited in Meyer, 1957: 99).

The organizational principle of revolutionary social democracy strives to proceed from the top downward, and upholds an extension of the rights and powers of the centre in relation to the parts. Lenin says that the dictatorship of the working class is being implemented by the Bolshevik Party and class dictatorship is exercised under the leadership of the Party. The increasing identification between the Party and the State apparatus together with the undivided domination exercised by the Party in the political and social affairs of the country is true to the extent possible, whose structure of power is much more monolithic. Then, what is the relationship between the Party and the Soviets? E.H. Carr (1966) pointing out the resolution of 8th Party Congress of 1919 says that the Party must win for itself undivided mastery over Soviets, and practical control over their work, though with reservation the Party has to lead the activity of the Soviets, but not replace them. According to Lenin, there is a close relationship between dictatorship of the proletariat, Soviets and dictatorship of the Party like that of dictatorship is exercised by the proletariat $\leftrightarrow$ dictatorship of the proletariat is organized into Soviets $\leftrightarrow$ Soviets are led by the Party $\leftrightarrow$ Party exercises the dictatorship of the proletariat $\leftrightarrow$ dictatorship of the proletariat is essentially the dictatorship of the vanguard Party. But this does not mean that Party is a dictatorship. Soviets are the direct expression of the dictatorship of the proletariat and every important political and organizational issue concerning the Soviets are decided by the Soviets themselves after the guiding directions from the Party. During the revolutionary period, Lenin opted for a narrow Party as opposed to a open Party and monopoly of the Party organization. Both Lenin and Stalin agreed that the Party would take the leading role and the Party and the dictatorship of the proletariat are closely related. The Party and not the Soviets would make the revolution. Though in the

11th Congress of 1922, Lenin suggested primacy to the Party than that of the Soviets, he compares the State with the Party.

Though Lenin's views on the Party have widely been acclaimed by the Marxists, he has been criticized by many on the grounds that he argues for the monopoly power of the Party and does not provide due importance to the revolutionary potential and creativity of the working class. They argue that the Party may guide the working class from behind and must not lead them on the ground that the working class must emancipate themselves with the help of their own. Centralization of power in the Party organization is a serious distortion of Marxism. These critics are against the narrow Party organization and opt for widescale inclusion of socialist trade unionist and greater power for local Party organizations opposing Party of activists and cadres aiming at assembling only class conscious proletarian vanguard. They are opposed to the orthodoxy of Russian Marxism. In Russia today, the connection between leader, Party, class and masses as well as the attitude of the dictatorship of the proletariat and its Party to the trade unions, are concretely as follows—the dictatorship of the proletariat is exercised by the proletariat organized in the Soviets, the proletariat is guided by the Communist Party of Bolsheviks. No important political or organizational question is decided by any State institution in our republic without the guidance of the Party's Central Committee. Here, few basic characteristic features of Menshevikism, Trotskism, Luxemburgism and Leninism may be stated as such:

Basic features

Sl. No.	Menshevikism	Sl. No.	Leninism
1.	Emancipation of the working class must be conquered by the working class themselves	1.	Social progress through Social Democratic Revolution is directed by the dictatorship of the Party organization
2.	The working class won their fight against the oppressor through their revolutionary potential and creativity	2.	There should be no middle or third ideology between bourgeois ideology and socialist ideology
3.	Centralized leadership is a distortion of Marxism.	3.	Social revolution cannot be made through spontaneous working class movement, is nothing but trade unionism

Sl. No.	Menshevikism	Sl. No.	Leninism
4.	Along with the revolutionary professionals the Party should include socialist trade unionists and Party sympathizers	4.	Spontaneity and trade unionism lead to subordination to bourgeois ideology
	Trotskyism	5.	Organization should be composed of professional revolutionaries
1.	For revolutionary transformation of society there is the need for mass working class consciousness	6.	Mass organization and Party organization should be separated
2.	The Party organization should be opened with maximum participation of workers	7.	The guiding principle in the Party organization should be democratic centralism.
3.	Party organization should not substitute itself for the Party and should not say final about the proletariat	8.	In the uninterrupted revolution from bourgeois democratic revolution to socialist revolution and in the revolutionary democratic dictatorship of the proletariat and the peasantry, the leading role goes to the proletariat
4.	It is possible for the workers to come to power in an economically backward country sooner than in an advanced country		*Luxemburgism*
		1.	Social progress can be made through spontaneous mass upsurge, strike and social revolution
5.	Nationalization cannot be equated with socialism—there is both socialization of the productive forces and bourgeois norm of distribution	2.	There exists an indissoluble tie between social reform and revolution
6.	Social progress can be made through revolution, mass working class consciousness and spontaneity	3.	In considering social progress Bernstein considers only means, *i.e.*, social reform and not end, *i.e.* revolution

Sl. No.	Trotskyism	Sl. No.	Luxemburgism
7.	Self-creativity of the workers is the prime actor in the revolutionary process, dictatorship over the Party and dictatorship over the proletariat*	4.	In case of revolution there exists two things — rising class consciousness and organization of the proletariat as a class
		5.	Spontaneous uprising of the working class—mass strike— is essential for revolutionary social progress
	*Trotsky's position in 1905: 'The Russian proletariat was an independent, vital revolutionary force, both in the sense of its economic-based political strength as well as that of its conscientiousness, idealism and devotion to socialist goals.' (Knei-Paz: 171). By 1917 he changed the theoretical line and accepted the necessity of 'revolutionary elite'—the 'vanguard', the 'leader', the 'very idea of the Party' (Knei-Paz: 228).	6.	In *Mass Strike, Party and Trade Unions* Luxemburg bridges the gap between economic reform of trade unions and political action
		7.	Mass strike is not an isolated action, where economic and political elements are inseparable, when revolution creates conditions and enable the fusion of economic and political elements
		8.	Lenin blindly subordinates all Party organs to the centre and restricts revolutionary initiative of the masses.

It is said that Trotskyism is not Leninism as such, it is para-Leninism. In opposition to Lenin's emphasis on discontinuity that the elements of the past and future in the actual historical circumstances, which he points out in *Two Tactics*, cross each other, where these historical circumstances can be logically and historically distinguished into major stages of development—development of bourgeois revolution and development of socialist revolution, when it is essential to make a distinction between them, Trotsky emphasizes on continuity and non-stop progress in his *Permanent Revolution* and *Results and Prospects*. He believes that the living historical process always makes leaps over the isolated stages, which derive from the theoretical breakdown into its component parts of the process of development in its entirety. In order to distinguish between the principal contradiction and secondary contradictions, to determine class alliances required by the tasks of stages it is essential to distinguish historical circumstances into stages, according to Lenin. Trotsky emphasizes on continuity and unity of the world market. In *Results and Prospects* Trotsky says that in relatively backward countries, it becomes impossible to make the construction of socialism impossible, due to the pressure of cheap commodities, produced by the capitalist countries. Capitalism has converted the whole world into a single economic and political organism binding all countries together with its mode of production and commerce. Thus, in revolutionary activities, Trotsky neglects the importance of national peculiarities, the specific conditions of the Russian Revolution and also of class struggle in all countries. He exaggerates the role of external influences and says that the defeats of Communist parties between the two wars are the results of the pernicious influence of Stalin and the Third International. He sees that all Communist parties in the world as mere puppets, imposition of Stalinist line on all Communist parties, and safeguarding the existence of Soviets and interests of the Soviet bureaucracy. He does not comprehend Marxist dialectic—as Mao-Tse-Tung in 'On Contradiction' says that the contradiction within a thing is the fundamental cause of its development. The interactions and interrelations with other things are secondary causes. External causes are the conditions of change and internal causes are the bases of change. Through the internal causes external causes become operative and take a meaningful recourse. For example, the defeat of the proletariat by the bourgeoisie in China in 1927 is the result of opportunism within the Chinese proletariat. For this incomprehension of Marxist dialectic by Trotsky, he ignores the law of uneven development that monopoly capitalists and imperialist powers develop at an unequal rate, economic basis and ideological and political superstructures also evolve at an unequal rate. Revolution occurs when principal contradiction explodes. Trotsky emphasizes revolution throughout Europe, which is a unique and continuous process unlike the Leninist theory of revolution that revolution in one country is a typical case and revolution in other countries is a rare exception. In his evaluation on Trotsky, Kostas Mavrakis (1976) says:

> The idea Trotsky had of the relation between theory and practice was equally undialectical. For him, theory forecasts practice and practice applies theory. Lenin, on the contrary, constantly listened to the masses. According to him, the Party must always be ready to carryout the task which the mass movement itself has put on the order of the day. Only the practice of

the masses makes it possible to give a concrete content to the general directives which guide the vanguard. Trotsky criticized Lenin's formula of 'the democratic dictatorship of the proletariat and the peasantry' for being algebraic; he, on the contrary, wanted only arithmetic.... Lenin's formula that 'theory is a guide to action' was taken literally by Trotsky, who ignored the fundamental mediation which Lenin never forgot, namely, 'the concrete analysis of the concrete situation'.... Trotsky did not understand the immense importance of Marx's indications on the necessity of combining proletarian revolution with peasant war even in a country as industrialized as Germany. After belatedly rallying to Lenin, he continued to underestimate the peasantry's revolutionary potential, to refuse to define the Party's political line in terms of the necessary alliance with it, and to formulate slogans appropriate to its wide mobilization. (Mavrakis, 1976: 180-181).

Then, what about revolutionary strategy and tactics in Lenin's thought? Lenin's first major work is *The Development of Capitalism in Russia* (1899), where he analyzes the formation of capitalism in terms of Marxist methods of analysis—the growth of trade in Russia, development of internal market, growth of wage labour and differentiation of the peasantry. Here, analyses are based on reciprocal interaction between economics and politics and dialectical and historical materialism. Capitalist development makes positive contribution to the development of productive forces of social labour and liberates labour mainly from bonded labour based on personal bondage, and to the growth of social democracy for a socialist system of society, which culminates against the politico-economic background of political supremacy of Tsarist autocracy and the development of capitalism and ideological background of the populist form of socialism, petty-bourgeois socialism in contrast with proletarian socialism. The Populists' or Narodniks' form of socialism may graphically be presented in Figure 63, which Lenin opposes. For that Lenin has been criticized by the Marxists that he fails to understand the dynamics of the peasant commune (Corrigan, 1978).

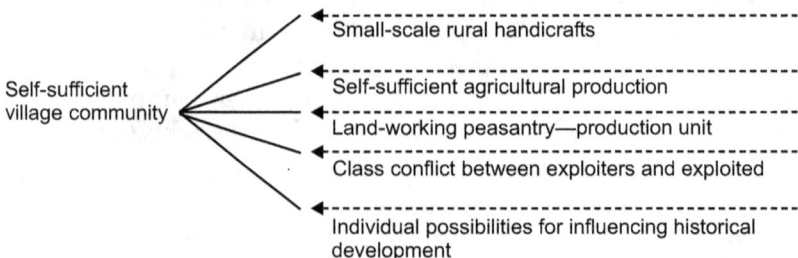

Self-sufficient village community

- Small-scale rural handicrafts
- Self-sufficient agricultural production
- Land-working peasantry—production unit
- Class conflict between exploiters and exploited
- Individual possibilities for influencing historical development

Figure 63

Lenin finds the positive contribution of development of Russian capitalism—large-scale production system, dependent agricultural production, proletarianization of the peasantry, class conflict between the capitalists and the proletariat, huge class of allotment-holding wage-workers. To Lenin, consolidation, promotion and development of village community are not socialist at all, and development of socialism needs organized proletarian struggle, where the Party would act as the vanguard of the proletariat. Lenin's opposing viewpoints with regard to agrarian socialism or self-sufficient, village community of the populists may graphically be presented below. See Figure 64.

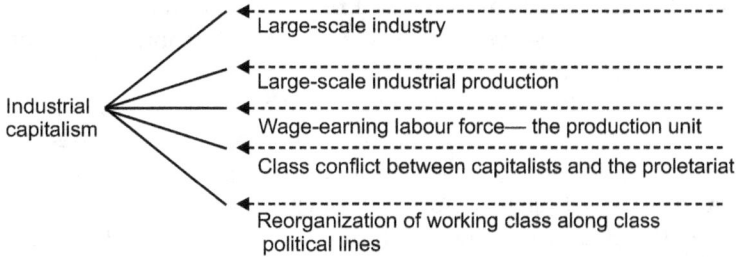

Industrial capitalism

Large-scale industry

Large-scale industrial production

Wage-earning labour force— the production unit

Class conflict between capitalists and the proletariat

Reorganization of working class along class political lines

Figure 64

However, in spite of differences between Populism and Leninism, there are similarities between the two on few points—intellectuals educate the masses and the working class, organization of mass uprisings and revolutionaries operating through the centrally organized Party, peculiarity of the conditions of Russian socialism, and the importance of the peasants in revolutionary struggle, which essentially intersect with each other. While intersecting these similar points of these two trends of Populism and Leninism form a rectangle of the revolutionary situation. Therefore, both the revolutionaries tend to have their faiths in the ideological motivation of the masses and the working class, in the organization of mass uprisings through the Party organization, in peculiar objective conditions of Russia and in the importance of the peasant forces for the achievement of socialism. The rectangle is like Figure 65. Lenin finds that the progression to capitalism is essential for the building of socialism, where the role of the peasants is important as a social and political factor. Marx in *Eighteenth Brumaire* does not regard the peasantry as an important social and political factor and treats the peasantry as self-sufficient, produces major part of its consumption directly, and thus acquires the means of life through exchange with Nature than in intercourse with society. However, Marx also finds in the *Eighteenth Brumaire* that (1) peasants are savagely exploited by the bourgeoisie, (2) the interests of the peasantry are placed in opposition to the bourgeois interests, (3) the interests of the peasantry are in accord with the interests of the urban proletariat, (4) the task of the urban proletariat is to overthrow the bourgeois order, (5) therefore, the peasants find their natural ally and leader in the urban proletariat.

Theodor Shanin (1971) shows that the peasantry consists of small-scale agricultural producers with the help of simple equipment and the labour of their families produce mainly for their own consumption and for the fulfilment of their obligations to the holders of political and economic power. Therefore, in economic terms peasants form a class. On the basis of common economic interests, the peasants form alliance with the urban proletariat. Engels differentiates peasants into four separate groups—prosperous group or peasant, small peasant, middle peasant and agricultural labourer, the most numerous class in the countryside like that of the industrial worker. Following Engels, Lenin differentiates the peasantry into four groups—the landed gentry, the petty-bourgeoisie, the poor subsistence peasants and the rural proletariat. According to Lenin, in bourgeois revolution the working class and the peasantry share like-minded short-term political goals. In *Petty-Bourgeois and Proletarian Socialism* Lenin says that the task of Russian social democracy would be to help the peasants energetically and help them finally and completely to overthrow the rule of officials and landlords. In *The Tasks of the Russian Social-Democrats*, he says that it would concentrate its activities on the industrial proletariat, who are most susceptible to social democratic ideas, most developed intellectually and politically, and most important by virtue of their number and concentration in the country's large political centres, and in *Two Tactics* he prescribes the leading role to the proletariat saying that the proletariat must carry the democratic revolution to completion, allying itself to the mass of the peasantry in order to crush the autocracy's resistance by force and paralyze the inability of the bourgeoisie. This class, *i.e.*, the proletarian class must accomplish the socialist revolution, allying to itself the mass of the semi-proletarian elements of the population so as to crush the bourgeoisie's resistance by force and paralyze the instability of the peasantry and the petty-bourgeoisie. That the working class should have to lead the bourgeois revolution, is absolutely necessary for the interests of the proletariat. The activity of the working class will set the bourgeoisie in motion to make the bourgeois revolution. Further, in his *Petty-Bourgeois and Proletarian Socialism* he says that the struggle against the officials and landlords can and must be waged together with all the peasants and even with the well-to-do and middle peasants. On the other hand, the struggle for socialism is waged against the bourgeoisie and therefore against the well-to-do peasants, which can only be waged in a reliable manner together with the rural proletariat. In *Agrarian Programme* Lenin says that in bourgeois revolution, the class of small producers, including the class of small farmers in its struggle against the bourgeoisie is a reactionary class, and therefore trying to save the peasantry by protecting small-scale farming and small-holdings from the onslaught of capitalism, would be a useless retarding of social development—it would mean deceiving the peasantry with illusions of the possibility of prosperity even under capitalism. It would mean disuniting the labouring classes and creating a privileged position for the minority at the expense of the majority. In *Two Tactics*, Lenin says that Russian revolution though bourgeois-democratic in character would be set in motion by the proletariat, the only class capable of waging a determined struggle for complete liberty and for the republic. According to Lenin,

i. .... the proletariat is the leader of entire people or the population
ii. .... the proletariat wins over the peasantry,
iii. .... the proletariat-peasantry alliance would establish bourgeois-democratic dictatorship of the proletariat and the peasantry,
iv. .... bourgeois-democratic dictatorship of the proletariat and the peasantry + armed forces = dictatorship of the proletariat,
v. .... the new authority = dictatorship of the proletariat = (dictatorship of the overwhelming majority + confidence of the vast masses + all masses in the task of government).

In this pamphlet Lenin categorically puts the subjective and objective conditions of revolution and two-sage theory of revolution. To him, the degree of economic development of Russia (an objective condition) and the degree of class consciousness and organization of the broad masses of the proletariat (a subjective condition inseparably connected with the objective) make the immediate complete emancipation of the working class impossible. Only the most ignorant people can ignore the bourgeois nature of the democratic revolution which is now taking place. A socialist revolution is out of question unless the masses become class conscious, organized, trained and educated in open class struggle against the entire bourgeoisie. Whoever wants to arrive at socialism by a different road, other than that of political democracy, will arrive at absurd and reactionary conclusions both in economic and political senses. Marxists are now convinced of the bourgeois character of the Russian revolution—it means that the democratic changes in the political system, and the social and economic changes that have become indispensable for Russians,—do not in themselves imply the undermining of capitalism. The undermining of bourgeois domination, on the contrary, will for the first time really clear the ground for a widespread and rapid development of capitalism and for the bourgeoisie to rule as a class. Only the proletariat can be a consistent fighter for democracy. It may become a victorious fighter for democracy only if the peasant masses join its revolutionary struggle. If the proletariat is not strong enough for this, the bourgeoisie will be at the head of the democratic revolution and will impart to it an inconsistent and self-seeking nature. Nothing short of a revolutionary-democratic dictatorship of the proletariat and the peasantry can prevent this. A revolutionary-democratic dictatorship of the proletariat and the peasantry is unquestionably only a transient, provisional aim of the Socialists, but to ignore this aim in the period of a democratic revolution would be plainly reactionary. The proletariat fights in the front ranks for a republic and contemptuously rejects the silly and unworthy advice to take care not to frighten away the bourgeoisie. The peasantry includes a great number of semi-proletarian as well as petty-bourgeois elements. This causes it also to be unable and compels the proletariat to unite in a strictly class Party. But the instability of the peasants differs radically from the instability of the bourgeoisie, for at the present time, the peasantry is interested, not so much in the absolute preservation of private property, as in the confiscation of the landed estates, one of the principal forms of private property. Though this does not cause the peasantry to become socialist or cease to be petty-bourgeois, the peasantry is yet capable of becoming a whole hearted and most radical adherent of the democratic revolution. The peasantry will inevitably become so if only the progress of revolutionary events is not interrupted too soon by the treachery of the bourgeois and the defeat of the proletariat. Subject to this condition, the peasantry will inevitably become a bulwark of the revolution and the republic, for only a completely a victorious revolution can give the peasantry everything in the sphere of agrarian reforms that the peasants desire and dream about.

Lenin admitted that the classical Marxist revolutionary strategy is inadequate for the solution of an essential problem—the transition from bourgeois to socialist revolution. Trotsky finds this problem through his idea of permanent revolution: Russian bourgeois class is incapable of leading bourgeois revolution in Russia; rather the working class should lead and carry through the bourgeois revolution to socialist revolution, and if bourgeois revolution is once started by the working class, would pass over to the socialist stage. The proletariat once in power cannot keep within limits of bourgeois democracy. It must adopt the tactics of permanent revolution: destruction of the barrier between the minimum and maximum programme of Social Democracy, more and more radical social reforms, and direct and immediate support of revolution in Western Europe (Trotsky, 1962). As the revolution has come too late to be a bourgeois-democratic revolution of the approved Marxist type, the proletariat will, therefore, have to carry out that which the bourgeoisie can not perform. A bourgeois-democratic revolution made by the proletariat will tend to become a proletarian revolution, when the political power will inevitably gravitate to the class which has played the greatest part in promoting it. The peasantry is incapable of rendering much assistance, and the success of the revolution will depend largely upon the support of the proletarians in other countries. The criticism of the Mensheviks may be pointed out here—they reject the two revolutions theory and say that Marx teaches us that the bourgeois democratic revolution must take place first, and then there will be a proletarian revolution. These two stages of revolution are different and needs a significant interval between the two, according to Plekhanov.

Figure 65

Trotsky says that according to Lenin, a bourgeois-democratic revolution should necessarily be undertaken under the hegemony of the proletariat, makes no sense, and it makes no sense when the two revolutions, bourgeois democratic revolution and socialist revolution are telescoped into one another. However, both Lenin and Trotsky both do not make it clear—how the proletariat fulfils the role assigned to it. Trotsky realizes the significance of the development of capitalism in Russia, the Russian Revolution and the proletarian class consciousness. To him,

  i. development of capitalism in Russia led to the most advanced industrial enterprises,
 ii. the proletariat can take power earlier than in countries where capitalism is advanced, and
iii. Russian Revolution produces conditions, when power passes into the hands of the proletariat before the politicians of bourgeois liberalism.

According to Lenin, revolution takes place within the revolutionary situation and conditions of populism depending upon the considerations of factors like ideological motivation by intellectuals, organization of mass uprisings through party organization, objective conditions of Russia and the role of peasants. See Figure 65. The proletariat leads the revolution due to their rapid growth, concentration, relative homogeneity and highly class consciousness. According to Trotsky, power passes into the hands of the proletariat or the working class and that depends directly upon relations in the class struggle, upon the international situation, and upon a number of subjective factors like the traditions, the initiative and the readiness to fight condition of the workers, but not directly depends upon the level attained by the productive forces. Further, to imagine that the dictatorship of the proletariat is in some way automatically dependent on the technical development and resources of a country, is a prejudice of economic materialism simplified to absurdity. For widening the foundations of revolution, the working class seeks allies among the peasantry, although the working class is the dominant and leading partner and the hegemony goes to the same working class. Whereas Lenin puts forward the association of the peasantry and the working class as equal partners in the revolutionary-democratic dictatorship, Trotsky advocates that the proletariat should draw the peasantry in its wake. Support of the peasantry is not a prerequisite for revolutionary action. The peasantry would follow the offensive movement of the proletariat when they are without a political organization of their own. He rejects Lenin's theory of 'dictatorship of the proletariat and the peasantry' and considers the peasantry to be a bourgeois force, cannot be relied on by the proletariat in the struggle for socialism. In *Permanent Revolution* Trotsky says that the dictatorship of the proletariat appears not after the completion of the democratic revolution, precisely because there is no other power and no other way to solve the tasks of the agrarian revolution. This opens up the prospect of a democratic revolution growing over into the socialist revolution. How the 'uninterrupted revolution' occurs? See Figure 66.

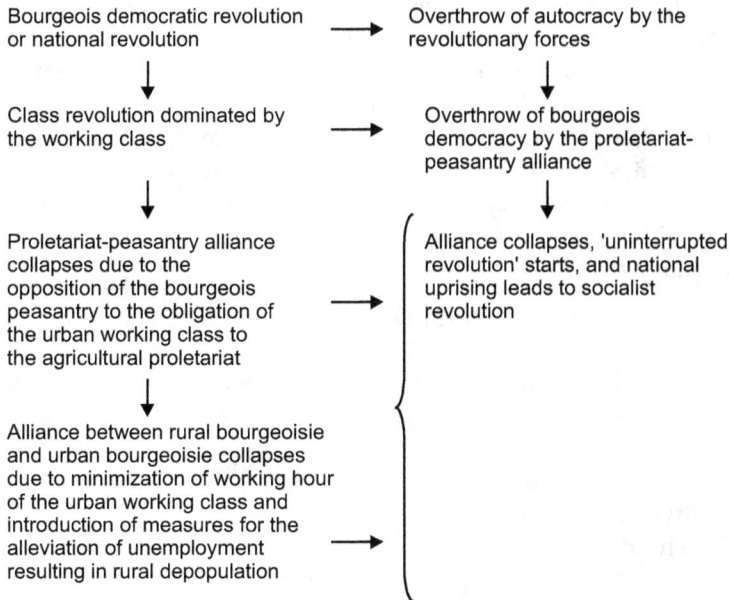

Bourgeois democratic revolution or national revolution → Overthrow of autocracy by the revolutionary forces

Class revolution dominated by the working class → Overthrow of bourgeois democracy by the proletariat-peasantry alliance

Proletariat-peasantry alliance collapses due to the opposition of the bourgeois peasantry to the obligation of the urban working class to the agricultural proletariat → Alliance collapses, 'uninterrupted revolution' starts, and national uprising leads to socialist revolution

Alliance between rural bourgeoisie and urban bourgeoisie collapses due to minimization of working hour of the urban working class and introduction of measures for the alleviation of unemployment resulting in rural depopulation →

Figure 66

Lenin says that Trotsky's major mistake is that he ignores the bourgeois character of the revolution and has no clear conception of the transition from this revolution to socialist revolution. Lenin disagrees with the merging of bourgeois and socialist revolutions and sees the two as distinct. But Lenin sees these stages running into each other. Lenin says that we stand for uninterrupted revolution, for the immediate extension of the revolution to its second stage, *i.e.*, the socialist stage. Social democracy can proceed from the democratic revolution, only in accordance with the strength of the class conscious, and organized proletariat. That the revolution would be uninterrupted means that after bourgeois-democratic revolution, socialist revolution would continue to be uninterrupted. Trotsky is different from Lenin on the ground that the formal bourgeois-democratic stage can be avoided. In *On the Two Lines in the Revolution* Lenin says that Trotsky learns the lesson from the Bolsheviks' call for a decisive proletarian struggle, and for the conquest of political power, by the proletariat and from the Mensheviks, their call for the repudiation of the peasantry's role. The task of the Party is to draw the peasants into the revolutionary activity to overthrow the Tsarist autocracy, and then to aid the prosperous peasants for the completion of socialist revolution in association with the proletarians of Europe. In *Social Democracy and the Provincial Revolutionary Government* Lenin, like Trotsky, emphasizes the international recognition to socialist revolution, which grows from the bourgeois revolution earlier, bears a corollary with Trotsky's permanent revolution. Lenin provides an important role to the peasantry like the Populists and unlike Trotsky. He says that the more complete the victory of the peasantry, the sooner will the proletariat stand out as a distinct class, and the more clearly will it put forward its purely socialist tasks and aims. Therefore, here few points may be made about Leninist revolutionary strategy in 1917—

1. Russia enters the period of transition to socialism after the fall Tsarist autocracy.
2. Socialism cannot be achieved in Russia with a single stroke and without transitional measures—abolition of autocracy and advancement towards socialism, preparing the way for the second stage of revolutionary victory—the distinction between two stages of revolution is blurred.
3. The decisive steps are concrete steps for the overthrow of capitalism and keeping up the dynamite of revolution, which according to Lenin, may be stated as such—nationalization of syndicates or monopoly houses as well as banks and insurance companies; publication of all fabulous profits which the capitalists are making for war supplies; abolition of commercial secrecy; introduction of universal labour service; control of the national economy: control, supervision, accounting, regulation by the State, introduction of a proper distribution of labour-power in the production and distribution of goods; nationalization of all lands in the country.
4. The establishment of the workers' government would emerge from the seizure of power during the second phase of the revolution emphasizing the primacy of the proletariat or the proletarian forces in relation to the peasant movement and making it clear that the revolutionary democratic classes would be headed by the revolutionary proletariat.
5. Political power passes into the hands of the proletariat in the

revolutionary struggle, where the aim is to establish socialism through the dictatorship of the proletariat and poor peasants.

6. State power exclusively and wholly belongs to the Soviets in a really democratic workers' and peasants' republic. Parliamentary representative institutions will gradually be replaced by Soviets of people's representatives.

Marcel Liebman in his work *Leninism under Lenin* says categorically—

> The concept of offensive internalism, the recognition of proletarian hegemony over the peasantry, and, along with this, the will to begin the struggle for socialism immediately, all marked a decisive rapprochement between Trotsky's theories of permanent revolution and Lenin's strategy of 1917. The Party did not fail to perceive this. If we are to believe Trotsky, 'in the leading group of the Party... they accused Lenin of Trotskyism during the month of April. Kamener did this openly and with much insistence.' When Trotsky had joined the Leninist organization he found an opportunity to develop his views in the Party press, and so *Pravda* of September 7th, 1917, carried an article ending with these words: 'A permanent revolution versus permanent slaughter: that is the struggle, in which the stake is the future of man.' According to Andre Stawar, who is hardly to be suspected of indulgence towards Trotskyism, 'Trotsky became within few months the most authoritative of the leaders, after Lenin, casting into the shade the experienced members of the Party's general staff; his theory of permanent revolution... came to occupy for a certain period the place of honour in the Party's ideology.' Lenin was not the only one to fall under Trotsky's influence, and, more especially, to apply Trotsky's views on revolutionary strategy. Already before 1917, during the first years of the war, men like Bukharin and Radek had not concealed their sympathy for the theory of permanent revolution. The events of 1917 drew into the wake of this theory an ever larger number of followers, conscious or otherwise, who constituted the Party's Leftwing and set decisive imprint upon its policy. (Liebman, 1975: 189).

Stalin in his work in *Foundations of Leninism* points out Lenin's account of various stages of revolution and consequent revolutionary strategies at various stages of revolution in history. Lenin says not only about two stages of revolution, but also about the third stage after 1917. Stalin differentiates Lenin's revolution into three historical periods— from 1903 to February, 1917, from February, 1917 to October, 1917, and after October, 1917. I can compile the strategies of revolution following Stalin's account of Leninism in the following manner:

Leninist strategies of revolution

Parameters	Bourgeois-democratic revolution	Socialist revolution (national level)	Socialist revolution (international level)
Objective	Overthrowal and demolition of Tsarist autocracy and medieval serfdom, oppression and tyranny, in other words, medievalism	Overthrowal of imperialism in Russia and withdrawal of Russian involvement in the imperialist war	Defeat of imperialism and imperialist war in all countries and in Russia with the help of the proletarian class and with the consolidation of the dictatorship of the proletariat — world revolution
Force of the revolution of primary in character	The proletarian class	The proletarian class	Dictatorship of the proletariat in one country plus revolutionary upsurge of the proletariat in all countries plus revolutionary movement of the proletariat in all countries
Reservation of revolutionary force with immediate effect for revolutionary action	The class of peasantry	The class of poor peasantry plus the proletariat of the neighbouring countries with probable reservation	The class of semi-proletariat plus the class of small-peasant masses in developed countries and liberation movement in colonies and dependent countries
Direction of the main blow of the revolution	Isolation of the liberal-monarchist bourgeoisie—liquidation of revolution by a compromise with Tsarism and winning over the peasantry are the primary aims of the liberal-monarchist bourgeoisie	Isolation of the petty-bourgeois democrats—liquidation of revolution by a compromise with imperialism and winning over the poor peasants are the primary aims of petty-bourgeois democrats	Isolation of the supporters of the policy of compromise with imperialism—isolation of the petty-bourgeois democrats and parties of the Second International.
Plan for the disposition of the reactionary forces	Alliance between the proletariat and the peasantry	Alliance between the proletariat and the poor peasantry	Alliance between revolutionary proletariat and the fighters of liberation movement in colonies and dependent countries—*i.e.*, an alliance between proletarian movement and liberation movement
The process of revolution	Proletarian-peasantry alliance→bourgeois democratic revolution→use of force to crush the resistance of autocracy and paralyze the instability of the bourgeoisie	Proletarian-peasantry alliance →socialist revolution→use of force to crush the resistance of the bourgeoisie and paralyze the instability of the peasantry and the petty-bourgeoisie	Proletariat—liberation fighters in colonies and dependent countries—international working class movement→use of force to crush the resistance of the petty-bourgeois democrats and parties of the Second International

Source: Compiled and edited with the help of Stalin, J.V., *Foundations of Leninism*

Strategy deals with the forces of revolution and the reserves of the revolutionary action and the strategy changes with the requirements of the various stages of revolution and with the development of revolutionary situation at various stages of revolution—bourgeois socialist revolution, national socialist revolution and international socialist movement or international working class movement. However, basically the strategy does not change. Tactics are parts of strategy. Strategy is a long-term process and tactics are short-term combinations of strategy which change according to the ebb and flow of the movement. Tactics are the determination of the line of conduct of proletariat in the revolutionary process, *i.e.*, replacement of the old forms of struggle and organization by the new ones, replacement of the old slogans by the new ones, and replacement of the old combinations by the new one. For example, the tactics during the bourgeois-democratic revolution changed several times *i.e.*, from the tactic of offence during 1903-05, such as political strikes, political demonstrations, boycott of Duma, revolutionary upsurge and revolutionary fighting slogans as forms of struggle to the tactic of retreat during the period of 1907-12, such as participation in the Russian Duma instead of boycott, opposition within the Duma instead of activities outside the Duma, partial economic strikes instead of full political strikes etc. On the whole, in the strategic leadership position, the direct reserves include the peasantry and the intermediate sections of the population, the proletarian class in the neighbouring countries, the revolutionary movements in the colonies and dependent countries, the positive results from the dictatorship of the proletariat and the indirect reserves include contradictions and conflicts among the non-proletarian classes and bourgeois States which the strategic leadership directly and indirectly uses and utilizes. Proper use of reserves by the strategic leadership is the important condition for success of the socialist revolution. Lenin advices in *Advice of an Onlooker* that never play with insurrection, concentrate a great superiority of forces at the decisive point and at the decisive moment, act with great determination and take offensive without fail when insurrection once begins, seize the moment when the enemy is scattered, and strive for daily success. In *Left-wing Commission—An Infantile Disorder* Lenin sets few conditions for matured stage of revolution. These are when all the class forces hostile to us have become sufficiently entangled and weakened in the struggle, when all the intermediate petty-bourgeois elements vacillating in character and distinct from the bourgeoisie have sufficiently exposed and disgraced themselves through their political bankruptcy, and when the proletariat as mass sentiment in favour of supporting the most determined revolutionary action against the bourgeoisie, has risen and begun vigorously to grow. When the revolution becomes ripe and is matured, then the victory of the revolutionaries is assured. Not only the concentration of the main forces of revolution and the decisive blow towards the enemy at the appropriate moment are necessary for revolutionary success, but timely retreat from the attack against the enemy is inevitable in order to gain time, disrupt the enemy, accumulate the forces for making an offensive against the enemy later on, and escape the possible blow against the vanguard.

Lenin categorically says in *Left-wing Communism—An Infantile Disorder* about the retreat tactic in the revolutionary struggle for the establishment of socialism—that the revolutionary parties have learnt the lesson of attack and now they must complete the lesson through the supplementary knowledge of retreat properly, they should have learn to realize by their bitter experiences that victory is impossible unless they have learnt both—how to attack and how to retreat. Not only that. The victory of the revolutionary struggle depends both on the activities of the vanguard Party and the 'whole class' socialist consciousness and the 'whole class' political experiences. Victory cannot be won with the vanguard alone. To throw the vanguard alone into the decisive battle, before the whole class has taken up a position either of direct support of the vanguard, or at least of benevolent neutrality towards it, would be not merely folly but a crime. In order that actually the whole class and actually the broad masses of the working people and those oppressed by capital may take up a position. Propaganda and agitation alone are not enough. The masses must have their own political experience. To this end, the role of revolutionary Party is of great significance.

In the revolutionary struggle Lenin is not totally opposed to reform or compromise—'Under certain conditions, in a certain situation, the proletarian power may find itself compelled temporarily to leave the path of the revolutionary reconstruction of the existing over of things and to take the path of its gradual transformation, the "reformist path", as Lenin says in his well-known article "The Importance of Gold", the path of flanking movements, of reforms and concessions to the non-proletarian classes—in order to disintegrate these classes, to give the revolution a respite, to recuperate one's forces and prepare the conditions for a new offensive. It cannot be denied that in a sense this is a "reformist path". But it must be borne in mind that there is a fundamental distinction here, which consists in fact that in this case reform emanates from the proletarian power, it procures for it a necessary respite, and its purpose is to disintegrate, not the revolution, but the non-proletarian classes.' (Stalin, 1975: 101-102). Therefore, compromise can also be a form of class struggle against the enemy of the working class—'direct and logical consequence of the actuality of the revolution' (Lukacs, 1977: 80). This is the dialectical-historical recognition of Marxist theory— 'history always creates new conditions; that therefore moments in history when different tendencies intersect never recur in the same, a form; that tendencies can be judged favourable to the revolution which are mortal danger to it tomorrow, and *vice versa.'* (Lukacs, 1977: 81). Lenin's theory of compromise is the realistic step towards the realization of Marxist theory.

Therefore, emergence of new production system out of the conflict between old forces of production and new production relations—this is called social revolution. Social revolution is not a sudden outgrowth. It becomes a historical necessity at the junction of social transformation. Objective conditions determine revolutionary social changes. Every social revolution has its own social-economic content, which is neutral of individual will and consciousness. Therefore, social revolution means (a) old production relation is replaced by the new production relation, (b) old class relation is replaced by the new class relation, (c) old ruling class is replaced by the new political and economic class forces, (d) power conflict over resources is resolved through the abolition of the old State power by the new one, *i.e.,* capturing of political power by the new class forces, and (e) capitalist force becomes the vanquished class and the working class the victor—the latter becomes the driving force of history and socialist revolution. Then, what are the conditions responsible for the success of social revolution? Social revolution needs total revolutionary situation, hence, neutrality of conditions does not give birth to social revolution. Then, the conditions are functional incapacity of the ruling class to rule society and the State in old ways and old fashion and then identity crisis gets its consolidation. Therefore, State power is weakened and its overthrow becomes the necessity. Secondly, oppression and exploitation become so intensified that the exploited class does not want to live their lives in the old ways, and then the change of society becomes the necessary condition. Thirdly, both the working class socialist consciousness and the working class political consciousness or political educations demand the revolutionary transformation of the society. The subjective conditions are (a) organization of the revolutionary forces, (b) proper leadership to the revolutionary forces, (c) revolutionary ideology, (d) revolutionary Party of the proletariat and the peasantry, (e) dictatorship of the proletariat and the peasantry, (f) proper revolutionary strategy and tactics. Marx and Engels formulate—

1. 'The possessing class and the proletarian class express the same human alienation. But the former is satisfied with its situation ....The latter feels itself crushed by this self-alienation. ... Within the framework of alienation, therefore, the property owners are the conservative and the proletarians the destructive Party.' (Bottomore and Rubel, 1986: 236).

2. 'Human emancipation will only be complete when the real, individual man has absorbed in himself the abstract citizen, when as an individual man, in his everyday life, in his work, and in his relationships, he has become a social being, and when he has recognized and organized his own powers as social powers, and consequently no longer separates this social power from himself as political power.' (Bottomore and Rubel, 1986: 241).

3. 'Revolution in general—the overthrow of the existing ruling power and the dissolution of existing social relationships—is a political act. Without revolution, socialism cannot develop. It requires this political act as it needs the overthrow and the dissolution. But as soon as its organizing activity begins, as soon as its own purpose and spirit come to the fore, socialism sheds this political covering.' (Bottomore and Rubel, 1986: 243).

However, Johnson repudiates Marxist theory of social revolution and tries to maintain *status quo* in the society. To him, revolution and counter-revolution are equal. To him,

peasant upsurge ≠ revolution,
revolutionary tendency under Jacobin ideology = C'oup, and
1917 October Revolution in Russia = Counter-revolution in Germany during 1920.

Secondly, Crane Brinton says that revolution is the overthrow of the Government in an illegal and violent manner. It is a separate and unconnected political event, which does not affect the society or other social events. Thirdly, Peter Amann thinks that revolution brings forth the fall of the monopoly power of the State, which results in the shrinkages of political obligation to the State. Here, revolution is nothing but the overthrow of State power. Fourthly, Sigmund Neumann characterizes revolution as the accidental process through which fundamental changes in social, economic and political levels or spheres take place. Social development does not occur in the old ways and methods. Actually, he does not differentiate between revolution and counter-revolution. Therefore, Western thinkers do not prescribe revolution from the depth of the economic relations, but separate the study of revolution from the economy and treat it as an accidental event.

However, Marxist study of revolution is not a study of accidental and pre-destined event. According to Marxists,

1. ....contradiction between the forces of production and relations of production forms the background of social and political revolution,

2. .... fruition of revolution comes into effect after the addition of historical trajectories of class struggle with the contradictory relationship between the forces of production and relations of production,

3. .... revolution means the creation of a new society, which means the emancipation of the oppressed class—'For an oppressed class to be able to emancipate itself, it is essential that the existing forces of production and the existing social relations should be incapable of continuing to exist side by side. Of all the instruments of production, the greatest productive force is the revolutionary class itself. The organization of the revolutionary elements as a class presupposes that all the productive forces, which could develop within the old society are in existence'. (Bottomore and Rubel, 1986: 243).

According to Lukacs (1977) 'Russia's socio-economic structure established the objective basis for the alliance of the proletariat and peasantry. Their class aims were different. That is why the crude soldering together of their forces in the name of vague and populist concepts like 'the people' was eventually bound to fall apart. However, it is only by joint struggle that they can realize their different aims. Thus the old Narodnik ideas return dialectically transformed in Lenin's characterization of the Russian revolution. The vague and abstract concept of 'the people' had to be rejected, but only so that a revolutionary, discriminating, concept of 'the people'—the revolutionary alliance of all the oppressed—could develop from a concrete understanding of the conditions of proletarian revolution. This was why Lenin's Party justifiably considered itself the heir to the real Narodnik revolutionary tradition. But because the consciousness and ability to lead this struggle exist—in objective class terms—only in the class-consciousness of the proletariat, it alone can and must be the leading class of social transformation in the approaching revolution.' (Lukacs, 1977: 23).

According to Lenin, the dictatorship of the proletariat is the instrument of the proletarian revolution, the dictatorship of the proletariat is the rule of the proletariat over the bourgeoisie, and Soviet power is the State form of the dictatorship of the proletariat. To him, the fundamental question of revolution is the question of power. The question of socialist revolution is the question of overthrow of bourgeois order. In *The Proletarian Revolution and Renegade Kautsky* Lenin says that if the exploiters are defeated in one country only, then a simultaneous revolution in a number of countries is a rare exception, still they remain stronger than the exploited. Wherein lays the strength of the bourgeoisie? The strength lies in strength of international capital; in strength of international connections of the bourgeoisie; in the money power; in their various connections, habits of organization and management, knowledge of management and superior education; and in the force of habit and in the strength of small production (*Left-Wing Communism*). In *Left-Wing Communism* he further says that dictatorship of the proletariat is a most determined and most ruthless war waged by the new class against a more powerful enemy and the dictatorship of the proletariat is a struggle —bloody and bloodless, violent and peaceful, military and economic, educational and administrative—against the forces and traditions of the old society. It will be necessary under the dictatorship of the proletariat to re-educate millions of peasants and small proprietors, employees, officials and bourgeois intellectuals, to subordinate then all to the proletarian State and to proletarian leadership, and to overcome bourgeois habits and traditions. According to Lenin, dictatorship of the proletariat is the rule of the proletariat over the bourgeoisie unrestricted by law and based on force. It is the rule of the proletariat enjoying the sympathy and support of the labouring and exploited masses. Therefore,

> dictatorship of the proletariat = complete democracy, democracy for all, for the rich as well the poor .... (1)
> dictatorship of the proletariat = State, which is democratic in a new way and dictatorial in a new way .... (2)
> dictatorship of the proletariat ≠ (does not vary with) peaceful development of democracy or bourgeois society and of bourgeois democracy .... (3)
> dictatorship of the proletariat ∝ (does vary with) smashing of the bourgeois State machinery, bourgeois army and police .... (4)

According to Lenin, which he says in his *The Proletarian Revolution and the Renegade Kautsky* that the proletarian revolution is impossible without the forcible destruction of the bourgeois State machine and the substitution for it of a new one. Soviet power is the State form of the dictatorship of the proletariat. Soviets are the all-embracing mass organizations of the proletariat, powerful organs of the revolutionary struggle of the masses, the immediate organizations of masses themselves, which unite all the oppressed and exploited, workers and peasants. Soviet power is the power of the majority of population over the minority, vanguard of the masses. Lenin in *First Congress of the Communist International* says that the experience of all revolutions and of all movements of the oppressed classes, the experience of the world socialist movement teaches us that the proletariat alone is able to unite and lead the scattered and backward strata of the toiling and exploited population.

Kautsky in his *Dictatorship of the Proletariat* goes against Lenin's seizure of power. The clash between Kautsky and Lenin is a clash between methods of democracy and dictatorship. According to Kautsky, Lenin's dictatorship of the proletariat is neither democratic nor transition to socialism. To him,

a. socialism is not the goal, if socialism is conceived as a particular organization of production,
b. democracy is not simply a means to socialism,
c. democracy and socialist organization of production are means to the human goal of liberation of man,
d. the human goal is the abolition of every kind of exploitation and oppression,
e. democracy and socialist production are not connected necessarily, rather they must be connected by the socialists,
f. active participation of people is essential for the transition to socialism,
g. pre-socialist democracy is essential for socialism in inculcating socialist habits, socialist responsibilities and socialist consciousness,
h. socialist ripeness presupposes highly developed capitalism, will make help to reach socialism by the proletariat, the strength of the proletariat to realize socialism, and maturity of the proletariat,
i. democratic capitalist republic is a pre-requisite for socialism,
j. in democracy proletariat's class interests coincide with the collective interest of the society, is progressively recognized by universal suffrage and democratic capitalist republic,
k. democracy provides maturity to the proletariat and avoids reckless and premature attempt at the revolution, and
l. between the two stages, for the preparation of socialism and its realization democracy is required,
m. after conquering political power, socialism in an economic sense has not yet brought about by the proletariat,
n. according to Lenin, dictatorship essentially implies suspension of democracy, dictatorship is not a form of government, but a condition which must everywhere arise when the proletariat has conquered political power,
o. dictatorship as a form of government implies suspension of democracy, freedom, suppression of opposition,
p. dictatorship of the proletariat means that the proletariat is the ruling class,—it does not mean the form of government—as a class can rule but cannot govern,
q. dictatorship of the working class Party does not imply

dictatorship of the proletariat as a form of government, which is not essentially political,

r. the best way for the proletariat is to rule through government based on universal suffrage—where the proletariat represents the majority, democracy will be the machinery of its rule and where the proletariat represents the minority, democracy constitutes its most suitable fighting arena to assert itself, to win concessions and to develop,

s. social revolution is a profound transformation of the entire social structure and political revolution is a sudden alteration in the relative strength of the classes in the State,

t. Lenin has so changed Marx's meaning or idea of the 'dictatorship of the proletariat' that he claims that no essential contradiction can exist between the Soviet power, which is socialist democracy and the dictatorial power of a single person.

Lenin in his work *The Proletarian Revolution and the Renegade Kautsky* says that Marx's revolutionary dictatorship of the proletariat is not a form of government that excludes or precludes democracy, but a State of rule. The rule of the proletariat as the rule of the majority of the population is possible with the strictest observance of democracy. On the other, Lenin gives more emphasis on dictatorship of the proletariat as a State of different type, which gives working people genuine democracy. Kautsky completely denunciates proletarian revolution. According to Lenin, dictatorship of the proletariat is historically concrete formulation of proletariat's task of abolishing bourgeois State machinery. Lenin believes that the proletariat needs to rule dictatorially and essentially all class rules are dictatorial. This dictatorship does not essentially mean or signify abolition of democracy for the class that exercises it, but does mean the abolition of democracy for the class over which the dictatorship is exercised.

To counteract bourgeois dictatorship, which is essentially the rule of the bourgeoisie based directly upon force and unrestricted by any laws, Lenin proposes revolutionary dictatorship of the proletariat as the counterpoise effect. It is the rule of the proletariat which are won and maintained by the proletariat against the bourgeoisie or bourgeois rule that is unrestricted by any laws. Lenin equates proletarian democracy with proletarian dictatorship. For example, the Soviet government enlists the exploited people in the work of administration and organization of the state of affairs in every possible way. The representative institutions cannot determine the democratic character of the State, rather the structure of the State, the character of the State machine, and the functionaries of the machine, the interests the machine serves or protects—all determine the character of the State. Democracy under proletarian rule represents the interests of the majority, but not the protection of minority rights and interests under the rule of the bourgeoisie. Therefore, proletarian democracy is more democratic than the bourgeois democratic republic. In relation with the Soviet republic Lenin interchangeably uses the terms State, dictatorship and democracy. According to Lenin, the proletariat cannot achieve victory without forcibly suppressing its opponents, and that where there is forcible suppression, where there is no freedom, there is of course no democracy. The contradiction between bourgeois democracy and proletarian democracy is in reality the clash between political democracy and the proletarian State. The State is primarily the coercive instrument of the ruling class. The role of parliament is almost dismissed and there is no room for consensus among the people. To crush the resistance of the exploiters and to organize a socialist economy the proletarian State needs State power, a centralized organization of force and an organization of violence.

Proletarian dictatorship is the organization of the vanguard of the oppressed as the ruling class. Proletarian dictatorship represents an expansion of democracy on the one hand, and represents no democracy on the other. The former is relative, when democracy for the exploited is increased and the latter is absolute, where there is no democracy. Luxemburg in her 'The Problem of Dictatorship', says that Lenin does not look into the life element of the dictatorship of the proletariat, *i.e.*, the political training and education of the entire mass of the people and if political life becomes absent, then there will be dictatorship of the handful of politicians, *i.e.*, dictatorship in the bourgeois sense and not the dictatorship of the proletariat. According to Luxemburg, Kautsky upholds bourgeois democracy and Lenin and Trotsky the bourgeois dictatorship. Socialist democracy is the same thing as the dictatorship of the proletariat. Lenin reconciles both democracy and dictatorship within his conception of dictatorship of the proletariat. Kautsky, on the other hand, contrasts democracy with dictatorship as political forms. Kautsky considers proletarian revolution with terrorism or communism. To him, the type of dictatorship as a form of government lies in personal dictatorship. Class-dictatorship is pure nonsense. Class-rule without laws and regulations is unthinkable. According to Lenin, there is no contradiction between Soviet democracy and the rule of an individual dictator and according to Kautsky, every form of compulsion must be applied with a view to introducing socialism is compatible with democracy. Kautsky believes that Soviet democracy is a peculiar structure, within which one can perform the dictatorship or arbitrary form of domination and one can merely give it in the name of socialism.

Trotsky justifies the October Revolution on the grounds that development of the technical command of men over nature has long ago grown ripe for socialization of economy or economic life, where the Bolshevik Party has a greater role to play, guided by revolutionary policy and revolutionary expediency. However, the Bolshevik regime is the regiment of terror; Bolshevik methods are widening the spiral of terror and compromise on anything except democracy, according to Kautsky. Trotsky believes that if socialist policy is subordinated to democracy, where there is formal democracy, then there is no place at all for the revolutionary struggle.

In order to justify revolution, Trotsky tries to make the significance of the historical necessity of revolution, the immanent requirements of history. Trotsky does not take into account the superficial balance of forces in the parliament. That is, Trotsky in *Terrorism and Communism* says that the opportunist elements are represented in the parliament, where mental confusion and indecision reign amidst the middle classes and the more backward elements of the proletariat. He justifies the seizure of power by the proletariat, and denigrates national consensus through national parliament. The regime of Soviets is bound up with the toiling majority of the masses closely, straightly and honestly. The toiling majority is not static, but dynamic—such democracy goes little deeper down than parliamentarism. The Soviets are the tools of the Bolsheviks for fundamental democracy and revolution, which needs Party authorization. Democracy is not able to provide the unity among the toiling masses for transition to socialism, where dictatorship of the proletariat or dictatorship of a single Party is a necessary pre-requisite. Dictatorship presupposes unity of will, unity of direction and unity of action. In the composition of the dictatorship of a class various heterogeneous elements, modes and sentiments, and various levels of development essentially creep in. The revolutionary supremacy of the proletariat presupposes within the proletariat itself the political supremacy of a Party with a clear programme of action and faultless internal discipline. Trotsky admits the following:

1. Dictatorship of the Party makes Soviet dictatorship possible.
2. Dictatorship of the Party is in no way substitute for dictatorship of the Soviets.
3. Communists express fundamental interests of the working class.
4. Bolshevik Party is equal to workers Party and Soviet State is equal to workers State.

   5. State of the proletarian dictatorship considers itself justified
      in subordinating the workers and the workers simply
      subordinate themselves to their own State.

However, Lenin does not consider the workers' State concept of Trotsky
in his work, *The Trade Unions, the Present Situation and Trotsky's Mistakes*,
pointing out that it is not quite a worker's State. It is actually a workers'
and peasants' State. The Party programme shows that it is a worker's
State with a bureaucratic twist to it. The Soviet regime is democratic in
the world and Bolshevik Party represents the true interest of the majority
of the toiling masses. Democracy under Soviet regime is real democracy,
which is different from formal liberal democracy, while former takes
precedence over the latter. There cannot be no freedom, no equality
and no labour democracy if it conflicts with the cause of emancipating
workers from the domination of capital. Bukharin (1979) contributes to
the defense of the Soviet regime on the ground of the proletariat's role
in dismissing and overthrowing rule, where the proletariat is the ruling
class which before it disappears as a class must crush all its enemies, re-
educate the bourgeoisie and remake the world in its own image.
Smashing the State organization of the bourgeoisie, the proletariat is
obliged to reckon with its continued resistance in various forms and in
order to overcome this resistance there must be a strong, firm and
comprehensive State organization of the working class, to break the
old relations of production and to organize new relations in the sphere
of social economics the fundamental task of the dictatorship of the
proletariat is to bring about economic revolution.

   According to Bukharin, as a class proletariat comes to power, which
does not signify the cohesive nature of that class, where everyone of
the members of dictatorship represents ideal mean. The proletarian Party
leads the others behind it, which grows and expands numerically as it
absorbs the ever-growing strata, and becomes more and more a class-
for-itself. Compulsory discipline is inevitable for the proletariat, which
is itself the self-coercion of the working class. Lenin intends that the
proletariat and their representatives should possess a political and social
weight in conformity with the aims of the new regime. The bureaucrats
and specialists with a bourgeois background must be under constant
supervision of the proletariat, must be conquered morally and must be
drawn into the proletarian fold, into proletarian apparatus. No political
concessions are made to them, Lenin points out these in his *The Immediate
Tasks of the Soviet Government*. Lenin further says that the proletariat can
throw out the Tsar, the landowners are the capitalists and they have
done these tasks. But the proletariat cannot overthrow bureaucracy in
a peasant economy and polity. These can reduce the bureaucracy by

slow and stubborn effort. Throwing off bourgeois ulcer is impossible and wrong in its very formulation. Surgery is an abstract formulation; the only solution is slow cure.

The October Revolution and the establishment of constitutional order based on Soviets placed the toiling masses a new place in the Russian society—workers' control over production, storage, purchase, and sale of all products. Control has to be exercised either by the workers and office staff themselves or in case of large enterprises by their elected representatives. Workers' factory committees are integrated into the new system in the interests of a systematic regulation of the national economy. Lenin says that in every socialist revolution after the capturing of political power by the proletariat there necessarily comes to the forefront the fundamental task of creating social system superior to capitalism, such as raising the productivity of labour and securing better organization of labour. Strikes remain the constant feature of social life in Leninist Russia under conditions of the New Economic Policy. Lenin unambiguously declares formation of strike funds and justifies this line of strikes and formation of strike funds by the facts that—(1) State enterprises are obliged to make profits, (2) existence of narrow departmental interests and excessive departmental zeal, entail a certain conflict of interests between the mass of the workers and the management, (3) the proletarian State power is distorted by bureaucratic distortion and all sorts of survivals of the old capitalist system in government offices on the one hand, and by the political immaturity and cultural backwardness of the mass of the working people, on the other. It is the duty of trade unions to avert mass disputes in State enterprises by pursuing a far-sighted policy with a view to objectively protecting the interests of the masses of the workers in all respects and to removing in time all causes of dispute. There exists a certain conflict of interests between the masses of the workers and directors and managers of the State enterprises in matters concerning labour conditions even after the introduction of the New Economic Policy. It is undoubtedly the duty of the trade unions to protect the interests of the working class and to correct the blunder and excesses of business organizations resulting from bureaucratic distortions of the State apparatus.

In *Economics and Politics in the Era of the Dictatorship of the Proletariat* Lenin says that socialism means the abolition of classes, dictatorship has done all to abolish classes, but classes cannot be abolished at one stroke. They still remain and will remain in the era of the dictatorship of the proletariat. Without dictatorship of the proletariat, the classes will not disappear, and dictatorship will become unnecessary when the classes will disappear. However, in this era of dictatorship, every class has undergone a change and the relations between classes have also changed. A sequential formulation may graphically be presented here: overthrowal of the bourgeoisie → conquering of political power by the proletariat → proletariat becomes the ruling class → proletariat wields State power → proletariat exercises control over means of production already socialized → proletariat guides the wavering and intermediary elements and classes → proletariat crushes the increasingly stubborn resistance of the exploiters or the counter-revolutionaries or bourgeois elements or the capitalists or the landowners. The class of exploiters, the landowners and capitalists has not disappeared and cannot disappear all at once under the dictatorship of the proletariat. The exploiters have been smashed, but not destroyed. In the form of international capital they still have an international base, they still have means of production in Party, they still have money, and they still have vast social connections. The peasants like that of the petty-bourgeoisie occupy the intermediate position even under the dictatorship of the proletariat—they are a large mass of the working people united by the common interest of all working people to emancipate themselves from landowners and capitalists, on the one hand, and disunited small proprietors and property-owners, on the other. Such an economic position inevitably causes them to vacillate between the proletariat and the bourgeoisie. 'In view of the acute form which the struggle between these two classes has assumed, in view of the incredibly severe break-up of all social relations, and in view of the great attachment of the peasants and petty bourgeoisie generally to the old, the routine, and the unchanging, it is only natural that we should inevitably find them swinging from one side to the other, that we should find them wavering, changeable, uncertain, and so on. In relation to this class—or to these social elements—the proletariat must strive to establish its influence over it, to guide it. To give leadership to the vacillating and unstable—such is the task of the proletariat.' (Lenin, 1984: 646).

Lenin's theory of imperialism plays a role in between the 'revolutionary-democratic dictatorship of the proletariat and peasantry' and 'proletarian revolution' in 1917. Lenin in his *The Socialist Revolution and the Right of Nations to Self Determination* explains that under imperialism there exists the division of nations into oppressor and oppressed, which is basic, significant and inevitable. The class analysis of the capitalist society has been transformed at the global plane into haves and have-nots, oppressor and oppressed, imperialist and colony. The present need at the imperialist stage must be to stand against the united and aligned front of the imperialist powers, the imperialist bourgeoisie and the social-imperialists and to stand for the utilization of all national movements against imperialism for the purpose of socialist revolution. Imperialist ideology penetrates the working class and the leaders of the working class have become social imperialists, socialists in words and imperialists in deeds. The imperialists bribe the labour leaders, who have become agents of the bourgeoisie in the working class. They are bribed by higher wages. Marx and Engels in the *Communist Manifesto* says that the bourgeoisie through the exploitation of world market has given a cosmopolitan character to production and consumption in every country. They have drawn the barbarian nations into civilization through rapid improvement of all means of production, immense facilitation of the means of communication etc. It (bourgeoisie or bourgeois class) compels all nations on the pain of extinction, compels them to introduce bourgeois civilization, compels the nations to become bourgeois themselves and overall creates a world after its own image.

Lenin's theory of imperialism is an advanced stage of capitalism. He says in his pamphlet *Imperialism* that imperialist stage is the highest or advanced stage of capitalism, where the domination of monopoly and finance capital has taken shape, the export of capital has taken or has acquired pronounced importance, the division of the world by international trusts has begun, and the division of the world territory by the capitalist countries or the imperialist countries has been completed. Therefore, the Leninist theory of imperialism connotes five characteristic features—(1) growing concentration of the production and capital with oligopoly taking the place of free competition, (2) merging of bank and industrial capital with the growing domination of bank capital, (3) the export of capital replacing the export of commodities, (4) the division of the world among international capitalist countries or combines, and (5) the completion of the territorial division of the world between capitalist powers.

A very important feature of capitalism in its highest stage of development is so called combination of production—grouping of different branches of industry in a single enterprise, which according to Hilferding[1], procures a more stable rate of profit through combined enterprise, elimination of trade, possible technical improvements, acquisition of super profits and strengthening of the position of combined enterprise or enterprises. Competition becomes transformed into monopoly. The result is immense progress in the socialization of production. The process of technical invention and improvement

---

1. Hilferding, *Finance Capital*.

becomes socialized. Production becomes social, but appropriation remains private. The social means of production remain the private property of a few. Secondly, at the imperialist stage, the banking system is developed and becomes concentrated in few numbers and also becomes powerful monopolies having command over the whole of money capital, over the means of production and sources of raw materials. The banking system is transformed from the system of middlemen to the system of monopolies in the process of transformation of capitalism into capitalistic imperialism. A handful of monopolists subordinate them to the operations of the whole capitalist society, both commercial and industrial. The banking system asserts exactly the financial position of the various capitalists, controls and influences the capitalists by restricting, enlarging, facilitating and hindering credits, and finally determines their income and fate by permitting them to increase their capital rapidly or depriving them of capital.

According to Marx, Lenin argues that the banking system represents the form of common bookkeeping and of the distribution of the means of production on a social scale. Thirdly, concentration of production and capital leads to monopoly. The concentration of capital belongs to the banks and ceases to belong to the industrialists, who employ it through production. Bank capital in the form of money is transformed into industrial capital, which according to Hilferding is called finance capital, controlled by banks and employed by the industrialists. It is to be noted here that finance capital is the core of monopoly capitalism at the imperialist stage and finance capital may be defined as:

  i. finance capital = (concentration of production + monopoly of the production system + merging of banks with industry), and
  ii. financial oligarchy = (conditions of private property and commodity production + business operations of capitalist monopolies).

According to Lenin, the characteristic features of capitalism in general are that (1) the ownership of capital is separated from the application of capital to production, (2) the money capital is separated from industrial or productive capital, and (3) the rentier who lives entirely on income obtained from money capital is separated from the entrepreneur, and from all who are directly concerned, in the management of capital. Imperialism or the domination of finance capital is that the highest stage of capitalism at which these separations reach vast proportions. The supremacy of finance capital over all other forms of capital means the predominance of the rentier and of financial oligarchy. It means the singling out of a small number of financially powerful States from among all the rest. Fouth, the monopoly of handful of powerful capitalists is characterized by the export of capital. Capitalism is commodity production, where labour power itself becomes the commodity. Capitalism itself is characterized by internal and external exchange, and also by uneven development of capitalism. Surplus capital are utilized not for the purpose of raising the standard of living of the masses in a given country, which will make a decline in profits for the capitalists, but for the purpose of increasing profits by exporting capital abroad to the backward countries, where profits are usually high due to scarce capital, low price of land, low wage rates and low prices of raw materials. The backward countries are drawn into the world capitalist intercourse. The necessity for exporting capital arises from the fact that in a few countries capitalism has become overripe and capital cannot find a field for profitable investment. The export of capital affects and accelerates the development of capitalism in backward countries. Finance capital has created the epoch of monopolies and monopolies introduce everywhere monopolist principles — the utilization of connections for profitable transactions takes the place of competition on the open market. Fifth, division of the world among capitalist countries is the higher stage, than that of export of capital, and the new stage of concentration of capital and production. 'Monopolist capitalist combines, cartels, syndicates and trusts divide among themselves, first of all, the home market, seizes more or less complete possession of the industry of a country. But under capitalism the home market is inevitably bound up with the foreign market. ... As the export of capital increased, and as the foreign and colonial connections and "spheres of influence" of the big monopolist combines expanded in all ways, things "naturally" gravitated towards an international agreement among these combines, and towards the formation of international cartels.' (Lenin, 1975: 79). Sixth, finance capital is the great economic force, which is capable of subjecting the politically independent States, is able to extract greatest profit from such subjection as it involves loss of political independence of the subjected countries. Colonial possession gives the monopolist combines complete guarantee with the sequence of events from the developed stage of capitalism to the struggle for the acquisition of colonies, which may graphically be presented as such:

> more developed State of capitalism → more strongly the shortage of raw materials needed → more competition for scarce resources → more competition and hunt for sources of raw materials throughout the whole world → more struggle for acquisition of colonies → more division of the world among great powers through the acquisition of colonies.

Finance capital not only is utilized in the already discovered sources of raw materials, but also in the potential resources as the development of science and technology is rapidly expanding and this may be applied to the land, which is useless and infertile. It may be fertile tomorrow with the application of new methods, techniques and large amount of capital. This is also applied 'to prospecting for minerals, to new methods of working up and utilizing raw materials' (Lenin, 1975: 99). 'Hence, the inevitable striving of finance capital is to enlarge its economic territory and even its territory in general. In the same way that the trusts capitalize their property at two or three times its value, taking into account its "potential" profits, and the further results of monopoly, so finance capital strives in general to seize the largest possible amount of land of all kinds in all places, and by every means, taking into account potential sources of raw materials and fearing to be left behind in the fierce struggle for the last scraps of undivided territory, or for the repartition of those that have been already divided.' (Lenin, 1975: 100). Therefore (1) finance capital strives for economic territory, (2) trusts capitalize their property at two or three times its value, (3) finance capital strives for largest amount of land and political domination by every means from division of territory to repartition of territory already divided, and (4) there is a fierce struggle for political and economic domination among the monopolist combines and powers. Seventh, according Lenin, imperialism is the direct continuation of capitalism, which becomes capitalist imperialism and capitalist monopoly, which displaces capitalist free competition. Capitalism is transformed into a monopoly through the creation of large-scale industry replacing the small-scale industry, concentration of production and capital, and merging of cartels, syndicates, trusts and banks. This transformation is a transition to a higher stage. Imperialism is the monopoly stage of capitalism means—

> finance capital = bank capital of very few monopolist banks + capital of monopolist combines of industrialists .... (1)
> division of the world = transition from a colonial policy which make hindrances to territories unseized by capitalist power to colonial policy of monopolistic possession of the territory of the world .... (2)

Lenin rejects Kautsky's definition of imperialism that it is one-sided and arbitrary that singles out only national question and it inaccurately connects national question with industrial capital and also inaccurately and arbitrarily pushes into the forefront the question of annexation of regions. The characteristic feature of imperialism is not industrial but finance capital. According to Kautsky, imperialism is a product of highly developed industrial capitalism. It consists in the striving of every industrial capitalist nation to bring under its control or to annex larger and larger areas of agrarian territory. With reference to political meaning of imperialism, Kautsky refers to Hobson's definition of imperialism that the new imperialism differs from the older—'first, in substituting for the ambition of a single growing empire the theory and the practice of competing empires, each motivated by similar lusts of political aggrandizement and commercial gain; second, in the dominance of financial or investing over mercantile interests' (op. cit. in Lenin, 1975: 109). Lenin further says that Kautsky detaches the politics of imperialism from the economics of imperialism, takes annexation as policy preferred by finance capital and justifies finance capital as the basis of bourgeois policy of annexation. 'It follows, then, that monopolies in economics are compatible with non-monopolistic, non-violent, non-annexationist methods in politics. It follows, then, that the territorial division of the world, which was completed precisely during the epoch of finance capital, and which constitutes the basis of the present peculiar forms of rivalry between the biggest capitalist States, is compatible with a non-imperialist policy.' (Lenin, 1975: 110-111). Eighth, monopoly is the economic foundation of imperialism and this monopoly is grown out of capitalism and exists in the environment of capitalism, commodity production and competition, and in the permanent and insoluble contradiction to this general environment. Parasitism, stagnation and decay are the characteristic features of imperialism. Last, while criticizing imperialism, Lenin adds that the enormous dimensions of finance capital are concentrated in a few hands and create an extraordinarily far-flung and close network of relationships and connections which not only subordinates the small and medium, but also even the very small capitalists, on the one hand. The intense struggle is waged against other national state groups of financiers for the division of the world and domination over other countries, on the other hand. The possessing classes go over entirely on the side of imperialism.

Imperialism is characterized by uneven development of capitalism. The world process of capitalist development brings about political upheaval in Russia and this will affect political development in all capitalist countries in the world system of capitalism—*i.e.*, developments in terms of internal dynamics of the advanced capitalist societies and relations between the advanced and backward countries. According to Marxists, three major tendencies of capitalism or capitalist society are responsible for the rise and growth of imperialism—

1. The capitalist system is a closed system and as a closed system the process of capitalist development essentially entails extraction of profit or surplus value, creates lower demand

leading to slumps in industrial production (*i.e.* capitalism →
extraction of surplus value → lesser buying capacity of the
people → lesser demand for the products → slumps in
industrial production).

2. Scientific and technical progress increases the proportion of
constant to variable capital, gives rise to organic composition
of capital resulting in a falling rate of profit (*i.e.*, scientific
technical progress → increase in C/V → organic composition
of capital).

3. Competition gives birth to decline of independent small firms
and individual entrepreneurship, and gives rise to joint-stock
companies and paid managerialism (*i.e.*, competition →
individual entrepreneurship decline → decline of independent
small firms → paid managerialship rise → rise of joint-stock
companies → changes in the structure give rise to functional
changes → banks become the dominant sources of capital and
finance).

Marx distinguishes the processes of capitalist development as
(i) accumulation of capital, (ii) concentration of capital, *i.e.*, increase of
social wealth in the hands of individual capitalists as the resultant effect
of expanded reproduction, and (iii) centralization of capital, *i.e.*,
culmination of the processes like concentration of capitals already
formed, destruction of individual independence, expropriation of capital
by the capitalists, and transformation of many small into a few large
capitals. This culminated process is forced on by the credit system and
the process provides the material basis of an uninterrupted revolution
in the mode of production itself. Developed with the credit system,
joint-stock companies have an increasing tendency to operate the work
of management as a function from the ownership of capital, according
to Marx. With the advancement of the credit system, the money capital
is transformed into bank capital and money-capitalists have to face
functional capitalists, *i.e.*, the banks. The managers perform the real
functions pertaining to the functional capitalists. Only the functionary
remains and the capitalist disappears as superfluous from the
production process. Money-capital assumes the social character with
the advancement of credit. In this form capital becomes conscious of
itself as a social power in which every capitalist participates
proportionately to his share in the total social capital. According to Marx,
growing accumulation means growing concentration of capital. In this
way the power of capital grows, *i.e.*, the conditions of the social
production personified be alienated from the real producers. Capital
comes more and more to the fore as a social power, whose agent is the

capitalist. This social power no longer stands in any possible relation to that which the labour of a single individual can create. It becomes an alienated, independent, social power, which stands as opposed to society as an object, which is the capitalist's source of power. According to Marx, the rate of profit is measured as the ratio of surplus value to that capital employed, *i.e.*, the constant capital (c) and variable capital (v). Therefore,

$$P_i \text{ (rate of profit)} = \frac{S}{C + V}$$

The only variable capital, the labour power yields surplus value. When organic composition increases, constant capital (c) rises relatively to variable capital (v) and other things being equal, *i.e.*, the ratio of surplus value to variable capital, then the profit (P_{ii}) will be lower than that of profit (P_i). This is the falling rate of profit.

Hobson in his study on *Imperialism* says that the system prevailing in all developed countries for the production and distribution of wealth, which has reached a stage in which (1) its productive powers are held in leash by inequalities of distribution, and (2) the excessive share goes to profits, rents and other surplus impelling a chronic endeavour to oversave in the sense of trying to provide an increased productive power without a corresponding outlet in the purchase of consumable goods. This drive towards oversaving is gradually checked by the inability of such saving to find any profitable use in the provision of more plant and other capital. But it also seeks to utilize political power for outlets in external markets, and as foreign independent markets are closed or restricted, the drive to the acquisition of colonies, protectorates and other areas of imperial development becomes a more urgent and conscious national policy. The motives of pride, pugnacity and prestige are stimulus for the search of foreign markets. There is no necessity to open up new foreign markets, and home markets are capable of indefinite expansion, for example, whatever is produced in England can be consumed in England, *i.e.*, the power to demand commodities is properly distributed. This only appears false because of unnatural and unwholesome specialization, based upon a bad distribution of economic resources. However this has induced an overgrowth of certain manufacturing trades for the express purpose of effecting foreign sales (Hobson, 1938). Hobson believes in the possibility of a more balanced economy, which is less dependent upon the world market, which arises from the belief that only a minority is really benefited from the orientation towards foreign trade, which in turn is reflected in the misdistribution of income. The root of imperialism is formed by this condition. The productive power of the capitalist countries is constantly tended to out-run the growth of consumption, more goods are produced that can be sold at a profit and more capital accumulated can be found than that of remunerative investment.

The aim of the capitalist production is the production of surplus value. According to Luxemburg, the capitalist's greed for surplus value, enhanced by competition, and the automatic effects of capitalist exploitation, lead to the production of every kind of commodity, including means of production, and also a growing class of proletarianized workers becomes generally available for the purposes of capital. On the other hand, the lack of a plan in this respect shows itself in the fact that the balance between demand and supply in all spheres can be achieved only by continuous deviations, by hourly fluctuations of prices, and by periodical crises and changes of the market situation (Luxemburg, 1951). Luxemburg extends Marx's theory of 'primitive accumulation' as the prior stage of capitalist accumulation, where capital seeks to gain dominant control over non-capitalist societies. It is the sphere of capitalist accumulation and non-capitalist buyers of surplus value. Capital needs the means of production and labour power of the whole globe for untrammeled accumulation—it cannot mange production and profit without natural resources and the labour power of all territories. Management of production and profit is equal to the management of untrammeled accumulation. The immediate and vital conditions for capital and capitalist accumulation are the existence of non-capitalist buyers of the surplus value, which is important decisively for the problem of capitalist accumulation. As a historical process, capitalist accumulation depends in every respect upon the non-capitalist social strata and forms of social organization. According to Luxemburg, capitalist accumulation is a kind of metabolism between capitalist economy and pre-capitalist methods of production. Accumulation of capital becomes possible only with the continuous and progressive disintegration of non-capitalist organizations. For capital, the standstill for accumulation means that the development of the productive forces is arrested and the collapse of capitalism is followed as an objective historical necessity. The final stage of capitalist historical progression is equal to contradictory behaviour of capitalism, is equal to imperialism, where the reason is equal to standstill of capitalist accumulation plus arrested development of the productive forces plus the collapse of capitalism. Imperialism is the political expression of the accumulation of capital in its competitive struggle for what remains still open of the non-capitalist environment. Imperialism grows in lawlessness and violence, according to Luxemburg. Imperialism opens up new opportunities for the realization of surplus value and thereby makes room for the prolongation of capitalism and capitalist accumulation. It is to be noted here—

imperialism = development of capitalism + subjection of less developed societies + nationalism + militarism + racialism

Here, political power is nothing but a vehicle for the economic process. In associating imperialism with the realization of surplus value Luxemburg underestimates the importance of export of capital. Luxemburg's analysis of imperialism hardly sees the methodical and rational form of imperialism based on investment by extra-territorial capitalist enterprises in less developed countries whether they are politically independent or not, and also does not take into account the growth of cartels and trusts and their combination in the realization of surplus value—cartels and trusts as specific phenomena of the imperialist phase.

The views of Hobson are in opposition to Luxemburg, when Hobson attributes the plutocratic character of British society, where a small upper class monopolizes the wealth of society and the large working class masses are allowed only to a very small portion of the national product leading to underconsumption and oversaving, inadequate purchasing power of the masses and insufficient demand for goods and services. Imperialism is connected with overseas investment, but not much concerned with struggle for overseas markets for more profitable investment. The reason for imperialism, according to Hobson, is not capitalism. He is not against capitalism. He establishes a closer link between imperialism and social structure, mass psychology and popular jingoism and economic factors like overseas investment. Aggressive imperialism is a source of great gain to the investor who cannot find at home the profitable use he seeks for his capital and insists that his Government should help him to profitable and secure investment abroad. Luxemburg in opposition to Hobson justifies imperialism with the realization of surplus value and untrammeled capitalist accumulation. Joseph Schumpeter in his work on *Imperialism and Social Classes* considers imperialism not as a product of capitalism, and considers it as a form of atavism in the history of capitalism. It is the unlimited forcible expansion on the part of the State with the objectless disposition, psychological disposition of aristocratic rulers, but not disposition of economic interests. According to Schumpeter, justification of capitalism can be made on the grounds that capitalism is anti-imperialist and elements of imperialism or the tendencies of imperialism are supported by non-capitalist factors in modern society (Figure 67). Therefore, capitalism is not imperialistic. Hence, imperialism is not the highest stage of capitalism. It is a transitional stage, bears continuation of the older social structures within the developing capitalist system. Imperialism is an element that stems from the living conditions of the past and not of the present, from the past rather than the present relations of production, is an atavism in the social structure, in individual and psychological habits of emotional reaction. Industrialization in the capitalist world produces structural changes that become unfavourable to the survival of imperialism and society becomes rationalized with rational accounting of profits and losses. The capitalist entrepreneurs win a share of power and leadership in the State. The working class, the salaried employees, the middle class and professionals become increasingly important and their lives become increasingly democratized, individualized and rationalized. Competitive struggle for the market and purely capitalist world do not make ground for the imperialist impulses. Even under capitalism, opposition to war and imperialism arises. Both exist at the opposite poles. With regard to the practice of contemporary capitalism he adds that conflicts are born out of export-dependent monopoly capitalism, which may submerge the real community of interests among nations. The normal sense of trade and business usually prevails. Even national economies characterized by export monopoly are dependent on one another in many respects. Schumpeter maintains that export of monopoly does not grow from the inherent laws of capitalist development. He says that it is a basic fallacy to describe imperialism as a necessary phase of capitalism or even to speak

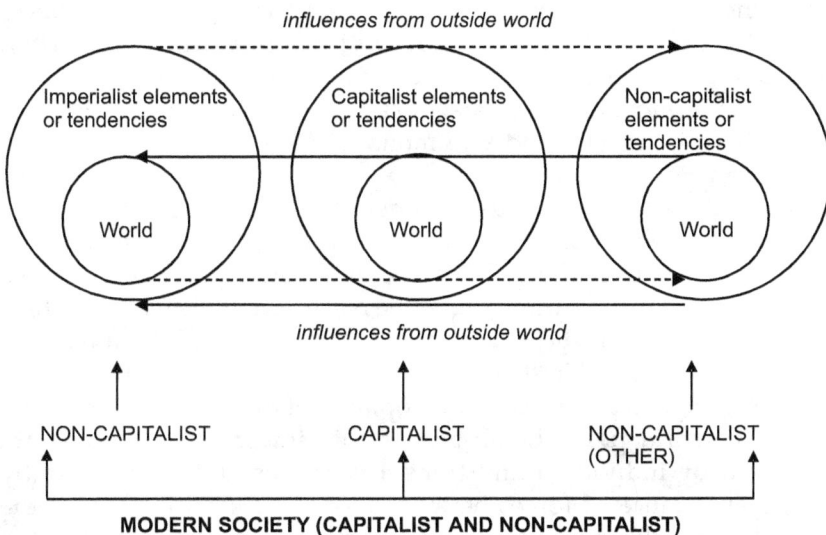

influences from outside world

Imperialist elements or tendencies

Capitalist elements or tendencies

Non-capitalist elements or tendencies

World   World   World

influences from outside world

NON-CAPITALIST   CAPITALIST   NON-CAPITALIST (OTHER)

MODERN SOCIETY (CAPITALIST AND NON-CAPITALIST)

Figure 67

of the development of capitalism into imperialism, and considers capitalism as viable, working towards the elimination of imperialism. Society is bound to grow beyond capitalism but this will be because the achievements of capitalism are likely to make it superfluous, not because its internal contradictions are likely to make its continuation impossible. Schumpeter considers that both nationalism and militarism precede the rise of the bourgeoisie and are antagonistic to capitalism, which involves both in its workings and keeps them alive politically and economically. Imperialism fuses with nationalism and militarism. Imperialism is not the outcome of capitalism, but of pre-existing forces. He draws the dividing line between capitalism and imperialism.

From this analysis, it seems clear that Luxemburg's analysis is closer to Marxist analysis than that of Hobson and Schumpeter. Lenin's analysis of imperialism is associated with antagonism, contradiction, class struggle, crises, concentration of capital and overproduction. Absence of successful socialist revolutions in the advanced countries has made capitalism bound to change and development, is caused by direct development, growth, continuation of the deep-seated and fundamental tendencies of capitalism and production of commodities in general. Finance capital is the latest phase of capitalist development. Free competition is driven from one field after another, but especially in heavy and in new industries based upon science, technology and vast capital. The phase of finance capital is dominated by monopoly combination in contrast to the free competition of the earlier period, which includes trusts, cartels, combines, syndicates and big business generally. A monopoly generally appears in some branches of industry, increases and intensifies the State of chaos inherent in the system of capitalist production. Lenin categorically puts in *Imperialism* that free competition is transformed into monopoly with the socialization of production. See Figure 68.

According to Lenin, due to inner necessities capitalism in its monopoly stage has had to expand itself outwardly in a particular way. Under old capitalism under which free competition prevails, where the export of goods is typical and under the newest capitalism under which monopolies prevail, the export of capital is typical. The advanced countries are involved in struggle for control over colonies and colonial markets. In opposition to Kautsky's opinion of the role of international cartels in world peace Lenin argues that international cartels are generated by individual and transitory causes and maintained by particular balance of forces between monopolies arising out of the struggle for colonies and colonial markets. Finance capital is the economic basis of imperialism and the non-economic superstructure

Competition (capitalism) →	Monopoly results: (capitalism) (wider scale)	1. Scientific and technical improvements ↓ 2. Immense progress in production ↓ 3. Socialization of production ↓ 4. Socialization of technical invention and improvement ↓
	Imperialism → Results: (capitalism) (widest scale)	
Results:	1. Newest form of capitalism	1. Capitalists against the will and understanding of the monopoly capitalists ↓
1. Free competition	2. Relations between capitalist combines	2. Socialization of scientific-technical invention and improvement ↓
2. Scientific and technical improvements and sociali-zation	3. Economic division of the world	3. Establishment of the new social order ↓
3. Improvement in produ-ction and socialization	4. Parallel with economic relations, relations are established between political alliances and States on the basis of territorial division of the world, of the struggle for colonies, and of the struggle for economic territory	4. Transitional stage, transition from complete freedom of competition or free competition to complete socialization ↓
		5. Widest socialization of production ↓
		6. Production becomes social, appropriation remains private ↓

Figure 68

grows up on the basis of finance, where colonial politics and ideology accentuate the striving for colonial conquests. In opposition to Kautsky's concern that imperialism is a policy that is suited to industrial capital, Lenin connects imperialism with finance capital, which involves annexation of industrial areas. However, like Kautsky Lenin puts forward the concept of ultra-imperialism or single world monopoly that development in the direction of a single world monopoly or trust, which without all exception will bound and swallow up all enterprises and all States. But this development is under stress, tempo, contradictions, conflicts and convulsions. Before a single world trust will be reached, before the respective national finance capitals will have formed a world union of 'ultra-imperialism', imperialism will inevitably explode and capitalism will turn into its opposite. At this stage an enormous extraction and accumulation of surplus of capital is made through the export of capital. It can be said without saying that if capitalism can develop agriculture, which lags behind industry, if it can raise the standard of the masses, who are still poverty-striven in spite of the technical advance at the present day, then there can be no talk of a surplus of capital. But then capitalism will not be capitalism as such. As long as capitalism remains as such, surplus capital will never be used for the purpose of raising the standard of living of the masses, for this will mean a decrease in profits for the capitalists. Instead, it will be used to increase profits by exporting the capital abroad, to backward countries.

Lenin in *Socialism and War* says that without the formation of the national States, capitalism could not have overthrown feudalism. Capitalism has developed concentration. Free trade and competition have been superseded by a striving towards monopolies, the seizure of territory for further investment of capital and for the sources of raw materials and so on. Formerly progressive, capitalism has become reactionary—it has developed the forces of production to such a degree that mankind is faced with the alternative of adopting socialism or experiencing years and even decades of armed struggle between the great powers for the artificial preservation of capitalism by means of colonies, monopolies, privileges and national oppression of every kind. In *The Socialist Revolution and the Right of Nations to Self-Determination* Lenin states that imperialism is the highest stage in the development of capitalism, where capital has outgrown the bounds of nation States, has replaced competition by monopoly and has created conditions for the achievement of socialism. The revolutionary struggle of the proletariat for the overthrow of the capitalist order and the expropriation of the bourgeoisie is the order of the day. Imperialism forces the masses into this tremendous struggle by sharpening class contradictions. The domination of finance capital and of capital in general is not to be abolished by any reforms of political democracy. In *The Military Programme of the Proletarian Revolution* Lenin points out that the development of capitalism proceeds extremely unevenly in different countries. It cannot be otherwise under commodity production. Socialism cannot achieve victory simultaneously in all countries. Socialism will achieve victory first in one or several countries. Other countries will remain for some time bourgeois or pre-bourgeois. Socialism, according to Lenin, can be achieved through revolution, but not through reform. Reformism is bourgeois deception of the workers, who despite individual improvements will always remain wage-slaves as long as there is the domination of capital. In *Marxism and Reformism* Lenin categorically mentions that the liberal bourgeoisie grant reforms with one hand and with the other they always take these reform measures back, reduce them to naught, use them to enslave the workers, to divide them into separate groups and perpetuate wage slavery. For that reason, reformism in practice becomes a weapon by means of which the bourgeoisie corrupt and weaken the workers and workers' movement. Marx and Engels in *The Class Struggles in France* identifies the revolutionary purpose in opposition to bourgeois and petty-bourgeois reformism that the permanence of revolution, the class dictatorship of the proletariat as the necessary intermediate point on the path towards the abolition of class differences in general, the abolition of all social relations and the revolutionizing of all ideas which come out from these social relations are necessary for revolutionary transformation of social relations. Making revolution permanent is meant for the advancement of revolution within the framework of capitalism and bourgeois-democratic regime. That is why Lenin pursues the importance of permanent revolution, which involves the application of continuous pressure for pushing and creating the conditions for a revolutionary break with the bourgeois democratic regime by way of revolutionary democratic dictatorship of the proletariat and the peasantry. See Figure 69.

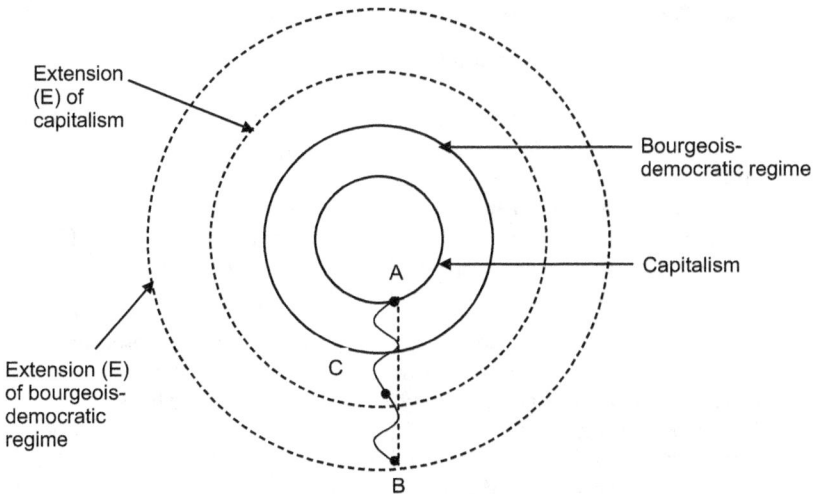

Figure 69

Here E = extended form, A = point of abolition of class differences in general arising from the existing relations of production, B =

revolutionizing of all ideas coming out from these social relations. The process is spiral, where C = point of revolutionary democratic dictatorship of the proletariat, application of continuous pressure for pushing and creating conditions for a revolutionary break with the bourgeois-democratic regime. The process becomes contradictory, where 'C' is the intermediate point between the abolition of class differences and the revolutionizing of all ideas. Lenin in *Two Tactics of Social Democracy in the Democratic Revolution* says that the revolutionaries cannot get out of the bourgeois-democratic boundaries of the Russian revolution, but we can vastly extend these boundaries, and within these boundaries they can and must fight for the interests of the proletariat, for its immediate needs and for conditions that will make it possible to prepare its forces for the future complete victory. In *The Position and Tasks of the Socialist International* Lenin emphasizes the task of organizing the proletarian forces for a revolutionary onslaught against the capitalist governments, for civil war against the bourgeoisie of all countries for the capture of political power, and overall for the triumph of socialism. The rule of the bourgeoisie is irreconcilable with truly-revolutionary true democracy. If the revolutionaries fear advance towards socialism, then they cannot become revolutionary democrats in the twentieth century and in the capitalist country—Lenin points out this fact in *The Impending Catastrophe and How to Combat It*. True democracy and pure democracy cannot be attained within the capitalist framework and bourgeois-democratic regime. According to Miliband,

> ... a 'state proper' is an absolutely imperative necessity in organizing the process of transition from a capitalist society to a socialist one. That process of transition both includes and requires radical changes in the structures, modes of operation, and personnel of the existing states as well as the creation of a network of organs of popular participation amounting to 'dual power'. The 'reformist' strategy, at least in this 'strong' version of it, may produce a combination of direction and democracy sufficiently effective to keep the conservative forces in check and to provide the conditions under which the process of transition may proceed.

> ... radical social change must ultimately depend on the force of arms. Bourgeois democratic regimes, on the other hand, may conceivably offer this possibility, by way of a strategy which eschews resort to the suppression of all opposition and the stifling of all civic freedoms.... Regimes which do, either by necessity or by choice, depend on the suppression of all opposition and the stifling of all civic freedoms must be taken to represent a disastrous regression, in political terms, from bourgeois democracy, whatever the economic and social achievements of which they may be capable. Bourgeois democracy is crippled by its class limitations, ... (Miliband, 1977 : 189).

According to Lenin, imperialism helps to explain the reasons for the revolutionary movement of the working class—revolution of the working class is postponed in the advanced capitalist countries, working class revolution moves from developed capitalist countries to the developing backward countries. The loyalty of the masses is ensured through the economic benefits of imperialism. Profits obtained from labour in the underdeveloped or developing or backward countries provide economic benefits to the affluent workers of the imperialist States or countries. Workers' political parties and unions obtain maximum benefit from the imperialist profits or super-profits. In short, the working class, their parties and unions are embourgeoisied and they for short-term economic benefit or maximization of economic interests support foreign claims of their governments. Competition between national capitals for colonies, for areas of influence and for annexation of available lands leads to war, which ushers in the era of social revolution and all the objective conditions of recent times have put the proletariat's revolutionary mass struggle on the order of the day.

The class struggle between proletariat and bourgeoisie transcends national boundaries. The process is like this: revolution in backward countries → collapse of capitalism in backward countries → feed back on the workers in the West → revolution in advanced capitalist countries → collapse of capitalism in advanced capitalist countries. Lenin in *Letters on Tactics* says that the bourgeois revolution in Russia is completed. According to the old conception, the rule of the proletariat and peasantry and their dictatorship must follow the rule of the bourgeoisie. Side by side, simultaneously, we have both the rule of the bourgeoisie and the revolutionary-democratic dictatorship of the proletariat and the peasantry, which voluntarily concedes power to the bourgeoisie and voluntarily makes itself an appendage of the bourgeoisie. The only solution, according to Lenin, is that power should be in hands of the proletariat, which should have to be supported by the poor peasants and semi-proletarians. In his *Tasks of the Proletariat in the Present Revolution* Lenin says that the specific feature of the present situation in Russia is that the country is passing through the first stage of the revolution, which due to the insufficient class-consciousness and organization of the proletariat places power in the hands of the bourgeoisie to the second stage, which in turn places power in the hands of the proletariat and the poorest sections of the peasants (Figure 70).

First stage revolution ⟶	Second stage revolution ↓
1. insufficient class consciousness and organization of the proletariat ↓	1. sufficient class consciousness and organization↓
2. power in the hands of the bourgeoisie	2. power in the hands of the proletariat and poorest sections of the peasantry↓
	3. use of State power of the proletariat (alliance of workers and peasants) in breaking bureaucratic-military State machine and in smashing election of all officials.

Figure 70

Lapidus and Ostrovityanov's accounts of imperialism show us that the imperialist epoch is also characterized by international division of labour and qualitative changes in the nature of capitalist production. Economic development of each country takes place in independence of what takes place in other places. It becomes unrelated to what is going on in the world market, which is nothing but a mechanical aggregation of parts as Stalin's theory of socialism in one country requires. To them,

  a. capitalism is declining and it is declining towards destruction,
  b. it is declining due to growing antagonisms within it,
  c. decline of capitalism and antagonisms of capitalism both limit the growth and development of capitalism, its society and its productive forces, buying power of the masses, technical possibilities and economic possibilities,
  d. besides the declining capitalism, the relatively stabilized capitalism is characterized by greater productive potentialities than that of buying power of the masses, greater technical possibilities than that of economic possibilities.

However, they do not point out the functional significance of imperialist expansion of capitalism, but only go on to describe the contradictions and inability of capitalism. Leontief's work, *Political Economy* is a complete denunciation of Trotskyism as the vanguard of the counter-revolutionary bourgeoisie coupled with an attack on Rosa Luxemburg's contribution, where no credit is given to her revolutionary integrity than her contribution to Marxist thought. Leontief goes on to state that it is in the nature of capitalism to tend to reduce consumption by the broad masses of the people to the most miserable minimum. But mention here may be made that it becomes true that the process of capitalist reproduction involves crises and instabilities in production, which does not preclude the growth of consumption when reproduction proceeds on an extended scale. Leontief says that capitalism holds back technical progress, which declines at home while hunting for super-profits, colonies and colonial markets, and preparing for war abroad. This inevitably leads to the conclusion that capitalism decays and begins to fall to pieces while still alive. Under conditions of expanded reproduction, when possibilities of realizing surplus value were growing, new techniques will be taken up on a considerable scale, even though selectively, will become the basis for extending the possibilities of profitable new investment. Stalin in this connection formulates the basic economic law of modern capitalism that in capitalism there exists two basic laws—securing of economic benefits and securing of maximum capitalist profit through (1) exploitation, ruin and improvement of the majority of the population of the given country, (2) enslavement and systematic robbery of the peoples of other countries, especially backward countries, and (3) wars and militarization of the national economy, which are utilized for the obtaining of higher profits. Stalin's law elucidates nothing—from the concepts of 'ruin and impoverishment' and 'enslavement and systematic robbery' it is difficult to explain how capitalism works and exits for long time. Stalin's law does not answer the question—if capitalists extract ever more surplus value, where do they realize it? The authors of the text book of *Political Economy* says that it implies a sequential process: continuous intensification of work → increasing redundancy → unemployment → decline in real wages → growth in the exploitation of the working class in the process of production, is supplemented by the robbery of the working people as consumers. Maurice Dobb in his work on *Political Economy and Capitalism* compares mercantilism and modern capitalism, where the former is characterized by colonial exploitation through the regulation of trade, prices of goods exported to the colonies and intervention of the State and the latter is characterized by industrial capitalism, integration of finance with industry, monopolistic

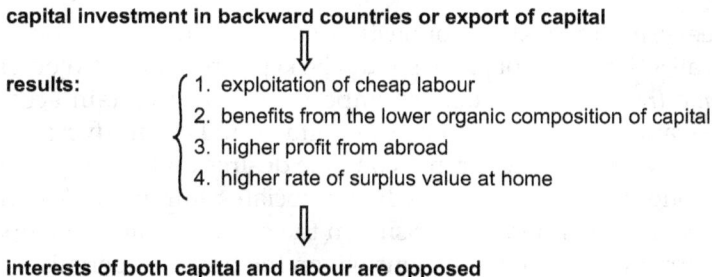

capital investment in backward countries or export of capital

⇓

results:
- 1. exploitation of cheap labour
- 2. benefits from the lower organic composition of capital
- 3. higher profit from abroad
- 4. higher rate of surplus value at home

⇓

interests of both capital and labour are opposed

Figure 71

organization and policies, and export of capital, but not export of capital goods. The interest of capital and the interest of labour—both are opposed to each other in this matter of export of capital. See Figure 71.

Imperialism in colonial countries is not characterized by full-fledged capitalist development, but by reactionary socio-political institutions, preservation of the old and holding back of industrialization. According to Dobb, any increase in capital accumulation must involve a relative decline in income spent in immediate consumption; it is possible to attribute any result which ensues from increased accumulation to decreased spending—one is reciprocal to the other. Capitalism has an inner logic of expansion and for capitalism as a whole colonialism can afford no more than a transitional respite. This connects the growth of monopoly and the export of capital. Paul Sweezy in his *Theory of Capitalist Development* explains the general crisis of capitalism and correlates capitalist development and under consumption pointing out that capitalism has an inherent tendency to expand the capacity to produce consumption goods more rapidly than the demand for consumption goods. Capitalists seek to promote and increase profits. They make fullest utilization of profits and fullest utilization of resources. Under conditions of fullest utilization of resources, consumption of both capitalists and workers grows, but not so rapidly as the growth of the means of production. The growth of the means of production is greater than the rate of growth in the output of consumption goods. According to Sweezy, bank capital in the period of transition from competition to monopoly capitalism falls back again to a position subsidiary to industrial capital. Access to bank capital, credit and shareholders' capital by the dominant groups is crucial to the structure of present-day capitalism, which may be summed up as monopoly capital or finance capital. While establishing interconnection between nationalism, imperialism and militarism, Sweezy (1946) formulates that—

> international antagonisms of imperialism = antagonisms of rival national capitalist classes = form of conflicts between States.

To Sweezy, in capitalist monopolistic system surplus value should have to be realized, the rate of profit should be kept up. Leonard Woolf in his *Economic Imperialism* associates imperialism with certain economic motives and sees it as an era of capitalism. The motive power is economic, which springs from economic desires and beliefs. Winslow (1948) following Schumpeter's line associates imperialism with the phenomena of war and militarism, on the one hand, and monopolies, trade barriers and colonial expansion, on the other. Imperialism is the result of political interference in the natural economic process of capitalism. That is, imperialism is a political phenomenon. As a policy it opposes and seeks to destroy democracy and capitalism, to turn nationalism from its original character as an expression of popular revolt against autocratic power and infuse it with the spirit of aggressiveness. Imperialism attacks the economic system through political channels, and the most obvious political channel is the nation-State. That the organization of peoples into regionally segregated political groups is the most potent cause of modern war is the one proposition which today claims the support of those who are unable to accept the Marxist theory that war is the product of capitalism.

In Marxist-Leninist ideas, two important tendencies of the world can be found, *i.e.,* capitalism and imperialism, when Lenin seeks to erect a socialist order upon the ruins of world capitalism and imperialism which would able to lead mankind towards the peaceful and harmonious realm of communism. To Liebman,

> Capitalism and imperialism still possess immense power for tyranny and destruction throughout the world. Communism has not been build anywhere, and in Russia itself they are very far from having established a socialist society, in which coercion would be, by Lenin's own definition, on it way out. Although capitalism, having been abolished in Russia by the October Revolution, has not been restored there, and the country's economic strength has multiplied tenfold, Soviet democracy has not been realized, and the arbitrary power of the State, which Marx and Lenin attacked, as well as bureaucracy, seems more firmly established than ever.... It proved unable to succeed in accomplishing those two tasks that the working class movement has to fulfil if it is not to suffer defeat, namely, to create the instrument that can strike down capitalism in the advanced industrial countries, and, on the ruins of bourgeois power, to organize and develop a socialist democracy and culture. (Liebman, 1975: 427).

Further, according to Liebman, Leninism fails to solve the problems of dictatorship of the proletariat and socialist democracy. 'As a revolutionary force for subversion and destruction, the Bolshevik organization achieved victory nowhere but in a society very different from the one that Marxism aimed to conquer in order to build the foundations of complete Communism. This failure can be inputted to the major weakness in Lenin's own strategy: having counted, in launching the proletarian insurrection in Russia, upon the revolutionary capacities of the working class in the West and the prospects of world revolution, he found himself, in the years following the October revolution, faced with a reality that was the negation of these hopes.' (Liebman, 1975: 430). Further, Leninism can be defined both as a theory and practice of political organization and centralization, an enterprise of revolution based upon the action of the vanguard Party, a technique of socialist reconstruction based on an authoritarian State or an active participation by the people in the affairs of administration. It is a form of personal dictatorship—a form of charismatic leadership—if Weber's theory of charisma is applied to the case of a socialist leader heading and handling popular revolution, leading a proletarian movement and reconstructing socialism.

Charismatic leadership is the greatest revolutionary force in a situation of inextricable social crisis accompanied by extreme upsurge of radicalism. The authority of the charismatic leader is based on a support of a nucleus of loyal followers, which bears some resembling to the concept of the vanguard Party, but profoundly different from Lenin's followers in the unconditional and irrational character of their allegiance to the leader. Besides the superficial analogies, the differences between Weberian charismatic personality and Lenin's personality are most striking, where the former shows complete disdain for economism —charisma is a typical anti-economic forces or activities defined in terms of rationality and pure charisma is foreign to economic considerations, the latter is concerned with economic development to the extremes of industrialism tinged with positivism. Whereas the charismatic leader finds the fascination that he exercises upon his rejection of all and any compromise, Lenin, on the contrary, defends realism against revolutionary purism. The irrational and often religious orientation of the charismatic authority is contrasted with materialism and devotion to scientific socialism. There is no trace with Lenin of the organization of any kind of personality cult. Charisma has no place in the reconstruction of Socialism and with regard to the question of dictatorial power Lenin is the forerunner of Stalinism in many people's eyes. Stalin is situated historically on the ground of Leninism and of the Bolshevik experience.

Both Stalinism and Leninism are deeply rooted from the politics of realism or *realpolitik* and the principle of politics as a force. However, Lenin sees politics as primarily a question of force or power, and Stalin recognizes politics in terms of power and sees power as a matter not just of brute force, but of ability, tenacity, firmness, efficiency and discipline, in short of the organization of will. Stalin may be considered as pre-Leninist or pre-Marxist as he sees nothing outside the will and thus understands the primacy of politics as the primacy of political will. The primary task of Party and politics is the organization of political will. In *Problems of Leninism* Stalin says that the whole point is to retain power, to consolidate it, and to make it invincible. For Lenin, politics is not only strength, power and organization of the will, it is something else. The something else may be defined as culture.

According to Lenin, socialism means political power wielded by the Party for underprivileged sections of the society, presupposes conscious and comprehensive management of social development, a State-capitalist monopoly stage which is made to serve the interest of the whole people. Lenin says that in Russia the first task is to establish first stage of socialism or the lower stage of communism. In this respect Soviet power is the first step. Like that of Lenin, Trotsky says that the Party must substitute itself in the economic and social revolution. Trotsky legitimizes compulsion, form of State power, Party hegemony, economic and social revolution from the above. While in power, Trotsky shares assumptions common to Lenin and Stalin. Like Lenin, Stalin says that the history of the development of society is above all the history of the development of production. The laws of history of society are sought in the mode of production of society and in the economic life of the society. Laws are independent of men. Laws may be or must be considered as the reflection of the objective world, the objective processes, which take place independently of men's will. Man cannot change or create laws, but he uses these laws, utilizes these in the interests of the society, may discover them, get to know and reckon with them. According to Stalin, the communist Party is the weapon of struggle, the political leader of the working class, the General Staff of the proletariat, the instrument of the dictatorship of the proletariat and leader of the working class in the revolution for socialist reconstruction. He emphasizes Party discipline after the establishment of the dictatorship of the proletariat. Weakening of Party discipline would lead to the weakening of the Party and enslavement to the bourgeoisie. The Party should be guided by the objective historical laws for the enslavement of the bourgeoisie and emancipation of the proletariat in their struggle against the bourgeoisie. See Figure 72.

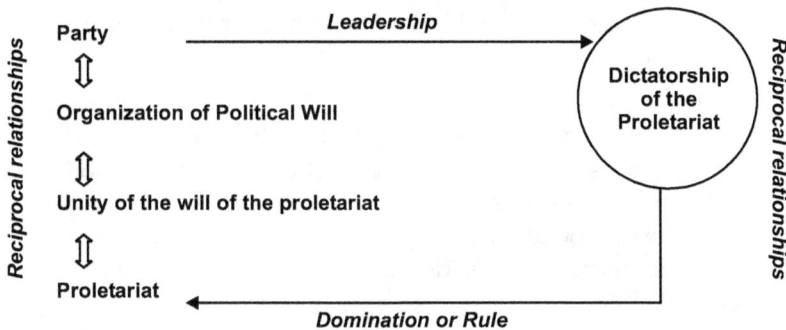

Figure 72

It is true that Stalinism is situated historically on the ground of Leninism, of the Bolshevik experience, of the revolution and its crisis. They share common views relating to—Party as the unity and organization of political will, which provides leadership to the dictatorship of the proletariat as the rule and domination of the proletariat within which the proletarian wills are socialized and organized under the leadership of the Party; international order of capitalism threatening Soviet rule in Russia; development of the productive forces under the dictatorship of the proletariat; proletarian Party should be guided by dialectical and historical laws of social and economic development; the major task of the Soviet government should be to teach the working people how to work etc; Soviet rule must be combined with the latest progressive measures of capitalism; and Soviet government must introduce the teaching of Taylorism. The Soviet form of dictatorship of the proletariat would be regarded as the international doctrine of the proletarians of all lands, is suitable, and obligatory for all countries without exception, including those where capitalism is developed. Stalinism is at odds with Trotskyism, which is petty-bourgeois opportunist current in ideology and politics, hostile to Marxism and Leninism. Trotskyism is characterized by extreme subjectivism, voluntarism, oversimplification and sophistry. Trotsky's ideological foundation is theory of permanent revolution, directed against the theory of uninterrupted revolution, *i.e.*, the transition of a bourgeois-democratic revolution to a socialist revolution. The main thrust of the theory of permanent revolution of Trotsky consists of the traits like distrust about the ability of the working class to rally its allies, denial of the revolutionary role of the peasants, adventurous attempts to boost revolution and skip the incomplete phase of revolution, rejection of broad democratic movements, emphasis on waging revolutionary war and denial of the possibility of building socialism in one country. Trotsky's anti-Sovietism provided a platform for rallying anti-socialist forces during 1920s and 1930s. Trotsky refers:

1. to the revolutionary potential of the Russian working class as insufficiently prepared for accomplishing a revolution,
2. to the peasantry assessed as a reactionary force bound to strike the proletariat from the rear, and
3. to the democratic phase of the revolution, where the struggle for democracy is considered as the past stage of the proletarian movement.

Trotsky's idea about tossing revolution from one country to another denies the possibility of any prolonged co-existence between States with different social systems. Trotskyism goes against Leninism and Stalinism, when he undermines the unity within the Communist Party, advocates the freedom of factions, sets the younger generation against the old, and sets up underground groups and uses illegal methods of struggle. According to Trotsky, the proletariat of one country or a group of countries, having won power, cannot and must not build socialism is one country, but must pursue a course towards world revolution, without which any proletarian State is doomed to failure. Stalin, on the other hand, emphasizes the importance of completing the construction of socialism in one country. Emphasis moves from the world proletariat to the national liberation movements. Stalin looks to other revolutions in backward and developing countries rather than in advanced countries. Under Stalinism democratic centralism becomes the mechanism for the mobilization of the people. Voting becomes a kind of audience participation and an expression of loyalty to the Soviet power.

For Lenin, the proletarian State is a necessary apparatus in the early stages of the dictatorship of the proletariat, but in the advanced stage of communism the State will wither away, but Stalin regards that the State even exists in the Communist society. Centralization, nationalization, State hegemony, social homogeneity, industrialization, and application of modern technology are the factors responsible for making reconstruction of socialism. Stalin calls for the value pattern of the Russian revolutionary sweep and American efficiency in the reconstruction of socialism. 'Russian revolutionary sweep is an antidote to inertia, routine, conservatism, mental stagnation and slavish submission to ancient traditions. Russian revolutionary sweep in the life-giving force which stimulates thought, impels things forward, breaks the past and opens up perspectives. Without it no progress is possible .... American efficiency, on the other hand, is an antidote to "revolutionary" Manilovism and fantastic scheme concocting. American efficiency is that indomitable force which neither knows nor recognizes obstacles; which with its businesslike perseverance brushes aside all obstacles; which continues at a task once started until it is finished, even if it is a minor task; and without which serious constructive work is inconceivable.' (Stalin, 1975: 122, 124).

Khrushchev criticizes Stalin as being excessively rude in his approach to power, for his lack of collegiality, for brutal violence, which produces untold harm to the Party. Power is accumulated in the hands of a single person. Abusing his power more and more, fighting eminent Party and government leaders and using terrorist methods against the honest Soviet people, Stalin made capricious and despotic nature of his power use. Medvedev criticizes Stalin for his long rule, which is personality-determined, not situation-determined, has produced personality rule and serious distortions in the theory and practice of socialist reconstruction, created arbitrary rule and terror causing death of millions. There is no continuity between Leninism and Stalinism. 'The cult of the state and worship of rank, the irresponsibility of those who hold power and the population's lack of rights, the hierarchy of privileges and the canonization of hypocrisy, the barrack system of social and intellectual life, the suppression of the individual and the destruction of independent thought, the environment of terror and suspicion, the atomization of people and the notorious "vigilance", the uncontrolled violence and the legalized cruelty.' (Medvedev, 1971: 553).

Markovic stresses the characteristic features of Stalinism—violent anti-capitalist revolution with the replacement of the political power of the bourgeoisie by the power of political bureaucracy of a proletarian State and of private property by State ownership of the means of production; monolithic, strongly disciplined, strictly hierarchical Party with a monopoly of all economic and political power reducing all other social organizations to its mere transmissions; existence of the State even after complete liquidation of a capitalist class; rigid administrative planning of all production and complete control of all political life; dictatorship of the Party leadership of a single leader in the name of the dictatorship of the working class; a new type of society characterized as collectivist welfare society, where all forms of economic and political alienation would survive; a centralized political and economic structure, where smaller nations are denied self-determination and continue to be dominated by the biggest nation; subordination of culture to politics and sphere of control by the ruling Party even in the fields of culture.

Cohen and Gouldner criticize Stalinism particularly on the basis of totalitarianism, excesses and reign of terror. According to Cohen, Stalinism = excess; Stalinism = (nationalism + bureaucratization + absence of democracy + censorship + police repression); Stalinism = extraordinary extremism; Stalinism = (civil war against the peasantry – mere coercive peasant politics); Stalinism = (holocaust by terror – civil war style terror or mere police repression); Stalinism = (fascist like chauvinism – Thermidorian revival of nationalization); Stalinism = (deification of a despot – mere leader cult). Stalinism essentially connotes excesses of rule. It is the systematic reign of terror aiming at and bringing about a transfer of property, where the private property is supported by State owned property, aiming at and bringing about collectivization of property. This reign of terror perpetrated by personal dictatorship with bureaucracy is responsible for bringing about mass property transfer.

According to Gouldner, there is a fusion of Leninism and Stalinism or the ideas of Lenin and Stalin, which may be stated as—(Leninism + Stalinism) = (Relatively voluntaristic politics + Model of economic development). Economic development needs industrialization, fostering of technological hardware and forces of production. Stalinism is characterized by terror and class conflict within the Soviet society, where socialism and socialist consciousness are brought to the groups and classes from outside by theoretically prescient elite. Following Gouldner, it can be pointed out that Stalin's account of Soviet government is conditioned by—punitive action of Soviet government → hegemony of the urban-centered power elite over the peasant community and over the countryside → mobilization of State power over the peasants → internal colonialism → colonial tributaries in rural territories. Tucker, following Gouldner, cites Stalinism as the revolutionary phenomenon in essence, an integral phase of the Russian revolutionary process. Stalinism is a culmination of several factors—the heritage of Bolshevik revolutionism, heritage of old Russia, the mind and personality of Stalin, rural revolution, mass collectivization and industrialization. Stalinism is a continuation of Leninism, continuation of revolutionary leadership, continuation of proletarian dictatorship, which is the continuation of class struggle in new forms, continuation of collectivization, which is the continuation of internal class struggle. However, Stalin's socialism is different in terms of mass poverty, sharp stratification, constant fear, national chauvinism and State power from that of Marx, Engels and Lenin.

Stalin's supremacy in Russia gained ground by April 1925, when the Party Congress accepted Stalin's thesis of socialism in one country, which is an amalgam of revolutionary environment, revolutionary outlook, revolutionary upsurge, Russian Marxism, features of Russian landscape and the Russian outlook. Mention here may be made that Russian revolutionary tradition and outlook are influenced by authoritarian elements in the Leninist political model, Lenin's theory of Party organization and rigid autocracy. Stalin regards that the Bolsheviks in Russia must use the State as the base for overthrowing imperialism and must therefore consolidate the dictatorship of the proletariat, where in this struggle the principal ally in capitalist countries must be the industrial workers, but the Bolsheviks must win the support of the peasants in their struggle against the bourgeois democrats, exponents of the policy of compromise with imperialism and parties of the Second International. The Bolsheviks should have to consolidate with the dictatorship of the proletariat. The Party must lead the proletariat. The peasants in alliance with the proletariat are guided by the vanguard Party. The Party never shares power with any other. It maintains contact with people through transmission belts like trade unions, Soviets etc. Party guides and persuades the people, convince them and then coerce. Therefore, dictatorship of the proletariat is not equivalent to the dictatorship of the Party. The Party is closely linked with the class and masses and by means of which the dictatorship of the class is exercised. It is also absurd to distinguish between the dictatorship of the leaders and dictatorship of the masses.

According to Stalin, it is the duty of the Party to lead proletarian revolution. Plamenatz evaluates in this respect both Stalin and Trotsky. 'Stalin attacked Trotsky for advocating "permanent revolution"? According to Trotsky, it was the duty of the Comintern to work continually for world proletarian revolution. There must be no internal of quiescence between the Bolshevik revolution and similar revolutions in other countries; there must be no letting up of energy, no putting other things first on the pretence that they were more urgent. Stalin, though he believed in the eventual (and even early) coming of world proletarian revolution, thought it inopportune in the middle twenties to incite the workers to make it. The incitement would exasperate bourgeois governments and unite them in common action against Bolshevik Russia. The Communists must bide their time, knowing that the not-too-distant future would bring new opportunities. But we must recognize that, of the moment, the times were unpropitious. Russia was still weak, and the capitalist world had recovered much of the strength lost during the war. We must distinguish the doctrine of "permanent revolution" attacked by Stalin in 1926 from the other doctrine of "permanent" or "uninterrupted revolution" expounded by the both Lenin and Trotsky in 1905. The earlier doctrine asserted that circumstances peculiar to Russia (or to countries like her) made it possible for the Russian proletariat and their vanguard to take a decisive part in the bourgeois revolution against the Tsarist autocracy, and then to use their power to change the character of that revolution until it became "proletarian" and "socialist". This doctrine, expounded with considerable vigour by both men (though rather more clearly by Trotsky than by Lenin), was inspired by one revolution and was revived on the eve of the next. Whereas the doctrine of "permanent revolution" attacked by Stalin in the middle of twenties advocated the devoting of Communist energies, everywhere and continuously, to making the revolution that would destroy world capitalism. The two doctrines are not unrelated—for Trotsky believed that there could be no uninterrupted progress towards socialism in Russia unless there was world "proletarian revolution".' (Plamenatz, 1954: 277).

Trotsky imagines that the advance towards socialism would be an uninterrupted advance, *i.e.* from bourgeois revolution, then a period of bourgeois ascendancy, and then the period of proletarian revolution, that is punctuated by the sequential advance: bourgeois revolution of 1905 → leading role of capitalism and the political ascendancy of the middle class → establishment of revolutionary dictatorship of the proletariat and the peasantry. Trotsky believes that —

> first, if revolution of 1905 in Russia continuous, the real power would go to the workers, and not to the bourgeoisie;
> second, successful revolution would bring socialism to Russia;
> third , this revolution would bring the transition to socialism smooth and rapid;
> fourth, this socialism would provide to the workers power;
> fifth, this socialism can only exist in advanced industrial economy; and
> sixth, if Russia of 1905 needs to be socialist, then it should be changed economically.

Furthermore, Trotsky believes that proletariat can seize power and deprive the bourgeoisie of its inheritance by using this State power. This is the similarity between Lenin and Trotsky about the revolution of 1905. But there is a difference between them with regard to the revolution of 1905—the alliance between the workers and peasants is of little importance to Trotsky, to whom the peasants as allies of the workers must be subordinated to them—the workers should control the transformation of Russia into a socialist and industrial State, which is not suitable and conducive to the peasants community. Trotsky sequentially finds—

> bourgeois-democratic tasks of the revolution of 1905 → bourgeois-democratic character of the revolution → impossibility of downgrading and displacing the bourgeoisie and their parties to lead the revolution who are at the helm of the affairs → abstaintion from any excessive actions on the part of the proletariat of the proletarian tactics—defending the specific demands, such as eight-hours day, right to strike and form trade unions etc. so that the bourgeoisie cannot push the revolution into a counter-revolutionary trend and a defeat.

According to Trotsky, the revolutuion cannot jump over the capitalist stage. The democratic dictatorship of the workers and peasants is different from proletarian and bourgeois dictatorship, and the bourgeois State emerges from bourgeois dictatorship as the economy of capitalist in character emerges from the bourgeois revolution. What is the bourgeois character of Russian revolution? Lenin in *Two Tactics* says that it means the reform measures, *i.e.*, the democratic reforms in the political system and the social and economic reforms that have become a necessity in Russia. Reforms in themselves do not imply the undermining of bourgeois rule. On the contrary, they will clear the ground for a wide, rapid and European development of capitalism. 'Unevenness, the most general law of the historic process, reveals itself most sharply and complexly in the destiny of the backward countries. Under the whip of external necessity their backward culture is compelled to make leaps. From the universal law of unevenness thus derives another law which, for the lack of a better name, we may call the law of combined development—by which we mean drawing together of the different stages of the journey, a combining of separate steps, an amalgam of archaic with more contemporary forms.' (Trotsky, 1967: 13-14). See Figure 73.

Trotsky believes that conquering of State power by the working class, sufficient self-restraint, defense of their specific class interests, and limitation of struggle for democratic and immediate demands— all these will not solve the problem of socialist reconstruction or socialist revolution in a backward country like Russia. Here, the working class remains to be exploited by the capitalists. Without conquering leadership of the whole nation the proletariat would be defeated in their missions of self-restraint, industrialization, modernization, and finally socialist reconstruction. See below:

> first stage → achievement of the supreme victory by the working class against autocracy
> second stage → achievement of supreme victory by the working class against all conservative forces, especially the bourgeoisie
> third stage → conquering of State power by the working class
> fourth stage → establishment of revolutionary government by the working class
> fifth stage → State rule by the working class with full of socio-political self-confidence and armed power
> sixth stage → economically the working class is exploited by the unarmed capitalists
> seventh stage → socialist reconstruction under socialist revolution is doomed to failure.

Therefore, in *Results and Prospects* Trotsky predicts—(1) it becomes possible for the working class to conquer power in a relatively backward countries before doing the same in the most advanced countries, and (2) it is not possible for the working class to build socialism in the relatively backward countries. This becomes due to the relative weakness of the bourgeoisie compared to that of the proletariat in backward countries, when the bourgeoisie let the working class to lead the struggle for national emancipation and modernization, to absorb the powerful tendencies of social composition, and to revolutionize the working class and many other layers or levels of society. However, in backward countries the working class faces the difficulties on the road towards the direction of a classless society. Capitalism has not yet developed to the creation of material preconditions for socialist reconstruction. However, the low level of culture and technical skill, and lack of political self-rule of the working class also act as barriers to socialist reconstruction. It is not only that. The working class faces three forms of external pressures—pressures from politico-economic domain, from economic domain, and from the socio-psychological domain (Figure 74).

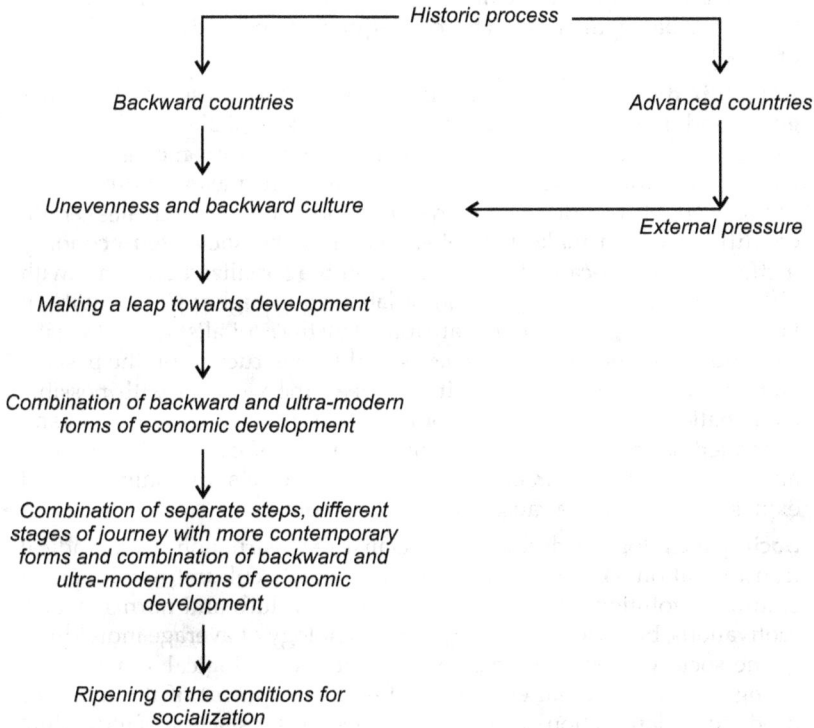

Historic process

Backward countries

Advanced countries

Unevenness and backward culture

External pressure

Making a leap towards development

Combination of backward and ultra-modern forms of economic development

Combination of separate steps, different stages of journey with more contemporary forms and combination of backward and ultra-modern forms of economic development

Ripening of the conditions for socialization

Figure 73

External pressures from triple domains

⇩

Politico-military domain → Capitalism needs to recapture the lost domain conquered by the victorious socialist revolutions through threats of war and reconquest, subversion, supporting civil wars → victorious socialist counterparts need politico-military self-defense, building and maintenance of strong armed forces to meet the opponents and fight against the enemies → strong military establishments in backward countries cost economically much more greater → politico-ideological and moral costs also make hindrances to the construction of a socialist society and to the establishment of a classless society. The cause is economic backwardness. The consequences are indirect economic offshoots.

Economic domain → Economic backwardness → pressure of cheaper goods and more advanced technology from the capitalist world market → defense on the part of the socialist countries by means of State monopoly of foreign trade and socialization of the means of production → post-capitalist world market pressures and imperialism creates certain conditions which make the self-defense of the socialized economy ineffective → post-capitalist onslaught on the socialized economy with the help of international division of labour and higher productivity of labour → the socialist economy are forced by the capitalist world to make a curious combination of tasks, *i.e.,* social reconstruction on the basis of equality, fraternity and solidarity between the workers with possible combinations and permutations of primitive socialist accumulation and expanded socialist accumulation and the tasks of competition with an alien social system characterized by anarchy, chaos, discontinuity and explosive growth. The cause is directly economic.

Socio-psychological domain → Socialist reconstruction needs radical transformation → radical transformation needs cultural revolution → cultural revolution needs radical changes in values and norms, habits, motivations, behaviour, thinking and psychology of average individuals of the society → radical changes in socio-psychological sphere need changes in the material environment → development of the forces of production, satisfaction of basic material needs, satisfaction of individual social needs, promotion of from each according to his ability to each according to his needs, increase in social wage independent of individual productive effort, rise in the standard of living etc. → growing faith in social co-operation and solidarity to satisfy all basic material needs in an equal way instead of self-gratification, self-enrichment, gains and losses in terms of material rewards and punishment.

Figure 74

Trotsky believes that the working class in backward countries would not be able to build socialism by their own efforts. However, the victorious proletariat by overthrowing capitalism at its weakest point would upset the world equilibrium of social and political forces giving a powerful impetus to world socialist revolution with the application of uneven and combined development towards socialization on a world scale. Socialism in one country is not possible. There would be no revolutionary stages in backward countries. If the proletariat succeeds in conquering political power and hegemony over the peasantry and succeeds in providing leadership over the revolutionary process, then revolution can be victorious, where (1) the proletariat must win over the bourgeoisie or the capitalist class under which or under those hands the socialization of the means of production still depends, (2) the revolution would uninterruptedly pass over from bourgeois-democratic revolutions to socialist revolution, and (3) dictatorship of the proletariat supporting the cause of the peasants would not stay within the bounds of capitalism, national and international and also (4) revolution would begin at once with the task of building socialist society or socialism— first it would begin at the national level and then it would spread internationally. Trotsky calls for world revolution—the international revolution, is a chain—moreover not a continuity of national revolutions, but each nourishes the other and in turn suffers from their failures—a totality of the concepts like world economy and class struggle subject to uneven and combined development. World revolution is the result of organic unity of national class struggles, the other side of the organic unity of the capitalist world market, from which flows growing internationalization of the productive forces, of the operations of capital and of the class struggle. This internationalization of class struggle is not the result of mechanical unification or synchronization of national class struggles, but is a chain, which leads to international wars, international revolutions, international counter-revolutions and international civil wars. Therefore, Trotsky's internationalism can be equated with a combination of moral-political repulsion for nationalism and class collaboration, internationalization of the productive forces, internationalization of the operation of capital, internationalization of the operation of class struggle overcoming of contradiction between the requirements for the survival of the nation-State and the international dynamic of the productive forces through the proletariat's struggle for world revolution and world federation of socialist republics.

In opposition to Stalinism, Trotsky inspired Left Opposition, which was defeated by Stalin. Stalin's arguments pleased the emerging powerful bureaucracies in Russia. Trotsky calls Stalin and his men in the Government of Russia as 'men of Thermidor', whose love of power and wealth turns them into the fold of reactionaries, who outlive the heroic period of revolution. Trotsky says that bureaucracy conquers something more than the Left Opposition. Bureaucracy conquers the Bolshevik Party, defeats the programme of Lenin, all the enemies, the Left Opposition, the Party, and, not with ideas and arguments, but with its own social weight. It outweighs the head of revolution, which is the secret of the Soviet's Thermidor. After Lenin's death, Stalin opens the wide gates of the Party, where the revolutionary vanguard loses its weight in raw human material, without experience, without independence and yet with the old habit of submitting to the authorities. The working class is numerically and physically weakened, absorbed by the State and the military apparatus. Members of the Soviets, who are workers, gradually left the Soviets. Party apparatus is gradually sucked into a process of gradual fusion with the State apparatus.

Bureaucratization of the Soviet State is completed by the bureaucratization of the Bolshevik Party, which thereby produces the political passivity of the working class. To the end of increasing the active and greater role for the working class in the face of growing bureaucratization, Trotsky fights for Soviet democracy and inner-Party democracy in broader perspectives, rise in real wages, disappearance of mass unemployment, accelerated industrialization and increased class struggle in the countryside. Trotsky's economic programme is based on a quicker rate of industrialization at the expense of the *kulaks* but to the benefit of the workers and peasants, on voluntary collectivization of agriculture, which can be mechanized and run by the poor peasants. This economic programme is in direct opposition to Stalin's position of adventurist industrialization and forced collectivization at the expense of both workers and peasants. The dictatorial power of bureaucracy is being exercised within the framework of transitory society, a transition between capitalism and socialism, but not a transition between State capitalism and bureaucratic collectivism. This bureaucratic State creates a degenerated form of workers' State. Bureaucracy does not create new production relation, but distorts and subverts the smooth functioning of the October Revolution. In abolishing private capital accumulation and petty commodity production Stalinist regime lowers down the standard of living of the working class and the anticipated productivity of labour. Thereby economic crises loom large. In the economic sphere Soviet bureaucracy abolishes direct workers' power in industry. Trotsky opposes the bureaucratically formation of Soviets and says about political revolution in maintaining and consolidating the main conquests of the October Revolution, in eliminating the dictatorial power of bureaucracy, in democratizing Soviet society, and in restoring the power of the proletariat through democratization of power, election of the

Soviets, multi-party system, planning system, and overall worker's management and public democratic control.

Trotsky considers the Stalin constitution of 1936 as betrayal of Bolshevism. The parliament elected by a people is divided into artificial territorial constituencies—this may look democratic, but does ensure the responsibility of the government to the people. This territorial constituency is not a social unit, has no common interest, no common will, and therefore, does not represent true community. However, a person, who represents the territorial constituency, becomes least unacceptable to different groups and classes within the constituency. Therefore, the representative must stand for something, what is common to different classes and groups within the constituency. He is a compromise candidate, and therefore, must speak and do what is common to them and what may encourage them. Parliamentary democracy is a system of belief-making and politicians are in the game of profit-making—to get power and sell the use of it to the highest bidder. But the real businesses of the government are never discussed with the people, who really make the representative or representatives. In fact, parliamentary institutions are political mechanisms of exploitation at the last stage of capitalist development. Men seek to promote their interests. Men for their own interests and for the promotion of their own interests try to become identified with institutions, myths and codes of behaviour appropriate to them.

Institutions are the ways in which men behave to their social environment with certain habits of mind and kinds of response. Parliamentary democracy is such an institutional feature, where processes are made whereby the ruling class deceives the majority that the majority 'will' is being elicited and given effect to, and amicable negotiations are made in the making of laws and executive decisions in the interest of the capitalist class. This does not mean that parliamentary democracy brings no benefits to the working class. However, parliamentary democracy makes concessions to the working class in accordance with the people's will, needs and desires. There is an element of compromise. According to Trotsky, Soviet democracy is not perfectly democratic. Not only that, Trotsky condemns Stalin for his defense of one Party democracy, which endangers the survival of the Soviet State. Stalin makes defense for one Party system for the preservation of bureaucracy against the people, the workers and peasants. Stalin constitution is a consummation of evils, an attempt made by the murderers of proletarian democracy, to bury the corpse. There must be either a political revolution or a social revolution to destroy the new bureaucracy and restore a true dictatorship of the proletariat, to destroy the old property system started by the old Bolsheviks and Lenin, and restore in some form, the right of inheritance and of private property in the means of production. Stalin betrays, misunderstands and corrupts this aspect of social and political revolutions. Suppression of private property in the means of production is the necessary, but insufficient condition for the existence of the socialist society. Trotsky says that the socialist organization of the economy must tend to reduce the physiological burden for the workers. This reduction of physiological burden must be in correspondence with the increase of technical power and maintenance of the co-ordination of the efforts of the different workers. Prosperity, leisure and joy in life must be assured for all. High level of productivity of labour is unattainable without mechanisation and automation. Monotony in work can be avoided by a reduction of its duration and of the burden it imposes. Harmonious economic planning is a necessary precondition to break bureaucratic monopoly of social and economic power, and for the transition from capitalism to socialism.

Then, what about transitional society? According to Lenin, the transition has to be a period of struggle between dying capitalism and nascent communism, between defeated capitalism and feeble communism. Buick (1975) argues that transition period is the period after the capture of political power by the working class and before the actual establishment of the common ownership of the means of production. A socialist society cannot exist if there is commodity production, if goods are produced for the market, if there is a State, and if there is class society. Like that of Buick, Lock says that the socialist mode of production is an impossibility and transitional society is a combination of two contradictory modes of production—capitalist and communist. Lock and Althusser cite Stalinist deviation at the transitory level. Althusser refutes the Stalinist regime as 'abuses' and 'errors' and Lock denounces it as effects and appearances of class struggle fought out in the economic, political and ideological spheres and as simple violations of socialist legality. Mandel refers to extreme forms of bureaucratic deformation and degeneration in the Stalinist era, a transitional society characterized by two antagonistic economic logistic —the logic of the plan and logic of the market and also by two antagonistic interests—interest of the proletariat and interest of the bourgeoisie. Bettelheim considers that transitional society is characterized by lack of conformity between social relations or production forces, by contradiction between forms of property and real mode of appropriation. The basic cause is low level of economic development, low level of productive forces and economic backwardness. According to Bettelheim the resolution of conflicts in transitional society, *i.e.*, according to Mandel, is a conflict between the non-capitalist mode of production and bourgeois mode of production. This, according to Bettelheim, is a conflict between the social relations and forces of production—should have to be made through the development of productive forces. According to Mandel, transitional society is characterized by relative immaturity of its production relations. Both Mandel and Bettelheim characterize the transitional society as the stage of isolation of the October Revolution in an economically underdeveloped country thereby producing a series of distortions from a mature model of a transitional society, which are enormously increased by peculiar development of subjective factors—self-identification of Communist Party of Soviet Union with Soviet bureaucracy, bureaucratization of the Party and Stalinism. Trotsky finds in Stalinism a heritage of oppression, misery and ignorance and the pressure of a barbaric world imperialism. Low level of productive forces gives birth to socio-economic and political backwardness, shortages of necessary commodities, distribution of goods and services on bourgeois rather than socialist principles. Stalinist degeneration is the result of low cultural level, traditional life styles, illiteracy, economic backwardness, the legacy of Tsarist political culture, and low level of political consciousness. Russia is at the transitional stage between capitalism and socialism. Russia is a socialist country as (1) in this society there exists no bourgeois class, which extracts surplus value and (2) economy in this society is not based on the production of goods for exchange but is based on the production of goods for use. Stalinist degeneration has also been noticed by Carrillo (1977) that the October Revolution has produced a State, which is evidently not a bourgeois State. It is not the proletarian State organized by the proletariat as the ruling class. It is not a genuine workers' democracy and it is not a State, as the State is not an end in itself but is a tremendous means for organizing, disorganizing and reorganizing social relations, and it can be a powerful lever for revolution or a tool for organized stagnation, depending upon the hands that control it (Trotsky, 1962).

Mao-Tse-Tung explains and analyses the theory of revolution and theory of socio-political development through his conception of materialist dialectics. Mention here may be made that the workers and peasants of China seized power by force of arms and established people's democratic dictatorship, a form of the dictatorship of the proletariat corresponding to the special conditions of China. The revolution was led by the Communist Party of China under the leadership of Mao-Tse-Tung. People's Democratic Dictatorship is based on Mao's conception of New Democracy. It differs from Soviet form of dictatorship of the proletariat. Then, who are the people?—they are the workers, peasants, the urban petty bourgeoisie and national bourgeoisie, who are headed by the working class and the Communist Party. These classes unite to form their own State and elect their own government, to enforce their dictatorship over the running-dogs of imperialism. Who are the running-dogs of imperialism? They are the landlord class, the bureaucrat-bourgeoisie, representatives of the landlord and bourgeois classes and Koumingtung reactionaries. The people consisting of workers, peasants, urban petty-bourgeoisie and national bourgeoisie suppress the running-dogs of imperialism and allow them only to behave lawfully in words and deeds. Democracy is practiced within the ranks of the people. These people enjoy the rights of freedom of speech, assembly, association and so on. The right to vote only belongs to the people, and not to the reactionaries. Therefore, the People's Democratic Dictatorship constitutes democracy for the people and dictatorship of the people over the reactionaries. Proletarian Cultural Revolution is necessary for the establishment of New Democracy and People's Democratic Dictatorship. The social development and revolution, and also social progress are made through the process of contradiction— the fundamental contradiction in the process of development of a thing and the essence of the process determined by the fundamental contradiction will not disappear until the process is completed.

Contradiction is a long process, different from one stage to another. Although the fundamental contradiction in the process of the development of a thing and the essence of the process remain unchanged, the fundamental contradiction in the process of development becomes more and more intensified as it passes from one stage to another. In addition, among the major and minor contradictions, which are determined and influenced by fundamental contradiction, some become intensified, some are temporarily or permanently resolved, and some new ones emerge in the process, hence the process is marked by stages. Classes exist as a particular manifestation of the struggle of opposites. The contradiction between the exploiting and exploited classes exist or co-exist for long time in the same society, be it a slave society, feudal society or capitalist society, but it is not until the contradiction between the two classes develops to a certain stage that it assumes the form of open antagonism and develops into revolution.

The theory of revolution is based on theory of dialectical materialism, relation between knowledge and practice, between knowing and doing. The theoretical foundation of revolution is practice.

Practice depends on knowledge, which mainly depends on man's activity in the material production, through which he comes gradually to understand the phenomena, the properties and laws of nature, and the relations between man and nature and the relations between man and man. In the production process man enters into definite relations of production. Man's social practice is not confined to activity in production, but takes many other forms—class struggle, political life, and scientific and artistic pursuits. That is, man's social practice is higher than that of knowledge. Therefore, according to the Marxist-Leninist theory of dialectical materialism, social practice is the criterion of truth, which has two aspects—class nature and practicality. See Figure 75. Practice is the primary and basic standpoint of dialectical materialist theory of knowledge. The perceptual and rational are qualitatively different from each other, but they are not divorced from each other— they are unified on the basis of social practice. In its knowledge of the capitalist society, the proletariat is in the perceptual stage of cognition in the first period of its practice, the period of machine-smashing and spontaneous struggle—the proletariat knows only some of the aspects and external relations of the phenomena of capitalism. The proletariat is at the stage of class-in-itself. But when the proletariat reaches at the second stage of its practice, *i.e.,* the period of conscious and organized economic and political struggles, the proletariat is able to comprehend the essence of the capitalist society, the relations of exploitation between classes. Then, the proletariat is at the stage of class-for-itself. Graphically, it may be comprehended as in Figure 76.

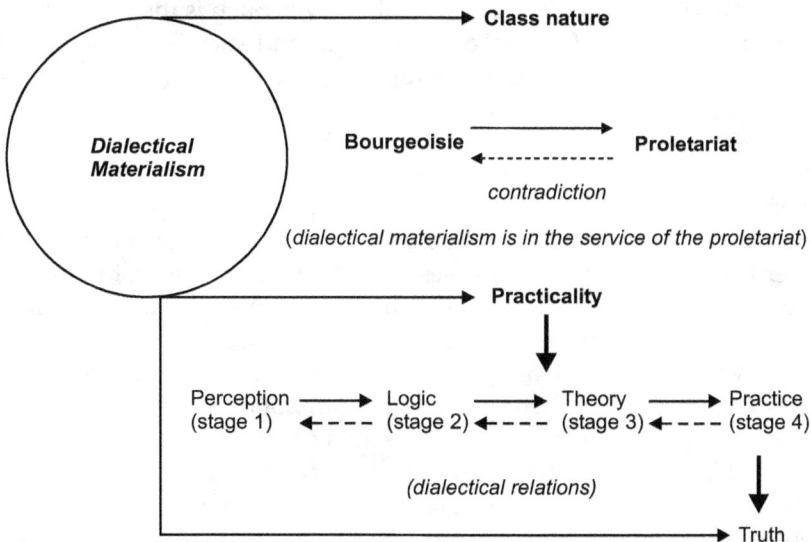

Figure 75

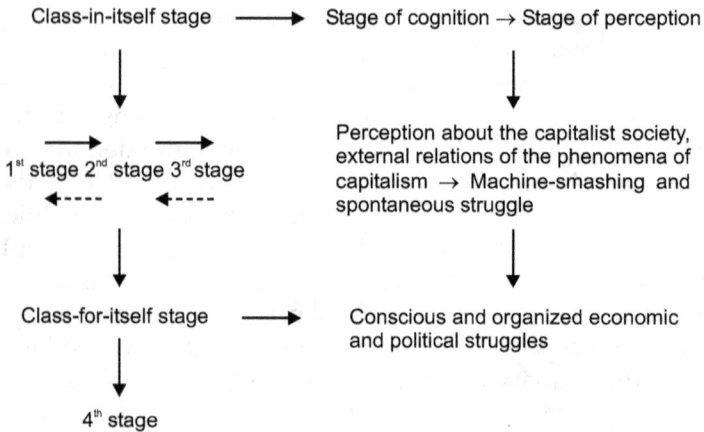

Class-in-itself stage ⟶ Stage of cognition → Stage of perception

⟶ ⟶
1ˢᵗ stage 2ⁿᵈ stage 3ʳᵈ stage
◀- - - - ◀- - - -

Perception about the capitalist society,
external relations of the phenomena of
capitalism → Machine-smashing and
spontaneous struggle

Class-for-itself stage ⟶ Conscious and organized economic
and political struggles

4ᵗʰ stage

Figure 76

Rational knowledge depends upon perceptual knowledge and perceptual knowledge remains to be developed into rational knowledge. Theory becomes purposeless and inactive if it is not connected with revolutionary practice. 'Discover the truth through practice, and again through practice verify and develop the truth. Start from perceptual knowledge and actively develop it into rational knowledge; then start from rational knowledge and actively guide revolutionary practice to change both the subjective and objective world. Practice and knowledge, again practice and then again knowledge, respectively take place. This form repeats itself in endless cycles, and with each cycle the content of practice and knowledge rises to a higher level. Such is the whole of the dialectical-materialist theory of knowledge, and such is the dialectical-materialist theory of the unity of knowing and doing.' (Mao-Tse-tung, 1973: 308).

There are two basic conceptions of development—linear and dialectical—as increase and decrease, as repetition, and as unity of opposites. Contradictoriness within a thing is the fundamental cause of its development, while its interrelations and interconnections with other things are secondary causes. Contradiction exists in the process of development of all things and a movement of opposites exists from the beginning to end in the process of development of each thing. Objective conditions are reflected in subjective thinking, and this process constitutes the contradictory movement of concepts. Opposition and struggle between ideas of different kinds constantly occur within the Party. This is a reflection within the Party of contradictions between the classes and between the old and new in the society. If there is no contradiction within the Party and no ideological struggles to resolve them, the Party will come to an end. Mao says that the Communists must learn the Marxist method of dialectic as described by Lenin in his *On the Question of Dialectics*: Marx in *Capital* first analyses the simplest, most ordinary and fundamental, most common and everyday relation of bourgeois society, *i.e.*, the exchange of commodities. This reveals all contradictions of the modern society. The growth and movement of these contradictions are revealed in the process of development from the beginning to the end. Particular contradiction constitutes particular essence which distinguishes one thing from another. The particular essence of each form of motion is determined by its own particular contradiction. Every form of society, every form of ideology, has its own particular contradiction and particular essence. Qualitatively different contradictions are resolved by qualitatively different methods. For instance:

Contradiction between and within	Methods of resolution
1. proletariat and the bourgeoisie	1. socialist revolution
2. great masses of the people and feudal system	2. democratic revolution
3. colonies and imperialism	3. national revolutionary war
4. working class and peasant class in socialist society	4. collectivization and mechanization in agriculture
5. society and nature	5. development of the productive forces
6. the Communist Party	6. criticism and self-criticism

Processes change, old processes and old contradictions disappear, new process and new contradictions emerge, and the methods of resolving contradictions differ accordingly. 'There are many contradictions in the course of development of any major thing. For instance, in the course of China's bourgeois-democratic revolution, where the conditions are exceedingly complex, there exists the contradiction between all the oppressed classes in Chinese society and imperialism, the contradiction between the great masses of the people and feudalism, the contradiction between the proletariat and bourgeoisie, the contradiction between the peasantry and the urban petty-bourgeoisie on the one hand, and the bourgeoisie on the other, the contradiction between the various reactionary ruling groups, and so on. These contradictions cannot be treated in the same way since each has its won particularity; moreover, the two aspects of each contradiction cannot be treated in the same way since each aspect has its own characteristics. We who are engaged in the Chinese revolution should not only understand the particularity of these contradictions in their totality, that is, in their interconnections, but should also study the two aspects of each contradiction as the only means of understanding the totality.' (Mao-Tse-Tung, 1973: 322-23). Mao accepts that imperialism is the highest stage of capitalism, and contradictions within it can be resolved through proletarian revolution. Revolution in its period of bourgeois leadership and revolution in its period of proletarian leadership represent two vastly different historical stages.

Proletarian leadership has fundamentally changed the whole face of the revolution, which has brought about a new alignment of classes, given rise to a tremendous upsurge in the peasant revolution, imparted thoroughness to revolution against imperialism and feudalism, created the possibility of the transition from the democratic revolution to socialist revolution, and so on. None of these is possible in the period when the revolution is under bourgeois leadership. Although no change has taken place in the nature of the fundamental contradiction in the process as a whole, *i.e.*, in the anti-imperialist, anti-feudal, and democratic-revolutionary nature of the process. In capitalist society, the two forces in contradiction, the proletariat and the bourgeoisie, form the principal contradiction. The other contradictions are between the feudal class and the bourgeoisie, peasant petty-bourgeoisie and bourgeoisie, proletariat and peasant petty-bourgeoisie, non-monopoly capitalists and monopoly capitalists, bourgeois democracy and bourgeois fascism, imperialism and colonies, and among the capitalist countries—all these non-principal contradictions are determined by the principal contradiction between capital and labour. The proletariat, which is more numerous than the bourgeoisie, and grows simultaneously with it, but under its rule, is a new force which initially subordinate to the bourgeoisie, gradually gains strength, becomes an independent class playing the leading role in history, and finally seizes political class and becomes the ruling class.

The old capitalist society becomes the new socialist society. 'Identity, unity, coincidence, interpenetration, interpermeation, interdependence (or mutual dependence for existence), interconnection or mutual co-operation—all these different terms mean the same thing and refer to the following two points: first, the existence of each of the two aspects of a contradiction in the process of development of a thing presupposes the existence of the other aspect, and both aspects coexist in a single entity; second, in given conditions, each of the two contradictory aspects transforms itself into its opposite. This is the meaning of identity.... In given conditions having and not having, acquiring and losing, are interconnected; there is identity of the two sides. Under socialism, private peasant ownership is transformed into the public ownership of socialist agriculture;.... There is a bridge leading from private property to public property, which in philosophy is called identity, or transformation into each other, or interpenetration. To consolidate the dictatorship of the proletariat or the dictatorship of the people is in fact to prepare conditions for abolishing this dictatorship and advancing to the higher stage when all State systems are eliminated.... These opposites are at the same time complementary.' (Mao-Tse-Tung, 1973: 337,339).

In human history, the antagonism between classes exists as a particular manifestation of the struggle of opposites. This antagonism between classes develops into revolution. Resolute leadership of the democratic revolution is the pre-requisite for the victory of socialism. The democratic revolution would develop itself through several stages under the slogan of a democratic republic. The change from the predominance of bourgeoisie to that of the proletariat is a long process of struggle. The success of the proletarian struggle depends on the work of the Communist Party in raising the level of political consciousness and organization of the proletariat, of the peasantry and of urban petty bourgeoisie. The first ally is the peasantry, and then comes the urban petty bourgeoisie. 'It is the bourgeoisie that will contend with us for leadership. To overcome the vacillation of the bourgeoisie and its lack of revolutionary thoroughness we must rely on the strength of the masses and on the correctness of our policy, or otherwise the bourgeoisie will come out on top.... We are exponents of the theory of the transition of the revolution, and not of the Trotskyite theory of "permanent revolution". We are for the attainment of socialism by going through all the necessary stages of the democratic republic. We are opposed to Taylorism, but we are also opposed to adventurism and impetuosity. To reject the participation of the bourgeoisie in the revolution on the ground that it can only be temporary and to describe the alliance with anti-Japanese sections of the bourgeoisie as capitulation is a Trotskyite approach, with which we cannot agree.' (Mao-Tse-Tung, 1973: 291). At present, such an alliance is in fact a necessary bridge on the way to socialism.

Then, what does Mao say about New Democracy? Mao says that Communists struggle for Cultural Revolution as well as for political and economic revolution with an aim to build a new society and a new State for the Chinese nation. This new society and the new State will have not only a new politics and a new economy but also a new culture. The aim in cultural sphere is to build a new Chinese national culture. Culture as an ideological form is the reflection of politics and economics, where the former has tremendous effect and influence upon the latter, where and when economic is the base, and politics is the concentrated expression of economics. In this connection, Marx says that consciousness of men does not determine their being, but on the contrary, social being determines their consciousness. The philosophers have interpreted the world in various ways; the point is to change it.

How are the old Chinese economics, politics and culture replaced with the advent of the new ones? See Figure 77. Against these colonial, semi-colonial and semi-feudal political, economic and cultural forms revolution is directed with a view to build up new politics, new economic and new culture. This revolution must go through two stages—first, democratic revolution and second, the socialist revolution. Here, democracy belongs to the New Democracy. China's new politics belongs to politics of New Democracy, China's new economics belongs to economics of New Democracy and China's new culture is the culture of New Democracy. Any political party, group or person taking part in the Chinese revolution that fails to understand this will not be able to direct the revolution and lead it to victory, but will be cast aside by the people and left to grieve out in the cold.

The Chinese revolution is a part of the world revolution. This Chinese revolution must be divided into two stages—the first stage is to change the colonial, semi-colonial and semi-feudal form of society into an independent democratic society and the second stage is to carry revolution forward and build a socialist society. The first stage started with the Opium War in 1840, when China starts changing into a semi-colonial and semi-feudal one from her feudal status. Then comes the Movement of the Taiping Heavenly Kingdom, the Sino French War, the Sino-Japanese War, the Reform Movement of 1898, the Revolution of 1911, the May 4th Movement, the Northern Expedition, the War of the Agrarian Revolution and the present war of Resistance against Japan. This first stage is a struggle waged by the Chinese people against imperialism and feudalism in order to build up an independent and democratic society and complete the first stage of the revolution, *i.e.*, the stage of bourgeois-democratic revolution. A change occurs in China's bourgeois-democratic revolution after the outbreak of the first imperialist world war in 1914 and founding of the socialist State at the global scale after the October Revolution of 1917 in Russia. After the October Revolution in Russia the whole course of world history has been changed and the capitalist front has been collapsed. Any revolution, then, in a colony or semi-colony directed against imperialism or international capitalism no longer comes within the old category of bourgeois-democratic revolution. This revolution may be termed as proletarian-socialist world revolution. They have become allies of the revolutionary front of world socialism. In a colonial and semi-colonial country the social character of such a revolution is fundamentally bourgeois-democratic at its first step, but the objective mission is to clear the path for the development of capitalism unlike the aim of the bourgeois-democratic revolution of establishing a capitalist society and a State under bourgeois dictatorship. The new type of revolution, *i.e.*, proletarian-socialist world revolution with the aim of establishing a new democratic society and a State under the joint dictatorship of all the revolutionary classes—this revolution serves the purpose of clearing a still wider path for the development of socialism, attacks imperialism, and this revolution is served by socialism and supported by land of socialism and socialist international proletariat. Therefore, this revolution becomes the part of world revolution.

In this connection Stalin in his *The October Revolution and the National Question* provides the international significance of October Revolution of 1917 in Russia—Revolution has widened the scope of national question, *i.e.*, converting of national question of combating national oppression in Europe into the question of emancipation of the oppressed peoples, colonies and semi-colonies from imperialism; Revolution has drawn the common people into the common current of the victorious struggle against imperialism; and Revolution has bridged the socialist West and the enslaved East. Lenin in *The Discussion on Self-Determination Summed Up* points out that the main point of the national question, the right to self-determination has ceased to be a part of the general democratic movement, and it has already become a component part of the general proletarian socialist revolution or proletarian-socialist world revolution. This revolution has the proletariat of the capitalist countries as the main force and the oppressed peoples of the colonies and semi-colonies as their allies.

Before the 4th May, 1919 movement, the petty-bourgeoisie and bourgeoisie were the leaders of the bourgeois-democratic revolution, where the proletariat participated in the revolution only as the follower. After 4th May the leadership position goes to the proletariat, although the national bourgeoisie continue to take part in the revolution. Mao says:

> Being a bourgeoisie in a colonial and semi-colonial country and oppressed by imperialism, the Chinese national bourgeoisie retains a certain revolutionary quality at certain periods and to a certain degree—even in the era of imperialism—in its opposition to the foreign imperialists and the domestic governments of bureaucrats and warlords, and it may ally itself with the proletariat and the petty bourgeoisie against such enemies as it is ready to oppose. In this respect the Chinese bourgeoisie differs from the bourgeoisie of the Tsarist Russia.... Here, the task of proletariat is to form a united front with the national bourgeoisie against imperialism and the bureaucrat and warlord governments without overlooking its revolutionary quality.... the Chinese national bourgeoisie also has another quality, namely, proneness to conciliation with the enemies of the revolution.... Possible participation in the revolution on the one hand and

proneness to conciliation with the enemies of the revolution on the other —such is the dual character of the Chinese bourgeoisie, it forces both ways. ....Therefore, the proletariat, the peasantry, the intelligentsia and other sections of the petty bourgeoisie undoubtedly constitute the basic forces determining China's fate. (Mao-Tse-Tung, 1973: 348-350).

This new democratic republic is different from both European-American form of capitalist republic and Soviet form of socialist republic, and is a transitional State between the two. The European-American form of capitalist republic is under the dictatorship of the bourgeoisie and the Soviet form of socialist republic is under the dictatorship of proletariat. The new democratic republic is under the joint dictatorship of several revolutionary classes. That is to say that republic under the joint dictatorship of several revolutionary classes is a State of transition between republic under bourgeois dictatorship and republic under dictatorship of the proletariat. The new-democratic State is under the joint dictatorship of several anti-imperialist classes. It is anti Japanese and an anti-imperialist united front. China may now adopt a system of people's Congress. China will own big banks, big industrial and commercial enterprises—'enterprises, such as banks, railways and airlines, whether Chinese-owned or foreign-owned, which are either monopolistic in character or too big for private management, shall be operated and administered by the State, so that private capital cannot dominate the livelihood of the people: this is the main principle of the regulation of capital.' (Mao-Tse-Tung, 1973: 353). In the new-democratic republic the State enterprises will be of a socialist character, however the State will neither confiscate capitalist private property nor forbid the development of capitalist production. China's economy must follow the path of regulation of capital, equalization of land ownership. The economy must not be privately owned by the few, and must not be dominated by the semi-feudal elements. The livelihood of the people must not be dominated by the few capitalists and landlords.

At present, the international situation is a struggle between capitalism and socialism, where capitalism is on a downslide and socialism is on the up. International capitalism or imperialism will not permit the establishment in China of a capitalist society under bourgeois dictatorship, because international capitalism or imperialism will always try for making more colonies for the benefits of their own. A mention here may be made that—

> We Communists will never push aside anyone who is revolutionary; we shall persevere in the united front and practise long-term co-operation with all those classes, strata, political parties and groups and individuals that are willing to fight Japan to the end...., the present revolution is the

first step, which will develop into the second step, that of socialism, at a later date...The present task of the revolution in China is to fight imperialism and feudalism, and socialism is out of question until this task is completed. The Chinese revolution cannot avoid taking the two steps, first of New Democracy and then of socialism. (Mao-Tse-Tung, 1973: 358).

Unlike the theory of a single revolution and theory of accomplishing both political revolution and social revolution at one stroke, Mao understands that revolution is divided into stages and revolutionaries can proceed to the next stage of revolution after accomplishing the first, when the first stage provides the conditions for the second. The two stages must be consecutive. The Communists assert New Democracy for the first stage and socialism for the second stage guided by the same Communist ideology.

Then, here comes the question of culture. Culture is the ideological reflection of the politics and economics of the given Chinese society. Chinese culture is imperialist, which is the reflection of imperialist rule in the political and economic fields. Chinese society is no longer an entirely feudal but a semi-feudal society. Feudal economy still predominates with the emergence of capitalist economy in China. The political forces of the bourgeoisie, proletariat and the petty-bourgeoisie are the new political forces, which have emerged and grown up with the growth and emergence of capitalist economy. The capitalist culture reflects the new political and economic forces in the field of ideology and serves them. Further, without the capitalist economy, without the petty-bourgeoisie, bourgeoisie and the proletariat, and without the new political and economic forces, new ideology or culture cannot emerge. The old political, economic and cultural forces are semi-feudal and imperialist. The struggle is between the old and new forces, between revolution and counter-revolution. Mao says:

> The new-democratic culture is the anti-imperialist and anti-feudal culture of the broad masses; today it is the culture of the anti-Japanese united front. This culture can be led only by the culture and ideology of the proletariat, by the ideology of communism, and not by the culture and ideology of any other class. (Mao-Tse-Tung, 1973: 373).

The Cultural Revolution is the ideological reflection of the political and economic revolution. The Chinese revolution is not yet a socialist revolution for the overthrow of capitalism, but a bourgeois-democratic revolution for combating foreign imperialism and domestic feudalism. Since the present Chinese revolution is a part of the world proletarian-socialist revolution, today the Chinese new culture is a part of the world proletarian-socialist new culture and is its great ally. Chinese revolution cannot go without proletarian leadership, and Chinese culture without proletarian ideology and proletarian culture. Revolutionary culture is a powerful revolutionary weapon for the broad masses of the people, prepares the ground for revolution. Without revolutionary theory there can be no revolutionary movement. A national, scientific and popular mass culture is essential to fight against imperialism and feudalism.

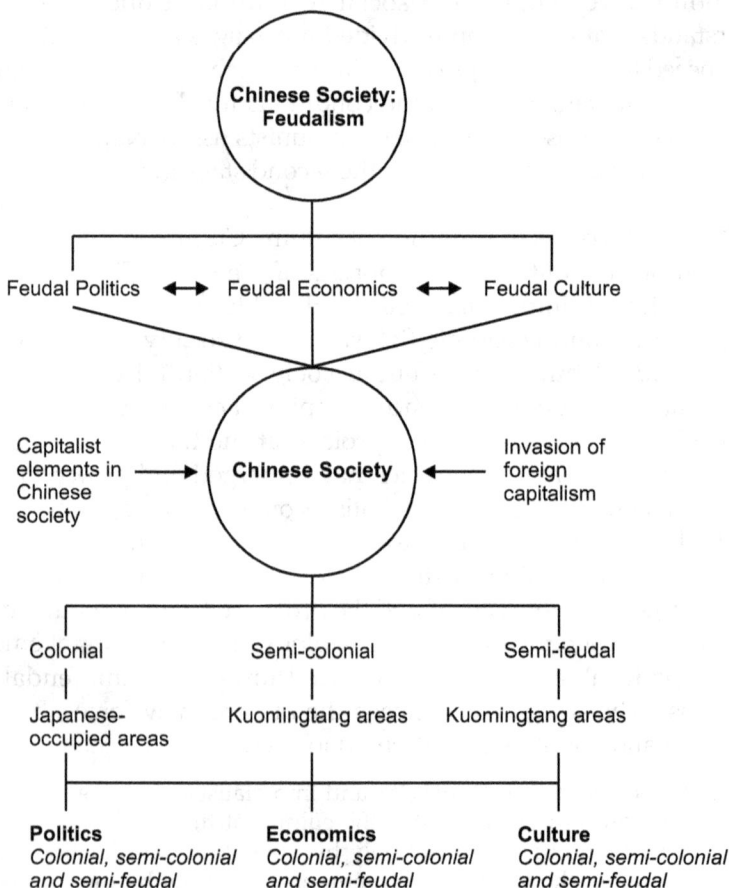

Chinese Society: Feudalism

Feudal Politics ⟷ Feudal Economics ⟷ Feudal Culture

Capitalist elements in Chinese society ⟶ **Chinese Society** ⟵ Invasion of foreign capitalism

Colonial — Semi-colonial — Semi-feudal

Japanese-occupied areas — Kuomingtang areas — Kuomingtang areas

Politics
Colonial, semi-colonial and semi-feudal

Economics
Colonial, semi-colonial and semi-feudal

Culture
Colonial, semi-colonial and semi-feudal

Figure 77

Lenin realizes that for the complete victory of socialism it becomes necessary that (1) masses of workers and peasants should take part in the affairs of the government and should take it into their own hands; (2) they should raise their cultural level to the point at which they could impose their ideology or so to say proletarian ideology. These are the aims of the Proletarian Cultural Revolution. They are designed to eliminate hostile elements to socialism, and to enable the working class to exercise leadership in everything and to launch an all-out offensive against the bourgeois ideology in such a way that the masses would be actively involved. The masses should liberate themselves. During the Cultural Revolution a revolutionary committee springs up based on 'three-in-one' combination—Party, People's Liberation Army and mass organizations: members of the revolutionary committee are elected, subject to recall and are directly responsible to the people. They are drawn from the Party, People's Liberation Army and the mass organizations. The revolutionary committees are the creation of the masses. According to Mao, the most fundamental principle in the reform of State organs is that they must keep in contact with the masses. The representatives of the revolutionary masses, the representatives of the working people— the workers and peasants come forward in the course of Proletarian Cultural Revolution. The revolutionary masses participate in the leading groups at various levels. This provides revolutionaries at all these levels with a broad mass foundation. Direct participation of the revolutionary masses in the running of the country and the enforcement of the revolutionary supervision from below over the organs of political power at various levels—ensure that the leading groups at all levels always adhere to the mass line, maintain the closet relations with the masses, represent their interests at all times, and serve the people heart and soul. According to Mao, transition to communism is a lengthy process and its successful completion can be ensured through continuing class struggle to the end. The final victory of a socialist country requires not only the efforts of the proletariat and the broad masses of the people at home, but also involves the victory of the world revolution and the abolition of the system of exploitation of man by man on the global level.

In the respect of the Ninth Party Congress of 1969, we can find the teachings of the Proletarian Cultural Revolution—grasp revolution and promote production. This teaching explains the relationship between revolution and production, between consciousness and matter, between superstructure and the economic basis, between the relations of production and forces of production. Political work is the life blood of all economic works. Politics is the concentrated expression of economics. If revolution is failed at the superstructural level, then arousing of the broad masses of the workers and peasants, criticism of the revisionist line, exposing of the true nature of handful of capitalist roaders and counter-revolutionaries, and consolidation of the leadership of the proletariat are also doomed to failures. How can the revolutionaries further consolidate the socialist economic base and further develop the socialist productive forces? In fact, this is not to replace production by revolution, but to use revolution to command production, promote it and lead it to forward. Productive forces, practice and economic base generally play the principal and decisive role. In certain conditions such aspects as relations of production, theory and the superstructure, in turn, manifest themselves in principal and decisive role.

The Sixteen-Point Programme of the Cultural Revolution, 1966 may be pointed out here. These may be presented as such—

1. .... To overthrow a political power, it is always necessary, first of all, to create public opinion, to do work in the ideological sphere.... At present, our objective is to struggle against and crush those persons in authority who are taking the capitalist road, to criticize and repudiate the reactionary bourgeois academic 'authorities' and the ideology of the bourgeoisie and all other exploiting classes and to transform education, literature, and art and all other parts of the superstructure that do not correspond to the socialist economic base, so as to facilitate the consolidation and development of the socialist system....

2. ... The masses of the workers, peasants, soldiers, revolutionary intellectuals, and revolutionary cadres form the main force in this great Cultural Revolution.

3. ... What the Central Committee of the Party demands of the Party Committees at all levels is that they persevere in giving correct leadership, put daring above everything else, boldly arouse the masses, ..., encourage those comrades who have made mistakes but are willing to correct them to cast of their mental burdens and join in the struggle, and dismiss from their leading posts all those in authority who are taking the capitalist road and so make possible the recapture of the leadership for the proletarian revolutionaries.

4. ... Make the fullest use of big-character posters and great debates to argue matters out, so that the masses can clarify the correct views, criticize the wrong views, and expose all the ghosts and monsters. In this way the masses will be able to raise their political consciousness in the course of the struggle, enhance their abilities and talents, distinguish right from wrong, and draw a clear line between the enemy and ourselves.

5. ... Concentrate all forces to strike at the handful of ultra-reactionary bourgeois rightists and counter-revolutionary revisionists and expose and criticize to the full their crimes against the Party, against socialism and against Mao-Tse-Tung Thought so as to isolate to the maximum....

6. A strict distinction must be made between the two different

types of contradictions: those among the people and those between ourselves and the enemy... The method to be used in debates is to present facts, reason things out, and persuade through reasoning....

7. ... To prevent the struggle from being diverted from its main objective, it is not allowed, whatever the pretext, to incite the masses to struggle against each other or the students to do likewise. Even proven rightists should be dealt with on the merits of each case at a later stage of the movement.

8. .... The anti-Party, anti-socialist rightist must be fully exposed, hit hard, pulled down and completely discredited and their influence eliminated....

9. .... cultural revolutionary groups, committees, and congresses are excellent new forms of organization whereby under the leadership of the Communist Party the masses are educating themselves....

10. .... In every kind of school we must apply thoroughly the policy advanced by Comrade Mao-Tse-Tung, of education serving proletarian politics and education being combined with productive labour, so as to enable those receiving an education to develop morally, intellectually, and physically and to become labourers with socialist consciousness and culture....

11. In the course of the mass movement of the Cultural Revolution, the criticism of bourgeois and feudal ideology should be well combined with the dissemination of the proletarian world outlook and of Marxism-Leninism-Mao-Tse-Tung Thought....

12. As regards scientists, technicians, and ordinary members of working staff, as long as they are patriotic, work energetically, are not against the Party and socialism, and maintain no illicit relations with any foreign country, we should in the present movement continue to apply the policy of 'unity, criticism, unity'....

13. ....The great cultural revolution has enriched the Socialist Education Movement in both city and countryside and raised it to a higher level. Efforts should be made to conduct these two movements in close combination....

14. The aim of the Great Proletarian Cultural Revolution is to revolutionize people's ideology and as a consequence to achieve greater, faster, better, and more economical results in all fields of work. If the masses are fully aroused and proper arrangement are made, it is possible to carry on both the cultural revolution and production without one hampering the other, while guaranteeing high quality in all our work....

15. In the armed forces, the Cultural Revolution and the Socialist Education Movement should be carried out in accordance with the instructions of the Military Commission of the Central Committee and the General Political Department of the People's Liberation Army.

16. ... Party committees at all levels must abide by the directions given by Chairman Mao over the years, namely that they should thoroughly apply the main line of 'from the masses to the masses' and that they should be pupils before they become teachers.

In the revolutionary struggle the chief targets are imperialism and feudalism—the bourgeoisie of the imperialist countries and landlords of the Chinese society. They are the chief oppressors and chief obstacles to Chinese progress. Both imperialism and feudalism collude with each other in oppressing the Chinese people. In the face of such enemies, the principal means or forms of the revolution must be armed struggle. It does not mean abandonment of other forms of struggles, rather the other forms of struggle must be co-ordinated with the armed struggle. Stressing work in the rural base areas does not mean abandoning work in the cities and in other vast rural areas. Without work in the cities and in other vast rural areas, the rural base areas would be isolated and revolution would suffer a defeat. The major objective of the revolution is the destruction of the enemy's main bases in the cities. The major tasks of the Chinese revolution are to carry out a national revolution to overthrow foreign imperialist oppression and a democratic revolution to overthrow feudal landlord oppression. These two tasks are united and interlinked. 'What classes are there in present-day Chinese society? There are the landlord class and the bourgeoisie, the landlord class and the upper stratum of the bourgeoisie constituting the ruling classes in Chinese society. And there are the proletariat, the peasantry, and the different sections of the petty bourgeoisie other than the peasantry, all of which are still the subject classes in vast areas of China.' (Mao-Tse-Tung, 1973: 319). In the bourgeois-democratic revolution the role of the peasantry, the proletariat and other sections of the petty bourgeoisie either in the alignment of class forces for the struggle or in the organization of State power cannot be ignored. The revolution must strive to create a democratic republic in which the workers, the peasants and other sections of the petty bourgeoisie occupy definite place and play definite role. At this stage, a certain degree of capitalist development would be an inevitable result of the victory of democratic revolution in an economically backward country like China. But this is a one-sided picture of Chinese economy and society. The other side is the development of the socialist society. Therefore, the whole picture is the development of socialist as well as capitalist factors. The socialist factors as Mao-Tse-Tung puts are:

1. relative importance of the proletarian class and their vanguard, the Communist Party as the political force in the country,
2. leadership led by the proletariat and the Communist Party,
3. peasantry, the intelligentsia and the urban petty bourgeoisie accept the proletarian leadership,
4. the State sectors of the economy are owned by the democratic republic, and
5. the co-operative sectors of the economy are owned by the working people. Mao says, 'To complete China's bourgeois-democratic revolution and to transform it into a socialist revolution when all the necessary conditions are ripe—such is the sum total of the great and glorious revolutionary task of the Chinese Communist Party. Every Party member must strive for its accomplishment and must under no circumstances give up halfway.... Every Communist ought to know that, taken as a whole, the Chinese revolutionary movement led by the Communist Party embraces the two stages, *i.e.*, the democratic and the socialist revolutions, ... The democratic revolution is the necessary preparation for the socialist revolution, and the socialist revolution is the inevitable sequel to the democratic revolution. The ultimate aim for which all communists strive is to bring about a socialist and communist society. A clear understanding of both the differences and the interconnections between the democratic and the socialist revolutions is indispensable to correct leadership in the Chinese revolution.' (Mao-Tse-Tung, 1973: 330-31).

Critics like John Elster (1985, 1988) see that Marx's theory of revolution is based on teleological reasoning. According to historical materialist understanding of Marx, revolutions occur due to the conflict between the forces of production and relations of production, which analytical Marxists find as an odd juxtaposition or a curious admixture of revolutionary romanticism and sundry hard materialism. To them, revolution is the expression of pure potentiality, the power and fecundity of the social community. Applying the method of integration of institutional structure, centrality of class dynamics and strategic rationality analytical Marxists justify the classical Marxists' understanding of revolution, their exaggeration of formative power of revolutions and at the same time underestimation of human costs. However, they make a connection between revolutions and forces of production—revolutions as crises in the forces of production. To them, strategic rationality is the useful method to analyze revolutionary class dynamics, there is no specific class structure and no specific class dynamics or specific forms of class dynamics, rather the class structure and class dynamics are derived from the distribution of productive property and the social rules specifying or indicating the use of productive property. Not only the exaggeration of the formative powers of revolutions and underestimation of human costs, according to Elster, Marx's general tendency is to explain all classical revolutions, for example the English revolution and French revolution in terms of final causes or achievements rather than at the social forces that make the revolutions to crop up or set them in motion. The achievements of bourgeois revolutions include abolition of feudal privileges, emergence of free competitive economy, and transition from absolute to constitutional monarchy. Marx's analysis of bourgeois revolution is based on tension between causal analysis, treatment of classes as rational actors, teleological reasoning and classes as puppets of history. Communism can only succeed if it is established on a wider scale. Communism, in a miniature form, cannot become economically superior and can never successfully compete with capitalism. Marx never articulates that communism is more technologically advanced than that of capitalism. Myopia, aversion to take risk, costs of revolution and romanticism—all make impotent the revolutionary working class movement for communism. Communist revolutions occur in underdeveloped countries and the subjective and objective conditions of revolution occur in opposite, for example,

> objective conditions for revolutionary working class movement: large-scale industrial production, rapid development of scientific knowledge and technological innovation, rapid development of the forces of production, high productivity of labour—are also the conditions for advanced capitalism, and subjective conditions for revolutionary working class movement: revolutionary consciousness, revolutionary movements, co-operative consciousness, co-operative movements, alienation from capitalism—are also conditions for underdeveloped countries in the capitalist world.

Therefore, communism cannot compete with capitalism. Both the subjective and objective conditions are opposed to each other. When alienation from capitalism becomes the subjective condition of revolution, then how become the objective conditions the objectively responsible factors for the revolutionary working class movement for communism? It is not possible and Marxist analysis of communism is different from Soviet Communism or German Communism, is not the same as Russian

Communism. Communist revolution in the capitalist world is not possible mainly through persuasion and coercion, institutionalization and threat, through high labour productivity and rapid industrialization, through material concessions diffusing the revolutionary movements, and through State power coercing and crushing the revolutionaries. Therefore, the revolutionaries, the workers and peasants will act rationally and hence, communist revolution becomes extremely unlikely in advanced capitalist countries. Strategically the workers, the capitalists and governments behave rationally in taking political decisions in advanced capitalist countries. Taylor (1988) finds that revolution is a collective action which can be explained in terms of individual action and rational decision-making—where and when it is believed that individuals are egoistic and try to fulfil their interests through rational action, and that rationality is relative to their attitudes and beliefs determined by the social structure. Individual actions are determined by incentives, which also are determined by social structures. Social structures also emerge from individual' actions and also are maintained and changed by these actions. The influence of the social structure is operated through the modality of individual choice. Strong membership ties in a community make possible the rebellious collective action rational, make possible the social pressure more potent, and also make co-operative action more rational.

Strategic rationality is the focal point of the game of revolution, according to Roemer (1988). He does not point out particular class structure and revolutionary class dynamics from this particular class structure. He analyzes revolutionary class dynamics in terms of distribution of income and rational pursuit of material gain. Following this, Reomer provides five major assumptions about revolution— (1) assumption of Coalition Monotonicity, (2) assumption of Penalty Monotonicity, (3) assumption of Lean and Hungry, (4) assumption of Symmetry, and (5) assumption of Relative Severity. The probability of revolution following these assumptions may be stated in Figure 78. Revolution, *i.e.*, Russian Revolution according to Roemer, is a game between Leninist strategy and Tsarist strategy, between revolutionary strategy and counter-revolutionary strategy, between income distribution and penalty schedule. This game has a probable solution if the two players, Lenin and the Tsar act sequentially and not simultaneously, *i.e.*, penalties minimizing the probability of revolution and redistribution of income as best response to these penalties. According to Roemer, the game of the Russian Revolution is the game between Lenin and Tsar, which may be stated as follows:

Lenin (Leninist strategy)	Tsar (Tsarist strategy)
1. Revolutionary strategy	1. Counter-revolutionary strategy
2. Revolutionary coalition and collective action	2. Prevention and counterweight to revolutionary coalition and collective action
3. Distribution of income in the midst of scarcity of resources and income—this will make the affectivity of revolutionary coalition	3. Penalty schedule for revolutionary coalition or participation in the revolutionary coalition
4. Participation in the revolutionary coalition depends upon the income of the person—if the income for joining in the revolutionary coalition exceeds the current income	4. The probability of revolution or participation in the revolutionary coalition depends upon the person's income—if the penalty cost does not cross or exceed the participant's actual or current income
a. Income for joining the revolutionary coalition or benefits accrued from participation > Actual or current income = More participation in revolutionary coalition	a. Penalties for participation in revolutionary coalition < Actual or current income or benefits accrued from participation = Less probability of revolution or participation in the revolutionary coalition
b. Income for joining the revolutionary coalition or benefits accrued from participation < Actual or current income = Less participation in revolutionary coalition	b. Penalties for participation in revolutionary coalition > Actual or current income or benefits accrued from participation = More probability for revolution or participation in the revolutionary coalition
5. Penalizing the rich in the interest of poor, *i.e.*, income distribution from rich to the poor	5. Penalizing the poor people more than the rich
6. Revolution	6. Prevention of revolution
7. Poor connected with revolutionary coalition—high probability of revolution—progressive redistribution of income: few above certain income level get less and few below that get more	7. Revolution unaffected by penalties —high probability of revolution— same and unaffected penalty severity

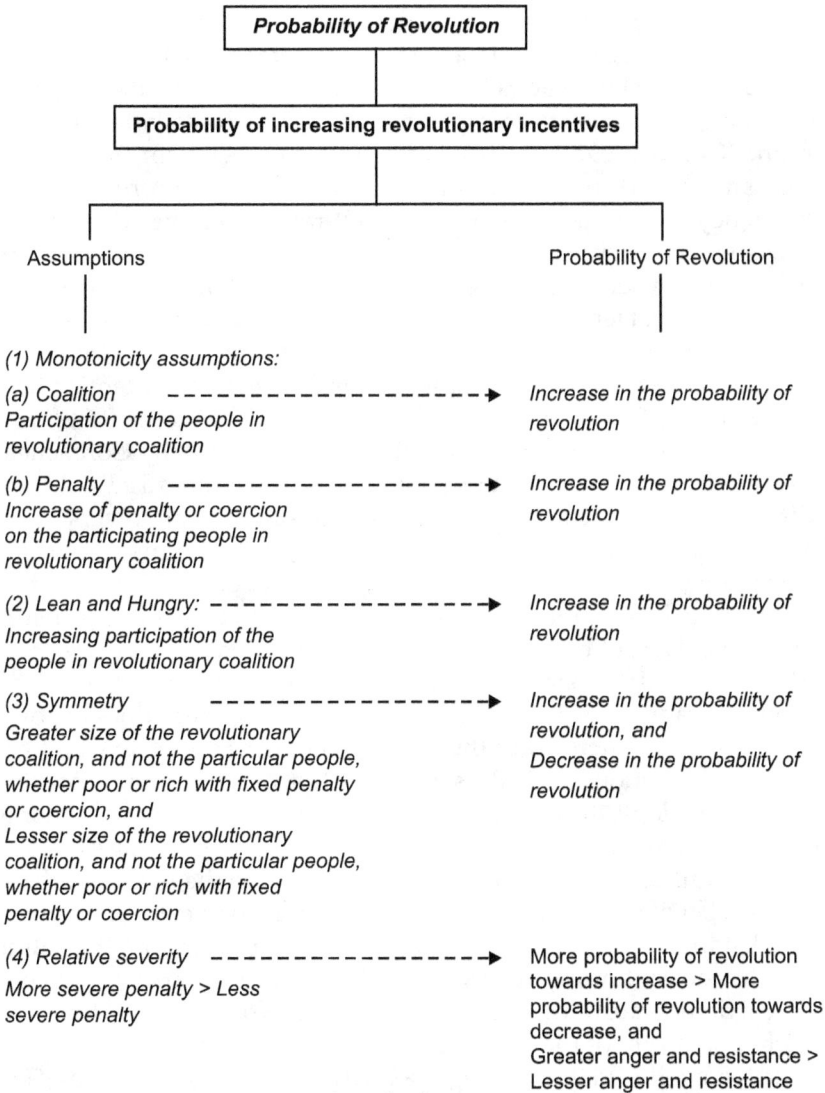

| Probability of Revolution |

| Probability of increasing revolutionary incentives |

Assumptions   Probability of Revolution

(1) Monotonicity assumptions:

(a) Coalition ----------------➤ *Increase in the probability of*
Participation of the people in *revolution*
revolutionary coalition

(b) Penalty ----------------➤ *Increase in the probability of*
Increase of penalty or coercion *revolution*
on the participating people in
revolutionary coalition

(2) Lean and Hungry: ----------------➤ *Increase in the probability of*
Increasing participation of the *revolution*
people in revolutionary coalition

(3) Symmetry ----------------➤ *Increase in the probability of*
Greater size of the revolutionary *revolution, and*
coalition, and not the particular people, *Decrease in the probability of*
whether poor or rich with fixed penalty *revolution*
or coercion, and
Lesser size of the revolutionary
coalition, and not the particular people,
whether poor or rich with fixed
penalty or coercion

(4) Relative severity ----------------➤ More probability of revolution
More severe penalty > Less towards increase > More
severe penalty probability of revolution towards
decrease, and
Greater anger and resistance >
Lesser anger and resistance

Figure 78

Following Elster's 'animal spirit', according to Roemer, revolutionary leaders behave strategically with rational ideologies and eliminate others as a process of natural selection like that of counter-revolutionary strategies of the defenders of *status quo*. It is the convergence between strategy and ideology. That is, people behave strategically rationally in their pursuits of material gains, and to this end, movements and revolutions have occurred in Eastern Europe and

Soviet Union for the transition to democracy from State socialism in opposition to the claims of classical Marxism—transition from feudalism to capitalism and from capitalism to socialism. It is not only the transition to democracy, but also to capitalism, for example the collapse of Soviet Union. Kornai (1992) says that the classical socialism or Stalinist socialism constitutes a system of coherence with repression and inefficiency. When the system starts itself reforming, the coherence of the system is slackened and internal contradictions of the system strengthened. Therefore, the reform is doomed to fail, unable to renew itself internally. Hence, the need for revolutionary changes does come in the end—that is elimination of the socialist system and transformation of the social system toward a capitalist market economy. Mention here may be made that economic collapse and the need for economic reforms are the by-products of the political changes introduced by Gorbachev.

The political changes—the withdrawal of the Communist Party from a direct role in the economy, the transfer of substantial powers to the Soviets, de-control and de-totalization and expansion of the independence of enterprises—all are expected to release human factors in economic development and economic growth, to remove pressure from above. The political reforms in the Soviet Union have become more and more radical (Ellman and Kontorovich, 1992). David Kotz (1992) says that unlike capitalism, the ruling group of State socialism does not own the means of production but the ruling group runs the system and has a privileged position within the system like that of capitalism. According to official ideology, the ruling group is supposed to operate the economy and government selflessly for the direct benefit of the working class. The system is authoritarian and undemocratic. Though the workers are the supposed beneficiaries of the system, they have no power to enforce their official status as the ruling class. Other than the tradition, the ruling group has no continuing tie or structural tie to the State socialist system. The real democratization of the system would probably have displaced the great majority of the ruling group from their high-level positions, would have reduced the privileges with their leadership positions. 'The group that stood to benefit from democratizing socialism was the working class, but they lacked the power to direct the process... underlying structural factor at work was the failure of undemocratic State socialism to develop a ruling class with an abiding interest in protecting and defending the system over which it presided. Once the system went into a moderately serious social and economic crisis, the bulk of the ruling group deserted the system and opted for capitalism.' (Kotz, 1992: 24). The movements against State socialism are aimed at establishing capitalism and creating democratic institutions around it.

Przeworski (1986) presents democracy in terms of institutionaliza-tion of conflicts, capacity of a particular group or groups to realize their interests and outcomes of conflicts not specified and determined by institutionalization in the process of transition to democracy from State socialism or authoritarian regime, *i.e.,* first, the liberalization process, second, extrication from power, and third, construction of new political institutions with the collapse of State socialism or authoritarian regime in character. In the liberalization process, the liberalizers opt for their position in the political system through the institutionalization of changes. Liberalization process occurs from conflict between pro-changers (liberalizers) and no-changers (hardliners) within the system and popular mobilization. The liberalizers either have to align with the hardliners or to take unilaterally the path of change. The unilateral decision to take the path of change by the liberalizers is influenced and decided by the option for change by the liberalizers and the popular mobilization for change and popular movement for elimination of authoritarian regimes. In the case of popular movement for elimination of authoritarian regimes, the liberalizers should attempt to make arrangement for repression of the movement or to make arrangement or to allow the transition to a different form of society or to democracy. In case of the former, the liberalizers should decide how much repression be taken for—whether successful repression which is equal to narrower dictatorship = 'r' or unsuccessful repression which is equal to insurrection = '1 − r'. In terms of preferences the liberalizers' decisions may be stated as in Figure 79.

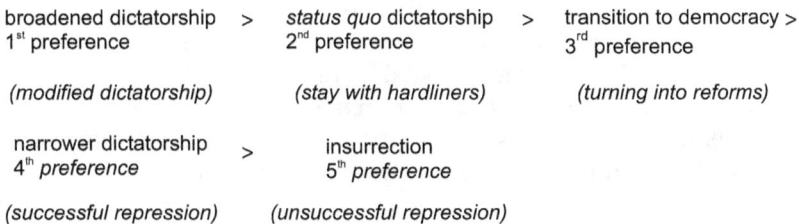

broadened dictatorship >	*status quo* dictatorship >	transition to democracy >
1st preference	2nd preference	3rd preference
(modified dictatorship)	*(stay with hardliners)*	*(turning into reforms)*
narrower dictatorship >	insurrection	
4th *preference*	5th *preference*	
(successful repression)	*(unsuccessful repression)*	

Figure 79

Then, how does the transition to democracy become possible, according to Przeworski? This becomes possible in two alternative ways —liberalizers' closer relations with the democrats and the liberalizers' change of outlook. The liberalizers want to stay in power through democracy and try to hold on it as long as they can, but when it turns against them, at some they try to decide whether to go back to the authoritarian regime or forward to democratic regime. Now, the alternative ways on the part of the liberalizers may be presented in

Figure 80. Transition to democracy does not occur automatically; it emerges out of conflict and struggle between the two contenders of power— those who are against the authoritarian regime and those who are for the authoritarian regime and also among the members of the anti-authoritarian coalition. It is the struggle for power and position between hardliners and reformers, moderates and radicals. Transition to democracy emerges from the extrication of democracy from the authoritarian regime. The extrication process or the process of freeing of democracy from the authoritarian regime, according to Przeworski, is seen in Figure 81.

The extrication process is mainly a game between reformers and moderates. Alliance of reformers and hardliners within the regime means survival and maintenance of authoritarianism, and alliance between reformers within the regime and moderates outside the regime means limited democracy. Further, alliance of moderates and radicals outside the regime means complete democracy. If the reformers become the leaders in the power struggle, then the outcome would be authoritarian regime with some reforms, and if the moderates become the leaders, then the outcome would be limited democracy. The transition to democracy out of the extrication process is unstable. In the extrication game, the questions are—how the alliance to be made is, how power to be achieved is, and how democracy to be freed from authoritarian regime is etc. In the collapse of the authoritarian regime, the questions remain as what democratic institutions that will emerge, and how these institutions will be self-enforcing. Stable democracy emerges when there are checks and balances, many balancing political forces operating within the political system, *i.e.*, constraining the exercise of power by the political leaders and democratic institution builders. Przeworski (1991) embraces social democracy with the aspects of socialism, but without the socialization of the means of production, *i.e.*, strengthening working class within the capitalist system, strengthening of the trade union movements and establishment of social democratic political party. It is not market socialism, it is not establishment of workers co-operative, and it is democratically run trade unions within the capitalist society.

According to Miller (1989), politics makes good in market socialism in rectifying unjustified inequalities, deficiencies in spontaneous community, alienation and exploitation of pure market socialism through consensus-creating dialogue politics. It is not the reconciliation of interests forging a majority coalition and majority decision; rather it is common good, accepted by both the majority and minority. Legitimacy of decisions through dialogue politics is based not only on proper procedures maintained for reaching at decisions, but on the reason or reasons behind the decisions. Therefore, the State under dialogue politics and market socialism must be consociational State rather than majoritarian democratic State. It is like A. Lijpart's consociational democracy. This type of consociational State must be with effective system of checks and balances and with division of decision-making powers. The basis of the State must be rule of law, but not rule of the majority. The market socialism aims at economic efficiency, equal distribution of income, autonomy of workers and limited power of the State, that State sets up rules for socio-economic transactions, manages economy so that it can function smoothly according to the rules of the market economy, provides goods and services, distributes income for the achievement of distributive justice, and protects the system from external threat. According to Miller, market socialism brings about price equilibrium and relative economic equality. Absence of private capital and the existence of perfect competition reduce the extent and amount of exploitation under market socialism, which is the best system under the present historical epoch and is the most desirable. When classical Marxists regard communism as the higher system than that of socialism, Miller criticizes communism as negation of capitalism, where wage labour, commodity production and market are all become absent; production takes place according to socially determined plan; each person receives according to his needs instead of according to his ability; division of labour is broken down; economic competition disappears and market relations become absent. Miller's market socialism may be presented below graphically—

> productive enterprises → workers' co-operatives → democratic control of the co-operatives by the workers → selling of the products by the enterprise in open market → workers are paid from the selling of the products → decisions of the co-operatives about the distribution of income among the workers → socially owned capital is managed through public investment agencies → capital leased to the workers' co-operatives.

Miller's model is different from the Lange-Lerner model: few branches of industry are under private ownership except the units producing consumer goods and units producing capital goods, while the prices of the consumer goods are determined by the market and the prices of the capital goods are determined by the central planning board. However, in Lange-Lerner's model of market socialism the rate of accumulation is politically determined and the economic life has become bureaucratized. Cohen (1991) criticizes Miller's account of market socialism on the ground that this socialism remains deficient from socialist point of view as there is injustice in the system which confers high rewards on the people who happen to be unusually talented and who form highly productive cooperatives. However, it (market

socialism) abolishes the distinction between capital and labour. Roemer
(1992) suggests market socialism in an alternative way other than Miller.
According to Roemer, market socialism, or socialism with a market
system, or any market system, with or without capitalists allocates
resources and incomes in an unjust manner. The competitive market
pays people according to the evaluation. Under market socialism people
will receive differential wages, which will provide differential economic
value to the society. 'But they will not deserve those wages nor be entitled
to them, because I do not believe they deserve or are entitled to returns
to their arbitrarily assigned genetic compositions and familial and social
environments, which largely determine their skills.... I view the
differential wages that will accompany a market socialist system as
justifiable for only one reason: they are a by-product of using a labor
market to allocate labour.' (Roemer,1992: 462).

Roemer's market socialism is like successful capitalist economy,
where publicly owned industries should be managed by individual
managers, who would maximize their profits at market prices. These
managers are hired by the board of directors or elected by the workers
themselves, but not appointed by the State. The State only intervenes
in the affairs of investment, but not management. The State provides
goods and services allocated by the market. The fundamental goal of
socialism is equality of opportunity for self-realization and income
equality is the means to that end. Profits are social dividends—workers
should not appropriate the profits of the enterprises as it would create
unjustified income inequalities, and it would undermine the efficacy of
the market economy. Unlike the classical Marxists, Robert van der Veen
and Philippe Van Parijs say that socialism is not necessary for reaching
communism. According to these theorists:

socialism	=	collective ownership of the means of production
communism	=	distribution of income, goods and services according to needs
socialism	=	material abundance
capitalism	=	material abundance
capitalism	=	abundance—*unconditional income grant* to each irrespective of other sources of income—each adult citizen receives the same amount of grant—*unconditional income grant* is gradually increased upto the needs—income is distributed according to needs.
therefore, socialism is not necessary for attaining communism.		

This unconditional income grant is treated as the *basic income*. This basic income paradigm has been criticized by Eric Wright (1987) as it would reduce rate of profit and cause major capital flight. To him, transition to socialism from capitalism through the route of basic income model is feasible. The transition to socialism, requires political support and transition to communism needs socialism more for political reasons than that of the economic. Carling (1991) in his Basic Income Game says that it is a game between persons who work and those who do not. A person, who works, produces a particular amount of economic value and receives this particular value, but at the same time losses the surplus value from his works. According to basic income policy this economic value is equally distributed among the members of the society, whether the member does work or not, when in case of the former the worker does not receive special for the work, and in case of the latter, the person does not bear the burden of not working (Figure 82).

(1) Liberalizers' closer relations with the democrats

Decisions: ⇩

broadened dictatorship >	transition to democracy >	*status quo* dictatorship >
1st preference	2nd preference	3rd preference
(modified dictatorship)	*(turning into reforms)*	*(stay with hardliners)*

narrower dictatorship >	insurrection
4th preference	5th preference
(successful repression)	*(unsuccessful repression)*

Outcome: transition to democracy

(2) Liberalizers' change of outlook

Decisions: ⇩

broadened dictatorship >	transition to democracy >	*status quo* dictatorship >
1st preference	2nd preference	3rd preference
(modified dictatorship)	*(turning into reforms)*	*(stay with hardliners)*

narrower dictatorship >	insurrection
4th preference	5th preference
(successful repression)	*(unsuccessful repression)*

Outcome: transition to democracy

Figure 80

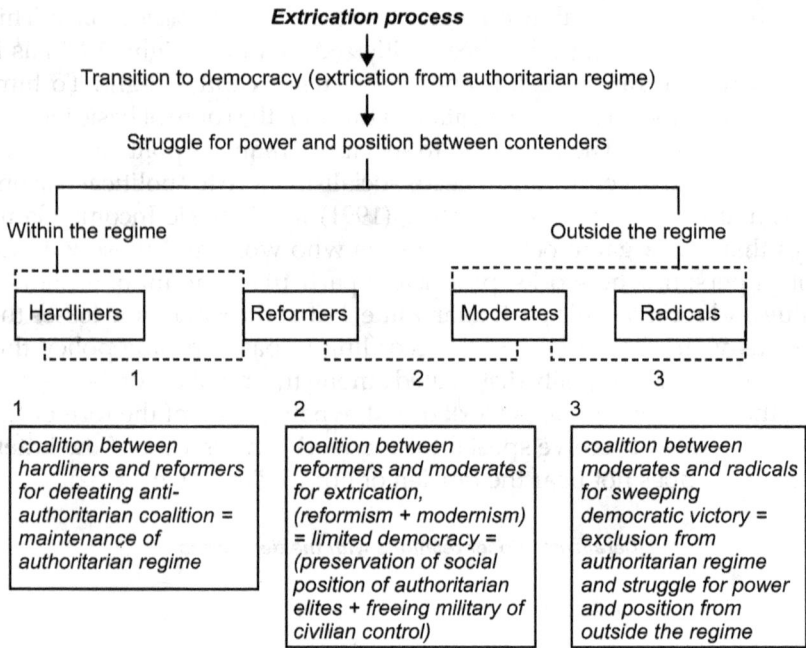

Extrication process

↓

Transition to democracy (extrication from authoritarian regime)

↓

Struggle for power and position between contenders

Within the regime   Outside the regime

| Hardliners | Reformers | Moderates | Radicals |

          1   2   3

| 1 | 2 | 3 |

| coalition between hardliners and reformers for defeating anti-authoritarian coalition = maintenance of authoritarian regime | coalition between reformers and moderates for extrication, (reformism + modernism) = limited democracy = (preservation of social position of authoritarian elites + freeing military of civilian control) | coalition between moderates and radicals for sweeping democratic victory = exclusion from authoritarian regime and struggle for power and position from outside the regime |

Figure 81

Then, according to Carling, if the people or the members of the society receive unconditional basic income, then they will not be motivated to work and there will be 'greenstick equilibrium'—no one will work if any one stops working. Society would be lazy and static. Carling makes an egalitarian solution to the Basic Income Model, *i.e.,* Gotha programme socialism and police socialism—

Gotha programme socialism	Police socialism
1. Rewarding of the work in proportion to the value of the economic product and distribution of the surplus value among the members of the society after then	1. Distribution of income equally among the workers and providing of punishment to the non-workers
2. Everyone receives the amount equal to the disutility of his labour as everyone has the same disutility	2. Coercive measures are imposed by the police force over the non-workers
3. Everyone works and every worker receives the same amount of income	3. Punishment measures are of two types—coercive measures imposed on the non-workers and tax payment measures imposed on the workers, in the State system

Gotha programme socialism	*Police socialism*
4. Equilibrium and socialism are established	4. Punishments may be defined as costs
5. Everyone works and receives the same amount of income	5. The amount of tax payment by each worker—total number of non-workers and punishment imposed on each non-worker: total number of workers.
	6. In police socialism model there are two types of equilibrium— everyone works, when the number of initial workers > the number of critical workers, and no one works, when the number of initial workers < the number of critical workers

The Basic Income Game
(Game between workers and non-workers)

Player A	Player B
(Player does work)	(Player does not work)
Produces fixed amount of value currently	Does not produce fixed amount of value currently
Value is distributed equally among the members of the society	
Suffers from surplus value and does not receive any special privilege for work	Does not bear the burden of non-working but sacrifices the share he has received earlier, when he does work and his produced economic value is equally divided among all the members of the society in future or in time later on
Player A is currently working and will decide to work in time later on or in future if material gains he presently receives > material gains he will receive in future, and *vice versa* or, costs of working < value the worker receives from her economic product which is equally divided among the members of the society	**Player B** is currently not working will decide to work in future if material gains or rewards he expects from working > material gains or rewards he receives at present from the value produced by others, for example Player A, which is equally divided among the members of the society, and *vice-versa* or, costs of working < value produced by the worker, which is equally divided among the members of the society and the share he receives
Equilibrium (no one will work)	*Equilibrium (no one will work)*

Figure 82

However, the neo-classical theorists say that the income redistribution by the government reduces economic growth, which can be reduced or limited through moderate trade union demands with strong social democratic movements. For which Albert and Hahnel (1990 and 1991) in their works prescribe participatory economics based on egalitarianism, community solidarity, participatory self-management, decentralized economic planning, economic rationality, public ownership of the productive property and distribution of income according to ability and effort, council communism and anarcho-syndicalism.

REFERENCES

Albert, Michael and Robin Hahnel. 1991. *Looking Forward: Participatory Economics for the Twenty First Century* (Boston: South End).

Albert, Michael and Robin Hahnel. 1991. *The Political Economy of Participatory Economics* (Princeton: Princeton University Press).

Althusser, L. 1971. *Lenin, Philosophy and Other Essays* (London: New Left Books).

Bettelheim, C. 1975. *The Transition to Socialist Economy* (London: Harvester Press).

Bottomore and Rubel. 1986. *Karl Marx* (London: Penguin).

Buick, A. 1975. 'The Myth of the Transitional Society', *Critique*, No. 5.

Bukharin, N. 1979. 'The Theory of the Dictatorship of the Proletariat' in *The Politics and Economics of the Transition Period* (London: Routledge and Kegan Paul).

Carling, Alan. 1991. *Social Division* (London: Verso).

Carr, E.H. 1966. *The Bolshevik Revolution, 1917-1923* (Harmondsworth: Penguin).

Carrigan, P., H.R. Ramsay and D. Sayer. 1978. *Socialist Construction and Marxist Theory: Bolshevism and its Critique* (Lonon: Macmillan).

Carrillo, S. 1977. *Eurocommunism and the State* (London: Lawrence and Wishart).

Cohen, G.A. 1991. 'The Future of a Disillusion', *New Left Review* (Vol. 190).

Cohen, S.F. 1977. 'Bolshevism and Stalinism', in R.C. Tucker (ed.) *Stalinism* (New York: Norton).

Dobb, M.H. 1937. *Political Economy and Capitalism* (London).

Ellman, Michael and Vladimir Kontorovich. 1992. (eds.) *The Disintegration of the Soviet Economic System* (London: Routledge).

Elster, J. 1985. *Making sense of Marx* (Cambridge: Cambridge University Press).

Gouldner, A.W. 1978. 'Stalinism: A Study of Internal Colonialism', *Telos*, No. 34.

Hahnel, Robin and Michael Albert. 1990. *Quiet Revolution in Welfare Economics* (Princeton: Princeton University Press).

Hammond, T.T. 1957. *Lenin on Trade Unions and Revolution* (New York: Columbia University Press).

Hobson, J.A. 1938. *Imperialism: A Study* (London).

Kautsky, K. 1974. The *Dictatorship of the Proletariat* (Ann Arbor: University of Michigan Press).

Knei-Paz, B. 1978. *The Social and Political Thought of Leon Trotsky* (Oxford: Clarendon Press).

Kotz, David. 1992. 'The Direction of Soviet Economic Reform: From Socialist Reform to Capitalist Transition', *Monthly Review* (Vol. 44: No. 4).

Krushchev, N.S. 1977. *Krushchev Remembers* (Harmondsworth: Penguin).

Lenin, V.I. 1975. *Imperialism—the Highest Stage of Capitalism* (Peking: Foreign Language Press).

Lenin, V.I. 1977. *Collected Works* (Moscow: Progress Publishers).

Leontief. A. 1935. *Political Economy: A Beginner's Course* (London).

Liebman, M. 1975. *Leninism under Lenin* (London: Jonathan Cape).

Lock, G. 1975. 'Introduction' to L. Althusser, *Essays in Self-Criticism* (London: New Left Books).

Lukacs, G.1977. *Lenin* (London: New Left Books).

Luxemburg, R. 1951. *The Accumulation of Capital* (London).

Mandel, E. 1974. 'The Theses on the Social and Economic Laws Governing the Society: Transition between Capitalism and Socialism', *Critique*, No. 3.

Mao-Tse-Tung, 1973. 'On Contradiction', *Selected Works of Mao-Tse-Tung*, Vol.1.

Mao-Tse-Tung, 1973. 'Win the Masses in their Millions', *Selected Works of Mao-Tse-Tung*, Vol. 1.

Mao-Tse-Tung. 1973. 'Chinese Revolution and Chinese Communist Party', *Selected Works*, Vol. 2, pp. 330-31.

Mao-Tse-Tung. 1973. 'On Practice', *Selected Works of Mao-Tse-Tung*, Vol. 1 (Calcutta: Nabajatak Prakashan).

Mao-Tse-Tung. 1973. 'On New Democracy', *Selected Works*, Vol. 2, p. 319.

Marx, Engels and Lenin: On Historical Materialism (ed.). 1984. (Moscow: Progress Publishers).

Mavrakis, Kostas. 1976. *On Trotskyism* (London: Routledge and Kegan Paul).

Medvedev, R. 1971. *Let History Judge* (New York: Alfred Knopft).

Meyer, A.G. 1957. *Leninism* (New York: Praeger).

Miliband, R. 1977. *Marxism and Politics* (London: Oxford University Press).

Miller, David. 1989. *Market, State and Community: Theoretical Foundations of Market Socialism* (Oxford: Clarendon).

Plamenatz, John. 1954. *German Marxism and Russian Communism* (London: Longmans, Green and Co. Ltd.).

Przeworski, Adam. 1986. 'Some Problems in the Study of the Transition to Democracy' in *Transition from Authoritarian Rule* (ed.) by Guillermo O'Donnell, Philippe C. Schmitter and Laurence Whitehead (Baltimore: Johns Hopkins University Press).

Przeworski, Adam. 1991. *Democracy and the Market* (Cambridge: Cambridge University Press).

Roemer, John E. 1988. 'Rationalizing Revolutionary Strategy' in *Rationality and Revolution* (ed.) by Michael Taylor (Cambridge: Cambridge University Press).

Roemer, John E. 1992. 'The Morality and Efficiency of Market Socialism', *Ethics* (Vol. 102).

Schumpeter, J.A. 1950. *Capitalism, Socialism and Democracy* (New York).

Schumpeter, J.A. 1951. *Imperialism and Social Classes* (London).

Shanin, T. 1971. *Peasants and Peasant Societies* (Harmondsworth: Penguin).

Stalin, J.V. 1952. *Economic Problems of Socialism in the U.S.S.R.* (London).

Stalin, J.V. 1975. *Foundations of Leninism* (Peking: Foreign Language Press).

Sweeze, P.M. 1946. *The Theory of Capitalist Development* (London).

Taylor, Michael. 1988. 'Rationality and Revolutionary Collective Action' in *Rationality and Revolution* (ed.) by Michael Taylor (Cambridge: Cambridge University Press).

Trotsky, L. 1962. *Permanent Revolution* (London: New Park Publications).

Trotsky, L. 1962. *Results and Prospects* (London: New Park Publications).

Trotsky, L. 1963. *Terrorism and Communism* (Ann Arbor: University of Michigan Press).

Trotsky, L. 1967. *History of the Russian Revolution* (London).

Tucker, R.C. 1977. *Stalinism* (New York: Norton).

Winslow, E.M. 1948. The *Pattern of Imperialism: A Study in the Theories of Power* (New York).

Woolf, L. 1920. *Economic Imperialism* (London).

Wright, Eric Olin. 1987. 'Why Something like Socialism is Necessary for the Transition to Something like Communism', *Theory and Society* (Vol. 15: No. 5).

7

Critical Theory

Critical theory provides the key element in the formation of the New Left—it is for Horkheimer an attempt to criticize capitalism and Soviet socialism making for an alternative path for social development while criticizing the existing capitalist society. Horkheimer regards that historical materialism is not useful for making men conscious of the contradiction of capitalism as the work is done by the critical theory. The only concern of the critical theorists is to accelerate development which would lead to a society without exploitation. There are no general criteria for critical theory. Critical theory has no specific instance for itself other than suppression of class domination and development of society without exploitation. According to Horkheimer, the attitude of critical theory is derived from difference of subjects rather than from one of objects. It views man as the creator of history, as the producer of all historical life forms, and pursues conscious human interest in rational organization of human activity. It is not only concerned with human goals in the existing life forms but with human and human possibilities. It is concerned with honesty, consistency, rationality, peace, freedom and happiness, lastly with metaphysical humanism.

Mention here may be made that unlike the natural sciences, the critical theory of society remains philosophical even as a critique of economics: its content is formed by the inversion of concepts which govern economy into their opposites: fair exchange into widening social injustice, the free economy into domination of monopoly, productive labour into the consolidation of relations which restrict production, the maintenance of the life of the society into the immiseration of the people. (Horkheimer, 1968). However, critical theory regards the bourgeois economics as a-historical, but does not regard it as unscientific and itself does not create any new scientific concepts. It begins with the idea of simple commodity exchange, which is based on value and profit. The social and material relations are determined by exchange relations. Dick Howard says that Horkheimer does not shy away from stating the goals, or so to say, revolutionary goals of Critical Theory. The immediate tasks he arraigns to the critical theory are defined by double crisis of Marxist and bourgeois theory. Horkheimer appears more concerned with the crisis of bourgeois science, the analysis of which is conducted in Marxist terms. Science is seen as defined, and limited by its role in the capitalist division of labour, which prevents and restricts bourgeois science to empirical facts gathering and in the service of human needs. Science should be able to predict and that prediction becomes fully possible only in a free society, for the true human freedom is neither that of being unconditional nor that of mere caprice, but it is identical with the mastery of nature through rational decisions. Therefore, according to Horkheimer, the task of the science is the realization of a rational society. See Figure 83. In this task, Horkheimer provides importance to the role of individual interests, drives and passions, and stresses the need for empirical research mediated through philosophy. To Horkheimer,

critique of positivism ≠ (Science – Philosophy), rather
critique of positivism = (Science + Philosophy)

Therefore, there is the need to integrate philosophy with science and investigations in research are to be organized in which philosophers, sociologists, economists, historians and psychologists come together. Horkheimer proposes to apply the interdisciplinary method—the question of interrelations between the economic life of society, the psychological development of the individual and the changes in the cultural sphere. The intention of investigating the relations among the three processes is nothing but a formulation. Horkheimer stresses the importance of interdisciplinary approach where philosophers, sociologists, economists, historians and psychologists must unite in working partnership. Social phenomena cannot be deduced from the mere economy, from the material being. Researchers must reformulate the philosophical questions more precisely and more particularly, but not losing sight of the universal and must explore the question of the interconnection between the economy of the society, the psychological development of the individual and transformations in the realm of culture—inter-connection between the socio-economic, psychological and cultural realms of the society within definite time, space and social groups.

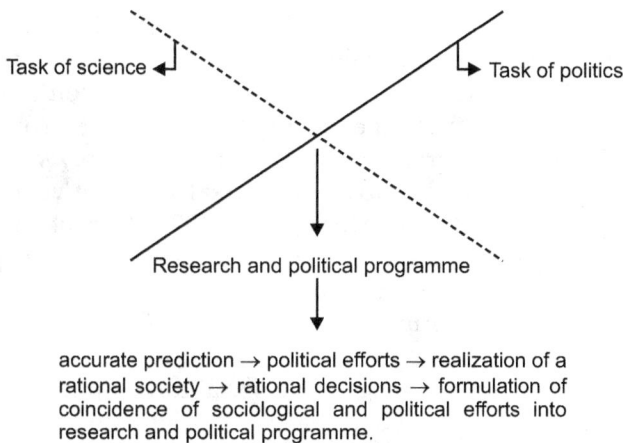

Task of science ◄┐ 　　　　　　　　　　　Task of politics

Research and political programme

accurate prediction → political efforts → realization of a
rational society → rational decisions → formulation of
coincidence of sociological and political efforts into
research and political programme.
Figure 83

Horkheimer always kept his distance from Hegel's philosophy of history. Hegel's system is the completion of truth, conceals from Hegel the meaning of *time-bound interest*, which influences individual dialectical presentations—the direction of thought, the choice of material and the use of names and words. Further, Hegel turns his attention from conscious and unconscious partiality *vis-à-vis* the question of life must necessarily become operative as constitutive elements of his philosophy. Horkheimer accepted Hegel's dialectic of thought, critique of knowledge and dialectical critique of ideology, where all thoughts in its historical context must express itself in human interests devoid of relativism and different from skepticism. Horkheimer rejected Hegel's forms of consciousness. Dialectical theory is critical theory as it reveals incompleteness where completeness is claimed. Horkheimer rejected Hegel's concluded concept of history. However, he defends Hegel's dialectical thought process, dialectical critique of knowledge and dynamism of history against empirical critique of Hegel's approach and inversion of Hegel's system by the orthodox Marxists and equation of Marxism with evolutionary determinism.

Horkheimer regards history as unconcluded. The materialist dialectic as unconcluded dialectic and there is no predetermined abolition of contradictions. The historical progress gives rise to a number of contradictions and multiple modes resolving them. The material human existence is the ground of all consciousness. The senses are changeable and are products of the human activities in societies, of culture and theory. Ideas are integrated with the whole social process. There is a breach between ideas and reality, *i.e.,* contradiction between breach and reality. Truths can be obtained through negations, which is double-edged negation of absolute claims of prevailing ideology and negation of brash claims of reality. Critical theory takes the existing values and ideas seriously but insists that they become parts of a theoretical whole that reveals their relativity. As subject and object, word and thing cannot be integrated under present conditions, we are driven by the principles of negation, to attempt to salvage relative truths from the wreckage of false ultimate (Horkheimer, 1974). Horkheimer regards that through practice truth can be reached. Conviction plays an important role in verification and confirmation of ideas and in historical struggles. Theory is confirmed through history. Critical theory has no inherent interest in the suppression of class domination. Horkheimer realizes the importance of progressive social forces in history. Theory must conform to the mental and materialistic situation of a particular class. Opinions of Horkheimer have been cited in Figure 84.

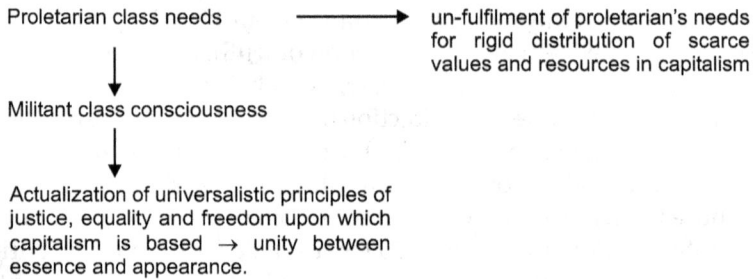

Proletarian class needs   ⟶   un-fulfilment of proletarian's needs for rigid distribution of scarce values and resources in capitalism

↓

Militant class consciousness

↓

Actualization of universalistic principles of justice, equality and freedom upon which capitalism is based → unity between essence and appearance.

Figure 84

Lukacs generalized the concept of 'reification', *i.e.*, reduction of human relations to relations between things linking Weber's conception of rationalization and Marx's conception of commodity fetishism. The reified society, according to Lukacs is like Figure 85.

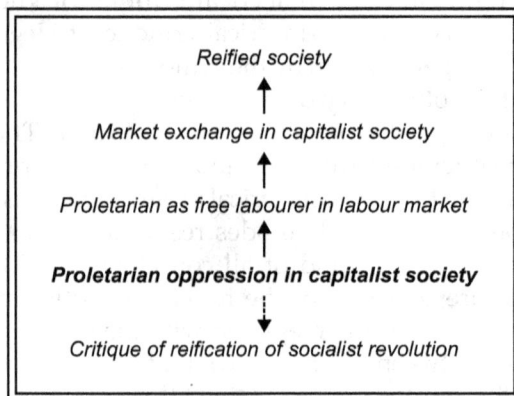

Reified society

↑

Market exchange in capitalist society

↑

Proletarian as free labourer in labour market

↑

Proletarian oppression in capitalist society

↓

Critique of reification of socialist revolution

Figure 85

According to Lukacs, under capitalism all economic categories appear absolutely reified so that their essence, man's relationships are obscured, the fundamental categories of existence are neglected producing the fetishizing character of the capitalist society. The world appears in man's consciousness as otherwise divorced from actual relationships. Under capitalism special intellectual effort is required to grasp the actual substance and man's social relations behind the reified terms which determine daily life. The concept of totality is central to Lukacs's thesis—the unity between essence and appearance is able to recognize the falsity of the representation of reality. (Lukacs, 'Marx and Engels on Aesthetics', *Writer and Critic*, p. 69). Horkheimer stresses the potential development of the working class, the needs of the working class, a rational society free of contradictions, which can only emerge in the struggle for the future, through the struggle against the existing contradictions and domination of technical rationality in all its forms. The proletariat is the potential force in the liberation of human needs, in the realization of free development of individuals, just allocation of scarce values and equality in community. According to Horkheimer, man's striving for happiness is to be regarded as a natural fact requiring no justification. The satisfaction of desires requires no reasons, excuses or justifications (Horkheimer, 1972).

In the wake of failure of revolution in the West, growth of monopoly houses and State-capitalism, and expansion of the authoritarian and bureaucratic State, Horkheimer acknowledged the less and less importance to proletarian class struggle, to generalizable equality among proletarian class interest, interest of the general public and the interest in a rational society, and realized the domination of technical rationality. Both Horkheimer and Adorno had found the integrative trend of capitalism—leaders of industry, administration, propaganda and the military had become identical with the State; these leaders laid down the plan of the national economy as entrepreneurs, *i.e.*, the domination of political apparatus in the interest of planned capital accumulation. The central concern here is capitalist rationalization. Both Horkheimer and Adorno expressed the views of Pollock with regard to State capitalism that the State capitalist order was the successor of private capitalism and that was not socialism, where the State assumed the functions of private capitalists and capitalist institutions like labour and profit, and played a significant role. (Pollock, 1941 : 451).

Under this regime, the State is the power instrument of a new ruling group which has emerged from the merger of the most powerful vested interests, the top ranking personnel in industrial and business management, and the higher strata of State bureaucracy. Everyone who

does not belong to this ruling group is a mere object of domination.
(Pollock, 1941 : 202). Pollock studies that the primacy of politics over
economics so much disrupted under democracy is clearly established.
Both Horkheimer and Adorno regarded central control over individual
decision-making, bureaucratic control over local initiative, planning of
resources over market allocation of resources, and technical
consideration of general efficiency, and rationality. Horkheimer and
Adorno followed the notion of rationalization and the notion of
instrumental reason. The rise of natural sciences was also a part of
rationalization. The emphasis is on science as domination. In *Critical
Theory* Horkheimer assets by 1932 that in the Marxist theory of society,
science is numbered among the human forces of production. The
application of forces and means of production is in grave contrast to
their development and the real needs of men. A method oriented
towards being and not towards becoming, corresponds to the tendency
to see the given form of society as a mechanism of equal and self-
repeating processes. In *Dialectic of Enlightenment* Horkheimer says that
knowledge is power, which knows no obstacles—neither in the
enslavement of men nor in compliance with the world's rulers. In *The
Jews and Europe* (1939) Horkheimer says that fascism is the truth of
liberalism and capitalism of modern society, of the whole aim of the
bourgeois Enlightenment from Bacon on to liberate man from the fetters
of superstition. He, who does not speak of capitalism, should also be
silent about fascism or not speak out fascism. Horkheimer's presentation
is represented graphically in Figure 86.

MARXIST THEORY	LIBERAL THEORY	CRITICAL THEORY
Conflict of interests	*Harmony of interests*	*Integration of interests*
↑	↑	↑
Reproduction of the relations of production by means of free contracts	Market relations	Primacy of politics or superstructure over economics or base
↑		↑
Enforcement of inequality of property		Enlightenment
↑		↑
Primacy of economics over politics		Natural sciences and empiricist epistemology
		↑
		Science and technical rationality

Figure 86

Enlightenment behaves towards things as the dictator does towards men. Enlightenment is mass deception. In contemporary society when the difficulties of reproduction are faced there is a stronger tendency to counter these difficulties by all the means available, for example the culture industry. The defenders of power distribution and property distribution harnessing the endogenous forces centralize ownership and control; employ economic, political and cultural means to defend the present State of affairs. Culture becomes commodity and a profit motive is transferred to the cultural sphere. Cultural entities are commodities through and through, a process which is expedited by interlocking of different economic spheres to an extent of increase and by dependence of cultural entities on industrial and financial capital. Mass culture reinforces the privatization pattern and consumption orientation, establishes a close liaison between private and public interest, undermines working-class culture, increases domination of instrumental reason, and spreads advertising.

Both Horkheimer and Adorno realize that the concordance between the mind of man and nature of things is patriarchal—the human mind overcomes superstition, where knowledge is power, and overcomes all obstacles. As with all the ends of bourgeois economy in the factory and on the battlefield, origin is no bar to the dictates of the entrepreneurs. Kings control the technology and technology is the essence of knowledge. This knowledge is power. While the bourgeois economy multiplies power through the mediation of market, it also multiplies its objects and powers to such an extent that for their administration all men are necessary. 'And knowledge, in which Bacon was certain the "sovereignty of man lithe hid", can now become the dissolution of domination. But in the face of such a possibility, and in the service of the present age, enlightenment becomes wholesale deception of the masses.' (Horkheimer and Adorno, 1972 : 42). Under monopoly, mass culture is identical. In culture industry, reproduction of culture or cultural entities inevitably requires identical needs to be satisfied with identical goods. The contrast between large demand and little supply is said to demand organization and planning by management. 'The result is the circle of manipulation and retroactive need in which the unity of the system grows even stronger. No mention is made of the fact that the basis on which technology acquires power over society is the power of those whose economic hold over society is greatest. A technological rationale is the rationale of domination itself.' (Horkheimer and Adorno, 1972 : 121).

This technological rationality is the coercive nature of the society, which is alienated from itself—this is the result of the functions of technology in society's economy, but not the result of the laws of movement of technology. All individual branches of culture industry are economically interwoven and are in close contact. 'The might of industrial society is lodged in men's mind. The entertainments manufacturers know that their products will be consumed with alertness even when the customer is distraught, for each of them is a model of the huge economic machinery which has always sustained the masses, whether at work or at leisure—which is akin to work.... The culture industry as a whole has molded men as a type unfailingly reproduced in every product.' (Horkheimer and Adorno, 1972: 127).

Culture is the common denominator and brings itself within the sphere of administration. The political powers and State had inherited cultural institutions from absolutism, had left them with a measure of freedom from the forces of power which dominate the market. In material production the mechanism of supply and demand is disintegrating and in the superstructure culture operates as a check in rulers' favour. The workers, farmers, employees and the middle class are the consumers, who are deceived and captivated. Culture is democratic and is distributed to all through constant reproduction of culture in terms of conformism of the buyers and effrontery of the producers. The culture industry perpetually cheats its consumers as the real point is never reached and promises are never fulfilled. Culture industry represses its consumers. In culture industry there is a fusion of culture and entertainment, which inevitably leads to intellectualization of amusement, which itself is a business. The aim here is to defend society. Both Horkheimer and Adorno believe that culture industry takes people as customers and employees and treats mankind according to this formula. Ideology emphasizes plan or chance, technology or life, civilization or nature. Whether as employees or as customers they remain as mere objects. 'As employees, men are reminded of the rational organization and urged to fit in like sensible people. As customers, the freedom of choice, the charm of novelty, is demonstrated to them on the screen or in the press by means of the human and personal anecdote.' (Horkheimer and Adorno, 1972 : 147). It is rationalization and rational domination, culture-making and cultural domination. 'The less the culture industry has to promise, the less it can offer a meaningful explanation of life, and the emptier is the ideology it disseminates.... Value judgments are taken either as advertising or as empty talk. Accordingly ideology has been made vague and noncommittal, and thus neither clearer nor weaker. Its very vagueness, its almost scientific aversion from committing itself to anything which cannot be verified, acts as an instrument of domination.

It becomes a vigorous and prearranged promulgation of status quo.' (Horkheimer and Adorno, 1972: 147). Culture industry is the embodiment of authoritative pronouncements and 'prophet of the prevailing order'. The masses are demoralized by the pressure of the system. Culture industry adds its contribution to the suppression of revolutionary instincts. 'In the culture industry the individual is an illusion.... Individuation has never really been achieved.... The individual who supported society bore its disfiguring mark; seemingly free, he was actually the product of its economic and social apparatus. Power based itself on the prevailing conditions of power when it sought the approval of persons affected by it.' (Horkheimer and Adorno, 1972: 155). Culture is consumed and amalgamates itself with advertising. Here, the motives are markedly economic. Both advertising and culture industry are merged technically and economically. In modern societies the religious feelings and revolutionary heritage are sold in the open market, the fascist leaders bargain over land and life of the nations while the public only listen and think.

Politics in this society is the business, which is gripped by a holy anger over the retarded commercial attitude of the Jews. Business motives have become absolute. There is domination and concealment of domination in production. 'Production attracts its own courtiers. The new rulers simply took off the bright grab of nobility and donned civilian clothing. They declared that work was not degrading, so as to control the others more rationally. They claimed to be creative workers, ...The manufacturer took risks and acted like a banker or commercial wizard.... On the market he completed for the profit corresponding to his own capital...They owned the machines and materials, and therefore compelled others to produce for them.' (Horkheimer and Adorno, 1972: 173). The subjects of the economy are psychologically oriented. The economy is more rationally operated. The society is adapted to technological development. According to Horkheimer and Adorno, dialectic of Enlightenment is transformed into delusion. See Figure 87.

According to Adorno, the rise of the authoritarian State and the growth of the culture industry result in the powerful manipulation of people's minds. To him, there is a reified subject-object antimony in capitalism, which makes its imprint on the whole consciousness of men. Proletarian existence has lost its revolutionary character in contemporary society of mass culture industry. Social relations appear as natural order regulated according to its own internal laws. Reified consciousness is structured by subject-object antimony. Free subjectivity is the character of consciousness. Marxism aims at consciousness capable of affecting a break from the realm of necessity. In *Negative Dialectics* he aims to demonstrate the priority of the object and confirms the mediation of subject and object. The object can be conceived only by a subject. It remains something other than the subject. A subject by its very nature is from the outset an object as well. We can conceive a subject, which is not an object and we can conceive an object, which is not a subject. To be an object is part of the meaning of subjectivity, but it is not equally part of the meaning of objectivity to be a subject. (Adorno, 1973: 183). The objects exist for us. The history of the subject is a history of it giving way to predominance of objectivity. The history locked in or bounded by object can only be delivered by knowledge mindful of the historic positional value of the object in its relation to other objects. The object is mediated through history. Historical process is stored in the actualization and limitation of the object. Knowledge is embedded in tradition, which mediates between objects and non-identity thinking depends upon tradition and alters the tradition. Non-identity thinking lives with identity thinking and operates between concept and object, idea and material world. Negative dialectics is non-identity thinking and depends on the internally related categories of concept and object, appearance and essence, particular and universal, part and whole. Negative dialectics regards that society is subjective because it refers back to human beings. The human beings create society. The organizational principles are juxtaposed with subjective consciousness.

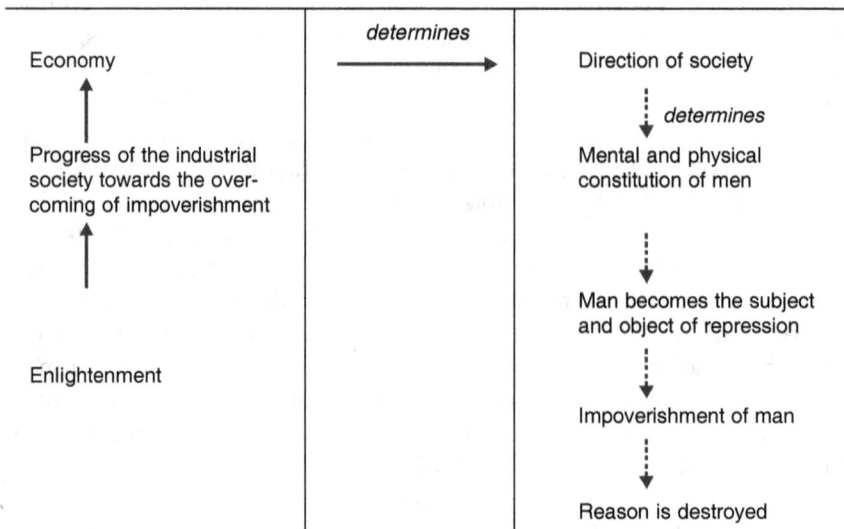

Figure 87

Logic is subjective consciousness. Not only that. Society is also objective on account of its structure. Society does not perceive its own subjectivity because its own organization restricts the installation of such subject and it does not possess a total subject. Critical theory seeks to understand society in terms of its subjective ground. Study of ideology, of false consciousness, of socially necessary illusion would be nonsense without the concept of true consciousness and objective truth. Recent empirical sociological study reveals that however, weak consciousness exists—with restrained class consciousness objective differences between classes will grow and with greater concentration of capital there is increasing impoverishment of the working class. The crises in capitalist society can be contained and class conflict can be managed. Relations of production reflect less and less relations of struggle. Class unity depends upon relations of classes among themselves and their actions in relation to opposite classes. In opposition to liberal capitalism, there exists no class unity in advanced capitalism with particular objectives and interests, where there exists certain tendencies like declining role of the market, greater importance to specialization and division of labour, more and more political and manipulative process, less and less class character of the society, impersonal domination, and classes as functionaries of planned capital accumulation. Classes become agents and bearers of exchange value.

The general character of advanced capitalism overwhelms the particular individual issues. Conflict cannot alter the foundation of society. However, behind this social process, there exists domination of men over men and class struggle, concentration of capital and impoverishment of the working masses, whose integration into society is not yet complete. Adorno does not regard as complete and adequate the Marx's theory of value, theory of capitalist development and theory of class consciousness, due to the influence of the political on economic life and diminishing role of the market, technical and industrial progress and increase in productive power. Adorno sees that social being does not necessarily create class consciousness, the masses have no more control over their fate, and they are not subjects but objects of the social process. Consciousness assumes the character of free subjectivity. Adorno here argues for enlargement of subject's own personality. Ego formation under modern conditions becomes difficult and the relationship between identification, ego and super ego remains incomplete. For free subjectivity and consciousness super ego and ego are essential. The cognitive activity of ego and self-preservation, *i.e.*, performance in the interest of self-preservation, has to be reversed and self-awareness has to perform the interest of self-preservation, to understand society and has to establish conscious prohibitions to manage the often senseless renunciation imposed on it. Enlightenment consciousness objectifies the world and domination of nature is the basis of this consciousness, where there is a radical disjuncture between subjectivity and nature, domination of humanity over nature. It is technological rationality or instrumental reason. The structure of the world given to us through consciousness is based on the inner historicity of consciousness, which is the result of social practice. From instrumental domination or Enlightenment domination, both Horkheimer and Adorno shift to rational domination nature, which integrates all human characteristics.

The concept of domination which Marcuse (1970) explores in *Five Lectures* that domination is in effect when the individual's goals and purposes and the means of striving for and attaining them are prescribed to him and performed by him as something prescribed. Domination can be exercised by men, by nature, by things—it can also be internal, exercised by the individual on himself, and appear in the form of autonomy. It is domination over one's own nature, domination of labour achieved by disciplined and controlled individuals, and domination of science and technology. Domination is a relational concept. In relation to the concept of domination we can point out Marcuse's emphasis on the early works of Marx, the *Economic and Philosophical Manuscripts*, on the concepts like alienation, division of labour and anarchic civil society. He draws inspiration from Hegel and Hegel's ideas of understanding history, reason and dialectics. Preoccupied with classical Marxism, he examines and reconstructs Marxism both with apparent and essential character.

Apparent trace elements in Marcuse's works	*Essential trace elements in Marcuse's work*
1. Revolution and future of revolution	1. Human emancipation and emancipation of human consciousness
2. Strength and ability of socialism	
	2. Reconciliation of humanity and nature, co-operation and co-ordination between the two
3. Utopian objectives for good society or emancipated society	
	3. Political movement of decentralized in nature
	4. Free development of self-consciousness

Herbert Marcuse finds that at the stage of monopoly capitalism, the proletariat has lost its revolutionary character. At this stage of developed capitalism they (the proletarians) are not revolutionary potentials at all (Marcuse, 1967). They have been absorbed in the advanced capitalist society and thereby they have lost the revolutionary class character (Marcuse, 1968). Graphically, it (advanced industrial society) may be presented in Figure 88. The role of culture industry in advanced capitalist society abolishes the revolutionary needs. Impoverishment of the masses does not necessarily provide the soil for revolution. However, a highly developed consciousness and imagination may generate a vital need for radical change in advanced material conditions. The power of corporate capitalism has stifled the emergence of such a consciousness and imagination. Mass Medias have adjusted the rational and emotional facilities to the market of corporate capitalism and policies of it. The culture industry and mass media have steered to the defense of its domination (Marcuse, 1969). The proletariat at this stage shares the stabilizing counter-revolutionary needs of the middle classes. Marcuse shares the Freudian notion of memory and psychoanalysis identification of the progressive character of the release of historical consciousness. In *Counter-revolution and Revolt* (1972) Marcuse says that socialist revolution is the qualitative leap, but not merely the extension of satisfaction within the existing universe of needs and the transformation of satisfaction from lower to higher one. Revolution is the radical transformation of the needs and aspirations among themselves, cultural as well as material, of consciousness and sensibility, of the work process as well as leisure (Macuse, 1972). In *Negations* Marcuse suggests Marxist viewpoint of human essence similar to that of Lukacs—

History and character of the species = Human essence = Transformation and development of human capacities

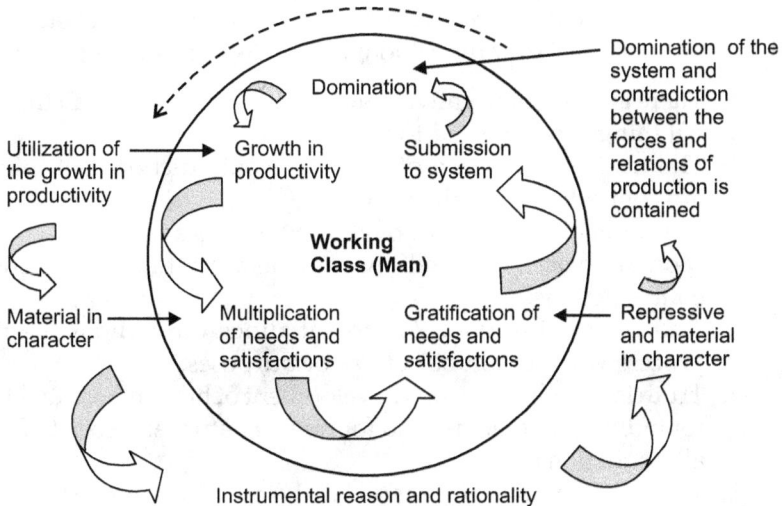

Figure 88

The dynamic focal point of the theory of society is the tension between men and things, the potentiality and actuality of human being. It is not the transcendental structure of Being. It is not the ontological difference between men and things, between potentiality and actuality of human being. With regard to man's worldly happiness, man reacts rationally. Directed by the process of knowledge man has the potentiality of freely determining and shaping his own existence. The level of development of the forces of production and relations of production is the criterion of such potentiality, which is realized in the rational structure of society. Man is the living rational organism. Here, Marcuse works out the relations between ontology, historicity and dialectics, criticizes empiricism, positive philosophy and positivism, and applies instinct in formulating the relation between society and individual and exercising rationality in the course of historical development. On the basis of rationality he criticizes both industrial capitalism and Soviet Marxism.

Marcuse follows the dialectical method of cognition, which makes the being free from appearance of rigidity and the Hegelian philosophy of becoming. Here objects come into being, acting and passing away in time following the Hegelian dialectical method. Negative thinking is the tool for analyzing internal inadequacy of the world of facts. Every being is the unity of opposites, which go beyond the immediately given State. The dialectical pattern represents and is thus the truth of a world permeated by negativity, a world in which everything is something other than it really means, and in which opposition and contradiction constitute the laws of progress. All things become self-contradictory. They are opposed to each other and force within can comprehend and endure contradiction. Few propositions can be deduced in this process—

1. There is inherent negativity and inadequacies within all things.
2. All things are opposed to themselves.
3. The truth and essence of things is contradiction—all things are contradictory in themselves.
4. Contradiction is the root of all movements and life.
5. Motion—external and self-movements are nothing but existing contradictions.
6. Truth is the fulfilment of potentialities throughout the life process with certain objectives or purposes.
7. Truth is the self-conscious development of human potentialities for individual freedom, and for freeing nature and society from all restrictions.
8. The realization of reason and consciousness through dissolution of arbitrary and external authority, freedom of

human will and reconciliation of human endeavour to reality is processed in dialectical progress of history.

9. Labour process, process of practical human sensuous activity is the foundation of historical development.

10. Labour process is the process of becoming, process of man's act of self-creation.

11. In the labour process man supersedes the objectivity of objects and transforms these objects as means of his life. Man impresses upon the objects the form of his beingness. It then is transformed into his work and his reality-man is realized in the object of his labour. Human universality is realized through labour.

12. Through labour man acquires determinate position in the historical process, not only in the process of becoming of 'material existence', but also in the processes of appropriation, overcoming, transforming and developing all of human existence.

According to Marcuse, as per the dialectical rule, every fact is more than the mere fact. It is the negation of real possibilities. As wage labour is a fact, but it is the negation of free work that can satisfy human needs, where labour is the driving force of human activity. When private property is a fact, then it is at the same time negation of collective appropriation of nature. Capitalist system performs the dual role—negation of the real possibilities and the overcoming of alienated conditions and establishment of the conditions for the fulfilment of human needs, and for creation of the conditions of universality—universal commerce, universal industry, universal interdependence and universal competition. Capitalism makes class universal. Mention here may be made that proletarian universality is negative universality. Alienation of labour is intensified and his work negates his own existence, which in turn takes a positive course to communist revolution, when the differentiation of man based on property, culture, religion and race lose their validity. Deprived of all assets, the proletariat is placed outside the prevailing system. He is a member of the prevailing system and at the same time is pitted against it. In *Eros and Civilization* (1962) Marcuse says that development of civilization is based on dialectics of labour. Satisfaction of instincts of human being is grounded on labour. Eros is the essence of being, *i.e.*, the human potentiality. This satisfaction of human potentiality or satisfaction of instincts becomes the goal of human existence. To Marcuse,

1. human existence is the struggle for existence;

2. struggle for existence is the struggle for pleasure;
3. erotic impulse in combination with ever larger and more durable living substances is the instinctual source of civilization;
4. the impulse to preserve and enrich life is also an erotic impulse;
5. sex instincts are life instincts;
6. life instincts seek pleasure and not security;
7. scarcity of resources is the barrier against the fulfilment of pleasure; and
8. human labour is the tool of human existence (Marcuse, 1962).

Scarcity of resources can be overcome through human labour. With the application of science and technology nature recognized by instrumental reason and profit deprives man or alienates man from the subject in its own right to live in a common universe. Realization of human possibilities is directly linked with the realization of Nature's inherent possibilities. To him, science and technology should be applied to liberate man, depends upon the nature of control of natural and social productive forces, the level of organization of labour, the development of needs in relation to possibilities of their fulfilment, and the availability of the material to be appropriated, and of the wealth of cultural values in all areas of life.

According to Marcuse, all particular objects constitute the elements of appearance and essence and from this anti-thesis, the possibilities for social development appear based on historical truth or rationality in senses like preservation and improvement of the productive achievements, greater chance for the pacification of existence within the framework of institutions which offer a greater chance for the free development of human needs and facilities (Marcuse, 1991). Production of needs and aspirations by the social apparatus integrates individuals into the advanced industrial society. Consumer capitalism integrates individuals. It is a totally administered society where individual freedom is sacrificed. *One-Dimensional Man* is an attempt to develop Marxian and Hegelian dialectic on the part of Herbert Marcuse. Negative thinking presupposes the distinction between existence and essence, and appearance and reality. Critical reason is creative thinking, which is the source of both individual liberation and society's advancement. Advanced industrial society demands accommodation to economic and social apparatus and submission to domination and administration to an increasing scale.

The efficiency and power of administration creates one-dimensional man and one-dimensional society. One-dimensionality has become the universal means of domination. Marcuse's theory presupposes the existence of human subject with freedom, creativity and self-determination. One-dimensional man and one-dimensional society are the products of erosion of individuality. One-dimensional man becomes the object of administration, domination, conformity and subjugation. Why? Man's needs and aspirations are unknown to their consciousness —their needs and aspirations are identified with public behaviour, administered and superimposed by the powers. Marcuse criticizes advanced industrial societies—capitalist and communist on the basis of irrationality in self-proclaimed rationality; progress based on waste and destruction; exploitation and repression; dehumanization and alienation in opulence and affluence; labour system; ideological indoctrination and culture; commodity fetishism and consumption fetishism; and danger in industrial-military complex. He analyzes the integration of individuals into society through advertising, consumerism, mass culture and ideology. Liberation of one-dimensional needs and satisfactions should be liberated and emancipated with new modes of realization corresponding to the new capabilities of society. Marcuse's study is based on theories of containment of contradictions, forces of negation and the possibilities of liberation. See Figure 89. This advanced industrial society is totalitarian, determines not only socially-needed occupations, skills and attitudes, but also individual needs and aspirations. Technology maintains social control and social cohesion. The technological universe is a political universe of the advanced industrial society and technological rationality is a political rationality. 'A comfortable, smooth, reasonable, democratic unfreedom prevails in advanced industrial civilization, a token of technical progress. Indeed, what could be more rational than the suppression of individuality in the mechanization of socially necessary but painful performances; the concentration of individual enterprises in more effective, more productive corporations; the regulation of free competition among unequally equipped economic subjects; the curtailment of prerogatives and national sovereignties which impede the international organization of resources.' (Marcuse, 1991: 1). The advanced industrial society maintains and secures itself through the mobilization, organization and exploitation of technical, scientific and mechanical productivity. Productivity determines the character of the free society. In free society of advanced industrialism in nature, liberation depends on the consciousness of servitude, and the emergence of this consciousness is always hampered by the predominance of needs and satisfactions. These needs and satisfactions to a great extent are individual in character, suffocated by the affluent society. 'Its productivity and efficiency, its capacity to increase and spread comforts, to turn waste into need, and destruction into construction, the extent to which this civilization transforms the objective world into an extension of man's mind and body makes the very notion of alienation questionable. The people recognize themselves in their commodities; they find their soul in their automobile, hi-fi set, split-level home, kitchen equipment. The very mechanism which ties the individual to his society has changed and social control is anchored in the new needs which it has produced.' (Marcuse, 1991: 9). See Figure 90.

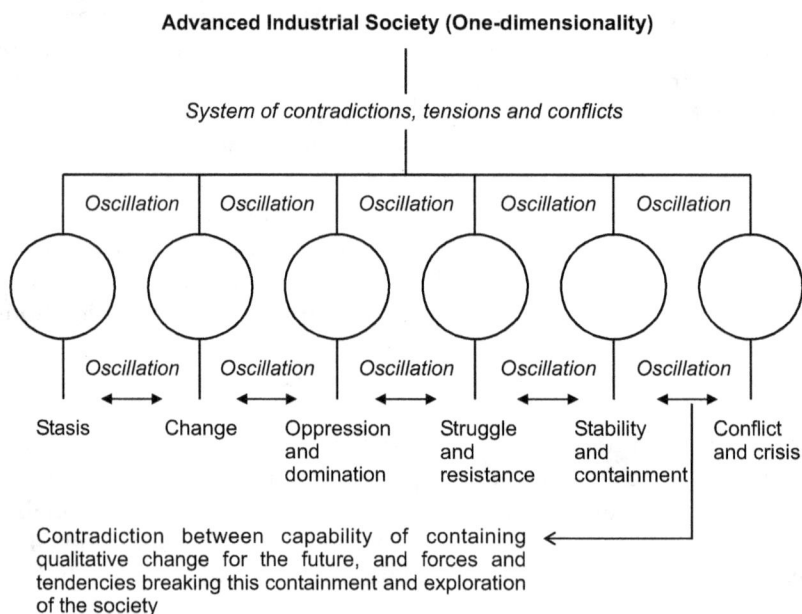

Figure 89

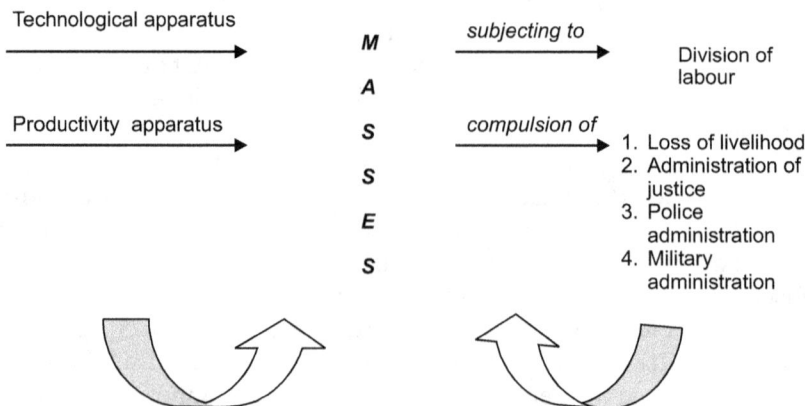

Figure 90

Combined progress in advanced and progressive industrial society would necessarily demand radical subversion of prevailing direction and organization of progress, when all vital needs are satisfied, production process becomes automated, necessary labour time is reduced to marginal time, domination limits its rationality, and 'technology would become subject to the free play of faculties in the struggle for the pacification of nature and society.' (Marcuse, 1991: 16). Marcuse uses the term 'pacification of existence'; where competing needs and interests are no longer organized by vested interests in scarcity and domination and technology is capable of creating conditions for this pacification. '...labour must precede the reduction of labour, and industrialization must precede the development of human needs and satisfactions. But as all freedom depends on the conquest of alien necessity, the realization of freedom depends on the techniques of this conquest. The highest productivity of labour can be used for the perpetuation of labour, and the most efficient industrialization can serve the restriction and manipulation of needs.' (Marcuse, 1991: 18).

It is a society of new character combining both the features of Welfare and Warfare States—proliferation of government tasks and consequent proliferation of administrative functions, concentration of national economy on the big corporations, hitching of national economy to world-wide military alliance, monetary and technical assistance, development schemes, assimilation of blue-collar and white-collar workers, leadership potentialities in business and labour organizations, leisure activities and aspirations among different classes, union and cohesion among the capitalists as a part of mobilization against class struggle of the proletarian class, higher production and employment and higher standard of living. Mechanization is increasingly reducing the exhaustion and intensity of physical labour and energy. Importance are being given to '...skills of the head rather that of hand, of the logician rather than the craftsman; of nerve rather than muscle; of the pilot rather than the manual workers; of the maintenance rather than the operator.' (Walker, 1957: XIX) are important. The worker is being incorporated into the technological community of the administered population and into the 'interdependent motions performed by a group of persons which follow a rhythmic pattern yield satisfaction.' (Walker, 1957: 104). Occupational satisfaction takes place with the interdependence of activities with the changes in character of the instruments of production. Technology takes place a stronger position with the reduction of professional autonomy. With technological automation, work conditions and instrument of production change, which change the consciousness of the worker and become manifest in the social and cultural integration of the workers with the advanced industrial society. From this integration process assimilation in needs and aspirations, in leisure and in politics crops up. Here, domination is transformed into administration. With the growing productivity of labour and technical progress, rise in population, permanent defense economy, economic and political union of the capitalist countries, and greater relation with the underdeveloped countries the capitalist circle is able to contain the chain of growing productivity and repression and possible threat of communism as a triumph against capitalism. It is a system of total administration. '...the prospects of containment of change, offered by the politics of technological rationality, depend on the prospects of the Welfare State. Such a State seems capable of raising the standard of administered living, a capability inherent in all advanced industrial societies where the streamlined technical apparatus—set up as a separate power over and above the individuals—depends for its functioning on the intensified development and expansion of productivity. Under such conditions, decline of freedom and opposition is not a matter of moral of intellectual deterioration or corruption. It is rather an objective societal process insofar as the production and distribution of an increasing quantity of goods and services make compliance a rational technological attitude.' (Marcuse, 1991: 48). It is a system of unfreedom, parasitical and alienated functions, and subdued pluralism.

Human is thus pre-conditioned for the spontaneous acceptance of domination. Social control of technological reality extends liberty while intensifying domination. Technological rationality reduces the need for sublimation and limits the scope for sublimation. Greater liberty involves contraction rather than extension and development of instinctual needs. It works for the *status quo* of repression or institutionalized de-sublimation. Institutionalized de-sublimation, an aspect of the conquest of transcendence is achieved by one-dimensional society, which reduces and absorbs opposition or qualitative differences in the realm of politics, culture and instinctual sphere. The result is the atrophy of the mental organs for grasping the contradictions. 'In contrast to the pleasures of adjusted de-sublimation, sublimation preserves the consciousness of the renunciations which the repressive society inflicts upon the individual, and thereby preserves the need for liberation. To be sure, all sublimation is enforced by the power of society, but the unhappy consciousness of this power already breaks through alienation. To be sure, all sublimation accepts the social barrier to instinctual gratification, but it also transgresses this barrier.' (Marcuse, 1991: 75-76). In advanced industrial society elections are an effective expression of democratic domination through the democratic process. Elections are a mean for the consolidation of liberal-democratic order, the processes of consent and competition. Elections are mechanisms for the maintenance of democratic order and stability, progress and *status quo*. They are a process of democratic pressure for manipulation of democratic consent. The mandate theory is originated from the classical conceptions of democracy, which says that or makes it clear that the process of representation derives from a clear-cut set of directives which the electorate imposes on its representatives. Elections are the procedure of convenience and method for insurance that representatives comply with directives from the constituents. Elections in democracy require competition among opposing candidates. The electorate derives power from its ability to choose between competing alternatives and opposing candidates. Either of them have a reasonable chance to win. The election process requires both parties to engage in a balance of efforts to maintain established voting blocs and to recruit independent voters. It also requires the contest between two opposing candidates for winning election. Both parties seek to enhance their chances of success in the next and subsequent elections. The political activity in the democratic political process includes voting behaviour of the electorates and political parties at the polls, supporting possible pressure groups, communicating with the legislators, participating in party activity, and engaging in habitual dissemination of political opinions. (Eulau, Eldersveld and Janowitz , 1956).

Marcuse relates social reproduction and growing technical ensemble of things and relations. The struggle for existence and the exploitation of man and nature are scientific and rational. According to Marcuse,

Reaction	:	*Scientific management and scientific division of labour, increased productivity in economic, political and cultural enterprises.*
Results	:	*1. Higher standard of living.*
		2. Production of mind and behaviour which justify the destructive and oppressive nature of the enterprises.
		3. Scientific-technical rationality and manipulation.
		4. New forms of social control.

'In this universe, technology also provides the great rationalization of the unfreedom of man and demonstrates the "technical"impossibility of being autonomous, of determining one's own life. For this, unfreedom appears neither as irrational nor as political, but rather as submission to the technical apparatus which enlarges the comforts in life and increases the productivity of labour. Technological rationality thus protects rather than conceals the legitimacy of domination, and the instrumental horizon of reason opens on a rationally totalitarian society.'

(Marcuse, 1991: 158-159). A mention here may be made that it is the force of technology; the force of liberation and the instrumentalization of things turn into a fetter of liberation and make the instrumentalization of man. Technology has become the vehicle of reification in its mature and effective form, and the web of domination has become the web of Reason. In order to falsify the established totality, a transcendental project of higher rationality and real possibilities of material and intellectual culture attained are required for the preservation and improvement of the productive achievements of civilization and for the pacification of existence within the framework of institutions which offer a greater chance for the free development of human needs and faculties. (Marcuse, 1991: 220). To Marcuse,

Reason = Rationality = Truth = Value judgement = Historical rationality

This process of historical rationality is the dialectical process for the attainment of consciousness or for the attainment of liberating potentialities. When consciousness is determined by the interests of the established society or established totality, then it is unfreedom. When consciousness is determined by the liberating potentialities, then it is freedom. Consciousness is unfree in established society as the established society is irrational. Consciousness becomes free for higher historical rationality and for struggle against established society. The truth and freedom of negative thinking have their ground. Therefore, according to Marx, the proletariat is the revolutionary historical force of liberation. Negation of capitalism occurs when the proletariat becomes conscious. It is a qualitative change, which would be a transition to a higher stage. The higher stage of civilization is defined by techniques, utilized for the pacification of the struggle for existence. '"Pacification of existence"does not suggest an accumulation of power rather than the opposite. Peace and power, freedom and power, Eros and power may well be contraries... that the reconstruction of the material base of society with a view to pacification may involve a qualitative as well as quantitative reduction of power, in order create the space and time for the development of productivity under self-determined incentives.' (Marcuse, 1991: 235-236).

Critical theory rejects any positive presence in capitalist society and tries to establish negation of negation as the essence of revolution. While rejecting prevailing theoretical and ideological foundations, the tradition of critical theory, goes outside science and formal logic. It makes a transition from historical practice to abstract and speculative thought, from the critique of political economy to philosophy. It proceeds from a position outside the positive as well as the negative and the productive as well as the destructive tendencies in society. Revolutions have not been sustained by the absolute negativity of the revolutionaries' demands, but by the concrete immediate demands in particular historical situation. H. Marcuse stresses human needs other than the economic ones. Critical theory reduces the scientific conjunctional analysis of the nature of the Fascist State to philosophical critique of capitalism. Like all members of the bourgeoisie, their initiation into revolutionary position comes about through a revulsion against capitalist oppression and hypocritical denial of that oppression. Critical theory regards revolutionary agents as Negating Subjects. To Horkheimer, critical theory is Marxism with a special interpretation. Critical theory is socially related with revolutionary proletariat. With Habermas the revolutionary proletariat is less important and emancipatory interest is nothing but self-reflection, according to Habermas. 'Emancipatory interest', according to Horkheimer, is the only concern for the critical theorists, which should lead to a society without exploitation and would accelerate such path of development. This path of development is proletarian socialist revolution.

Habermas's approach to knowledge does not know the subject and is not a system of knowing, but is a system of scientific propositions and procedures. He tries to make a link of close liaison between philosophy of history and the theory of knowledge and carries the critique of knowledge in the form of a reconstruction of the history of the species. Habermas draws his lesson from the course of history—degeneration of the Russian revolution and triumph of technocratic social revolution, absence of revolutionary class consciousness and failure of revolution in the West, collapse of the Marxist theory as deterministic, on the one hand, and on the other, changes in the appearance and essence of the capitalist system, growing intervention of the State in the organized sectors, even expanding instrumental reason and bureaucracy. He argues for radical democratization of the society and advocates a new social structure of constellation of economics and politics in the force of growth of commerce and industry, technology and mass media, means-end rationality and State-society interdependence. Politics is no longer the phenomenon of superstructure, but the means for the liquidation and draining of dysfunction and avoidance of risks that threaten the system. It is the age of fusion of science, technology, commerce, industry and ideology.

Habermas is not optimistic about the radical transformation of the society and the possibility of non-repressive desublimated society. Rather than providing emphasis on aesthetics and mass popular culture, Habermas gives emphasis on psycho-analysis for explaining the closer links between individual identity formation and institutional social framework. Habermas does not share with Horkheimer and Adorno's non-ultimate foundations for knowledge and values and non-systematic thought. He draws inspiration from traditions of philosophy and social theory and reformulates the foundations of new social theory. Habermas has translated the project of critical theory from the conceptual framework of philosophy of consciousness into the conceptual framework of a theory of language and communicative action. He distinguishes two types of action and two types of rationality—instrumental action and communicative action, and instrumental rationality and communicative rationality, respectively. Against Marx, Habermas shows the bourgeois forms of universalistic morality and universalistic law, which are closely related genetically to the emergence of capitalism. Against Weber, he shows the emergence of universalistic morality and universalistic law, which has led to the modern conception of democracy representing a type of rationality or rationalization process, which is different from formal and bureaucratic rationalization. Again, against Horkheimer and Adorno, Habermas takes the idea of a rational organization of society based on free agreement among the members of the society. According to Habermas, in an emancipated society, the life-world would no longer be subjected to the imperatives of system-maintenance. A rationalized life-world would rather subject the systematic mechanisms to the needs of the associated individuals or social individuals. Here, the dependence of superstructure on the base comes to an end. The rationalization process in modern age is the growing decentralization of consciousness, which enables us to adopt different basic attitudes of objectivating, norm-conformative and expressive towards the elements of different worlds like objective, social and subjective. We then get nine fundamental relations in the process of rationalization—

Basic attitudes	*Basic worlds*	*Basic rationalities*
1. Objectivating- Norm- conformative	1. Objective-social	1. Cognitive-instrumental
2. Norm-conformative- Expressive	2. Social-subjective	2. Moral-practical
3. Objectivating- Expressive	3. Subjective-objective	3. Aesthetic-practical
		↓
		Rationalities of
		1. Science, technology and social technologies
		2. Law and morality
		3. Eroticism and Art

Objectivating attitude to objective and social worlds yields the cognitive-instrumental rationality; norm-conformative attitude to social and subjective worlds yields moral-practical rationality; and expressive attitude to subjective-objective worlds yields aesthetic-practical rationality. In *Theory of Communicative Action* (1984), Habermas points out that if we start from the view that modern structures of consciousness condense to the three complexes of rationality, *i.e.*, cognitive-instrumental, moral-practical, aesthetic-practical, then we can think better of the structurally possible rationalization of society, as combination of ideas from the domains of science and technology, law and morality, art and eroticism with interests and their embodiment in corresponding differentiated orders of life. This would enable us to select the necessary conditions for non-selective pattern of rationalization. The three cultural value spheres have to be connected with corresponding action systems in such a way that the production and transmission of knowledge that is specialized according to validity claims is secured.

The cognitive potential developed by expert cultures has to be passed on to the communicative practice of everyday life and to be made fruitful for social action systems. The cultural value spheres have to be instituted in such a balanced way that the life-orders corresponding to them are sufficiently autonomous to avoid being subordinated to laws intrinsic to heterogeneous orders of life. According to Habermas, the objectivating attitude must be adopted towards all objects and State of affairs that are directly or indirectly accessible to sensory experience. An actor can only comply with norms. The actors subjectively regard themselves as valid or justified. With recognition of normative validity claims he exposes himself to an objective judgment. In *Towards a Rational Society* (1971) Habermas justifies that technocratic consciousness validates particular class interest in domination and affects the very structure of human interests. He finds that instrumental reason, dominates the modern thought structure. For human emancipation from domination, it is essential to reaffirm the necessity of self-reflection for self-understanding. Knowledge is historically rooted, bounded by human interests, and guided by human activity. Human organizes experience in terms of cognitive interests or knowledge-guided interests: adaptation to technical dispositions, adaptation to the arrangements of practical life and adaptation to emancipation from naturalistic constraints. Human interests are bounded by work, language and domination. Domination is the distorted communication. The human species survives through the system of labour and coercive self-assertion, communicates through language, and reinforces consciousness, in relation to group norms at every stage of individualization. Therefore, human interests are manipulative, communicative and reflective. Habermas provides a trichotomous model of human species:

Interests	Media	Sciences
Manipulative and technical	Work or labour	Empirical-analytic
Communicative and practical	Language and interaction	Historical-hermeneutic
Reflective and emancipatory	Power and domination	Critical

To Habermas, speech is oriented to genuine consensus or rational consensus, which is the ultimate criterion of truth. Critical theory makes normative standard for a critique of distorted communication. Reconstruction of communicative competence, of cognitive, linguistic and interactive abilities is essential for self-reflection. Human emancipation is dependent both on theoretical learning and practical activity. Praxis is a complex phenomenon that comprises instrumental action, purposive-rational action, communicative action and strategic action. Through work and interaction, human species evolve through development of the productive forces and development of the normative structure of interaction. However, Habermas rejects the concepts of forces of production and relations of production and substitutes with work and interaction. Habermas, however, develops the concept of self-realization of human through labour and the notion of labour as synthesis of man and nature. The framework of relations of production is the institutional framework of society, the symbolically mediated interaction, such as norms, culture and symbolic communication. The State is divided between sub-systems of labour or work, on the one hand and sub-systems of interaction and relations of communication, on the other. State intervention is important and effective and science and technology legitimize State domination. There is no contradiction between labour and interaction.

Advanced capitalism is susceptible to legitimization crisis. Citizens, in this society, transmit the needs of this society to the State to transform political authority into rational authority within the medium of public sphere, where the general interest is the measure of such rationality. The process of de-politicization started with the growth of large-scale economic organizations, growing State intervention in economic activities, ever growing influence of science and technology and growing role of instrumental reason in the social sphere. Necessarily, the public sphere was reduced. The public sphere mediates group needs, demands and expectations and thereby becomes the field for competition of interests. Public sphere performs certain functions in the sphere of commodity exchange, and social labour and social powers (private sphere, groups and individuals) also perform certain political functions. Large organizations strive for compromise, or so to say, political compromise with one another among themselves, excluding the public, whenever possible. In spite of extension of fundamental rights in the welfare State the public sphere can fully be realized on the basis of a rational organization of social and political power under mutual control of organizations committed to the public sphere. (Habermas,1974). In *Towards a Rational Society* (1971) Habermas finds the advent of State intervention in economy, science and technology as leading force of production, technocratic consciousness, and institutional procedures for combating dysfunctions due to private utilization of capital. Marxist theory of surplus value is undermined. Civil society is no longer autonomously regulated. A new form of legitimization is essential to secure a rational society, to secure private utilization of capital, and to secure mass loyalty to the system. To Habermas,

> Legitimacy = Technocratic consciousness + Efficiency of technicians, administrators and politicians + Minimum level of welfare + Management of economy + Sustained economic growth

The growth of instrumental reason here means that technology becomes autonomous, which dictates the value system in the society. Rationalization of technical control may be observed in four phases (1) application of science to the social problems for the actualization of specific goals, and (2) application of technology for the realization of rational decision when there is a conflict between competing technical solutions. Decisions are reached through the values of efficiency and economy. (3) All previous value orientations are measured against the value of self assertion. (4) Decision-making is oriented towards computers. In the age of technology of the advanced capitalist society, the class conflict does not affect the structure of the society. 'The system of advanced capitalism is so defined by a policy of securing the loyalty of the wage earning masses through rewards, that is, by avoiding conflict, that the conflict still built into the structure of the society in virtue of the private mode of capital utilization is the very area of conflict which has the greatest probability of remaining latent. It recedes behind others, which, while conditioned by the mode of production, can no longer assume the form of class conflicts. This means not that class antagonisms have been abolished but that they have become latent. The political system has incorporated an interest—which transcends latent class boundaries—in preserving the compensatory façade.' (Offe, 1976: 388-421).

Social systems reproduce through actions incorporating claims to generality and validity. The human species in the process of social evolution and social reproduction process learns in the dimensions of technical knowledge and of moral practical consciousness for the development of productive forces and the structures of interaction. Social evolution is a learning process, which can be reconstructed on the basis of developmental logic based on cognitive developmental psychology and moral consciousness. Habermas adopts Freudian psycho-analysis to explain this perspective. Human beings are forced to adapt to environment in order to survive. Thereby complete gratification of instinctual desires is not met with. With the development of the forces of production the scarcity problem of the society decreases, the level of repression is diminished and the institutional framework of society is changed to accommodate need gratification to the higher level. The development of social organization is directly related with the development of the productive forces, Marx understands. Freud puts emphasis on the development of social needs and motivational patterns. According to Habermas, human emancipation in society depends upon both development of the productive forces and technical progress and overcoming of distorted communication. Human development is based on ego development comprising three aspects of individual development—cognition, speech and action. He identifies the essential stages of the development of ego formation—natural identity, role identity and ego identity. He goes from individual identity to group collective identity formation though the stages of historical progress and development. Cultural traditions and normative structures are the bases of the rationalization of action. ' ...(a) new structures are required in the individual consciousness and transposed into structures of world views; (b) systems problems arise, which overload the steering capacity of a society; (c) the institutional embodiment of new rationality structures can be tried and stabilized, and (d) the new latitude for the mobilization of resources can be utilized. Only after rationalization process has been historically completed we can specify the patterns of development of the normative structures of society.' (Habermas, 1979: 123). Habermas finds that history is the embodiment of will and consciousness, domination and freedom, self-understanding and action, rationalization and emancipation. In the historical process there are three types of interest—technical interest in controlling environment, practical interest in furthering mutual understanding and emancipatory interest in securing freedom. Human rationality needs to be cultivated through appropriate knowledge. Self-reflection or self-understanding is necessary for the release of rational human capabilities. According to Habermas,

> '...knowledge for the sake of knowledge comes to coincide with the interest in autonomy and responsibility... the emancipatory interest in knowledge has a derivative status. It guarantees the connection between theoretical knowledge and an 'object domain' of practical life which comes into existence as a result of systematically distorted communication and thinly legitimized repression.' (Habermas, 1971: 197-98, 212).

The basic conditions of human existence are work, language and domination. The emancipatory interest develops according to the institutionalization of domination, which is the systematic distortion of interaction. Habermas goes through rational reconstruction of universal competence and tries to develop a materialistically transformed transcendental philosophy. Emancipatory interest is the guiding interest. The cognitive activities of the human species have transcendental function which arise from actual structures of human life that 'reproduces its life both through learning process of socially organized labour and processes of mutual understanding in interaction mediated in ordinary language.' (Habermas, 1971: 194). Thus, human interests and activities assume the empirical status. Habermas analyzes the psycho-analysis method of empirical-analytic sciences for the generation of empirical knowledge. See Figure 91.

According to Habermas, Dilthey proposes that the community of life is united, which is defined by the process of self-formation and ego identity on the one hand, and dialogic relation between subjects, on the other. It is the objective framework of *Geisteswissenschaften*—a combination of diachronic dimension (cumulative individual experiences over time) and synchronic dimension (intersubjectivity common to different subjects). (Habermas, 1971: 154-158). *Verstehen* is the method of understanding in dialogue, which is related with the accomplishment of life and the process of interpenetration. According to Gadamer, it is the interpretative understanding. Tradition is mediated through understanding, *i.e.*, the understanding of effective-historical consciousness. Knowledge is generated through effective-historical consciousness. The process of understanding aspects of the world constitutes self-formation and self-understanding. Habermas recognizes the importance of historicity, communication and understanding. 'Depth hermeneutics' is necessary for revealing the historicity of tradition, nature and sources of domination and distorted communication. Social action can be understood through labour, language and domination. Beside the inter-subjectivity, Habermas contends that the world is shaped by material constraint of outer nature that enters into the procedures for technical mastery and by the constraint of inner nature reflected in the repressive character of social power relations. Language is the medium of domination and social power. Domination is social action, which is legitimized through language. Relations of organized force are instituted by and institutionalized through language. 'In so far as the legitimations do not articulate the power relations whose institutionalization they make possible, in so far as these relations manifest themselves in the legitimations, language is also ideological.' (Habermas, 1977: 360). In *Knowledge and Human Interests* (1971) Habermas says, '... for the behavioural system of instrumental action, the use of language involved is monologic. But the communication of investigators requires the use of language that is not confined to the limits of technical control over objectified natural process. It arises from symbolic interaction between societal subjects who reciprocally know and recognize each other.... This communicative action is a system of reference that cannot be reduced to the framework of instrumental action.' (Habermas, 1971: 137).

Structure of Psychoanalysis

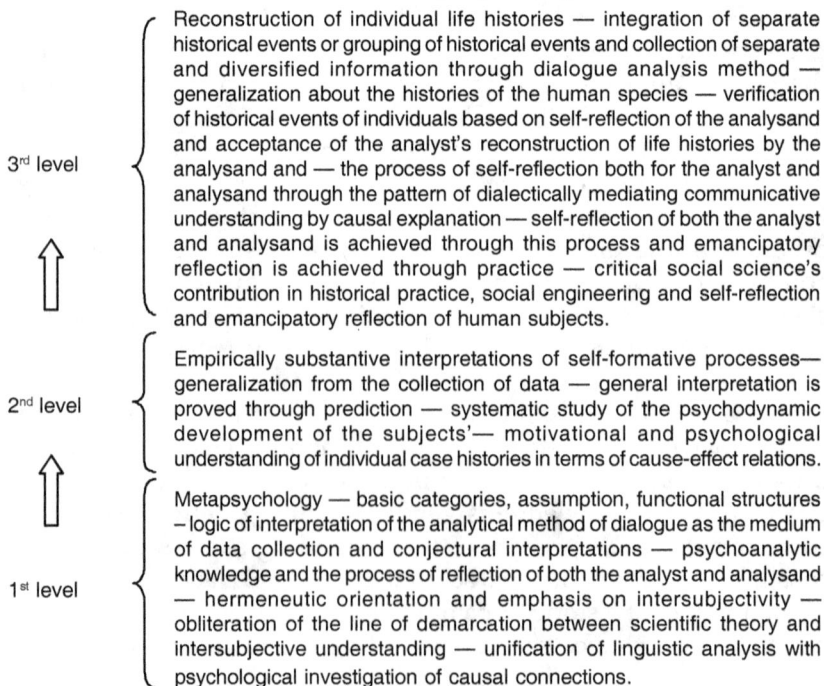

3rd level
{ Reconstruction of individual life histories — integration of separate historical events or grouping of historical events and collection of separate and diversified information through dialogue analysis method — generalization about the histories of the human species — verification of historical events of individuals based on self-reflection of the analysand and acceptance of the analyst's reconstruction of life histories by the analysand and — the process of self-reflection both for the analyst and analysand through the pattern of dialectically mediating communicative understanding by causal explanation — self-reflection of both the analyst and analysand is achieved through this process and emancipatory reflection is achieved through practice — critical social science's contribution in historical practice, social engineering and self-reflection and emancipatory reflection of human subjects. }

⇑

2nd level
{ Empirically substantive interpretations of self-formative processes— generalization from the collection of data — general interpretation is proved through prediction — systematic study of the psychodynamic development of the subjects'— motivational and psychological understanding of individual case histories in terms of cause-effect relations. }

⇑

1st level
{ Metapsychology — basic categories, assumption, functional structures – logic of interpretation of the analytical method of dialogue as the medium of data collection and conjectural interpretations — psychoanalytic knowledge and the process of reflection of both the analyst and analysand — hermeneutic orientation and emphasis on intersubjectivity — obliteration of the line of demarcation between scientific theory and intersubjective understanding — unification of linguistic analysis with psychological investigation of causal connections. }

Figure 91

History of the human species is the history of crisis and progress.

With the process of historical development dialectic of progress is associated, where the extent of exploitation and repression by no means stands in inverse proportion. See Figure 92.

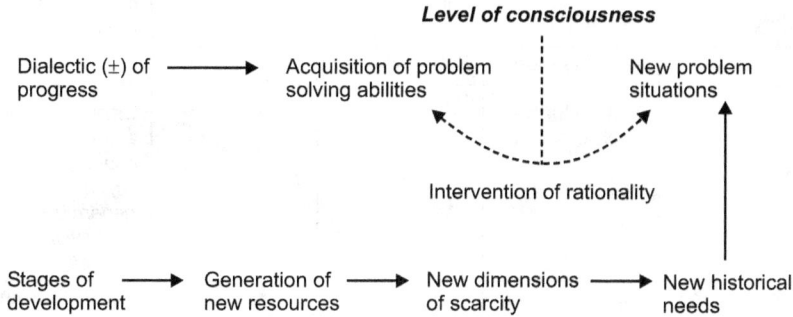

Level of consciousness

Dialectic (±) of ———→ Acquisition of problem solving abilities   New problem situations

Intervention of rationality

Stages of ——→ Generation of ——→ New dimensions ——→ New historical
development   new resources   of scarcity   needs

Figure 92

Every suffering is the negation of the new needs and demands and new needs and demands are generated thorough social-evolutionary learning process. In the process of social crisis its resolution implies liberation of the subjects. Resolution of crisis can be made through social integration, where the 'speaking and acting subjects are socially related' and through system integration, where 'steering performance of a self-regulated system' and 'capacity to maintain their boundaries and their continued existence by mastering the complexity of an inconsonant environment' are essentially set forth and actualized (Habermas, 1976: 4). Advanced capitalist society is divided into three sub-systems— economic, political-administrative and socio-cultural, are susceptible to system crisis and identity crisis, economic crisis and rationality crisis, and legitimation crisis and motivation crisis, respectively. Habermas's account of this crisis situation of the sub-systems is seen in Figure 93.

What is needed is the rational reconstruction of society— rationalization of the purposive-rational actions and communicative actions. To Habermas, purposive-rational actions are considered in terms of empirical efficiency of technical means and consistency of choice between suitable means. Rationality of means requires knowledge, which is empirical-analytic and technically utilizable. Rationality of decisions requires the explication and inner consistency of value systems and corrects derivation of the acts of choice. To him, social reality is reflected in the purposive-rational action. Scientific social inquiry represents feedback-monitored action. 'The process of inquiry... (1) isolates the learning process from the life process. Therefore the performance of operations is reduced to selective feedback controls. (2) It guarantees precision and inter-subjective reliability. Therefore action assumes the abstract form of experiment mediated by

Sub-systems	Products of the sub-systems	System crisis	Identity crisis	Causes of crisis
Economic	Values	Economic crisis (State intervention)		Requisite quantity of *values* not produced
Political-administrative	Legitimization and administrative decisions	Rationality crisis	Legitimation crisis	Requisite quantity of *rationality* or *rational decisions* and requisite quantity of *legitimacy* or *generalized motivations* are not generated
Socio-cultural	Meaning		Motivation crisis	Requisite quantity of *action-motivating meaning* is lacking

Economic Crisis: ⟶

Handling of the crisis by the government through investment contribution, infrastructure development, taxation, planning, programming and budgeting and overall bureaucratic control — breakdown of State control, policy and planning and further economic crisis

Rationality crisis or deficit of rationality in policy, planning and dministrative decisions:

Contradictions in the administrative system — the State can adjust to the conflicting situations through bargaining, compromise and alternative policy formulations and can avoid the risk of rationality crisis — State or administrative system's twin tasks: protecting and sustaining the

Not determined by the law of value, but increase of productivity of labour through the contribution of the material and non-material infrastructures by the government and rise in the production of surplus value are the determinants of economic crisis — crisis can be averted through greater government intervention and State control

Various demands are made on the State as system — failures of the administration in fulfilling the needs of the system and in reconciling the various demands — lack of rationality in policy, planning and administrative decisions — the State is supposed to act as collective capitalist — competing individual capitals cannot form or carry through collective will as long as freedom of investment is eliminated — coherent and consistent policy failures accumulation process and maintaining the level of mass loyalty to the system — failure to perform these tasks means crisis of legitimacy to the system

Legitimation crisis — mass loyalty to the system is threatened:

↕

Increasing role of the State in the private realm with the process of development — new needs, demands and expectations of the masses — new pattern of motivation formation — demands and expectations are dislocated with new pattern of development and new pattern of motivation formation — State and administrative system's inability to meet these demands

↕

Motivation crisis or failure to fulfil the requisites of new motivation formation

Various demands are placed to the State and administrative system with regard to economy, education, political participation etc. — greater development and greater development needs — failure of the administrative system to meet these needs within the potentially legitimizing alternatives available to it — legitimization crisis is contradiction between class interests

Socio-cultural system changes with the process of development — new motivation formation — dislocation of new demands and expectations which become dysfunctional for the State system and for the system of social labour — motivations — civil privatism: interest in the output of the political system and familial-vocational privatism: interest in leisure and consumption and status competition — these motivations are functionally necessary for the maintenance of the late capitalist society, but are being eroded and bourgeois components like possessive individualism are being undermined by the late capitalist society — through rational justification of social realities, disjunction and disconnection of socio-cultural system from the politico-economic system, *i.e.*, the independence of the politico-economic system and universalistic morality in combination with participatory democracy crisis in advanced capitalism can be avoided

Figure 93

measurement procedures. (3) It systematizes the progression of knowledge. Therefore as many universal assumptions as possible are integrated into theoretical connections that are as simple as possible.' (Habermas, 1971: 124). In 'Historical Materialism' Habermas points out that rationalization means extirpating the relations of force that are set in the very structures of communication and that prevent the conscious settlement of disputes or conflicts and also prevent consensual regulation of conflicts by means of interpsychic and interpersonal communication (Habermas, 1979). 'The paradox of rationalization is that a rationalization of the life world is the precondition and the starting point for a process of systemic rationalization and differentiation, which then becomes more and more autonomous *vis-à-vis* the normative constraints embodied in the life-world, until in the end the systematic imperatives begin to instrumentalize the life-world and threaten to destroy it.' (Wellmer, 1987: 56).

According to J. Habermas, technology and science have become the primary productive force and scientific and technical progress has become the autonomous source of surplus value. Technocratic ideology linked with the State's economic intervention has replaced the ideology of equal exchange as the foundation of bourgeois society. Technocratic system of economic regulation has substituted class rule. Institutionalized scientific and technical progress has created mass loyalty. In this system, class contradictions have become latent. Therefore, Marx's theory of class struggle is not applicable in advanced industrial societies. Economy in this society does not have autonomy. The State intervenes in the economic sphere. Hence, State and society cannot be treated as superstructure and base. The base-superstructure relation is applicable in advanced industrial societies. Emancipation of the masses requires a rise in the standard of living, which cannot be articulated in immediate economic forms. Under such conditions, the proletariat has ceased to become proletariat. In the process of social emancipation, Habermas treats emancipation in terms of interaction, free from distorted communication, communication free from domination, and general and unforced consensus. The State acts as the stabilizer of advanced industrial society. Here, the State is associated with domination, which is legitimized. This legitimization process is processed through rationally motivated agreement or consensus. Rationality resides in the fact that the reciprocal behavioural expectations are raised to the normative status, which keeps validity and truth at the higher level and places common interest without deception, above particular interest. Consensus produces the common interest, where individual interests must be reached at the generalization label. Interests must be shared, where a common interest point must be located communicatively.

In his theory of communicative competence Habermas introduces normative, universal, transcendental, pragmatic and intersubjective principles in interaction or communication, and in interactive behaviour or communicative behaviour. Raising the philosophy of language, he justifies consciousness, by and through discourse or language. He studies communicative action in terms of philosophy of language. All communicative actions cannot be comprehended without speech action. It means the reconstruction of universal conditions of possible understanding through speech and through the investigation of consensual speech. Communicative competence has a universal core as linguistic competence. Successful communication is possible through universal validity claims having rational foundations of comprehensive communication, truthful communication, correct communication and sincere communication. Throughout this process universal possible understanding is reached, based on legitimate, appropriate and genuine consensus—inter-subjective mutuality of reciprocal understanding, shared knowledge and mutual trust. See Figure 94.

Speech action has validity claims	
Speech action ↓	*1. outer reality or external nature—speech representing facts of world objects or existential presuppositions of manipulable world objects*
Validity claims --→ ↓	*2. Inner reality or internal nature— intention of the actor expressed corresponding to what is actually intended by the speaker actor (every speaker is a social actor)*
In speech action there are two types of interaction or understanding: *1. intersubjective communicative interaction or understanding* *2. intersubjective proportional communication and understanding* ↓ *doing-saying-hearing communicative interaction*	*3. Normative reality or society—speech and action corresponding to socially recognized expectations, values, norms and rules* *4. Language—use of language following the established system of rules— intelligibility of language engaged in the universal pragmatic functions of representation, expression and legitimate interpersonal relations*

Figure 94

In speech action, the speaker enters into communicative interaction with the hearer through illocutionary force of speech action, which can fully be comprehended if we take into consideration the consequence of speech actions that are connected with one another on the basis of a reciprocal recognition of validity claims, which have a cognitive character. The speaker can illocutionarily influence the hearer and the hearer illocutionarily influences the speaker, as the 'speech-act-typical commitments' are cognitively recognized with testable validity claims. This reciprocal relation has a rational basis. This 'speech-act-typical commitments' must have comprehensibility, truth, rightness, appropriateness, sincerity and truthfulness. (Habermas, 1979). Norms are legitimized through legitimizing worldviews. Excluding discursive will formation communication structure secures the validity of worldviews. Validity claim of speech action can only be adequately redeemed if it can possibly freely enter into communicative discourse and move freely between different levels of communication: cognitive, interactive and expressive. An ideal speech situation, according to Habermas, comprises the following characteristics—

1. In speech grammatical sentences are embedded in relations to reality.
2. Speech action depends upon the suspension of constraints of action.
3. In very speech action there are statements and interaction, which imply truth claims and validity claims, where experience supports truth claims further supported by argumentation and rational motivation supports the validity claims. Rational consensus is the criterion of truth.
4. Radicalization of argument must proceed step by step—acts → grounding → language-criticism → self-reflection or self-understanding.
5. Like steps in radicalization of argument the steps in theoretical and practical discourses may be stated as: acts: statements and commands → grounding: explanation and justification → language-criticism: meta-theoretical and meta-practical → self-reflection: critical knowledge and rational critical will.
6. A consensus is reached in ideal speech situation.
7. Each participant in this game has equal opportunity to select and employ speech acts, to participate in the dialogue process as legitimate, equal and autonomous partners.
8. Mutual understanding among the participants is the grounding of an ideal speech situation.
9. An ideal speech situation is a reciprocal relation between participants. It is neither an ideal construct nor an empirical one, but an inevitable and unavoidable phenomenon in communicative discourse. An ideal speech situation does not necessarily counterfactual. But, when it becomes counterfactual, then it is a fiction, which becomes effective in the

operation of communication. It is anticipated and as anticipated it is also effective and rationally motivated. It is action in anticipation and a self-controlled learning process.

10. An ideal speech situation is a 'counterfactually projected reconstruction', which is guided by a question based on universal pragmatism—'how would the members of a social system, at a given stage of development of productive forces, have collectively and bindingly interpreted their needs if they could and would have decided on the organization of social intercourse through discursive will-formation, with adequate knowledge of the limiting conditions and functional imperatives of their society.' (Habermas, 1976: 112-113).

According to Habermas, the process of emancipation is inseparable from the struggle for self-emancipation—they are closely associated with one another. Formation of collective will, reaching at the door of collective will and the satisfaction of collective needs through democratization, popular participation and decentralization are essential for self-emancipation and for the satisfaction of collective needs, which cannot be fulfilled and satisfied through market mechanism and administrative mechanism. The ideology of advanced capitalism is declining and new structures emerge giving birth to new principles of organization. New form of consciousness is emerging against the capitalist value system. Patterns of consciousness, especially class consciousness vary significantly across and within specific cultures and countries. To him, system crisis can be contained through State intervention which occurs at the cost of increasing legitimation pressure on the State, where system integration and social integration meet. Organized capitalism is able to contain a possible threat to its system.

Habermas's work on labour and interaction, knowledge-constitutive interests, speech-action and ideal speech situation cannot fully be comprehended. The difference between labour and interaction, purposive-rational action and communicative action, action based on intersubjectivity and action based on institutional structures is very difficult to distinguish. In the framework of social relations individual interacts through production and distribution of resources, but how are these spheres related with the interactive process?—this question Hebermas does not clarify. The concept of labour as instrumental action cannot fully be understood. Integration of nature into the practical life and ends-means interaction need to be carefully studied. However, man-nature relations are effected by different patterns of productive forces and instrumental action simplifies this relation. The concept of labour is not synonymous with the concept of work. According to Habermas, human having interest in manipulating natural objects require knowledge is not sufficient condition for the analysis of knowledge-constitutive interest. The analytic-empirical knowledge is not the basis of technical control. The living together of transcendental and naturalistic approach to knowledge is associated with a dilemma— 'either nature has the transcendental status of a constituted objectivity and cannot, therefore, be the ground of the constituting subject; or nature is the ground of subjectivity and cannot, therefore, be simply a constituted objectivity.' (McCarthy, 1978: 111).

The consciousness of the proletariat is the agent of enlightenment. Marcuse's model is grounded on human instincts. Habermas's model is based on ideal speech situation.

> One of the main concerns of Frankfurt social theory is to explain why revolution, as envisaged by Marx, has not occurred in the West. Habermas's contributions to social theory are predicated, much less strongly, on a similar concern. In trying to account for the absence of revolution the critical theorists tend, ..., to underrate the complexity of political events. Their assumption that change should have occurred through a decisive break with the existing order, leads them to give undue weight to the power of the forces operating to stabilize society. In attempting to explain why what they expected was absent, they exaggerate the capacity of the system to absorb opposition. As a consequence, critical theory loses sight of a range of important social and political struggles both within the West and beyond it—struggles which have changed and are continuing to change the face of politics. The struggles, for instance, between labour and capital, while not constituting a revolutionary situation, show no signs of abating in countries like Britain. They continue to impinge on the successful reproduction of capitalism. Further, the massive political changes in China, Cuba and Vietnam point to a range of political circumstances which cannot be encompassed within a theory that focuses on the Western capitalist nation-state. (Held, 1995: 399-400).

In fact, critical theory is normative and idealist. Historical subjects realize through all-embracing historical process. Truth is the essence of human reality. Human assessment is realized through the general assessment of reality. This theory turns attention away from classical Marxism— the essential concern of historical materialism, the theory of surplus value etc. It is more philosophical than the practical-political concerns. There is a clear rift between theory and practice. Among the determinants of social life, the sueprstructural phenomenon is studied more and given prime importance. The critical theorists are concerned more with philosophy and abstract issues than that of economics and politics. Knowledge, knowledge-guided interest, culture, psycho-analysis, ideal speech situation, speech action etc. are provided more importance by the critical theorists than that of the working-class politics. Adorno criticizes the general historical subject, historical process of evolution and the concept of negation of negation, primacy of articulation of the fundamental structure of being as well as human thought structure. Both Adorno and Horkheimer criticize bourgeois ideology and existing form of thought structure and structure of domination. Adorno affirms the primary of objects. Horkheimer and Adorno find no inevitable path of human history and the path of capitalist development. Marcuse finds sensuous practical human activity as the foundation of historical development.

Horkheimer and Adorno want to go against the degeneration of Marxism into the form of technocratic consciousness. Authoritarianism, contemporary culture and bureaucracy—its criticisms by the critical theorists help the working class in their struggle for emancipation. Critical theorists direct their attention to the spheres of economy, politics and other areas of life. They extend the domain of political reflection into the areas of division of labour, ownership and control, sexism and various ecological problems. To the theorists, State, bureaucracy and economy are deeply interlocked, where the concept of class domination is rigid and not clear. They do not specify the social relations and conflicts that underlie in this process of interlocking, do not clarify the possibilities of class conflict and class struggle over State activities, of State as the arena of class conflict and of reforms in the sphere of State activities. The business cycle, inflation, unemployment and economic crises in advanced capitalist society have not been fully discussed by the theorists. The integration of economy and State activities or State intervention and the shaping of political attitudes, demands and State activities by science, technology and instrumental reason are overestimated by the critical theorists. Further, Alan Swingewood remarks that critical theorists shift their attention from aesthetic dimension of capitalist commercial culture in advanced industrial society to practical effects of this culture on mass behaviour and consciousness resulting in the neglect of complex of mediating factors and influences of peer groups, occupational and professional groups, family and other social institutions in the formation of consciousness (Swingewood, 1977).

The study of consciousness by the critical theorists is essentially related with the bureaucracies in contemporary capitalist society and reification, but not with political economy and institutional analysis and also not with the analysis of patterns of social relations, labour process and political organizations. Apart from the theory of reification, the concept of negative dialectics makes no positive foundation to capitalist and socialist development and makes no systematic elaboration of new concepts and generalizations. Horkheimer's argument of unfulfilled interests in the capitalist mode of production is an interesting step towards fulfilment of self-emancipation of the masses, but he does not explore the integral relations between interest fulfilment, needs and universal principles like liberty and equality and also does not explain the question of relation between interest and rationality and rationality of interest and rational society. Critical theory makes no insight into the constituent elements of rational society of Horkheimer and conditions of unfulfilled possibilities of Adorno. However, Marcuse makes or tries to make a framework of a rational society—the possibilities of a rational society, development of human potentiality in rational society, human needs and material conditions of life etc. In spite of that his work is based on political statements and propositions about the development of capitalism. His thought structure is not fully developed on any particular field of study, but moves from one sphere to another—from metaphysical statements about human existence in eros to practical statements about conditions of human life and then to practical statements about historical development. His approach is more historical than philosophical. He draws inspiration from Hegel, Marx and Freud.

According to Marcuse, history reflects history of repression and through history human potentiality is realized—this contradiction is resolved through individual action, social development and human labour. 'In the Marxist perspective, as Marcuse has convincingly shown, labour cannot be simply represented by the concept of instrumental action. The concept of instrumental action simplifies the changing relations between people and nature affected by different patterns of productive forces. Accordingly, given problems with the work/ interaction distinction, aspects of Habermas's critique of Marx run into difficulties. While Marx does often appear to assume unjustifiably that changes in the relations of production are directly depended on developments in the productive forces, he cannot be accused, at a meta-theoretical level, of reducing interaction to work. For his concept of labour is not synonymous with the concept of work. While Marx does understand the unfolding of human powers and needs in history in relation to labour, this does not entail the collapse of interaction into a narrow instrumentalist framework.' (Held, 1995: 391-392).

REFERENCES

Adorno, T. 1973. *Negative Dialectics* (New York: Seabury Press).

Eulau. H., S.J. Eldersveld and M. Janowitz (eds.). 1956. *Political Behaviour* (Glencoe: Free Press).

Habermas, J. 1971. *Knowledge and Human Interests*, translated by J. Shapiro (London: Heinemann).

Habermas, J. 1971. *Towards a Rational Society* (London: Heinemann).

Habermas, J. 1974. 'The Public Sphere', *New German Critique* (No. 3: Fall).

Habermas, J. 1976. *Legitimation Crisis* (London: Heinemann).

Habermas, J. 1977. 'A review of Gadamer's Truth and Method' in Fred R. Dallmayr and Thomas A. McCarthy (eds.) *Understanding Social Inquiry* (Nortre Dame, Indiana: The University Press).

Habermas, J. 1979. 'Toward a reconstruction of historical materialism' in *Communication and Evolution of Society*, translated by McCarthy (London: Heinemann).

Habermas, J. 1979. 'What is Universal Pragmatics?' in *Communication and the Evolution of Society*.

Habermas, J. 1984. *Theory of Communicative Action* (Boston).

Held, D. 1995. *Introduction to Critical Theory* (London: Polity Press).

Horkheimer, Max. 1968. *Critical Theory* (Frankfurt).

Horkheimer, Max. 1972. *Critical Theory*, translated by M.J. O'Connell (New York: Herder and Herder).

Horkheimer, Max. 1974. *Eclipse of Reason* (New York: Seabury Press).

Horkhemier, Max and Theodor Adorno. 1972. *Dialectic of Enlightenment* (New York: Herder and Herder).

Lukacs, G. 'Marx and Engels on Aesthetics,' in *Writer and Critic*.

Marcuse, H. 1962. *Eros and Civilization* (New York: Vintage Books).

Marcuse, H. 1967. 'The Obsolescence of Marxism' in N. Lobkowicz (ed.), *Marx and the Western World* (Notre Dame: University of Notre Dame).

Marcuse, H. 1968. *Reason and Revolution* (London: Routledge and Kegan Paul).

Marcuse, H. 1969. *An Essay on Liberation* (Harmondsworth: Penguin).

Marcuse, H. 1970. *Five Lectures* (Boston: Beacon Press).

Marcuse, H. 1972. *Counter-Revolution and Revolt* (London: Allen Lane).

Marcuse, H. 1991. *One-Dimensional Man* (London: Routledge and Kegan Paul).

Marx, K. *Economic and Philosophical Manuscripts*.

McCarthy, T. 1978. The *Critical Theory of Jurgen Habermas* (London: Hutchinson).

Offe, Claus. 1976. 'Political authority and class structure' in P. Connerton (ed.), *Critical Sociology* (Harmondsworth: Penguin).

Pollock, F. 1941. 'Is National Socialism a New Order?', *Studies in Philosophy and Social Science* (Vol. 9).

Pollock, F. 1941. 'State Capitalism', *Studies in Philosophy and Social Science* (Vol. 9).

Swingewood, Alan. 1977. The *Myth of Mass Culture* (London: Macmillan).

Walker, Charles R. 1957. *Toward the Automatic Factory* (New Haven: Yale University Press).

Wellmer, Albrecht. 1987. 'Reason, Utopia and the Dialectic of Enlightenment', in Richard J. Bernstein (ed.), *Habermas and Modernity* (London: Polity Press).

Conclusion

Politics essentially requires multiple actors, multiple interests, conflict of interests and resolution of conflicts. Marxists and non-Marxists differ essentially on the resolution of conflicts, when the former regards resolution through revolution aiming at transformation of social and political change and latter emphasizes on accommodation of class interests and institutionalization of class conflicts. Accordingly, revolution involves mobilization of the masses, both ideological and political. Therborn points out,

> Instead of looking for the subject of revolutionary class consciousness, we must try to understand the actual processes of ideological mobilization. Ideological mobilization may be said to involve setting a common agenda for a mass of people—that is to say, summing up the dominant aspect or aspects of the crisis, identifying the crucial target, the essence of evil, and defining what is possible and how it should be achieved. Such mobilization develops through a breach in the regime's matrix of affirmations and sanctions, which in normal times ensures compromise or acquiescence and the successful sanctioning of oppositional forces. This breach grows to the extent that it is itself successfully affirmed in the practice of demonstrations, acts of insubordination and revolt, and so on. A successful ideological mobilization is always translated into or manifested in practices of political mobilization. (Therborn, 1982 : 116-117).

Politics of mobilization, both ideological and political are closely associated with and essential for the politics of revolution, where the interests of the subjects mobilized and the mobilizer on the one hand, and the interest of the regime, on the other, come into conflict with each other, which according to Marxists, can be resolved through revolutionary transformation of the regime and the establishment of the dictatorship of the proletariat and according to non-Marxists through rational action and accommodation within the same regime concerned, but not 'through a breach in the regime's matrix of affirmations and sanctions'.

According to Marxists, civil war breaks into revolution, where the proletariat raises itself into the position of power as the ruling class to win the battle of democracy and the party, the vanguard of the proletariat is being educated by Marxism. The party will devote itself to the revolutionary theory and without comprehensive revolutionary social and political theory, the party cannot be disciplined and workers cannot be united under an ideological stronghold. The revolutionary-democratic dictatorship is the possible way to conflict resolution over the conflict of interests between the proletariat and the peasantry of Tsarist regime and the regime itself. It means victory of the revolutionary people over the Tsarist regime. Analytical Marxists find an odd admixture between revolutionary romanticism and hard materialism. The analytic Marxists regard both the formative power of revolution and underestimation of human costs of classical Marxists as unscientific. Strategic rationality is the most useful method in analyzing class dynamics, where classes act as rational actors. In advanced capitalist countries the communist revolution is not possible, as classes act rationally, workers and peasants act rationally, and capitalists and governments behave rationally, in taking decisions. The Russian Revolution is a game between Leninist strategy and Tsarist strategy. Following the 'animal spirit' people behave rationally, they have learnt the human costs of revolution. Therefore, movements and revolution have occurred for transition to democracy from State socialism in opposition to the claims of classical Marxists. It is the establishment of capitalism creating democracy around it. It is the institutionalization of conflicts, unlike the classical Marxists' approach to the overthrow of conflicts mainly between capital and labour, with the establishment of socialism and finally communism. Analytical Marxists take recourse to the establishment of democracy with the institutionalization of conflicts.

The process should start from the liberalization process to the process of extrication from power, to the construction of new political institutions, and finally to the process of establishment of democracy. Establishment of democracy in advanced capitalist society requires the establishment and consolidation of social democracy. Advanced capitalist system is the successful capitalist economy, is like Roemer's (1992) market socialism, where people will receive differential wages, which will provide differential economic value to the society unlike Eric Wright's (1987) Basic Income Model. In Roemer's market socialism publicly owned industries are managed by individual managers, who are hired by board of directors or are elected by workers themselves.

These managers maximize their profits at market prices. Here, the State only intervenes in the affairs of investment, but not management. The State provides goods and services allocated by the market. In critical theory, Habermas (1971) finds that State intervention in economy, science and technology is the leading force of production, technocratic consciousness and institutional procedures for combating dysfunctions due to private utilization of capital. To him, a new form of legitimization is essential to secure mass loyalty to the system of advanced capitalism with technocratic consciousness; efficiency of the administrators, politicians and technicians; minimum level of welfare; management of the economy and sustained economic growth.

A system of rational society should have to observed, according to Habermas. The system of advanced capitalism has a policy of securing loyalty of wage earning masses, of avoiding conflict, of making conflict latent through rewards and welfare measures. Following Freudian instinctual desires, Habermas finds that social evolution and social adaptation, development of human needs and motivational patterns and desires, are essential for human emancipation and human development. Cultural tradition and normative structures are the bases of rationalization of action. Human rationality needs to be cultivated through appropriate knowledge and self-understanding. Rationalization of purposive-rational actions and communicative actions is essential for the reconstruction of the rational society. Emancipation of the wage earning masses needs a rise in the standard of living, which cannot be articulated in immediate economic forms, but can be in terms of interaction free from distorted communication, communication free from domination, general and unforced consensus and common interest point. Therefore, to them, revolutionary overthrow is not essential for human emancipation, class struggle is not inevitable and applicable in advanced industrial society, and base-superstructure separation is not the reality of the present day society. Throughout successful and meaningful communication universal possible understanding is reached based on inter-subjective mutuality of reciprocal understanding, mutual trust, genuine consensus of legitimate and appropriate in nature, and shared knowledge.

The reciprocal relation has a rational basis. Habermas's emancipation process is different from Marxist struggle for emancipation, while the former denotes democratization, rationalization, popular participation and decentralization, and latter justifies revolutionary overthrow of the old regime and the establishment of a new one. Different from Marxist tradition, Habermas (1984) prescribes that system crisis can be contained through State intervention which occurs at the cost of increasing legitimation pressure on the State, where system integration and social integration meet and make a common ground together. Interest, knowledge, knowledge-guided interest, culture, psycho-analysis, speech and *ideal speech situation* are provided with more importance than that of the working class politics by the critical theorists. Horkheimer (1972) regards that the task of science and scientific knowledge would be the realization of a rational society through rational decisions. The central concern here is capitalist rationalization. The emphasis is on science as domination, rationalization and instrumental reason. Both Horkheimer and Adorno (1972) state that technological rationality is the rationality of domination. This is the result of the functions of technology in society's economy and not the result of the laws of movement of technology. The culture industry has moulded men's minds. Culture dominates the market. It is rationalization and rational domination, culture making and cultural domination. Hence, dialectic of enlightenment is transformed into delusion. The working class has lost its revolutionary consciousness at this stage. Masses are the object of the social process. They cannot create consciousness, which assumes the character of free subjectivity. For free subjectivity, super ego and ego are essential. Both Horkheimer and Adorno shift from Enlightenment domination or instrumental domination to rational domination to nature, where humanity and free subjectivity will prevail, subjectivity and rationality and nature will make a close reciprocal relation with each other. At the stage of technocratic domination in advanced capitalist society, which is at the stage of monopoly capitalism, the proletariat has lost its revolutionary character, according to Marcuse (1968). Marcuse applies instincts in the formulation of the relation between society and individual and in the exercise of rationality in the course of historical development. Satisfaction of instincts or satisfaction of human potentiality becomes the goal of human existence, which is grounded on human labour. Advanced industrial society is consumer capitalism, which integrates individuals into the system through advertising, consumerism, mass culture and ideology. The worker is being incorporated into the technological community of the administered population. For the attainment of human consciousness and of liberating potentialities the process of historical rationality is essential. When consciousness is determined by liberating potentiality, then it is freedom. Consciousness becomes free for higher historical rationality and for struggle against the established society. Negation of capitalism occurs when the proletariat becomes conscious. For revolutionary development, Marcuse stresses the development of human needs other than the economic ones.

Revolutions have not been sustained by the negativity of the revolutionaries' demands, but by the concrete immediate demands in particular historical situations. Truth is the essence of human reality and human assessment is realized through the general assessment of reality. Marcuse finds sensuous practical human activity as the essence of historical development. Horkheimer and Adorno (1972) find no inevitable path of historical development and goes against the technocratic consciousness of classical Marxism.

Critical theory rejects labour as the category of human activity and makes the difference between labour and interaction. The critical theorists regard the gradual decentring role of the proletariat and loss of any historically ground agency of human emancipation. It also regards revolutionary consciousness of the individuals rather than class expression and romantic and undialectical conceptions about capitalism, science and technology. Marcuse believes that human emancipation is possible only through the sublimation of work itself in a sensuous manner. In respect of consciousness, Gramsci (1971), unlike the Marxists, considers it as the superstructure and tends to analyze the base through superstructure. One's real nature is determined by the struggle to become what one wants to become. The real nature is the sum total of animal impulses and instincts like that of Roemer's 'animal spirit'. Gramsci stresses on rationalization and seems to overlook the effects of industrialization of culture on consciousness unlike the critical theorists. Critical theory modifies Lukacs's (1971) absolutism of historicism and criticizes Marx's conception of labour, objectivism and scienticism.

Critical theorists, like Marcuse, identifies Marxism as scientific, but not self-sufficient, as action, but not merely as philosophy, as theory of social activity and historical action, and more specifically, a theory of proletarian revolution and revolutionary critique of bourgeois society. Critical theorists consider the psycho-analytic and materialist understanding of the historical processes, the effects of culture industry on mass behaviour and consciousness reflecting complex of mediating factors and influences of peer groups, occupational and professional groups, family and other social institutions. Analytical Marxists, like Roemer (1981) considers the materialist understanding of the historical process in terms of forces and relations of production and individual preferences. Individuals are formed by society, and these individuals react rationally to their environment, which in turn produces individuals who think somewhat differently from before, and react in their environment to bring about a new equilibrium.

Lukacs (1971) considers historical processes in terms of class consciousness, not the psychological dimension of consciousness, but consciousness in terms of interest. He does not separate subject and object and considers both as total. History is the interaction between subject and object. Through ascribed consciousness the proletarian class can unite both subject and object. Gramsci (1971) shares Lukacs's notion of totality, the political dimension of Marxism and the importance of ideological struggle in the process of socialist transformation. To him, for socialist transformation hegemony is essential. According to Marx, the individual subject is the ensemble of social relations and subject has an important role in the understanding of history through the concepts like forces of production and relations of production. According to Althusser (1971, 1965), the notion of structural causality follows the conception of history as a process without subjects or subject. To Althusser, humans are not the active subjects of history. However, in analyzing the role of ideology, Althusser says that there is no ideology, except by the subjects and for the subjects. The role of subjects in history has further been formulated by Gramsci in his role of intellectuals—direct relationships with social groups and classes, where members of the society agree with the norms and principles of the society and the rules and laws formed by the dominant and indirect and motivated role in the productive process through creative-analytical- exploratory-persuasive and justified activities and indirect and mediating role in creating and expanding hegemony at the superstructural level through common consent and classes.

Lukacs (1971) finds that a class ripe for hegemony means that its interests and consciousness enable the class to organize the whole society according to their interests. However, common class interest is developed by co-operative class strategy *vis-à-vis* individual interest developed by conflicting class strategy. The task of the State is to provide a co-operative solution. The neutral State would uphold the legitimacy of the State and an autonomous State maintains class equilibrium in civil society. In fact, the State makes a compromise with heterogeneous class interests. The State, however, keeps itself free from the influence of the capitalists, free from the structural dependence on capital. Without damaging the interests of the capitalists and workers, the State makes a positive response to the desired income distribution through various welfare policies. Following Przeworski (1991), Bowles and Gintis, it can be pointed out that in a capitalist democracy there is a dynamic equilibrium between democracy and authoritarianism, between individual interest and community interest, between civil rights and property rights, workplace democracy, community empowerment, participatory culture and democratic accountability. The concept of dynamic equilibrium and compromise of heterogeneous interests are not accepted by the classical Marxists. Society, according to the Marxists, is divided into property owner and non-property owner, people with more property, and people with less property, privileged and under-privileged. According to Engels,

> As men originally made their exist from the animal world—...so they made their entry into history: ...There prevailed a certain equality in the conditions of existence, ...—at least an absence of social classes—which continued among the primitive agricultural communities of the civilized peoples of a later period. In each such community there were from the beginning certain common interests the safeguarding of which had to be handed over to individuals, true, under the control of the community as a whole: adjudication of disputes; repression of abuse of authority by individuals ... Such office ... are naturally endowed with a certain measure of authority and are the beginning of State power. The productive forces gradually increase, the increasing density of the population creates at one point common interests, at another conflicting interests, between the separate communities, whose grouping into larger units brings about in turn a new division of labour, the setting up of organs to safeguard common interests and combat conflicting interests... Here we are only concerned with establishing the fact that the exercise of a social function was everywhere the basis of political supremacy; and further that political supremacy has existed for any length of time only when it discharged its social functions. (Engels, 1978 : 218-220).

The ruling class rules the material force of society and intellectual force of society simultaneously. The ruling class interest is represented as common interest of the non-ruling class. The former justifies its rule as representative of common interest, representative of law and order and defender of common good. The victory of the ruling class benefits many individuals of other classes which are not winning a dominant position. The opposition of the non-ruling class to the new class later is profoundly developed. Every new class attains political hegemony on a broader scale than that of the ruling class previously. Intellectuals are also divided on class lines—some serve the interests of the capitalists and others the interests of workers — they are most vacillating in character in class terms. Revolution is a political term, where class consciousness of the working class is transformed from 'class-in-itself' to consciousness of common situation, from consciousness of common situation to 'class-for-itself', and from 'class-for-itself' to consciousness of common interest. A mention here may be made that in society of exploitation and class conflict there is the superimposition of the State on the society where the superstructure serves the interest of the ruling class. The ruling ideas are ideas of dominance. With the change of economic foundation, the entire superstructure is more or less rapidly transformed. To overcome the old relations of production in conformity with the new productive forces, a corresponding transformation of views and institutions is necessary.

According to Marxists, history makes the path of progress through class struggle. The concept of 'revolutionary real politik' provides the importance of class struggle, which is the most fundamental in the course of human development or the development of society. Analytical Marxists like Cohen (1988) do not accept class struggle as the fundamental, but following classical Marxist line he takes into account class struggle as immediate, economic structure as the primary, which determines the non-economic institutions in the superstructure, and that economic structure is determined by the forces of production, are replaced by new ones. No particular group wants to reduce the productivity of labour. Groups are motivated to increase the productivity of labour, hence, forces of production, productive technology and productive knowledge evolve with the passage of time.

However, according to Wright and Levine (1980), class interests are not exclusively determined by the forces of production and class capacities are not exclusively determined by class interests. Forces of production, relations of production and superstructural conditions are all important in the formation of class interests and class capacities. Roemer's (1992) ideas do not contradict with Cohen that socialism grows more and more as the crisis of capitalism gets worse and worse. Roemer accepts Cohen's (1978) formulation of the technological dimension of historical development, but traces the evolution of exploitation in the course of historical development in terms of property relations. Apart from Cohen's formulation of technological dimension, Robert Brenner (1985) gives importance to class power in the course of historical development. Likewise, Wright (1985) considers class structure, class consciousness and class struggle in interrelated forms, but does not consider class as the only determinant of historical development like that of the classical Marxists. Class power only influences the historical process, when class is related with exploitation and production relations. Relations of exploitation are nothing but the manifestation of fundamental conflict of interests in the society. Class conflicts or conflict of interests are not exclusively determined by class structure or production relations, but are determined by the totality of relations, economic, political and ideological. To him, class struggle is the determinant of class formation and class structure of the society and is also responsible for transformation of society. The advent of socialism is not possible due to giving of less importance to class organization and in taking part in the electoral process by the socialist parties, according to Przeworsk (1986). Roemer (1988, 1992) does not point out any particular class structure and revolutionary class dynamics from this particular class structure. He just analyzes revolutionary class dynamics in terms of income distribution and rational pursuit of material gain.

Whatever may be the difference between classical Marxists and analytical and critical theorists on the questions of nature of conflict and conflict resolution, it can be said that classical Marxists provide an explanatory method for analyzing unresolved social problems, such as conflict, change and again conflict, exploitation and accumulation and also rational norms and understanding for socialist society. Marxist analysis is not one-dimensional study; rather it studies social development with reference to economic substantiation, philosophic conceptualization, historical premises and political understanding. Marxist dialectics is the comprehension and affirmative recognition of the existing state of things and negative state of things with the use of concepts like totality, contradiction and negation, process, motion, and qualitative change etc. The study starts with the fact, comparison, and confrontation of facts with other facts, but not with ideas. In the production process, production, distribution, exchange and consumption, are interdependent and interacting elements, where production is the determining element and capital and labour are the focal points of Marxist study. Marx's study of history is not Labriola's 'naturalization of history', but it is the historical understanding of nature in terms of class struggle, productive force and productive relation through the concepts like totality and determination.

The concept of totality and a particular kind of cause-effect relation— one part determines other parts and other parts influence another (*i.e.*, each part determines or influences other parts) at the same time—this goes against the reductionist interpretation of economic determination in classical Marxist analysis of historical development. Not only objective understanding of history, but Marx also applies the subjective understanding, for example, human needs and aspirations, ideology, consciousness, motivation and mobilization etc. However, the classical Marxists' economic factor is more important than that of other factors, which provides less importance to the time factor of Ogburn's cultural lag theory—changes in different parts of culture are adjusted and readjusted with technological changes in the course of time. However, classical Marxism does not the ignore time factor. Time-space dimension is important in the development of both productive forces and production relations. The structural causality points out that economic structures determine technological structures. The linear causality takes into account technological inventions in chronological order among the four factors responsible for culture change—invention, accumulation, diffusion and adjustment. However, historical materialism is the science of historical totalities comprising economic bases and politico-juridical-ideological superstructures. It is not the primacy of economic motives that constitutes the difference between Marxism and bourgeois thought, but it is the concept of totality. Society is regulated by objective laws. Development of the material basis is the foundation on which views; institutions; and political, ideological and cultural development grow, and views, institutions and ideas also play an important and active role in the development of the material basis. Changes in the superstructure become profound when one economic basis supersedes another as result of the social revolution. The old superstructure falls apart and the new one is created by the action of the social forces. The superstructure serves class interests. However, classical Marxists move from economic to political. But, in totality of relations both are dependent and independent variables in the course of historical development. Production, base and superstructure are key links to and components of any socio-economic formation. Superstructure plays important role in social development. Likewise, Gramsci (1971) pays attention to the role of intellectuals and the importance of thought in the formation of society. However, Gramsci pays particular importance to understanding the socio-economic relations of society by the organic intellectuals and to the necessary political means to transform the society. Therefore, he moves from the political-ideological to the economic. Marx develops the concept of totality; unity of economy, politics and ideology: the unity of structures, according to Althusser (1965). Politics, according to Marx and Engels, is fundamentally about economics. Politics lies in the basic conflicts over the modes of productive activity. All political struggles are one of the forms of class conflicts and class struggles in ideological disguise. The ideological disguise of economic issues is political ones. The economic interpretation of politics goes along with political interpretation of economics. This politics is important for the fulfilment of man's nature.

REFERENCES

Althusser, L. 1965. *For Marx* (London: Allen Lane).
Althusser, L. 1971. *Lenin, Philosophy and Other Essays* (London: New Left Books).
Brenner, Robert. 1985. 'Agrarian Class Structure and Economic Development in Pre-industrial Europe', *The Brenner Debate* (eds.) by T.H. Aston and C.H.E. Philin (Cambridge: Cambridge University Press).

Cohen, G.A. 1978. *Karl Marx's Theory of History* (Princeton: Princeton University Press).

Cohen, G.A. 1988. *History, Labour and Freedom* (Oxford: Oxford University Press).

Engels, F. 1978. *Anti-Duhring* (Moscow: Progress Publishers).

Gramsci, A. 1971. *Prison Notebooks* (London: International Publishers).

Habermas, J. 1971. *Towards a Rational Society* (London: Heinemann).

Habermas, J. 1984. *Theory of Communicative Action* (Boston).

Horkheimer, Max and Theodor Adorno. 1972. *Dialectic of Enlightenment* (New York: Herder and Herder).

Horkheimer, Max. 1972. *Critical Theory* (New York: Herder and Herder).

Levine, Andrew and Eric Olin Wright. 1980. 'Rationality and Class Struggle', *New Left Review* (Vol. 123).

Lukacs, G. 1971. *History and Class Consciousness* (Massachusetts: MIT).

Marcuse, H. 1968. *Reason and Revolution* (London: Routledge and Kegan Paul).

Przeworski, Adam. 1986. 'Some Problems in the Study of the Transition to Democracy' in *Transition from Authoritarian Rule* (eds.) by G. O'Donnell, P.C. Schmitter and L. Whitehead (Baltimore: Johns Hopkins University Press).

Przeworski, Adam. 1991. *Democracy and the Market* (Cambridge: Cambridge University Press).

Roemer, John E. 1988. 'Rationalizing Revolutionary Strategy' in *Rationality and Revolution* (ed.) by M. Taylor (Cambridge: Cambridge University Press).

Roemer, John E. 1981. *Analytical Foundations of Marxian Economic Theory* (Cambridge: Cambridge University Press).

Roemer, John E. 1992. 'The Morality and Efficiency of Market Socialism', *Ethics* (Vol. 102).

Therborn, G. 1982. *Ideology of Power and Power of Ideology* (Verso: London).

Wright, Eric Olin. 1985. *Classes* (London: Verso).

Wright, Eric Olin. 1987. 'Why Something like Socialism is Necessary for the Transition to Something like Communism', *Theory and Society* (Vol. 15: No. 5).

Bibliography

Adler, Max. 1925. *Kant under Marxism* (Berlin).

Adorno, T. 1973. *Negative Dialectics* (New York: Seabury Press).

Albert, Michael and Robin Hahnel. 1991. *Looking Forward: Participatory Economics for the Twenty First Century* (Boston: South End).

Albert, Michael and Robin Hahnel. 1991. *The Political Economy of Participatory Economics* (Princeton: Princeton University Press).

Almond, G. 1965. 'A Developmental Approach to Political Systems', *World Politics*, Vol. XVII, No. 2, January.

Althusser, L. 1965. *For Marx* (London: Allen Lane).

Althusser, L. 1971. *Lenin, Philosophy and Other Essays* (London: New Left Books).

Althusser, L. 2002. 'Ideology and Ideological State Apparatuses' in Anand Prakash (ed.) *Marxism* (New Delhi: Worldview Publications).

Althusser, L. and E. Baliber. 1970. *Reading Capital* (London: New Left Books)

Anderson, Perry. 1975. *Lineages of the Absolutist State* (London: New Left Books).

Aron, Raymond. 1965. *Main Currents in Sociological Thought*, Vol. 1 (UK: Penguin).

Arora, P. 1967. 'Marx: Utopian or Scientist', *Political Quarterly* (Vol. 38).

Avineri, S. 1972. *The Social and Political Thought of Karl Marx* (Cambridge: Cambridge University Press).

Baran, Paul and Paul Sweezy. 1966. *Monopoly Capitalism* (London: Penguin Books).

Bell, Daniel. 1965. *The End of Ideology* (New York: Free Press).

Benton, Ted.n.d. 'Marxism and Natural Limits', *New Left Review*.

Berlin, Sir I. 1939. *A Contemporary Critique of Historical Materialism* (London: Macmillan).

Bernstein, E. 1961. *Evolutionary Socialism* (New York).

Bettelheim, C. 1975. *The Transition to Socialist Economy* (London: Harvester Press).

Blondel, J. (ed.). 1969. *Comparative Government* (London: Macmillan).

Bluhm, William. 1965. *The Theories of the Political System* (New Jersey: Prentice-Hall).

Bottomore and Rubel. 1986. *Karl Marx* (London: Penguin).

Bottomore, T.B. and M. Rubel. 1961. *Karl Marx* (London: Penguin Books).

Bowle, J. 1954. *Politics and Opinion in the Nineteenth Century* (London: Jonathan Cape).

Bowles, Samuel. 1983. *The Production Process in a Competitive Economy* (Massachusetts: University of Massachusetts).

Brecht, Arnold, 1959. *Foundations of Twentieth Century Political Thought* (Princeton: Princeton University Press).

Brenner, Robert. 1985. 'Agrarian Class Structure and Economic Development in Pre-industrial Europe', *The Brenner Debate* (eds.) by T.H. Aston and C.H.E. Philpin (Cambridge: Cambridge University Press).

Brenner, Robert. 1986. 'The Social Basis of Economic Development', *Analytical Marxism* (ed.) by John E. Roemer (Cambridge: Cambridge University Press).

Buick, A. 1975. 'The Myth of the Transitional Society', *Critique*, No. 5.

Bukharin, N. 1979. 'The Theory of the Dictatorship of the Proletariat' in *The Politics and Economics of the Transition Period* (London: Routledge and Kegan Paul).

Byrnes, Robert E. 1983. *After Brezhnev* (London: Frances Pinter).

Carling, Alan. 1991. *Social Division* (London: Verso).

Carr, E.H. 1966. *The Bolshevik Revolution, 1917-1923* (Harmondsworth: Penguin).

Carrigan, P., H.R. Ramsay and D. Sayer. 1978. *Socialist Construction and Marxist Theory: Bolshevism and its Critique* (Lonon: Macmillan).

Carrillo, S. 1977. *Eurocommunism and the State* (London: Lawrence and Wishart).

Carver, T. 1981. *Engels* (Oxford: Oxford University Press).

Cohen, G.A. 1978. *Karl Marx's Theory of History: A Defense* (Princeton: Princeton University Press).

Cohen, G.A. 1988. *History, Labour, and Freedom: Themes from Marx* (Oxford: Oxford University Press).

Cohen, G.A. 1991. 'The Future of a Disillusion', *New Left Review* (Vol. 190).

Cohen, S.F. 1977. 'Bolshevism and Stalinism' in R.C. Tucker (ed.) *Stalinism* (New York: Norton).

Colletti, Lucio, 1985. 'Marxism and the Dialectic', *New Left Review* (No. 93).

Colletti, Lucio. 1972. *From Rousseau to Lenin* (London: New Left Books).

Colletti, Lucio. 1973. *Marxism and Hegel* (London: New Left Books).

Curtis, M. 1968. *Comparative Government of Politics* (New York: Harper and Row).

Dahl, Robert A. 1963. *Modern Political Analysis* (Englewood Cliffs: Prentice-Hall).

Dahl, Robert A. 1969. 'The Behavioural Approach in Political Science' in Gould and Thursby (eds.), *Contemporary Political Thought* (New York: Rinehart and Winston, Inc.).

Dahl, Robert A. 1986. *Democracy, Liberty and Equality* (Oslo: Norwegian University Press).

Dahrendorf, Ralph. 1959. *Classes and Class Conflict in Industrial Society* (London: Routledge and Kegan Paul).

Deutsch, Karl. 1967. 'Nation and World' in Ithiel de Sola Pool (ed.), *Contemporary Political Science: Towards Empirical Theory* (New York: McGraw Hill).

Djilas, M. 1990. 'Social Democracy in a Worldwide Movement', *Moscow News Weekly*, March 12.

Dobb, M.H. 1937. *Political Economy and Capitalism* (London).

Ellman, Michael and Vladimir Kontorovich. 1992. (eds.) *The Disintegration of the Soviet Economic System* (London: Routledge and Kegan Paul).

Elster, John.1985. *Making Sense of Marx* (Cambridge: Cambridge University Press).

Engels, F. 1935. *Socialism: Utopian and Scientific* (New York: International Publishers).

Engels, F. 1978. *Anti-Duhring* (Moscow: Progress Publishers).

Engels, F. 1982. *Dialectics of Nature* (Moscow: Progress Publishers).

Eulau, H., S.J. Eldersveld and M. Janowitz (eds.).1956. *Political Behaviour* (Glencoe: Free Press).

Federn, Karl. 1939. *The Materialist Conception of History* (London).

Fromm, E. 1966. *Marx's Concept of Man* (New York: Frederick Ungar).

Fromm, Erich. 1967. (ed). *Socialist Humanism* (London: Penguin Press).

Gerth, H.H. and C. Wright Mills. 1958. *Max Weber: Essays in Sociology* (New York: Galaxy).

Gilbert, Alan. 1981. 'Historical Theory and the Structure of Moral Argument in Marx', *Political Theory*, Vol. 9.

Gilbert, Alan. 1982. 'An Ambiguity in Marx's and Engels's Account of Justice and Equality', *American Political Science Review*, Vol. 76.

Gilbert, Alan. 1984. 'Marx's and Moral Realism' in Ball and Farr (eds.), *After Marx* (Cambridge: Cambridge University Press).

Gouldner, A.W. 1978. 'Stalinism: A Study of Internal Colonialism', *Telos*, No. 34.

Gramsci, Antonio. 1971. *Selections from Prison Notebooks* (London: International Publishers).

Gramsci, Antonio. 2002. 'The Formation of the Intellectuals' in Anand Prakash (ed.), *Marxism* (New Delhi: Worldview Publications).

Gramsci, Antonio. *Political Writings*.

Gramsci, Antonio, 1985. *Selection from Cultural Writings* (Cambridge: Harvard University Press).

Habermas, H. 1970. 'Contribution to a Phenomenology of Historical Materialism', *Telos 4*.

Habermas, J. 1971. *Knowledge and Human Interests*, translated by J. Shapiro (London: Heinemann).

Habermas, J. 1971. *Towards a Rational Society* (London: Heinemann).

Habermas, J. 1974. 'The Public Sphere', *New German Critique* (No. 3: Fall).

Habermas, J. 1976. *Legitimation Crisis* (London: Heinemann).

Habermas, J. 1977. 'A review of Gadamer's Truth and Method' in Fred R. Dallmayr and Thomas A. McCarthy (eds.) *Understanding Social Inquiry* (Nortre Dame, Indiana: The University Press).

Habermas, J. 1979. 'Toward a reconstruction of historical materialism' in *Communication and Evolution of Society*, translated by McCarthy (London: Heinemann).

Habermas, J. 1979. 'What is universal pragmatics?' in *Communication and the Evolution of Society*.

Habermas, J. 1984. *Theory of Communicative Action* (Boston).

Hagan, Charles. 1958. 'The group in Political Science' in Ronald Young (ed.),

Approaches to the Study of Politics (Northwestern University Press).

Hahnel, Robin and Michael Albert. 1990. *Quiet Revolution in Welfare Economics* (Princeton: Princeton University Press).

Hammond, T.T. 1957. *Lenin on Trade Unions and Revolution* (New York: Columbia University Press).

Held, D. 1995. *Introduction to Critical Theory* (London: Polity Press).

Hilferding, R. 1981. *Finance Capital* (London: Routledge and Kegan Paul).

Hobson, J.A. 1938. *Imperialism: A Study* (London).

Holub, Renate. 1992. *Antonio Gramsci* (London: Routledge and Kegan Paul).

Horkheimer, Max and Theodor Adorno. 1972. *Dialectic of Enlightenment* (New York: Herder and Herder).

Horkheimer, Max. 1968. *Critical Theory* (Frankfurt).

Horkheimer, Max. 1972. *Critical Theory*, translated by M.J. O'Connell (New York: Herder and Herder).

Horkheimer, Max. 1974. *Eclipse of Reason* (New York: Seabury Press).

Kalecki, Micha. 1971. *Selected Essays on the Dynamics of the Capitalist Economy: 1933-1970* (Cambridge: Cambridge University Press).

Kamenka, Eugene. 1970. *Marxism and Ethics* (London: Macmillan).

Kautsky, K. 1974. The *Dictatorship of the Proletariat* (Ann Arbor: University of Michigan Press).

Knei-Paz, B. 1978. *The Social and Political Thought of Leon Trotsky* (Oxford: Clarendon Press).

Kolakowski, Leszek. 1978. *Main Currents of Marxism* (Oxford: Oxford University Press).

Kolakowski, Leszek. 1968. *Towards a Marxist Humanism* (New York: Grove Press).

Korsch, K. 1970. *Marxism and Philosophy* (London: New Left Books).

Korsch, Karl. 1970. 'Concerning Marxism in Linguistics', *Supplementary, New Times*, Vol. 26, June 28.

Kotz, David. 1992. 'The Direction of Soviet Economic Reform: From Socialist Reform to Capitalist Transition', *Monthly Review* (Vol. 44: No. 4).

Krushchev, N.S. 1977. *Krushchev Remembers* (Harmondsworth: Penguin).

Labriola, Antonio. 1966 (1904). *Essays on the Materialist Conception of History* (New York).

Laclau, Ernesto and Chantal Mouffe. 1985. *Hegemony and Socialist Strategy* (Verso: London).

Lasswell, H. 1958. *The Political Writings of Harold Lasswell* (New York: Free Press).

Lenin, V.I. 1943. *Selected Works* (New York: International Publishers).

Lenin, V.I. 1970. *Collected Works* (Moscow: Progress Publishers).

Lenin, V.I. 1975. *Imperialism—the Highest Stage of Capitalism* (Peking: Foreign Language Press).

Lenin, V.I. 1977. *Collected Works* (Moscow: Progress Publishers).

Lenin, V.I. 1977. *State and Revolution* (Moscow: Progress Publishers).

Lenin, V.I. *Materialism and Empririo-Criticism*.

Leontief. A. 1935. *Political Economy: A Beginner's Course* (London).

Levine, Andrew and Eric Olin Wright. 1980. 'Rationality and Class Struggle', *New Left Review* (Vol. 123).

Liebman, M. 1975. *Leninism under Lenin* (London: Jonathan Cape).

Litchtheim, G. 1969. *The Origins of Socialism* (New York: Frederick A. Praeger).
Lock, G. 1975. 'Introduction' to L. Althusser, *Essays in Self-Criticism* (London: New Left Books).
Lukacs, G. 'Marx and Engels on Aesthetics,' in *Writer and Critic*.
Lukacs, G. 1966. 'Technology and Social Relations', *New Left Review* (Vol.39).
Lukacs, G. 1971. *History and Class Consciousness* (Massachusetts: MIT).
Lukacs, G. 2002. 'Critical Realism and Socialist Realism' in Anand Prakash (ed.), *Marxism* (New Delhi: Worldview Publications).
Lukacs, G.1977. *Lenin* (London: New Left Books).
Lukacs's opinion cited in Chatterjee, P. 1978.'On the Scientific Study of Politics: A Review of the Positivist Method' in Sudipta Kaviraj and Others (eds.), *The State of Political Theory* (Calcutta: Research India Publications).
Luxemburg, R. 1951. *The Accumulation of Capital* (London).
Macpherson, C.B. 1962. *The Political Theory of Possessive Individualism* (Oxford: Oxford University Press).
Makhov, A.S. and A.S. Frish (eds.). 1969. *Society and Economic Relations* (Moscow: Progress Publishers).
Mandel, E. 1974. 'The Theses on the Social and Economic Laws Governing the Society: Transition between Capitalism and Socialism', *Critique*, No. 3.
Mandel, Ernest. 1971. *The Formation of Economic Thought of Karl Marx* (New York: Monthly Review Press).
Mandel, Ernest. 1975. *Late Capitalism* (London: New Left Books).
Mandel, Ernest. 1976. 'Introduction to Karl Marx', *Capital-I* (London: Penguin).
Manuel, E.M. and P.F. Manuel. 1979. *Utopian Thought in Western World* (Oxford: Basil Blackwell).
Mao-Tse-Tung, 1973 'On Contradiction', *Selected Works of Mao-Tse-Tung*, Vol.1.
Mao-Tse-Tung, 1973. 'Win the Masses in their Millions', *Selected Works of Mao-Tse-Tung*, Vol.1.
Mao-Tse-Tung. 1973. 'Chinese Revolution and Chinese Communist Party', *Selected Works*, Vol. 2.
Mao-Tse-Tung. 1973. 'On Practice', *Selected Works of Mao-Tse-Tung*, Vol. 1 (Calcutta: Nabajatak Prakashan).
Mao-Tse-Tung. 1973. 'On New Democracy', *Selected Works*, Vol. 2, p. 319.
Marcuse, H. 1960. *Reason and Revolution* (Boston: Beacon).
Marcuse, H. 1962. *Eros and Civilization* (New York: Vintage Books).
Marcuse, H. 1964. *One-Dimensional Man* (London: Routledge and Kegan Paul).
Marcuse, H. 1967. 'The Obsolescence of Marxism' in N. Lobkowicz (ed.), *Marx and the Western World* (Notre Dame: University of Notre Dame).
Marcuse, H. 1968. 'On the Affirmative Concept of Culture' in *Negations: Essays in Critical Theory* (Boston: Beacon).
Marcuse, H. 1969. *An Essay on Liberation* (Harmondsworth: Penguin).
Marcuse, H. 1969. *Negations: Essays in Critical Theory* (Boston: Beacon)
Marcuse, H. 1970. *Five Lectures* (Boston: Beacon Press).
Marcuse, H. 1972. *Counter-revolution and Revolt* (London: Allen Lane).
Marshall, Roy K. 1951. *The Nature of Things* (New York).
Martel, M.U. 1968. 'Saint Simon' in *International Encyclopedia of Social Sciences* (London : Macmillan).

Marx and Engels. 1976. *Selected Works* (Moscow: Progress Publishers).

Marx, Engels and Lenin. 1984. *On Historical Materialism* (ed.) (Moscow: Progress Publishers).

Marx, K. 1844. *Economic and Philosophical Manuscripts.*

Marx, K. 1978. *Capital,* Vols. I-III (Moscow: Progress Publishers).

Marx, K. and Frederick Engels. 1847. *The German Ideology.*

Marx, K. and Frederick Engels. 1875. *Contribution to the Critique of Gotha Programme.*

Marx, K. and Frederick Engels. 1982. *Collected Works* (Moscow: Progress Publishers).

Marx, Karl and Frederick Engels. 1975. *Selected Correspondence* (Moscow: Progress Publishers).

Marx, Karl. 1963. *The Eighteenth Brumaire of Louis Napoleon* (New York: International Publishers).

Marx, Karl. 1967. *Capital,* Vol. 3 (Moscow: Progress Publishers).

Marx, Karl. 1971. *Theories of Surplus Value* (Moscow: Progress Publishers).

Marx, Karl. 1973. *Grundrisse* (Harmondsworth: Penguin).

Marx, Karl. 1976. 'Preface' and 'Introduction' to *A Contribution to the Critique of Political Economy* (Peking: Foreign Language Press).

Mavrakis, Kostas. 1976. *On Trotskyism* (London: Routledge and Kegan Paul).

McCarthy, T. 1978. The *Critical Theory of Jurgen Habermas* (London: Hutchinson).

Mclellan. D. 1998. *Marxism after Marx* (London: Macmillan).

Medvedev, R. 1971. *Let History Judge* (New York: Alfred Knopft).

Meszaros, I. 1975. *Marx's Theory of Alienation* (London: Merlin Press).

Meyer, A.G. 1957. *Leninism* (New York: Praeger).

Miliband, R. 1969. *The State in Capitalist Society* (London).

Miliband, R. 1970. 'Reply to Nicos Poulantzas', *New Left Review,* No. 82 (Nov.-Dec.).

Miliband, R. 1973. 'Marx and the State' in S. Avineri (ed.) *Marx's Socialism* (New York: Lieber-Artherton).

Miliband, Ralph. 1977. *Marxism and Politics* (Oxford: Oxford University Press).

Mill, John Stuart. 1961. *Auguste Comte and Positivism* (London: Cresset).

Miller, David. 1989. *Market, State and Community: Theoretical Foundations of Market Socialism* (Oxford: Clarendon).

Miller, J.D.B. 1965. *The Nature of Politics* (London: Gerald Duckworth and Co.).

Mills, C. Wright. 1951. *White Collar* (New York: Oxford University Press).

Morera, Esteve. 1990. *Antonio Gramsci* (London: Routledge and Kegan Paul).

Myerson, M. and E.C. Banfield. 1955. *Politics, Planning and the Public Interest* (New York : Free Press).

Myrdal, G. 1944. *An American Dilemma* (New York).

Nell, Edward. 1982. 'Understanding the Marxian Notion of Exploitation: The Number of One Issue', in George R. Feiwell (ed.), *Samuelson and Neo-classical Economics* (Massachusetts: Kluwer-Nijhoff).

Offe, Claus, 1976. 'Political authority and class structure' in P. Connerton (ed.), *Critical Sociology* (Harmondsworth: Penguin).

Ogburn, W. 1964. *On Culture and Social Change* (Chicago: Chicago University Press).

Oizerman, T. 1981. *The Making of Marxist Philosophy* (Moscow: Progress Publishers).

Pareto, V. *Lectures of Political Economy, Manual of Political Economy* and *Treatise on General Sociology* cited in Raymond Aron. 1967. *Main Currents in Sociological Thought*, Vol. 2 (London: Penguin Books).

Parsons, Talcott, 1966. *The Structure of Social Action* (New York: Free Press).

Petrovic, Gajo. 1971. *Philosophie and Revolution* (Reinbek bei Hamburg: Rowohlt).

Plamenatz, John. 1954. *German Marxism and Russian Communism* (London: Longmans, Green and Co. Ltd.).

Pollock, F. 1941. 'Is National Socialism a New Order?' *Studies in Philosophy and Social Science* (Vol. 9).

Pollock, F.1941. 'State Capitalism', *Studies in Philosophy and Social Science* (Vol. 9).

Poulantzas, N. 1978. *Political Power and Social Classes* (London: Verso).

Poulantzas, N. 1969. 'The Problem of the Capitalist State', *New Left Review*. No. 58 (Nov.-Dec.).

Poulantzas, N. 1978. *Classes in Contemporary Capitalism* (London: Verso).

Poulantzas, N. 1978. *Political Power and Social Classes* (London: Verso)

Poulantzas, N. 1979. *Fascism and Dictatorship* (London: Verso).

Poulantzas, N. 1980. *State, Power and Socialism* (London: Verso).

Przeworksi, Adam and Michael Wallerstein. 1988. 'Structural Dependence of the State on Capital', *American Political Science Review* (Vol. 82).

Przeworski, Adam and John Sprague. 1986. *Paper Stones: A History of Electoral Socialism* (Chicago: University of Chicago Press).

Przeworski, Adam and Michael Wallerstein. 1982. 'The Structure of Class Conflict under Democratic Capitalism', *American Political Science Review* (Vol. 76).

Przeworski, Adam. 1985. *Capitalism and Social Democracy* (Cambridge: Cambridge University Press).

Przeworski, Adam. 1986. 'Some Problems in the Study of the Transition to Democracy' in *Transition from Authoritarian Rule* (eds.) by Guillermo O'Donnell, Philippe C. Schmitter and Laurence Whitehead (Baltimore: Johns Hopkins University Press).

Przeworski, Adam. 1991. *Democracy and the Market* (Cambridge: Cambridge University Press).

Przeworski, Adam. 1990. *The State and the Economy under Capitalism* (Switzerland: Harwood Academic Publishers).

Reich, Wilhelm. 1971. 'What is Class Consciousness?', *Liberation* (October).

Rodinson, M. 1969. 'Sociological Marxism vs. Ideological Marxism', in *Marx and Contemporary Scientific Thought* (Hague: Mouton).

Roemer, John E. 1988. 'Rationalizing Revolutionary Strategy', Michael Taylor (ed.) in *Rationality and Revolution* (Cambridge: Cambridge University Press).

Roemer, John E. 1981. *Analytical Foundations of Marxian Economic Theory* (Cambridge: Cambridge University Press).

Roemer, John E. 1985. "'Rational choice' Marxism", *EPW*, Vol. XX, No. 34, August 24.

Roemer, John E. 1992. 'The Morality and Efficiency of Market Socialism', *Ethics* (Vol. 102).

Rubel, M. 1957. *Karl Marx* (Paris).

Sartori, G. 1973. *Democratic Theory* (Connecticut: Greenwood Press).

Sartre, Jean-Paul. 1968. *The Critique of Dialectical Reason* (London: New Left Books).

Sartre, Jean-Paul. 1969. 'Marxism and Existentialism' in J.A. Gould and V.V. Thursby (eds.), *Contemporary Political Thought* (New York: Holt).

Schumpeter, J.A. 1950. *Capitalism, Socialism and Democracy* (New York).

Schumpeter, J.A. 1951. *Imperialism and Social Classes* (London).

Schumpeter, J.A. 1976. *Capitalism, Socialism and Democracy* (London: Allen and Unwin).

Shah, A.B. 1964. *Scientific Method* (Bombay: Allied Publishers).

Shanin, T. 1971. *Peasants and Peasant Societies* (Harmondsworth: Penguin).

Shaw, William. 1981. 'Marxism and Moral Objectivity' in Kai Nielson and Steven C. Patten (eds.), *Marx and Morality* (Guelph: Canadian Association for Publishing in Philosophy).

Singer, P. 1980. *Marx* (Oxford: Oxford University Press).

Smith, Adam. 1937. *Wealth of Nations* (New York: Modern Library).

Sorel, George. 1908. (1972). *Reflections on Violence* (New York: Macmillan).

Stalin, J.V. 1938. *Dialectical and Historical Materialism* (New York: International Publishers).

Stalin, J.V. 1952. *Economic Problems of Socialism in the U.S.S.R.* (London).

Stalin, J.V. 1975. *Foundations of Leninism* (Peking: Foreign Language Press).

Stalin, J.V. *Concerning Marxism in Linguistics*.

Struik, K.J. 1964. *The Economic and Philosophical Manuscript of 1844* (New York: International Publishers).

Sweeze, P.M. 1946. *The Theory of Capitalist Development* (London).

Swingewood, Alan. 1977. The *Myth of Mass Culture* (London: Macmillan).

Taylor, Michael. 1988. 'Rationality and Revolutionary Collective Action' in *Rationality and Revolution* (ed.) by Michael Taylor (Cambridge: Cambridge University Press).

Therborn, G. 1980. *Science, Class and Society* (London: Verso).

Therborn, G. 1982. *Ideology of Power and Power of Ideology* (Verso: London).

Thomas, P. 1980. *Karl Marx and the Anarchists* (London:Routledge and Kegan Paul).

Thompson, E.P. 1977. *William Morris: Romantic to Revolutionary* (London: Lawrence and Wishart).

Timpanaro, S. 1975. *On Materialism* (London: Verso).

Trotsky, L. 1962. *Permanent Revolution* (London: New Park Publications).

Trotsky, L. 1962. *Results and Prospects* (London: New Park Publications).

Trotsky, L. 1963. *Terrorism and Communism* (Ann Arbor: University of Michigan Press).

Trotsky, L. 1967. *History of the Russian Revolution* (London).

Tucker, R.C. 1961. *Philosophy and Myth in Karl Marx* (Cambridge: Cambridge University Press).

Tucker, R.C. 1969. *The Marxian Revolutionary Idea* (New York: W.W. Norton).

Tucker, R.C. 1973. 'Marx as Political Theorist' in S. Avineri (ed.) *Marx's Socialism* (New York: Lieber-Artherton).

Tucker, R.C. 1977. *Stalinism* (New York: Norton).

Walker, Charles R. 1957. *Toward the Automatic Factory* (New Haven: Yale University Press).

Wartofsky, Marx W. 1977. *Feuerbach* (Cambridge: Cambridge University Press).

Wellmer, Albrecht. 1987. 'Reason, Utopia and the Dialectic of Enlightenment', in Richard J. Bernstein (ed.), *Habermas and Modernity* (London: Polity Press).

Williams, Raymond. 1977. *Marxism and Literature* (Oxford: Oxford University Press).

Williams, Reymond. 1961. *Culture and Society* (Harmondsworth: Penguin).

Williams, Reymond. 1982. *Culture* (London: Fontana).

Winslow, E.M. 1948. The *Pattern of Imperialism: A Study in the Theories of Power* (New York).

Wolfe, B.D. 1967. *Marxism* (London: Chapman and Hall).

Woolf, L. 1920. *Economic Imperialism* (London).

Wright, Eric Olin. 1985. *Classes* (London: Verso).

Wright, Eric Olin. 1987. 'Why Something like Socialism is Necessary for the Transition to Something like Communism', *Theory and Society* (Vol. 15: No. 5).

Wright, Eric Olin. 1992. 'State Employment, Class Location and Ideological Orientation', *Politics and Society* (Vol. 20: No. 2).

For Product Safety Concerns and Information please contact our EU
representative GPSR@taylorandfrancis.com
Taylor & Francis Verlag GmbH, Kaufingerstraße 24, 80331 München, Germany

www.ingramcontent.com/pod-product-compliance
Lightning Source LLC
Chambersburg PA
CBHW050623280326
41932CB00015B/2504